THE FAMILY IDIOT

Volume Five

Translated by Carol Cosman

Jean-Paul Sartre

THE FAMILY IDIOT

Gustave Flaubert

1821–1857

The University of Chicago Press • Chicago and London

Originally published in Paris as volume three, books one and two, of *L'Idiot de la famille: Gustave Flaubert de 1821 à 1857*, © Editions Gallimard, 1972.

The University of Chicago Press, Chicago 60637
The University of Chicago Press, Ltd., London

© 1993 by The University of Chicago
All rights reserved. Published 1993
Printed in the United States of America

02 01 00 99 98 97 96 95 94 93   5 4 3 2 1

ISBN: 0-226-73519-2 (cloth)

Library of Congress Cataloging in Publication Data

Sartre, Jean Paul, 1905–80
  The family idiot.

  Translation of: L'Idiot de la famille.
  Includes bibliographical references.
  1. Flaubert, Gustave, 1821–1880. 2. Novelists,
French—19th century—Biography. I. Title.
PQ2247.S313   843'.8[B]   81-1694
ISBN 0-226-73509-5 (v. 1)
  0-226-73510-9 (v. 2)
  0-226-73516-8 (v. 3)
  0-226-73518-4 (v. 4)
  0-226-73519-2 (v. 5)

∞ The paper used in this publication meets the minimum
requirements of the American National Standard for
Information Sciences—Permanence of Paper for Printed
Library Materials, ANSI Z39.48-1984.

CONTENTS

TRANSLATOR'S NOTE

I would like to thank Michael Lucey for his help in preparing this volume for publication.

CAROL COSMAN

BOOK ONE

Objective Neurosis

The Problem

Thus far we have tried to understand Flaubert's neurosis from within, to reconstruct its protohistorical genesis, its history, and to discover the *subjective* teleological intentions it constitutes and by which it is structured in turn. When I call these structuring intentions *subjective*, I mean of course to select and designate only those arising from his particular—originally familial—situation which have meaning with respect to his particular case and, when applied to an "unspeakable" but disturbing anomaly, integrate it with what he himself calls a "particular system made for one man alone." We have seen his neurosis develop, in short, on the well-defined terrain of passive activity, which also conditioned it. And we have distinguished two discrete elements in it, which can be separated only through discourse. The primal disturbance and stress, a self-defensive reaction attempting to enclose the disturbance and to dissolve it, or at least to neutralize it, and which through this very attempt (through the general mobilization of lived experience it requires and its dialectical relations to that throbbing discomfort it encloses, hardly digests, then suffers as its motivating, and unforeseeable, determination), finally produces the greatest possible disruptions in the area of *habitus* and conduct. We thus perceived Flaubert's neurosis, intentional and suffered, as an adaptation to illness, bringing in its wake more disturbances than the illness itself. Yet though we have enumerated these disturbances according to Gustave's own testimony, we have not tried to *evaluate* them. In other words, we have indeed seen that, far from suppressing the anomaly, they reinforced it, and even in a way *constituted* it, by making Gustave a man profoundly different from other men. But lacking a system of values, we have been unable until now to decide objectively whether the neurosis harmed Flaubert—and to what degree—or whether, to the contrary, it was useful to him.

Certainly there is no lack of objective structures, and we have used this as our starting point. There is the institutional whole, a product and expression of certain infrastructures; there is historical contingency, which, conditioned by that whole, goes beyond it even while preserving it by reviving its internal contradictions; there is the Flaubert family, a metastable result of certain structures and history, whose disequilibrium—common at this period—bears witness at once to the survivals of the past and the difficult advent of a new order. Finally there is the father, both rural and urban, both feudal and bourgeois, a man of science, therefore agnostic at this period when faith, slain by Jacobinism, attempts a rebirth without great success and manifests itself in the new generation as a dead loss, a diminution of being with nothing to counterbalance it. But these abstract and general determinations are already highly particularized in the familial intersubjectivity of the Flauberts: that famous father, nervous to the point of tears, that "done me wrong," a good-natured or fearsome tyrant; that mother, burdened forever by the death of her mother, outdoing herself in wifely servility, adoring her husband as a spouse and even more as a substitute father; the gloomy atmosphere of the Hôtel-Dieu—all this contributes to enriching institutional determinations and to surpassing them toward the concrete history of an irreducible micro-organism that cannot escape historical contingency but suffers it and totalizes it in its own way. And, above all, we have had to imagine that concrete whole—the rise of the bourgeoisie refracted in one particular daily life—as it was lived in ignorance and panic *by a child*, by a constituted product of this social cell, a son of man, predestined even before conception, who surpassed these conditionings blindly, in the dark, toward his own ends, and consequently ran up against alien objectives that an *other* will had imposed on him and that he internalized despite himself as if they were *also* his. Ignorance and passive constitution, the devoted coldness of the mother, and that second weaning, the sudden disaffection of the father—or what was felt as such—then, the jealousy and exasperation of a kid caught between given incapacities and the familial ambition he had already internalized: that nest of vipers could not be untangled; it had to be *lived*, to be obscurely constituted as a *subjective* determination. And Gustave's subjectivity manifests itself precisely in this, that the only tools at his disposal for understanding himself and those around him are symbols (the curse of Adam, the paternal curse), myths (fatality, the ultra-Manichaeanism that consecrates the

4

victory of evil over good), false constructions (Achille conceived as usurper, Achille-Cléophas sometimes identified with the Devil), and fantasies of resentment (connected to that cruelty he calls "meanness" in his youth and which Sainte-Beuve will call sadism in his critique of *Salammbô*, but which, as we have seen, is rather a *variety* of sadomasochism connected to the problem of fiction and incarnation). Thus, the attempt to demonstrate the objective conditions of neurosis in the institutions and historical existence of the Flaubert group has been futile, and we are forced to state that well before the crisis of 1844, indeed from early childhood and throughout that adolescence I will call *preneurotic*—for in it we see future disturbances emerging and gradually taking shape—Gustave does not react to the *objective* aggressions explained by his real situation but to the coded interpretations he gives them, which originate in the prefabricated schemes of his subjectivity. Any attention Achille-Cléophas might pay to Achille will appear very early on as a frustration diabolically premeditated by the symbolic father, that dark Lord, and Gustave's response will be the *literary* hatred that makes him write *Un parfum à sentir* or *La Peste à Florence*. At the *collège*, his comrades' innocent gossip or inopportune smiles strike him as the murderous cruelty of the multitude scandalized by his anomaly. Against this thorough but dreamed ostracism—he actually seems to have enjoyed real popularity and even a certain prestige—he defends himself with passive ecstasy. In other words, this preneurotic and perfectly subjective behavior (which might, strictly speaking, be called neurotic, and is subjective since it seeks in stupor a purely imaginary compensation understood as such) is a defensive reaction to an erroneous, hyperbolic interpretation of the real situation, whose strictly symbolic aspect is dictated by preconstituted schemata. Thus not only is the induced behavior a modification of subjectivity, but the inductive determination, though it appears to be a simple perception of the objective event, is a subjective evaluation of that event. We might say that everyone shares this condition, and it is true: to perceive is *to situate oneself*; so in any case there is a dialectic of internalization and externalization. The important point here, however, is proportion: while a part of the object is revealed as it is, by revealing to us what we are (that is, our relation to it and our anchorage), we can hope, at the end of an extended quest, to achieve that reciprocity of position (the object defining us to the same degree that we define the object) which is the truth of the human condition. In Gustave's case, subjectivity gnaws away at the objective and leaves it only enough exteriority for it to transmit its inductive power to the phantasms that digested it. His effort is entirely to desituate himself.[1]

We have therefore followed his preneurotic life until the explosion of his neurosis and have restrained ourselves from objectively evaluating his behavior; we have preferred to *understand* him, to study his behavior with regard to its ends, and to conceive of that behavior as a response to *experienced* situations rather than declare it *aberrant* in comparison to "real" stimuli or to the behavior of others. Indeed, in principle it is impossible to determine what is *reality* without invoking a system of values. Who is more adapted to the real: Gustave, who uses every means possible to try to interrupt his legal studies because he knows deep down that they will lead him to take up a profession, thus to become that abhorrent "bourgeois"? Or Ernest, who was also a romantic and thoroughly despised "philistines" but never nurtured the intention to escape his class; who climbed skillfully, flexibly, each rung of his career ladder, beginning as prosecutor in Corsica and ending as a parliamentary representative; whose primary concern, when asked for the letters of his deceased friend for publication, was to expurgate them? For a psychiatrist, for a bourgeois analyst—and they are all bourgeois—Ernest is the very type of the adult: social, sociable, adapted to his task and even to the evolution of French society. Those practitioners are too well trained to deny Gustave his exceptional personality, but for them he remains a man to be cured. Maybe so, but *of what?* None of them, of course, would dream of preventing him from writing. They might look for slight behavior modifications, that's all. But to what end? So he could go to Paris more often? Live there? Spend all his nights in the Muse's bed? Write different books? Get elected someday to the Academy, like his friend Maxime, the photographer? Would they try to make him acknowledge that he is bourgeois whatever he does, and that his struggle against his class, lost in advance, is simply wasted effort, a futile waste of his talents? He does tear himself apart. And Joséphin Soulary is certainly more adult, stronger, more reconciled, when he admits, with an amused smile: "What do you expect? I am bourgeois." I am reminded of the advice given by a psychotherapist to one of my friends who liked young boys: "My dear man, you must choose: become a passive homosexual or try heterosexuality." Should Flaubert be told, "My dear man, you must choose: *be* consciously the bourgeois you have

1. That is, to destroy or conceal the relation of reciprocity.

under your skin, become the great poet Soulary, or go over to the people, work in a factory and despise your class of origin by becoming one of the exploited"? This is a contemporary solution and was not possible earlier, as we know. In other words, it is totally impossible to relive Gustave's neurosis *sympathetically*, to grasp its origins and intentions, to affirm *with him* that it allows him to live, therefore to be faithful to his ultimate ends—and at the same time to evaluate it from the outside in the name of a doubtful concept of normality.

There is indeed neurosis, however, as Flaubert himself admits. Ten years of "epileptiform" attacks, hallucinations, anguish, extreme nervousness, and near sequestration. This is what he calls "my nervous illness." We have seen its meaning: that sacrificial choice to be a man-failure, and beneath it the negative theology of "Loser Wins," which reestablishes hope in the depths of this desperate soul. There is no doubt that in response to an emergency situation (an emergency for him, as he had been made, as he was making himself) this illness saved him from the worst. But *at what price?* For the disturbances are incontestable. And invasive. Although he always understood, in some obscure way, "just how far he could go." But ask yourself: this man wanted only to write. If he is writing, what does it matter to him, basically, if he is sometimes compelled to have convulsions on his couch? We cannot judge his forced seclusion as would a man of the world, a politician, or a soldier. If there are *damages* and we must evaluate them, we have only one scale of measurement available, the one he himself accepts. The illness removes him from the law and assures him the freedom to write—quite simply, the freedom of leisure. He says so, and that is not in doubt. But *without the illness*, more torn perhaps, more unhappy but more adapted, wouldn't he have *written better?* While claiming to serve his supreme end, art, didn't the neurosis subtly degrade him? Didn't it make him a second-rate artist when without it he could have aspired to be first-rate?

This evaluation, which seems to use criteria acceptable to Flaubert himself and reestablishes us, or means to reestablish us, on the terrain of objectivity—on the terrain of the work as an assessable object—is what Maxime attempted after his friend's death. According to him, Gustave was a writer of very great talent. Without his illness *there is no doubt* he would have been a genius. Despite the quarrels that divided them after 1850 and until Flaubert's death, this affirmation is of interest because Du Camp knew him before his crisis at Pont-l'Evêque and seems to have sincerely admired him at that time. *Novembre* had touched him; he found himself in it, strangely enough.

7

And of these two friends, the future member of the Academy is the one who experienced the other's superiority. He sensed a withheld strength, an explosive power in Gustave that would soon become manifest. After the first attack, Maxime went frequently to Rouen and thought he could see a certain *deficit*. Gustave was in a panic, he feared he was going mad, was dying. In the midst of his cozy life, the slightest vexation plunged him into a frenzy. This was the least of it; he lost all interest in external events, no longer even read newspapers, lived in a dream from which he could rouse himself only with difficulty, and, above all, he *didn't change any more*, like a clock forever marking the time of the accident that destroyed its mechanism: the same readings, often grossly obscene, the same behavior, the same witticisms.

It must first be observed that Maxime's judgment is secretly dictated by the name he gives Flaubert's illness. He calls it epilepsy, a somatic ailment which nonetheless has formidable effects on one's mental life. In other words, the amateur physician's diagnosis already involves the certainty of a psychic *deficit*. In those days there was no conception of the existence of neuroses. Moreover, the system of evaluation proposed by Du Camp is hardly used today: the contrast between genius and talent has a historical background (to which we shall return) that implicates Providence; it was abused during the Romantic period, and the generation of 1830–40, to its misfortune, inherited it. We do not reject the distinction out of hand because we want to form our own estimation in accord with Gustave, who, like all his contemporaries, made ample use of it.

Still, this type of estimation presupposes that Flaubert's works should be judged by Maxime's aesthetic criteria, which are no longer acceptable. Du Camp, of course, has the right to apply them, provided he knows that in passing judgment he is judging himself, as we all do. But in 1970 it is impossible to make those aesthetic criteria our own. Gustave's work, he tells us, could have been better than it is. It reaches a certain level and never goes beyond it. The fruit did not fulfill the promise of the flower. This judgment is revocable, however. It was, and is, revoked daily: first—even before it was formulated—in 1857, by the thundering success of *Madame Bovary*;[2] later by the generations of Zola, of Daudet, and of Maupassant. In other times, Flaubert was out of fashion: Valéry didn't like him; some critics

2. A novel that Maxime didn't much like or didn't understand— though he thought it worthy of appearing in the *Revue de Paris*.

tried to demonstrate that he wrote badly; literature was following other paths and defined style differently; but *Madame Bovary* was not condemned for the reasons Maxime proposed. And that period ended in its turn. Gustave is now back in favor, and the new novelists see him as their precursor; they admire him for his justifiable concern in the mid-nineteenth century with the problem they consider essential, that of language, which puts in question the very being of literature. Again a revocable judgment that will one day be revoked and whose revocation will in turn be annulled. In short, like all great bodies of work, Flaubert's has a history that began in the author's lifetime and has not approached completion. Every negation of a negation enriches it and leads it toward its *potential evolved truth*, an ideal totalization that can be imagined only at the end of history, if words still have any meaning. And every negation is merely Flaubert's *situation* by a literature that redefines its objectives and the means of reaching them.

As for Maxime, he is out of the game, swallowed up along with his ideas. He is still, however, of some interest: he *alone* posed the question of damages. And on what does he base his daring assertion that Gustave, without his "epilepsy," might have written better? On a critical appraisal of the novels? No, on the man's behavior.[3] The text is clear: Flaubert is living in a state of permanent distraction, the present does not interest him, does not touch him. As a result, he remains immutable. Conclusion: *he has nothing to say* simply because *he refuses to draw his inspiration from lived experience.*

This negative judgment issues from a positive aesthetic. When Flaubert, sullen and peevish, was dozing on his horse or camel, Maxime, lively, watchful, was scrutinizing the countryside, slipping out of the saddle and photographing the Nile or the Pyramids; to him we owe the first photographic reporting on the Middle East—his claim to immortality. This achievement presupposes an admirable dual adaptation to reality: not only can he organize himself to realize his dreams—the dreams of his generation—but he manages to fix them, to reproduce them, and to offer them to those who have remained in France, by skillfully using an instrument that has just made

---

3. But the appraisal of the works is an underlying assumption, the point of departure, and the final term of the estimate of Gustave's behavior which is denigrated in the name of what it *might have been*. An absurd proposal: How can we know what it might have been without the crisis? But Maxime is too shrewd to show his hand: he claims to have us judge the works on the basis of their author's behavior. How could this woolgatherer, this enervated, abnormal fellow reach the heights in his works?

its appearance, the newest product of technology. An aesthete, he has understood the possibilities of using a modern piece of equipment to capture *as an artist* the most ancient monuments. Thus he claims to be the permanent contemporary of his time, and nothing is lost on him: he internalizes immediate reality as lived experience and re-externalizes it as a work of art. Inspiration comes to him in the course of things; he bathes in it and lets it penetrate him.

A profoundly bourgeois conception, as we shall soon see. The artist, according to Maxime, is not concerned with depicting man in the world, with rendering in each of his books the totalizing relation of the macrocosm to the microcosm; in each of his works he seeks to *detail* a *particular* novelty. By the same token, he affirms his faith in progress, not the progress of art as form but the progress of its content, which will be enriched by all political or technical innovation. The bourgeois cry out for such an art, which would be both anecdotal and present in the social and scientific evolution; they want a high-toned literature to make an inventory of *their* world and reflect back to them the constant improvements that will nourish in every reader the great *necessary* myth of creative evolution. But to the extent that this conception remains without principles for Maxime, it establishes the foundations, several years in advance, of what will later be called the art of journalism.

But if in order to write you have to be on the look-out, to be tuned into both history and its footnotes, to live with your times, to be informed, Maxime had of necessity to condemn Flaubert and to declare that his illness had cut him off from the world, had made him incapable of *observing* and *feeling*. This is the very type of false condemnation, or, if you will, falsely objective condemnation, because it clings resolutely to the exterior of its object—by rejecting a priori situational reciprocity. Maxime's notion of genius is supreme attention to the real, contemporaneity itself as it is lived; this means the work will be inspired by new needs that industry—strange as it may seem—hatches in man solely for the purpose of satisfying those needs. According to these observations, genius would be the normal thing. This conception, which is well suited to the bourgeoisie of the Second Empire, is—taken at face value—merely an incomplete idea and hence false. Assuming that the writer gives an account of his own period as he experiences it through his own facticity, how can he adopt his anchorage as a point of view without probing more deeply and redefining it in terms of the class struggle? How can he vaunt the bourgeois century without showing the progressive constitution of a proletariat that is its truth? And a writer of 1860, of course, will not be expected to discover that truth by some blinding intuition and then make us see it, then use it to denounce us. No, but simply not to be inferior to his public, to M. de Girardin, whose prophetic reaction we saw at the time of the revolt of the *canuts*, to the notables of 1848, who after the June massacres clearly understood the dangers of universal suffrage and, having abolished it, judged it safer to put themselves in the hands of a "strong man." The ruling class has no desire to share this farsightedness, or at least this anxiety, with its writers. The Nile and photography—that is the fantasied alliance, the past revived by ultramodernism. But the author is urged to stop there, not to reveal the other dimension, labor, not to refer with his camera, an egg laid effortlessly by modernity, to the factory, to machines, to the worker— even to denounce his "barbarity," as a bourgeois conscious of himself as such would take it upon himself to do. Even after 1871 and the massacres organized by Thiers with the plenary approbation of the ruling and middle classes, the bourgeoisie was aware of its fundamental hatred of those spoilsports, the exploited, but its writers were not allowed to mention it. That would be to acknowledge that classes exist, and that relations of production arouse in the individual, as a member of his class, what might be called an affective a priori. So Maxime will gloss silently over real history, peopling his books with flat figures animated by flat sentiments—by emotions that seem uniquely born of human nature, meaning of course bourgeois "nature" (an abstraction created by its constitutive relations with the working classes) and its progressive transformation by modernity. Yet those relations are never revealed for what they are: the singular determinations of a fundamental and hidden affectivity, which is our real way of living our anchorage *among men*, in a class, in a particular milieu, in a social "stratum" defined at the core of this class by antagonisms aroused by the division of labor and its resulting conflicts. Maxime's "modernism" will serve the mystifications organized by his masters, since he makes modernity a state of the soul sustained by the benefits of a heartless industrialization. And when he judges Flaubert in the name of that pliant, loquacious, and untruthful art which, beneath its perpetual adaptation to *gadgets*, hides a profound and deliberate maladaption to the social world and its contradictions, an inert lacuna, a rigid non-will hidden by the darkness of the depths, it is the bourgeois public that judges Gustave through Maxime and reproaches him, finally, for having failed to write a literature affirming the values of his class. Apart from the fact that it is difficult to condemn a writer for never having undertaken what he refused to undertake even in his first works, Maxime's bourgeois monarchic conceptions (which will find their public under Napoleon III) represent, crudely speaking, the doctrines of hack writers who have vanished without a trace. Perhaps he thought these doctrines were in conflict with Romanticism; but he did not perceive that Romanticism, by means of a rigorous dialectic, had already been challenged, surpassed, and preserved by a new determination of the Objective Spirit first revealed—*precisely*—by Flaubert (and at the same time by his contemporary, Baudelaire, as well as—although less clearly, we shall see—by Leconte de Lisle, their elder by three years, and of course by the Goncourts), that it was enriched and developed during the second half of the century until it found its theorist and hero in Mallarmé, then died of senility after the Symbolist decadence. Maxime would be unwitting witness to this fecund *deviation* of literature; he would not see the clear evidence that all the *good* works between 1850 and 1880 were born—directly or indirectly—from this new current. Always seeking the master stroke that would make him rich, trying to write and sometimes writing a best-seller, enjoying, or imagining that he enjoys, a large audience—in proportion to his compromises—he aspires to communicate with his reader and succeeds easily; yet this facile victory conceals the most important *literary fact* of that half-century: the divorce—unique in history—of the writer from the public. This event will be experienced *as a drama* by all the "artists" of the period, and their works, behind a facade of deceptive serenity, bear witness to it.

In order to assess the *damages* of the neurosis, it is therefore necessary, though not sufficient, to confine our research to the domain of literary production. We must, moreover, refrain from imagining this production in terms of norms that claim to be transhistorical and are actually just the product of another moment in history or, at the same moment, of another social stratum having other interests and other internal relations with the bourgeois class. The only possible principle is the one that Flaubert continued so lucidly to recall throughout his long correspondence: critics must judge the work of art by the artist's intentions, that is, in terms of his initial project, which itself depends on a structured set of aesthetic norms. Gustave obviously does not require his judges to have a subjective sympathy for the phantasms of his subjectivity; he is demanding an objective criticism, rigorous in its *comprehension*, that would grasp in the finished work the principles of the enterprise implicitly inscribed in it, and appraise what the artist did in terms of what he intended to do. For—as we shall see more clearly as we go along—all literature, as a historical determination bound to contingency and to tradition, defines its own subject; that is, it demarcates and isolates a certain sector for cultivation by the structures it generates, and in this connection it discovers a new use of language, its instrument and raw material. Or, if you will, it understands *linguistic being* in a new light; starting with an original goal, it assigns it real *possibilities* never before envisaged.

Considering Flaubert from this point of view, we shall suggest that what Maxime would call his *deficit* is merely the organization of a neurotic instrumentality intended to give him the means to "make art" according to the principles he has established. Certainly not by deliberate choice, but because he *found* them within himself *already adopted*. The *rejection of immediate reality* is not, as Maxime insinuates, a lesser presence in the world due to a psychoneurotic sclerosis of his adaptation to the real. It is the firm determination never to be inspired by the event; in other words, it is the intention to purify inspiration. Inspiration born in the course of events sometimes seems dazzling but in fact remains variable and hazardous, obscured by passions; it comes from chance, and chance kills it. Sullied by the materiality of life, the work issuing from such inspiration is itself hazardous and bears the traces of original filth. This does not mean that the artist cannot *utilize* immediate reality. He can recount the sad story of the Delmarre couple or the life of a group of young men between 1846 and 1860. But he keeps his distance from the events he retraces; he is not inspired by them because his subject lies elsewhere; he handles them from afar, modifies them at will, and assigns them the job of incarnating the nonimmediate in the contemporary world. The incarnation is imperfect because the real subject has nothing in common with the plot; yet this imperfection must persist and become meaningful allusively, referring to a silent totality all the more present as it continually calls attention to itself, given the impossibility of *rendering* it, as the whole which, canceled by the singular determination, resides in each of its parts. When writing *Madame Bovary*, Flaubert shares with Louise his deep desire as an artist: *to appear* to treat one subject but in fact to be treating another, quite different in quality and scope, or not to treat it at all, by which he does not mean writing to say nothing, but writing to say, Nothing. This is the role of the immediate in *Madame Bovary*: to symbolize, strictly speaking, to allude to the macrocosm or the void that is its equivalent, and above all to distract attention, to fool the reader, and while the reader is absorbed

13

in reading a contemporary story, to inject him with an ancient, eternal poison *through style*. For Gustave the subject of literature is given a priori. He would say later to George Sand: one does not write what one wants. And it is true; Maxime does write what he wants, or almost, but this is not writing. The content of the work cannot be provided by the course of things, a succession of opaque and trivial singularities, nor can it be provided by caprice. The only *possible* content, for Flaubert, is the judgment the adolescent made of the world at the end of childhood, which was always the same despite the various ways he expressed it: "The earth is the realm of Satan"; "At a quite early age I had a complete presentiment of life"; "I believe in the curse of Adam." In short, the worst is always certain, I believe in Nothing. The Delmarre woman never interested him for herself. But he charged her and all her petty world with developing before our eyes that obscure a priori, human life as he perceived it at the end of his childhood.

In reality, Flaubert knows the grayness of the quotidian; this world is *not enough* to be truly assimilated to Hell. But we have seen why the task of the artist is to *represent* it by a totalizing tightening of its slackened bonds, by imperceptible additions, by discreet eliminations, as if it were that perfection. The content of the work will thus be its form: the world must be reproduced as if it were the work of a freedom whose goal is to realize radical evil; this presupposes that everything, of itself and beneath the level of action joined to all other things, must lead to the worst. And this enterprise requires such rigor in the writing, such a multiplicity of connections between the elements of the narrative, such adroitness at offering glimpses of the savage and menacing All through every part, and then at suppressing each one so the totality can manifest itself stripped bare and reveal in the final instant that it is quite simply nothingness. Such effort, care, and calculation are required that radical evil is merely an ethical designation of that other absolute norm, beauty. And as evil cannot identify with being as being, which is simple positivity, or with nonbeing, which taken as such is nonexistence pure and indescribable, it must reside in the dialectical movement between the two: the nonbeing of being expressed by the being of nonbeing. *The nonbeing of being* is the prophesied result of totalization when still in progress, the meaning of the narrated story while there are still characters to live it and while it is still sensed through their tumultuous passions. Totalized, being identifies with the void, and evil is not that ultimate, colorless, odorless, tasteless void but allows itself to be glimpsed at every step of the totalizing narrative; this happens when, through the reciprocal determination of the parts by the All grasped as the rule of unification by the annihilating future (fate), and of the All by the parts (the part, by managing a painful disappearance *as part* so that the All should be manifest in its radical unity, becomes the symbol of the All taken as permanent disappearance), the violent, massive and variegated multiplicity of the present denounces itself, in the heart of its permanent affirmation, as having no substance other than an eternal and featureless void. Evil is that gnawing contradiction at the heart of being, that discovery in every being, when it invests all its forces in persevering, that it is merely an illusory modulation of nothingness and, in sum, the futile contention of that truth sensed in the rage and turbulence of passions.

The being of nonbeing is the raw material itself of the work as fiction; it is *appearance*, which is diabolical because the being of nothing, always borrowed, relative to being, suddenly shows us the disturbing, vampirizing power of what is not. In this sense—as I have demonstrated elsewhere—absolute evil is none other than the imagination. But in the Book as Gustave conceives it, appearance reveals its borrowed being and its nonexistence at the moment when being, in the course of the narration, is itself revealed as appearance. Hence being, maintained in the fictional setting, can no longer challenge appearance the way truth challenges error. Quite to the contrary, the two strata of appearance reinforce and challenge each other, and the work remains in suspense like a nightmare that would at the same time be true. The extraordinary purpose of art, in Gustave's view, is *to manifest* the ineluctable slippage of being toward Nothingness through the imaginary totalization of the work; *at the same time* its purpose is to preserve indefinitely, by that regulated illusion which is the work, a sense of endlessness in this slippage, fixing it through the restraining power of words whose permanence assures us *in the imaginary* that it will never reach its end and will always remain ineluctable, irreversible but *unachieved*. Thus the nonbeing of being—which is realized, according to Flaubert, only at the end of an exhaustive totalization symbolized by the anecdote—is signified by the being of nonbeing, which confers upon it in the work a perfect but imaginary *atemporality*. Temporalization (Gustave's worm in the apple) is exhibited in the work that denounces it, like destiny or a fatal slippage toward the worst: it is a fundamental structure of the *Subject*. But at the same time the work enfolds it in its calm eternity. So that the temporal, maintained, sustained at every moment of the Book by

15

a continuous creation, manifests itself during reading as a byproduct of atemporality. The work is born of an interference in which two movements annul each other: being slips into nonbeing, and this very nonbeing saves it by vampirizing it. Flaubert's sadism is thus unleashed. This is not just a transparent display of the nothing at the basis of being; Gustave adds insult to injury by subjecting being to nothing: he compels it to take the little substance and permanence he concedes it from the imaginary.

The sole problem, the sole concern of the artist as Flaubert conceives of him, is therefore art, by which I mean the set of procedures that allow putrefying being to be preserved in the alcohol of nonbeing. The *idea*—the totalizing conception of the work and hence the unique subject of literature—has always intoxicated Flaubert. For this reason, no particular circumstance is at the source of his writings. Breughel's *Saint Antoine,* the *Saint Julien* of Rouen Cathedral, are *already* works of art, and of the kind he would wish: they are totalizing. No doubt he *encounters* them, they impress him; but this is because he *recognizes* them. They provide him with what the formalists call the form of content, that bit of unformed matter without which the idea would vanish. Standing before that picture, before the stained glass window, his fervor is engaged because the object grasped—itself imaginary—spontaneously offers him the thing that gives meaning to *any* great work (in his eyes): a circularity of being and nothingness, in which nothingness must triumph over being although that is the source of its false substance. A circularity that is *unthinkable, unspeakable* (at least directly) and essentially *irrational* (merely one of its charms for Gustave), and that can be expressed only in the work—a center of unrealization which is already in itself a hybrid mixture of being and nothingness. In other words, the meaning of the work of art is to give—indirectly and in the imaginary—the only form of existence possible to that inchoate idea which, Gustave tells us in *Mémoires d'un fou,* is confused with his life. In short, the form of content will be quickly found. What is *essential* are the techniques of creation, its procedures and directed inventions, all the manipulations that aim—blindly—at *making visible* what cannot be thought and in this way introduce into other minds an inchoate thought, the meaning of the work, a lingering phantom they cannot confront, a perpetual and disturbing incitement to conceive of something inconceivable that escapes them the moment they think they've grasped it. But these aesthetic means are themselves almost impossible to find. Indeed, as their purpose is to render the irrational, they are by nature inac-

16

cessible to reason; and the idea cannot help to define them, for without them it would have no existence, remaining latent or vague to Flaubert *unless* he has discovered a way to embody it. Hence the young author's alternating enthusiasm and discouragement, then his bitterness, finally his despair; for the idea—immutable in itself—is nothing (being, stripped down, the unthinkable idea of the nothingness of being). When Flaubert is carried away with excitement, it's because he thinks he has found the lens to refract it; when he abandons his project in disgust, it's because the idea proves elusive. The techniques weren't good enough: for lack of appropriate treatment, the anecdote has shriveled and is reduced to its particularity.

In short, Maxime has understood nothing. For Gustave, the work's meaning and content are given in advance. So what's the good of living? Life is disruptive; its tepid passions and petty cares could distract the artist from his true task, which is to perpetuate the wreckage of the world through *style*. And, indeed, why *change*? What is there to change since his task is fixed? The refusal to seek inspiration in the event, which is clearly formulated in the first *Education* ("it merely refers to itself") must be accompanied by the refinement of a defensive lens against any alterations. Art requires a *guaranteed immutability*. First of all, living distracts us; the main thing is, we must think only of the means to construct the irrational object that will indirectly suggest the unthinkable idea; in fact, we must think only of style. From this point of view, convinced that he is aiming too high for his feeble powers and that, lacking taste, he might destroy himself if impotence doesn't silence him first, Flaubert thinks he hasn't a minute to lose. Writing to Louise one day, he expresses his amazement: how could Leconte de Lisle, an artist, fritter away two years in tempestuous and disappointing love affairs while he forgot his art? Gustave's stupor will provoke laughter; it is typical of him, however. Why love when the artist's only concern is to write, and style, an absolute point of view, is constantly slipping away? "Think of style," he says to the Muse, "think of it always." He could be a believer speaking of his God. That is what it is, and even worse: for that uninterrupted meditation on language is pursued in anguish, in disgust; this Christian believes he is damned. His only chance for salvation is time. A time that is uniform and empty of all content, that smacks of boredom, whose every moment is like the last, a time that he can put to good use for inventing the form adequate to his unique subject, which was fixed since adolescence and yet never treated.

On this level, perspectives are reversed. Like Maxime, we wonder whether Gustave's neurosis did not hamper him in his work as a writer. Shouldn't the question be, rather, whether it was *useful* to him? I don't mean that kind of immediate appeasement procured subjectively by certain neurotic *stresses* to the detriment of psychic integrity. I am wondering about the *objective* results of his "nervous illness": doesn't it furnish him with the *means* to write *Madame Bovary?* I have said that art, according to Flaubert, requires a *consolidated immutability.* It is not enough to reject the accidental and think only of the very essence of beauty, of the means of capturing its light; you must be *protected from changes.* This is something no choice, no decision, even in the form of a vow, can provide. I cannot commit myself in relation to myself; and the vow not to change, even as it is made, invokes the possibility of being broken, which becomes *my* permanent possibility and perhaps my vertigo, my temptation. And then, even when I for my part would be faithful to the pledge, who can guarantee that a change in my moods or taste will not be the result of external forces? Immediate reality seeps in everywhere: How shall I defend myself against it? Making vows is all very well—no sooner said than done; they take you off, tonsure you, and shut you up in a monastery. But that commitment has meaning only in a religious society: it is integrated by a constituted body, by an *Order,* and this order is entrusted with recalling the commitment, with imposing it in case of failure; in short, the order takes responsibility for that commitment, and the new recruit must internalize it as an *other will,* or the *will of the Collective,* sustained by the constraint of the serial, by the constraint of the sworn group, if need be by bodily constraint. The newcomer is protected against the outside by high walls, against himself by the simple fact that it is much more difficult to leave the Order than to enter it. In these communities, mystic flights are often merely rebellion turned inside out by the consciousness of its impossibility. For Flaubert, an agnostic who wants to devote himself in solitude to a profane occupation, the only conceivable equivalent to constraint is neurosis as a suffered option. The public solemnity of vows—which helps to make them irreversible—is here replaced by the publicity of scandal: the declared unworthiness of the Flaubert son protects him from temptation, compels his sequestration. The illness itself, six months of bed rest, the irregular, always imminent return of the attacks, defends him against himself and confines him to his room; the will of the family is substituted for his own: Doctor Flaubert personally forbids his return to Paris. Finally—as he so often repeated!—this profound upheaval has killed him; his heart is dead:

18

even if he wanted to, he would be incapable of falling into the amorous senility that doomed Leconte de Lisle. "I am not made for pleasure." Opportunities can proliferate, but for this phantom, void of his affective substance, they will never again be tempting. Public commitment, *other* will, prohibitions, bodily constraint, high defensive walls—all replaced by his neurosis. And, like a monastic order, it is easier to enter than to leave. Beginning in January 1844, Flaubert is nothing more than a mediation between the idea that ravages his life and the style that must indirectly render it.

The question of "damages," however, has so far been answered only in part. It has, if you will, shifted its ground. It seems evident that Flaubert's conception of art requires the immutability of the artist. But isn't this conception of art itself neurotic? Let us not forget that the desire for immutability seems to have long preceded his aesthetic ideas. When he stoutly declared to Ernest that he was and would remain the same, he was fifteen years old and still relied upon his spontaneity as a "poet." At that period—and during the following years—the young man was engaged in a struggle against his fate. And the primary goal of this clearly affirmed "immutability" was not to serve his artistic vocation but to give him symbolically, and preserve for him, the inert present of inanimate matter *against time*, which would perforce change him into a prosecutor or a notary. Couldn't it be said, then, that immutability—the refusal to live the life others wanted to impose on him—was a singular and primitive neurotic goal; that he desired it, or believed he was afflicted by it, to escape the paternal curse and because it satisfied his obsessive desire to be a mortuary figure, a dead man, a being beyond life; that before a suffered exis it was a role, and far from being required by art as a condition of its possibility, it was, on the contrary, immutability as a neurotic attitude that imposed on Gustave a conception of art to justify it? Indeed, for that which is immutable, a totalizing art that rejects life becomes the *only possible*; and so immobilism, dissembling its identity as primary cause, poses as the indispensable means of attaining beauty.

Shouldn't we consider, indeed, that in *L'Education sentimentale* and in his correspondence Gustave presents as aesthetic *norms* certain *factual* determinations encountered in psychoneuroses as definite symptoms, some of which even seem to belong to the psychotic universe? His refusal to change is accompanied by a refuse to live, to adapt himself. Isn't that impassive witness, the artist, the final incarnation of the Old Man—a role so favored by Gustave—or of that other role,

19

the dead man? And haven't his morbid passivity and pithiatism made him choose the Imaginary as a permanent milieu *against the Real*, even before he decided on his vocation? In this case the *subject* of art—the oneiric world and the directed dream of a continuous annihilation of being—merely provided the expression of a neurotic option prompted by resentment and an unrealizable desire for compensation. Isn't there an obscure, *unthinkable* nucleus in this breachless circularity of being and appearance? We might say he *rationalizes* in the form of aesthetic, hence in some way universal, imperatives that "system made for one man," whose profound finality—to mask his anomaly and escape the paternal curse—is strictly *singular*.

In a way, this interpretation is irrefutable. Neurosis is the subjective—at least as it is lived by the neurotic. And while *maladaptation*—which is essentially psychotic—does not characterize neurotic disturbances and isn't a symptom *required* for their clinical definition, neurosis always implies a certain refusal, a break with the real. This is what happens in the case of hysterical disturbances, which alone concern us here. When Charcot was teaching at Salpêtrière, hysteria was seen by his students as a *refusal* that was somatized through spasms. But we know today that this brutal and manifest refusal represented the only response that uneducated, often illiterate subjects could offer to questions raised in the course of things. By studying this same neurosis in the most cultivated circles of Vienna, Freud proved indirectly that the spasms were merely extreme and *meager* reactions to the permanent aggression of objectivity. In the most intelligent patients, these symptoms did not appear—and today it seems that with the general rise in the level of culture, they have nearly vanished. Hysteria becomes characterized, to the contrary, by flexibility and docility, by an incontrovertible comprehension of the real and by an *apparent* adaptation to objective situations. But this adaptation is deceptive: the patient deciphers questions posed by his surroundings and events at hand in terms of a fundamental intention of *rupture*. If the intention is given at the outset, it proposes the rupture as long-term objective: the patient will espouse the real to the point where he can detach himself from it by a role that at once embraces and neutralizes it. He investigates the traps that history and the environment might conceal only so as not to be discovered when he focuses on believing in the role he is playing. Of course, the game and the investigation—when the neurosis is in place—happen simultaneously: the role as it is now interpreted is merely an adaptation already passed, surpassed—however valid it still might be in its general features—and the investigation is prospective; the patient sniffs out ambushes, and in this search he is already outlining his future response, the character he will try to interpret. In Flaubert's case we might say that, although unfamiliar with either of these illnesses, he orients his *neurotic* pithiatism toward the imitation of the kind of *psychotic* refusal of reality associated with schizophrenics.

The trouble is that *Madame Bovary*, incontestably the work of a neurotic, is in no way *in itself* a *neurotic work*. Writings certainly exist that in themselves bear witness to disturbances in the mind of their creator; these are often deeply interesting documents, of brilliant and terrible beauty, but revealing to the reader—even if he understands nothing of psychiatry—the disturbing universe of mental pathology. I am referring to that vast collection of what we might call "morbid literature," journals, narratives, memoirs, tales and stories, very few of them published and remaining for the most part in the archives of psychiatrists or psychiatric hospitals. Haunted by phantasms, loaded with symbols, torn by obsessions that generate the work and yet rip its texture, sometimes simplified by a pathological geometry or hyperlogic to the point of extreme poverty or to a strange elegance that throws us into discomfort, sometimes obscured by the richness of an autistically structured thought that can render them unintelligible to everyone and primarily to their author, these productions are in themselves symptoms. Their ambiguity will seem clear if we compare them to patients' drawings, which are better known to the general public. Such drawings do have clinical value for the psychiatrist; they reveal to him the morbid schemes and hidden intentions that structure a patient's psychic life. During treatment they can in turn confirm the diagnosis and the cure by the progressive disappearance of a symbol and hence of the obsession or inhibition expressed by it. But these drawings are often exhibited as though they were the canvases of a "normal" painter. Then, although visitors instantly *perceive*—in a state of estrangement[4]—the *other thought* present in the style of drawing and self-proclaimed in all its otherness, they cannot help being sensitive to the *aesthetic* character of the productions. This is not surprising, for in most cases the drawing bears witness to a rupture with the real and to the choice of the Imaginary, even as the artist's pencil allows the neurosis or psychosis to act as a totalizing idea in Flaubert's sense. So it is with pathological writings, although

---

4. Because that *other thought* designates, beyond rationalizations, *their own*—which is, in each of us, at once other and the same.

the difficulty inherent in using linguistic signs rarely permits them to be entirely beautiful. The evolution of the Objective Spirit is such that in our day the best of these productions are integrated into literature, which is defined for us as a hermeneutics of silence rather than a rigorous construction according to rules. It does not much matter that the literary is incomplete or incoherent if its allusive value is incontestable.

But while the essential quality of Flaubert's works is undoubtedly *allusion*, his works do not fall into this category. They are finished products, wrought, polished, up to the standards of his time—*first-rate*. In other words, what they first reveal is rationality as the rule of literary praxis. No doubt the essential goal of this achievement is to "render thought indirectly through form." Be that as it may, it is there in its density, its irreducibility, making *Madame Bovary* what its author wanted: a *natural being*, like a tree or a landscape, which new generations accept as they would *things* of the urban or rural world, and institutions. And this can never be said of "morbid works"—even the most beautiful—for even as they fascinate us they unravel before our eyes. Their essence is that inconsistency which does not allow them to stand alone; incomplete, confused, ambiguous, their "vibrating disappearance" is effected in the very process of reading as an attempt at recomposition, and leaves us face to face with pure horror. Such horror is the *meaning* of Flaubert's novels, but their density prevents them from dissolving. Thus the literary object *is composed* through us, during the reading, and is posed for itself in its unity. As a result, the horror is never present, it haunts the book without becoming visible; always intended, it escapes. For that very reason, *Madame Bovary* as a work does not fall into the categories of the pathological; by itself it refers neither to the subject who wrote it nor to his obsessions. Pathological writing is continually transparent to subjectivity: hence it offers us the horror of living but doesn't convince us directly. Flaubert's work is classical because it convinces us of that horror without bringing us up against it. And we can be sure that this is how it seemed to the public of 1857, who would never have accepted it otherwise.

If neurosis defines itself as the more or less radical choice of subjectivity—and this is indeed its function for Gustave—it offers no means of escape from that subjectivity; and the work issuing from it must be morbid, must mark the singularity of its author without becoming the *singular universal* that self-evidently wins our adherence, for singularity touches us by designating us through its aesthetic universality

to precisely the degree that universality masks subjective idiosyncrasy. Indeed, neurotic writing is masturbatory: its only end is neurosis itself, and the intention to communicate is absent or reduced to
its simplest expression.[5] And while Flaubert's relation to the public
may be poor a priori, while he may write *in the absolute* rather than for
readers, his works are unreal determinations of objectivity. He wants
to produce centers of unrealization that escape him, little metaphysical events that close up and turn against him—and not to assemble
words that would reflect his neurosis to him alone. In other words, it
is quite true that Gustave's intentions are neurotic, and that they are
aimed primarily at his idiosyncratic subjectivity. But it is also true that
he has produced an objective work that presents itself to the reader
as a singular universal. It seems we have come to an impasse: Is it
conceivable that the return to the subjective could in practice result in
the production of an object in the social world? And it hardly matters,
in this case, that the object is imaginary since it is, as such, a *real*
determination of the society. Are we to claim that in this case, quite
by chance, neurosis is counterbalanced by talent? That means nothing. First of all, talent is indefinable: that "gift" is revealed only in the
work; it is the very success of the work projected a posteriori onto the
subjectivity of the author. Then, too, it is a metaphysical virtue, in
Comte's sense of the term, the abstract explanation of a shift from the
subjective to the objective by a power analogous to the soporific virtue of opium. Even this absurdity would be less manifest if the imagined author, a mixture of the objective and the subjective, attempted
to emerge into objectivity by expressing himself. But if he is neurotic,
if he writes to satisfy his neurosis, it is subjectivity he is aiming
at—and the incommunicable; then talent becomes providential grace,
or, better yet, the *miracle* by which God would transform this systematic subjectivization into objectivity, and would transform the
refusal to communicate into communication. For at the extreme we
would have to conceive of a schizophrenic turned toward absolute
autism and, *thanks to talent*, offering to share with the reader the pure
asocial nature of his autistic thought. This is inconceivable since in
this case writing is merely a means used by the illness, an effort to
steal language from others and use it to take refuge in an inexpress-

---

5. Still, if you like, communication continues to exist, misunderstood and indirectly
intended; in effect, the neurosis attempts to infiltrate the very consistency of the words,
but that consistency and otherness of language come naturally from the fact that language came to him through others and he remains *spoken* by them. The neurotic does
not connect this *consequence* to its primary cause.

ible self. Talent—like *exis*—would, if it existed, contain a communicative intention that would be denied and shattered by the systematic rejection of all communication and the quest for that absolute point at which lived experience, heavily charged with social desires, would realize them by ridding itself of all intersubjective conditioning, primarily by rejecting the distinction between the possible and the real, as we do in dreams. It may be asserted that we write to free ourselves of our neurosis, and that talent, in this case, is the good fortune that allows such a deliverance by projecting it into the world, inscribing it there. But this solution is merely wordgames, and a vicious circle at that: we would write to detach ourselves from the subjective, but how can we do this if we haven't already taken our distance? And what would be the significance of the neurosis-talent dichotomy, reminiscent as it is of the abstract opposition between reason and the passions introduced by classical philosophers? Talent, if it existed, would be spoiled from the first by neurotic infiltrations, and so would be ever more resistant to itself the more it was dazzled by the "unspeakable" illuminations of neurosis. Why should one go through hell, then, to express what is in theory inexpressible, not as an inert determination escaping verbal expression by its very nature, but as a fundamental refusal to be made rational, fixed, and displayed through a systematic effort of expression? And what *would* that talent *express*? For literature flushes out words hidden in things and feelings; but if there are no words, or if they are stolen and used against speech as obscure talismans, what can this literary probing lead to? We can name only that which demands a name; in a word, if neurosis issues in a *work*, then talent, a view of the mind, has nothing to do with it, and we must seek its explanation in the neurotic process as a whole.

And even that would not suffice. We can easily demonstrate—and we have done so—that for Flaubert, fame and literature were, at first, merely neurotic phantasms closely linked to that other phantasm, the paternal curse, and that in order to write and to be reborn (a secondary and phantasmatic desire), and equally to escape the arid wisdom of his father, he chose to go deeper into subjectivization and *realize*, through a memorable crisis, the principal themes of his preneurosis—old age, the infantilism of regression, the rejection of change, a break with the real, and living death—as a set of suffered prohibitions that condemned him to sequestration and to dreaming. We know too that at that time he was rationalizing and universalizing his neurotic qualities by using them to build a system of aesthetic norms, which amounted to defining *his task*. Defining it but not accomplishing it:

24

until 1848 it remained more a dream than an enterprise. Hence two related questions: How does he shift to execution—that is, how does he objectify the subjective, which is a way of turning his back on subjectivization? And since he always remained faithful to his values, that is, to the transposition of his neurotic phantasms into canons of art and style, how could the work that was the issue of this fidelity become integrated with the Objective Spirit? In other words, how could one man's madness become a collective madness and even the *aesthetic justification* of his times? For in our investigation to this point we have not yet succeeded in generating the *writer* Flaubert from Gustave the family idiot, who dreamed of writing but also imagined he was a musician without understanding anything of music. Which means, of course, that his writing—at least until and excluding the first *Education*—remained incantatory and masturbatory, whatever its quality. But this also reveals new difficulties. To be a writer is not only to write words in a notebook, it is to be published and then read. To be a *famous* writer, as he became from one day to the next, is to create scandal but also to arouse admiration and enthusiasm. These apparently opposite reactions have the same meaning: the resistances of certain social strata (today we can define them by class, socio-professional milieu, residential area, age, sex, etc.) are accompanied by a new awareness in others, and the intensity of the awareness to resistance bears witness to the aptness of the work, its topicality. It was unexpected, of course: the most enlightened public merely expects the reprise of the same works under other signatures. But when it appears, it wounds to the quick or reveals the need it has fulfilled. And when the fulfillment far surpasses the scandal—as was the case with *Madame Bovary*—there is *at once*, of course, *misunderstanding* (we shall see Gustave in the next volume labeled a realist and shouting his rage) and, beneath these errors of interpretation, readers and author discovering their *synchronism*.

But if the public demands to recognize itself in the work, the writer would have to live the most typical or, as the Americans say, the most "popular" common experience. With more or less distance, to be sure, and *in his own way*. This would be his only chance to produce what *in any case* a work must be: a singular universal. The singularization of the universal (the idiosyncratic internalization of the external in and through the author's experience) produces in the reader the universalization of the singular. This means he understands that particular experience through the obscure abstract generalizations that refer him to his own particularity. But how is it conceivable that a

25

neurotic work, produced by a patient as a means of subjectivization, could disclose to the reader anything other than a singularity that is posed for itself *against the universal,* and consequently presents itself during reading as the absolute Other, crying out to the public: *"You are not me* because *I don't want to be you"*? Perhaps, despite everything, we feel distantly touched in that slime resting on the bottom of every pond. But the explicit refusal to communicate, which characterizes the neurotic (or psychotic) work, serves as a pretext to each of us to refuse in turn to be *affected* by alien phantasms. The work seems to be closed in on itself, meant only for itself, limited despite certain beauties to the complacent exposition of a case. The interest we bring to it, then, limited as it is, can only be objective and documentary: "There are people like this." Yet it will quickly fade—a clinical study will be more compelling; it describes symptoms, isolates the illness, classifies it in one of the great psychoneurotic categories, and in some cases attempts at least a conjectural etiology. In short, it is informative. A morbid work, *experienced* neurosis, is not informative; it is merely upsetting. Assuming that, under exceptional circumstances, it holds one's attention for a moment, can we imagine it has anything to teach us? It would have to create a certain need in the public that it alone can fill, *and at the same time* specialized readers—writers and "artistic people"—would have to see it as a revelation of the true meaning of their enterprise and appropriate it to surpass it toward their own ends. Two impossibilities: the neurosis, by posing its singularity in the work, deprives itself of the means to transform itself into the required Objective Spirit; boxed into the present, it cannot in principle initiate a future cycle. Yet today's reader may find it to his liking: historical circumstances—too numerous to indicate here—have caused us, as I have said, to prefer the infinite to the finite and consequently the incomplete to the complete, the monster to the pure product of art. But it is unimaginable that our great-grandfathers in 1857 could have recognized themselves in a morbid book, or that a neurotic, offering himself as such in his writings, could have enlisted followers and changed the form, the content, the meaning of literature.

We return to our point of departure. In 1844 Gustave is locked into his neurosis; his intention to write is the neurotic consequence of the Flaubert family's disequilibrium, being structurally half-bourgeois, half-rural, with the relation to the father predominant. Achille-Cléophas's death clearly diminishes the adverse pressure on his son. But he is far from being cured: he loiters and daydreams, literature as a neurotic demand is manifest to him as a prohibition, and condemns him to impotence. We could not, moreover, reconcile the decreasing frequency of the attacks or even their later disappearance with a perfect cure: Gustave is a hysteric and will be one all his life. His life is organized around his neurosis to such an extent that it sometimes seems to him, in his hours of discouragement, that far from sacrificing his life to art, art serves him as an excuse not to live. The principles and norms of his aesthetic, moreover, seemed a short while ago merely a transposition of the chief intentions of his hysteria. It is the particular system "made for one man," and therefore incommunicable; it is the sequestration Flaubert attributes in his last years "to the fear of living"; it is the absolute pessimism and frantic misanthropy whose origin is not knowledge of the world or men but a certain "presentiment," the basic condition of neurosis, which is itself the product of a preneurotic *universalization* of the original (hence familial) situation. Unable to denounce or change it, the child masks it to himself (and masks his anomaly) by seizing upon radical evil as the ruling principle of human relations. This self-defensive reaction to the ostracism he believes he suffers is finally just the abstract thought of the negative: Is it possible to derive from it a system of norms, a synthetic and concrete idea of artistic labor, a form as imperative, a content as requisite? No, *that cannot really happen*; morbid universalization is here falsely objective and can generate neither rule nor content; at most it can delude itself by generating symbolic and sado-masochistic narratives in which everything is arranged to show vice rewarded and virtue punished. Moreover, Flaubert's radical misanthropy—often translated by that dream of dying unknown, *his very name* forgotten— may not prevent him at other moments from desiring glory (he imagines it as a way of debasing the human race); but I contend that it creates in him, from adolescence on, a pathology of communication which deteriorates until his project of writing. Hence this paradox: Gustave's neurosis could produce, *strictly speaking*, only neurotic works that would have repelled the public of 1850. Yet *because of it*, between the ages of thirty and forty he wrote a book that is dense and full, with an aesthetic rigor (not classical, however, since the "form of its content" is a draining away and it owes its beauty to the union of these opposites, the "marble" stability of the sentence subservient to the sliding toward death, or, if you will, the immutable charged with representing both immobility and movement) that imposes itself on the public and, for the writers of his time, initiates a future cycle, though the norms of the new art are still unclear (for until his preface to *Dernières chansons*, which is not even very good, Gustave never

27

wrote about those norms publicly) and, *just because of that*, as if a concrete task were to be invented and achieved. This book, a concrete reality posed to the public as an enigma—because its mode of production remains unknown—becomes, as do all great works, institutional. Gustave, of course, is not the one who institutes it (as the normative determination of a certain sector of the social imagination); whoever its author, this operation does not belong to him; by a profound affinity with his time, he merely provides the means of the consecration. And his integration into that totality called the *Objective Spirit* of his society provokes a totalizing transformation of that organism, which must be altered from top to bottom to assimilate him.[6]

This paradox can be explained only if we assume that a work by itself transcends the stage of neurotic complacence and contains the structures of objectivity. But, being the issue of that *subjectivization* characteristic of neurosis, it can in fact generate in itself only the elements of *false objectivity* (for example, pathological universalization). Its author, then, is incapable of accomplishing this transcendence and objectifying himself in it as a singular universal, furnishing the public with a critical mirror held up to contemporary society. The public itself, in this particular case, is the agent that transforms this false witness into a true witness of his time. And since the work's objectivity remains false *in principle* (there is nothing to prevent panoramic consciousness, immobilism, and radical misanthropy from being mistakenly adopted with the resulting familiar contradictions), its truth—its power to express the times—can come to it, through an external qualification which it internalizes, only from the times themselves. In other words, its false objectivity will become true in its very falsity if the various social strata that constitute its public see its past and present circumstances *with false objectivity*. But this is not all. There is no society based on the division of labor and on exploitation that does not have an objective but false idea of itself, in particular when that idea is produced by the ruling classes as their self-justification and as the edifying mystification that the exploited classes must be made to swallow. We call this unreal but quite rigorously constructed totality *ideology*. Can we say that all ideology is a collective neurosis? To do so would be to abuse a rigorous concept. This abuse, moreover, would serve no purpose; in other times, with other ideologies, morbid works have gone unnoticed, unremarked, slip-

6. This is not a matter of organicism, as you might think. I shall clarify my views on this subject further on.

ping into nothingness before awakening the slightest resonance. And such public indifference results when the norms of art imply the rationality of the work. In the age of Voltaire and the Encyclopedists, the idea of beauty imposed by a combative bourgeoisie whose most potent weapon was critical reason suggests a rigorous construction, rules based on rationality rather than custom, communication between author and reader, the final objective of the universalizing enterprise, which is the aesthetic agreement (a universal determination of sensibility pathos-demand) of all readers. By the same token, art was defined by health, normality, the equilibrium of the artist, and even without making this negative consequence explicit, it was agreed that a madman cannot be an artist since madness *makes no concessions*. At that time, as in many other times, a morbid work hadn't the slightest chance of being read; furthermore—whatever it might be—it would bear witness neither to the miserly and conscientious bourgeois busy making their pile, trying to find the laws of mercantile capitalism by conceiving of them as rules of the economy *in general* and on the model of natural laws, encouraging scientific research with a view to its future practical utility, and combating customary privilege by substituting analytic positivism for history; nor to the aristocrats, whether traditionalist or enlightened, skeptical and sometimes even cynical, who would initiate the Revolution even before the third estate. They read Nerciat, they enjoyed Faublas because that superficial eroticism is a *rational* diversion; but de Sade's black, profound eroticism found no public because the books it produced, despite the undeniable beauty of their extravagance and the radicalism of the questions they raised, manifestly fell into the category of neurotic works.

This society, however, is fueled by false ideas: the idea of nature, of human nature, of natural law, is false; the fundamental conception of a bourgeoisie conceiving of itself as a universal class is false. The public of 1850 must have not only an erroneous notion of the structures of its society and its origins; in the cultivated strata of the society those errors must be of a *neurotic* sort and manifest in themselves underlying affinities with Flaubert's neurosis. Only in this way will Flaubert's neurosis, even in its systematic subjectivization, bear witness to those errors. Going one step further we can say that Gustave's malady will allow him to be objectified in representative works only if it appears as a particularization of what must surely be called a *neurosis of the Objective Spirit*. Not only does Flaubert's deviation become the measure and expression of a certain loss of direction of the com-

29

munity on the sociocultural level, but in the objective neurosis in which he participates the young patient finds general aims that surpass his own and give them universality; even his abstractions will a priori find their flesh and blood, their concrete substance, in the multiple determinations of the multitude. The tools of his creation, the techniques and especially that "taste" he has coveted, everything that seemed to escape him in the preneurotic state he will have the good fortune to fix *in objectivity* not only as products of a culture going off the deep end but also as the still unnoticed or unexplicit means of objectively structuring his works. In other words, if his neurosis is the result of an objective illness, the work resulting from it doubly escapes neurotic subjectivization. As testimony, its truth expresses the false collective testimony; as irreducible novelty, it derives from the objective realm—especially from the works of contemporaries— methods that will endow it, at the very least, with that rigorous and non-neurotic necessity, aesthetic unity, and will consequently transform it into a singular imperative.

At this stage of our investigation we are compelled to reverse the terms and ask ourselves if art does not affirm one of its historic moments—that very moment fitting to the second half of the nineteenth century—through the neuroses of Flaubert and the great authors of his generation. In this case, instead of conceiving of Flaubert's art and its normative principles as the result of his neurosis—which brings us back to a pure subjectivization contradicted by his work— shouldn't we conceive of Gustave's neurosis as a product of art-to-be-made, its pathological aspect originating in the impasses of art already-made and its objective requirement—its meaning being that for art to be possible, these impasses must be surmounted—a requirement which, by the very nature of those impasses, will never be satisfied except by neurotic inventions? In Flaubert, art would become neurosis to survive its contradictions by an illusory surpassing and *hold on* until the general movement of the society has surpassed but not resolved them. In this case we would have to seek, at the core of subjectivization, elements of objectivity that, far from arising from the neurosis, would take possession of it, penetrate it, direct it in the name of a transcendent finality—a finality that is external, even in the very core of neurotic immanence—but without any *personal* agent. In contrast to the Father's curse—which is a factor of subjectivization since the subject grasps it at the heart of lived experience as an *other* will and relates it to a well-defined person—a teleological and normative system would be organized in and through

Flaubert's mental troubles without, however, leaving the realm of the anonymous and without being defined other than as the surpassing required by the objective contradictions of literature. In mentioning this rigorous structuring—and the transcendent imperative: if you want to write *today*, you must go crazy—in conjunction with the curse of Achille-Cléophas, an idiosyncratic and purely familial fact, whose consequence is a particular and purely subjective neurosis (which can, strictly speaking, be conceived of as a mode of Flaubert's intersubjectivity), I wanted to indicate the complexity of the problem. Indeed, if we must accept the hypothesis that Gustave's subjective neurosis is the internalization, and then the reexternalization, of *art-to-be-made* as a contradictory set of impersonal imperatives, we would be equally compelled to take account of familial structures and the will of the symbolic Father, which are the determining factors of Gustave's neurosis in its *other* guise as an irreducible singularity. What relation can be established between these two types of conditionings? And how can the same illness *at the same time* be valid as a solution to social antinomies and as an individual issue? We have witnessed the genesis of the Flaubertian aesthetic, and we have seen in its principles—immutability, panoramic consciousness, impersonalism, an identification of beauty and evil—the rationalization and universalization of a self-defensive system that at other moments acknowledges it is "made for one man." If we must now admit that when he chose—during the preneurotic period—to reward his exile with literary glory, he released an objective process that directs the internal evolution of his malaise and ineluctably transforms that malaise into neurosis because art, to remain vital and survive this thankless period, needs neurotic ministers, we are faced with two contradictory interpretations of the attacks ravaging Gustave's existence. The first supports Maxime: immutability, the rejection of immediate reality, and the principle of panoramic consciousness (speaking only of those fundamental determinations originating exclusively in the structures of the Flaubert family for the sole purpose of elaborating a defensive strategy—when all is already lost) offer themselves as false aesthetic norms; art, defined and conceived exclusively for Gustave's individual salvation, loses all its substance, which is a considerable impoverishment. In the second hypothesis, art, as a function of its very impossibility, transforms Gustave into that chosen vehicle by which literature, already half ship-wrecked, will be saved and brought into port. The neurosis is thus *positive*, appearing to be the only means conceivable in 1850 by which something like art might be possible,

31

despite its new impossibility and especially *because* of that impossibility. Flaubert would then be a martyr, his difficulties requisite and his life *exemplary*. The erroneous principles at the origin of his aesthetic system by no means represent—as Maxime would have it—abstract, empty rules, a sort of artistic Eleatism, but should be imagined—starting from its *results*, from *Madame Bovary*, for example—as the substructure necessary to a new and concrete conception of literary art and its object. Flaubert's Catharism would then appear as the monastic rule that imposes itself for half a century on respectable writers. Can these contradictory interpretations be entertained at once? We cannot say as yet. Whether one *can* accept them together or not, however, they *must* certainly be taken at the same time; for without the first, how do we explain the attacks, the sequestration, the stupor, the conduct of failure? And without the second, how do we explain *Madame Bovary*?

To conceive of the strange reciprocity uniting the singular and the collective in Gustave, we must first define what we call the Objective Spirit and its neurotic determination. In what follows we shall see the exigencies and contradictions of literature during this period, the questions it raised for the Postromantics, and the reason why the only responses possible, not only for Flaubert but for his contemporaries, were psychopathic. We shall then endeavor to return to Gustave and determine *to what extent* and *how* the insoluble problems of art are at the heart of his troubles: how these can be—despite apparent contradictions—a neurotic response both to a subjective malaise and to the objective malaise of literature. Only by this method shall we perhaps manage to discover whether Flaubert's illness produced a mental deficit of some kind or whether, to the contrary, it was the means for him to accede to *literature-to-be-done*, more precisely, *to do it*.

The Objective Spirit

Let us avoid any misunderstanding. At the beginning of the twentieth century, the long literary dream that began with Gustave at age twenty was completed with the last of the Symbolists. At that moment many young writers who wanted to preserve the heritage of the preceding generation and go beyond it toward a new classicism, influenced by the strange attitude of their fathers and older brothers, decided that neurosis was the necessary condition for genius, as Gide wrote of Dostoyevsky. But this post-Symbolist generation was judging conditions necessary to the work of art according to those art demanded of their immediate predecessors. In this sense they were attesting to the fact that between 1850 and the end of the century you had to be mad to write. Quite true: their ideas only confirm my own. Only I cannot accept their *generalizing*, as if the meaning and function of literature—for the individual and society—were not constantly changing in the course of history; as if, depending on the period, art did not recruit its artists according to different criteria. It *is* true that from 1830 on, for reasons I shall enumerate, some of which are still valid today if less virulent, neurosis was the royal road to the masterpiece. But this doesn't seem to me to have been the case in the eighteenth century, and even less so in the seventeenth. In those times the author was chiefly required to be a "respectable man," integrated into the society as long as he strictly observed certain rules. In this case, neurosis can exist—it does in Rousseau,[1] who may even have

---

1. Obviously, Rousseau's psychopathic state is a direct source of the *Confessions* (he had to defend himself against a conspiracy) and provides some of this autobiography's dominant themes. *Rousseau juge de Jean-Jacques*, on the other hand, can be described as a *morbid work* because it cannot be understood without reference to the author's illness. It should be observed, however, that that work, like the *Confessions*, is determined by the obsession with conspiracy. And conspiracy *did exist.* Not in the form of a rigorously

been psychotic, and probably in Pascal—but it is utilized *indirectly,* the writer writes *against his illness,* in spite of it, as Rousseau did, and not by virtue of it. In other authors it is certainly harmful: without it they would have done better or done more. In still other cases it takes its toll in different areas and so spares the literary realm. Every man, of course, is a totalization that is temporalized, and nothing can happen to him that does not affect him, one way or another, in all his parts. The point is that in integrated societies the psychoneurotic element, if it exists, is never regarded as the artist's aim, and even less as the reason for his art. I have said elsewhere that genius is a way out, the only one left when all is lost. I say so again, specifying that

---

organized cabal but rather as a tacit agreement between men who knew and understood each other well enough without direct contact or even correspondence, and certainly without a leader, to conduct a well-organized campaign; when one of them came out into the open and struck, the others knew what they had to do. This is what gives the *Dialogues* their true dimensions; though the aggression is obviously exaggerated, its reality must never be forgotten. And I would contend that the three autobiographical works (in which I include *Les Rêveries*) are written *against* Rousseau's psychopathic state because they have a *double* aim: first, of course, to show his true self to readers, who might then judge fairly the calumnious accusations leveled against him; but also to *know himself.* Whence the profound states of heart and soul that were as yet unknown in Europe; whence the dialogue form, in *Rousseau juge de Jean-Jacques,* which has been foolishly cited as the onset of mental disintegration, when, quite to the contrary, this fiction was a guarantee for Rousseau of the distance necessary to all reflexive knowledge. As for the motive of this effort to know himself, it was doubtless from the outset a quest for *serenity.* He would find serenity in part in the "Promenades," having accepted his fate. Thus, these three works together constitute at once a speech for the defense and the most sustained, the latest effort to grasp the meaning and value of a life in its fleeting, elusive flow that is often masked or deformed by the ravings of a suspicious soul. If the *Confessions* were merely an apology, we would long ago have ceased to read it. And in this sense we could speak of the work as neurotic: in it Rousseau would surrender to his phantasms. But this book is still alive after two centuries because it also contains the opposite tack: the author *wants to use it to see clearly* how to defend himself also against himself, and the apology finds its best arguments—even without using them explicitly—in that extraordinary, purifying investigation and in the decision to say *everything.* Thus—taking into account that other works offer rigorous *objective* contents—we can say that the admirable tension of style and ideas are generated in Rousseau not by his troubles but by his struggle against evil. He is a man of the eighteenth century, a citizen of Geneva, a doubly reasonable man attacked in his reason, who turns that reason on his adversary and, just as he appears to surrender to madness, devotes himself to the difficult enterprise of cleansing his understanding of the morbid infiltrations that might infect it. If literature was enriched by these invaluable works, which for the first time in centuries deliver up lived experience candidly, we owe this not only to the author's sensibility, but also above all to the work of a reason that does not abdicate. Thus the illness is the source of the work only to the degree that Rousseau engages in single combat against it. And the normative principles that define the writing—and the whole book in its composition—are, in their rigorous rationality, the opposite of a neurotic art.

this way out is not neurotic and usually even allows one to spare oneself a neurosis. In a word, when literature does not appeal to psychopathology, neurotic accidents do not take place, or, if they are produced in an author, this fact—of prime importance for understanding the individual—is annulled in the Objective Spirit because it is a matter of chance, a non-meaning in relation to the meaning of that cultural moment. And although the substitution of one form for another is made *by men* and motivated by discomfort (there is a contradiction between the earlier form and content that asks to be treated in the present), there is no reason why this discomfort, which is of a specifically cultural order, should be experienced *neurotically, unless* the particular structures of the historical moment require it.

And this is precisely what happens around 1850, a moment in which the condition for creating art is to be neurotic.[2] Not in just any way but in a specific way, which we shall attempt to define; the objective movement that transforms culture on the basis of deeper transformations—but also as a function of traditions and laws proper to the cultural sector—produces such strict and contradictory norms that the contemporary moment of art cannot be realized as a determination of the Objective Spirit except in the form of *art-neurosis*. This does not mean that the works will be neurotic but that literary doctrines and the "poetic arts" will be, and that artists will have to act, or actually be, neurotic. And because of the dual nature of the literary act, reading, while it is taking place, becomes the public's brief, induced neurosis.

This cannot be understood without several general clarifications regarding the Objective Spirit. We may well wonder if it isn't dangerous to preserve this suspect notion still bearing traces of its origins in Hegelian idealism. But there is some use in reviving it and indicating the instrumental function it can perform in the perspective of historical materialism. In fact, the Objective Spirit—in a defined society, in a given era—is nothing more than culture as practico-inert. Let us understand, first of all, that at the origin of culture is work, *lived, actual* work insofar as it surpasses and retains nature in itself by definition. Nature is the given environment during a specific period, and work reveals this environment as simultaneously that which presently exists *and* the field of possibles that can be made use of to give

---

2. Edmond de Goncourt: "Imagine, our work—and perhaps this is its originality—is dependent upon nervous illness." Cited by Bourget, *Essais de psychologie contemporaine*, vol. 2, p. 162.

that environment a new being consonant with the goal fixed by the worker, in short, with a certain condition, called the environment, that does not yet exist. Thus work is by itself antiphysis; its definition is to be antinature nature, which is precisely the essence of every cultural phenomenon. It seeks knowledge in order to transform, which implies, elementary as the work night be, that for the worker it bears witness to a type of exploitation, to a regime and the class struggle, ultimately to an ideology. And for the worker himself immersed in this exploitation, work itself redounds upon him as an enemy force; being praxis, hence an illuminating surpassing of being toward an end (a surpassing of raw material toward the production of a change within the practical field), work is the internalization of the external and the reexternalization of the internal. As such, it is lived experience and consequently reveals both itself—as imposed, for example, and remaining external even while internalized—and, through it, the fundamental human relations proper to this mode of production (the kind of reciprocity established on the level of its concrete labor, the kind of nonreciprocity generated by the division of labor and possibly by the resulting exploitation). Moreover, this work is accomplished by means of an instrument—that would alone suffice to define society and man's relation to nature, at once antiphysis (which appears on the level of carved stone) and nature appearing beyond antiphysis on the level of carved stone) and nature appearing beyond antiphysis and in it (even at the level of automation) as its internal and external limit, continually displaced. By the use he makes of it, the instrument therefore becomes the worker's *organ of perception:* it reveals the world and man in the world. Thus the most elementary praxis, insofar as it is actual and lived from the inside, already contains as an immediate condition of its later development and as a real moment of that development, *in the living state,* an intuitive, implicit and *nonverbal* knowledge, a certain direct and totalizing yet wordless understanding of contemporary man among men and in the world, hence an immediate grasp of the inhumanity of man and his subhumanity, the first seed of a *political* attitude of refusal. On this level all thought is given, but it is not posed for itself, and so in its extreme compression it escapes verbal elaboration. I have said enough about it, however, to make it clear that superstructures are not the site of this revealing but merely the upper levels of elaboration in which this practico-theoretical knowledge is isolated, posed for itself, and systematically made explicit, hence becoming theoretico-practical. Here we must take reflection as a starting point, for reflection shapes lived experience according to its own ends, though that experience is originally unreflected and becomes reflected according to certain rules that themselves issue from certain reflexive needs. In other words, in the totality of praxis reflection isolates the moment of theory, which has never existed alone but only as a practical mediation determined by the end itself. Recourse to language thus becomes necessary. And language, on the one hand, isolates and transforms into a finished product the knowledge that existed implicitly in the worker's act. It provides names and hardens in the form of defined structures all the elements that have interpenetrated in the cultural revealing of work (mode of production, relations of production, institutional whole, mores, law, etc.). Named and thus perpetuated, these fragments of the real becoming fragments of knowledge are thereby falsified. Through this quality of false knowledge they come close to being a nonknowledge, which also exists on the elementary level of the living actualization of praxis—that set of opinions arising from pathos that are proffered, at this higher degree of elaboration, as learning from experience. In fact, these extrapolations are inseparable from lived experience, and they form, if you will, class subjectivity. After processing they will become the clearest of what we call ideologies. Thus, along-side false knowledge, whose origin is a practical and nonverbalized knowledge, ideologies that impose themselves on the worker—ideologies of his class, of the middle or ruling classes—are introduced or reintroduced into him in the form of recipes explicitly presented as a verbal exposé or a related set of determinations of discourse that would illuminate his condition and offer him the means to tolerate it. This involves chiefly, of course, a conception of the world and of men formed by the ruling class in taking possession of its environment through the systematic exercise of power, and inculcated—by familiar means—in the working classes as though it were a universal ideology, or a body of knowledge. In the worker, of course, these ideologies come into permanent conflict with *his own* ideology—which issues communally, like a myth, from his hopes, his despairs, the refusal to accept his condition as an inevitable destiny—and they have the upper hand as long as working-class ideology is not *verbalized*. Were it to be so, moreover, it might encourage a sudden awareness but might just as easily retard it: class consciousness appears only at the end of a theoretico-practical effort that aims at dissolving ideology into knowledge as much as possible. I will merely cite as an example the slow emancipation of the worker in the nineteenth century. Between 1830 and 1840, his ideas were so effectively confused that *L'Atelier*, the first proletarian newspaper, insisted on Catholicism, or at least Theism, in face of the Jacobin bourgeoisie who had deprived the worker of the consolation of God. He set his knowledge in the practical realm against alien ideologies—as did the Canuts in Lyon; when wages were lowered, he rebelled. But as soon as the revolt was either victorious or suppressed, he could think explicitly about this knowledge only through alien ideologies, words and phrases that did not apply to it—quite to the contrary—and that distorted it while claiming to articulate it.

Thus, elaborated ideologies are quite distinct from that intuitive and immediate constellation I have just described, which involves an implicit ideology spun around a kernel of knowledge, accompanied by myths and a system of values tacitly applied by agents who have never articulated its basis. Not only are these elaborated ideologies distinct from it but they are in conflict with it by providing immediate and nonverbalized thought with translations that conceal it from itself. Yet it will be observed that the force of these inadequate systems comes from their inertia. Primitive and immediate thought is none other than the practical behavior of the worker insofar as it discloses in order to effect change and is necessarily accompanied by a nonpositional consciousness of itself; this presupposes a constant "syntony" of that tacit body and the real, whence its perpetual flexibility. It must exist as an act and as part of an act, or it does not exist at all. In other words, it issues from work and vanishes with it. On the other hand, *verbalized* value systems and ideologies remain in the mind, or at the very least in the memory, because language is matter and because their elaboration has given them material inertia. Written words are stones. Learning them, internalizing their combinations, we introduce into ourselves a mineralized thought that will subsist in us by virtue of its very minerality, until such time as some kind of material labor, acting on it from outside, might come to relieve us of it. I call these irreducible passivities *as a whole* the Objective Spirit. And this definition has no negative intent, no voluntary deprecation. In a society of exploitation, of course, these structured wholes are harmful to the exploited classes to the extent that they are introduced into everyone from the outside and recast in the memory as ramparts against any sudden awareness. But taken in themselves they simply manifest this necessity: matter is the mediating element between men to the same degree that through their praxis they become mediators between different states of matter. The Objective Spirit is culture itself but only in accordance with its becoming the *practico-inert*. That is valid for all its aspects, as much for the mode of production, defined by that particular wrought matter which is the instrument, as for relations between men as they are established as *institutions* and become lived institutionally. And the relational mode of wrought matter to the agent is, as I have proved elsewhere, imperative. Every object produced presents to me its directions for use as an order ("Shake contents before using," "Slow, school zone," etc.). We understand that even if, as frequently happens, the sponsor of the object in question finds his interest in the imperative form—which guarantees the proper usage of the thing—he is not the source of that form. Strictly speaking, he can present his advice only in the form of a hypothetical imperative, such as: "If you want to use this object, you must . . . ," and so forth. For the real relation between men is actually reciprocity, which excludes orders. But whatever the object produced—even a machine—the utilization that Society or any such group recommends by way of it necessarily passes *through* and consequently undergoes the transformation imposed on it by the practico-inert. Its directions for use become an inert discourse participating in the inertia of matter. As such it imposes itself on the agent as *not to be* modified by any subjective intention—not because it represents the universal in the face of the particular, but because the practical seal imposed on the raw material participates in its materiality and is introduced into everyone as an inert thought that belongs to no one but must be preserved, whose practical consequences must be derived and applied on pain of seeing the practical thing burst out. In the internal structure of this thought, in any case, we encounter material inertia (for example, in a particular and mechanical relation between premises and consequences). In sum, it represents at once the beyond of matter here present and a kind of materialization of that beyond. And if there have always been men to give orders, they should rather be considered transmitters. Besides, the "master" who commands, and usurps the inorganic minerality of the commandments given by the object, clearly plays an inorganic role in relation to the slave, and his orders obviously issue from a stone mouth, his own. Indeed, he commands as a function of his mineral being, of his interest, which is something imperative, and he augments its status as thing by depositing it into that other thing, discourse. In our view, the Objective Spirit represents culture as practico-inert, as the totality to this day (in any day) of the imperatives imposed on man by any given society.

But for our purpose, which is to study Art-neurosis as a historically specific determination of the Objective Spirit, it is preferable to imagine only a sector of that spirit: the elaborated unity of ideologies, cosmogonies, ethico-aesthetic and confessional systems as they manifest themselves as the structuring of a discourse. We have no reason to consider them in themselves, as ideas that are institutionalized, but should consider them rather as they pose to language the question of their adequate expression, and thereby define literature in the abstract as a work of material production. We are at the top of a hierarchy, and thoughts seem almost dead. But they are merely exhausted along the way: they are neither reflections nor byproducts of an infrastructural, unthinking reality but must simply be seen as the last avatars of total ideas, mute and practical, that are merely one at the outset with the act of work, of appropriation and exploitation, or a hundred other acts. This explosive combination of values, verities, ideologies, myths, and mystifications, contradicting each other insofar as they emanate from classes and—within classes—from different social strata, nonetheless poses itself as a multiple and contradictory comprehension of our species as the product of its history, of present circumstances, and of the future that it is preparing for itself "on the basis of prior circumstances." Enclosed in writing, it has become canned thought. But written language, by lending its material and institutional reality to those "expressible" thoughts, has bent them to its laws. Intellection—and likewise comprehension—is surely a synthetic surpassing of signifying materiality toward signification. Nonetheless, that surpassed matter is preserved in the act that transcends it, and it both limits and determines that act in spite of itself. Materialized in writing, culture—at this level—burdens thought with its own weight and does not derive its permanencies from a firm and sustained but still lively intention; quite to the contrary, they are the passive aspect of the idea. I am speaking, of course, of the written thing, and I am well aware that no judgment on it is ever definitive. Posterity will return to it and situate itself by situating it in new circumstances. Still, certain internal articulations, certain structures— manifest or implicit—are unvarying. Consequently, living thought as a surpassing is at once aroused, advanced, and retarded by that opacity to be surpassed which is precisely the idea as written, "thing-a-fied." Indeed, this written idea has set its seal upon matter, but matter has in turn invaded the idea-seal, infected it with its heteronomy, better known as the principle of exteriority. It has broken the interiority of the original thought—a translucid presence of the all in the parts and the parts in the all—and substituted the *letter* in its place by penetrating even its minutest aspect with an external scattering. The idea becomes a thing: once imprinted, its tendency to persevere in its being is precisely that of the thing. When the library is deserted, thought dies; the thing alone remains, made of paper and ink.

Writing operates on a dual principle: one person writes, the other reads. Without the reader, nothing is left, not even signs—for their only function is to guide the project of transcendence. We might almost speak of an abstract virtuality, which does not come from the book itself but determines it from the outside insofar as it becomes the object of various intentions: of the librarian who arranges a catalogue, or of future readers who promise themselves that "one day" they will read or reread the work. These considerations lead us to several conclusions.

1. *The Objective Spirit*, while *never* on the side of pure lived experience and free thought, exists *as an act* only through the activity of men and, more precisely, through the activity of *individuals*. As far as we are concerned, it is clear that without readers it simply would not exist. On the other hand, in the intimacy of a room, in classrooms or libraries, millions of people read millions of books, each of which contains references to other works not consulted at that moment. A detotalized totalization is thereby effected; each reader totalizes his reading *in his own way*, which is at once similar to and radically distinct from the totalization that another reader, in another town, another neighborhood, tries to realize *with the same book*. From this point of view, the multiplicity of individual totalizations (they are not all related to the same book but to different sectors of written knowledge, many implicitly referring to each other) seems irreducible. It would take too long to explain here how, despite the apparent atomization, this set of circumstances continually effects an exhaustive totalization without a totalizer. My point is, rather, that following generations will make today's lived present into a totality that is past, surpassed, still virulent in certain ways, and readers, individually or as a group, vaguely sense this. So they feel they must work their particular synthesis of one detail of a sector of knowledge in the stable and inherently dated milieu of accomplished totality. And this totality—as it appears to them, an invisible unity of the diverse, a transcendence that destroys their present immanence, a future that eradicates experience in men's hearts as it is being lived in the name of experience to be lived by future readers—represents for each of them the totalitarian objectivization of each one's particular efforts

41

of acculturation. In this future objectivization, whose meaning is still unknown and which, as such, is aspired to only through empty intentions, they find their ineffable objective unity: it makes them, for themselves, representatives of *the times*. But as their praxis at this moment is reading—an effort, indeed, of acculturation—these living times that have already been fixed and described appear to them in their cultural aspect (the limits of knowledge, unresolved problems, areas of ignorance, established convictions to be revoked by the future). Seen from another angle, this is precisely the Objective Spirit of the age, an imperative constellation, unlimited but finite, whose thought cannot yet emerge.

2. However, although a gaze is needed to restore it by making it readable today, the Objective Spirit is characterized on this level by its position *outside,* not the present product of an effort of thought but first and foremost *in books,* in the writings of *others.* In this sense its materiality expresses at once its alterity (in relation to the reader) and its pastness (it bears a date, *it may already be dated;* recent works may be better informed, it may be challenged six months from now by works as yet unpublished). In any event, reading is an attempt to transform a thing into an idea. The eye must recover the ideative act of the other through its vestiges, gather up the scattering of signs, and discursively *recompose* according to learned codes what may formerly have been the object of flashes of intuition. Our concern, for the moment, is with the double character of the Objective Spirit, which can be a surpassing toward the idea *in us* only if it is *outside,* as worked matter. The guarantee of its permanence is its status as thing: it does not exist, it *is,* and the only dangers threatening it come from outside, from great natural forces and social disorders. And when I transform the thing into an idea by reading, the metamorphosis is never complete; it is an idea-thing penetrating me because the reality of that hybrid being which I alone can revive is necessarily outside me as thought frozen in matter, and because that thought, even as I make it mine, remains definitively *other,* thought surpassed by another who orders me to revive it. Furthermore, the idea I appropriate is also, I know, appropriated by other readers at the same time; these are people I don't know, who are not like me, and who surpass the same material toward similar but perceptibly different significations. Thus every lexeme remains *within me* external to me to the extent that I perceive it as enriched by a thousand interpretations that escape me; the book, a finite mode of the Objective Spirit, appears both internal

and external in relation to the reader. Reading is an internalization according to definite procedures, but the sentence is never entirely soluble. Its indestructible materiality derives at once from the frozen rigidity of the *vestige* and from its multiple relation—for every reader —to others. In other words, its *virtual* extension to a whole public and its current connections with *series* or readers or *groups,* or the two together. In this sense, writing gives us a glimpse of society as one of the elements of its essential duality. Or, if you will, the exteriority of writing makes it appear to every reader as a *social object.* This, indeed, is *what it is.* If apprehended in its relations to the seriality of readings, it seems to be a *collective,* a real index of social detotalization. Through it we measure the *separation* of individuals in an envisaged society; its mystery represents the false union of readers, each of whom is unaware of the other's thoughts. In our societies this may be the result of the creation of mass culture; in this case, as the words penetrate the person reading, that person internalizes *his own solitude* in the face of an impenetrable block of exigent sociality, without considering that this sociality is nothing but the detotalization of a collectivity as lived socially by each of its members. In short, the social opacity of the book and its institutional character refer quite simply to an indefinite number of other solitudes. In this way, the book as *collective* is, in a sense, a *sacred* object; its "numinous" character is manifest most clearly when we imagine it in its occasional relations with uniformed people who read very little. When they approach a work— recommended by others whom they trust—they treat the text as if it were composed of *carmina sacra,* according it the same *respect.* In effect, they are dimly if inarticulately aware that by absorbing those little pointed black splinters we call words, they are about to swallow society whole.But they also know that it will remain *outside* as the collective character of the book, even as they are trying to install in themselves the content of the work as *knowledge.* Thus, through its exteriority the duality becomes a trinity: the relation reader-author refers to the usually serial relation among readers. The profundity of an *idea* I have *read,* as I have retained and understood it, *is others:* those significations that I have not grasped but that I know to have been awakened by the gaze of others as *underlying structures* of the legible object. Profundity is therefore an abstraction that haunts me, especially if I know and lament the gaps in my education, and it is an intention that misses its mark insofar as it *escapes me* in certain respects. It is a way of isolating myself with respect to society *grasped through its culture;* moreover, this abstract but present profundity defining the work in its objectivity comes to me as an imperative: I *must* understand what the author wanted to say as best I can, and in its totality, to the extent that others have exalted the meaning of the work and made those ideas-things incandescent. Obviously I will not complete this task—I know that well enough, and how far I get depends on my education, my greater or lesser degree of familiarity with abstractions, the time I have at my disposal, etc. But the imperative is to push as far as I can, to become integrated with new social strata; when I can go no further, the mysterious residue represents the unfathomable, indefinite social realm, or, more precisely, seriality.

If the work refers to a group—and it must be a sworn group—the imperatives are much more rigorous. For a young communist, the *Manifesto* of 1848 is at once the work of Marx, an objective description of reality, and the theory-practice that creates the unity of the Party to which he has just given his allegiance. The individual aspect of the work, its relation to the dead author, tends to be effaced (as does the relation of Carnot's principle, or some other discovery in the natural sciences, to the living man who invented it). On the other hand, the second characteristic is sustained and exalted by the third: the *processes* articulated by Marx and Engels, the events presented and illuminated by the class struggle, are not purely and simply facts for this neophyte. They are *also* facts and perhaps *primarily* facts, as we have just seen, insofar as knowledge absorbs such thinkers and eliminates them, but they are also what he *must* understand to realize a total integration with the group; and furthermore they are practical considerations which *must* illuminate his understanding of the current politics of his Party and his individual tasks. The book is structured as a collective to the extent that any group is necessarily penetrated by seriality (it may be that students or young workers meet regularly to read the book and discuss it. Only *this evening* the young man has gone to his room and reads without friends or witnesses). But while this ambiguous structure reminds the isolated reader *in this fashion* of his present solitude, it defines it not as a real and permanent state but as both a product of bourgeois society (therefore as a yoke to be thrown off) and a danger: all alone, I have no one to stop me from making a mistake. I must try to read as if I were *everyone together*. It is my vow—my commitment to the Party—that determines my reading; the book restores the group as the normative determination of my activities.

All these remarks, of course, derive from the fact that the work, something inert, continues to *be-there* passively, the way an object in motion continues to move indefinitely if nothing comes along to stop it. And the work presents itself to everyone in the name of that inertia as having existed before the current act of reading, existing elsewhere, in other libraries, and living on after the present reading. The book, whatever it is, and whether it conveys fact or fiction, virtually gives us the assertoric itself in the imperative form. Indeed, I distinguish two imperatives: the first—crude, obscure and solitary—is linked to seriality. We *must* read the Goncourts because everyone reads them and we should be able to discuss them; so we also *must* understand and judge them. The second imperative, which refers to the platoon and its unity, is the imperative of freedom—at least in principle. But in both we see that comprehension is not defined in each reader by the free play of his possibilities and the quiet recognition of their limits; rather it is required, and when at the end of his resources the reader halts midway, he feels guilty and regards his limits not as factual givens (linked to the empirical conditions of his intellectual development) but as a moral fault and a premeditated failure (in the past he *could* have learned more, even today he *should have been able* to concentrate more, to ask more of his intelligence— and of course none of this is true). In other words, when human intentions are addressed to us through worked matter, materiality renders them *other;* inert but indelible, they designate us as *other* than ourselves and our fellow citizens. Human reciprocity is broken by the mediation of the thing, and the frozen intention that summoned us *as others* can have only the structure of obligation. Thus the Objective Spirit—which is culture as practico-inert—can address itself to us, even in literature, only as an *imperative.* This is its very constitution, and it cannot be changed, even if we accomplish the task of intellection or comprehension prescribed to us, because of the indestructible residue of materiality that remains in us after reading, and which we apprehend as a failure or an unjustifiable halt in our mental operations. The Objective Spirit reveals our finitude and compels us to regard it as a fault.

These remarks, of course, are not meant to restore reading—or the transformation of the thing-idea into an idea-thing—into its plenitude. The syntheses of recomposition are in fact accomplished according to objective rules (the structures of language, the author's explicit and implicit intentions, the judgments on the author made by other authors we have already read, etc.) *and,* simultaneously, according to the idiosyncratic *habitus* of a singular internalization (oneirism, resonances, bad faith, ideological interests, etc.). As a result, the work, apprehended by a developed—at least partially closed—individuality, is never entirely taken for what it is; it is read in the light of the historical moment and of the cultural means at the reader's disposal (which indeed rank him in one social stratum or another); and at the same time the act of reading serves as a pretext for each reader to relive his own history and perhaps the primal scene. Be that as it may, under this subjective camouflage the skeleton of imperatives remains, directing the readerly thoughts as much as and more than they seem guided by the reader's oneiric (and purely factual) compliance.

3. This would be of little importance if, in the sector concerning us, the Objective Spirit as it is fundamentally materialized did not manifest itself to readers as the disparate contiguity of works belonging to all social categories and all periods. As soon as this atemporal juxtaposition is internalized and realized in me, it becomes explosive. I may have chosen *these* books and tried to digest them to satisfy my singular needs; as a systematic resurrection, reading constitutes me as the objective mediation between the cultural past and present, and between different conceptions to which contemporary works appeal. By awakening *meanings* through a totalizing movement whose source is my personal unity, I provoke collisions of ideas and feelings, and by lending them my time and my life I exalt and exacerbate innumerable contradictions. Now, given our earlier descriptions, we already know that these contradictions are written in stone: they are rooted in the inertia of thesis and antithesis. They coexist outside me in the pure, nonsignifying being-there of the thing; internalized, they are revealed through my subjectivity, but still retain the rigidity that characterizes them on the outside. We are not, in effect, dealing with a flexible and fluctuating confrontation with an idea, which in a practical totalization would set the all against the part and the parts against each other. There is no whole; only disjunctures, contradictory theses, whose authors were often unaware they contradicted each other since they were unacquainted. Thus the oppositions are at once rigid and without real consistency, not having been generated by a rigorous totalization. The operation proposed to the reader here is the reverse: he must totalize and surpass toward a synthesis starting from those given contradictions revealed in contingency. I say he *must* totalize because, as we have seen, every idea of the Objective Spirit imposes itself as a demand as soon as it is invoked. Furthermore, when two ideas-demands are manifest at the same time in a

reading, these contrary imperatives imply a third imperative: to reconcile or transcend toward a synthesis, to integrate these notions
gleaned somewhat at a random into the organic unity of a totalization
that produces and surpasses them, and will itself be an imperative.
Thus the Objective Spirit, an external-internal reality whose source—
as far as we are now concerned—is the dual aspect of writing, is
characterized both as a sum of inert demands and as a supreme, ubiquitous imperative that summons the reader to dissolve contradictions
in the unity of an ongoing totalization. I say "ongoing" because the
Objective Spirit renews itself: every day it is enriched by new books,
new demands. And these new writings can very well become integrated into one or another personal totalization effected by readers.
But they can also set themselves against any such a totalization. In
this case, everyone must get back to work again and break the determinations (the negations, the limits) of his totalization with respect
to the new work and its silent demand, so it can be included. And as
the number of books published each day far surpasses the individual
possibility of totalizing written culture, the perpetual addition of new
material has the effect of preventing the totalization from closing in
on itself and being transformed into a tranquil totality. This is what
we will call the life of the Objective Spirit, a material detotalization
internalized as a demand to be totalized which contradicts that dream
of stone, totality in inertia, by the constant and nullifying appearance
of new productions. The Objective Spirit of an age[3] is at once the
sum of works published during a specific period and the multiplicity of totalizations effected by contemporary readers. As we know,
thoughts are living things. They are born of original thought, which
is merely practical behavior as it reveals the environment from the
totalizing perspective of its reorganization. When thoughts are in libraries, they are petrified by writing and therefore dead. The reader
recomposes them, yet he does not reach the profound and naked life
of the root-thought; the *lived* reality he confers by internalizing them
cannot be a return to thought before writing: it assumes the written
word and can merely animate the graphemes by binding them together in an interior synthesis. In this sense he is still distancing himself from primal spontaneity; his own personal, practical field is not
defined by needs and physical dangers but is composed of books and
words, and his work is the perpetual stirring up and reorganization
of this field on command. Yet his practical thoughts are indeed spon-

3. I am, of course, defining it only in the realm of writing.

taneous in that they represent his conscious behavior (reflexive or unreflected) as a reader. Hence, whatever the content of the Objective Spirit as canned thoughts, we can say that every cultivated reader formally intuits it—totalizing it in the abstract—insofar as that intuition simply illuminates the multiple aspects of reading.

Awakened significations do not demand only to be understood or even totalized: these engraved signs refer to the universe, to our being-in-the-world, and primarily to our conduct. We are led back to the real environment, full of surprising traps, that we left behind upon entering the library. Knowledge and ideas are—more or less directly—practical; so it is through our personal praxis that we must try to accomplish this veritable totalization demanded by books (through techniques, ethics, religions, etc.). Action, being the totalizing of doctrines, thus transforms us; we become representatives of a past or future group that we intuit behind the imposed practico-inert idea, or a group we will form by winning it over to our practical totalization. For the Objective Spirit tells us, contradictorily but imperatively, who we are: in other words, what we have to do.

We are chiefly concerned, however, with a category of specialized readers who read in order to write. In them, literature plays the role of recruiting officer. No doubt their choice to become writers represents a subjective way out of their difficulties and problems. We have seen this in Flaubert's case. But just as you can become a shoemaker for accidental reasons and through particular events, and those reasons and events do not alter the objective need to know how to repair shoes according to current techniques and use an awl *properly,* so every reader who reads in order to write will discover literature as it is in his time even before deciding to be an apprentice author. In short, none of them, in any age, invented or reinvented literature. We might say that it is reinvented in them as an obligation to write from the starting point of literature already written. In every historical society in which an individual decides to be a writer—whatever the outcome—literature is given to him primarily as a totality he chooses to enter. This totality, of course, is not given to him in all its details, by which I mean in all works of literature; quite the contrary, the individual's approach to the All is variable. We have Flaubert's totality, Proust's—which might be called "highly literate"—as well as that of the young shepherd whose writings were published by *Les Temps modernes,* who had read only almanacs, newspapers, and a few books by Victor Hugo. Yet none of them *invented* literature for his own ends. It existed, and each of those would-be writers, according to certain features of what I call literature-already-written, deemed it advisable to enter an apprenticeship and become a representative of literature-to-be-written. So literature seems to be a practical activity and manifests itself by the existing results of that activity, literary works, which the aspiring writer reads differently than a simple reader, in order to discover through inspection of the finished product the rules that aided its production and which he wants to know for his own use.

The difficulties he encounters are therefore of several kinds.

a) He reads each properly literary work as an All that defines literary activity. And as his major project is to write and the work read is a piece of writing, that writing becomes an obscure organization of imperatives he must assimilate that will provide him with rules. Early in his apprenticeship he does not envisage *originality*, or rather he conceives it as the production of a new work according to the old rules. For in some obscure way he feels new, of a new generation conditioned by the more or less profound changes of the society into which he was born. He imagines, therefore, that he will be original in any event through the new content he will give his books, for in them he will speak, according to tried and true methods, of new matters revealed to him by this set of circumstances. None of this is clear to him, but perhaps if he can treat a subject particular to *his time* by applying authorized rules, he will write a universal and singular book. Singular in its subject; universal in its formulas. In other words, conditioned by his prehistory and his protohistory he is in contradiction with the general rules of his profession (or the prevailing way of life), yet the imperatives engendered by the practico inert are not diminished, and he fails to realize that his personality is no longer quite syntonic with past methods. The contradiction, moreover, varies according to periods and persons: in some it is veiled; in others it is visibly explosive. This problem, in short, recapitulates the generational struggle.

Thus, whatever the subjective motivations of the choice, *written* literature—that determination of the Objective Spirit—must be considered in every case the objective reason for the choice to write, for its continuation through other pens.

b) When reading is done *with* the intention of writing, it is prospective. Seeking and revealing in the narrative itself the norms that led the author to produce the work being read, it presents them to the

49

future man of letters as aesthetic requirements and at the same time as formulas he will later apply. But more importantly, that conception of art read between the lines or sometimes clearly articulated by the author determines the adolescent in his future being, revealing to him and imposing on him a certain status. It defines the public to whom he must address himself, the kind of relationship he will have with it; and by so doing it classifies him, assigns him a rank in society, defines his powers. In this conception, literature defines its subject; not only does it sketch out themes he will have to develop, but by this very choice it orients his subjectivity, dictating feelings, emotions he will cultivate in particular, determining whether he must establish the predominance of reason over affect or, to the contrary, throw himself into passion, subject the reasons of reason to the reasons of the heart. A book read from the perspective of writing another book paints a portrait of the future artist which is none other than that of a dead author becoming the young reader's major imperative and his destiny. A few biographical details will do the rest; their very inertia will serve as a prophecy, surpassed, preserved, and surpassed again. Indeed, in this realm of the Objective Spirit the life of a writer is a book or a chapter, printed matter. It is set in words that perpetuate it, lending it with their material passivity a perennial quality that makes it both a particular affirmed essence—which its inert permanence tears away from that author's first affirmation and transports, moment by moment, as pure matter in itself—and an exemplary existence, a model to be imitated, through the reading of an adolescent who wants to write. It is not surprising that literature presents itself to the young reader who awakens it as form and content, a subject to be treated, a way and style of life, finally as the underlying determination of his idiosyncrasy—the all in the form of an imperative. It appears as a totality in any era we single out; economic, social, and political conditions—historical circumstances—assign to the writer in one fell swoop his subject, his level of life, his place in society. These different features are together symbolic, and by *articulating each other* they reveal the place that a given community assigns to writing— its status and meaning, or, if you will, its public. It is, in fact, crucial whether the literary thing addresses itself to certain people or to everyone, to one class or another; this relation to the public is a fundamental given on the basis of which we can establish *what there is to say*, and *why*, and *by whom*. Thus through a literary work, whatever it is, the young reader grasps as his future a global and past reality he *must* restore. Naturally, this apprehension of the Other as a future self to be engendered often remains obscure—unless the author being read took care to articulate his poetic art; norms exist, they are guessed, but only through a vague intuition, opening the door to the apprentice-writer's phantasms and also his mistakes. Be that as it may, things will gradually become clear; it doesn't take long for an adolescent, especially if he continues his higher education, to grasp classical *order* as an irreducible whole (the social order, the order of life, the order of creation), and to detect in the "century of Louis XV," beneath an apparent disorder, the writer's vigorous struggle against the powers that be—which implies a change of public and determines a new kind of life.

c) Everything would be fine if the function of literature were not in a constant state of flux, often from one generation to the next, as a function of the continual transformations of our historic societies. In the feudal centuries, despite extreme diversity in production, certain constants may be observed to which the reader could refer for his own peace of mind. For Ronsard and Racine, for example, the notion of glory is the same: the eternity of the work and the poet remain explicitly linked to the permanence of the monarchy. Only later does one write for the "happy few" of the future, or hope to "win on appeal"; the classical poets, like those of the Pléiade, mean to win glory in their lifetime, by the king's grace. The sovereigns succeeding him need merely take up his literary choices along with his scepter and all his other attributes, for these are a dead man's final wishes and worthy of respect.

From the beginning of the eighteenth century, however, history accelerates; the public is continually transformed—generally growing but sometimes strangely retracting—and after the execution of Louis XVI, kings are an uncertain guarantee. In other words, the inert contiguity of books in libraries masks the upheaval that revolutions effected in all domains, and consequently in the written thing, which is merely the indirect projection of living culture in the *practico-inert of writing*. Doctrines *succeed one another:* they merely express the brutal transformations of the *objective* place and function which those societies in a permanent state of revolution assign to literary art. For the writer-apprentice who devours everything as it appears, these changes affect even the prose of his predecessors, those living authors who are still producing and who, addressing themselves to other readers, have other principles and other rules of life. If there were at least *progress* in the art of writing, historical duration would be restored, there would be no occasion to revive in the distant past the exemplary works and lives of the Greeks or Latins. Unfortunately, *beauty does not make progress:* we can conceive of it, indeed, only as a strict relation between form and the "form of content." Temporality, moreover, was long conceived as a process of degradation: the ancients were the best; after them, decadence began. An author could do no better than imitate them. This conception—familiar to the seventeenth century, abandoned by the bourgeois of the eighteenth century—was almost taken up again by the first generations of the nineteenth century, for quite different reasons. In sum, beauty seems nontemporal; and if there were temporalization, it would be a degeneration. These ideas—one, though illusory, seems to issue from authentic structures of the beautiful; the other is merely the projection in 1830 of political pessimism on the literary plane—exalt and actualize apparent contradictions that never really coexisted in time. For the young bookworm, Theocritus, Shakespeare, and Hugo, as manifest through their works, are all equally present. Hence, the aesthetic conceptions made manifest in their works clash violently. And how is he to choose among them since they all participate equally in the beautiful? Even if one accepted the pessimism that makes temporality a form of degradation, these contradictions, no longer caught in the abstraction of a moment, would nonetheless remain insoluble. By granting the ancients—farthest removed from our concerns—an aesthetic perfection he denies to Hugo, who speaks directly to him of his daily life, his hopes, his enthusiasms and his sorrows, the adolescent might always condemn "modernism," that is, any literature speaking to the contemporaries of today's world. Even as one would revive antiquity in the middle of the first industrial century, our lives would flow by in silence and the earth swallow them up, with no bard deigning to fix our passions in words—so different from the passions that moved Ulysses or a Sicilian shepherd—or to capture the flavor of our world. In fact, things did not go quite so far. A young reader of 1835, a future writer, becomes intoxicated with Hugo, Vigny, Musset; he finds in Goethe's *Faust* the mandate to totalize the universe; he may rank them inferior to Virgil, but despite this rigid, abstract judgment they speak to his deepest feelings.

Does he therefore take them as examples, making their essence, affirmed in their books, his imperative and his fate? That would seem the logical thing to do; although they are all still living, he comes immediately after them. But this is just why they contend with each other inside him when he internalizes them. These writers, sons of the Empire, were directly engaged with the seventeenth and eighteenth centuries, which they envisaged through the revolutionary outcome and from the viewpoint of the restored monarchy. For a young reader of 1835, their junior by ten or fifteen years, the situation is more complex. As he reads them, these writers reveal past centuries as they saw them, but he preserves—through that fissure characterizing the appearance of a new generation—a permanent possibility of becoming engaged directly with Voltaire, Corneille, and Homer; he need merely read them. Hence the challenge is challenged. In his direct relations with past authors, the apprentice-writer discovers them to be *different* from the image given him by his older brothers, living literary figures. As if there were two Voltaires—the Voltaire of *Rolla* (and many other works) and the Voltaire who wrote *Candide*. Indeed, Musset, desolate at having nearly lost his faith, thought *hideous* the man who concluded his letters with the phrase "Crush the Beast." But as we have seen with Gustave, if the Post-romantics regret the consolations of religion, they are nonetheless freer on this ground, and more bourgeois besides. When they read Voltaire directly, they find in him a relation to Christianity and a strain they can accept. So they are simultaneously for and against Voltaire. Thus the future writer is imperatively charged by every masterpiece he reads to reproduce in his century, through other masterpieces, the literature that produced those great books—as totality (art, social function, public, meaning and subject, life). But every imperative is contradicted by another established in him with equal rigor when he shifts from one author to another. He must call Boileau—as Hugo does—a "has-been"! But if he reads *Art poétique,* he must bow before such taste and call him the "legislator of Parnassus." Boileau will be judged by Hugo and Hugo by Boileau, and the result will be a vacillating uncertainty that charges the future work with being romantic through a negation of the classics, and classical through the *recovery and envelopment* of Romanticism and its works in the name of rules and taste, in the name of a monarchical order definitively rejected by contemporary society. The trouble is that every literary form is internalized as a commandment, the reader is penetrated with contradictory and frozen imperatives—that will be, for example, *Gargantua, Phèdre, Candide,* the *Confessions, Hernani,* each work becoming in the course of reading a singular imperative ("Create the society and consequently the public that will demand such a work from you and give you the kind of life that will allow you to produce it"). If you read for the sake of reading, eclecticism is possible, strictly speaking, but not comfortable. The reader will respond to these multiple contradictory demands simply with resignation; they will continue to clash *in him and through him,* and while letting it happen he will not feel obliged to unify them—an obligation he does have, however, since the demands he has awakened are addressed in him only to himself. But things are quite different if he reads for the sake of writing. In every work, art as a whole affirms itself; none appears relative to a society, to a particular period, although it is entirely conditioned by it. Thus whatever he reads, the literary thing in him becomes a total demand: it induces him to write but demands that literary art as a whole should be manifest in each of his future writings—a totality present in each partial production—in such a way that this art requires him to be inside it. This is not a matter of either reconciling or explaining through historical relativism: the elements of these multiple contradictions being imperative, their surpassing in a unifying synthesis appears to be the absolute demand of literature *in this future writer.* Let us say that from this point of view, surpassing is writing. The demand to write, the distant and fixed summons art extends from the depths of the future, is merely the determination of a future enterprise by the recomposition of a past and reified activity. But this summons—expressed at the time by the words "vocation" and "genius"—is also past literature demanding to be reproduced whole in every future work. This means that every work read, by demanding to be reproduced as bearer of this totality, is challenged by others as much as it challenges them. Thus the literary imperative is double: the new work must restore the beautiful as the all of which it is a part through the ancient canon; it achieves the synthetic surpassing of contradictions, the artistic totality will be manifest in it only as a totalization (through concrete texture and not through doctrines) of all those dead totalities. Insofar as the objective reason for this future activity is none other than the internalization of past literature, writing is not *just writing anything.* The meaning of the totalization to be attempted is objectively outlined as a solution to the revealed contradictions; the surpassing, of course, can only be invented, but in a way it will be from a perspective strictly defined by those contradictions themselves and so participating in their passive materiality. Thus in every age a sketchy outline is given of *what must be done,* given the imperative oppositions we internalize. Not just beginning with these, moreover, but also as a function of the place contemporary society reserves for the writer *compared* to the place literature already written claims for him through internalization. In other words, literature as a vocation induced by reading demands of the chosen writer that he affirm the literary thing through a new totalization—whether a drama, a novel without the slightest aesthetic commentary—which defines the society, the public, and the place of the writer in the social fabric. But two principal factors can make this definition impossible: on the one hand, the contradictions can be such that no rational synthesis can surpass them; on the other hand, the situation created for living literature by the contemporary society can enter into conflict with the situation that is manifest to the apprentice writer as a synthetic demand of written works, so that the rational synthesis of these works, were it to be found, could not be lived as a *real condition*. But as I have just shown, the literary form and content of an era are inseparable from the real situation of the writer in society, and consequently from the function this society actually assigns to literature. From this perspective, the real task of the future writer, which imposes itself on him as a surpassing of contradictions read, may seem to him more or less incompatible with the conditions of life which contemporary society imposes on the artist and with the type of readers it offers him. This arises from the fact that every cultural sector is on its level the expression of the total society and at the same time develops according to its own rules, that is, from the *practico-inert* produced in it to this day. When these two oppositions are manifest *together*, when the objective imperative appears as a "you must" which no "you can" comes to sustain, this objective will lose none of its intransigence—indeed, its source lies in the materiality of the Objective Spirit. Yet those it solicits can satisfy it only in the dream, by a series of *unreal* behaviors with no correspondence to the objective structures of society and the possibilities they *actually* offer the writer. Hence the chosen writer's need to unrealize himself in order to write. At the same time, other determinations may compel the public, or one part of the public, to become unrealized in order to read (or to read to become unrealized); and this being the case, we could imagine that the Objective Spirit of the age, in contradiction to the general movement of the living society, would compel the future author to despair of his vocation and in the end renounce it; or force him to unrealize himself through the supposition that he has resolved the insoluble contradictions posed by written-literature, and by this resolution to play *as a role* for his own benefit the character demanded by the Objective Spirit and unwanted by the real society. He is, as we can see, doubly driven to neurosis. But that

55

neurosis is itself objective, it is a *way to write;* a doubtful, suspect way, but unique. If the cultural practico-inert outlines a neurotic condition for the future artist as a sham, though a necessary subterfuge for producing *works in this time,* this necessary unrealization may be envisaged as an art-neurosis to the extent that art is not only the practico-inert set of works produced but the set of behaviors aimed at producing new ones. We need merely recapitulate briefly the givens that situate the future Postromantic writer in the culture between 1830 and 1850 to demonstrate that neurosis—we shall see more precisely what kind of neurosis—is an operational imperative for him. We will then be able to return to Flaubert—who lived those demands, as did all his contemporaries—and we shall try to establish the relationship that unites art-neurosis as a determination of objectivity to his subjective neurosis.

TWENTY—TWO

The Literary Situation
of the Postromantic Apprentice Author

Let us place the apprentice author in adolescence, surrounded by books from the municipal library or the library in his parents' house. He has already read a great deal; literature has become its own inducement: now he reads in order to write. Let us follow him from century to century to see the models and norms he revives. Let us attempt to determine whether those rules are compatible with the historical circumstances in which he finds himself (he is educated under Louis-Philippe but will write under the Second Empire), whether they are mutually compatible, and whether he manages to discard some and modify others or to combine all of them into a sort of synthesis in his works—a synthesis which, taking my cue from literature-already-written, I shall call literature-to-be-written.

A

I shall quickly gloss over the literature of the seventeenth century, although our future author had a systematic knowledge of it (that is, he studied it at school). The result of that knowledge is indeed ambiguous; he may know Racine *better* (yet even this should be questioned) but regards him as an author read at school—an author who is quite dead and accessible only through scholarly techniques. So the "great" authors of the seventeenth century seem to guarantee that beauty—as the unity of form and the form of content—exists, or, at least, has existed. But just as certain primitive and polytheist religions suggest the existence of a prehistoric monotheism (or at least a privilege accorded to one God, Uranus), which has lost its real content while preserving the absolute right to found Creation (though it is no longer consulted), so Racine, Bossuet, and others stand as proof—long since become an abstraction—that a work can be made beautiful. But they

57

are reread hardly at all. They have a central importance (the Romantics are embarrassed to mention them). And they may be at the origin of literary vocations. But the apprentice of 1840 rarely rereads them. Flaubert respects them; in his youth he often surprises Maxime by ardently defending them; but he hardly looks at their work, with the possible exception of Boileau, who in Gustave's view lacks the "palate" for taste but offers judicious recipes (as a first step). Yet there is a sixteenth-to-seventeenth-century author, a foreigner, Shakespeare, who is perfectly beautiful as well as alive. For Gustave learned to read Shakespeare *through the Romantics*. In contrast to the classics, Shakespeare represents rather well the type of Romantic drama the reader's older brothers try to realize—in vain, apart from Musset. Here we have the first literary challenge: the classical authors are dead gods, and Shakespeare is a living God.

The eighteenth century is the beginning of living literature. Of course its authors are dead, but they all have something to say to our apprentice. He doesn't know everything, he has read some works and biographies. Through this practico-inert material he receives the following imperative: *be the kind of writer we were.* What are the features of this model? Certainly they vary enormously from Lesage to Rousseau; but considering the general movement of history, we can establish *grosso modo* a list of major requirements.

1. The Objective Determinations of Eighteenth-Century Literature as an Activity

I propose that this literature is negative, concrete, practical, and that it struggles throughout the century, in a hundred different ways, to win its autonomy.

It is *negative*, or, still better, the literary expression of *negativity*. For its goal is to ensure the reign of analytic reason against historical privilege. Its purpose was not immediately clear; originally, these authors, the oldest of whom were born in the previous century, claimed only to be inspired, as were their predecessors, by healthy reason. But they were all influenced by the great upheaval of ideas that disturbed the seventeenth century's calm at its end, and so in their hands analysis, like it or not, became an instrument of criticism and demystification. And science is none other than reason itself, constitutive and constituted; not even its product, but its dynamic. We cannot, therefore, imagine the slightest opposition between science and litcrature; quite to the contrary, the shift from one to the other is easily accomplished. And both have political consequences: the struggle against prohibitions that keep men in ignorance is a more or less direct struggle against the regime. And we see the writer offer his services to men of science: as a political act Voltaire articulated Newton's theory to the French; he put his style at the service of the physicist; as a political act Diderot and his friends wrote the *Encyclopédie*; as a political act Chénier meant to write a cosmogony. At the time, mathematicians like d'Alembert found themselves to be writers without even knowing it, and literary men devoted themselves quite naturally to research on fire, on the chemical elements. Science, despite remarkable progress, was still in the early stages of its development; hence it was possible for a man of letters to articulate the most recent discoveries "in fine language" without falling into vulgarization. Certainly the divorce between technical or mathematical language and so-called "literary" language had begun, but the fault line was still invisible. United by the same politics, science and literature sometimes seemed to merge, and at other times the distance between them was easily negotiated, with the sole difference that the scientist's invention, positive in itself, could be negative only indirectly, whereas critical negativity is constantly present in literary works. These in themselves, however, while remaining works of beauty—with respect to taste—can take a scientific turn, as does *The Spirit of the Laws*. For the human sciences are still virgin territory. It is left to the literary man or the philosopher to speak of man. And, indeed, from the beginning of the century, literature laid claim to the realm of philosophy—the great writers called themselves philosophers. They were not philosophers, however, except insofar as they tried to unify scientific laws by notions as complex as that of nature and, anticipating the forthcoming discipline of Anthropology, judged themselves capable of treating human nature. Human nature, unvarying and universal, restored to the bosom of nature, was the *subject* of a literature that aspired to be philosophical. This is the very type of a false synthesis. The unity of nature can come only from God; for many, indeed, the notion of nature was refurbished by these people to disguise beneath the supposed unity of the creation the infinite dispersal of a mechanistic materialism which, simply by being articulated, would lead to the stake. In the same way, the unity of human nature as a structured totality implies its creation; but hidden analytic enzymes gnaw away at this splendid whole and atomize it: man is no more than a dance of molecules governed externally by the laws of association, which

presuppose the application of the principle of inertia to lived temporality. Yet those deceptive totalizations are not merely precautionary
measures; the writers believe in nature, in human nature. Just as they
preserve in spite of themselves a little of their childhood faith. Or as
if, beyond the results of analysis, they sensed a movement of the still
future spirit that would bind these multiplicities of indivisible elements into an internal unity of dialectical synthesis. A vestige of the
past, a presentiment of the future, *human nature*, an issue of the re-
gulating idea of analytical operations and the observations of moral-
ists, was a common ground upon which writers could encounter the
powers-that-be and confront them. Man—*nature* for the first, *creature*
for the second—is originally good, either because he issues naked
from the hands of God, who wished him to be fallible and finite but
not radically bad, or because he emerges in the center of the macrocosm as a *pure* product of great universal laws. Taking no blame from
prelates or princes, literature seizes upon human goodness and uses
it as a negative weapon. If everyone were equally pure, equally good
at the outset, privileges could no longer be explained by the superiority
of *blood.* By affirming our original purity against Boulainvilliers, that
wicked author who defended the aristocracy, literature established
that society alone is responsible for the inequality among men. It
based its argument on these principles, on the permanence of human
nature, and borrowed from the jurists—who took it from Roman
law—the notion of natural right, which itself becomes a weapon, a
limit to the arbitrary: this far and no farther.

In short, eighteenth-century literature—that *already written* literature our apprentice writer devours, and whose underlying unity he
perceives despite the diversity of literary figures—has only one subject: man in the natural world and in society. But this seemingly contemplative and positive subject conceals a *political* campaign against
religious dogmas, aristocratic privilege and absolute power. And the
man it describes and claims to find everywhere, even under the pompous garments of a great lord, is in fact bourgeois man. Or rather man
as he must be conceived by the bourgeoisie around 1750. That man,
of course, is neither true nor false: he is one of the pillars of the ideology formulated by the bourgeois at this period when, possessing
economic power in the form of merchant capitalism, they try to assure
his free development by seizing political power. "Human nature," a
deadly weapon against privilege, is actually a *negative* concept. Moreover, it is a class concept. But the writers are not entirely conscious of
that; the utterly Cartesian rejection of history demands the negation

of acquired rights—they are fully conscious of that. But as literary men-cum-philosophers, they see it *first* as the triumph of reason, that is, of the nontemporal and of universality. Bourgeois by birth, they think of serving not the interests of their own class—which, mingled with the more disadvantaged classes under the label of third estate, considers itself the universal class—but those of all humanity. And the *positive* names they give their weapons mask the fact that the very essence of literature resides at this time in a systematic effort to compel language, used according to the rules of taste, to manifest and transmit the corrosive acid of negativity. For the adolescent of 1840 who devours those finished products, the books of the eighteenth century, literature imperatively manifests the subject to be treated as an exhaustive totality of man and the world; but this uncertain imperative tends of itself to disintegrate, to allow mechanistic materialism to be glimpsed behind it.

Literature is concrete. The Church and the secular power prohibit a direct attack on principles and a public substitution of the new ideology for the feudal one. The dogmas of theology and the principles of absolute monarchy, though directly challenged, cannot be called into question again without mortal danger. The writer will therefore denounce them indirectly and through their consequences, in other words, in everyday issues, through "affairs" arising almost daily. By denouncing judicial errors, for example, he makes the reader responsible for drawing conclusions and condemning the corrupt justice of the Ancien Régime that makes those errors possible. But to show the innocence of men like Calas, the inquest must be taken up point by point, and literature must be forced to express the most concrete facts, of the sort found in a police report, without renouncing its own rules. Thus the great battle between analytic reason on the one hand and dogma and privilege on the other is translated by a new flexibility in "literary" language that must be capable of accounting for everything, even the trivial, without losing its quality. Eighteenth-century literature imposes itself on the reader of 1840 with this imperative: show the course of things, describe and discuss events; there is no longer any such thing as a *noble* subject, the literary domain must be the critical and detailed narrative of the human adventure. We have already understood that the *conquest of style* in the eighteenth century not only is characterized by an extended vocabulary but implies a general secularization of writing. To the Postromantic reader, the systematic pursuit of secularization seems to be a sacred imperative of the preceding century. Literature must be extended into the realm of quotidian banality without contravening the rules prescribed by taste, whose observation defines the work of literature.

Literature is practical. The preceding observations suggest that the reader of 1840 perceives literature as *in essence active.* In fact, it exercises its negativity on particular events because it is unable to contest the general principles of the regime; it throws itself into the daily scuffle, takes up the cudgels, and sides with the bourgeoisie in the struggle against the aristocracy. Its arguments have real efficacy to the extent that the rising class appropriates and internalizes them as bonds between its members (as the means to dissolve seriality in favor of groups). On the other hand, the writer's social responsibility—so often denied in the nineteenth century and even in our own day—cannot be doubted: this is a decision of the government, not of the writer. Thus literary action is two-pronged: it structures the bourgeois class by gradually creating the main ingredients of its ideology; and it puts the writer in danger. This time, the imperative can be summed up as follows: always write in such a way that your work is an act.

Literature asserts its autonomy. This is a paradoxical consequence of the preceding observations, and we shall soon see why. But first we must understand that the writer—his life or liberty always at risk—asserts the right to express his thought even when faced with imprisonment or the seizure of his books. But since freedom of expression is not recognized as a universal right of citizens, he claims that right not as a citizen but in his capacity as writer and in the name of literature. For literature has defined its subject, which is simply man in the world; in the absence of any anthropology, it can, in its contradictory totality, pose as man's thought about himself, as the systematic expression of knowledge and the *imago* as these will be determined in their capacity as *universals* deriving from human nature taken in its generality. Literature claims the right to fulfill its function, which is to reveal to men the pure thought of universal man regarding himself and the world. And as this universal man is arguably everyone of flesh and blood once delivered from the false ideas that circumvent his judgment, literary autonomy can be nothing but the right to express man's image and knowledge of himself *in their original purity,* that is, by stripping them of all the imposed ideologies that conceal them from view. Eroticism—one of the predominant themes of the period, at first worldly and presented as an agreeable entertainment of good society, then becoming increasingly dark, and finally revealing the asocial despair of perversion—appears throughout the century as an increasingly deflected and repeated effort to tell the truth about sex. By claiming autonomy, literature stands on its own: it would serve no party nor submit to any dogma; it refuses—unlike the classics—to reflect the social *order* in which it is produced, because it does not judge that order to be good—any better than any other—and seeks to bear witness to man in the state of nature. It will describe the structures and mores of its times, of course, but in order to contest them. Literature lays claim to its permanent autonomy insofar as it stands for beauty in the service of truth, and for it there is truth only in the unchanging universality of the concept. It is noteworthy that in the eighteenth century autonomy is requisite, rather, by virtue of literary content, the ahistorical thought permanently formed by our species, and must be represented to us only by virtue of formal qualities. It is truth, or what they take for it, and not beauty that establishes the sovereign right of authors; and the backbone of the argument is that since man has always possessed that immediate thought of himself which is the immediate correlative of his carnal existence, literature cannot fill his mind with subversive ideologies and is limited to structuring that which has never ceased to be. Through such structuring, however, beauty is reintroduced as the only presentation worthy of truth. Thus literary autonomy defines itself as the body of true thought made manifest according to the norms of beauty. By this assertion, in any case, literature *stands on its own* for the first time since the century of Louis XIV.

Paradoxically, just when it sincerely believes it is freeing itself of dogmas and ideologies, it is actually engaged in revealing to the bourgeois their own ideology, and that ideology, gradually conquered and composed, finally becomes the sole content of literature. Analytic reason, the rights of man, individualism, the rejection of history and of an encumbering religion—these are the themes of literature and of embattled bourgeois thought. The bourgeoisie agrees to condemn all forms of society—when Rousseau bids them do so—provided that universal judgment weakens the constricting feudal regime. It is perfectly happy to affirm the legal equality of all men if that truth can shake up acquired rights and privileges without touching real property. The bourgeoisie sincerely admits that eternal man is expressed by a pure and eternal thought, for, as we have seen, it regards itself as the universal class, thus confusing man with bourgeois man. And when the writer fights for freedom of expression, it supports him all the more forcefully, since without suspecting it he does not claim from the sovereign the right to publish just any thought but precisely that of the bourgeois class. In claiming this right for their own caste, moreover, the literary men find as a direct consequence that they are demanding this right for anyone, that is, for the entire class that bore them. How, indeed, could we imagine a society in which only writers would have the right to speak? Thus, in the course of the class struggle, which reveals its true face in the eighteenth century when literature believes it is self-sufficient, the writer is limited to destroying the ideology of the politically dominant class only to clear the way for the ideology of the class with economic power.

Yet if their struggle against the powers-that-be is supported by an interested bourgeoisie, the writers, by pride of caste, see it as a harsh battle *for full powers*. It might be expressed in these terms: *if it is literary*, an exposition, whatever its content, must escape every jurisdiction but that of taste. Flaubert will later sum up the meaning of their enterprise when he repeats this aphorism: "That which is well written cannot be harmful." By fighting for its autonomy, literature means indeed to escape the common law: writers alone have the privilege of saying *everything* provided they say it *well*. In a way, they nearly reached their goal at the time of Voltaire's triumph and death. They did not win the right to speak for everyone, but through dearly won tolerance they alone in Europe could speak out. In this situation we find the seeds of a divorce: they are regarded by the class that reads and supports them as its spokesmen, while they take themselves as spokesmen for the human race. But this danger is still veiled, for two reasons: first, bourgeois ideology is still negative, and literature serves it only through its negativity; and then, although literature takes on a growing importance in the life of society, it does not yet question its being: far from taking itself as an absolute, it still considers itself a human activity.

If the young Postromantic reader opens a pamphlet by Voltaire or a biography of Voltaire, he cannot help discovering autonomy as a major imperative. If he writes, literature is affirmed through his work as the pure expression of human nature beyond *any ideology*. And since knowledge of man (analytic reason) is clearly distinguished here from ready-made ideas, imposed dogmas, prejudices, and pseudorational justifications, literature presents itself to the future writer as the ultimate human activity. This young bourgeois, breaking with his class and enchanted by *Candide*, is unaware that the eighteenth century, frozen in books, is proposing to him that the noblest of tasks lies in serving the interests of his class and refining its ideology for the consumption of all social groups. This mission, of course, is offered to him in 1840 as a work of destruction that awakens his negativity, while bourgeois ideology, elaborated, completed, has become positive and conservative since its rise to power. We shall soon return to this hidden contradiction.

2. Objective Determinations of the Writer as Person

Literature in the eighteenth century seems in its very essence to be engaged in the violent political struggle between the various classes. It chose its place; its discourses are in part acts, and beneath the blooms of rhetoric it secretes acids: its rational violence precedes and announces the inevitable violence of weapons. Consequently, it has a double mission, and so does its public. On the one hand are the timorous, conservative bourgeois, whom fear, interests, and an abiding fascination range on the side of the aristocracy, and whom the writer must *convince* by destroying the arsenal of arguments entrenched by those forces. And here we must add the aristocracy itself, which is far from homogeneous. Certain noblemen, the minority, could be won over; but others, the indomitable, can be *demoralized* by reducing their "thought"—an impoverished and *defensive* doctrine—to a few vicious circles in which they thrash about helplessly. On the other hand are the majority of the bourgeois, long since familiar with analytic reason through their economic activities, who are won over in advance. They must simply be allowed to internalize a destructive argumentation that, taken again as a whole, will be altogether a sudden awakening and an aggressive arming.[1] This duality of the reader provokes a characteristic *tension* in the works and even in the style of the writers. Those who can be shaken up or won over must be addressed in their own language. Let them reach the end of the argument—which repudiates or torments them—through a form that seems familiar to them, that seems to preserve the graces and superannuated nobility of the *grand siècle!* Bourgeois readers, on the contrary, accustomed by their business affairs to rigor, conciseness, precision in language, demand a new style that "calls a spade a spade," a style that Boileau claimed to create but really didn't. Since both groups must be reached, a style will gradually be forged, surpassing and resolving this major contradiction, finding its perfect realization in *Candide* and in the first vol-

---

1. A sudden awakening that is only partial, of course, since it is born above all from the ongoing struggle. The bourgeoisie awakens to consciousness of the hindrances and constraints that might paralyze it in its praxis, but at the same time it takes itself for the *reality* of the third estate, that is, for man.

umes of the *Confessions*. These two works differ in every respect but their inner tension.

Style thus seems of paramount importance though it is itself a trap, or, more precisely, a kind of bait. But at the same time its tension manifests the social position of the writer himself. The son of bourgeois, a bourgeois himself and living as such, he is the interpreter of his class. But for that very reason he is often coddled by the reformist minority of the aristocracy. These people imagine themselves "enlightened"; like the Marquis of Argenson, they have a sense, from midcentury onward, that the worm-eaten edifice of the monarchy is about to collapse; many of them secretly desire the advent of a regime that—as in England—would preserve their privileges while permitting the bourgeois elite to share them. The writer, as representative of that elite, is the first to be privileged. Of course, no one dreams of ennobling him *by rights;* but he benefits from a de facto ennoblement that is hard won and always contested. He dines at the table of lords at a time when the most celebrated musicians are taking their meals in the kitchen. He speaks to noblemen with respectful familiarity; some abandon him at the first sign of danger—like the noble friends of Voltaire at the beginning of the century, when the Chevalier de Rohan had him beaten—and others will be his faithful friends and protect him against the strictures of government. To this must be added the favor of certain monarchs. The meaning of all this is clear: sensitive to the fame of several authors, Frederick and Catherine try to make them their public relations men, or if you will their publicity agents. Problematic connections that will, however, be binding, for good or ill: Voltaire will cover up several of Catherine's murders and dub her the "Semiramis of the North" before an astonished Europe.

Such an attitude might seem treasonable today. We may well ask, what are these bourgeois doing among their class enemies? Why accept and even solicit the favors of an aristocracy when their role is to dismantle it? In Voltaire's century things are not so clear-cut. First of all, class conflicts are initially somewhat masked by national unity. Among the bourgeois, those who will eventually become the regime's staunchest opponents were raised with respect for institutions and privileges; their fathers were proud of *their* noblemen, whose accomplishments and virtues brought them indirectly a kind of prestige. They inculcated that humble pride in their sons. Thus the struggle between bourgeois and aristocrats—at least until the coronation of Louis XVI—was not perceived as "class against class," as our own social struggles are often characterized. Besides, the bourgeoisie as a whole accepts and even insists upon the monarchical regime. Its disputes with the nobility are not meant to overthrow royalty but to further its ambition to become the *political* class *under the kings' rule,* that is, to substitute its influence for that of the privileged. In other words, the bourgeoisie needs a cover, and the idea of establishing a Republic either doesn't occur to it or seems horrifying. From this point of view, the "treason" of its intellectuals, far from offending the bourgeoisie, seems to serve its interests. It considers writers its delegates to the sovereign: they will introduce bourgeois ideology into those higher spheres that seem most receptive to it; they will exhort them to govern according to reason, to suppress privilege, to appoint bourgeois ministers. The monarchs, of course, hear a different refrain: for them, the writer primarily has publicity value and secondarily is an entertainer—at best, a friend of inferior condition with whom one can occasionally discuss the sciences or the fine arts.

The writer himself is unconscious of his real situation. The very ambiguity of his position in relation to the aristocracy more easily rewards his dreams of grandeur. He maintains a profound admiration for the nobility, as does every bourgeois, and feels quite dazzled to be "received" by a number of privileged families. At the same time, he is not unaware that his principal objective is to destroy privilege, hence to undermine the very basis of that prestigious aristocracy. He claims to love the *man* in the duke or prince who protects him; he scorns, or claims to scorn, the caste spirit of all his titled enemies and its resultant stupidity. Thus, communicating "man to man" with a lord who is interested in physics or chemistry and invites him to his laboratory, lifted out of his class by the favor of kings who receive him, alone among other bourgeois in the intimacy of kings, he can regard himself seriously neither as a bourgeois—since he doesn't lead a bourgeois life—nor as a lord—since he has no title. But as he finds himself, or believes he finds himself, on equal footing everywhere, he considers himself classless, someone who is part of an elite marginal to the institutionalized elite, and at the same time a representative of the human race in its purity. Indeed, if he communicates with dukes, princes, and bourgeois—who occupy such varied positions— he thinks it can be only insofar as they are men and he himself is a man. And if he differs from them all, it is because their prerogatives and responsibilities initially mask their humanity; the writer, by contrast, who communicates with them only by detaching them from their particularities to *recall them to reason,* to universality, is quite simply a man. A man without quality, without social determination; a man

67

who cannot be identified with one class and is sworn by his nature to bear witness to human nature for all the strata and classes of society while belonging to none. Of course, these authors do not all claim that humanity is originally good, but there isn't one who doesn't recognize a destiny in it, a vocation—which is happiness in virtue—and the power to *progress*. In this sense their interpretation of their own social situation remains in perfect accord with the idea they have of literature. And that is understandable: in the realm of culture, as in many others and particularly in literature, conditionings are circular. Thus the idea these authors have of their social being becomes the subject of their literature; and reciprocally, their critical enterprise and negative use of analytic reason condition their conception of literary art and of themselves.

Be that as it may, these bourgeois pull the wool over their own eyes. First of all, they are always and everywhere much more bourgeois than men; one of the surest reasons for Voltaire's disgrace in Prussia was that he profited from Frederick's wars to line his own pockets with what today would be called the black-market currency exchange. Second, their class tolerates their excesses only because it is on its way up, still oppressed, and needs them to rationalize its destructive enterprise. They are negative because in these historical circumstances the action of the bourgeoisie can only be *politically* negative. I remember a time when the Soviet Union was living under threat, and in the midst of disorders, civil war, and foreign intervention it had some difficulty providing itself with institutions, which remained abstractions without firm underpinnings; this was in 1920. At that time the political friends of the Soviet Union willingly tolerated all outside literature, no matter how scandalous to them, because their aim was to weaken the bourgeois democracies and so to *demoralize* the bourgeoisie. Many writers among us believed then that the Russian revolution was going to bring about a cultural revolution and sanctify the creative freedom of literature. Simply put, the first objective of that beleaguered country was to defend the conquests of socialism, and it demanded of those on the outside the systematic exercise of negativity. This became clear when central power was consolidated and industrialization began. From that moment, everyone had to *construct*, and literature within the Soviet Union was summoned to help the politicians build the edifice of socialism, in other words, to become edifying. Outside, negativity remained—the enemy still had to be fought—but its place was severely reduced; it had to vaunt the greatness of the worker, of communist man. In search of such positive heroes, Soviet, communist, or communizing literature strained more and more each day to achieve positivity. That is understandable: a class in power (even when it is the dictatorship of the proletariat) desires a class literature, and those literatures—despite irreducible differences—have a common feature, which is that the critical function, having predominated during the struggle, quickly atrophies.

Thus that pure and free man, protector of the humble, respected friend of the powerful, conceals beneath the abstract positivity of virtue an inveterate, merciless, ultimately black negativity. A young dreamer of 1840 couldn't help seeing him as a prestigious model: in the simplicity of his mores and the dreaded power of his pen, wasn't the writer an aristocrat superior to the real aristocracy? Didn't he show in all his actions and in the smallest details of his life that to be a man and to write are one and the same, or, conversely, that literature is the only truly human activity? Yet, as we have just seen, the image is false. Although his self-representation is erroneous, however, the eighteenth-century writer does not find himself in a neurotic situation. The error, here, is *normal*. It is simply a false interpretation of specific givens that could not otherwise be understood. It is perfectly true that between his flogging and apotheosis, Voltaire struggled mightily to win superior status. It is also true that this status, grudgingly granted, challenged, revoked and reestablished, could not escape a certain indeterminacy, and could not conceivably be institutionalized. The most famous of these authors, moreover, while bourgeois in origin and responsible for condensing the negative elements of bourgeois ideology, rarely rubbed elbows with people of their own class; they saw princes and sometimes kings, and more frequently they saw each other. And what a triumph for them in what today we would tend to describe as treason: they denounced privilege without respite, and *for that very reason* they were coddled by the privileged. They did not overestimate their importance, but they were unaware that it derived from that bourgeois public which silently took up its arguments and turned them into weapons—and that the profundity of their writings lay not in them but in their class.

B

Such, then, is the first model proposed by the *Objective Spirit* to the young man who revives old books under the reign of Louis-Philippe. It is an imperative summons: literature is the highest form of human activity, its autonomy is the very expression of our freedom; it can be exercised only by a small number of the elect, who are the equals of kings; be of this elite and risk scandal, prison, or renounce writing. What could be more tempting? And yet, can the apprentice author between 1830 and 1848 adopt this conception of literary art without falling into sudden and unwonted contradictions?

The proposed *imago* must fascinate him, certainly. If he has chosen to write, it is probably to compensate for some maladaptation, a slight inferiority; and here it is declared that he will be the first among men. Literature, in him, discloses that superiority, exhorts him to surpass everyone; through it he learns of the triumph of the dying Voltaire and of Rousseau transported to the Pantheon. He might not have asked so much of it on his own; his desire is expanded by the internalization of the cultural practico-inert, which gives its objective structure to a vague, indecisive aspiration and transforms it into a relation to the world, into a claim that extends to the whole society, and into this commandment: seek glory.

The masterpieces of the eighteenth century are certainly his parents' delight. These are *their* books, which situate them as *others* with respect to the new generation. The adults read them, reread them almost on the sly; under the Restoration this was a clandestine form of opposition. The young man admires these works to the extent that he still admires his father. He finds them a bit dated, just as his admirable progenitor seems a bit aged, just as he discovers in him a stagnant, repetitious, unraveling life. And those well-thumbed works that used to provoke muffled laughter over his head, that were part of the paternal library kept under lock and key, seem somehow familiar—seen before, read before—even without being opened. In a word, they are like family. Besides, several years earlier they were involved in an unfortunate business. Voltaire is not only the author of *Candide*, he wrote bad tragedies. And these tragedies are defended by the older gentlemen against the new theater: at the opening of *Hernani* the "codgers" were applauding Voltaire, and as a result he grew old overnight, becoming the weapon of reactionaries. When a child dreams of writing, it is always to some extent in opposition to the gentlemen who visit with his father; and since those gentlemen, who bear no resemblance to Calas in prison and even less to the chevalier of La Barre, are the guardians of the eighteenth century and its "philosophers," it is also in opposition to *accepted* literature that this young reader wants to write.

That is not such a problem, however. Voltaire is the only one whose work lies partly covered with dust. As for the others, either you read everything they wrote, or the one or two of their books that have remained wonderfully vivid, like the *Confessions*, which offer themselves as imperative models and as a pledge of hope to every reader between fifteen and twenty years of age: you must, therefore you can write that. But *especially* when these old books are dusted off and opened, the reader perceives that they are not at all what he imagined. The reader of 1840 finds a common, inarticulable, diabolical thought in them that both frightens and attracts him. This is because they are the product of "the spirit that always denies." In other words, the spirit of negativity. That happy rationalism suddenly discloses a desperate pessimism. Marivaux is a *dark* author, and this can be understood by reading *Les Fausses Confidences;* Voltaire is dark also: the serene moral of *Candide* rests on a moderate but thoroughgoing pessimism. And as for Rousseau, that persecution maniac who really was persecuted, what image does he give of man and society? Where does he find salvation—save in solitude and escape? Moreover, the late fruits of the century are venomous and reflect on all the rest: *Les Liaisons dangereuses, Les Infortunes de la Vertu.* Each of these books in its way, one discreetly, the other candidly, pushes negativity to its limit and poses the fundamental question of that atomizing and individualist ideology: Are human relations possible? Can there be any relation between one atom and another but that of exteriority? For a young man of the nineteenth century, individualist or not, whose thought was built on the postulates of his class—mechanism, psychological and social atomism—that is the question. Since atomism introduces exteriority everywhere, can there be a connection of interiority between two persons? And if not, how can we communicate? Thus, as something reborn, the book is a bottomless abyss, for as soon as it is awakened by a gaze, it contains the imperative of negativity in inert but aggressive form. As if that radical negativity were the basis, means and content of literature. There is nothing more terrifying than a century that opens up and allows a glimpse of an abyss of pessimism. There is nothing more dizzying than to see evil and misfortune in the depths of that gulf of the *past* as inert claims on the living reader.

In fact, the terror is exaggerated. If there indeed exists a "dark literature" in the literature of the eighteenth century, it cannot be considered central. The optimism of the authors, save toward the end,[2] is

2. And it must be noted that de Sade and Laclos are not bourgeois. De Sade's thought, in particular, expresses through notions borrowed from bourgeois "philoso-

sincere. And it is not their fault if philosophical atomism transforms societies and every man's thoughts into archipelagos. We must see this nascent individualism that first reveals its negative aspect as an extenuated translation—on the ethical and philosophical plane—of *real* property, property rights, and above all the behavior of appropriation.

It is really the Church, the Congrégation, the emigrés and their literary lackeys who have denounced the atrocities of those great deceased figures; this impious literature smacks of heresy. The child well knows that his parents responded to these public accusations with a simple smile, that they were not quite atheists, or very rarely, but that they did very well without God, whether or not He existed, and would not call pessimistic an ideology that seeks to be rigorously secular. The difficulty arises here from the difference in generations. The bourgeois parents, dechristianized by Jacobinism, are proud of their separation from the Church and their abandonment of dogmas, at least of those that seem most absurd. This accounts in part for their acknowledgment of the dead authors who disabused them. The children know only how to think; after all, they were raised in the Catholic religion: baptism, first communion, confirmation *at the very least*, which weakened the parents' position and caught them out in a blatant lie; and then, unable to crush in their young pupils the agnosticism inculcated quite early by their families, the priests usually managed to worry them. They would remain worried all their lives. And finally, they read the Romantics—to whom we shall return—and they all know *Rolla* by heart. Voltaire's *hideous* smile is not simply a toothless grin to them; it expresses the abject satisfaction of a demoralizer who succeeded in his crime and happily sees faith fall from our hearts. The new generation, too, thinks this grimace *hideous*. First of all because in their time they loved Musset. And then, though pushing unbelief still further than did their older brothers, who themselves asked only to fall to their knees, the younger generation regret their agnosticism, making it one of their grievances against parents and even grandparents, thus against Voltaire and his contemporaries. This doesn't prevent them from admiring him: they reproach him for being right. I will suggest that a future writer—between 1830 and 1850—sustains *ambivalent* relations with the literature of the eighteenth century.

Curiously, he fully accepts the frightening negativity that caused

---

phy" the bitter despair of a nobility that has a presentiment of its destiny. Louvet's eroticism, on the contrary, remains superficial, optimistic, and good-natured.

the death of God only when he sees it as the source of literary *autonomy*. For it was lost under the Revolution and the Empire; when the bourgeoisie in power fought against all of Europe and also against domestic factions, its bards took it on themselves to celebrate it anyhow. In short, to some degree out of fidelity to itself, literature became positive and reserved its negations for the enemy. But during its first triumph, when it sold itself to a military man who bled it dry but imposed internal order, the bourgeois class showed its gratitude to *literature* by sinking it under the weight of its own prohibitions. There was only one bourgeois genius, Constant, a rather nasty fellow; negativity passed into the overthrown class: *literature* exiled itself, not so much stubborn in its negations,[3] at least in its great works, as determined to find an alternative ideology, a monarchist thought which, rather than refute bourgeois thought, would envelop it and thoroughly digest it. Around 1840, exile does not mark the loss of *autonomy* in the eyes of the young; to the contrary, with the concurrence of retrospective illusion, it seems to be its consecration since great writers accepted it to maintain their independence. In any event, that is the lesson a young author learns at this time from the great books of the preceding century: *autonomy* must be the fundamental condition for the existence of a *modern* literature. What was conquered will never again be lost: literary art makes its own laws. On this level, the meaning of autonomy—presenting itself as both an inalienable essence of the literary thing and an imperative addressed directly to the future writer through the books he reads—begins to shift. It is merely a beginning, and in the course of the same period we shall see the avatars of this basic notion. Indeed, for the young bourgeois of 1840, the aristocracy is reversed. Consequently, the struggle of the eighteenth-century writer, instead of being grasped for what it is—a dubious campaign issuing in defeats and victories always of a doubtful nature—is illuminated in his eyes by its final term, the reversal of privilege. From this perspective, kings and the nobility look like paper tigers; the writer, by contrast, whether imprisoned or exiled to England, appears, with the help of retrospective illusion, already imbued with his future victory. Considered from this angle, he seems superior to our kind; his fame and the favor of kings raises him above the bourgeoisie; his writer's vocation puts him above the aristocracy since he unmasks the absurdity of their privileges and is proceeding to destroy that arrogant class foolish enough to fête him. Conceived

3. Especially in the second period of the Empire.

retrospectively, autonomy, far from being a stake in the game, seems rather the first sketchy outline of what I have called above panoramic consciousness. To speak of human nature and nature, a writer must come out of nowhere, have no roots, possess, in short, a clairvoyance unobscured by any prejudice—which is impossible for anyone, predisposed as we invariably are by the biases of family or immediate concerns. In a word, merely to be naked man, rather ingenuous perhaps, with common sense and some judgment, would require being more than a man; to speak of society without having our discourse conditioned by it, as indeed such a man would do, one would have to be situated above it and observe it from outside. This, think our apprentice writers, is granted the man of letters, who finds himself classless, sometimes the equal and friend of the monarch, sometimes captive or hunted, and sometimes, in his modest dwelling, the conscientious crafter of style. For them, autonomy is necessarily tied to nontemporality. To be the witness of his time, the writer must detach himself from historical duration; eternity is only for those who are eternal in advance.

The authors of the eighteenth century are in part responsible—unwittingly, to be sure—for this misunderstanding. Didn't they claim to write about human nature as universal and unchanging? Didn't they contrast it, in its perfect purity found in all people equally, to the monstrous deviations produced in us all by societies based on inequality? Yet while all of them, even Rousseau, had the weakness to frequent the great and the vanity to believe they were members of an elite, they never stopped seeing themselves as men living among their fellows and threatened by the same dangers. In the *Confessions*, Rousseau addresses the reader as "his fellow, his brother"; persecuted, vilified, he appeals to the judgment of those who read him; Voltaire invents Micromégas, a superman from another planet, to show the absurdities of contemporary society. But in other stories he gives the same job to the Ingénu, or to Candide, who are merely men or even at the very bottom of the social hierarchy, buffeted by all the waves of history, powerless, culturally impoverished, with no weapon but good sense. For men of letters at that time had no need of panoramic consciousness to know the first givens of our nature; they practiced, or believed they were practicing, an analysis that reduced aggregates to their elements. The error of these people was to confuse our being-in-the-world with our existence-in-society. In the first case, it is true that the universe surrounds me and that nonetheless analytic reason has the power to penetrate it effectively; this is because, at least in macrophysics, I can stand outside the experiments I make. In the second case, however, since I am a son of man and a man myself, I cannot make a single judgment on my own species without its being secretly conditioned by my condition, my family, my traditions, and my times. In this sense, the young reader who dreams a hundred years later of surveying the human race is more conscious of the problem than they were. Only instead of understanding that this problem has no solution, he commits the error of forging one—which is impossible—and consequently of imposing on himself, in the name of autonomy, an *untenable attitude*. Of all the inventions of the preceding century, he retained only Micromégas. The prerogative to write belongs only to interstellar travelers who were not born on this earth.

The misunderstanding comes primarily from the fact that autonomy seems to him *given*, once and for all—it cannot be otherwise since these books, sometimes so foolishly free, exist as determinations of the Objective Spirit, and their authors have found glory—whereas autonomy cannot exist unless it is conquered anew each day. It does not belong to them, it is the outcome of their grandfathers' battle. *Yes, it is an imperative*, and this means they must find their own and wrest it from the prevailing powers by a daily struggle; but when in *Candide*, in *Jacques le Fataliste*, in the *Lettres de la Montagne* they read passages of surprising license or stunning boldness, they imagine, wrongly, that their authors have broken through the gates for all writers from now on. Freedom of expression seems *given* to them simply because it is *dead*. In those libertine or reckless books one enters at will; to write others with the same audacity requires a struggle, as is clearly exemplified in England, where the most obscene intrigues and the crudest words are tolerated on the stage in our day from dramatists *up to and including Congreve*.

Whom shall they struggle against? Here we find the reappearance of the misunderstanding that is inevitable when one epoch, with its blinkers, tries to understand another. It is all the more excusable in this case since the writers in question were fooling themselves. We know that they thought they were expressing the claims of man when their pens were really serving the bourgeoisie. The autonomy that was won, lost, and won again was the right not to say everything but to forge and articulate the ideology of the bourgeois class according to the rules of taste. In a modern society—since the Renaissance—when the writer and the press (if there is one) have claimed freedom of expression, it has never been an abstract insistence on saying anything at all but the concrete demand of a social stratum or class which, under the cover of this undefined freedom, attempts to articulate openly its particular ideology and substitute it for the ruling ideologies of the age. Politicians catch on to this immediately, and journalists are quick to take advantage; only men of letters remain naive. And if the young people of 1830 to 1850 do not recognize their papa's ideology, *their ideology*, in the works of the preceding century, it is because the bourgeois have changed a little in the meantime. In taking power, the bourgeoisie suppressed some of its ideas and elided others, such as equality, the foundation of universal suffrage; indeed, of the ideas it kept, most shifted from negative to positive except for one, which did the reverse (as we shall see below), the idea of human nature, good insofar as it helped to reverse privilege, bad when it became necessary to justify new inequalities. Thus, for the young bourgeois who reads during the reign of Louis-Philippe, the ideas of his grandparents as he discovers them in books bear a certain resemblance to each other and some affinities. But their virulent antagonisms, Voltaire's scolding of Rousseau, the lively literary quarrels that animated the century mask their strict dialectical unity. Behind the exuberant efflorescence he can't see the rigidity of systems, and behind the systems he can't see the unique structure of which they are merely diverse expressions. Moreover, as the most advanced positions of the great writers provoked counterattacks from authors who supported the regime, all mercenaries but not all bad, the young reader gets completely lost. The autonomy claimed by the authors was the right to say everything and to accept no rule but *taste;* which must be understood as meaning the right to criticize everything, to spare no abuse, no privilege, even putting the Church or the monarchy on trial. In other words, the bourgeoisie demands from its writers a systematic critique of the regime, the rigorous application of the spirit of analysis to all the structures of this corrupt society. But as he cannot grasp the unity of the multiple, the young man discovers through his readings only an incredible diversity of genres and subjects, thesis and antithesis: *everything*, he thinks, is treated here. But he understands this to mean *anything*, pro and con, the idea and its negation. In a licentious book he sees only licentiousness—what audacity! And he does not relate this to another work on the history of religions, save in its equal audacity. It seems to him, finally, that the subjects treated in these works are less important than their consequence, which is the extension of the literary realm. In other words, far from thinking that the literature of the eighteenth century would be so autonomous as frankly to articulate the corrosive ideas of the bourgeois class, he begins to think that the writers choose the most libertine themes just to assure the formal autonomy of literature, continually risking scandal and imprisonment as they do so, and because literature can be entirely itself only if it rejects the external constraints of religion, politics, or respectability and accepts no laws but its own: the pure aesthetic norms of writing.

After all, this young man is a bourgeois of the nineteenth century. The Objective Spirit is composing itself in him through the resurrection of that practico-inert, printed matter. But this operation is performed within the framework of historical circumstance and under its guidance, which of course determines its meaning. And after 1830 the bourgeoisie openly took power; having become the ruling class, it required a class literature. So it will allow its writers to live off a portion of surplus value provided they elaborate and reflect in their works its new ideology—individualism or the sublimation of real property and its consequence, incommunicability; social atomism as the sublimated expression of the forces of mass culture and as the systematic destruction of the notion of class; exteriority as the universal relation between men and the assimilation of human events to physico-chemical facts; and the corollary, the assimilation of economic laws to the laws of nature, freedom as the extenuated sublimation of the principle of free competition, the utilitarianism or puritanism of interest, noninterference of the state in private affairs, absolute distrust of human nature and a complementary absolute confidence in the forces of order, etc. Their task—and the task of all "thinkers"—is therefore quite specific: to defend their class on two fronts, maintaining the principles of formal democracy against the crushed but revanchist aristocracy; turning the entire arsenal of analytic reason against the proletariat to prevent their leaders from making them believe they constitute a class; refashioning in novels the irksome austerity of utilitarianism, masking its sordid reality with an exemplary exalting of the immensity of the work undertaken and the bosses' spirit of sacrifice; making the bourgeois, in short, a positive hero. If this attempt succeeds, its most important consequence will therefore be to assure the ruling class of what Gramsci calls its "hegemony" over the whole society. This means that the exploited classes, having internalized the ideology of the ruling class, will invent reasons to accept their exploitation and become its accomplices. The class writers see themselves entrusted with another task, which is marginal to this central mission: they are ordered to produce diverting works, light entertainments to prompt smiles or dreams. That too is a new fact: for the first time in human history, the class in power demands of its writers a literature of consumption.

And this literature appears on cue. The big newspapers created the serialized story in 1836 to increase sales. Nothing could be more surprising to our apprentice writer; he observes that this new invention has the immediate result of considerably enlarging the circle of readers. But he is annoyed to see great writers like Balzac contributing serialized stories alongside superficial entertainers like Dumas *père*, or writers with no talent at all like the cynical Eugène Sue. Moreover, considering the grandfathers' hard-won autonomy, the serialized story is an unforgivable literary crime: through it, literature *becomes useful;* the novelist becomes doubly productive. Hitherto he has produced capital only for his publisher; now he produces it for the owners of the press as well. The subordination of literature to the material interests of a newspaper is alienation, pure and simple; novels are commissioned, then written, to make people read a daily paper. Would it be better, then, if instead of diverting the bourgeoisie the writer were to serve it by reflecting its ideology? Hardly. The lesson young people thought they had learned from the authors of the eighteenth century is that art is not made to be used. Thus, between 1830 and 1850 something would be accomplished that the writers of the Restoration had unconsciously begun: the writer's break with his public. And this break—almost unperceived while the older writers are so productive and widely read—will be accomplished by those young bourgeois who so far have done nothing but read in order to write; in a way, the reasons for it are already in place at the time he is reading Rousseau and Voltaire while the bourgeois spectators are handing the honors to Emile Augier. This divorce, already experienced but unacknowledged, now appears to them a necessary consequence of the aesthetic enterprise; the two are so closely bound together in their view that the break indeed seems to belong *to the very meaning* of the work, as if it were being written expressly *not to be read.* This line of Paulhan's—which I cite from memory—sums up their point of view rather well: "There are two kinds of literature: bad literature, which is widely read, and good literature, which is not read." But they might not actually have considered the bad to be literature. Since good literature affirms *as an imperative* the necessity of rejecting the public, it can exist only as a result of this rejection, and so there is no other "bad" literature deserving of the name.

Why does this break present itself as normative rather than as a special event? It is something we must examine with even greater attention since we find here a fundamental element of the objective neurosis. In general we can say that its primitive structure comes from the fact that autonomy presents itself as an imperative—insofar as their gaze awakens that practico-inert, eighteenth-century culture—just when the "natural" readers of their future works are revealed to them as a class public. But let us look more closely.

a) Just when the bourgeoisie takes power, these young bourgeois are given this double commandment as a determination of the Objective Spirit: literature must affirm itself beyond all social divisions as the pure idea of man and the world expressed through written words; the literary work can be produced only by an elite, affirmed as such to the extent that it is identified with no single class, not even its class of origin. The error here stems from the fact that the alleged elite was writing a *class literature* in the eighteenth century; but this error is objective, inevitable, for the malice of those great dead authors was never to set bourgeois against aristocrat but to set human nature against the monsters produced by society. As a result, the unity of function and rank of those who exercise that malice (put differently, of function and medium) requires that future writers *become reborn through a transcendence of class.* The notion of transcending class is central here, and we know its source: the favor of kings and princes seemed to detach from their class both the petit-bourgeois Diderot and the haut-bourgeois Voltaire. A hundred years later the meaning of royal favor, grasped through the practico-inert of written history, has changed: it seems no longer the cause of the apparent transcendence of class but rather its effect. Such royal favor would appear to sanction the genius of those who have broken the barriers of their class and, rising to the level of universality, have shown themselves to be the equals of sovereigns. And of course the monarchs recruited the best authors. But when they invited them to their palaces or engaged in correspondence with them, they chose them expressly *because they were bourgeois* and could serve as intermediaries between the monarchy and that class whose economic power was becoming formidable. Thus transcendence of class is the central imperative: one *must* become classless in order to write. But just when this becomes imperative for future writers, there is no longer a way to do it. Certainly the citizen-king can give a peerage to poets. But no one is fooled: this bourgeois distinction can flatter one's vanity for a moment, but it does not separate the writer from his class any more than does the ribbon of the Legion of Honor. *Quite the contrary:* by these rewards—accorded for services rendered—the ruling class signals to its artists that it *acknowledges them as its own.* A prime example is Victor Hugo, who was *doomed* as a poet in 1848 and was only saved by Louis Bonaparte's coup d'état. From this point of view, transcendence of class will be realized symbolically *by negation:* one ought to reject the benefits of the regime and begin by vowing never to enter the Académie française. This rejection, of course, has no *real* value, and above all no efficacy. Neurosis surfaces when the Kantian "You must, therefore you can" is not respected. If rebirth is obligatory and impossible, if the writer must and cannot detach himself from his class of origin, and if a violent *need* to write exacerbates this contradiction, a solution will certainly be found, but it will not be realistic or even rational. On one point, however, success is conceivable. Since the literary function is defined by autonomy, the young writer must vow to serve no ideology, specifically bourgeois ideology, whose utilitarianism challenges the very possibility of autonomous sectors—everything must serve. Autonomy must steel itself against this challenge: a work of the mind must serve nothing and no one. From 1850 onward, autonomy is radicalized in those young, overheated brains. In the eighteenth century, literature obeyed only its own laws; reinterpreted after the June revolution, the formula becomes something slightly different: literature must be its own end. Nonetheless, an objection may be raised that its subject remains identical: it must speak of man. That's true. At least it would be true if our young men read nothing but the works of their grandfathers. We shall soon see that they also read their older brothers, and we shall notice that the themes of the different generations interfere with each other. In any case, from 1715 to 1789 literature announced itself as negativity. When the apprentice writer revived the old books, this negativity, despite the occasional semblance of something positive, was immediately striking; it became his mandate. The trouble was that it had lost its meaning and its object. Indeed, through it analytic reason, the real weapon and thought of Science and the bourgeois class, was affirmed by flexing its muscles against the inherited privilege of history, against history itself. Now that the bourgeois class is in power, analytic reason appears to be its reason. It is responsible for mechanism as well as psychosocial atomism, the dominant segments of bourgeois ideology. And analytic reason has dissolved the very notion of class and reduced social groupings to aggregates of individuals. What can a writer do with it? Feudal privilege is already abolished: what good is it to set oneself against a vanquished, ruined aristocracy? As for turning that formidable instrument against the bourgeoisie itself, that is totally impossible; mechanism and atomism would merely be rediscovered, for these are its "natural" products. In fact, reason of this kind can intervene and dislocate the complex relations—traditional, human, in any case synthetic—on which feudal property is built; it is helpless against *real* property, that is, against the naked relation of the individual (a social atom) to the *res* as inert materiality. To succeed in unmasking bourgeois domination, another point of view would have to be adopted, and another kind of reason. And since the negative tool belongs organically to the bourgeoisie and can be used only to reproduce the ideology of that class, absolute negativity springs from the past century and imposes itself as the very condition of literature just when the writer, if he really wants to transcend his class, finds it impossible to wield.

b) For the same reasons, just when the writer rejects ideologies, he is denied exact knowledge. We have seen that despite the developments of science, the author of 1750 is still a "gentleman": he knows Newtonian physics, can articulate it in his own language, and often pursues laboratory experiments himself. There is a difference, of course, between the scientist who writes and the writer who practices scientific methods, but not a radical one; communication between them is always conceivable, and in any case relations of *confraternity* are established. By the middle of the following century, relations between the writer and the scientist are no longer the same: the sciences have made such progress that it is useless to describe them in literary language, and besides, it is usually impossible without falling into vulgarization. The various disciplines have adopted their own languages, and in the clarity of their symbols, the precision of communicated information, and their concision of exposition these languages have an "elegance" that has no connection to "style" or literature in general. Moreover, the culture of our future writers can be pushed quite far,[4] but it will never allow them to consider science an activity that belongs to *them* and can be practiced on a par with the specialists. This impossibility is known quite early: in secondary school, everyone displays his "aptitudes." From this time on, the literary option may be chosen against science and out of spite; in any case, it is maintained and defined outside it. The movement of analytic reason constructing its knowledge can no longer be the object of literature—that

---

4. Louis Ménard, for example, was also a chemist.

would be a *paraphrase* (like Louis Bouilhet's *Les Fossiles*). So not only does the critical exercise of negativity make no more sense in 1840, but the domain of knowledge—a systematic product of analytic nega-tivity—no longer belongs to literature. We can even speak of a certain opposition between science and literary art: not that the latter, in gen-eral, challenges science (we shall see that it does that too, but under the influence of the Romantics); simply, literature chooses a *non-scientific* domain as its arena of knowledge. That is, if it exists; since reason is entirely employed by the bourgeoisie to provide it with theoretical and practical knowledge, hence an ideology, the nonscien-tific domain must be conceived as *external to the rational*. But just as that moment, and in contradiction to it, the former rigor of the dead writers of the preceding century becomes imperative within the nor-mative notion of autonomy; even if the content of scientific thought is inimical to any transposition, its form imposes itself on future writ-ers. Whatever its subject matter, literature must make itself scientific through the utilization of *exact methods*. The contradiction here is pro-found since we are dealing, in short, with an application of the meth-ods of scientific reason to a nonscientific and perhaps nonrational subject. Is nonknowledge to be treated as knowledge? If the content of the work is nonknowledge, is there even an affinity between aes-thetic rigor—which according to the classics is a norm of literary cre-ation—and the rigor of the exact disciplines? Let us not imagine that this is a matter of subjective fantasy. This absurd problem is the result of the objective divorce of literary art and science. There was a com-mon ground in the eighteenth century, and the two kinds of rigor could to some degree reflect each other. The situation is revived through reading as an imperative just when that ground no longer exists, when the high development of science *rejects* literature, when the division of labor, pushed ever further, makes the scientist and the writer two *specialists*. Later, naturalism will offer a new synthesis of these oppositions. For the moment there is none. Literature *to be writ-ten*, flung in the direction of imagination, poses for itself the question of its relation to *truth*. Certainly for the first time since the high Middle Ages: neither the intellectuals and revolutionaries of the Re-naissance, nor the great classical writers and prerevolutionaries of the eighteenth century, had any doubt about the veracity of a master-piece, or even its efficacy, whether the issue was overthrowing a re-gime or chastising morals. But at the very moment when literature is confronted with the problem of its fundamental subject, the unbeliev-able success of experimental methods makes writers wonder whether they will not acquire new rigor by the scientific use of pure imagination. The same writers, moreover, to the extent that they still seem to think the fundamental subject of their art is human nature, wonder whether they can establish its laws through technical rigor and precision of *observation*. For without knowing it they are the victims of a myth of bourgeois ideology which, giving the lie to experimentalism—now held by scientists to be the imperative of science—bases practical knowledge on the accumulation of observations. This myth is *empiricism,* the inevitable consequence of associationism, of mental passivity, made necessary by its reduction to simple elements effected by analytic reason throughout the past century. At the outset the apprentice writer must take on the bourgeois status of a "man of experience," one who has seen and retained a great deal, a status in contradiction with his extreme youth and even, we shall see, with the imperative of impassivity that is soon to be revealed to him. Since, moreover, this conception of knowledge as accumulated passively[5] has no truth, the apprentice finds himself in the presence of two impossible alternatives: to learn the objective laws of the imagination and govern it according to these rules (even though art always implies the free play of the imaging function), or to pose at the outset as a specialist in human nature, the knowledge of which is merely the sum of accumulated observations.

At the very moment, however, when literature is trying to borrow the methods of science, and clarity, conciseness, precision, and rigor are apparently becoming aesthetic norms of the construction of the literary work, the resuscitated eighteenth century continues to make imperative rules of art defined by the *taste* of the period. In themselves, the rules of taste are already inimical to the set of norms art seems inclined to borrow from the systematic search for truth. Those norms, indeed, are merely applied to the work from the outside. It is desirable, of course, to be concise—and Pascal long ago complained of "not having the time to make it brief." But beyond the fact that conciseness cannot, ultimately, appear as an *absolute* obligation, as though in all cases a work should be as short as possible,[6] conciseness

5. There would be every reason to study this idea of *experience* as accumulated knowledge and to find out if it isn't *one* of the extenuated expressions of the process of economic accumulation. That process is certainly at the source of the myth of Progress, which is impossible to determine qualitatively but is on firm ground in areas of quantitative accumulation. And experience can be considered in each person as the progress of the individual.

6. Always as brief as possible. But that "possible" allows so many factors to be taken

nonetheless defines the work from the outside; the work reduces it-self to the negative rule that prohibits prolixity. It does not permit the literary work to be constructed or evaluated, except formally. From examples in our own culture we could say that there are many differ-ent kinds of conciseness: that of Jules Renard, which derives from a systematic purging of the sentence and could be expressed as follows: "Under any circumstances, as few words as possible"; and that of Proust, who economizes neither on words, nor on incidents, nor on parentheses but assigns a precise function to every element of his sentence and rejects anything that does not enhance the unity of the verbal whole. How are we to choose? *Taste*, as manifest in the eigh-teenth century, is constituted by rules that determine the work from within, that is, from its internal relations; in this sense norms are not only prohibitions, they facilitate the production of a work of the mind. No doubt the rule of the three unities and the obligation to write a tragedy in alexandrines can seem *external:* the intimate bond uniting laws dictated by a Greek philosopher with the living principle of Racinean tragedy is not immediately apparent. That bond is the impossibility of reconciling contrary passions (passional *rights*), and consequently the impossibility of *living*. But it doesn't take long to see that the rule was not observed at the beginning of the seventeenth century, and that tragedy internalized it by realizing its own rigor.

If drama's stage is the world, conflicts can become diluted, solu-tions can seem unexpected, coming from *elsewhere.* The three unities are required, on the contrary, to condense space and time in such a way that the characters, alone and naked, without mediation, with-out intercession or escape, confront each other in the most perfect state of abandonment and die by each other's hands. In a general way, the genre defines its rules in the classical centuries by acquiring depth, and those rules are simply the synthetic schemes that allow it to become totalized and radicalized in every particular work. But for this very reason *taste*, as it reappeared in 1850 for the future writer, looks like an empty demand of totalization. With the exception of a few laggards, no one is writing tragedies in verse or epistolary novels anymore. And the norms that presided at the birth of *Bajazet* or of *Les*

---

into consideration, if the work in question is a literary one, that the rule of conciseness is no more than a corollary to style in the end. Mathematical elegance, by contrast, demands the most extreme conciseness whatever the circumstances and without other considerations. But this lies within the exact sciences and is a *logical* necessity that derives from the goal and its methods. It remains external to the work of art.

Liaisons dangereuses cannot be applied to future works. On the other hand, as future works are not yet born, they have no form or meaning; their aim is not yet known—especially since literature, taking itself as its own end, is no longer certain of its subject. Thus the *taste* of 1750 is not suitable a hundred years later; even in 1750 it was a strange and unstable composite in which the royal rules of the seventeenth century were at once proclaimed by authors and eaten away by the diastases of bourgeois negativity, while other norms, derived from more recent genres or those in progress, were added surreptitiously to the first. And the *taste* of 1850 does not exist except as an imperative postulation requiring future works to engender their own rules, which must remain accessible to all. Between 1830 and 1850, literature affirms its autonomy, but it is unaware of its current essence, its objectives, and its own laws. It does know that *knowledge* has been severed from it. And that it has the choice either to constitute itself as autonomous knowledge by applying itself to plumbing the depths of feelings, or to make itself the site of nonknowledge.

c) The fame of Voltaire and Rousseau, the beauty and internal tension of their works, and their social privileges come from one and the same source: the essence of literature is fundamentally *communication*. Whatever their strictly aesthetic pleasure in crafting language to the height of expressiveness and purity, the sentence they are fashioning is destined for others; it is primarily conceived to be understood, and as I have shown it must be addressed on the one hand to the aristocracy, to win it over or unsettle it, and on the other to that vast public we have called bourgeois, which they confuse with unprivileged humanity. So for them the vast power of a word resides in those thousands of readers who are going to take hold of it and establish it as a guiding scheme for their understanding or a singular rule of their sensibility. And when the young Postromantics revive it in their turn, its profundity—a practico-inert determination—comes from the collective comprehension and adherence it evoked in all those now dead minds. Inert, because of the annihilation of that first public for which the work was destined, inexhaustible beyond materiality, this profundity seems to them an essential property of verbal matter. But for us it is clearly just the residue of that vast vanished intercommunication that at the time had as much the effect of dissolving the sentence in the idea as of isolating it and preserving it for its unique beauty. Thus literature already written reveals its chasms—its significations insofar as *several* diverse publics have simultaneously seized upon them—and cannot help presenting communication as an imperative; it says to its young reader: *write to communicate.* From communication, and from it alone, will come the glory he seeks; through his works he will shape the taste of his readers, and they in turn will judge him by what he tried to do.

Unfortunately, this very clear order is signaled to the Postromantic adolescents just when they have understood their real situation: they are making their appearance at a moment when there is no public to be found. Of course, people read a good deal. Even more than they did in the preceding century. But the Romantics live on, the bourgeoisie forms its literary cadres, and there is an ever-growing class literature. Autonomous literature has lost its public. For the first time in history those young souls harbor a brutal separation between writing and communication. In fact, there is only one public: the bourgeoisie. And the writer has nothing to say to it unless he renounces autonomy and enlists in the service of class ideology. So this imperative is a dead letter. Or rather, it takes hold in these young minds and acts negatively by fueling their constant, vague anxiety. Be that as it may, the refusal of the new generation is clear: they will not write to be read. This decision will take a hundred forms in the course of the century; in the beginning there will be the grim, impassioned will not to publish. We have seen it in Flaubert and have tried to explain it by subjective reasons. But objective reasons are equally strong, and the prefaces he writes to his adolescent works suggest he is conscious of this: he only rarely fails to insult his philistine readers. This writer, like Baudelaire and so many others, is tortured by the contradictory desire to be read and to have no readers. Later, the works will be allowed to appear but protected by smoke screens: the meaning of written sentences must be wrapped in a propitious obscurity to discourage the unworthy. From Flaubert to the last Symbolists, one thing is certain: the artist accepts only other artists as his readers. Does this mean that he writes for them? Not even that. In a way, the refusal to communicate tends to transform the literary object into something incommunicable. A hundred years earlier, language was a perfect instrument that rendered thought in all its nuances and transmitted it intact. Now, the triumph of the bourgeoisie puts communication in question: there are *several* languages, and there is no common language between the writer and this public. The reason is, of course, that the attitude of the autonomous man of letters and that of the bourgeois utilitarian are irreconcilable. But one quickly comes to the conclusion that discourse is unsuitable for transmitting everything; the new literature will have to bend that imperfect instrument, making it allusive or discarding it altogether. In the age of communication, the work is merely written speech. But when the public is nowhere to be found, silence counts as much as the Word.

The other consequence of the writer's denial of *his* society is that, more or less discreetly, he considers the public to be inessential. Communication, which used to constitute the word and confer upon it its functional reality as sign, is surreptitiously removed from the intentional structures of literary discourse. Certainly men are allowed to participate in that permanent celebration of art which is each particular work: they *can* approach it when it is finished, and they can read it at their peril. It is like touching a relic: in the best case it communicates the sacred in the form of a particular grace reserved for you alone; otherwise, nothing happens, you adore without being implicated. A relation of reciprocity between author and reader is, of course, out of the question, as it would be between a holy thighbone and a believer. Literature is no longer *dual*; it exists in itself as the pure product of the author, with the authorized but in no way obligatory participation of a public that is never the aim of the writing. This conception can be maintained only if language is granted a certain substantiality, at the very least a being independent of interlocutors. Language must, if you will, be preserved not only in its materiality but in its signifying structures, in its intentional surpassing of its raw material understood as the movement of one speaker toward another through matter, preserved even if neither speaker actually exists. And in a way this is just how the linguist sees it today, as a system of signs having a conventional origin and internal relations independent of any concrete locution. But while studying language as constituting its own rules and imposing itself on its interlocutors, the linguist today is not unaware that his research is intentionally abstract, that language is an abstraction in relation to a particular language, which exists only insofar as it is spoken, though it must be spoken as it is. The point of view that tends to impose itself as an imperative on the Postromantic future writers is that the word in its concrete fullness, possesses a resonant and visual beauty that is the very expression of its materiality, as well as a signifying depth born of the coexistence of multiple semantic levels, sometimes superimposed in strata, sometimes—depending on the sentence—present all at once in a multiplicity of interpenetration; and the writer needs no duality to make the word render up all its flavor and good sense. He needs only to deploy verbal units in such a way as to highlight the synthetic unity of visual beauty and multiplicity of meaning for every vocable. Once the thing has been made, whether it is printed or not, read or not, it remains. In itself and for itself. Not for others. Let us be more precise. Francis Ponge shows us a monkey—after our species has disappeared in some disaster—hunched over a book, a strange and futile object, which he holds in his hands and examines without discovering what to do with it. This alarmist hypothesis is never far from the minds of 1840; humanity is a mortal species. Leconte de Lisle, for example, willingly destroys it in the heating or cooling of the planet. But for these young people, this quite predictable wreckage in no way detracts from the eternity of the work. Provided the orangoutangs take care to preserve the books in hothouses, the meaning of sentences in all its ambiguity and beauty will remain unwitnessed, as the unseen flower pours out its secret perfume "in absolute solitude." The "thingness" of the signifier would be inconceivable if it did not impose itself on the future writer *as a reality*. Not only as the consequence of his denial of the public, but above all because words in old books seem to be things that signify by themselves and in their materiality. Revived by those young men, the sentences of Voltaire and Diderot are offered not as *written* by an author just for their eyes, but initially and expressly as *not* meant for them. All those letters, all those pamphlets, all those apologetic memoirs, all those defenses, some of them written in prison, are read *after* the writer's *death*, when they have already reached their actual destination—which was contemporaneous—and did or did not obtain the desired effect. In this sense the young Postromantic feels superfluous, even when inspired by Beaumarchais's prose: a dispute over money was involved, it festered, hence those magnificent letters, and the matter was straightened out. The file is closed, the dirty linen has been washed in the family—the family, in this case, being the eighteenth century drawing to its close. The reader of 1840 is admitted, but he is merely a useless troublemaker since those letters have already reached their intended readers (certain authorities, members of parliament, the bourgeois elite). Better, they understood; all of Paris laughed at these libels and kept them alive for several weeks, like a chain linking Parisians together. And this understanding *remained:* we know how those pamphlets were received, we know the details of the Guzman affair, the importance of the written thing really had its effect, the admiration aroused by certain lines, certain movements of the pen. In 1840, little as he might care about it, the young reader knew almost as much about it as we do. He did care about it: an apprentice man-of-letters sees the prefiguration of his own fate in that celebrated writer's life. He was opening books *already* read, reading sentences *already understood,* which had *already* produced their real effect. Those graphic signs were part of literary culture as a practico-inert revealed by *books* written *about other books;* as a result, they were manifest as the material structure of signs: the sentences were long since deflowered. By men now dead. The young writers of 1840 *were reading what was already read.* The "already read" could not fail to qualify every word of the text as an irreversible and eternal determination. But at the same time the Postromantics knew that those readers in knee breeches and white stockings, so near and yet so far away, had died unaware. Indeed, what remained of them, apart from a few bones, was *in books.* Unless one of them deserved special mention, their only determination was anonymity: they were retained and wholly defined by masterpieces, by the success reserved for the *Confessions,* for the *Mariage de Figaro;* in short, by the impact these works had on them. Thus literature is posited as self-sufficient: the *already understood* is affirmed and isolated, cut off from its first readers who are cast into anonymity by death. This same death gives that graphic sign its inert materiality. Since its audience is deceased, the act of intellection or comprehension has been extinguished as the synthetic surpassing of raw material toward the signified; it remains inscribed, however, as the past surpassed, preserved, and perpetuated in the printed thing. That inert past qualifies it and gives it the false unity of this seal: an act that has vanished as praxis, that is preserved by its material traces and the false unity it gives to the dispersal of raw material. Didn't every heart beat faster when those schoolboys opened the "famous" *Candide* or the "admirable" *Juliette* for the first time? A pyramid of readers, dead from base to summit, with a living, inessential comrade on top, guaranteed the work which had long since internalized that valorization, presenting itself with the imperative: *admire me.* To be sure, these observations are valid at any period. But there are those periods when history slows down, when the difference between generations, while always real, is not translated into violent oppositions. And others when history accelerates, when in rebellion against one's parents one goes in search of a grandfather or great grandfather; in these periods crystallized readings superimpose or establish themselves as the practico-inert signs of the book, and the distance between the most recent readers and the first is such that those earlier readers crumble to dust and reside only in the anonymous valorization incorporated by the work. This is the case in 1840; too many major events have separated the old, defunct authors from their successors: the Revolution, the Empire, the Restoration, the triumph of the bourgeoisie under the July monarchy, the substitution of industrial capitalism for commercial capitalism. A young reader reads those glorious monuments of the past with a certain reserve, he does not entirely surrender to them. So these are posited as self-sufficient, and former readings exist in them as strata— at once clearly separated and undetectable—that comprise its profundity and ambiguity, even as the admiration provoked in former times is incorporated in them and, reawakened, presents itself to new readers as a singular imperative issuing from the work itself. Thus the old books, once the new products of literary craftsmen, tend increasingly to resemble things. As a blotter absorbs ink, they have absorbed the diverse and contradictory thoughts of a changing public, and now they put forth those thoughts as their own qualities without indicating their provenance. The most resistant of them, which are made the object of a unanimous consensus, at least for a time, are discovered as if they were fragments of nature, a familiar countryside or continent. In short, the source of the curious notion that replaces literary duality with the unity of the creator and the work, positing the work as a manufactured object existing alone and self-sufficient, is the simultaneous disappearance of the author and his contemporary readers, which has broken the *dual being* of literature-already-written. That literature now seems to have the unity of an objective reality whose significations, already a hundred or a thousand times revived and surpassed toward the signified, certainly seem *capable* of being revived anew but to have no need of this inessential reactivation to exist *as an act for no one*, or for God, and in eternity. The triumph of the practico-inert is the source of Postromantic illusion; what is concealed is that by resting the sign on the quasi-total suppression of the interlocutor, the illusion bears a truncated relation to the absolute. For there is no doubt that the literary absolute does exist, but it must be sought in the *dual* totalization of author and reader by the manufactured object, signaling that the moment of the work's full existence is the moment of reading. Unable to understand this necessity—since they denied reciprocity as a bond between the author and the bourgeois public—the future writers of the Postromantic era considered themselves ephemeral and inessential as readers, as authors they thought themselves demiurges working in the absolute. But the rigor of this dialectical development—based on false but imposed premises—leads them still further; for if the work is self-sufficient, if, as was first said at the time, it shuts itself off to its creator and somehow sets itself against him, the demiurge himself is merely a necessary means of the work—once finished, he effaces himself before it. This theme will sound throughout the second half of the century. At the outset, the book in its inhuman perfection solicits the sacrifice of its all too human author; in this inert demand we see one of the roots of impassivity as an objective norm of the period, which we shall later examine. In the end, demanding that the tragic poet preserve anonymity in his lifetime and until the end of time, Mallarmé embodies the ultimate meaning of the writer's inessentiality when he dreams of a great tragedy that would portray before the assembled people, like the medieval passion plays, the mystery and fatal contradiction of man plunged once again into the rhythms of nature. Thus conceived in the eighteenth century as a critical requirement, formulated by the writer in the name of the social function he attributes to his art but politically sustained by a still victimized rising class that makes negativity its chief weapon, literary autonomy finds itself taken up again and reaffirmed in the middle of the following century and invested with new significance because of the triumph of the bourgeoisie and the consequent divorce of the writer from his public. Refusing to serve, to be integrated into a class literature, the work becomes its own end; it stands on its own in an inhuman solitude, resting on the related suppression of reader and author.

The final contradiction to which literature as the *Objective Spirit* of the eighteenth century condemns its specialist is secondary but no less striking. If literary writing is not dual, and if the writer must produce without counting on the favor of a public that is nowhere to be found, writing must on no account become a profession; in other words, work in belles-lettres will be *noble* if the worker does not live off his writings. It is therefore imperative that he provide for his material independence. And that can only be done in three ways: by practicing a secondary profession that will allow him to earn his keep, by accepting a pension or sinecure from the state, or by being wealthy enough to live on the income from his capital. But it must be observed that these three solutions—which define the new position of the writer in society—all contradict the imperative of the preceding century. Indeed, in 1750 the autonomy of literature required that the writer belong nowhere.[7] A hundred years later that same autonomy can be safeguarded only if the man of letters affirms his independence

7. As we have seen, this was an appearance based on the necessity of writing on "human nature" in general.

as an author by exaggerating his class condition. He will be a petit-bourgeois, a poorly paid civil servant or teacher; unless—since patronage disappeared with the aristocrats—he bases his refusal to write for his class on the acceptance of the meager donations accorded him by the *apparatus of that same class*. Otherwise, living on a bourgeois fortune, he will be qualified to deal with human nature or any other subject outside of class only by his wealth, itself based on the complex relations of production which in this era defined relations between the classes, and particularly bourgeois property. In other words, he can write about *everything* and quite independently (with no need to please his bourgeois public or even to publish), *provided* his thought—inasmuch as it more or less clearly expresses his position—is suffused with bourgeois ideology.

Considering merely the imperatives of the eighteenth century as they are refracted through the circumstances of 1850, we see that literature poses questions to future writings that do not admit of rational answers. The movement of history propels the art of writing into insoluble contradictions. In the eighteenth century, literature knew itself to be pure negativity and so affirmed simultaneously its autonomy and its universality "beyond class." This was its profound illusion; it was in fact a class literature in that writers, born bourgeois, practiced negation for the sake of the bourgeoisie, and falsely positive "human nature" symbolically represented the negative ideology of a class that still had to undermine the defensive constructs of its adversary. That inevitable illusion had in part to do with the position of the writer and the subject he had to treat and in part with one of the essential aspects of literary activity, masked after 150 years of virulence by the "classical century" and rediscovered through social conflict: negativity. Autonomy and negativity are fundamental literary imperatives that were gradually defined in the course of the centuries and could not disappear, *provided they were understood correctly*, without the collapse of literature itself. For this double reason the writer announces that he is "classless" to his successor, who feels he is the product of the triumphant class, the same class that supported the pamphlets of his predecessors. The real situation is the reverse of this mirage. It was in the eighteenth century that the writer—usually unwittingly but not always—created a class literature; he did not perceive it as he was absorbed in the struggle against particularisms *in the name of universality*. In 1840 the adolescent, having decided to write quite probably to escape his family and hence his bourgeois condition, interprets the imperative of autonomy as a strict prohibition against creating class literature. Now, this is the era when the triumphant bourgeoisie, resting its power on the routing of the aristocracy, presents itself to young bourgeois as a rigorously closed totality where one can sometimes rise but never leave except through failure. The refusal of these prisoners, however, is sincere. The imperative of autonomy shows them literature as a demand for classlessness; and by that very fact it serves their intentional evasion. The trouble is that any *real* class transcendence is actually impossible. Which—going no further—reveals to these apprentices the impossibility of literature itself, insofar as it would refuse to be a class literature. Of course this revelation is quite particular to the era: the young bourgeois finds support neither in the sullen nobility, who stand aloof from culture, nor in the proletariat, whose nature he does not understand and whose class consciousness is still obscure. Later, other kinds of class transcendence will be possible: the bourgeois will be seen through the eyes of peasants or workers, and without necessarily being a child of the working class, it will be possible to adopt their point of view. The result will not be a literature of class but rather a literature of *alliance,* linking the petit-bourgeois intellectual to the proletariat. Another possibility, realized more or less consciously with the beginning of naturalism, would be for a writer writing for the bourgeoisie to conduct an effort of radical demoralization in its very heart, to depict the bourgeoisie as it should see itself. This time the writer is an agent or accomplice, if you will, of the exploited classes, expressing not their vision but rather, thanks to the inner distance he owes to their existence, a kind of sudden negative awareness of bourgeois reality, in himself and others. Maupassant's *Bel Ami* is one example. This literature cannot be called a class literature, though it does not leave bourgeois terrain. Influenced at a distance by the conditions of life lived by the masses, it tries to show—without real principle—the contradictions of bourgeois ideology as well as its refutation by daily life. In this sense, literature preserves its autonomy. But in 1840, not having found a real support that allows him to transcend his class *in the work* (if not in the writer), the young bourgeois can base autonomy as a *real* demand of the literary object only on an *ideal* classlessness or, as we shall see, on a conduct of failure. This first contradiction is at the basis of all others: the break with science and the effort to integrate scientific rigor; the rejection of analytic reason and the justified fear of thereby reserving for literature the single domain—suspect and decried—of the irrational; the necessity and impossibility of retrieving the use of negativity; the rejection of communication and transformation into the allusive creation of the incommunicable; the search for glory colliding with the scornful rejection of the only possible public; the obligation to live as a bourgeois to safeguard independence and to write nonbourgeois works. All these contradictions rest on the historical movement that makes the bourgeoisie, considered a *negative* class, the dominant class imposing its order as a positive absolute.

C. The Older Brothers

Had the works of the eighteenth century, dead and revived as imperatives, been the sole determinations of the Objective Spirit, the situation of a future writer in the middle of the last century would have been neither easy nor enviable. But in the meantime, literature had produced other imperatives that contradicted those earlier ones and were contradicted by historical circumstance, making things even more complicated. Between 1789 and 1815, as we know, literary autonomy suffered an eclipse. The bourgeoisie fought to keep power and imperiously demanded to be served. At first the writers did so voluntarily, which meant that despite everything they were sacrificing themselves as authors to the triumph of their class. In other words, the specialists in human nature consented, in combat, to write militant works of class literature. So that under the Empire, when the military dictatorship presented bourgeois demands as orders or prohibitions, exploiting and censuring, the muzzled and dazed writers did not recognize behind this tyranny the dictates of the bank and big business. Autonomy, conquered and lost, could reestablish itself only *against the bourgeoisie;* it would take refuge in the aristocracy and would reward itself with intermittent exile. Significantly, the greatest writer of the Empire was the monarchist Chateaubriand, and his fame with the bourgeois public of France was confirmed by *Le Génie du christianisme,* a defensive but effective campaign against Jacobin dechristianization. The Voltaireans were not won over, but the generation of 1840 never forgot that adept defense, which glossed over questions of dogma and the real existence of the Almighty to assert that Christian aspiration toward the infinite was the source of the finest monuments of art and literature. For the first time, negativity, losing its practical power of continuous corrosion, became negation. Beauty, born of dissatisfaction, contested the real in its entirety and bore witness to the Christian impulse toward the other world and the hidden God. Other defensive themes were energized. History, reconsidered, challenged analytic reason: compact, indissoluble, by reconquering temporality it legitimized if not all privileges at least the principle of monarchy; reasons of the heart, restored through the beauty of style, happily challenged those of Reason. Napoleon let things take their course, becoming annoyed at times; this new writing favored one aspect of his complex politics, for he certainly wanted to disarm the religious opposition and reintegrate the old nobility into society.

True Romanticism, however, does not date from this period. The paradoxical situation of literature-in-the-process-of-inventing-itself, borne by circumstance to the side of the conservative class, fully affirmed itself only after 1815, when the Allies, faute de mieux, restored the old king, Louis XVIII, to the throne and for fifteen years gave the appearance of power to the exiled nobility. I have indicated in the preceding volume some of the hopes and disappointments the provincial apprentice artists found in Romanticism. I shall quickly summarize the features relevant to our present discussion that marked the generation of the Postromantics from 1830 on. Paradoxically, literary autonomy shifts to the young Romantics just as bourgeois freedom of expression is severely controlled. When the Congrégation is spying on citizens even in their homes, the new poets and novelists can say *what they want*. There is some friction, of course: a few plays are censored and then the censorship is revoked. Just enough of it to make this autonomy too appear to be overcome. But the truth is that these newcomers can say anything because they are attempting to express the thoughts of the rulers. Let us be more precise. The politically dominant class at this period thinks nothing, has forgotten nothing, has learned nothing. But if it is desirable for that class to win the favor of other social strata and isolate the bourgeoisie, it must have a new ideology. Not the ideology of the *Old* Regime, which fell into ruin in the childhood of Louis XV and was effectively dismantled by the bourgeoisie; but quite the contrary, a set of ideas and myths that represent the Restoration as the original and new surpassing of the bourgeois reign by a new order. In short, writers would like to be the *public relations men* of the restored monarchy. Just as Voltaire and Diderot were for the despots of the Enlightenment. The difference is that they don't claim to represent the other classes of the nation in the corridors of power. The *tension* so manifest in the works of the preceding century has disappeared in the works of the new writers: they write for the king, the aristocracy, the repentant part of the bourgeoisie, and in a few cases—though they are not easily reached—for the popular masses they call the people, who are precious allies against the class that exploits them. And, by the same token, against the impenitent bourgeoisie, against the whole class with rare exceptions. This aristocratic literature must be *practiced* by aristocrats. Here again, only in reverse, we find the imperative link between autonomy and the transcendence of class. An adept government might have profited from the situation to attract the ambitious men who so spontaneously devised its publicity. But these rulers are forbidding and closed, and above all distrustful. They hardly encourage the writers. Yet literature will be made high and low, without the transcendence of class; the best authors are poor gentlemen encouraged by the bourgeois defeat to break ranks. Even Hugo is a Royalist on his mother's side. The Romantics, however, certainly do not refuse to earn their living with their pens—far from it; it's of little importance to them whether the abject bourgeoisie reads their works, which are full of condemnations of the bourgeoisie along with considerations that will in part escape it and, if dimly understood, would very likely demoralize it. But at the same time they are transforming the profession of writing, or rather they are denying that writing is a profession. Remunerated or not, it is a gentleman's activity. Therefore it is the opposite of *work* as the bourgeois practices it, as he imposes it on the disadvantaged classes. This does not mean that they refuse to craft their works carefully—although most of them claim to write a poem or a play in one night, mingling ink with the tears they shed. Rather they contest the goal of labor proper to bourgeois societies, which is to accumulate capital and, for the exploited, to reproduce their life. In other words, these gentlemen and assimilated gentlemen reawaken the soldier's contempt—their fathers' and older brothers'—for productive work in its vulgar aspect. Once again it is a matter of objective imperatives. More than one person will be found to imagine literature as a successor to the military profession. According to this view, the aristocrat—essentially a soldier—risks his life to kill the enemy and ravage a foreign country. Literature must be characterized by that generosity, that gift of oneself, and if this substituted activity is no longer essentially destructive, it manifests itself in any case through *unproductive* works—which are thereby inherently destructive to the class enemy, the bourgeois—and, neglecting the utilitarianism of the rabble, aspire only to serve king, religion, and fatherland. The poor bourgeois children who around 1840 delight in *Les Nuits* by Musset, in *Eloa,* and even in *Les Orientales,* will thus be victims of an objective delusion.

96

In the light of works of the preceding century, Romantic nobility seems opportunely to reaffirm the autonomy of art. Yet, while the truth of its behavior essentially refers to this affirmation, it continues to say the opposite. In the eyes of these aristocrats, it isn't literature that recruits and defines the writer everywhere according to its requirements, that is, according to those of the Objective Spirit; rather, it is really the writer that defines literature. Writers view literature as the natural activity of the aristocracy. When the aristocracy is not doing battle, it is singing. And no one can imitate it—except a few providentially chosen bourgeois who deny their class. And then the essential characteristic of the poet, generosity, belongs only to the military elite who inherit it by blood from their numerous ancestors who have died for the king. Consequently, the very idea of bourgeois literature is nonsense; no one can write unless he is a gentleman by birth and sometimes, with the help of God whose designs are inscrutable, by sensibility. This pseudo-autonomy is effaced and unmasks a class literature. The nobility alone has the privilege of writing; and its works, expressing its generosity in their very texture, have only one purpose and subject: the manifestation of a neo-aristocratic ideology. The bourgeois of Voltaire's century did the greatest harm to the Ancien Régime, which would otherwise still be standing: thus the license to write is now revoked. Not by government decree, but by producing works it would be beyond their reach to write, and by disqualifying self-styled authors who are not in a position to write such works. The harsh struggle that ended with the victory of Romanticism at the first performance of *Hernani* is political as much as literary; it is less a question of opposing the new doctrine to the old than of tearing the pen from the hands of the bourgeoisie. Tragedy, born under absolute monarchy, is condemned because it is bourgeois at its origin and because it became thoroughly bourgeois with Voltaire; by rejecting it, the new writers reject the public as well, which still has a taste for it—Jacobins all, muzzled but solidly clinging to their position and in no way repentant. What fun if they still want to fight! By producing a Casimir Delavigne, they prove by themselves that tragedy is not worth an hour's trouble, and, in the presence of the generosity of Romantic dramas that encompass the whole world, they unmask despite themselves the avarice, the sordid economy of means, that in the very construction of the tragic work betrays the baseness of their utilitarianism.

The adolescent of 1840, son of a notary or a physician, is in perfect accord with the new authors who denounce the narrowness and false

97

rigor of the tragedies his father still enjoys; for there are plenty of other reasons for that denunciation—which we shall not go into—and many other aspects of that vast European event we call Romanticism. At the same time, unfortunately, he is learning that he has been condemned without recourse. Bourgeois, bourgeois by birth, raised in bourgeois ideology, he can do anything but write. These noblemen, who have lost so many of their plumes, tell him that art is the unique privilege of their caste and resumes all others. In our century, Charles Maurras had the charming idea of proscribing our culture to the Jews, who were not, of course, capable of detecting the incomparable *quality* of Racinean verse. A matter of race, to be sure; the stupidest Frenchman could be sensitive to that alexandrine line "Dans l'Orient desert, quel devint mon ennui"; the most intelligent Jew might understand the meaning but could not grasp its power. For the texture of the line was specifically French; moreover, eternal France was incarnate in it, as the whole allows itself to be glimpsed through the part. The Romantic enterprise, at the outset, is not unconnected to this wretched ruse. More adroit and audacious, however, it is not content with showing the bourgeois older works beyond their comprehension; it *produces* works that are in essence inaccessible to it—race is not invoked here, but rather blood. And even as they think they have plumbed the depths of their older brothers' works, the young Postromantics sense some elusive but ubiquitous resistance that indicates their permanent exclusion. They will write only by obliterating their bourgeois sensibility—and that is an impossible task. In other words, the imperative of the eighteenth century could be summed up in these words: "Transcend your class if you want to write; the privileged will help you leave your class, and through the exercise of critical negativity you will soon raise yourself above the privileged themselves." And now the works of their elders, incorporated by readers into the Objective Spirit, throw this proscription in their face: "You will not write anything since you are not an aristocrat." The imperative and the proscription contradict each other. Not entirely, however; in both cases *real* transcendence of class is impossible. The triumph of *Hernani* is soon followed by the death throes of Romanticism, the July Revolution. The poets survive and adapt, but the class they claimed to represent falls into ruin. Above the bourgeoisie there is nothing; so future writers might just as well place themselves ideally above the ruling class and declare gratuitously that they constitute a new aristocracy. Instead of being defined by a status, and instead of grounding that dignity in an institution, they will ask their activity as artists to define them in their social being. Many of Flaubert's contemporaries could claim as their own that sentence he wrote in a letter to Louise: "We artists are the Good Lord's aristocracy." In its bizarre fashion, this sums it all up. The Good Lord's aristocracy—an odd turn of phrase for an agnostic, but justified by usage. This aristocracy, in short, is untamed and, in a way, asocial since it is recognized by no one *but* the artist; indeed, even supposing the bourgeoisie should value *art* above all else, and the real aristocracy should no longer deny the common people the right to be writers, it would be no less evident to either that the artist belongs to the bourgeois elite, that he is, if you will, a superior bourgeois. This is so true, and the future authors are so conscious of it, that especially after 1870 they will claim—as we have seen—a privileged place beside the men of science but *within* the bourgeois class: Know how to honor your great men, they urge the bourgeois. But even then, having arrived at a clear knowledge of their class reality, they cannot renounce their fantasy. They will have two simultaneous conceptions of themselves. First, as the most outstanding of their class, they will be an enlightened group advising the politician and guiding men (over the years, experimental knowledge has replaced empiricism in their mythology), yet their conception of themselves, modeled on the psychological atomism of the past century, does not allow them to base this new idea of science on the valid notion of mental activity; in short, for the first time they will accept a theoretico-practical function in society.[8] At the same time, they will

8. What is involved, from this point of view, is an attempt by the petty bourgeoisie (the liberal professions) to impose itself on the haute bourgeoisie as its mentor by means of its intellectual capital. An enterprise doomed to failure as long as society views property and technical authority as inseparable. The haute bourgeoisie will use the petty, but the center of decision making will not be displaced. Only with the appearance of monopolies—on an international scale—will the attempt again be made, with good chance of success, by the *technocrats*, those whose knowledge and teamwork put them in a position to impose decisions. In any event, the first effort, prompted by the war of 1870 and the Commune, had the effect of giving the Third Republic a petty bourgeois facade. For a long time it was the Republic of the radicals, and Thibaudet—seeing only appearances—regarded it as the "Republic of the Professors." In fact, politics were conducted under the direction of certain pressure groups closely linked to large-scale industry and banking. But mystifying as it was (men of science couldn't put a word in), this pretense of democracy had the effect of a certain class movement—property owners summoning technicians—thanks to which petty bourgeois literary men again believed in the transcendence of class. They were rising through the middle classes, they were going to find themselves at the summit, psychological advisers to the manufacturer and the banker. An illusory transcendence of class, but more modest in its ambitions and more realistic than the dream of being beyond class or

remain aristocrats in a primitive state, elevated directly by that God in which many of them are not able to believe. But in 1840 the future writer, despairing of his true condition, can think of himself only in phantasmatic terms. And the phantasm—though in fact it exists only aroused in them and by them, in particular in the movement of internalization we call reading—originates neither in subjective caprice nor in the pride of certain individuals; it is an objective determination engendered as an inert norm by the underlying opposition and superficial collusion of an imperative (tear yourself away from all classes, survey society) and a proscription (commoners are forbidden to write). Historical circumstance would have it that the insolent class which formulated the proscription through its class writers should simultaneously be struck down; its interpreters, however, novelists and poets, pursue their trajectory as solitary and glorious luminaries and so seem to represent only themselves—or, better, art. Thus their prestigious career seems in itself an invitation to join them at the heart of a new aristocracy whose origin is no longer birth but a certain conception of literary activity. Since their works—even while adapting to new conditions—continue to base the essence of literature on aristocratic imperatives (generosity, feudal loyalty, writing conceived as a gift or as a prayer, the solitude of contempt, stoicism, etc.), to equal them it is enough to adopt their principles and, systematically rejecting bourgeois ideology, to become a *self-made* aristocrat by writing for a defunct aristocracy.

This is why the literary apprentices find themselves suddenly confronted by the normative system their older brothers used to define the essence of their art, a system whose meaning is clear to the younger brothers: here are the rules to be observed so that literary activity may *by itself* define its agent as an aristocrat. In fact, if honestly inspected, these rules (unlike autonomy, for example) have no connection with the essence of the written thing; they define *one* class literature based on class conditions that originally determine their authors. But their social and particular character is concealed by the historic collapse of the class whose real power and domination they are supposed to express.

---

coopted by the aristocracy. The petty bourgeoisie is suffused with bourgeois ideology and even sees to keeping it in working order; besides, while capitalists are defined by profit and alone decide its uses, they concede to the middle classes a portion of surplus value, which determines a real connivance between the liberal professions and the factory owners, and even a kind of homogeneity in mores, in any case a reciprocal porosity.

At first the Romantic writer takes the side of power, of the restored monarchy before 1830 and its supporters, the nobility. This means he looks down on French society with a royal gaze and, like his peers, the princes and dukes who surround the throne, sees everything from above. Such is Chateaubriand. And Vigny. And Hugo before him. Such is that foreign poet, Goethe, bourgeois by birth but minister of a principality. It is notable that this is an imperative already encountered in the literature produced by the eighteenth century: Take the larger view! But the truth soon hits home: Romantic panoramic consciousness flagrantly contradicts the consciousness of the "philosophes." First of all, they were discovering the whole society from an asocial point of view; institutions and customs were seen through the eyes of Micromégas. The century hesitated: Should one tear oneself away from all of humanity to discover its objective nature through the inhuman eyes of reason, or, on the contrary, should one inhabit human nature, seize it from within and challenge in the name of man the inequality produced by institutions? In any event, the writer tried to glide *without support* in this dogmatic naïveté, which is not excluded by negativity, like that Kantian dove that dreams it would fly better if air did not exist. By contrast, Romantic panoramic consciousness, initially less naive, is sustained by blood, birth, rank, royal favor, the interest of the great, in short *by class*. On the one hand, this is what gives it reality: the ruling class gazes on what is beneath it. But this is also the source of its limits. By *situating* himself, the poet rejects the negative radicalism of the "philosophes"; he remains beneath princes and king, beneath God. He will express not man's view of himself but the rulers' view of the people and sometimes, when God inspires him, the point of view of the Almighty as the Church defines Him. In any event, the vision expressed in the work cannot help being hierarchical: the social body is envisaged from the perspective of the extravagant generosity that characterizes the nobility and the art that expresses it. And thought itself, a reprise of old ideas generated by old interest, will be necessarily synthetic. Such, indeed, was the defensive thought of the class in power in the eighteenth century; it protected privilege from analysis by trying to present it as the organic product of history. At that time, analytic reason was an irresistible force easily overpowering the argumentation of the rich. They themselves were convinced of the powers of analysis, and the dialectical notion of synthesis, though always in existence, had not yet been discovered. With the return of the emigrés, this notion gains currency; by a curious irony, the bourgeois

101

revolution engendered it in the Objective Spirit of German philosophy as the sole means of understanding the history it was simultaneously making and denying. The young Romantics have not read Hegel; they are not in a position to turn the dialectical weapon against the bourgeoisie. Nor are they content, however, to ameliorate the tactics of the privileged and their watchdogs; weary of fighting a rearguard action, they shift to the offensive, borrowing from medieval Catholicism the idea that the created world is an organic totality that manifests itself entirely in each of its parts. Thus meaning will be preserved for social inequalities, which are simply a hierarchy of points of view on the universe, whose synthetic unity the most elevated grasp explicitly, though that universe is also wholly present, if roughly and indistinctly, to those on the lowest level. For the poet, the issue is not to *demonstrate* this organicism but simply to *prove it through beauty.* In other words, the subject of literature is the world as it is revealed to the gaze of the king. And beauty is not born of a strict observance of rules; it has nothing to do with taste, that negative determination. It appears in the world and in the work as the strict relation of the parts to the whole and, in the framework of the totality in process, as the internal union of the parts themselves. The beautiful work, by its very existence, manifests the world; being total, it invites us to seize the world through an ample, totalizing gaze whose movement and boundary the work itself provides.

We immediately grasp the purpose of this aggressive beauty; it would not take long to show how the idea of totality appears in Europe's Objective Spirit with the Holy Alliance. But it must also be noted, in the specific case we are dealing with, that totalization is the very function of panoramic consciousness, especially when it belongs to the master, an ample gaze taking in the goods he tallies up. Wouldn't those "tours of the world" so often repeated by his older brothers seduce the young bourgeois who dreams of writing? And since being an artist or a gentleman is the same thing, wouldn't the totalizing work impose itself on him as *his imperative task?* He will raise himself up to the summits occupied by the great, now fallen, and look down on the hills and plains with an aristocratic gaze.

This prescription—impossible to follow, as we know—sets in relief a harsh conflict that is going to tear the Postromantics apart. In the eighteenth century, autonomy was the power to *say anything,* to push analysis to the end, only taking care not to violate the rules of taste. The power claimed by the Romantics, and which they are easily accorded, is the power to *say all*—the all. Which is just the opposite.

For the eighteenth century, as we have noted, does not solely or even especially require the panoramic surveying of human societies or their contemplation by some astonished Martian. It is characterized above all by a negative and patient thinking that eats away at self-styled irreducible aggregates and doesn't stop until it has finished, having reduced them to their elements. There is an endless disassembling— of things, institutions, the arguments of adversaries—and when nothing remains but disconnected pieces, no one is left to reassemble them. That is the purpose, moreover, and by producing in place of an object the indivisible atoms or simple ideas that constitute it, analytic reason means to show that there are no bonds between beings or the component parts of a system but the bonds of exteriority. For the rest, if objects whose parts are united by bonds of interiority really exist, each essentially modified by the existence of the other so that their real unity is not reducible to the sum of analyzed elements and every element is essentially different, depending on whether it is envisaged within the system or considered in isolation, then analytic thought remains dumb and blind. It cannot even conceive of what is at issue, and in the presence of an organic totality it will decompose it like the others, killing it unwittingly. Analytic literature, the patient thought of the slave, enters into the minutest details because it can decompose the most majestic constellations only by reducing them to irreducible molecules, and until it runs up against the indissoluble or indivisible, its work is not finished. *To say anything*, the demand of literary autonomy in the century of Voltaire, is therefore to examine everything, to gauge everything, to put everything to the test: nothing will be negligible, and if surveying wholes is sometimes a good thing, their component parts should often be examined through a magnifying glass.

To say all—this is the demand of the master. A synthesizing gaze surveys the world, summing it up, totalizing it, attentive to its larger structures and noting their meaning, their internal bonds with the whole. For these operations, the search for detail is useless; it would destroy everything. But the master, in considering the parts, must never lose sight of the whole, for the parts must be understood in relation to the whole. So one must be truly a master, and this synthesizing assumption must be indistinguishable from the act of appropriation. Puntilla, for example, wishing to make his valet Matti admire the beauty of nature, does nothing more than assemble his property around him. This endlessly repeated act is based on an optimism of possession: the world is good because it is mine. Despite rage, despair, and other more profound states of discomfort I shall soon take note of, Romantic synthesis bears the optimism of the proprietor. Actually, the proprietor is the *other*, the king; these writers are poor gentlemen, which is why Romantic autonomy is a lie; the truth of this literature is alienation. That does not prevent it from being beautiful; nor does it prevent those young bourgeois of 1840 from confusing the imperatives of master and slave in the books they are currently reading, and from dreaming that they in their turn can create a sublime work that *will say all*.

And how are they going to manage it? What instrument of thought do they have at their command? In fact, they have nothing but the analytic reason their fathers inherited from their grandfathers and with which they were inculcated, whose negativity can no longer serve them but lends the progress of science an incomparable prestige. Consequently, the diastases of analysis eat away at the totalizations they sketch out—and, conversely, analytic procedures, reassembled for a moment by these unstable syntheses, reveal their radical negativity and arouse a fundamental pessimism in these young men. The cosmic totalizations of their older brothers did not depend on *another* reason or on another conception of the rationality of the real; the dialectical idea was in the air, but they had grasped only its appearance. Thus the totalities they produced in their works were not based on reason but were justified by the decisive choice of the irrational. With all the force of their greatness they ranged themselves against the rationalists who had guillotined their fathers, against the Jacobin cult of reason and the Supreme Being, against the corruption of reasoning that led Louis XVI to his death and the royal house to the edge of doom. Since reason and revolution were one and the same thing, these young men crushed the vanquished revolution and ridiculed reason with the same contempt. Yet the worlds they depicted were neither follies nor dreams, for they had chosen to conceive them according to the unreason of Church and State. But the Postromantics, those young malcontents, brothers and sons of scientists, jealous of science, antibourgeois, perhaps, but *reasonable*, could not believe in those harmonious worlds when they wanted to enter them. Agnostic, hostile to the Bourbons who had just taken flight, they had no valid motive for adopting this angle of vision; and the poisons of analysis dissolved those false totalizations against their will. Beauty remained, however, doubly imperious since it demanded to be admired in the finished work and to become the rule for the work to be written. In other words, the imperative subject of literature remained the totalization of being. Yet when the future authors envisage that totalization from the perspective of the exhaustive work to be produced, analytic reason suddenly seems an insurmountable obstacle. Or, rather, the unity of the creation is deconstructed and allows a glimpse of infinite scattering. In the preceding century bourgeois prudence, as we know, invented the hybrid concept of nature, whose apparent unity refers to the act of the Creator but simultaneously conceals both the exteriority belonging to "natural" events and mechanistic materialism, the ultimate conclusion of analysis. The idea of nature had been shattered, mechanism had triumphed. As long as they were reading specific pamphlets, the detailed libels of the eighteenth century, the young bourgeois were amused by analytic negativity; they went no further than the author himself and contested with him the statement of fact he denounced. But when the synthetic unity of the created world became the imperative subject of literature-to-be-written, they attempted to totalize their knowledge, and this unification, bearing on the results of analysis, caused them to rediscover mechanism, the only analytic theory of the universe. By their very efforts they were lost, strangers to themselves, atomized, an absurd swarming of molecules in the midst of an infinite and senseless agitation. Thus the Romantic imperative haunted them, inciting their abstract, optimistic attempts to unify the world through a regal gaze, and those attempts, by promptly disintegrating, left them in the presence of a cold nothingness that drew its unity from their failures and affirmed itself as the endless eternity of disorder. This entailed social decline: the future author, one moment a gentleman and a believer, fell back into the unbelieving rabble, into the bourgeoisie; this bitter tumble proved the impossibility of realizing his fantasy and *making himself* an aristocrat through his literary activity. To manage that, he would have needed other principles, other beliefs, another history from the outset, in short, he would have had to be *well born*. Is he going to give up? No; that would be to renounce writing. He is caught between contradictory imperatives.

French Romanticism is not, however, all optimism. Its works are war machines; even their serenity is combative. The disappearance of negativity should not fool us—it is not a master's weapon. A certain positivity is concealed in these authors by absolute negation, which should be understood not as an activity but as a permanent attitude; and the object of that negation, rarely named, loser today, perhaps winner tomorrow, is the bourgeois. He is not criticized any more than his works are systematically undermined, one by one; he is *abolished*, once and for all, by sovereign decree, as a lord would do having the power of life and death over his subjects. So the upsurge of pure negation in this young literature transforms the critical act that was enterprise and work into a negative fiat, which strikes down without destroying. This attitude is all the more rigid as the writer feels less sure of himself. Absolute negation is at bottom only the reaffirmation of a right to which he is in no way certain of being entitled: the right to reestablish a healthy hierarchy on the subordination of the reconstituted Third Estate to the other two estates.

This right, as we have seen, is the very basis of literature for the French Romantics. But no sooner is it affirmed than it is challenged, and literature with it. First of all, those young aristocrats, born for the most part in France under the Revolution or the Empire, have become partially bourgeois through childhood; not, of course, like the following generation, who are bourgeois to the hilt. Education more or less secretly supports them in the idea that they have an ineffable but incomparable *quality* from birth, and that this is the basis of their duties—above all feudal loyalty—and of their *natural* superiority. Under the Empire, however, instruction and amusement were bourgeois; in the absence of princes of the blood and the royal court, mores became bourgeois. These young men experienced all this and internalized it. They have a bourgeois side that must be constantly dominated, repressed by a tense denial which in its negative immobility is the subjective analogue of the absolute negation expressed in their books. That is not too difficult: it will be enough to show the positive counterpart by straining a little at the sublime, at nonchalant insolence, at everything that manifests an inalienable superiority. Alfred de Musset's charming caprices in his early poems serve the sole purpose of affirming themselves, regal and gratuitous, over the destruction of that painful accumulation of norms and customs, bourgeois literature. His poem on the moon locates beauty in flippancy and scandal, for only an aristocratic nature can be flippant and thus mock the rules; but the sovereign gratuitousness of the work results in shocked incomprehension by the lower classes.

That part of themselves made bourgeois by childhood, however, allows them at the same time to better comprehend their situation and history than do the pure aristocrats, the emigrés. They *communicate* with those masses they scorn, or force themselves to scorn—much more easily than their younger brothers will be able to do, and much more profoundly than they do with their true lords, the princes. As a result, well before 1830 they judge that in the uncertain combat waged by the two enemies since 1815, every chance of victory belongs—at least in the long run—to the new bourgeoisie. This latter class, as they well know, holds the purse strings and can asphyxiate a regime or foment and finance a Revolution at will. By the same token, they take the measure of the incompetence and foolishness of their class with a sadness much more real than their flaunted despairs. Yet they choose it by choosing themselves. This means that from the advent of Charles X, they have chosen failure. For it is Romanticism—and not its bourgeois successors—that has for the first time put failure at the heart of literature as its innermost substance. Their sort of failure, however, does not contain the desperate darkness of the Postromantic shipwreck. They deck themselves out in sacrificial robes; indeed, it would be possible for them to abandon that class clinging to its doom and desert to the ranks of the conqueror—just as Lafayette did in his time. They do not, however. For the internal relation that underlies the aristocracy, as mysterious as the blood bond and no doubt deriving from it, is the unconditional fidelity of vassal to lord, and of both to the king. And so opting for the nobility within themselves and outside them, in society, they assume an ethic and a fate. Devotion to a lost cause, accepting its doom for oneself—this is precisely what is called generosity, an extravagant virtue denied on principle to the bourgeoisie. This lucid consent to their own doom manifests their greatness and the unhappiness of the times. The only virtue in the face of bourgeois utilitarianism is that unconditional, almost military devotion which defines a man as an indissoluble synthesis by the choice of his death. Or, if you will, which defines the human condition not by being-as-deferral but by the voluntary and deliberate assumption of his being-to-die.

An ambiguous notion; indeed, accepted failure established the basis for greatness and manifested the irreducible quality of blood. In other words, for those writers who participated in the general *embourgeoisement*, there was no other way of proving the superiority of their birth. The prior acceptance of collective shipwreck, far from being purely negative, as resignation would be, for example, can be considered essentially *positive*. It *actualizes* that pure virtuality conferred by *birth*; it manifests the irreducible superiority of the writer-aristocrat over the bourgeois, who not only is incapable of following him on the road to greatness and sacrifice but even lacks the means to comprehend this dramatic humanism. At the same time, it reveals—surreptitiously and in quite a different way from the bourgeois litera-

107

ture of the eighteenth century—the preeminence of the aristocrat-writer as opposed to the aristocrat who does not write. Received by the nobility, the bourgeois author in Voltaire's time refused to enter that class and continually denounced its privileges; the supremacy of the Romantic writer is that he is a superaristocrat. The aristocracy, in effect, hastens blindly to its doom by compounding its errors; the writer, who is clairvoyant, assumes the historical faults of others while fully understanding their consequences; his class bond is stronger than theirs. But he denies this supremacy, which condemns him to solitude, in order to be merely the equal of his brothers. It is not hard for us to believe that this conscious denial only enhances his value. So much so that he comes to the point of detaching himself from his class through the production and illustration of an aristocratic ideology, which, by dint of being given the lie by the real actions of the nobility, finally—as he recognizes—has become imaginary. As a result, the ethic of failure is generalized and at the same time individualized. It is generalized as humanism because certain authors, like Hugo, extend it to the people—the nobility's natural ally, it was then thought, against the bourgeoisie. Flaubert said: "I call bourgeois anyone who thinks meanly." Hugo would have said: "I call aristocratic anyone who thinks nobly." Moreover, under the influence of bourgeois individualism these gentlemen personalize this beneficent failure. It defines their life, giving it a literary interest; the failure of love and its immediate consequence, inspiration, symbolize loyalty to the class that will soon be vanquished and the moral greatness that is its direct result. Nothing makes us so great as a great sorrow; this is false, sorrow is abstract, it is a deficiency and a rationalization. But in the framework of consensual failure it becomes the individually lived symbol of the internal connection linking assumed frustration to greatness; or, better, greatness grasped only in assumed frustration which is surpassed toward transcendent plenitude—God, King, Beauty. If sorrow enhances us, it does so because it raises us above the commonplace, that is, above ourselves; thus loyalty unto death raises us, in the midst of shipwreck, above man; greatness is a surpassing. At issue here is not an anomistic surpassing that is essentially unlimited but one that is defined by the unsurpassables toward which it aspires—monarchy, religion. In this sense, such a transcendence must be seen as a *tension* between the surpassed being and the unsurpassable objective. For the Romantic, this tension is *experienced* aristocracy.

In this sense, the Romantic conception of literature tolerates neither analysis nor the realistic inventory of institutions, instruments, or men. Its subject is dual; it must reveal the created world, present in each of its parts, in its harmonious totality, bearing witness to God's omnipotence and his goodness. But at the same time literature must present this very world of happiness and order in the light of a harsh and particular failure, of a tumultuous, inexplicable disorder that is produced as the very contradiction of this universe—the best possible—and at the center of being. The nobility being of divine right and situated at the summit of the social hierarchy as the exaltation of human nature, its shipwreck gives the lie to every theodicy. However, the world thus denounced in its injustice nonetheless remains a rigorous and perfect synthesis whose beauty reflects the creative act of the Almighty, his infinite generosity. For the man about to perish who tells us about his shipwreck and also about the wreckage of the human elite he is part of, the world has not ceased to be a magnificent gift nor God to be good. It is characteristic of the Romantic hero to gaze on that beauty, that goodness, with despairing eyes. It is he who has hit upon the idea of dying in the midst of a superb summer night and of speaking to us, in his death throes, of the sky without sparing us a single star. And the odd feeling he awakens in the reader is that he is the cursed one, the excluded, the *desdichado* of a strange universe that possesses neither the right nor the means to this excommunication. Quite the contrary, the light of failure reveals in nature and men a certain wild and desperately fascinating sweetness: everything is enhanced by the grandeur of this dying man. Like the tenor in *Tosca*, he never loved life so much. Upon leaving the world he grasps its pure beauty, its sacred depth. What is it, then, that keeps the reader from being horrified at the thought of his failure and from judging the splendor of the world a final decision? Precisely that this failure unto death is *consensual*. And this acquiescence born of loyalty, of feudal honor, with a flick of the finger makes everything return to order. The greatness of the aristocrat does not lie in his power or in his calm enjoyment of worldly things, but in his sacrifice to the king. Not only in quiet times and when order prevails everywhere, but above all in the disorders of a foreign or civil war; he is the man for these disorders, risking his life to stop them. Not so long before, the French nobility, as cavalrymen, were charging in a body toward English archers, who calmly slaughtered them. If the number of the nobility's dead were great enough, it could say: all is lost save honor. In other words, its sacrifice effaced the defeat, became the spiritual order of that disorder. Going still further, we would add that disorders of whatever sort are necessary to the majestic harmony of the creation.

And the creation is fashioned so that man may surpass himself in it, so that the aristocrat may affirm himself as the supreme order by succumbing through generosity and fidelity to the disordered attacks of the enemy. In 1830 and for several years afterward, the last Romantics in that supreme disorder, the liquidation of the aristocratic class, saw the magnificent and supreme exaltation of the nobility; it gave up the ghost, and through its splendid demise affirmed the supremacy revealed only in disasters. Mission accomplished. Historically, of course, the adventure of the last aristocrats hardly resembled this mythical story. They had lost power by pushing their king into bad politics; and the affair of the emigrés' billion does not testify to the "extravagant generosity" attributed to them. But the aristocratic writers hardly care; those poor gentlemen were not coddled by the great; their ideology, which they kindly offered, was hardly endorsed in high places. In short, they celebrate feudal loyalty but they do not consider themselves the liege lords of those rich fools. Let them croak. The Romantics, while continuing to glorify the greatness of aristocratic failure, will quietly adapt to the bourgeois society that made their fame and would benevolently open the doors of the Académie française to them. There will be a few losses—Musset, for example, a member of the Académie but a hopeless alcoholic. But as a group these poets of defeat won their cause; they do their utmost to represent the politically vanquished class in glory and honor; they will bear witness—in their public character—to its servitude and its greatness. In short, they will *be* the aristocracy in the eyes of the bourgeois who honor it in their person, and they will *recount* it in their books, which will be in themselves marks of fidelity and consequently of good actions. Under these conditions, it is understandable that the myth of failure in its first form does not disturb the optimism of Christendom. God willed it: in this decisive proof he will recognize his own people; the bourgeois by definition must triumph, for utilitarianism is their doctrine and their most effective weapon; nobility, being the gift of self and generosity, must by definition perish—at least as a power. Thus, everything is in order. But isn't it a monstrous world where the bourgeoisie reigns? How can God want to deprive the earth of its best men and compel calculation and the love of profit to reign? Well, the aristocracy has not been physically liquidated; the nobility, without power but not without property, remains among the vanquishers as an example to follow. Better yet, it produced the intellectuals who represent it and depict it to the people.

God, moreover, is not always present. Musset and Vigny often lament the Jacobin dechristianization: they were brought up without faith. But those who committed this crime are certainly the bourgeois, or those of their parents who were victims of the bourgeois contagion. Insofar as these poets received the ideology of the common people in spite of themselves, and carry the bourgeois beast inside them as a second nature, they are no longer capable of believing and are desolate over it. As aristocrats by blood, they are believers— a nobility without God is inconceivable since it exists by divine right. And if failure through fidelity is to receive its reward when order is finally reestablished, there must be a Heaven. Thus faith is part of the system; moreover, the nobles who do not write are distinguished by their devotion. This contradiction could seem embarrassing if the act of fealty by which these poets manifested themselves in their greatness through solidarity with their class, with its misfortunes as well as its virtues, were not precisely the *poem*. For by means of the poem they tame the bourgeois beast within and without; for how could it produce verse? Isn't the bourgeoisie's essential question "What good is it?" The Romantics paved the way for the idea of art for art's sake by saying, precisely, that their poems were not *good for* anything. Not that they would deny their ethical dimension, quite the contrary; but they saw in them chiefly the supreme generosity of their class, making a gift of its failure. The need to *give* its sufferings to God, to its peers, to the people, cannot come to the poet from that prosaic bourgeoisie that will make Béranger *its* bard. And the need—honorable as it is—would not suffice without genius. That belongs only to aristocrats; in these noble intellectuals it represents the *actualization* of the aristocracy. But it cannot exist—save in the "people" as a collective—unless measured *by blood*. For these authors, a genius is a man above men, he must be *born* such; these intellectuals do not allow, of course, that he can be a genius as a result of the particular configuration of his brain. Yet Gall had gone over that ground—and so had phrenology. There will be scholarly confusion between "birth" and so-called *constitutional* traits. At any rate, genius cannot be an accident; and if it remains a disposition of the soul rather than a hypertrophy of the brain, this proves the existence of God. When approaching their desk, all these writers know that they are poets *by divine right*. So they write abundantly, in a frenzy, finishing in the morning, after a wild night, what they began the evening before. In a word, they are *inspired*. Inspiration is God speaking in the ear of the chosen man. Unless it is the superior nature of that man which, exalted by events, passions, surpasses itself in the greatness of the

111

poem. The great Romantics leave room for some doubt; they do not choose between the two. It is flattering, of course, to be the mouth-piece of the Almighty, but this is just being a medium; and it isn't bad for the poet to be gifted, to speak by himself, and for inspiration to be the spontaneity of superior souls. From our point of view it amounts to the same thing: in this harmonious world, the poet's "windfalls" are not accidental—indeed, there is no place for accident. They are *gifts* whose source can only be the Creator, illuminating his creation for man. After that, it hardly matters whether these gifts are made one by one to the people through the intermediary of a prophet whose words are whispered to him, or whether this "vatic poet" received once and for all as a divine gift, even before his birth, the inclinations that will permit him at will to speak in the name of God. In this antibourgeois literature, everything is a *gift*; the writer makes that gift, the masterpiece—failure rewarded—because he received that other gift, genius, the *power* to show man the world—again a gift—which is manifest as an act through inspiration.

Hugo repeats this to anyone who will listen. Lamartine would not contradict him, although he is fond of likening political meditation to religious meditation. How so? In prayer too, inspiration is necessary. Others, though lamenting the contagion of unbelief, or the eternal silence of Heaven, believe in God while they are writing and imagine they have demonstrated His existence through their works—by the simple fact that they were possible—because it is an *a priori* requirement of their literature. And when they reproach their fathers and bourgeois society under Napoleon for having failed to give them faith, they call themselves the victims of a mutilation; but at the same time they are certain that the Creator, in whom they cannot believe, exists and serves as a guarantee of the beauty of their works, as Descartes's Creator guaranteed truth.

For the young men of 1840, the new beauty of Romanticism was manifest through that double imperative: to admire, to take the torch from the hands of their older brothers and continue the march in the same direction. But no sooner had they internalized these works through their enthusiastic reading than the second imperative decomposed within them, leaving them in a daze. Literature-to-be-written announced itself to them, through literature-already-written, as inherently a triumph born of failure. Indeed, the link between art and failure was introduced into the Objective Spirit of the nineteenth century by the Romantics and remained part of it until its final years. But the optimistic and rewarded failure they were given as a model was the failure of *others*, not theirs. These young products of a triumphant class felt in no way bound to the vanquished whom their fathers had just overthrown. So where do they get that obligation of fidelity which constituted the ethical foundation of French Romanticism's aesthetic norms? Taught by their parents the meaning of the Three Glorious Days of July 1830, they judged all the more cruelly the incompetence of those noblemen blinded by resentment and stubbornly clinging to outdated prejudices, given that they were not of the same party. In other words, the defeat of the aristocracy seemed to them at once a necessary consequence of its anachronistic aims and a sanction merited by its politics. Of course, they would have liked a nobility of blood to tear them away from the bourgeoisie, or, lacking that, their activity itself to lift them above all classes; but the real nobility did not arouse their admiration. Being untitled, they did not feel its failure from within and could not experience the need to surpass it through a work expressing its proud beauty. Quite to the contrary, the merits attributed to the vanquished class seemed to them pure hagiographic inventions. These people were neither generous nor faithful; returning in the supply carts of the foreigner, they had set upon France and pillaged it like an enemy country. In a way, the dishonorable fall of Charles X marked for these young bourgeois the end of the literature of high sentiment; certainly bourgeois utilitarianism could not make them believe in it, and the privileged, by showing themselves for what they were, drove home to them that the sublime was not of this world any more than generosity, and that the work of art was not a gift.

Yet the work-as-gift does exist; the Romantics invented it, the bourgeois youth of 1840 gorged themselves on it. And more generally, the bourgeois public adopted it. We may well wonder how that puritanical and serious class, whose only motive was self-interest and whose only objective was profit, could allow itself to be won over by Romanticism, which forced on it an image of man that was unrecognizable. The answer must be, first of all, that the best and most numerous readers of the time were women and young men—both of whom are less integrated: the young men because they are learning about the world and not yet reproducing their life, which gives their thought for a time a certain obvious suppleness of contour; the women because they are as much victims as accomplices of a system that oppresses them, and because, while sharing the principles of their class, they do not hesitate to betray them. As for the men, the haute

113

bourgeoisie did not read, any more than did the barons of the late Middle Ages. But there were enough readers in the middle classes, who were all the more divided as the elected regime kept them from voting. Guardians of culture, living on surplus value but consisting primarily of passive citizens, they were at once in solidarity with the great capital that made them a living by paying for their services, and in masked conflict with a plutocracy that deprived them of political power. The more aware members of the petty bourgeoisie would join with the workers to proclaim universal suffrage and the Republic, but the great mass often regretted the overthrow in 1830 of the legitimate aristocracy, whom they judged preferable to the reigning bankers. At least they knew that the bankers were commoners like themselves, and their tyranny consequently a usurpation; they were less bitter obeying those perceived as another species and superior by blood. For these readers, the great Romantics did not do too badly by throwing in their lot with Voltaire, and this fellow feeling was less a result of the eclecticism of the readers than of their essential contradiction. And in a general way the bourgeoisie could not be consoled for having guillotined its king. It retained a vague yet profound consciousness of its culpability; it was afraid of finally achieving that power it had clamored for; despite twenty-five years of revolutions and victories it had not forgotten that it formerly represented the lower classes of the nation. In a way it continued to regard itself as the *third estate*, and had the vague feeling that far from having overthrown its masters, it had lost them in an incomprehensible catastrophe; and now—contrary to its nature—it had to make decisions alone instead of executing those of others. In short, there was a bourgeois desertion, and the dream of this dreaming bourgeoisie was to find a *good* aristocracy.

Of course, we mustn't exaggerate the importance of these fantasies, the residue of the Ancien Régime's ideology. The bourgeois were stepping up industrialization, transforming feudal properties in the countryside into bourgeois possessions and then concentrating these holdings—in short, they were achieving world conquest. And against those vague nostalgias they wielded a well-constructed ideology based, apparently, on science, and a formidable weapon, analytic reason, which had belonged to them in their own right for two centuries. That was the reality; the remorse and the regret were part of the dream. But their reading of the Romantics was a directed oneirism, a way of dreaming that God exists and that man is defined by greatness. They took all the more pleasure in it as the caste that had oppressed them under Louis XVIII, a class now dismantled, was no longer dangerous. And such fantasmagoria did not prevent them from demanding bourgeois authors who would write a class literature.

Be that as it may, this *consensus* gave Romanticism an ambiguous character that was imposed on the future authors of the subsequent generation. That fealty, that devotion to a lost cause, that greatness—were they to be seen as the traits of man as he should or could be, or simply as an invitation to the dream? What was given in that literary gift? Exemplary but true images that allow the reader to surpass himself toward the sublime, or quite the opposite, as consolation for an abject world, a means of escaping into the unreal and inventing what reality *might have been* if God had created the universe and man had been good? Of these two hypotheses, the second is the newer at this time and will have greater consequence; if it were to be adopted, for the first time in literature the imaginary would cease to be a means of attaining the true and become, *against truth*, the fundamental objective of literary art. *Zadig, Candide, Jacques le Fataliste, Adolphe* all lie in order to tell the truth. *La Mort du loup, Ruy Blas, Les Burgraves* lie in order to lie. In fact, the Romantics believed they were depicting reality relatively unembellished. Hugo's sublime and serious hero, always cursed, always saved, was someone they knew well because he was themselves. But for these young bourgeois who judge men according to their parents, it is incredible that Hernani, who kills himself on the eve of his marriage in order to save his honor and respect the sworn faith, should be taken seriously as a typical representative of human nature. Especially because around this time, and for reasons I shall soon indicate, the bourgeoisie had once more changed its opinion of our species. Until the time of the Reformation, in opposition to an aristocracy that declared itself good, the common classes had conceived our nature as universally bad. Oppressed, hopeless, they denied the superiority of blood in the name of equality in evil. In the eighteenth century, on the verge of winning their struggle, the bourgeoisie refuted the racism of the noblemen with the concept of the noble savage and the equality of all in goodness. After the Revolution there was another reversal: since the bourgeoisie imposed order by force, all men are bad; the nineteenth century will be pessimistic. This new determination of the dominant ideology did not escape the adolescents of 1840; at school it is good to be one of the "blasés," to be cynical, to be scornful of man and his base needs. So Romantic works, despite their authors' intentions, will be regarded as revolutionary; they are the first to contrast the fragmented ugliness of the real to that harmonious and created totality which is none other than pure imagination making its own laws. In this case, the autonomy of literature might well become the autonomy of the imaginary.

But if the first hypothesis were true, if Romantic man is a *realizable* model—and that is just what his creators say—he cannot in any event serve as an example to these young bourgeois. First of all, where would they find situations that require sublime acts? How could these *collégiens*, these students, offer their lives to an amorous old duke or, as false grandees of Spain, preside over a council of ministers? For most of the Romantics, as we know, greatness is only for aristocrats. But even those who, like Hugo, see in every man a possible aristocrat, the circumstances they create—so that their heroes might grow into it at their ease—are themselves *aristocratic*. Ruy Blas is a valet, certainly, therefore a man of the people and no bourgeois; but for this valet to have occasion to show the spiritual strength of a prince of the blood, his master must live at the Spanish court and require his help in resolving improbable intrigues. Thus, whatever their opinion of this literature, the young readers feel it legislates against them; greatness, generosity, the chivalric virtues are clearly denied them, whether because they are men or because they are bourgeois. It seems that part of the violence that took place in the secularized lycées under Louis-Philippe between 1830 and 1840 was chiefly caused by the impossibility for these students beset by Romanticism to situate themselves both as bourgeois and as representatives of the human race. They disguised themselves as pirates and carried loaded pistols in their belts, trying to realize the convergence of extraordinary circumstances that would have allowed them to surpass themselves. But they sensed that this cheap finery would not change them, that they would not escape their reality as young bourgeois, products of the bourgeois family and promised the circumscribed circumstances of a bourgeois life. But to the extent that Romantic greatness exalted them, they experienced this impossibility as a civil imprisonment, the consequence of an unjust condemnation. At the same time, their parents' pessimistic ideology made them reject Romantic models as culpable impostures; man is bad, that's all there is to it. Then what is the source of the emotion, the exultation aroused by their readings? Didn't they have a deep desire for greatness? And what was this desire worth? Did it prove that virtue was possible? And in this case weren't they victims of the ideas and mores given them by their fami-

116

lies? Perhaps the ubiquitous desire to surpass the self through generosity, a characteristic vow of human nature, was prohibited *for them alone* by their bourgeois second nature? In this case, they were damned. Or perhaps it was a desire without any object; perhaps man, enclosed in his finitude, boxed in by his particular interests, desires this surpassing simply because he is incapable of it. In which case this mirage desire would be derisive; through it, not content to define himself by the baseness of his interested calculations, man would denounce that baseness in vain and condemn it stupidly, since nothing else is possible and Heaven, the sole acceptable source of judgment, is mute. Finally—this is the least unhappy solution—without God or freedom, rigorously conditioned by events and situations, it may be that we are worthy only through the totally unrealizable desire to be *other, elsewhere,* or rather, considering our confused aspiration in its clearly negative aspect, quite the opposite, through our *dissatisfaction* with the world and ourselves. These thoughts revolve in the heads of the schoolboys of 1830. Some of them kill themselves, not because of Romanticism, as has foolishly been claimed, but because the Romantic attitude and faith were prohibited. That is the true *mal du siècle.* Gentlemen created a class literature, one of whose chief aims was to rejoin the aristocracy to the people by expunging the bourgeoisie through a negation of principle. The class that sustains them goes under, the bourgeois take power, and their children internalize through reading the poisoned works that deny them implicitly on every page. And just as the Restoration convoked or reassembled the writer-aristocrats, so the July Revolution, by bringing bankers and manufacturers to power, engendered literary vocations among the bourgeoisie. The gentlemen will continue to write—less and less, except for Hugo, who will keep changing but will never stop crushing his successors with his lofty image of man. But their young bourgeois successors will enter the career of writing disgusted with themselves, and all their writings will be governed by this vague disgust; whether evoked by their class being or human nature, they do not know. From the outset, however, it is certain that falling from aristocratic hands into the hands of the bourgeoisie, literature as an imperative demand of the Objective Spirit has *lost* its subject. All the young men who want to write are incited to it by those *practico-inert* objects, the books of Voltaire, Diderot, Rousseau and, simultaneously, those of Byron, Vigny, Musset, Goethe, and Hugo. But without renouncing autonomy and creating a class literature, the moment has passed for turning the analytic weapon against the enemy. And without deceiving themselves, the moment has also passed for repeating the Romantic theodicy and showing the greatness of man at the heart of creation. These young men literally know only how to write. That is why the works of the Romantics, by showing them the grandiose failure of the nobility and its moral victory in the midst of defeat, awaken some echo within them, revealing to them another failure, their own. Without a public, without a subject, the literary cause is lost in advance; these future writers *start out losing* and they know it. But there is no greatness in this misfortune, which might be called defeat in triumph. When their class was struggling, when the outcome was doubtful, its writers were unwittingly in solidarity with it. Now that it has won, its authors do not want to serve it though they are its products and know it well enough. Unlike the Romantics, who sought collective failure through fidelity to their class, the initial defeat of these young men particularizes them and cuts them off from the collectivity that engenders them; they are still bourgeois, but isolated. They are lacking in everything, and above all in *tradition*. That is what allowed the authors of the eighteenth century to innovate prudently, staying within the framework of classicism; that is what allowed a work to be judged according to the rules of taste. But the history of the preceding hundred years was so violent and harsh that *a number* of literatures were formed in the Objective Spirit and imposed themselves on the reader of 1840 with contradictory imperatives that could not be surpassed toward any rational synthesis.

D. The Neurotic Solution

Let us take as a starting point these contradictions as they were lived in the middle of the nineteenth century; and since there is no rational transcendence, let us examine the irrational solution they delineate, which determines the kind of writer these young men must become and the kind of work they must produce.

1. Absolute-Art

Throughout the works of the eighteenth century, autonomy seems to be an objective status of literature. A class literature, to be sure, but as that class is combatant, autonomy here represents a pure, combative negativity; it asserts itself as an institutional imperative, inseparable from analytic reason, the chief weapon of the bourgeoisie, whose ultimate outcome must be mechanism, that is, dissolution taken to its logical conclusion.

The same notion, after a period of eclipse, reappears in Romantic literature. But its function is no longer the same and its meaning has changed; it is now merely the obligation of aristocratic writers to impose the ideology of their class. Beneath the positive idea of synthetic totality, of creation, that ideology conceals two negations—one compensatory, the victory-failure of the nobility, the other fixed and absolute, the radical condemnation of the bourgeoisie.

These two imperatives, reanimated by reading, are intertwined and give literary autonomy an instable and circular content; for that autonomy is based on analysis, whose function is to reduce everything to its elements, and on the aristocratic synthesis that establishes totalitarian unities on the unity of the creating fiat. Thus the project imposed on the future writer is forever to depict the creation in his work as the production of a harmonious whole, and forever to eat away at it with the worm of analysis, whose self-imposed task must be to reduce it to mechanistic dispersal. But this final term of the dissection is not the ultimate theme of the work, though the analysis cannot be carried further; indeed, through the coexistence of the two imperatives, neither of which destroys the other, the totality is no sooner atomized than it is revived and once again subjected to analytic diastasis. So this double, contradictory autonomy somehow demands of the young bourgeois would-be writer the *literary* disclosure of the nothingness of being and the being of nothingness—which reflects, with the *hysteresis* proper to cultural works, the antagonism of two classes, one of which is on the way to its demise. The general theme suggested by literature-to-be-written is the reduction of the world as totality to nothingness, and the reestablishment of that totality as appearance. Behind this perpetual movement, however, a third term is concealed, for totality, an optimistic but mortal instrument of the aristocracy, is realized on the literary suppression of the bourgeoisie; thus totalization by the master, while devoured by servile negativity, destroys the slave and his labor by a fixed, total, irreducible negation. No literary works after 1850 are without the skeletal structure of this triple antagonism. Revealing it, as I have just done, we can say that it *offers no meaning:* the slave denies the master, who does away with him, that's all; or, if you like, the creation is reduced to mechanism, which is reduced to the absolute void from which the creation is reborn. Meaning cannot come from these contradictions, which coexist only because their spatial contiguity as *practico-inert* de-

119

terminations has effaced the historical temporalization that produced them *successively*. A meaning *must* emerge from these antagonisms, and the future author is bidden to provide it through his work. He is free to choose it, provided that he integrates all contradictions in the aesthetic unity of the object produced.

The freedom to choose, without ever being entirely suppressed, is nonetheless singularly reduced by imperatives *exterior* to the first. Other historical circumstances have in effect produced new determinations of the Objective Spirit which, in the trinity comprised of totality, negativity, and negation, tend to demand the predominance of absolute negation. For these young bourgeois, the autonomy of literature is the fundamental requirement of that cultural sector and the primary reason for their choice to write; and yet at the moment when their class triumphs and demands positive books, that autonomy seems to them merely a way of gilding its utilitarian morality with a little idealism. As a result, these future authors have broken with the readership of their own class even before they have written, meaning that by 1840, they have broken with the public pure and simple. Consequently, negativity and the spirit of analysis, instruments that were so effective in the previous century, seem suspect to them; when they yearn to make use of them, they run up against objective resistances arising from the fact that these are the tools proper to their class, and they will not appropriate them without being appropriated in turn. As a result, the human subject of their books—if there is one—will no longer be the man depicted by Voltaire, Diderot, or Rousseau himself; he will no longer contain that "human nature" defined by analysis thanks to social and psychological atomism. But the young writer offers no substitute; in any case, nothing new occurs to these young minds spoiled by analysis. Romantic man, in effect, could not seduce them for long. In 1840, Romanticism is dead, as witness the failure of *Les Burgraves;* for Romantic man represents a synthetic totality, and as good bourgeois they could not refrain from dismantling him despite themselves. Yet by vanishing, the hero made them ashamed of themselves, of their class of origin. The aristocratic authors' contempt remains in them as the great mute negation hidden behind Romantic frenzy. They have contempt for themselves without knowing why. And this contempt becomes their sole greatness since it raises them above themselves. This contorted attitude, the internalization of absolute negation, must be held without respite. But which do they scorn in others and themselves, the bourgeois or the man? First, surely, the bourgeois. These unhappy young men have internalized the contested but ubiquitous and scornful gaze of another, nearly moribund class; they are cut off from themselves by this gaze of failure and death that reveals only bourgeois utilitarianism and the spirit of analysis—ethical and epistemological norms *already familiar* to them. But the bourgeoisie rejects the "people," that vast national unity invented by the monarchy in the interest of propaganda. It knows the working classes, which it exploits, fears, and dislikes, and which its resident thinkers attempt to reduce to the swarmings of individuals; it takes itself for the universal class and now proclaims that classes are abolished. Consequently, its younger sons see *bourgeois man* everywhere; for it means to impose bourgeois *nature*, on the ethical and psychological level, on the individuals who each day, constrained by the wretched poverty spawned by industrialization, make "free" individual contracts with it. The bourgeoisie teaches them, it teaches its own children that this "nature" is truly the essence of the species, that like good bourgeois, the workers, too, seek their interest, competing with each other for employment just like businessmen or entrepreneurs, and that—like bourgeois, maybe more so—they are individually *envious* of the prosperity of others. The fact is that human nature is bad; it must be restrained by rigorous institutions and its weaknesses supported by real property. Raised in these principles—without much questioning them—the young bourgeois have no difficulty extending their contempt to the universe. This is made even easier by the fact that the world is bourgeois—or at least it is expressed only by bourgeois voices—from 1830 on. If man is bourgeois, these children have contempt for the bourgeois in themselves as the definition of mankind. And that contempt, despairing at its lack of support, extending from their class of origin to their race and back again to their class, having acquired a sufficient degree of mystification to follow the path to the universal, will be called *dissatisfaction* by the most realistic. On the one hand it is the verification of what exists and could not be otherwise (In whose name would they contest this nature, these natural laws, and the society that issues from it?); on the other hand it is the global and harmless negation they inherited from Romanticism, defeated in advance, without principle or privilege in this real domain. Nothing else is even declared possible—How would they dare to affirm such a thing when they were raised in unbelief, in agnosticism, or in a superficial religion practiced to give the poor a reason to live and subjected by the lycée student as a matter of major concern to triumphant bourgeois analysis? They may even think, like Laplace,

121

that everything had to be this way from all eternity. In short, they say nothing; they simply live out an impotent denial of the whole world, whose meaning is: I *am not* part of it, I do not *recognize* myself in it. These boys in no way consider themselves fallen gods who remember the heavens; they remember nothing at all. They deny that being, such as it is, *represents* them (in their eyes, in the eyes of others); they claim not to be incarnate in it, not to be objectified in it as bourgeois or as men through work. And this claim, which by itself would be consciously futile, assumes in their eyes the substance of an imperative because it is contiguous in them with autonomy as the rigorous requirement of literature and gives it, ultimately, its content.

Autonomy, the necessary means of writing in 1850, the arrogant exercise of the privileged aristocratic gaze in 1830, appears *in any case* to the new generation as art for its own sake. This *obvious* characteristic of literature-to-be-written represents to them the eternal imperative that their fathers and grandfathers misunderstood *and* originality, since it will be *their* task to obey it. Yet if art has no end but itself, if it disappears from the work when asked to serve, if its major imperative condemns utilitarianism—without even referring to it—and along with it all human ends, then this calm and thorough negation, this perfect inhumanity, can be revealed only to the dissatisfied, who exhaust themselves condemning the world but lack the power to leave it. In other words, in this period as in any other, art defines its artist. No one can accede to it who is not first discontent with everything; indeed, if he has made the slightest accommodation to real society, he will not even think of tearing himself away and will attempt to make a place for himself in it, to objectify himself through productive work. Conversely, absolute negation as perpetual dissatisfaction will be merely an insubstantial whim and will not be raised to ontological dignity insofar as it will not be incarnate in a work whose absolute nihilism—without being the overriding goal[9]—is its immediate and necessary condition. Thus, while the subject of a literature that is posed as its own end is yet undetermined, one thing is certain: its autonomy is not experienced at this time as the necessary status of a social activity, nor even as the result of the writer's permanent struggle against the powers that be; it is an affirmation of art as the *only absolute,* hence the condemnation of all *practical* enterprise—aiming at any

9. To pursue in a work of art a direct enterprise of radical negation, to make it the *goal* of art, is to give it an end other than itself. But if art is pursued *for art's sake,* the affirmation of the beautiful implies negation of the real.

objective, at a given date, in a given society. Absolute-art produces its own temporality—as an inner temporalization imposed by the work on the public. But the refusal to serve, sustained by the young authors' internalized, aristocratic disgust for bourgeois activities, immediately rises above practical temporality. In other words, there are only eternal works, and those that are not eternal *at their inception*, even if distinguished by some purely aesthetic quality, can *in no way* be called works of art.

But while this notion of absolute-art is generated by the interference of the aristocratic imperative with several other imperatives we have enumerated, while it is based indirectly on contempt, or perhaps because it is, the work-to-be-written does not seem a gift to the new generation and does not demand any generosity of the artist. Absolute negation in these youngsters comes, in fact, from the bourgeois certainty that generosity is a mirage, a booby trap invented by the nobility for its conquerors; they looked for and found interested motives behind generous actions. Besides, to whom would the work be given? The only *real* public is the bourgeoisie, who want a class literature. To be *given* a disinterested work, they would at least have to imagine accepting it, which is by definition impossible. And why give anything to men when you have contempt for them all, and when the novel or poem expresses absolute negation, its author's regret at belonging to humanity?

The fact is that the work is not a *donation*, it is not addressed to anyone, and when Musset *gives* his sufferings to readers, these young puritans are horrified by his striptease. This is the same literary current that will soon account for the success of the idea, now outdated, that literature is a form of prostitution. At that moment, turning its negation against itself, literature would condemn itself because it would eventually be read. No, the author is not generous; what he seeks in art, and in the rigorous impersonality of the work, is his *personal* salvation. His refusal to be man will become objectified in the inhumanity of absolute-art: the inaccessible beauty of his product will turn the negative into something positive.

Thus the notion of the panoramic *overview* takes on a third meaning generated by the other two. In the eighteenth century, the writer must survey society because—in his own eyes—he escapes class determinations and finds himself thereby representing human nature "without foreign additives"; through the Romantic overview, the writers of 1830 reaffirm the superiority of the aristocratic, and the lofty gaze they level on other classes restores the hierarchical society

123

in which by divine right they occupy the highest rung. The former believe they are surveying society and declare their solidarity with all men; the latter are and want to be inside it but in first place; in solidarity with their class and with it alone, they protest that exemplary man exists only as an aristocrat, and that the other ranks are merely rough drafts of humanity. In both cases, such a panoramic overview does not dehumanize; on the contrary, it allows the author—though in rather different ways—to express the human in its plenitude. Man of the eighteenth century is simply by definition what Romantic man rejects; in 1840 this internalized contradiction produces uncertainty and disgust in the young men who are ready to go on duty; consequently, the panoramic overview becomes a metaphysical rupture of the writer with his race. Denying human nature in himself, he takes an artist's overview of the world, that apparent totality which breaks up into molecules, and of man, that stranger who inhabits it. What he discovers, we surmise, is universal nothingness—as the noetic counterpart of his attitude of absolute negation. The contradiction of this attitude is that he claims simultaneously to make himself an aristocrat (therefore the best of men)—a notion borrowed from the Romantics—and to sever his ties with humanity. And this contradiction is attributable not to subjective motives but to the coexistence in the practico-inert of two determinations of the Objective Spirit that are internalized through reading in the same mind in which they are united, opposing each other through bonds of interiority. As if the young reader had concluded that in order to *make himself* aristocratic, he had no choice but to escape from his own nature through absolute-art. As a consequence, absolute-art expresses the point of view of the absolute on the world. A point of view that is resumed in the absolute of negation.

Yet the most basic requirement of the new art is impossible to satisfy. In the first place, the idea of absolute negation is a contradiction *in adjecto*. The existence of an object or a quality in a determined sector of being, and in relation to another object or another sector, is denied. Moreover, negation is merely the formal and judicial aspect of negativity, which is praxis, destructive work. It is logically admissible, for example, that one class can deny the privileges of another class or its rights. And this is precisely the source of negation as an attitude: the writer-aristocrats, by their contempt and the positive aspect of their ideology, deny the humanism and humanity of the bourgeois. But transposed to the young men of 1840, pushed to the limit and decreed a priori a literary requirement without the support of a

124

social class, or at least a social stratum, negation becomes absolute at the moment it ceases to express an external view of the object, and it no longer signifies anything but the subjective effort of those young malcontents to take their distance in relation to the class that produced and sustained them. A futile effort, obviously, and one that leads to the denial of *everything* in the name of nothing. Indeed, the Postromantics' condemnation extends to the totality of the world: they want to expose it, beneath the mosaic of appearances, as nothingness. But *in relation to what* can this world, which in any case exists, be regarded as a lesser being and finally as that nothingness, vanity of vanities, which must be its ultimate secret? If it were in relation to God, who represents the total plenitude of being, that negation would be conceivable; but precisely for that reason a Christian would ascribe to it only a *relative* meaning: *in relation* to God, the world is nothingness; but in itself, and to the extent that it was the object of the Almighty's creative act, it is impossible to deny it a certain reality. If, on the other hand, God is not at issue, and if nihilism is applied to the world in itself, negation becomes absolute but now signifies nothing; and, as we know, those young agnostics no more claim to compare the world to a Creator than to judge the bourgeoisie through the eyes of the real aristocracy. The purpose of a work of art, according to them, is to manifest the inconceivable. Nothingness is not only the disintegration of the totality into molecules whose movements are governed from the outside by laws of exteriority; it is at the same time the condemnation of mechanism in the name of that impossible totality. Thesis, in effect, would be merely the application of bourgeois thought to the mendacious syntheses of history and religion. But if antithesis were reformulated and now defined mechanism itself as nothingness (a *nothing* without unity) even while destroying it, the writer would attempt to retain in himself that *arrested* double movement and present it as the world's negation of itself. Art, then, sets itself an unrealizable task: it will have to hide the real antinomy of thesis and antithesis and give it its purely fictive solution in beauty—in this case in the flaunted cult of appearance, of that which denounces its own lack of reality.

These young writers, when they aspire to that overview, have never meant it to be a real activity. In any event, overview is impossible, as we know, since we are fixed in space. But they know it as well. They have never dreamed, like philosophical dogmatists, of acquiring by that "distancing" an absolute knowledge of being. And although they like to speak of mystical ecstasies, they have not tried to envisage distancing as a real transcendence, a real ascent toward that absolute term, the God of believers. Their scientism, the sad fruit of the surprising progress of science, deters them from regarding philosophy as a rigorous discipline; rather, they have seen it as an auxiliary of art. The free play of ideas gave a broader foundation and some guiding schemes to the free play of imagination. And as for mysticism, apart from the fact that they lacked faith—the result above all of the progressive laicization of all sectors of human activity—they could not espouse the elevation of the mystic *in any case*. Indeed, if the mystic in his dark night has the feeling of progressively shedding the mundane determinations of his finitude, passions, language, and even imagination, it is because his enterprise has only one purpose: to offer himself to God so that He might penetrate him and suffuse him with ecstasy. He isn't the least concerned with leaning over and looking down to contemplate terrestrial nothingness from above. The negative is merely a means of ascesis; the end is pure positivity. And if, on the contrary, he returns to our world, he does so in order to regard it with the utmost seriousness and to help his brothers, as did John of the Cross and Theresa of Avila. Instead, our young men, caught between negativity and nothingness, frustrated by faith, convinced of the truth of scientism but hardly attracted by its austere theories, elevate themselves only to take their distance from the world and to embrace it in a single negative view. Having taken up literature in order to escape their fathers, naively persuaded that it could treat only lofty sentiments, they have seen those sentiments disappear and have understood in their disappointment that literary art was the terrain dreamed of for the totalization of their rancor and the assuaging of that hatred of man provoked by the Objective Spirit. But since they must elevate themselves without any source of support or lifeline, and without any real destination, they cannot help knowing that their ascension is fictive, or, rather, that they are embarking upon it without considering its strict impossibility, and even *against* it. And this is precisely why they define the imaginary as a permanent recourse against the impossible.

For these young men, literature opens an emergency exit; the imaginary being beyond the impossible but without its own consistency, its objectivization in the work will give it the consistency it lacks. In view of the work, and by virtue of it, they insist on their unconditional condemnation of the real by absolute negation as an unreal negation whose virulence comes, in fact, from *their choice of unreality*. In other words, literature imposes itself on them through the Objective Spirit as having no domain but the antireal, or pure unreality, pitting itself against the palpable world. Only in this way can they give a certain efficacy to the various ruptures imposed on them by their situation and the determinations of the Objective Spirit. In the name of autonomy they had to break with the public just when contrary imperatives were compelling them to break with man, then with the world. In short, with the totality of the real. And yet they remained what they were: young bourgeois of thc middle class, supported by their family or practicing a "liberal" profession. So they had to choose: either nothing had been produced—because nothing could be produced—except in dreams; and so literature, insofar as it demanded these ruptures, had become *impossible*. Or the choice of the imaginary, insofar as it represented the common signification of that behavior, was an effective and revolutionary step. The Postromantics chose the imaginary *so as to be able* to write.

But the necessity of this choice represents in itself an element of objective neurosis. Let us examine what it means. In the first place, rupture with the real—which is equivalent to condemning it—cannot be lived except as a permanent refusal to adapt; the artist must deny the aims of the race and society in himself and others as much as possible. And as he does not always manage to do so, the refusal must be imaginary. Similarly, he is required to lose the ordinary comprehension of objects, acts, and words to the same extent that absolute negation compels him no longer to share common aims. But this incomprehension does not come—as with the philosophers of the Platonic cave—from a superior knowledge that would in itself degrade the superficial activities of men in the name of their underlying essence and the essential goals of humanity, or even from a demand for deeper knowledge of them. Outside this incomprehension there is nothing: it confines itself to manifesting things in a state of estrangement precisely because of the refusal to integrate them into a real system. The point, in short, is to live in a permanent state of slight depersonalization, sometimes sincerely felt, sometimes maintained in the form of a *role*. In this state, if it can be sustained by external assistance, the writer must put himself and the world between parentheses; he does not intervene, he abstains. Consequently, things lose their weight of reality and sensation loses its "seriousness"; this is a subtle way of "realizing" absolute negation by reducing the universe to a series of apparitions untested by praxis and which—by their nothingness of being, the total absence of any coefficient of instrumentality or adversity—are finally equal to *appear-*

127

ances. Since art must be the supreme negation, the content of the work will be that desubstantialized, invisible universe of the imaginary. And in order to obtain the suppression of being in the interest of the pure, unreal apparition, the artist will have to receive his impressions *as if he were imagining them*. This is called the *aesthetic attitude*, the rigorous requirement of a literature that claims its full autonomy just when the bourgeoisie wants a class literature. With this attitude the artist unrealizes himself and at the same time derealizes the world. And as art is posited for its own sake through him, these strategies must in themselves imply a reversal of the usual set of values, making appearances worth more than realities and any apparition valued in proportion to its quantity of nonbeing. Thus the autonomy of art in 1850 can be obtained only through the nonreality of the artist and the content of the work, since these show us the nonreality of the world or the subordination of being to appearance. This may mean that the techniques of art are used to destroy the real, to present it in the work as it appears to the aesthetic attitude. Or it may mean that the artist can turn his back on reality, a strategy particularly favored in the Symbolist period for the purpose of choosing the imaginary and even attempting an oneiric literature. The chief thing, in one form or another, is the valorization of nonbeing. Around this time, the reason for writing is to resurrect vanished civilizations, to contest quotidian banality by an exoticism often entirely fabricated in Paris. Everything that is no longer there, that is not there, that is fixed in a permanent absence, is good provided one has access to the resurrected object solely through imagination. There is nothing accidental in the widespread vogue of Orientalism, the translation of sacred Indian songs, the recurrent presence of antique Greece—works on Greek history and art proliferate—but it is more dead and distant than ever. Writers thus hoped to escape their element and wanted that ancient, exotic culture to remain savage and inaccessible, its unassimilable originality revealing itself in the very heart of reading to be an image beyond all images, making palpable the nothingness at the very heart of imagination as the limit imposed on it by absence and death.

Absolute-art, an objective determination of literature-to-be-written, imposes the rupture with being on its future ministers from the outset. They cannot write without a metamorphosis which, unable to call itself by name without exposing its neurotic nature, announces itself *objectively* as an *ordination*. But the comparison is misleading: a religious order is an institution that sustains the vocation of the neophyte against the exterior and often against himself; in addition, for a believer, and above all in eras when faith is a positive bond between men, a young man *leaving the world,* in what is actually a negative moment, believes he is turning toward the full positivity of being. But when literature makes itself the absolute, that absolute can be only an absolute of negation. Thus the *vows* of the writer commit him only to himself and are posited by themselves as always revocable. In other words, they will be irrevocable—which is a necessity—only if the artist is unable to revoke them. The fact is that his first negation or renunciation of the world is not supported by any community and, far from being a source of integration, reveals exile and solitude as his imperative lot; on the other hand, this negation is not transformed into negativity—or the patient and joyous work of undermining—or into the gateway to positivity (the neophyte's access to the primary truths of the supernatural plenitude of real being). It must remain radical negation. And the supreme dignity of the work—a false positivity—lies in its vampirization of being (and primordially language); its fabric is, and must remain, *imaginary.* Therefore the artist can choose to show our world or a possible world in the brightest colors; the imperative simply demands that those colors, in one way or another, denounce their own nonbeing and that of the depicted object. In other words, absolute-art demands a suicide swiftly followed by genocide. And together these operations—one subjective, the other objective—can only be *imaginary.* Absolute-art requires *entrance-into-literature* the way in certain times and places *people entered into religion.* But as this conduct is purely fictive for the writer, it could be called his *entrance-into-the-imaginary-realm.* The Objective Spirit demands that he choose unreality as a rigorous refusal of the real (which he may subsequently depict, but as the real refused); but since this option *is itself imaginary,* its precariousness is evident to the author and denounces him as a traitor to art, possibly forever, indeed as a traitor to himself *unless* that precariousness has the consistency and irreducibility of a neurosis, or a suffered option. Of course neurosis as a *solution,* as the only possible support for the vow of unreality, is not imposed by the imperatives of 1850; those demand simply that the artist become *other than man,* that he attain this state through an ascesis and maintain himself there. But in this impossibility born of contradictory demands, neurosis emerges as a possible solution. And it amounts to this fascinating suggestion: let us behave as if all those insurmountable difficulties were resolved; let us, indeed, start from this solution, leaving to our bodies the task of finding and living it; let us write *beyond* the negative convulsions of our decrepitude.

2. *The Absolute as Beyond Failure*

This disturbing profile of the neurotic suggestion, which can be glimpsed behind the contradictions of the Objective Spirit, will be all the more fascinating in that it defines itself as the sublimation of failure, and as such the future author is *already* acquainted with it as a factual state to be assumed and a radical imperative. In other words, the entrance-into-literature presupposes the *real failure of the author* (ratifying the rupture of the new author and his real public), *the failure of man* (the first imaginary vow, whose objective stimulus is the failure of the aristocracy presented by Romanticism as its essence), and *the failure of the work itself,* not in the sense that its author may have botched it but rather that literature-impossibility can be manifest as such only through works which contest its being as they are contested in their singularity. We shall see how this triple failure can be realized only by a neurotic situation.

a. The Failure of the Artist

The failure of the artist on this first level does not yet signify the impossibility of defining oneself by a masterpiece. It is rather a matter of some previous disappointment: as a child, an adolescent, the future author was inclined toward literature-to-be-written by literature-already-written, which imposed a choice of works suggesting both a calvary and a triumphal march, the two notions for once not mutually exclusive. The poet makes good use of his personal suffering: he *gives* it, and the public returns it to him as an *eternal determination of the Objective Spirit.* This salutary pain impresses by its universal singularity; that is what allows it to be given to following generations as singular universality, as a framework to internalize for their affective life. As for the author, those young men understood that he too gradually became a determination of the practico-inert, death presenting itself as the completion of the process, and that his glory resided in this thorough integration reserved for him by society, producing books on his life and his works that transform him into a material idea as well, a permanent determination imperative for the newcomers' acculturation. But just when literature-already-written was leading him on that royal road to glory, that burial begun in early childhood with the chance for the famous author to hear his own funeral orations pronounced on street corners during his lifetime, the poor boy was confronted by a demand born of historical circumstance: the necessity to break with the entire public. Of course, he can dream that the burial will be deferred, that he will first be unceremoniously entombed and later exhumed by his descendants, who will bear his ashes to the Pantheon. But at the same period, disgusted by the triumph of their class yet too immersed in its ideology to envision its replacement by a classless society—one without individual property—these young bourgeois are induced to see social time as an involutive process. There was the golden age—fabulous Antiquity— then the bronze age; we are now entering the tin age. How can one hope that a humanity which is daily more degraded will be more capable in the future of rendering homage to the masterpieces that it failed to recognize when it was less wretched? This contradiction means that they are writing for glory, knowing full well that they will have it neither posthumously nor during their lifetime. To *deserve* literary glory, in 1850, is to write in such a way that it is denied a priori and forever. Needless to say, two solutions suggest themselves—and one is compromise. Rejected on principle, it is in fact more or less ubiquitous; they will not compromise on the work, but if, contrary to all expectation, it finds some echo, they will be quietly content. The other solution is intransigence itself, or neurosis; like the work, glory is an imaginary *reality*. What should it be attached to? Everyone is free to decide for himself. But only this second solution can conceal that contradiction *in adjecto* from the artist: he writes to detach himself from his class, the object of his radical contempt, and he demands, directly or indirectly, that this class grant social status, glory, to this detachment.

These remarks apply equally to his permanent project of *class transcendence*. Nearly the same contradiction is involved. First of all, we know that in this period of bourgeois dominance, he is writing to create a new aristocracy, in which he obviously participates and which defines itself through its works; and at the same time, conscious that a real class rests on the division of social labor governed by the instruments of production and institutionalized, he understands that he lacks the means to impose himself as an aristocrat. And the other imperative that designates him as a writer orders him to detach himself from all of humanity by the work that denounces the real in the name of unreality. Being unable to renounce either of these determinations, moribund demands imposed by reading, he thinks of himself either as a medieval scribe (a member of the upper class, at least in appearance, since it then possessed vast goods, a share of the temporal power, and imposed its own ideology on all classes), which

131

makes no sense—for every conceivable economic, social, and historical reason; or else as a knight of nonbeing, a baron of nonhumanity, which is self-destructive since admittedly, in this case, he is fully realizing his human nature even as he has succeeded in radically undoing his membership in the human race. Shall we say that he escapes antinomies if he confines himself to stating the superiority of nothingness over being and of the inhuman over man? Indeed he dreams of it, and around this time a rough notion of the superman appears, though still cautious and veiled, with whose later avatars we are quite familiar. But that superiority itself is not really conceivable. The superman as he will be imagined at the end of the century has at least the logical coherence of pursuing the human enterprise in its most general terms; he, too, is praxis, and his goal is the dialectical surpassing of oneself and one's situation. But if the first rough sketch of superhumanity simply defines people who put human nature in themselves (and outside them) between parentheses, and whose goal is to rank the unreal as the absolute negation of reality, no comparison is possible between them and real society absorbed in its praxis. They are neither superior nor inferior, but *other*. But it is impossible for these artists denied by their public to *persist* in solitude and obscurity unless they experience that failure and exile—art's a priori requirements—as the source of their fundamental superiority. They will find no way out of the vicious circle and will shift from one conception to the other, dissatisfied with both.

This is especially the case as that superiority remains *oneiric* and as their social reality is perfectly defined by their class of origin, their economic and political status, their mores, and even, as we shall soon see, by the dominant ideology. They belong for the most part to that stratum of the middle class called, at the time, the *capacités*. Their parents and friends mostly work in the liberal professions; living on a barely adequate portion of surplus value, these "enlightened" bourgeois would like to rise to the propertied class and participate in political power—although, whatever their responsibilities, they are among the *salaried* in the sense that their services are remunerated by a "salary" fixed in advance or by "honoraria" equally defined at the outset. Nothing could be clearer under the July monarchy, since political power belongs to the rich and serves exclusively to enlarge their fortunes behind the facade of liberalism. The *capacités* find themselves in a vicious circle: you need power to become rich, you must be rich to exercise power. In short, these mid-level bourgeois demand that the property qualification for the vote be lowered from two hundred to one hundred francs. This is a far cry from universal suffrage. These orderly people abhor subversion; in the early 1830s they learned of the existence of a working class, the rabble, and refuse to testify too energetically to their own discontent for fear the rabble should take it as a pretext to shake up the very foundations of society. These bourgeois have not understood, moreover, that the possession of capital makes bankers and manufacturers a class distinct from their own; they imagine that there are no more privileges, except political ones, and that the wealthier, their class brothers, are simply the luckiest. Against such blind accident, which according to them favors undeserving individuals, they vaunt their culture and their specialized knowledge; this is the very basis of their demands, the knowledge at their disposal which—for the good of the whole society—makes them fit to govern. Guillemin says, rather aptly, that "their little Fronde is not entirely unlike the Parlements under Louis XV and Louis XVI." How many of them are there? The adult males—those who would vote if the property qualification were lowered by half—number at the most two hundred thousand. With their wives and children, we have perhaps eight hundred thousand souls, perhaps a million. The Knights of Negation belong to this miniclass—one-thirtieth of France. They share its culture, its mores, and its discontent. Indeed, they will turn that discontent against the working classes under the Third Republic. Flaubert will say, "I am easily worth twenty electors from Croisset" because his father, under Charles X or Louis-Philippe, more discreetly implied that his *professional capacity* as a physician made him the equal of at least twenty rather illiterate and titled squires. The striking thing, then, is that the primary demand out of which they would be artists had its origin in the general dissatisfaction of their class. They have a respectful contempt for big banking and big business because before 1830 their fathers, those "enlightened" men, felt the same contempt along with the same respect. They share these sentiments because they have acquired the paternal culture—whether or not it is modified by the choice of a new specialization. In other words, the acquired culture is transformed in them into radical negation because it becomes conscious of its dependence the moment it affirms its universality. Clearly, their choice to write goes beyond the discontent of their class; far from claiming political rights, they condemn those futile disturbances—as they condemn all human actions—and deliberately set literature against them as a rigorous enterprise of *depoliticization*. They thereby reject at the outset their best public—their own class—by declaring quite simply

133

that they will not serve its enterprises and become the Voltaires of the petty bourgeoisie, taking up arms against its superiors. They will demolish the powerful by analysis, but neither more nor less than the weak and disadvantaged. Analytic activity, defined in the light of that dead totality, Romantic man in the bosom of creation, no longer aims at destroying privilege; rather it seeks to demonstrate, through psychosocial atomism and the systematic reduction of lofty sentiments to interested motives, that the human race, benighted or enlightened, is everywhere made of the same stuff, of nothingness. To study the functioning of bourgeois society, moreover, much more than analytic reason would be required, and in a way these new literary men have remained at the stage of pure negation for lack of another kind of reason, another tool. No matter; although the choice to be apolitical and opt for an imaginary transcendence of class was determined in each of them by the singularities of childhood, that choice nonetheless particularizes the discontent of the professional class and carries it to an extreme. The superiority of culture is lived by their fathers and brothers as negativity to the extent that it challenges a social order that does not acknowledge it; in the young Knights of Nothingness this superiority becomes supremacy. They do not ask that it be recognized through the bestowal of advantages; they affirm it as an incontestable absolute, which they base on the annihilation of the human race. It is another choice: by dreaming, they are already surrendering to what others try to conquer by practical negativity; but this choice—in itself neurotic—is the direct expression of the class demand they claim not to apprehend. The apolitical stance and unrealization seem the shortest roads to the realization of culture as a set of unprescribable norms superior to everything, even to the human race that produced it. So just when they seem to turn their backs on it, these young men are prey to that original negativity which torments the social stratum from which they have come, and their class being is thereby affirmed by the very movement that would allow them to transcend it. An obscure and unrealizable desire, it is the petty-bourgeois professionals whom they attempt to raise in their person above big Capital as the aristocracy of the universal, of nonbeing. It is not that they have lost interest in the class struggle; rather, they transpose it and pursue it by other means. All the more bound to the middle class as they think they are leaving it behind, if they achieve that coveted glory—which is for the moment inaccessible, for the reasons I have mentioned—their triumph will rebound on them and, without in any way altering the infrastructural contradictions, will favor their conscious awareness and their emancipation. We shall return to all that; the story of these men and their destiny can be understood only through the evolution of the middle class. This will allow us in our final volume to broach a difficult problem that has never been dealt with: what is the *class-being* of a writer born into the professional class who produces *Madame Bovary?* For the moment, it suffices to note this new contradiction: the writer of nothingness makes himself bourgeois by expressing in his own way the point of view of his class of origin when he believes he is becoming radically detached from it.

Yet that is not enough; he must lay it on thick, and we have seen that at this moment of the vanished public, he can deny the bourgeois only by becoming bourgeois. He doesn't write to be read, so he must assure his independence by means of income property or a profession. But these revenues or that job will obviously not raise him to the level of the governing plutocrats but will ensconce him firmly in the petty bourgeoisie. A little later, in the time of Villiers de l'Isle-Adam, the same literary current will produce more radical artists, who will indicate their aristocracy of negation by assumed poverty, by refusing to do anything in that bourgeois world except write works all the purer for never being read. But that reaction, which is perfectly logical, is somewhat alien to the first generation of Postromantics. For them, poverty may be the "milk of the strong," but it is best avoided; the work will be purer and more disinterested if one can draw on other resources to live. Moreover, part of its essence is *not to be merchandise,* and this is best signaled by *not selling* it, or at the every least not writing it for that purpose. If some publisher publishes it, that is his business, but the author must not count on it; without readers he affirms himself as an aristocrat by his rejection of a literature of consumption. No longer a *gift,* the work has at least preserved the Romantic character of gratuitousness earlier linked to generosity of spirit, now signaling the freedom of its creator. More accurately, the work *in itself* at once suppresses and reabsorbs author and reader into itself. Literature being dual, one of the terms cannot be suppressed without the other disappearing; thus the book stands unwritten, unread, a substantiation of culture, like a column in the desert beneath the silent sky in which, perhaps, lies hidden its only worthy reader. But *in relation to the writer* and *while he writes it,* the work seems to be the product and objectivization of a *gratuitous act,* which might be understood—or almost—in the sense Gide will later give it.[10] That gratuitousness is essential to the Postromantic, it is the very basis of his aristocracy; writing *for nothing* and *no one,* he belies the maxims of utilitarianism by his free activity, done for its own sake ("nothing comes from nothing," "no one does anything for nothing"), and by the same token he manifests his essence, which is in principle non-bourgeois, since the bourgeois is defined by self-interest.

So the writer necessarily becomes bourgeois: he must live, he will live modestly. Not, of course, like the best paid of his class (barring exceptional circumstances); for that he would have to have social ambition and give himself over completely to lucrative work. But often by means of a poorly paid job—as a bureaucrat, a civil servant, a teacher in a private institution. His disgust for the "lower classes," however, compels him to stay *outside* them, even in semidiscomfort, distancing himself from the "bohemian," whom he regards—as Barrès does later—as merely an intellectual of the proletariat. He looks after his appearance, seeks decent lodging by economizing, if he must, on food; he compensates for the paltriness of his means by the dignity of his bearing—sometimes to the point of pomposity. Thus, not only his salary but his characteristic budgetary choices define him as a petty bourgeois, or, if you will, situate him concretely at a lower level of the middle class. Unlike the working class, the bourgeoisie typically choose at this time to sacrifice food—that vulgar need—to expenses of a *social* nature, that is, to *appearance.* On this level of the middle class, relations are eminently those of politeness and ceremony, being directly conditioned neither by manual labor, which is exercised in general on inanimate matter, nor by the search for profit; thus when the writer concerns himself with his attire and his bearing, he is only doing what is required of him by his employer (the director of some private institution), his boss (his immediate superior if he is a civil servant), or his clients (if he gives private lessons). This compels him to live his bourgeois condition fully in every detail of daily life and, in order to avoid useless friction, meekly and deferentially to carry out the orders of employers or civil servants who certainly know themselves to be, and want to be, bourgeois and who regard him in terms of his salary and his work. The contradiction

10. Let us say rather that a writer of 1900 can imagine an ethic of the gratuitous act for one reason only: because he transports into the domain of praxis the gratuitousness that half a century of tradition has assured the work of art. And difficulties will come precisely from that transposition; what is suitable to the work—because literary duality can be abstractly suppressed—cannot be suitable to the act.

136

here is that what he takes for a *role* is really the inevitable result of his class-being. He trims his food budget, he thinks, out of an artist's austerity in order to reduce to the minimum his membership in the great social enterprise of survival; on this point he is compelled to share the most vulgar of human ends, but he will do only what is necessary, never more than that. Thus he experiences the restrictions imposed by his class-being as the *choice made by an artist*. Similarly, he perceives his ceremonious politeness, the restrained deference all subordinate employees are expected to observe toward their superiors, as a challenge to the social order: his restrained obedience, he thinks, is a way of *keeping his distance* from the representatives of bourgeois society. He resembles the Christian who renders unto Caesar that which is Caesar's out of a greater devotion to God. Except that God, at least by virtue of the sacred bond of those early communities, was wholly positive. Absolute-art, on the other hand, is entirely negation. In other words, their life is similar in every detail to the lives of the petty bourgeois of the same social level because it is conditioned by the same objective determinations. It is, of course, distinguished by that impassioned and profoundly solitary activity, writing. Writing for art, for God, for the self, for nothing, against everyone. But, save in rare moments of devastating lucidity, far from considering themselves petty bourgeois who write (which would raise extremely complex questions to which we shall return in the final volume of this work)* and therefore exercise an activity which in 1850 is found to belong to their class insofar as it comprises the *capacités*, they regard themselves as aristocrats (or supermen) who have become petty bourgeois in order to write. In a way, this illusion contains elements of truth. It is *true* that they are defined above all as *individuals* by the choice to write, by the internalization of the culture of the *capacités*, literature-already-written projecting into the future the imperatives of literature-to-be-written. But given the variety of circumstances, this choice, which is a specific instance of the great choices possible for their class—at *this* time, at the end of *this* history, and in *this* set of circumstances—far from raising them above it, merely confirms their anchorage. Everything, even the *gratuitousness* of the work undertaken, finds its basis in a certain exis of the "enlightened" classes; certainly, for several centuries the bourgeoisie has been demanding a "class literature" that the writers declined to give it. This relates to the way in which the rising class finds its particularity

---

*A volume that Sartre was never to write.—Trans.

in the obstacles set against it by the aristocracy, and in the intermittent favors dispensed by a royal power determined to maintain a social equilibrium that favors royalty. But at the same time the bourgeoisie regards itself as the universal class, and proudly affirms that it is virtually single-handedly producing sons who are specialists in universality. And although that universalism is itself a weapon, and its relations with science, law, and art are fundamentally practical, the bourgeoisie must devote itself to assimilating its own culture as that culture reflects its universality in terms of class and seems to be at once its own thought and human thought in general. Consequently, its overt and, to some degree, real attitude toward the cultural whole is disinterested curiosity. Let us say simply that this disinterestedness can also be explained as a form of self-interest, since by studying man and nature this class aspires to become conscious of itself and, as the source of all knowledge and all artistic creation, to *deserve* the political power still denied it. Be that as it may, tradition in 1840 is specific, going back through the classical centuries to the Renaissance, and through the Italian influence even further back to the Florentine fourteenth century. Although it might allow for practical applications, culture taken as a whole serves no particular interest; one acquires it or enriches it *for its own sake,* to know men and to know oneself, to be finally—beyond social distinctions—fully human, universal as bourgeois. This tradition is called humanism, and before any specialization the *capacités* devote themselves to "doing the humanities." Thus the gratuitousness of literary activity— while it may be conditioned by an aristocratic imperative and constitutes a debasement of Romantic generosity—finds the true basis of its possibility in humanistic disinterestedness, which it merely takes to the extreme, to the moment when, in the name of the work, it is turned against man himself.

We have already understood that the new writers have every interest in denying the disinterestedness that allowed them to conceive of art established for its own sake on the death of man. We understand, therefore, that the bourgeois is always defined by action, whose only motive is self-interest. Generalization is easy: the definition will be extended to *man in this era* and sometimes to human nature. Thus the artist will have to regard the disinterestedness inculcated by his fathers as an antihuman or superhuman attitude, whereas quite obviously a class in the process of expansion, which claims to devote part of its time to cultural activity outside any self-interest, is necessarily led to produce its own specialists of disinterested activity. The contradiction here is that the writer, in order to affirm both his aristocracy and the autonomy of absolute-art, must cut all his ties to his own class and exhaust himself trying not to see the social conditionings that allowed him to become what he is.

The neurotic aspect of this attitude is obvious: for these young men, writing is not simply a matter of producing a work, it is *playing a role*. And certainly a writer of any era, if he wants to recover his being—if he takes himself seriously—is obliged to play the role of writer, great as he might be otherwise. But in general these little dramas are epiphenomena; they are played in drawing rooms, Academies, more rarely in intimate circumstances, and above all the author doesn't need them in order to write his work, any more than a doctor needs to play the role of doctor in order to cure his patient.[11] It can even be said generally that if a certain complacency with the author's image as Creator is glimpsed in a book just written, it will mar the work. In the case of the Postromantics, the contradictory imperatives of literature-to-be-written are such that the only way they can produce a work is perpetually to play the role of writer. Indeed, they do nothing unless they set the absolute autonomy of art against the interested passions of man. The contention is that man, as he is, is incapable of writing. Thus, as they are living the same life as their neighbors within their class, they will write nothing themselves unless they raise themselves permanently above what they consider to be "human nature" and establish themselves—against their real condition, which is defined by their salary, their employment, their mores and their human relations—as an unacknowledged aristocracy. And since the objective of their literature is to establish its autonomy through the absolute negation of the world, along with the human race it contains, they cannot even conceive of their subject without constituting themselves in their daily lives as a pure panoramic consciousness, external to the world and to human nature. We must understand that it wouldn't be enough for this metamorphosis to take place in nocturnal solitude, when they finally take up their pens, for it would then yield only pure, abstract and empty negation, which is not the work itself but rather its meaning and its unity. If they want to fill that empty demand with the tumult of sounds and colors that

11. Of course I understand that he needs to adopt a certain attitude to inspire confidence in the patient. Protective playfulness or calm authority, sometimes extreme, are frequently adopted. But such behavior is meant to persuade the *other*; moreover, it is not indispensable, and can be adopted without inner conviction. And, in any event, the important thing is the diagnosis and treatment.

139

will constitute the texture of their work and become manifest as that which must be totalized by its abolition, they must confront their daily lives from morning to night and envisage those lives as capable of providing the work's content. Not because they are immersed in it and it provokes emotions and acts but, quite the contrary, because they do not participate in it at all, as if they were *someone else*, a man living it in their place, and as if, contemplating it from the point of view of death, they were discovering its nothingness. For them, of course, it is a matter of maintaining by day the aesthetic attitude that will finally allow them to become once more, at night, artists *in action*. But while the writer easily adopts this attitude in total inaction, like a tourist before a landscape to which he is unattached by any bond of labor, it becomes practically *impossible* the moment he is involved in human relations or an enterprise. For it effectively implies the dereal-ization of perceived objects and their reduction to simple appear-ances, whereas at the same time activity reveals the irreducible reality of the practical field. Therefore, the writer of this era must *simultane-ously involve and disinvolve himself* in his family, at his office, in the street, and as that cannot really be done, he must be resolved to *play-act* one of the two attitudes. He will no doubt manage to simulate listening or acting, and lead his life as if interpreting a role, in order that he might devote all of his reality solely to the intimate reflected gaze. In this case life is the dream, and truth resides in the frozen quietism of the contemplating consciousness. But the urgency of practical tasks, their difficulty, the complexity of human relations, the distasteful matters endured during working hours, the aggressive-ness of a boss, the conspiracy of subordinates, everything that endan-gers the petty bourgeois dignity of the Knight of Nothingness must continually be faced, and that leaves hardly any time to catch his breath or cut his losses. The writer *really is* that worker humiliated by a rebuff, that employee afraid of losing his position, that bashful lover. The humiliation, the anxiety, the pains of love are *true;* they suggest the *true* character of one petty bourgeois, and they *truly* ex-press the general movement of his class—its claims, its struggles, its ideology, and its system of values—as well as the singular history of his life. His *reality* is human; the writer disappears, and what remains is an angry or frightened man—who by definition cannot be an artist. In order to preserve the continuity of the function of writing, the only solution is to playact for oneself, and for oneself alone, the sublime indifference of the artist. You flank the all too human bourgeois with an imaginary double, whose chief traits are being-outside-the-world, solitude, the nonqualification and love of beauty conceived as totality-abolition. In a word, the young Postromantic *unrealizes himself as an artist*; this means that he takes all the blows, bleeds, suffers fully the wounds to his self-esteem, and pretends he hasn't been hit. Yet a little leisure is needed to take on this role; the artist can manage it only if the pressure of the real lets up a bit. When that isn't possible and the event hurries him along, his recourse is retrospective reconstruction. He can falsify his remembrance by claiming that a certain offense did not even disturb him; in this case the unrealization involves a trick of memory. And he has just as much license to acknowledge that the affront took him unawares and affected him unduly at the time, but that today he kids himself about it and merely savors the scene evoked "as an artist"; in this case, the reflection itself is unrealized. In any event, in 1850 as in other times, art defines its artist; it assigns him a fundamental objective, a function, a place. The misfortune of the young elect, in this era, is the contradiction between the arrogant program imposed by the demand that panoramic consciousness should detach them from the race, and, if this program is to be accomplished, the obvious need for them to become still more firmly entrenched in their class and to adhere completely to their "petty bourgeois" condition. There is no doubt, however, that if one wants to write, *that* is the literature which must be written; and reciprocally, the art of 1850 can be made only by *those* artists. The only trouble is, the Aristocracy of Nothingness does not exist and cannot exist. And at the same time, recruitment for it is being done in the middle classes. These young men, scarcely out of the ranks, understand the original failure of their literary generation; transcendence of class, dehumanization, panoramic consciousness, impassivity, the preconditions of their activity *are not realizable.* Yet art is to be made and must be made by *them.* They will not know glory since no one will read them, and besides, even if it should come through misunderstanding or compromise, it would be a stinking glory, fouled by the infamy of the readers who would confer it. Yet these writers have the obligation to create immortal works. They will have no money, which facilitates the transcendence of class and allows the artist to maintain the aesthetic attitude. Yet true solitude and the leisure it provides are indispensable to anyone who wants to bear witness in his books to absolute negation. They will not replace the defunct aristocracy; those who do not read them—that is, all Frenchmen—see them only as middle-class bourgeois, living on a modest income or a small salaried position. It is their duty, however, to raise themselves above the bourgeoisie, mistress of the world, and make it ashamed of its shabby quest for profit by producing that unheard-of luxury which no nobility could create by itself, a masterpiece, a gratuitous and perfectly useless splendor. Such is the first insurmountable obstacle, and their first failure. But by the same token, the primary objective structure of the neurosis seems beyond these antinomies, like a solution by means of the irrational. We must imagine, of course, that the newcomers throw themselves into literature with a passion all the more frenzied as they have chosen it as their only way out. They will not renounce it. More precisely, at this midpoint in the century its summons has a resonance so extraordinary, it demands and promises such marvels, that although one can certainly fail to hear it, anyone who does has no power to escape. Isn't it a question of *creating* nothingness out of uncreated chaos? Since this elect group perseveres, the difficulty must be turned around: for lack of *being* an artist—which is required to produce the work of art[12]—one can employ that strategy dubbed *acting as if*. In principle, the expedient is not even unreasonable; it is used in teaching the sciences and sometimes even in research: "Act as if the problem were solved." But in this case it is simply a matter of provisionally leaving aside an objective determination to forge ahead, without losing sight of one's omission and with the intention of returning to it subsequently with new knowledge. The "act as if" proposed to the young *littérateurs* of 1850 is far more serious, for it concerns themselves. Since one must be a proud aristocrat, and gloriously survey the world in order to be an artist and create according to the rules of *this* art, *let us act as if we were*. Let us play the extravagant liberality of the nobleman, the cosmic meditation of the brahman, the calm temerity of the genius already crowned with glory; let us approach absolute-art as imaginary supermen, let us conceive and execute the work out of our fictive greatness, let us really make the demands that correspond to our false capacities. Perhaps the *Book* will issue forth at the end of this drama, precisely because we have had the audacity, by deliberately taking ourselves for *others*, to demand incredible wonders of ourselves—which we would never have dared in our right minds; perhaps because in the infinite void inside us there are answers to all demands, and it is enough to take courage and solicit them. This is the procedure suggested by the Objective Spirit. It must be noted that the neurotic element does not

12. This is true only in France in 1850. Elsewhere, it is usually the work that qualifies its author.

reside in the drama itself but in the actor's belief in his character. Indeed, if we assume that the role is played coolly and, as Diderot would have it in his *Paradox*, without the slightest emotion, the self-styled artist, knowing it's a game and remaining aware of his actual personality, will never be bold enough to "work with genius." If he wants to become fully mobilized and produce new sounds, he must perch on the summit of his pride and take himself truly for the man he pretends to be. In this sense, the objective neurosis is perfectly recognizable: it is the requisite autosuggestion and, consequently, pithiatism. We have seen above that absolute-art required the artist's break with reality. This divorce reminded us of certain psychotic attitudes—schizophrenia, for example, in which, by means of a false severity, or at other times by means of delirious imagery, the patient "disengages" and loses contact with the environment and his own body. This is true. But what proposes itself to the young authors does not at all correspond, in fact, to a psychosis; they believe in their derealization, but it is acted. More accurately, one of the chief characteristics of this objective hysteria is that it will imitate the schizophrenic's attitude toward the world *by believing in it*. The complexity of the neurotic solution—and its greatest chance of success—comes from the fact that unrealization, before being a strategy for these future authors, was defined by literary imperatives as a judgment against the real and prescribed as a norm of artistic activity; this involves reducing reality to nothingness by affirming the being of appearance, or cultivating oneiric imagery not despite but because of its unreality. Thus, when the young writer unrealizes himself as the artist, he becomes more at one with the imperative content of his work, which must be the unreal, or the derealization of reality. His role favors it, and he is better at inventing the unreal (or derealization) because he is unreally an artist or a derealized bourgeois. He would, in short, produce images to the second degree. And these are required by absolute-art because of their double dose of nothingness. Conversely, unrealization being a cardinal norm of art, the author will have no scruples about unrealizing himself as an artist. Quite the contrary, as absolute negation is the foundation of future creation, derealization, the aesthetic norm of the work, becomes an ethical value for the person who wants to write. To deny oneself by playing a role is, in some way, to deserve to create. Be that as it may, the ethico-aesthetic norm of unrealization is born of a primary failure: the impossibility for the young elect actually to fulfill his assigned office.

143

b. The Failure of Man

The failure of the artist, though transformed into a neurotic kind of ethico-aesthetic norm, can be regarded as originally suffered. By awakening the imperatives of the Objective Spirit, the young bourgeois reader becomes designated by contradictory imperatives, unites these contradictions in the explosive notion of the artist, and can merely record the permanent explosion which renders that notion *unrealizable*. The intention to unrealize himself in order to surpass those contradictions comes to him only afterward. By contrast, the intention of failure is primary in his life. By this I do not mean that it is in fact preceded by knowledge of the irreconcilable demands of art, but simply that the intended solution does not *come after* an experienced failure, that it is the failure itself grasped as a *reality to be produced*. In the second half of the century, the vatic poet becomes the cursed poet. Poetry is defined negatively by the infirmity of the poet considered as man, and his poetic vision is spoken of only allusively; we only see the albatross—that vast bird of the sea—pitted against other men and, in a general way, against reality; he becomes "clumsy and . . . ugly," he is ridiculed, he is the *cripple* who flew away. But the failure of man—his powerlessness to live the ordinary life—is expressly given as the *necessary result* of his victory as a poet: his giant wings prevent him from walking. In this form, the failure is still *suffered*. But wouldn't the converse be true? Doesn't the poet make himself into a cripple in order to prove to himself that he can fly? Indeed, Baudelaire belittles his cursed poet even more when in his study of Edgar Allen Poe, published in 1852, he replaces this still noble anathema with the simple word "jinx" [*le guignon*], which recurs, moreover, as a *title* of a poem published in 1855. In that poem a famous distinction is made which will be taken up again by Mallarmé. First, there are *great* poets, socially recognized, celebrated, and otherwise irreproachable. Upon their death, these poets find "celebrated sepulchers." And then there are others, who are headed "toward an isolated cemetery"; they are not read, they have no luck, that's all. But must one be read to be certain of having produced unseen beauties?

> Many a jewel sleeps enshrouded . . .
> In shades of forgetting
> Far from pickaxes and probes.

The objective reason for this transformation of the theme is simply the existence of Victor Hugo, whose fame is vast and incontestable,

and who is admired, or initially admired, by all the new writers—
Flaubert, Leconte de Lisle, Baudelaire, Mallarmé. Without Hugo, it
would be a closed case: poetry would be identified with Malediction; every poet is cursed, every cursed man is in a way a poet.
This is Baudelaire's original impulse, moreover, as he writes in
"Benediction":

> When, by pronouncement of almighty powers,
> The Poet appears among us in this tired world,
> His outraged mother, racked by blasphemies,
> Clenches her fists to God, who pities her.

Aside from the fact that they satisfy a certain neurotic resentment
and that "breach" he spoke of—born of his mother's remarriage—
these lines succeed in showing us the poetic genius *actualizing himself*
through hatred, rancor evoked by the elect in spite of himself. Cursed
by his mother, scorned, tortured by his wife, virtually lynched by the
mob, the poet finally becomes himself and cries out:

> Be praised, my God, who gives us suffering*

But Hugo is there, full of genius, celebrated, accepting with dignity
the honors they beg him not to refuse, but also capable of preferring
exile and solitude to any compromise; Hugo is a political party all to
himself, the party of the republican opposition to the Empire. France
does not follow him, but his books are in great demand, and the Emperor has assured him more than once that he would be welcome
with open arms if he returned. *Therefore*, one can be a poet without
invoking a mother's curse. From these painful findings a new conception is elaborated. On the models of Baudelaire and of Theophile Gautier, who troubles no one as he is neither cursed nor a genius, there
are two sorts of poets: those whose work is at once a perfect poetic
and social success, and those who can be defined only by the radical failure of their social and aesthetic ambitions; on the muddle of
their life they construct a poetic world that will be unacknowledged,
and they will never know if it was viable. Moreover, Baudelaire consoles himself by thinking that language, the vehicle of communication, can exist *by itself* when it is determined as the bearer of the
incommunicable.

*From "Benediction," trans. Stephen Stepanchev, in *An Anthology of French Poetry
from Nerval to Valéry, in English Translation*, ed. Angel Flores (New York: Anchor Books,
1958).

> Many a flower pours out with regret
> Its sweet perfume, like a secret,
> In utter solitude.

Secretly, to be sure, we infer that he prefers the funeral marches a cursed poet plays for himself alone, on a muted tambour, to the great public prophecies of the vatic poet. This confirms the revision of lines 12 and 13 of "Le Guignon," for indeed he had first written:

> Many a flower pours out in secret
> Its sweet perfume, like a regret . . .

The idea was simple: the secret was simply a result of the fact that the poem was not read, that the flower was growing at the bottom of a desolate cliff. When he inverts the terms, we understand that he is going much further: the true poem is in essence incommunicable; its very being—a determination of discourse, which is made to communicate—is *in itself* a regret. In a way, it is more beautiful when it does not yet exist. The revision quite simply defines the new poetry. But a few years later, Mallarmé—in complete literary confusion—takes the idea of "Le Guignon" and radicalizes it. There are great poets, "beggars of the sky's blue," who bound above the dazed human cattle. Those beggars *also* find greatness in failure: they suffer terribly in the night marches, getting drunk with the happiness of seeing their blood shed. But this failure is grandiose: "They are defeated by a powerful angel"; and in their very lifetime, when they sing, "The people kneel and their mother rises," "They are consoled, sure and majestic." There is Hugo once more, cursed to some degree because he is a man, despite everything, but triumphant because he possesses some kind of superhuman power. As for the others, whom he "drags along in his wake," they are *his brothers;* but they are scoffed at, "derisory martyrs of tortuous accidents." Accidents of life and especially, as we shall see, accidents of words, which must be excluded, and which a toss of the dice, the poem, will never abolish, being accidental itself. Therefore, they lose on all fronts: "if one blows on his bizarre trumpet," children will make us laugh "aping its fanfare." The only possible ending is suicide:

> When everyone has spat scorn in their faces . . .
> These heroes, worn out by a bantering wretchedness
> Go and ludicrously hang themselves from the street lamp.
> ["Guignon"]

No mercy: they have failed in everything, their work and their existence. And if they are scorned, it is not that they are reproached for being poets but rather for being failed artists and failed men. That is certainly the fate Mallarmé feared for himself at the time, so much so that he was haunted by the idea of suicide. Yet does he *entirely* believe in this perfect shipwreck? Let us note, first of all, that these grotesque characters are the *brothers* of the "beggars of the sky's blue," and that they participate in their insatiable quest. They, too, have bitten into the idea's bitter fruit. The hero, moreover, worn out by bantering wretchedness, who is going to hang himself from a street lamp, is not Mallarmé but Gerard de Nerval—the allusion is clear. Can we imagine that Mallarmé saw Nerval as merely a ridiculous Hamlet,[13] the victim of bantering wretchedness, blowing on a bizarre trumpet? Not really; Mallarmé simply radicalizes failure. The public laughter, the bizarreness of the trumpet, the suicide are needed for that triumph (which no God will guarantee) and beauty, attained at last, to be manifest in the heart of the grotesque as a "mystery." The poet defines here a new Ars poetica, a simple radicalization of the Postromantic aesthetic which we shall have occasion to discuss below. Certainly the pessimism that emerges around 1850 with the first Postromantic generation is accentuated with the following generations, and failure, a notion already present but sometimes implicit at the beginning of this literary current, becomes the very foundation of the artist's life and work, *with no compensation.* The vatic poet now condemns himself by his very success; the cursed poet is still too pompous—a prophet in reverse, that's all. You can deny the real only if the real begins by excluding you; in order to succeed in this game of "Loser Wins," the poet must be at once despoiled of his poetic *aura* and of his human dignity. Let us take it one step further: literature is by now the only career still open to these failures; they enter it, and precisely because they have failed in all human endeavors, they make a pitiful mess of their work. These repeated failures do not even deserve pity; yet those shabby works are the only way for us to glimpse, through their gaps, a vision of unrealizable beauty. That is all we can ask of them: to be *allusive,* to bear witness to an absence. "Advise me, my dream, what to do?"

> Take in at a glance the virgin absence scattered in this solitude and, as one gathers in remembrance of a place one of those magical, still unopened waterlilies that suddenly spring up, enclosing in their hollow whiteness a nothing made of unspoiled dreams, of happiness that will not be, and holding my breath in fear of an

13. "Worn-out heroes" have replaced the "shamed Hamlet" of the earlier version.

apparition, flee with it—silently rowing backward little by little, so that the illusion may not be broken by the shock, nor the lapping of the visible bubble of foam rolling in my wake throw at anyone's arriving feet the transparent resemblance of the abduction of my ideal flower.[14]

On this level, fixed negation gives way to an extraordinary dialectic of nothingness.

But what becomes evident at the end of this literary movement can also be found at its beginning, between 1840 and 1850, already implicit and sometimes quite explicit. Literature is feminine, it is already a last resort, the choice of incapacitated, unvirile men. Conversely, *because of that* it is great, it is all. For man is in principle a failure whose only mirror and unique perpetuation is the work, that radical and sublime failure. Thus choosing art and entering literature find their motivation from the outset and their final justification in the failure of practical life. That has always been true. Writing presupposes in principle not, certainly, neurosis but an essential maladaption to society and to the daily course of affairs. That is even truer in the 1840s, and for the young bourgeois whom literature-already-written will induce to write, the original determination can be only a familial malaise, hence an obscurely experienced social malaise. Is this reconcilable, however, with the dramatized transcendence of class that makes the writer an aristocrat or a superman? Certainly; first of all, pride is the mediating factor: writing is a means of overcompensating. But even so, the literary imperative demands that the artist's absolute superiority be based on his incapacity. This curious but strict requirement has the effect, first of all, of facilitating the drama: if aristocrats are in essence failures, a failure will be able, with some conviction, to play an aristocrat. All the more so since yesterday's literature, Romanticism, placed the greatness of man in his consensual defeat. But absolute-art demands much more of its ministers; it can be established only on a radical and *involuntary* failure. This must be briefly explained.

Absolute-art, the exaltation of autonomy in the age of the absent public, initially requires the overview, that radical negation of the bourgeoisie and finally of man by breaking with all human ends, which will henceforth be *considered* from a vantage point of aesthetic estrangement and no longer *shared*. This implies that the artist is no

14. Mallarmé, "Le Nenuphar blanc," *Poèmes en prose* (Bibliotheque de la Pléiade), p. 286.

longer connected *as man* to those objectives which, in sum, define the human race in its practical intersubjectivity. And the future writer—whom literature-already-written evokes by giving a future to his malaise—comes to art as a young bourgeois, discontented, of course, with his circumstances and his class, but bourgeois even in that discontent. The consequence is clear: he is the first target of the radical, unconditional condemnation of the bourgeois—and finally of man—issued by art-to-be-done. No doubt he hopes for class transcendence through the work, and perhaps he already hopes for dehumanization; but what art-to-be-done first reveals to him is that class transcendence through the work is impossible. It is not sufficient to condemn the vulgar nature of the bourgeois within himself by words or outbursts of temper; as long as it remains within him, as long as it has not been broken by events, it will prevent him from writing a single line of real literature. This is a new contradiction, and absolute-literature is once again betrayed by its own demands; we have seen and we shall see that it requires masterpieces from the writer even as it removes his means of creating them. At present, the man it chooses, it's only possible *author*, is condemned in advance even in his good will, therefore absolute-literature reveals him to be falsely chosen. In effect, this unfortunate bourgeois, who wants to detach himself from his class by inventing himself through a work, conceives the access to art and creation *in a bourgeois fashion* as an *enterprise*. In other words, aristocracy is his aim, and art is the unique and rigorous means of entering it. In short, this young man in desperate need of distinction is not much more distinguished than Monsieur Jourdain, the bourgeois gentleman. He wants his work to be *useful*—if not to the public or to humanity at least to himself; he makes his salvation the purpose of an *activity*. But art is not useful to anyone, not even to the artist, at least insofar as he is a man. This good young man who dreams of writing because he is an unhappy bourgeois can only write class literature; he is even fated to do it by his inner contradiction which, as long as it remains what it is, defines him by a distancing from within the bourgeoisie that allows him to see and depict it. But he has not lost an underlying solidarity with his class, for that contradiction has not destroyed the *spirit of enterprise* in him, and he shares with his social setting if not particular ends at least that bourgeois (human) trait of leading a practical life defined by an end. In vain does the pseudo-veritable artist—if such a man exists and our young man meets him—explain to him that art is never a means; if the apprentice is convinced, he will make literature his end. And there he is again, defined by a

149

purpose, by a praxis. Let us imagine his touching efforts, his systematic ascesis. Since writing is henceforth his absolute end, he will divest himself of his bourgeois identity with the intention of writing; patiently he registers in himself the mores of his class, the customs and ideas that define it, and savagely attempts to root them out *in order to write*. And—aside from the fact that nothing is achieved by this false ascesis, which denies in theory a class characteristic that only a real transcendence of class can destroy—the enterprise is poisoned from the outset by the *bourgeois spirit of interest*. "It is in my interest to divest myself of my bourgeois identity if I want to write; it is in my interest to nullify, at least, that respect for money I discern in myself, even if I cannot entirely uproot it. Finally, it is in my interest to make myself capable of attaining that objective, the work. I am trying to disencumber myself of superficial bourgeois qualities, but I do so by preserving and utilizing the very intention that produces and sustains them—the *practical* intention as it uses an end to define the means it must *utilize*, the possibles judged as useful and those rejected as useless and harmful." In other words, literature-to-be-written indicates that it is not *productive* of an aristocracy, and that, quite the contrary, to create it one must first be an aristocrat and essentially have cast off all *finalism*, replacing any teleological intentions with pure gratuitousness, a substitute for generosity, as the source of all creation. But even as it demands these qualities of the artist it prohibits him from making the slightest effort to acquire them; that would be excessive, and the unhappy candidate would turn forever in the infernal circle of means and ends. It would be a mistake, in effect, to understand literary autonomy in 1840 as if that autonomy were meant to be the artist's absolute end. Taking these imperatives in the strict sense, absolute-art, the *dated* expression of this autonomy, claims to be *its own end*. In other words, in the era of *art for art's sake* (an expression not adopted by everyone at the time but which from our vantage point says effectively what it means), the true artist must be free of all personal teleology. Art is not the artist's end, it is its *own end*, and the writer (or sculptor or painter) is merely the unique possible mediation between this inhuman imperative of beauty and its objectivization through works conceived as centers of derealization. But the servants chosen by the beautiful, who are bound to its objective manifestations, must in no instance or under any pretext aim to detach themselves from the human condition by the deliberate self-mutilation of excision from the teleological system that defines man as praxis on the basis of his needs and interests. They must be this way—that's all. And since everyone is born with a prefabricated destiny which society orders him to accomplish, since everyone from the outset is trained like a beast by the qualified representatives of his class, who inculcate practical finalism and the suitable ideology, in other words, since no one is gifted for art—even someone who dreams of creating—and since you cannot *make yourself* an artist without becoming despite yourself a simple artisan of class literature, there is only one solution, which is the very solution that a little later becomes the salutary effect of the "Jinx": the only writer *possible* is found among the losers of the society. When a man has not been able to ingest the ruling ideology or learn several conditioned reflexes that form the basis of his adaptation to class interests and his particular interests, when those mental infirmities—denied, of course, by his family—have led to disaster just when his "start in life" was being carefully arranged; when he suddenly finds himself, without wishing it but after a long period of malaise, in the ditch, rejected by his class and by humanity, who continue blindly to shuffle along the paths of history as usual; when he has understood, despite himself, that our alleged ends are ruses of nature or society, then this unfortunate may be an idiot, but also, perhaps, one of the chosen. And perhaps—who knows?—both at once; at least that idea is beginning to gain currency. In other words, the birth of the artist through art, whose minister he becomes, demands—like a religion—this prerequisite: social death. Art, that absolute, that supreme value, can be served as a cult only by the infirm and the useless—and no one is an artist without giving stunning proof of his incapacities. Christian ideas can be glimpsed, of course, behind this conception: beauty, as a divine fulguration, strikes most frequently the humble and deprived; conversion is merely a new vision of the world grasped through the secular failure of the convert. The religious convert, however, reviewing his life, sees its humiliations and defeats as the effect of a Providence that claimed him entirely for the service of God. The aesthetic imperative, considered by itself, offers no reference to providential action; beauty has no worldly efficacy since its fundamental character is *not to be*. Every artist is free to choose his interpretation when he turns his dead eyes toward his past life. It may be chance that *jinxed* him, fortuitously. Or God may choose not only His priests but also the priests of beauty. Or again, the only ministers of His cult, even if they doubt Him, may be the artists, the elect. The fact is, these interpretations remain subjective, and they are variable and hazy as well. The same person shifts from one to the other unwittingly; everything depends on his history, on

151

the present circumstances, and the poisons injected into him by language. The constant in this literary current, however, is the arrogant attempt to interpret this necessary denuding positively, to seek in the psychophysiology of the period reasons for grasping this required *less* as the veiled expression of a *more*. Pride, here, concurs with logic, which effectively demands an explanation: how can genius, that superabundant plenitude, issue from the void, since the chosen man is nothing but discarded humanity? We shall see the appearance, first in the Goncourts, I believe, then in all the writers until Mallarmé, of the idea that the artist is prevented from acting by a hypersensitivity due to the extreme fragility but also the exquisite quality of his nervous system. The nerves: an ambiguous fact, borrowed from recent discoveries of medicine. If they merely transmit stimuli to the brain and responses to the muscles, they are doing an adequate job; the man of action is adapted to his task; when he surrenders himself wholeheartedly to the enterprise without letting himself be surprised by the event or distracted by an appreciation of value, he is said to "have nerves of steel." If the nerves, on the contrary, make their presence felt, are surprised, panicked by events, and if they vibrate for a long time, transmitting the *affective* essence of the situation instead of sending practical information to the central nervous system and relaying back orders to the peripheral system, action is no longer possible. Failure is therefore assured. But in its place is born a sorrowful understanding of man and the world. From this time on, the artist's failure is conceived as a feminization of literature. It will not be the task of the retarded and the simpleminded, but of that new category of chosen people: feminine men. And Caroline Commanville is merely obediently repeating a myth solidly established by the writers of the time when she writes of her grandfather: "A man of eminently strong character, very active habits, he had difficulty understanding the nervous and somewhat feminine side that characterizes all artistic constitutions." [15] Yet those feminized men were for the most part misogynists. They reproached women—judged at the time, like them, to be unfit for masculine work—for making poor use of their rich sensibility: woman is in heat and wants to be fucked. In other words, sex and its needs bind them to the "seriousness of sensation," so they experience only passions or *practical* feelings—vitiated by a teleology of sexual origin, by what we would call today *libido*—the alleged idealism of which, far from raising them above the species, engages them more

15. *Correspondance*, vol. 1, *Souvenirs intimes*, p. xxii.

profoundly in human relations. This attitude of the Postromantic writer and his ambivalence toward the feminine condition throws into relief the paradox of his position. He reproaches women, in short, for the normal development of emotional life which they owe, according to current thinking, to their "nervous organization"; in other words, he reproaches them for desiring, taking pleasure, loving, suffering, despising, becoming impassioned by a cause or a man. These various emotions, in conjunction with many others and bound in general to the most basic demands, are the abiding and real forms of pathos encountered in every human being, regardless of gender; and if his "nervous temperament," his early history, or any other factor makes him hypersensitive, this will be translated by the increasing number and intensity of these reactions, which will finally overwhelm him. Yet the Postromantic writer who claims hypersensitivity clearly rejects the passions and emotions that would chain him to reality and prohibit him from surveying the world. He considers his "commitment to nervousness" the reason for his failure, and at the same time he claims impassivity. Obviously, then, his affectivity has suffered a radical transformation, and while it is the source of his incapacity to act, it manifests itself uniquely through *aesthetic* reactions determined by unreality as such: the reading of a written work, the conception of a work to be written, or the derealizing contemplation of the surrounding world. This conception of the nervous organization complicates things enormously, first of all because such a definition of the hypersensitive temperament strongly resembles the definition of insensitivity. Indeed, the Postromantics are not known for their human warmth, since clearly they want to raise themselves above the human condition. As for aesthetic sensitivity, they demand it, of course—it is the sole virtue required by these men without qualities to the extent that the imperative of art makes it a condition sine qua non of their election. But how shall we understand its relation to failure? Must we imagine that such sensitivity comes to them *first,* as a direct and lived relation to unreality, that it has deterred them from acting and plunged them into a contemplative quietism, whose object of contemplation is, naturally, imaginary? In this case, failure disappears, replaced by election; there are men who act and others who dream. But how shall we explain the fact that a human sensibility, tied to that organized matter we call the nervous system, a set up for relaying information and orders evoked by the real environment, can sometimes of itself turn toward the unreal alone and refuse to accept any inductor but that which does not exist? This would rest on an assumption that the

153

problem is resolved. Or shall we grant that the artist's affectivity, his subtle sense of harmonies and correspondences, his tact, his taste, his precise feeling for proportions and the pleasures he derives from the derealization of the world are merely residues of a defunct sensibility that was formerly vibrant and passionate, like that of women, only more so? And that this affectivity was entirely turned toward the real but exhausted by some jinx, by incredible misfortunes and sorrows all the more acute as it was so receptive, finally killed by the increasing harshness of misfortune, yet losing neither its depth nor its delicacy, unrealized as imaginary pathos, as imaginary emotiveness, set in motion solely by products of the imagination? This conception has at least the double merit of explaining the initial failure by an overabundance of feelings and passions, an obstacle to any concerted action, and of presenting the artist's sensibility as the result of a history rather than as a natural gift. The artist had a big heart pulsing with tears and blood; that organ has died bit by bit, and in its place was grafted its exact but imaginary replica. This would explain how these writers demand at once the most exquisite "affects," the most profound emotional upheavals, and impassivity as the two simultaneous requirements of their art. Admittedly, there is no proof that the death of the real heart suffices to produce—almost automatically, you might say—the birth of the imaginary heart, or, if you like, that the cult and love of the beautiful can be engendered from the wreckage of a real and passionate life. It is more likely—if we renounce the hidden optimism of this interpretation—that the desensitization which sometimes follows an excess of suffering, far from provoking the aesthetic attitude, is lived as an indifference to everything. In this case, of course, the negative aspect is manifest: attention to the world and oneself is diminished, so that the real is slightly distanced. But this rupture of affective syntony implies no positive counterpart; anorexia—in the sense that Gide used it in his last years— far from being a path toward beauty, deflects any interest in beauty. For although in certain respects—the raw material itself and human praxis totalized—the work of art is transhistorical, and although our relation to it is unrealization, it never yields itself except in a cultural context that defines the human for real men of a certain society. For this reason, whatever its content, whatever its aim, it interests us only to the extent that we are caught in the real meshes of human relations, in passions and conflicts that express a certain reality of man in the social universe that deviates, mutilates, oppresses, alienates, and mystifies him but is *his own* world, the one that produced him, that he produces each day, that he loves and hates, that he wants to change but not eliminate, the only world in which he recognizes himself. If someone detaches himself from human violence, if he loses his power of hating and loving, the work of art, from his point of view, ceases to bear witness to man.

These remarks are not intended to condemn a priori the works that issue from the postulation of inhumanity characteristic of the writers of the second half of the nineteenth century. Some of these works are, on the contrary, among the finest in our literature. My concern was to show the uncertainty in which these young authors find themselves, at the time, with regard to the actual signification and function of the dehumanizing failure imposed on them. The literary imperative reveals their radically and uniquely negative character by commanding them, from the very first, to be rejected by men and cast out by society despite their efforts to be integrated. No ascesis, no spiritual exercises, thereby rising gradually above the human race; literature is not an enterprise, that's all there is to it. This arid aspect of negation is not unproblematic to the eligible writers; to compensate for it with some positive element they hastily erect that absurd notion of the "nervous temperament," an artful, materialist ersatz of the gift. But as we have seen, their theory remains vague; when they try to be specific, it founders. They preserve it to protect themselves; the shift from failure to genius escapes them. And then, it is not so convenient to be rejected by a whole society—unless you are a criminal or a fool, two solutions these petty bourgeois refuse a priori and which, in any case, do not facilitate the ascent to Parnassus. These young men are not at all on good terms with their families, through whom they have the unsettling experience of their class. But finally, for the moment, they are ending or about to end their secondary studies, and no one dreams of casting them beyond the pale. Yet they are sure of it, they *want to write*, they are candidates for absolute-art. What will happen if the jinx spares them, if it neglects to persecute them, to deliver them gasping to their mother's curses, to the derision of the crowd? Where will they find the strength to undertake and achieve a work if they remain in the ranks, mediocrities among the mediocre? So they are plagued by two contradictory fears: one inspired by the literary imperative, which demands absolute failure without softening it with any promise, any hope, in other words, a degradation that is repulsive to them; and the other, which comes to them from their well-entrenched situation—they are mostly the sons of good families—and from their melancholy certainty of never being banished from the community. They are rather cynical, moreover, these former school-boy "blasés"; the time of Byron and the great exiles is past. These two anxieties result in a tension that will determine their behavior. Here again, the option is not subjective; everyone will particularize it by internalizing it. We are dealing with a determination that is not imposed but *proposed* as a means of turning away from insoluble difficulties. Today this solution has a name, which it did not have in 1850—the *conduct of failure*. By this we mean a behavior with two objectives, the more superficial being to reach a definite goal and the more profound being to fall short of it. The first is the object of a formulated intention, one that is quite conscious; the second, implicit but equally intentional, is the very meaning of lived experience, the false taste of our decisions and efforts, a prophetic aura at every moment of the enterprise, making it seem "lost in advance" and provoking a pessimism that discourages us from doing everything possible, a sudden, stubborn memory multiplying omissions; and if that isn't enough, the error *that must not be committed* which offers itself, a brief madness, glaringly evident, as the most economical means of realizing our project. The agent is no dupe; he is constantly warned of the principal intention by the experienced inequality of what he wants to do and what he does. But since the chief occurrence of failure must be *unmerited*, the essential structure of this double conduct implies that he be deliberately *inattentive* to the real intention and to the information of lived experience, to the same extent that he focuses *the most extreme attention* on his decision to attain the objective—which he counts on missing—and on the motivations that have led him to take that decision. In subjective neuroses, the conduct of failure is tied to the givens of one's protohistory, which profoundly condition it. Outlined by the objective neurosis as a solution to the insoluble problem of election, it is not attached to any unfathomable idiosyncrasy and presents itself as an abstract determination of activity. It is a defense against the two dangers that threaten the candidate for the situation of artist. On the one hand, if he is persevering, it should lead to that exile whose victim he fears he will not be. He will undoubtedly exclude himself by repeated failures that will reveal his incapacities to the "capable." But since the characteristic feature of this behavior is to gloss over this intention to lose and to emphasize the intention to win, the young man will grasp his defects as the effect of his impotence or of *another* power, his consistent bad luck, and he will see his underlying intention, interpreted with respect to his superficial decision, as the jinx itself slipping under his skin and guiding

156

him from within toward his doom. From this point of view, the essential interiority of his basic intention not only will not hinder him but will render him a tremendous service, provided that—playing on the contradiction that structures this behavior—he can regard it as the existence of an alien and irresistible power in the depth of his subjectivity. In fact, the jinx has no meaning unless it is internalized. It is not an external curse but an intimate and negative virtue, the *incapacity to be man*. The conduct of failure is of interest to the future artist only to the extent that the essence of man seems to him to be praxis. If, for example, humanity could be *accomplished* in contemplative quietism, in calm transcendence, recourse to failure would no longer make any sense, and quite to the contrary, action would become the characteristic feature of an inferior race. But after the victory of the bourgeoisie, man's virility is characterized by the breadth and success of his enterprise. These puritans want nothing less than the conquest of the earth; it is a matter of accumulation, in this era, of pushing industrialization to the extreme—giving the country its new infrastructures—and extending *real* property to the countryside itself, increasing concentration within the framework of ruthless competition and opening new markets on every continent. Thus the bourgeois considers himself—beyond his utilitarianism, which is a rather timid, conservative ethic—a builder of empire, which he is *too*. He hasn't read Darwin, but he considers competition a process of natural selection that eliminates the weak. Consequently, when his enterprise succeeds, he ranks himself among the *strong*. If he were really concerned with literature, he would ask its writers to replace the old, false images of him that he himself hasn't been able to discard with the image of the conqueror who knows how to take risks, the man with nerves of steel, hard on himself and perhaps on others, but who takes the world on his shoulders and gives work and bread to the lower classes of society. Indeed, after 1870 this wish will be granted by all the writers who opt for class literature, by the Ohnets, the Hervieux, the Bernsteins; at the beginning of our century, businessmen will be thrilled to see themselves represented in a successful play under the name of *Samson*. In short, man is action. To be detached from the race, one need merely be incapable of acting. Yet his incapacity must not be explained by defects of character, by bad habits, handicaps, hesitations or inhibitions, in short, by contingencies, serious accidents that would have destroyed from the outside certain aptitudes of the candidate for inhumanity that properly belong to our race and which, without some accident, some unexpected event in his child-

157

hood, he too would have possessed. He would be judged, in this case, as a man who had no luck and whose development was arrested too soon. Or as an invalid, a badly disabled veteran. If he must really show that beneath his human envelope he is a stranger to humanity, he must bear witness by his failure that action is *by nature* alien to him, and that it makes no sense in his view. His practical actions—which, like everyone's, are legion—must indicate by their stiffness, by some mistake (sometimes just barely avoided, often not too serious) that they are merely automatic behavior, the result of harsh training, or imitations he attempts out of fear of displeasing or the desire to be loved; but he does not know, *literally,* what he is doing. In other words, he is not lacking any particular quality, or even a set of qualities, but simply "practical sense," in the usual meaning of the term; he understands neither human ends nor the relation of means to ends, and he does not share the motivations common to all members of the race. In fact, no one knows—he doesn't know himself—why he is like this, "born in exile," an "intruder," a "stranger," etc. Maybe he is gifted from the start with a contemplative sensibility (which, as we have just seen, would again make the aesthetic attitude an a priori). He may be so lucid that all the great human mystifications are dissolved in him as soon as they have penetrated. It may be just an accident of the void, of that inert lacuna inside him, that practical relations between ideas, between feelings, simply cannot take hold. In any event, he uses a permanent failure to announce that he fulfills the negative conditions for being an artist; at least that is the neurotic proposition made to him. It would be up to him, if he accepts it, to give the proposition a concrete meaning arising from his personal singularity.

The conduct of failure therefore has the advantage of seeming to be a deserving effort, which the real, in short, *denies*. Inhumanity is not the object of an enterprise, it is not the goal of an action, but it is verified, by contrast, in the impossibility of acting, a double negation—internal and external—which the candidate can only *verify*, perhaps even in desolation. Clearly the conduct of failure, if permanent and nuanced, is a permanent denunciation of the real—in interiority—and it is manifest in the very flavor of lived experience. In this sense, the more complex and more radical conduct the literary imperative demands of the artist, the imaginary rupture with *all* of reality (a hysterical imitation of schizophrenia), can find in this fine-tuned shifting of phase an excellent springboard, perhaps the only one that allows him at any moment to break through the hoop, like Banville's clown, and jump into the unreal. The conduct of failure is by itself the perpetual igniting of derealization.

But at the same time it is an exemplary vigilance. One must *avoid success* under any circumstances. This vigilance allows one to avoid the other danger: the imperative demands, in effect, but promises nothing, and the candidate may sink into subhumanity with no compensation. In a way, the failure of the man would be hurtful if it were too *real*, if, for example, it were translated by financial ruin (bad management of a fortune) or loss of employment (the *manifest* incapacity to fulfill imposed tasks). For in the final analysis, to be dead to the world and to contemplate it from above, you must at least be alive; and that means, as we have seen, being integrated. In other words, aesthetic disintegration requires a modest but real integration. And that integration in turn—as the economic basis of the whole enterprise—must be forgotten or denied by the artist. Forgetting, a convenient solution, is possible especially when the author lives off his income property; if he must work every day, it is more difficult. In this case, as in many others, we can give ourselves through appropriate behavior an inner feeling of constant maladaptation (I know neither who I am, nor why I'm in this office, nor what I am doing here, and so I grope in the dark and do not act); this is a feeling of failure as a negative and constitutional determination without even the distant risk of real catastrophe—insolvency or loss of employment. To put it simply: you will only truly make a mess, in a noticeable way, of trivial matters—for example, relations with peers or minor undertakings. In relations with superiors or in responsibilities that define the salaried job or position, the vigilance of failure permits success, or at least no loss, provided it is accidental and inadvertent. Such behaviors are automatic and meaningless, the consequence of uncomprehended drilling, but despite their rigidity *it just happens* that they produce the required results. Failure, here, is not manifest in the behavior that attains its objective on its own but in the candidate-artist's inability to be involved in what he is doing, in the divorce that has cut him in two, his lower half reduced to a mass of conditioned reflexes, his upper half merely an inert lacuna tinged with ennui and estrangement. The failure of love, on the other hand, can be radical and catastrophic; it is not dangerous. One begins by investing woman with the infinite, by seeing her as a recourse against *dissatisfaction*, all the while knowing quite well but forgetting what will later be discovered in disappointment and disgust. Failure in love, lived in the most complete bad faith, will therefore be employed to show the future artist that it is constitutionally impossible for him to sustain relations with human beings. Well directed, this failure can be accompanied by scornful disillusionment: the author discovers the silliness and vanity of those relations; you have to be blind or base, like men, to believe in them, to establish and persist in them. Thus the failure of the artist allusively provides its positive counterpart, the possibility that the ridiculed or disappointed lover is precisely a being superior to humanity; and the failure of love will result in a postulation toward immutability, the refusal to fall back into these denounced illusions. On this level, however, vigilance must be strict. You have to keep your ambivalence toward failure, deriving from it above all a feeling of depersonalization and estrangement—the surprise at not being man and the risk of being less than humanity—coupled with the vague if indecisive hope of being too great to fit the human condition. At this moment, moreover, the inhuman reveals its relative being: it would not be if our species did not exist; the artist is a man too great to be man, something he divines through his sufferings and his humiliations as a failed man.

The conduct of failure is therefore an action that is veiled and disguised as passion because it claims to suffer the results it intends to obtain. But in itself it has all the essential features of activity: in effect, it means to obtain an end—the destruction in itself of all possibility of action—by an appropriate combination of means. The demonstration of his incapacity is originally aimed only at the candidate himself; it is up to him to persuade himself. The public is involved in certain cases only as mediator, so that its conviction should reinforce the future artist's.

It is clear that this comportment can only be lived, at the very least, in total bad faith. Of course, it would be crowned with success if it were accompanied by belief, which leads us back to pithiatism. In any event, it is a role that aspires to found art, as the totalizing representation of the nothingness of life, on a definition of the artist by his incapacity to live. It is proposed on the horizon as the irrational solution to the panoramic overview required by literature and the real anchorage of men who make that desituation impossible. In this sense, it is not proposed to contest *others*—whether bourgeois or simply men—but to ruin fictively in the artist himself, and for him alone, his class-being or his membership in the race. Here his failure is nothing short of man perpetually and futilely denied. This can only be understood, moreover, in the context of a still more radical wreckage, that of literature.

c. The Failure of the Work

In the mid-nineteenth century, literature-to-be-written imposes a curious destiny on its future authors: they will affirm their vocation as artists only if literature contests itself in their works and reveals its impossibility in their failure. This, of course, is the result of the contradictory imperatives awakened in the Objective Spirit by these young readers and exacerbated by historical circumstances. These conflicts of norms, seen from the outside, could simply be said to culminate in rendering all purely literary activity provisionally impossible except when it is prompted by outmoded principles or aimed at constituting a class literature. But it is one thing to situate oneself outside a historic moment and view its structures with serene objectivity, and quite another to live it blindly, with all the force of our elemental passions, or, if you like, on the basis of previous circumstances. For these discontented young men, mad with pride and intoxicated by their readings, who stake their entire lives and their salvation on literature, to learn that literature is impossible cannot mean that it must be renounced but the reverse, that its value and being reside in that impossibility. And one of the most striking aspects of the objective neurosis is their need to regard as their essential possibility a behavior they know to be impossible. An irrational position but an objectively indispensable one, for without it the great works of the second half of the century would not exist. We must examine this position more closely.

A work of the mind exists only as an intersubjective objectivity: it is *actualized* by the conjugal relationship of writing and reading through its materiality as a written thing. And as we have seen, that relationship appears to be severed for the new apprentice writers simply because literary autonomy affirms itself just when the bourgeois class definitively comes to power. In fact, there will be no true rupture, but the future writers think they are bound to reject their only possible public, which is their class. The work to be written presents itself, therefore, as a being-in-itself, independent of author and reader, owing its ontological consistency only to its beauty. It seems thereby to contain the principle of its own failure, since it is denied that consistency a priori. Literature-to-be-written, then, already contains the crazy, futile prescription to hypostasize the Word and make it a solitary inhuman monument. All would not be lost, however, if God existed—that privileged reader would give the works of man an absolute value. But for these children of the Jacobin bourgeoisie, God does not exist. At least nothing is known of Him. Thus the original failure of the work is that without an audience of men it falls back into nonsignifying materiality, yet it is created by an author who, without bothering about them, addresses himself over their heads to a witness whose existence he denies, or whom he claims to know nothing about. As if the absolute reality of a literary production—the beauty of being-in-itself—resided in its conjectural relation to a Being who is not, or who escapes us, and consequently as if that reality were on principle escaping not only the reader but the author himself, who never knows whether his product *is*, or who *acts as if* that object *possessed some being*, all the while aware that it possesses none. In 1850 the given or always possible failure, a priori, of literature-to-be-written is determined by the contradictions of another sector of the Objective Spirit, the current bourgeois religion. Autonomy and non-communication effectively compel one not to write, or to write for God; it is *for God* that flowers exude their perfume in utter solitude. Consequently, agnostics must address themselves *in secret* to that supreme reader, in short, they must *believe* as writers in what they deny as men and, even more curiously, in their works. And atheists locate the whole worth of literature in its failure: the work is sacred because it demands, in full knowledge, a guarantee that does not exist, because it is a religious ceremony—and even a solemn sacrifice—to Nobody.

The very content, moreover, of literature-to-be-written denies it the being-in-itself it demands since its meaning must be the absolute negation of the real, that is, of being. This identification of being and reality was not philosophically rigorous during this period, since philosophers were attempting to construct that negative theology which still poisons us today and were basing the *being* of God on his absence of all reality. But literature-to-be-written is constrained—by its new use of imagination—to posit the nonreal as its domain by asserting the being of appearance over the nonbeing of reality. Or, as I said above, to represent the nonbeing of being by determinations which it brings to the being of nonbeing, its raw material. In other words, the choices of the imaginary and of absolute negation condition and contradict each other. Absolute negation, as the radical denial of all that exists, articulates itself as the demand for derealization and thereby makes the author into an imaginary. But it thereby passes into unreality as well and becomes the unreal negation of being. The contradiction here is that negation could find its plenitude only if it existed *as an act*, if it were incarnate in a praxis of destruction, and at the same time its condemnation of the real makes the pure unreal the essential value, thus compelling it to present itself as nonrealized as well. This is the sense in which for Mallarmé the most effective bomb is poetry. Against the real and consequently particularized destructions of anarchism he set the harsh, universal, and intentionally ineffective abolition of the world by language, and of language by itself.

We know that absolute negation operates on two planes. On the plane of facts it must produce the world as a created totality that it may be devoured by mechanism; on the ethico-religious plane it must show the nothingness of mechanism starting with the creation, nonbeing claimed in vain as the only possible meaning of man. This is, in effect, addressing the privileged reader to inform him of his own nonexistence. The major objective of literature-to-be-written is to teach God that He doesn't exist. To win the being-in-itself it requires, God must eternally exist to elevate the nonbeing of the work—finally, His own nonbeing—to the dignity of *being-beyond-being*, and at the same time He must be forever dissipated by the dissolving effect of the work and forever vanish in the last line of the final page. The conflict, here, is between the a priori designation of the uniquely worthy interlocutor and the a priori meaning of the message that denies that interlocutor's existence; hence that new structure of failure for the work itself, the ambivalence of the imaginary. The work is radically and deliberately imaginary, from top to bottom, because the only absolute is a desperate negation of being; the work *is only imaginary*, even as a work it *does not exist*, it has no status, it floats. In this sense, the imaginary, in positing itself for itself, demands to be the flower of evil, or, rather, absolute evil. First, because its totalization in the work is the negation of God and the denunciation of the wretchedness of man without God, therefore radical pessimism. Then, because that pessimism, a venom hidden by the concrete organization of the work, is not the expression of human abandonment *for man* but quite the opposite, a negation of man himself, a denunciation of the odious absurdity of human agitations addressed to the nonexistent Creator. The work, as a hateful denial of the human, must *do harm*. Finally, because this objective of literature, although required a priori, is in essence unattainable. This negation of negation is not an affirmation but, to the contrary, a reinforcement of the negative principle; nothing is worse than impotence in evil, especially if that impotence is intentional and opposes the fundamental intention to do harm without abolishing it. In fact, that absolute negation must acknowlege itself through the work as nothing, since it has being only as nonbeing and cannot reach the world it claims as its goal without losing its aesthetic status as *appearance*. It thus leaves intact what it denies; as a result, the claimed artistic creation becomes a kind of aping, the imitation of a creation that did not take place. The writer lies for the sake of lying, and his unattended lie self-destructs. His assigned mission is to act as though he is revealing what is, even while representing what is not. And he himself must be half-fooled by this mystification and offer us a diabolical image of our world, which is in truth merely the inconsistent outline of *another* universe that will never exist.

Thus in the work itself, whatever its beauty (the rigor of imaginary totalization), literature-to-be-written claims to be a shipwreck because its imperative choice of autonomy and unreality implies that it has a *being-in-itself*, and that this being is merely a mystification. But even under these conditions the work cannot exist, for it can only be a masterpiece, and even as it demands the artists' rigor in totalization, literature-to-be-written deprives them of any way to follow its orders.

We shall note, first of all, the most obvious contradiction: the artist is called upon to found his aristocracy or his superhumanity on his incapacity to live, or, more precisely, to take pleasure and to act. Action in all its forms is *alien* to him; only on this condition can he attempt to write. But what will the accomplished work be if not the result of an activity? To be sure, this determination of praxis—like all others—has its particular structures; it is a matter not of satisfying a need, of gratifying a real desire, of modifying the structure of our practical field but of producing, through the organization of a discourse, a center of unrealization. Be that as it may, the motivations are there, the concrete end, which is the finished work in its totalizing unity and its complexity; the raw material, language, presents itself as a field of possibles, with its primary instrumentality and its coefficient of adversity. From this starting point, the end will recruit its means, the means will define the end. There is no doubt we are dealing with an enterprise. Yet the work must in no way seem to be a *practical* result. To those who will soon be its authors, it claims never to be a *product:* it will shine through its gratuitousness, issuing from that "gratuitous act" which is not an act but a nontemporal creation. This contradiction finds its origin in the literary conceptions of the preceding generation; moreover, the Romantics had resolved the difficulty even as they posed it. The generosity of the artist rests on the inexhaustible generosity of the divine; he does no work because God inspires him. Once again, the death of God is going to plunge the Postromantics into insurmountable conflicts. Sacred inspiration disappears along with Him, in effect, hence art-to-be-written loses not only its privileged reader but its only valid author. God was giving God that unique text, the world, to read, and the writer was merely a mediator between the absolute Word and the absolute Gaze. In a way, the Word and the Act were parallel attributes of the creation. If He no longer exists, what disappears is that essential feature of the work, a *renewing of the creation*, which makes it visible to the Creator. And that occurs at the very moment when agnosticism bases its aesthetic requirements on this denied creation; if the artist is no longer a medium, the beauty of his work must issue from the *rigorous* totalization it effects in the imaginary. Inspiration will have to be rejected a priori, since it is not guaranteed by the Almighty; the Holy Dictum from above must not be confused with the vulgar babbling provoked below by our all too earthly passions, in particular by our anguish, which could have ethico-aesthetic value only when posed as the reactions of being to the trials inflicted by Providence. And disappearing along with the inspired writer is genius, which is nothing other than a *given* power actualizing itself in that beautiful prophetic delirium, the masterpiece. In other words, the book—which was the gift of a gift— loses its natural and divine character (it was the simple result of *endured* trances) and demands to be a manufactured product in which the author's labor is inscribed—like a piece of merchandise—just when absolute-art condemns all human enterprise and consequently will not allow "artistic writing" the status of an enterprise. Yet neither genius nor inspiration disappear for all that; contested by literature-to-be-written, they remain the norms of literature-already-written. The masterpiece of the past, as a *practico-inert* demand, claims to have been the manifestation of inspired genius. For the future writer in 1850, genius now signifies nothing, its meaning is confused; *and yet* Homer and Shakespeare *are* geniuses, they *must* be acknowledged as such. This has the immediate consequence of a priori devalorizing the new art that is no longer directly bound to inspiration, just when it affirms itself as absolute and finds its superiority in its unconditional purity. Unless, that is, to the extent that literature-to-be-written is conditioned by previous circumstances even as it denies them, inspiration and genius cease to haunt the new artist as *what ought to be;* without this happening, the masterpiece is by definition impossible—

to which, by its arrogantly consensual failure, literature-to-be-written bears witness. Either absolute art is itself defined as self-conscious, therefore reaching a splendid maturity, and at the same time as the degradation, the *decadence*, of art. Or it finds its superiority in failure, which at once proves the necessity of the work and its impossibility. The neurotic solution will be to *believe* the contrary of what one *thinks*. The moment they use irrefutable arguments to deny themselves the means to create a masterpiece, they surreptitiously disqualify those arguments whose principles belong to bourgeois ideology, to the agnosticism inculcated by the Jacobin fathers. So they artfully maintain that the absolute work, the failed masterpiece, is a true masterpiece *elsewhere* (outside the world, outside of time, or in the future grasped as *contemporary* compensation for the present). Or—we shall return to this—it may be a masterpiece *in unreality*.

Literature-to-be-written presents itself, nonetheless, as a *work to be executed*. Writers will carve the marble of discourse, they will chisel, produce enamels, cameos; they will be "good workers" in inlay work, in goldsmithery. That can only be done according to the rules. If the artist is an artisan, he must learn the formulas of his art. Therefore, the antique notion of *taste* returns to obscure that of genius. But aside from the fact that the work remains condemned and thereby even repugnant,[16] on what basis is taste to be established? In the classical centuries, it was nothing other, really, than a set of norms claiming to manifest the homogeneity of the writer and his public. In fact, it marked the subjection of art which, failing to recognize its negativity, was produced in the bosom of a socially inferior class and took on its laws as a function of the demands of the dominant class. In the seventeenth century, bourgeois negativity is concealed, *taste* translates in the aesthetic domain the unstable equilibrium the absolute monarchy tries to establish between the nobility and the bourgeoisie. Around 1680 this system is overturned: negativity reveals itself, literature claims its autonomy but can exercise its destructive action only in the framework of originally aristocratic norms, which still dissimulate the fact that they are outmoded. In short, there is no taste without a lofty public whose rights are recognized a priori by the artist; I would even say there is no taste without a perfectly integrated society—even provisionally—whose state apparatus has full coercive

---

16.   Je t'apporte l'enfant d'une nuit d'Idumée!
        Noire, a l'aile saignante et pale, déplumée . . .
        . . . accueille une horrible naissance.

powers at its disposal. The apparent homogeneity of the artist and his public derives from the fact that, instead of thinking he is superior to that public, he offers it his work as an act of submission; negation is only in the work. Or, more precisely, in its content.

How can *taste* be recovered when the rupture between the writer and the public seems an accomplished fact, when the first disqualifies the second above all for its lack of taste? Worse still, when the author as a product of the bourgeois class finds in himself the same lack of taste he denounces in it? Caroline Commanville naively observes:

> My uncle corresponded less than anyone to what is called an art-
> ist. Among the peculiarities of his character, one contrast always
> surprised me. This man, who was so preoccupied with beauty in
> style, and who gave form such a high if not primary place, was
> very little concerned with the beauty of things in his surround-
> ings. He chose objects and furnishings with heavy or graceless
> contours that might have shocked the least delicate, and he had
> none of that taste for curios so widespread in our time.

At the time she is writing these lines, the bourgeoisie is devoting a conscious portion of surplus value to cultural activities; it is "refined." The future authors of 1850 were another species: all, or nearly all, of them counted on art to detach them from the puritanism and vulgarity of their milieu; but they had no intention of surrounding themselves with art objects, giving their life an "artistic style"; they were too encumbered by their education even to conceive of the idea. Their only purpose is to combat the *bad taste* of the bourgeoisie around them and *within them* by the production of works of *good taste*. But as taste—good taste—was the norm of the useless, they accepted the confusion of usefulness with bad taste (or the mere absence of taste), and thereby abandoned the practical field around them to ugliness. And as the practical field reflected to each person his own objective image in the very way it is determined, they had to reinternalize that objectivization as the foundation of their subjective *imago;* consequently, ugliness invaded them, became their deepest aspect, the being-in-class on the basis of which they produced their lived determinations and, especially, their works. Those works, then, presented themselves, insofar as they were works to be written, as ugliness denied and surpassed. But that transcendence of ugliness, preserved as the content of the work, was not sufficient to generate the canons of beauty. It could be only a savage negation of their *natural* attribute—of their first custom —without signposts, without coordinates, without even the suspicion of a path toward a positive and concrete construction. Quite the contrary, their complicity with ugliness, their way of not even seeing it *except* where creative work was concerned, deprived them of that cultural springboard at the disposal of creators in happier times when the arts respond to each other, and when the distinction between the useful and the beautiful is not so clearcut (when one can write, for example, that the beautiful is the elaboration of the useful, or that architecture must be functional). Beauty, far from being a certain relation between man and *all* his products in a given society—allowing the future artist to be familiar with it from childhood—appears to the Postromantics to be an ineffable Beyond of ugliness, a pure negative abstraction that cannot provide any rule. Thus *taste*, which should orient their labors and become the law of their creative activity, seems to them above all an absence. It can become manifest in them only negatively, like something missing, a lacuna; this is eminently logical, for by contesting genius and inspiration, artists are led to claim for their work criteria that are unsuitable for them insofar as these rules express a *previous agreement,* whereas all other life presents itself as the *consequence of a rupture.* Thus, just as they preserve genius and inspiration in themselves as imperatives—those determinations of literature-already-written and especially of Romanticism—so, when they see creation as a methodical labor, they find at their disposal only the outmoded norms of classical literature. At the same time they understand that those norms are inapplicable as such; modernity must have its own *taste.* But it is precisely that taste which is denied them since the modern work must break with tradition, or rather verify that this tradition was broken by history and must therefore provide its own rules. It is a vicious circle: if taste is always the singular law generated by the work in the process of its own creation, the work would have to be already written, or at least its fundamental structure known, to provide any guidance. Of course, it might seem easy enough to break out of this circle and imagine that the tool is forged in the forging. But this becomes conceivable only when the idea of taste has ceased to torment the writer, when the search for the beautiful has given way to the systematic investigation of the literary domain, and the notion of the work to that of experiment, adventure, etc. In 1850 *there must be an order,* and it must be at once invented and preestablished. That order, furthermore, is the order not of the real but of the imaginary as such, and there is nothing to prove that it is not, by itself, unreality. Inspiration, work, gratuitousness, practical enterprise, genius, taste—these cardinal categories of art-to-be-created contradict each other and are in themselves contradictory; faced with the work to be accomplished, the new artist experiences an empty tension that prevents him from even conceiving its rules, its meaning, the means to forge it—which he calls *impotence*. This is not an accidental state in 1850, it is the attitude that represents the candidate's only chance of becoming an artist. Indeed, it manifests the impossibility of art by denying inspiration, and the artist may be none other than the painful incarnation of that impossibility.

> . . . a book, plainly, in many volumes, a book that is really a book, architectural and thought out, and not a collection of chance inspirations, however marvelous . . . I will go further, I will say: the Book, persuaded that at bottom there is only one, attempted unwittingly by anyone who writes, even Geniuses. The orphic explanation of Earth, which is the sole duty of the poet and the literary game . . .
>
> . . . I shall succeed, perhaps; not in writing that work in its entirety (to do that, you would have to be God knows who!) but in showing a fragment of it executed, making its glorious authenticity shine through, indicating all the rest for which one lifetime isn't enough. In proving by the finished portions that this book exists, and that I was aware of what I could not accomplish. (Mallarmé, *Autobiographie* [1885], written for Verlaine [Bibliothèque de la Pléiade, p. 663])

In fact, there is one requirement revealed by the new literary object which at first sight could serve as a rule: that totality which sacrifices itself for its own sake must realize its self-destruction with scientific rigor. When the writer relied on inspiration, he took everything that came along pell-mell—diamonds and ashes. Agnosticism prescribes a rigorous labor for future authors: they will construct their works in such a way that chance is excluded. This imperative, moreover, conforms to their underlying intention: against chance, which made them so absurdly born into *this* class, in *this* milieu, and defines them by the contingency of lived experience, they will make themselves born anew, as inhuman aristocrats, through their works. These fortuitous offspring of a whim will objectify themselves through the creation of an unreal that excludes chance. Style must be the point of view of the *absolute* for them, *not only* because it expresses the overview of pride but also because it represents chance excluded from language. Should a paragraph, a sentence, a word be dispensable, all is lost: the work does not "take." This means that every element of the discourse must maintain at all levels the greatest *possible* number of intentional relations with all other elements and with the signified

169

totality. Moreover, no relation can be established between them unless it has been expressly sought by the creative intention; this corollary implies nothing less than rejecting as nonartistic everything that Gide will later integrate into the work and label "the Devil's part." Those creators who will have known how to exclude from creation every fortuitous combination and radically multiply premeditated combinations will thereby have proved their *necessity*. Would they have been able to banish chance from their books if they themselves had not been subject to it, at least for the duration of the writing, if the movement of creative totalization had not, through a kind of reciprocity, simultaneously produced the author as a seamless unity, as a pure dynamic conception of the whole producing its parts and manifesting itself in them, this whole itself being unreality totalized through the discourse? Thus the artist seems—ideally in this case—to be the absolute master of a universal combiner, whose purpose is not to unify the diverse by establishing a more or less conventional system of equivalences but to totalize the multiple by producing it as a multiplicity of the aspects of a whole according to a synthetic law of generation and integration. On this basis, chance is ugliness regarded as the residue of reality at the core of systematic unrealization. The "Devil's part" mentioned above, insofar as it is constituted by the relations established between the parts of artistic discourse outside the creative intention, can be conceived in 1840 only as a renaissance of the real at the core of constructed unreality.

In this sense the pure artist seems, yet again, to be the opposite of the man of action. The latter, for practical reasons, tries to produce a particular modification in the real world, which he knows to be ruled by chance, where his anchorage is chance as the basis of his singular existence. In this sense action itself is a matter of chance; it is the facility, as a fortuitous given, that determines the motivations of action, its end, its means, its style, and in a general way its practical perspective. Born of chance events, action cannot be undertaken either *for* or *against* chance; rather it represents a dialectic of the contingent and the necessary, as Hegel effectively demonstrated. And in the course of his activity the man of action learns the necessity of contingency and the contingency of necessity. In other words, far from trying to exclude chance, he attempts both to guard against it and to make use of it. Everything depends on the relation of the unforeseen to the proposed end—that is, essentially, of external contingency to internal contingency—and not on the unforeseen *as such*, for reality presents itself to enterprise as a variable but always definite relation between the foreseeable and the unforeseeable. But let us not forget that there are foreseeable chance events, that the calculation of probabilities, to introduce a certain order in this domain, does not suppress chance but, quite the contrary, is based upon it. Therefore, when we plan a political operation or construct a machine, for example, it is less a question of eliminating contingency as such than the opposite, of admitting it and reducing its coefficient of adversity to the minimum. Should human society have suppressed its divisions and realized a socialism of abundance, it would still, at the core of its internal necessity, be constituted from its original contingency, not by suppressing it but by integrating it into its order. Even in that event it would be nothing but a singular universal, deriving from its history a radical idiosyncrasy that would be the internalization of its facticity, in other words, of its contingency grasped as necessity.

The man of action, a real person, works with reality; his production—which is wrought matter—cannot appear in the physical world without maintaining infinite relations with the full range of materiality through the mediation of man and with the full range of men through the mediation of materiality. But the artist himself must choose to be the unreal lord of unreality. He does not, therefore, aspire to *one* particular end, whose realization *in the physical world* would depend on possibles as such; his objective, even through a work that seems a particularization of the imaginary, is to manifest the unreal in its rigorous totality. In fact, by unrealizing himself as a panoramic consciousness, he has denied his anchorage, his facility, the contingency of his all too human ends; in other words, this chance being has made himself into a desituated, hence universal, witness to imagination as a rigorous totalization. When imagination renounces its subordinate function, the detection of possibles in a practical perspective, it places itself beyond all impossibility, and by the same token beyond chance events; its free play is confused with the most implacable necessity. Since anything is now possible in this domain, every image can and must be the product and expression of the imagination as a totality in practice, essentially as the absolute negation of the real. Chance disappears along with reality. Even if it is thought *necessary* to represent it in the work, it will figure there as destiny, as another face of necessity. Thus the plenary freedom of the artist, son of his works, is reflected to him by the inflexible necessity of his poem or his book, insofar as imagination as a regulated totalization was incarnate in it.

Yet through this requirement of literature-to-be-written, absolute-art as the absolute negation of the real is driven to deny itself absolutely as reality. Apart from the fact that imagination is not that "world-beyond-the-world" it claims to be, and is distinguished, on the contrary, by its essential poverty, its determinations must be capable of inscribing themselves in a wrought matter, language, whose inertia will assure their permanence. So the artist finds himself once again faced with an essential contradiction: the work is the product of a labor involving words; these elements of language are determined at once by a history—which, however rigorous, seems to be a matter of chance—and by structural relations that define them in terms of one another, a complex constellation in which necessity is born of contingency and contingency of necessity. Furthermore, the writer, to the extent that he would be an artisan, is neither above language nor outside it: he is *inside,* and his relations to discourse are the very expression, on the linguistic level, of his facticity. His speech recounts his history even if he claims to use it for other ends. Not only to the extent that his relations to words in general are determined by familial conditionings and by his primary, basic choices, but also to the extent that the verbal material he has at his disposal is defined by his situation, whether social, national, geographical, or whatever. So once again he becomes chance, plunged to a level where contingency and necessity are in opposition, passing into or mutually conditioning each other. As a result, the enterprise of writing recovers the status of action. At this time, certainly, writing differs from human activity in many respects, and in particular from work as the reproduction of life. First of all, it does not serve the aims of the species and is intended to denounce their futility. In addition, far from making use of language as a means of communication, writing attempts to steal it away from men, to derealize it. Nonetheless, the absolute work, the totality of self-destruction signified *by a certain discourse,* must be imposed on the artist as his aim, and must be attained by the means at hand. And in their contingency those means refer to the author's facticity and denounce him as a chance being whose determination to write is a matter of chance even in its fundamental necessity, for it is conditioned by his protohistory and, through that, by the opacity of his birth, of a contingent anchorage in a defined society. And facticity, of course, represents the necessity of our contingency, but the projected work consequently reveals the contingency of its necessity. In other words, the author, a product of chance even in his effort to detach himself from chance, can be objectified only in a work subject to chance. "Every thought is a Toss of the

Dice." Yes. But a toss of the dice will never abolish chance—that would be impossible since to toss them you have to accept the reign of chance you claim to abolish. And even when you turn up four aces together, they are merely a fortuitous combination. Chance invades everything; through this sinister caricature of inspiration, *some* words come and attract others, in keeping with rules whose necessity is burdened by contingency and which are, in any case, external to the artist's aesthetic aim. Between the elements of discourse, which, though subjected to derealization, are real determinations, equally real bonds are instituted, despite the author or unbeknownst to him, that go beyond literary intentions and yet give a depth to the work or else, to the contrary, short-circuit its intentional significations. The only means of surpassing the antimony of contingency and necessity will be proposed by literature *in our century:* the writer must envisage his work as the *particular* purpose of his *action* and must accept unconditionally, though not without control, the collaboration of chance. But this makes the book a human enterprise which in part escapes its author and precisely because of that reflects his facticity as much as his freedom. To seekers after the absolute in 1850, this resignation seemed inadmissible. If style accepts the concurrence of chance, a double drama unfolds: the failure of man through the failure of the work, and vice versa. Thus literature-to-be-written, even as it is designated *absolute,* is shown to be impossible to write. And here again we encounter that despairing imperative of absolute-art: You must, but you cannot.

This time we've come full circle; art reveals its radical impossibility: "Nothing will have taken place but the place, some minor splashing to disperse the empty act . . . which, if not through its lie, might have founded perdition in those regions of vagueness where all reality is dissolved." Must we give up? No; literature-to-be-written requires that newcomers exhaust themselves at the task to bear witness by their ever-punished zeal that failure is a cipher, that the shipwreck of every work is an *allusion.* To what? To being-beyond-being? To the supremacy of nonbeing over being? In fact, to both at once. In consensual failure there are elements of a game of *Loser Wins,* but the most radical unrealization is to be found as well. The work seemed at first a determination of the real, whose meaning was the negation of all reality (it was a real center of unrealization); now it seems this meaning has turned on it to engulf and dissolve it: the work itself passes into unreality and can exist only as imaginary. Isn't totalizing rigor in itself, as the rule of imagination and an exact coincidence of creative freedom and necessity, merely a postulate[17] of our imagination? The book denies itself in order to sever all contact with reality. Yet books must be written and always fall short so that the artist can affirm, through his zeal and his assumed failures, the importance of that imaginary pole.

An unlivable situation, unless one is slightly insane. Surpassing the idea of failure, the artist will be able to support himself only by becoming the man of impossibility, or the Lord of the impossibility of man. He dreamed of writing out of *dissatisfaction,* as we have seen; now dissatisfaction must be turned against the work itself and become radicalized through its negation. What is left? An absolute negation that cannot be *lived* and *affirmed* as such but constitutes itself as the meaning of lived experience; it has been completed by the revealing of its own impossibility, that is, by the unreality of the work that should have made it manifest. So the artist, master of allusion, will live allusively as well, seeking to subtly deny everything around him, himself included, in the name of a total unrealization which he can bring about neither through the work (to *present* the unreal to God, who is not) nor through lived experience (to be devoured by the dream, to be no more than an image without real support). On this level, curiously, the writer, contesting reality in each of his perceptions or behaviors, once again finds negativity, the real basis of literary autonomy, which will *in fact* give him the power to write; yet he exercises it in the name of absolute negation. So he does not acknowledge it as a pure freedom of transcendence which lays the foundations for the sign and claims no foundation itself; rather he designates one of its products, nothingness, as a necessary foundation, which is itself hypostasized and reified. Indeed, the false relation between negativity and nothingness, the radical inversion that makes nonbeing, as the surpassing of everything (hence as the surpassing of nothing, or as surpassing surpassed and consequently *realized* as being), into the meaning and justification of an annihilation *in progress,* which is none other than existence, praxis as producer of instruments and work. This subversion lived as life's allusive relation to absolute nonbeing, this *false* illumination of life by death, or, if you like, this way of grasping life as the analogue of a continuous death, is the objective neurosis itself insofar as contradictory literary imperatives compel the artist, merely by living, to fashion the servile work of resentment as the permanent expression of the lofty stoicism of the

17. In Kant's sense of postulates of practical reason.

masters. This neurotic behavior is necessary; without it, literature-to-be-written would be revealed in its pure and simple impossibility. But since the unreal is the only *value*, since the work must be a super-human effort and crowned by failure, since that failure itself is a value as it allusively reveals the grandeur of the artist and of art—their impossibility—and hence the grandeur of the persevering artisan who serves the futility of his effort and for that very reason pursues it until death, *he is therefore allowed to write books*, provided the dissatisfaction that produces them is sustained and continues to denounce them, and the artist sees them as nothing but allusive shipwrecks. In fact, the idea of allusion-literature found its expression only much later, at the end of this neurotic process, and in the last Knights of Nothingness it became visible as a discreet rupture with their predecessors. With Leconte de Lisle in mind, Mallarmé responds to Jules Huret:

> I think there should be nothing but allusion. The contemplation of objects, the image taking flight from the reveries aroused by them are the song. The Parnassians themselves take the thing whole and show it, hence they lack mystery; they withhold that delicious joy the mind feels when it believes it is creating. To *name* an object is to suppress three-quarters of the pleasure of the poem, which is made for guessing it little by little: to *suggest* it, that is the dream. It is the perfect use of that mystery which constitutes the symbol . . .

Here he treats poor Huret with kid gloves. What must be suggested, in fact, is an object that is the precise figuration of nonbeing, "the rose, missing from every bouquet." And this conception, rigorous and precise enough here to establish an Ars poetica, though less self-conscious in the writers of the preceding generation, is nonetheless at the root of their works. It is found in various forms in Flaubert, in Baudelaire, in the Goncourts, even in the Parnassians. No doubt Leconte de Lisle and sometimes Flaubert seem in search of adamantine rigors, they "take the thing and show it," at least apparently. What they suggest is not the object of the work, nor its particular meaning, but the cosmos, all and nothing dialectically linked, divined through the "thing" as its perpetual shipwreck and its unique ambition, the *raison d'être* of the book or poem, and the reason for their nonbeing. The rather heavy architecture of the "thing"—a residue of the imperatives of literature-already-written—is lightened by the dead gaze that contemplates it and by the distant flight of that absence, the World, an imaginary totality of self-destruction that should be seen

175

behind every line, like the whole in each of its parts, and which is sensed in them only as an inert lacuna, failure. In other words, the victory of the unreal.

Permission to engender a work comes solely from what I shall call the ambivalence of failure. For by self-destructing, the objective posed and not attained reveals the increasing role of nonbeing. The end in itself is already a contesting of reality, since it is manifest in a surpassing of the practical field and can be realized only by a reshaping of that field. Thus, as I have shown elsewhere, the real reveals itself by that nonbeing which is the practical future, the end proposed as something *to be attained*—therefore, as not yet being—by the reorganization of what already is. In the mid-nineteenth century, that relation, which constitutes the fundamental structure of the project, is at the source of every endeavor, including the endeavor of writing. The reshaping of the real, however, the synthetic unity of means as it defines the end, is offered in principle as *possible*, as *realizable*. In this sense the *reality* of the future is made manifest to us, although the future organization of the field has not yet shifted from nonbeing to being by way of the subjective behavior we enact in order to accomplish our enterprise. But what if the future should be nothingness?

It is on this conviction, as I have shown in the preceding volumes of this work, that these writers base their constructions of the practical jokes that suddenly, for one moment, conjure up nonbeing in the place of aspired being by spoiling perception envisaged as praxis. Their roles are distributed in advance and can be defined, with regard to the perpetrator of the joke, as the realization through the other of a desired but unrealizable neurosis,[18] something that cannot be conceived without an effort on the joker's part to identify with his victim and enjoy, through the victim, the disarticulation of the real. Consequently, the victim makes evident for the Other the teleological intention of consensual failure: the intention to increase brutally the part of nonbeing in the world and, at the collapse of being revealed as appearance, to elevate nothingness—the negation of all that being offers in evidence and which exists unperceived and unforeseen—to a new ontological status, making it the *absolute*. In other words, nothingness is compelled *to affirm* itself as *that which stands behind being* and is not only nonbeing but being-other-than-being, which can take place only on the ruin of all human conduct, on the failure of praxis

18. The practical joker, moreover, often presents really neurotic traits (mythomania, etc.) which do not in themselves constitute the conduct of failure.

and the disappearance of man as a practical existence *in his own eyes*.

Since this is the teleological meaning of intentional failure, the Knights of Nothingness must perceive the work as a practical joke. This is the only way they can produce it. Yet a distinction must be made. Much later, around the middle of the twentieth century, when writing was definitively recognized as dual, a *black* humorist—like Genet—could regard himself as a joker, consider the reader his dupe, and make the literary object a trap; he achieves failure *through the reader*, and in this failure beauty becomes that absolute, the work negating itself, self-igniting, falling into ashes, with being emerging from the abolition of a booby-trapped language as an infinite and dizzying void. In this case, the shipwreck of the reader is the writer's triumph. But in 1850, and for many decades thereafter, the writer's rupture with his public is not conceived as a war to the death initiated by the writer; it is manifest as a pure and simple abstention. Again, Mallarmé beautifully summed up thirty years of literary history when he declared: "I believe that poetry is made for the pomp and supreme ceremonies of a constituted society that has a place for glory, something people seem to have lost. A poet's attitude now, as then, when *he is on strike against society*, is to push aside all the corrupt means available to him. Any proposal is inferior to his conception and his secret work."[19] Therefore, the poet goes on strike: for lack of a community that acknowledges his aristocracy, he refuses to work for just any public—that is, for his own class. He does work, however, for himself alone, in secret. Which is going on strike by work-to-rule. And Mallarmé's words at the end of the century echo those of the young Flaubert at its midpoint: "I write only to please myself." We know, in fact, that Mallarmé refuses to distinguish the poet from the writer; when the latter tries to expunge chance from his sentences, he is working as a poet, prose does not exist. In short, the rupture is thorough, mechanical: no contact; an abyss, an unbridgeable gap between literature and society. So the writer, wrapped in his solitude, must be practical joker and dupe *at the same time*. In other words, writing is impossible without that neurotic behavior, the writer's conduct of failure. Everything is clear, everything is inscribed in the object: the rupture with the bourgeois public—born of the conflict between a victorious bourgeoisie and an autonomous literature—leads to absolute negation, to art constituting itself as an end *against* reality. This negation cannot be realized as Parmenidian being with-

19. Bibliothèque de la Pléiade, p. 870. My italics.

out disqualifying all enterprise, including the work itself. And under these conditions, either the work does not happen or it takes on a new aim: to be made *so as not to happen*, so as to manifest by its very impossibility the triumph of the unreal, of reality negating itself even in the literary enterprise of unrealization. In this sense, since the writer refuses any witnesses but himself, he keeps to himself the crazy evidence the practical joker can evoke only in his dupe: the dizzying moment of beauty will be that same moment when the "impeccability and impossibility"[20] of his work will burst into pieces, suddenly revealing the essential imperfection of beauty and the a priori impossibility of all perfection. But for the joke's sake that impossibility must be masked, the literary enterprise must always seem possible and must be attempted as a function of its possibility, just as the false sugar cube is dropped into the cup because it seems real, soluble. Thus the impossibility of literature can only be the secret essence of its evident possibility; these two qualities must be inseparably and dialectically linked. Which implies that the writer is himself and another. As *dupe* he believes that chance can always be expunged from language given the appropriate methods; and his conviction comes to him from language itself, a trick object that would suggest its exclusion of contingency and attain its exemplary essence if only some artisan were to concentrate on tightening its internal bonds. As *practical joker* the author throws himself into that formidable task only to expose its impossibility; that is, he attempts to prove to himself, once and for all, that he himself, a product of chance, cannot expel chance from that contingent environment, language, and that all thought, like the false sugar cube, is falsely universal, since even as it is enchanted by the necessity of its content it "proffers a toss of the dice."[21] The work must be written to misfire and to demonstrate that the greatness of literature lies in its unreality, that consequently the greatness of the poet and his aristocracy issue from his real failure and from his unrealization as an imaginary author of an impossible masterpiece, dissatisfaction and the shift to the imaginary here being inseparably linked. So he must be himself and other, his truth residing not in himself but in that other who directs him. He must double himself, play the role of himself, believe in it, and let himself be governed by the other. In other words, the only possibility of satisfying

20. Terms used by Mallarmé to designate the works of the Parnassian poets.

21. In other words, whatever its objective reality (in the Cartesian sense), thought *is* itself a toss of the dice in its formal reality—and the contingency of the latter reacts on the necessity of the former.

the contradictory imperatives of literature-to-be-written lies in accepting the proposition of the objective neurosis, that double game whose origin and end both reside in the dissatisfaction that hoists it above the real by the infinite loftiness of its demands. This double game has meaning and will achieve its goal only if accompanied by *belief*; in this sense, it is neurotic because that double and dogged belief is necessarily a product of autosuggestion. One must be able to incarnate the dupe trustingly, and put oneself in a state of hysterical *distraction* in relation to that other who guides one toward one's doom "like a bad angel." *Other* simply because he is *unrecognized*. One must persuade oneself that the goal of art is to disqualify the real by inscribing in it a center of perfect unrealization, the *Book*, whereas there is no goal but the final shipwreck, the total unrealization, beyond the impossible, of man as artist and of the accomplished—and failed—work as a perfect and dreamed work. In addition, one must be able to effect a subtle breach of trust and, while affirming the identity of being and reality, to steal from reality any ontological consistency and define absolute being in terms of complete unreality. This is scarcely conceivable, barring a directed misunderstanding that intentionally confuses being and the irreducible presence of fact on the ontic level; while on the ontological level, being and value are confused, which allows us to designate by the same name that which is real but has no value and that which is not but should be. This confusion, if well maintained, will allow any sleight-of-hand; in particular, the being of the real (of what *is*) will be disqualified in the name of the being of the unreal (of what *is not*, on principle—the norm). And conversely, by gratuitously assimilating the totality of the unreal to fundamental value, everything that is not will be made to pass without distinction for what should be, indeed, for that which refuses to degrade itself as reality so as to preserve its normative purity, and consequently for that which, eminently, *is*. As a result, the artist, that unhappy lover of the impossible, is consecrated by failure; endlessly repeated failure guarantees his value and consequently his being, the portion of deserving nonbeing which the nonrealization of the work and so of himself expands in the inert lacuna of nothingness (grasped as what should be). This pithiatic tour de force—a first elaboration of the negative theology that has made such ravages in our century—cannot perpetuate itself without a perpetual and devastating tension. Even given this tension, the real constantly threatens to overturn the formulations; if art is impossible, isn't the so-called artist "a bourgeois who busies himself with literature"? Once this point of view is entertained for a moment, everything changes; writing is a futile *activity*, and furthermore, since there have been *masterpieces*, there is no proof that literature reveals its demand and its radiant impossibility in every failed work. On the contrary, the author alone would have to be held responsible. The author or his times. This morose lucidity is all the more inevitable as the writer of the 1850s, disconcerted by contradictory imperatives, has covered over but not suppressed the strong, simple motivations that trigger his choice to write: a firm resolution to accede through genius, through fame, through authentic masterpieces to the upper class and to be reborn an aristocrat; a passionate desire to lead the noble life of the great Romantics. These frustrated demands incline him to bitterness, to bad temper: he runs the risk of judging his sad present condition in the name of his ambitions and realizing the extent of its fraudulence. This must be avoided at all costs, for it would be the death of genius—and in vain. The only result of this disenchantment would be the decision never to write again. Therefore, *enchantment* must be maintained whatever the cost; for this reason, the neurotic state—which allows one to live through it without making the effort to sustain it—seems a kind of grace.

A gloomy enchantment. A long, solitary, dark dream pursued by a man of resentment in hatred of men and himself, the objective neurosis proposes his *subjectivization* as the only means of escaping the impassable contradictions of the times. The choice of the unreal and that of subjectivity are one; there is surely no question of sinking into egocentrism, for these people do not like themselves at all. At the most we might speak of a negative narcissism in some. But the essential thing is to reject the rigidity of oppositions—because they are the structures of the real—by derealizing oneself. In short, we are dealing with a spontaneous imitation of autistic thought; as the contradictory imperatives are not surpassed, they are unceasingly made to absorb each other and transformed into vicious circles; the writer constructs a logic of nothingness that shifts from the realization of the unreal to the unrealization of reality, making impossibility the basic condition of any enterprise. He thinks on several planes, in several voices: on the surface, he attempts a masterpiece because it is always possible to write one; less superficially, he undertakes it because it is impossible and to dream of it. The work, misfiring, is the dross of the dream; underneath, however, the foolish, mute hope of possessing genius persists, of succeeding at the impossible and winning glory despite "the strike against the public." The work, *bound* to fail, at a certain level finds its full value *in the imaginary*, and its high dignity, sanctioned by failure, derives from the fact that it is a dream; the poet falls headfirst into the unreal, which closes around him. But on another level he regards it, without admitting it, as wholly successful: dissatisfaction alone, he thinks—the lot of great artists—prevents him from seeing beauty in it; he is Moses on the outskirts of the Promised Land: later or elsewhere, others will enjoy what he has sown and could not reap; he bases his merit on failure. As a result, the aesthetic is transformed into the ethical, greatness consists of sacrificing oneself unreservedly for causes lost in advance. But merit is demand: What if suddenly winning, just when you thought you had lost, were the reward? If the jinx were merely the visible aspect of election? Depersonalization, rupture with the real, solitude, hypostasized language, misanthropy, self-hatred, the conduct of failure, the quest for the impossible—these neurotic traits are merely the *means of writing*, that is, *of ensuring the continuance of literature* in a time when, far from finding his freedom in literary autonomy, the writer is alienated from it and writing is challenged with every piece, when the possibility of writing a work can no longer be assumed, when faced with the scandal of the elusive public and contradictory imperatives, the basis of art must be sought in irrationality. Of course, this is merely a passing moment; imperatives will change, the movement of history will render obsolete certain unresolved contradictions, others will issue from other circumstances and be surpassed by more rational inventions. Meanwhile, with no public and no God, no guarantee, no freedom or rule, the writer must *persist* in creating works *for no one*, attaining universal singularity through masturbation. It is the tenor of the times: there will be no literature or it will be perpetuated by the neurosis of literary men. For in this iron century, writers could not write if they knew what they were doing; to be sure, whatever the period, they never do know entirely, and we have seen how the eighteenth-century writers were writing a class literature while imagining they are transcending their class by means and for the sake of literary autonomy. But in 1850, blindness is an imperative; the best is obviously *proposed* by neurosis, namely, hysterical distraction. In short, we have seen authors in every era who played the role of writer, but it was an effort to recuperate the self, nothing more. In the mid-nineteenth century, the only way to succeed in the *practical* enterprise of writing was to *play* the role of writer without respite. Not just any man of letters but one who defines himself through unsurpassable oppositions and therefore perceives himself as unrealizable, hence a pole of unrealization. It is this *character* who, in opposition to his "character," de-

181

fines a new beauty based on the nothingness suggested in allusive works, with the failure of art its form and the failure of the human race its content. The author must slip into this skin and stay there if he wants at once to hide his praxis of writing and give it, in the unreal, the unity it requires and does not provide for itself. The crux of the problem—to which we shall return, for it is what will bring us back to Flaubert—is to know *to what extent* it is necessary to *believe* in this character. In subjective neurosis, in effect, the subject can declare, as Gide does: "I am playing myself." But barring a perfect coincidence, which when it exists, as in Gustave's case, must itself be explained and constitutes the basis of the problem, no one can truthfully declare that this silhouette, transcending the possible as a surpassing of objective counterfinalities, is entirely himself. At issue here is a writer-being, an anonymous and authorless figure that everyone must invest with his own life. Among actors there are some who will be good, others bad; some will be spontaneous because those objective determinations synchronize with their imago, providing it with a skeletal structure; and others, even excellent actors, will play it cold or will make a "composite" because, as they say in the theater, they "are not in character," or they "do not feel it." Here, "genius" will depend on the coincidence of the subjective and of the subjectivization proposed by the objective neurosis. It is on that level, in the mid-nineteenth century, that the question of the relationship between the individual who writes and the society that produces him arises. As we shall see, a thorough answer is forthcoming.

3. The Historical Moment

We do not write merely for our own amusement. At least the "advance guard" of every generation has a sense of urgency that varies in quality according to the time and place. This is the result of a stressful contradiction between the imperatives of the Objective Spirit and those of the historical moment. In the case of the young writers of 1850, there was almost an antinomy between the social situation and literary requirements. We have just seen that the major requirement of art was the autonomy of literature. For a certain number of writers, literature *must* be posited as self-sufficient and have no end but itself. And it seems that during this period, when the majority of works—not their own—were placed in a historical context, social facts directly or indirectly acted upon them and gave them another meaning. If we therefore imagine literature both in its own essence of the period and from the point of view of a hybrid and historical essence that had just been brought to it on the tide of events or, according to some who were not exclusively writers, had too eagerly courted an initially reticent audience, we find a contradiction. So we must indicate within which pseudo-literary history—and social truth—these writers are creating "true" literature, indeed, what accounts for their sense of *urgency*.

Texts of the proponents of art for art's sake abound, which would suggest that their sacred mission is less to conquer new terrain for art than keenly to defend terrain already acquired. To the extent that they take into consideration industrial and scientific development, they all share the same terror: that one day art will no longer exist, destroyed by civilization in the process of establishing itself. Leconte de Lisle, for example, denounces "the monstrous alliance of poetry and industry." He writes: "The hymns and odes inspired by steam power and the electric telegraph, and all those didactic circumlocutions having nothing in common with art, would prove in my view rather that poets are becoming by the hour more and more useless to modern societies." And this is echoed by his friend Louis Ménard[22] in *Lettres d'un Mort:* "What place is there for Art in a society that devotes all its time to exploring the infinite field of science and industry?" It is not just a matter of "pure" science—for the Knights of Nothingness will certainly see that its purity (science for science's sake) is comparable to their own—but *applied* science. Flaubert writes to Du Camp: "In the preface to *Chants modernes* you talked a lot of discreditable rubbish, you celebrated industry and sang the glories of steam power, which is idiotic and too much like Saint-Simon by half. Not satisfied with such depravities, you are now going to contrive administrative literature." According to the art for art's sake group, there is a fatal deformation of art by the very people who "make it" by treating it as the means to *something else*. This will kill it.

For there is such a thing as "bourgeois" literature. It disgusts them but may kill them yet. Beginning in 1835, theorists with art in mind, like Victor Cousin and the disciples of Quatremère de Quincy, gave declining Romanticism an aesthetic doctrine that corresponded to what we call art for art's sake. We know that those four words can be found in Cousin's writings. And Quincy had already defined art un-

22. Louis Ménard was a chemist.

der the Empire as the interpretation, and not the imitation, of the beautiful by means of ideal forms that are found only in our mind. Its purpose, he says, is to please, and therefore it is alien to morality. But in the face of these theorists, whom Flaubert readily judges to be stupid and full of excellent intentions, the press after 1838, profiting from its precarious freedom, transforms the public's relation to the writer into a matter of profit. The first *Revue de Paris*, the one edited by Buloz in 1839, introduces the novel to the periodical press. In 1836, *Le Siècle* and *La Presse* create the serialized novel. It is a triumph: newspapers proliferate; at the same time, Girardin puts in paid advertisements, and the newspaper—and consequently the literary works that appear in it—is industrialized. The greatest authors are accused of padding; Balzac, serial writer par excellence, speaks one day of the "ten or twelve literary marshals of France. . . , those . . . who offer a certain commercial surface for exploitation." An anti-Romantic *bourgeois* literature is established with Ponsart, Augier, Jules Sandeau. For them, art should *moralize*. They condemn passion in the name of utilitarianism. After an early Romantic parry, Alexandre Dumas *fils* does the same.

Engagée literature had its theorists—republicans, socialists, or followers of Saint-Simon. These last are the most specific: since humanity is perfectible, the mission of art is to cultivate the sentiments that perfect it. They are indignant at the inutility of contemporary art. In the first issues of the *Revue encyclopédique*, Pierre Leroux drafts an *Adresse aux artistes* demanding their commitment in rather vague terms. His personal action is more important, since he managed to break George Sand's attachment to Romanticism. Thanks to him, that moralizing bourgeois woman would proclaim herself a *socialist* until, and *excluding*, the Commune. This time the artist was required to make *modern* works, like Du Camp; but in quite a different sense (oppositional), Fortoul denounces "art for art's sake" as the basis of Romanticism, which should have known how to adapt itself to the social movement after our "regeneration" (1830). Louis Blanc is of the same opinion. From the liberal Catholics we get the same tune: "The old world is dissolving," writes Lamennais; "the religion of the future projects its first rays on the expectant human race and its future destinies. The artist must be its prophet." These sentences should not be taken as simple maxims; they express social forces powerful enough to convert Victor Hugo and Lamartine to social art. The conversion of Hugo, unanimously considered the leader of the Romantic school, was a hard blow to the theorists of autonomous art, all the more so when later, from Guernsey, the vatic poet himself turned against art for art's sake: "Art for art's sake can be beautiful, but art for progress' sake is more beautiful still." [23] The apprentice authors of the second half of the century could not regard this defection as anything but treason. They understood it, however, for it was exile that gave it such a distinct coloration. The attitude of the aging Hugo—alone on his island—seemed admirable to them, and they found it something of a temptation to socialize art and finally destroy it for good reasons. There was something frightening in this temptation, contradicted by the imperatives of the Objective Spirit; artists discovered that they were their own enemies, and all of them at one time or another had thought, as did Michelet, whom they admired, that art was dead and history had killed it.

All the more so as history hardly spared them either. After the Revolution of 1848 there was 2 December and the Empire. The press lost the little "freedom" it still enjoyed. All of journalism suffered from it: the literary press disappeared, replaced by a popular press devoted to social gossip, of which Villemessant's *Le Figaro* was the best example. If they did not want to lose their "dignity," writers held themselves aloof; in short, they threw themselves back on the side of pure art, but again, this was merely a defensive move. There was great danger of losing all talent; it was *urgent* to *defend* oneself by seeking isolation. All the more so as social art, represented especially by the exiles, was transformed in France into that monstrosity, governmental art. The emperor sent brief congratulatory notes to the moralistic writers. writers. To Ponsard: "Persevere, Sir, as your success obliges you to do, in that path of morality that is perhaps too rarely followed in the theater." Sainte-Beuve lets himself be tempted; in 1870 we find in the papers of Napoleon III a secret note he addressed to the emperor recommending a cultural politics under the pretext of giving help to poor authors, namely, suggesting to him ways of directing writers toward morality. This time the risk was real: the Goncourts, Flaubert, and Baudelaire perceived it in 1857; morality took revenge and put them on trial.

Everyone, however, including the Romantics, determined that Romantic art was dead—Romantic art, which for the new writers represented "freedom in art." Those young people could not believe in

---

23. [Sartre attributes this to] Victor Hugo.

its demise. They had gathered into themselves its practico-inert demands and attempted to renew or revive it. Banville writes the "Ballad of His Regrets for the Year 1830":

> O Poetry, O my dying mother,
> How your sons loved you with a great love
> In this Paris, in the year 1830 . . .

This cult of the past consigned those young aristocrats to the corner of reaction. But the original reason was that they were suffocating. For the same reason they regrouped around the last Romantic, Theophile Gautier. They read his preface to *Mademoiselle de Maupin,* in which he was the first writer to proclaim and insist on art for art's sake; there again, a risk, a display. Flaubert rather liked him but mistrusted his "intellectual whorishness."[24]

For the writers of 1850, the *urgency* lies in their feeling that all of literature is in mortal danger. It demands, in short, to live. And to live *through them;* there isn't a moment to lose. The historical moment, therefore, gives a very specific meaning to the imperatives of the Objective Spirit: it's a matter of urgency that they be applied, for the life of literature is its autonomy; these are remedies for an era when writers have not found their public or go on strike against it. All of them, from Flaubert to Mallarmé, are convinced that they are living in a time of transition, that the future may see the rebirth of a public; so the remedies of art for art's sake are *provisional,* though they cannot even conceive of what the art of the future will be. They set to work, then, bucking the prevailing winds, without knowing just what they are looking for, unable even to define the beautiful. "The Beautiful," say the Goncourts, "is what your mistress and your servant instinctively find abhorrent"; and Flaubert, in conversation: "The Beautiful is what vaguely excites me."

Thus around 1850, certain young Frenchmen, most of them around thirty years old, find themselves caught between the objective imperatives of the literature of the age, whose primary requirement—almost its only requirement if we look closely—is autonomy, and those of the historical moment. Among these writers are Theodore de Banville, Barbey d'Aurevilly, Baudelaire, Bouilhet, Flaubert, Fromentin, Gautier, the Goncourts, Leconte de Lisle, Louis Ménard, and Ernest Renan. They all know each other, or will do. They will certainly not be part

24. Gautier, with Du Camp and Cormenin, founded the *Nouvelle Revue de Paris.* In a foreword to the first issue in October 1851, Gautier speaks of attaching himself to the "contemporary movement."

of the same school. Each has different ways of serving a similar goal. Their first contact with literature-already-written has revealed to them its identical and already contradictory demands. And when they entered the world, they found the same enemies of art, sometimes in themselves, which gave their choice of writing its special urgency (they had to *stick to it* all their lives, art was entrusted to them), while the contradictions of the Objective Spirit had to be resolved instead by a definitive farewell to impossible literature. For they *must* write. Yet each speaks of his literary task as his duty; they must all necessarily adopt a neurotic attitude, sincere or affected, which constitutes, in sum, a failure syndrome. That neurosis, which each has sensed in the others, is confirmed by its *communication*. It becomes, in a sense, their milieu. And for a moment they have come to believe that writers in their day truly write only for other writers. But since literature is dual, despite what they say, it was not true at the time that their neurosis had to be consolidated by simple communication among themselves, the neurotics. On strike and readerless, these authors must find a vast public following for themselves in spite of everything. It is thus fitting to denounce the final illusion of these author-actors: if contemporary readers denied those works which deny the public, they would fall into an oblivion from which posterity alone, in the best case, would redeem them. Yet, as we know, literary history took another course. These black authors with their atemporal aspirations were read *in their lifetime;* not all were renowned, but none died in obscurity; the first work Flaubert published—and surely the most radical, the blackest—made him instantly famous with a resounding success. We can conclude, then, that numerous and structured groups of readers recognized their books, that is, recognized themselves in them. What were these readers like? And doesn't neurotic writing find its guarantee in neurotic reading? We would have to believe, then, that this denied public accepts these negative works because to some extent it denies itself. For just when the young apprentice authors had finished their apprenticeship and were about to publish their first works, the revolution of February 1848 and the coup d'état of 2 December changed human relations and the class consciousness of the bourgeoisie.

4. *The Newfound Public*

The July Revolution—unlike the Revolution of 1789—seemed less the overthrow of one class by another than simply the inversion of the relations established by the Restoration between the two dominant classes. They still shared power, but the archaic aristocracy was sinking, while the newly arrived bourgeoisie continued to rise; their irreducible opposition does not prevent a certain community of interests. The bourgeoisie, moreover, whatever it does, does not like to show its hand; it needs a "cover" that will be not only the Orléanist monarchy but, if need be, the landed gentry. It keeps the aristocracy *in reserve* while it continues to fragment it by the concentration of goods and extension to the countryside of *real*, or bourgeois, property.

In a France of 75 percent peasantry and in the midst of industrial development, the writer's public cannot be recruited from among the disadvantaged classes, who are deliberately kept illiterate; his public will be encountered, if it should exist, among the two dominant classes. Again, let me be specific: the aristocracy as a whole—despite the high culture of certain of its members—is in a sulk over modern literature and "modernity"; it is absorbed in its ideology, which is religious, and when reading it prefers to turn to the classics or to those Romantics who speak to it of its greatness. The bourgeois will become more refined in the course of the century; for the moment, they are not great readers: their spouses inform themselves of what is coming out when they have the time and when they are allowed to read novels. Neither the retail business nor administration—whatever the choices of individuals—are likely to provide a sufficient public for the Knights of Nothingness. These people have no interest in literature, or if they bother with it, they have their favorite authors, Paul de Kock, Béranger, the serial writers. Certainly the works of neurotic-art will gradually penetrate these various milieux, yet they must surmount some resistance, and this cannot happen unless they first find a relatively homogeneous group that is directly receptive to them, in which they will be conveyed like a contagious disease by readers who at the outset represent the most favorable terrain for their "internalization." On this level, propaganda can be reduced to simple propagation; the work *is communicated* because the carriers of the germ communicate among themselves. But other social sectors each represent a *threshold* which the work cannot cross unless its diffusing agent develops a certain level of activity; for communication itself is impeded by internal fractures due to social fissures. All this is based on the assumption that the group originally designated by the work—without the author's knowledge—is qualified to serve as mediator.

And this group does exist. In the service of the rich, whether they live off their private income or profit, another social aggregate has developed which extends from those whom Guillemin calls, for good reason, the semirich to lower civil servants and retailers. Its unity is above all negative, since with rare exceptions the only common feature is their status as unproductive workers who nonetheless do not derive their resources *directly* from the exploitation of the proletariat. That broken, pluralistic unity is rather effectively marked today by calling this group the "middle class."

In the case of neurotic literature, the milieu defined by the work—insofar as writing implies reading *in spite of* the artist—is obviously the upper stratum of the middle class, formed by what was then called the *capacités*. These were professionals defined by their function in bourgeois society and consequently by their kind of remuneration, their relation to capital and to private income, their economic behavior, their budgetary options, their political power. In general, we can say that they exercise the *liberal professions* with more or less success, and that they are doctors, engineers, architects, lawyers, scientists, teachers, etc. These are social individuals who produce, transmit or utilize concrete knowledge to ends that theoretically concern the whole of society but in fact are of interest mainly to the propertied classes. Since the link between knowledge and power is plainly evidenced around 1840 by the dialectical conditioning of industry by science and science by industry, it seems clear that the *capacités* are the technicians of practical knowledge. Practical knowledge would be a pleonasm if it did not seem, at the time, that certain industrial applications were merely indirect or accidental consequences of the development of *pure* or theoretical knowledge. These practitioners haven't any employers, unless they are engineers or civil servants, yet it must be observed in the latter case that their employer is the State, that is, *grosso modo*, the apparatus of the ruling class. The others, so it appears, receive no *salary*. What unites them solidly, despite the diversity of their functions, is that the body of employers grants them a portion of its profit, and the aristocracy a portion of its income from property. Thus their employers, though not private persons, nonetheless exist: the dominant classes *as a whole* support them as their salaried workers through individuals who pay for their services with fees. Thus they live indirectly from the labor of workers and peasants, since they receive a part of the produced wealth through the intermediary of those who appropriate it directly. These remarks suffice to demonstrate the solidarity that connects them organically to private income and capital. If some among them take it into their heads to

189

play the rebel, it is strictly as individuals; besides, they are used to dissimulating their rebellion which, as events of the time would suggest, is never radical even when it decides to show itself. The very exercise of their functions, which constitutes their social being, is done in absolute dependence on the dominant classes, which solicit them, request them, impose on them the need for continuous progress in extending and deepening their knowledge, and if necessary do not hesitate to aid their research with financial support. For this reason, although they serve as intermediaries between the dominant classes (the physician, for example, if he has a good reputation, cares for the spinning-mill owner in town as well as for the lord of the manor in the neighboring countryside), the internalized imperatives of the bourgeoisie win out, in them, over those of the nobility. Competition implies progress—go forward or die!—for which they are the technical agents. Thus the practitioner, even in his pride, even in his probity as a researcher and in what he calls his disinterestedness, is eminently conditioned by his double clientele; he builds his knowledge on the absolute recognition of private property and the social order that guarantees it, a principle in which the two dominant classes think to find a permanent basis for agreement, although it is interpreted differently by each of them. But once this principle is adopted, the professional more eagerly takes the side of its bourgeois interpretation; he is not unaware that since the development of Italian and Flemish cities, the progress of science, technology, and the arts has steadily been linked to that of the bourgeoisie. And he is even more cognizant of the fact that since the July Monarchy the disciplines involving concrete knowledge, solicited by the needs of industry, have continued to progress, and that if ever the aristocracy should regain power, those disciplines would fall into the stagnation that followed the defeat of Napoleon I. Thus, around the mid-nineteenth century, science became bourgeois, which does not mean that its content is class knowledge but that it is linked to the rising class by a dialectical relationship of reciprocal conditioning. Although the practitioner lives above all on, and for, surplus value, as soon as he earns more than he spends he buys lands in order to resemble the squires, who fascinate him; so he is found living at the same time on a salary bestowed by the two dominant classes as a whole *and*, to a lesser degree, on private income. This petty betrayal of his bourgeois master is translated in fact by a real betrayal of the aristocracy; indeed, even as he claims to seek the feudal way of life, he is advancing the process of *embourgeoisement* and the concentration of real property. In short, he is the genuine intermediary, the double agent. The enlightened elite, indeed, deserves the name of upper-*middle* class, not only because it provides the producer with the *means*—direct or indirect—of lowering costs by intensifying production, but, more particularly, because it serves to mediate between the two dominant classes and, through its family relations—numerous and ramified—between the haut bourgeois who no doubt issued more or less recently from the intermediary classes, and the petty bourgeois, who occupies its lowest rank; between the town, where the enlightened elite resides, and the countryside, from where it more or less recently came.

This double character—mediation, knowledge—qualifies the elite to adapt the ideology of the dominant class to the transformations of society; negative in the eighteenth century, bourgeois humanism must become positive in the nineteenth century when the bourgeoisie has taken charge. Until the Revolution, the bourgeoisie took itself for the social setting in which men mutually acknowledged their equal possession, beyond negligible variations, of that universal essence then called human nature. On the one hand, the bourgeois class, mistakenly assimilating the third estate, claimed to contain within itself the quasi-totality of the French; on the other hand, its *practice* demanded instruments of universal usage provided by the exact sciences. The circulation of merchandise led it to demand that tolls and internal divisions everywhere should be replaced by a radical homogeneity of time and space.

For this reason, the theory of bourgeois universality, or, what amounts to the same thing, the theory of human nature similar in all times and places, was not produced by the ship owners, bankers, or big industrialists of the period. If the dominant ideology in a society of class divisions is that of the ruling class or the rising class that will soon rule, this does not mean that such a class produces its ideology whole cloth; we can say, perhaps, that it provides the basis of that ideology by its false consciousness of its praxis, insofar as that praxis refuses to acknowledge and reveal itself to others for what it is. But to become stabilized, to resist the contradictions that emerge both within and outside it, out of its own social divisions, to transform itself into a general conception of the world and man in the world, this ideology must be elaborated; such work is no more suitable to the slave traders of 1750 than to the barons of the thirteenth century. In both cases it is up to the intellectuals to take on this task. The medieval Church—ideology and class, ideology become class—teaches the feudal barons, who do not know how to read, to see themselves as they are not, not to see themselves as they are; it instructs the peasants to regard their poverty as a providential trial. In 1750 the elaboration of humanism was the business of scientists, practitioners, architects, engineers, lawyers. For their praxis was valid only in the setting of universality. If they happen to encounter man as a certain object of their specialty, they will treat him as a universal: for a physician, for example, it is highly important *before* any work is involved to know whom he is dealing with—rich man or poor man, noble or commoner, lower civil servant or highly placed appointee; his fees will depend on it. But in the exercise of his profession it matters little, at least in principle, whether the patient belongs to one social class or another; the symptoms are what count, a set of visible manifestations that *always* correspond to the same illness. Thus universality—demanded by commerce and *produced* by and for the labors of practitioners—implicitly and quite independently engenders a humanism, which is the abstract acknowledgment of the equality of men with regard to care given them or instruments constructed for their use. On this level the issue is still one of a logical consequence and has no real conceptual content. When the *capacités* of the eighteenth century outline the idea of *human nature* on this basis, they use knowledge to establish an ideology, that is, a specially constructed nonknowledge in its unity as a "model" and in its dismissal of multiplicity in order to realize the phantasmatic projection of universality—as the purpose and rule of conceptual knowledge—onto the terrain of social and political struggle. The ideology of the universal in the eighteenth century could be summed up by these four principles: (1) There is such a thing as human nature and all men participate in it. (2) All men are good. (3) Man is doubly universal because he engenders the universality of the concept through reason—which means that scientific truth is accessible to all *in principle,* or, as Descartes said a century earlier, good sense is the commonest thing in the world—and because he figures as a universal object in theoretical and practical knowledge. (4) Consequently, all men are equal, since none is by definition more human than others; all men are brothers, which defines their way of *realizing* their common belonging to human nature in their original goodness; all men are free, which means that no particular shackle should prevent them from manifesting their human essence in its integrality, that is, in its full universality.[25]

While the bourgeoisie remains in opposition, optimistic humanism can sustain itself without great difficulty; at that time it represented, *as negativity*, all the social groups whose work or the concrete demands of life brought into conflict with the relations of feudal production, that is, with the institutions of the Ancien Régime. In a divided society, universality is never anything but negative: it challenges real divisions in the name of a demand for universalization. Equality, a natural right claimed by all against the privileged, existed within the third estate only to the extent that the privileged *denied it equally to everyone*. Therefore, humanism has yet to come, it remains to be accomplished; it is the task of man and seems to be the simple negation of a negation: remove all obstacles, sweep away particularisms and prerogatives, and human nature will affirm itself if only it is allowed to become manifest in its plenitude and goodness. Optimism, here, is tied to nonbeing: what exists is worthless, but it is the fault of a handful of men; this confused present can be challenged in the name of what is to come, which is none other than the advent of the human. At the same time, what is to come is none other than what already is: it is a question not of *making* man but of *releasing* him, for whatever his camouflage, human nature was always his essence and has in all times and places remained the same in everyone; and this will be revealed once the usurpers have been chased out.

The subsequent lacerations are well known; from the time the reign of man had begun to the great days of the Constituent Assembly, the haute bourgeoisie, taking account of natural inequalities, replaced de facto equality—a simple consequence of the formal universality of concepts—with the *right* to equality, which led to the division of equals into active and passive citizens without changing the conceptual framework. A muddled and egalitarian petty bourgeoisie, along with the *Sans Culottes* whom Lefebvre called a "Popular Front," briefly succeeds in establishing universal suffrage against the advice of the propertied class and its electors, defining the *formal democracy*

25. The reader will have already understood that for convenience's sake I was using the word "ideology" here in the Marxist sense of the term. But that practico-inert determination is unconnected to the practice of post-Marxist philosophers, who seek the truth from Marxist philosophy and whom I called ideologues in the *Critique de la raison dialectique* to indicate than they attempt to elaborate in detail a philosophy they did not create.

that makes the right to vote—the political right to intervene in public affairs—a strict consequence of the presence in every man of man's essence, or human nature. This outrage doesn't last long: once Robespierre is overthrown, the haute bourgeoisie again takes charge, and the Constitution of the year III suppresses the right of the poor to intervene in the affairs of the rich. On this point, shortly before the Constitution was accepted, Boissy d'Anglas defined its meaning in these concise terms: "A country governed by property owners is a country with a strong social order." Which essentially gives the abstract concept of *human nature* a concrete content that is property itself. Would this sudden injection of an empirical synthesis into what was hitherto only a pure thought of the universal—or, to take the words in their Kantian sense, the sudden transformation of an *analytic*, therefore a priori, judgment, "Every man is man," into a synthetic, a posteriori judgment, "Only property owners are men"—would this explode the concept of man altogether? In effect, while continuing to affirm, among other things, that man is *zoon politikon*, the great majority of Frenchmen are denied the political dimension. But in the first place, in 1795, the recourse to property had merely negative virtues—at least apparently; it was used against the madness of the murdered Montagnards, and in great part it guaranteed the nation against the muddle-headed irresponsibility of the have-nots. It is desirable simply to distinguish the heads of families—who wanted to preserve and extend their holdings to deed them to their sons, and who will consequently maintain the social order that is indispensable to the security of business—from the crowd of those who, having nothing to lose, would risk ruining the nation with their temerity. The issue, in short, is one of a practical and judicial evaluation. And, in the second place, if the *rich* seemed at the time like fully empowered men, perfect representatives of human nature in its ethical flowering insofar as this is not a simple concept but also a value, then the crowd of the excluded is composed not of submen but of *potential men:* each is capable of being humanized, for there is no law to prevent him from becoming a possessor and thus acceding to wisdom—the crown of humanism. In this new society, where property has replaced "birth," nothing is prohibited a priori. To anyone. In short, under the Ancien Régime, *humanity* was denied the great majority on principle; now everyone *can* acquire it. By this sleight-of-hand the ideology of the "universal class" can preserve the external trappings of humanism. It disguises the fact that the new society is built by thrusting the great majority outside of humanity; it conceals from the submen the harsh truth that it produces their subhumanity and prohibits them from escaping it—with some exceptions—because they are necessary to the construction of the social edifice. A hypocrisy made easier by the fact that the proletariat as a class is still embryonic. Thus God's will or economic laws—conceived as natural laws—have made it such that rich and poor *coexist* in human societies. But the relation that unites them remains one of simple contiguity. Even if some distressed souls declare—inspired by that fool, Rousseau—that property is theft, they grasp only one aspect of the question; for them, the rich produce the poor, which is, strictly speaking, reparable; they fail to see that the poor produce the rich by creating wealth for them, which has the direct consequence of forcing a choice between man and private property. In any event, to make property the basis of eudaemonism, the full flowering of human nature, is to define the human on the basis of the nonhuman, that which is on principle external to the species. These speculations, moreover, came to a quick end: the bourgeoisie, uncertain of itself, wanted a cover and lived in the shadow of a military dictatorship.

From 1830 on, therefore, the task of the professionals is to restore humanism and base it on private property. A task made all the more difficult as bourgeois society is now *incarnate;* civil and foreign wars, the Napoleonic cover, the defeat and the Restoration had preserved, despite everything, its veil of negativity. It was not yet what it might have been. Under the July Monarchy, the incarnation is achieved, the veil falls. Indeed, during the first thirty years of the century, with the development of manufacturing, the idea of private property continued to grow in importance and to erode "human nature"; moreover, it was divided: private income represents stability, profit represents progress, its condition and consequence. From this last point of view, the role of *goods* becomes positive: these are no longer simply the lead soles that provide ballast for "respectable folk" and oblige them to be balanced in their judgments; they are in themselves the driving force and glorious destiny of the owning class, which, obliged to increase its goods just to keep them, finds itself launched on conquering the earth, remodeling nature, ensuring the progress of humanity's knowledge and power. Internalized by the property owner, property becomes his most intimate *conatus* and his sacred leavening. At the same moment, the bourgeois is astonished to discover his product and his secret: the proletariat. The shock is so great that he hesitates. More especially as the legitimists tell him so straight to his face: a social order built on such poverty will not long survive. After the rebellion of the Canuts, two tendencies emerge. The first is pessimistic, probably out of lucidity. In 1831, Casimir Perier declares flatly: "The workers must come to know that there is no remedy for them but patience and resignation." Fine. But then no one is capable of being *humanized*—with a very few exceptions. There are only perpetual submen. Let us not forget that of 21,000 born in the workers' slums of Lille, 20,700 are dead before the age of five. For the survivors, these are the statistics provided by Baron Dupin: of 10,000 worker conscripts, 8,980 are discharged, on an average, as unfit for military service. If they don't die, the children go to work in the factory eight hours a day from the age of eight. How can you urge patience under these conditions without convincing these submen that they will be whole men in another world, in heaven? Guizot, successor to Casimir Perier, understood this very well; beginning in 1833, he entrusted the Church with the supervision of primary education.

Indeed, this is a return to an ideology of the privileged, to the ideology of the Ancien Régime *minus* its optimism. The bourgeois—we shall return to this—not being bourgeois by divine right and persistent in his denial of the existence of class divisions, can justify and explain a necessary but illegitimate inequality, strictly speaking, only by recourse to economic laws—conceived as laws of nature, hence inexorable, with no conceivable relation to justice or injustice—by injecting aristocratic optimism with a fatal Manichaeanism. This is how it goes: On earth everything is bad. Let us give up humanism and put ourselves in God's hands; He will realize *elsewhere*, if he so desires, the impossible equality of men. Montalembert will sum up this doctrine in September 1848, in one of his speeches:

> Social interest demands the propagation of religious instruction . . . [because] the teaching of the Church can be summed up in two words: abstain and respect. Yes, these two words sum up its social and political action . . . We have taught the common people no longer to strive for their share of celestial happiness, and so they claim happiness on earth. And they will be happy at our expense, just wait and see . . . What is the problem today? To arouse respect for property in those who are not property owners. And I know of only one formula for arousing such respect . . . to make them believe in God, in the God of the catechism, in the God who dictated the Ten Commandments and condemns thieves to eternal punishment.

A policeman-God, perfect: thanks to him, on this earth the bourgeois will be forever rich and the people forever poor, which is necessary for the accumulation of capital. But *by what right* do the bourgeois consider themselves the beneficiaries of this regime, since for the most part, if we look into their family histories one or two generations back, they are newly rich, or the sons of the newly rich? Take Decazes, for example, with a purchased patent of nobility and few means: the prefect of police in 1815, a duke and peer by royal grant and founder of Decazeville, the owner of coal mines and forges, the *direct* creator of a proletariat of miners and metallurgists. Yet this ignoramus was made nobility. And what about Laffitte, a nobody, president of the Bank of France in 1814, a simple landowner who based his right to property only on his mania for finding pins on parquet floors? What about all those speculators, all those acquirers of national holdings who, under the Revolution or the Empire, founded their wealth on the despoiling of their former masters? What about the Perier family, and Casimir Perier himself? Borrowing the aristocracy's doctrine for instilling patience in the working classes, the bourgeoisie condemns itself: in the name of this ideology, all bourgeois are interlopers and usurpers, in short, illegitimately rich. Above all, religion establishes *landed* property, for thereby the lord of the manor, through his human relations, becomes more refined in contact with those lands that God created by a gift and which the property owner receives as a gift in exchange for homage or through inheritance; it cannot justify portable property—the naked relation of man to thing—nor, most certainly, profit. So it is prudent not to use it excessively. One will go to mass very publicly, and disseminate the faith through religious instruction. But all those newly rich, the sons of Jacobins, are dechristianized from childhood because their fathers had understood that religion—which formerly condemned lending at interest under the name of usury—did not legitimize transfers of power and condemned the lay purchase of property confiscated from the Church.

It was therefore necessary to choose a different way, to patch humanism up a bit as the true legitimation of the bourgeois dictatorship. There is a glaring contradiction, moreover, between that gloomy Catharism and the confidence the bourgeoisie has in itself and in its destiny. True, the people were restless during the first years of the reign, but a few warning shots sufficed; they lie low after 1835, and their barbarity is more or less forgotten: they must be persuaded that

197

all is for the best. In sum, the class ideology must be optimism. The same Guizot whom we saw at his advent especially preoccupied with giving religion to the people is not the last to switch allegiance and combat the humanitarianism of those one calls "social romantics" in order to vindicate bourgeois humanism. He declares in '46 that the country, "tranquil in its principles, in the moral interests so dear to it, tranquil in its great moral existence . . . , carries on its daily business peacefully." Are there no more submen? Certainly not! The worker is no longer constrained to resignation: "Get rich by saving." Therefore, every human being can be *humanized;* it is enough for him to *deserve* human nature through patience and economy. As a result, the ruling class boasts in its wake a humanism slightly tainted with feudalism. The manufacturer "foresees the needs of Society, assuring work to the working class and making himself loved like a true father to his family." This paternalism of Gay-Lussac finds a woebegone echo, after the days of June 1848, in a speech by the industrialist Sevaistre, majority deputy:

> The chiefs of industry have [always] regarded their workers as their family, and what sustains them in an often difficult career is precisely the inner satisfaction of providing a living, and sometimes even comfort, for numerous workers.

You read correctly: with a wage of two francs a day, some workers do live in comfort. To be sure, these workers are flocking toward the condition of man; if they want to accede to it, that's up to them—all they have to do is save. The mill owner Grandin pushed such optimism still further: "Far from seeing child labor as a form of sordid avarice . . . it [should] often be acknowledged as an act of generosity on our part." Generosity—the basis of aristocratic ideology—this is how the capitalist bourgeoisie attempts to annex it. Timidly, it's true: child labor in large-scale industry is *often* generous, nothing more. The exploitation of peasants by the squires of the Ancien Régime was *always* generous. To complete this pastoral image, one notion is still missing, that of progress. It will be quickly elaborated; when they consider the path taken from the creation of the railroad to the opening of the Suez canal, the bourgeois class and the *capacités* marvel. It will be enough that a single inspired spokesman fix in words the capitalists' astonishment at what they take to be their work. Among the candidates I will cite only one name, Maxime Du Camp, a slightly tardy chorister of "modernity" (this was under the Empire, in 1854, and optimism was the rule). In *Chants modernes,* he writes:

> Know the past but sing of the future.
> The golden age is very near, we may be touching it . . .
> Sing of freedom, love and progress . . .
> In a hundred years soldiers will be laborers,
> Generals will be directors of our factories,
> With howitzers we shall make machines . . .

In the preface he writes: "We are the century . . . that found applications for steam power, electricity, chloroform, the helix, photography, electroplating . . . and we must concern ourselves with the Trojan War and the Panathenaea? . . . We are that people who are giving birth to the future."

To please the new masters, Maxime tells them what they want to hear: the bourgeois is the agent of progress.

The truth is that Maxime is celebrating in these lines what might be called the official ideology. The bourgeois is devoted to progress, he sacrifices himself to his large family, the proletariat; scientific discoveries and their technical applications, which characterize the bourgeois regime, will free man from his last remaining chains, at the end of a long process of evolution, by bestowing opulence on the most disadvantaged. Thus the social order will still be based on property, but if authority reverts by right to the big property owners, small property will proliferate. An excellent expectation—not of the future worker's real condition but of the future avatars of bourgeois ideology even as the dominant class reeks of optimism. Here we find the principle of the radical-socialist program—at least until 1914—and that of our present slogans of "Societies of Abundance." *Official* ideology: the dominant class wants it to inspire political speeches and editorials in the daily press as much as works of propaganda—what I was calling class literature or, if you will, authorized literature. But if the bourgeoisie attempts to hide the wall of money behind the wall of discourse, that slightly inane discourse, it *does not believe* in what it says, in what is said in its name. When they read Maxime's *Chants*, the chief reason for their skepticism is historical—we shall return to this, the days of February and the coup of 2 December. But those very people, who in the calm before the storm presented Louis-Philippe with this flattering image as his reflection, hardly believed it themselves. The reasons for their mistrust are obvious. First of all, capital could care less about the proliferation of small ownership; everyone recognizes the need for a poor proletariat whose members individually possess only their strength for work; if they were property owners, why would they sell their strength like a piece of merchandise?

And mindful of the celebrated Ternaux, mill owner from Sedan and hero of industry, the manufacturers know perfectly well that they buy machines to reduce costs, that is, to reduce wages. Since 1830, wages have continued to decline—they will rise again much later, under the Empire, when industrial progress will once again place value on manpower, and especially under the Third Republic until 1914—but as a result the working class becomes a dreaded adversary. Its strikes are successful, the class struggle intensifies, and the manufacturers under Louis-Phillipe, without clearly comprehending the process of accumulation, are entirely conscious of increasing their profits through the pauperization of the workers; they are even convinced that capital requires the *absolute pauperization* of the proletariat—a notion even blacker than an already black enough reality (exploitation, relative pauperization). How could they believe in the general progress of the human race, how could they evoke it among themselves with a straight face? The proof of their skepticism is their energetic refusal to hear of literacy for the disadvantaged strata of society. As a future property owner, it would be good for the worker to be able to read; as long as he remains merchandise, what need does he have for human knowledge? Moreover, they expend the same vigor opposing not only any intervention by the State in favor of the proletariat, but also the cooperative organization of manual workers. On 25 August 1830, La Fayette declares, addressing the national guard: "Any demand on us to intervene between employer and worker on the subject of fixing wages, the length of the work day, and the choice of workers will not be admitted, being formulated in opposition to the laws that have consecrated the principle of free industry." Yet the State, in their opinion, must be interventionist. But in only one instance: "It is"—as Thiers says—"obliged to assure the protection of the manufacturers." The beneficiaries of this one-way intervention do not conceal its meaning from themselves: the new barbarians must be maintained in their barbarity. Any association of workers would have the effect of diminishing their competitive rivalry in the labor market and, hence, of slowing the decline of wages by replacing competitive atomization with the unity of a monopoly. Therefore, it must be prohibited; the cost of the worker will thus fall by itself to the lowest level under the double impact of mechanization and competition in the labor market. That is what the employers want, and *they know it*. Wages must be kept at the lowest level; and this can be done only by consistently maintaining an overabundance of manpower, *in any case* by a technological unemployment supported by the acquisition of new and continuously perfected machines, in short, by technical inventions. In other words, they are conscious, at this time, that progress *operates to the worker's disadvantage*. And that is why they were so violently opposed to the humblest demand of the working classes in 1848: a recognition of every man's *right to work*, which would absorb unemployment and make the price of human merchandise rise on the labor market. In short, they know what they are doing. How can they stand it? Are they cynical? Rarely. Do they feel guilty? Not in the least. They replace a subjective consciousness of their inhumanity with the objective knowledge of natural inhumanity: the economy is ruled by strict laws, as inflexible as those that govern physical phenomena; you must bow to them if you want to produce wealth; should you try, moreover, to escape them, you would ruin yourself to no one's profit and at great harm to the workers, who would be thrown into the street if the factory closed its doors. In this purely negative sense, people are apt to speak of the boss's solidarity with his employees. But if classical economics—by presenting the structures that a society has *given* itself as external laws—allows manufacturers a clear conscience, the set of practices they believe it establishes does not authorize them to share Maxime's bleating optimism: the world is like this, so be it. But the unavoidable consequence is that it is quite black, and man, a product of the world, a slave to its laws even if he declines all responsibility, is no longer so untarnished himself.

As much as the bosses sometimes vaunt their generosity, they do not believe it for a moment. Or perhaps just for the time it takes to make a speech. For it is contradicted by their real morality, which is produced through them by capital in its phase of accumulation: utilitarianism. In a competitive period, generosity is a forbidden luxury. It is not a matter of consuming the goods of this world, and still less of giving them; they must be produced and accumulated, which for the boss himself implies a puritanical austerity, the practice of abstinence. As for his relation to wage earners, Gay-Lussac defines it as clearly as Marx will do later, but without seeing any harm in it: "The manufacturer has nothing else to do . . . but buy manpower and, when it is bought, dispose of it." Hard on himself and on others, his only human relation to his employees and to himself is *to economize*. Privation, saving, all those negative virtues are rigorously opposed to the economy of the gift, which is expenditure and sometimes squandering. The sole form of generosity a boss can permit himself is not to have any, to reduce his way of life as much as possible and pay the lowest possible wages in order to reinvest in his enterprise, enlarge it, and thereby support the greatest number of working families on ever lower wages. For all these motives, the bourgeois may read Du Camp and be amused by his enthusiasm, thinking that this good purveyor has delivered precisely the goods they ordered, but they do not allow themselves to be taken in by what he tells them. This optimistic modernism is not their ideology. Indeed, it is no one's ideology; its only possible utility is as a diversion.

Must we then return to the pessimism of Casimir Perier? No, for it offers no exit. Taking it literally, the bourgeois would be led to become truly conscious of his class and of the practical relation of that class to other classes. And this he cannot do without revealing that secret shame of the bourgeoisie which is the proletariat, its product, perhaps its destiny. And if it is revealed to the working class that its condition has a remedy other than resignation, it will undoubtedly be led to despair and revolt, in short, to the contrary of the desired outcome. Above all, the dominant class *needs* an ideology. In other words, it needs to think about itself and legitimate its power. This means that it must be provided with a *false consciousness* of itself so that it might conceive of the order it sustains as conforming to the nature of man and things, in short, as the best possible order and not a perpetuated disorder. By ideology, to be sure, we must not infer a philosophical system, a rigorous construction—even one based on false premises—and not even a vague, loose constellation whose content would be common to all individuals of a certain class. We are dealing, in fact, with a group of relations between terms defined only by their reciprocal oppositions, or by a "differential" that determines each one by the others insofar as its sole essence resides in its difference from this or that other term and, as a result, from all. This differentiation as the reciprocal determination of the pair appears as a form (formal duality) on a foundation constituted by the totality of differentials insofar as each one can be differentiated from others only by affirming itself as constituted by its difference from the paired form that stands out against the whole. What is involved is a false, *nonsubstantive* totality of matrices and operative schemes, without any concrete individuation of the All or of the twinned relations. It is, if you will, less a thought than an abstract model of thoughts, which, when produced, can be absolutely anything, provided their skeleton and vertebrae are the differential relations that engender the terms on the level of the model. This means, first of all, that these thoughts can be indefinite in number and vary from one individual of a certain class to another and even, at times, within the same individual. And, second, that the essence of the creations spun from this model is not prescribed by it; we must understand that the differential whole can generate, depending on the situation, a general view of the world and of man in the world, a particular judgment on a historical circumstance, a myth or whole mythology, a system of values, a deontology, etc. In other words, the model does not dictate one's restriction either to the realm of facts or to the normative; fact and norm will share a certain relational structure which, in its abstraction, is on this side of the distinction between being and ought-to-be, although it is produced, in fact, for the always normative needs of a justification. We are dealing, in short, with a device constructed and internalized in such a way that it is, if not impossible, at least very difficult to formulate a thought that is not a specification of the model, and still more difficult to shift from an idea structured by these schemes to ideas that would not belong to the system. The main thing is that these differential relations, meaningful only in relation to each other, continually reverberate from one scheme to the other and from each of them to the totalized whole, so that thought, once caught in these grids—though surpassing them each time toward a concrete creation—has no way out. On this basis, social individuals can produce concrete systems that vary infinitely and can even conflict with one another as concrete determinations—as, for example, Diderot's and Holbach's conceptions of nature conflict with Voltaire's; yet the operative schemes are the same, and behind them the differential articulation of structural relations. This *false consciousness*—this filter of thoughts—common to all individuals in a class, which springs from their inability to achieve a true class consciousness as such, and whose teleological intention is to render that consciousness impossible, is not produced in its reality, with its powers of diffraction, refraction, astringency, and deviation, etc., by the simple historical praxis of class. At most we can say that this praxis has created favorable conditions, an exis which, as an intentional attitude, gives *meaning* to future ideology. In fact, in its first stage, the embryonic state, it posits itself as a *need*, which is self-contradictory since it is both *a thirst for knowledge* and a profound appetite for *nonknowledge*. The reference to knowledge is primary, not only because human reality is praxis and knowledge is a necessary disclosure of the field of possibles, of the structures of being based on its transcendence toward being-to-come, but also because, whatever its social being, the living human is a *being in question*, or, which amounts to the same thing, exists as a putting-in-question of his own being. These two determinations are, moreover, inseparable: praxis necessarily assumes the putting-in-question, and, reciprocally, the putting-in-question is not originally the search for a theoretical knowledge but the *practical* quest for a recuperation of the self as a living being, reproducing its life by an action on an environment made of hostile things and other living beings who (a rarity) contest that action by the simple fact of their existence. Thus, the social individual must be able to see himself as able to act; he acts to the (variable) extent that he can see himself.

But the appetite for nonknowledge is equally fundamental; concrete life—that of the free, practical organism—enfolds a comprehension of the self, as a response which surpasses and preserves the question in itself and excludes, as it is lived, that other type of response, objective knowledge. In other words, understanding as the self-adherence of the person in question differs from knowledge, which is distancing and a formulation of the question through discourse; for that implies that the person in question, in response, presents himself to himself *as another*, or as he is viewed by others. As far as our study is concerned, the knowledge of the social individual should designate him in his own eyes as a class individual, as he is viewed by the members of other classes and, specifically, through the eyes of the exploited, who find the secret of his being in exploitation.[26] In a more general way, man's being-in-question—that is, his being-in-danger in the world and society—determines in him a priori a denial of any question. All good reasoning offends, says Stendhal. We must go further: given that the question, as the ontological structure of human reality, is the origin of thought, that very thought is frightening—unless it makes itself entirely technical. To think is not to *put ourselves* in question but to condemn ourselves to discover, sooner or later, directly or indirectly, that being put into question is

26. Conversely, the understanding the exploited have of their needs and their poverty is a restraint rather than a prod to conscious awareness. "Submen conscious of their subhumanity" will regard themselves as submen only if they grasp themselves through the praxis of the boss, who dehumanizes them and justifies that dehumanization by secretly assigning them a natural inferiority. This presupposes the denial of all hope, and particularly the denunciation of Lamartine's optimistic lie, the "misunderstanding that separates the classes." A misunderstanding can be dissipated; the exploited still have a chance for happiness. But class consciousness—or an objective awareness of oneself—cannot be formed unless the exploited discover that there is not the slightest misunderstanding between the classes. This means that the boss is *forever* the destiny of the exploited, and the only choice for the working class is between an impossible resignation and the radical overthrow of society. Such consciousness develops slowly among the proletariat of the nineteenth century because at the outset it requires shame and despair as its primary determinations.

the practical foundation of our being, and that it cannot be suppressed, whatever the answers, since we, as both questioners and questioned, supply the very questions that serve us as the basis for new ones. The *denial of knowledge,* however, cannot be posited in the form of a *deliberate will to ignorance.* In this case, putting things in question would manifest itself in broad daylight as something that bears no response. The appetite for nonknowledge will offer itself as such only by admitting that it is based on the question as a fracture of being; and, hence, it presents itself, to the contrary, as conditioned by an already constituted body of knowledge.

The question doesn't exist, or no longer exists, because all the answers are already given: man is not a *for-itself* but fundamentally an *in-itself,* susceptible to being known in his objectivity and his exteriority. This knowledge, already acquired, can be exploited, strictly speaking, or developed to practical ends, but there is no more specific problematic of human reality. The question—today suppressed by the answer—arises only from our original ignorance; in this sense, we do not differ ontologically from other objects of our knowledge: for the Ancients, physico-chemical nature posed questions to which science provides answers. That, of course, fails to recognize the fact that the universe questions us only because we, the questioned-questioning, are at the source of every question. But above all—and this is what interests us here—in this way nonknowledge is presented as already constituted knowledge. And as knowledge exists in other domains— particularly science and its corollary, technology—the denial of the question implies that man's nonknowledge of himself is presented as a concrete body of knowledge, the direct consequence of true knowledge. This appears clearly in 1840, for example, when child labor is discussed in the Chamber of Deputies. The industrialist Grandin thanks the *"true men of science"*—his own terms—who have shown that the employment of children was often an act of generosity. Assuming that men of science had raised their voices on this issue— these men would have been, of course, economists, sociologists, and physicians—they would, *as such,* have been incapable of demonstrating that using six-year-old children in the textile mills was in itself *"generous."* The economists may have calculated the resources that capital derived from this underpaid manpower, while the sociologists and physicians may have pointed to the depredations wrought by this practice in working-class families and in those young, fragile, rapidly growing organisms. Ethical and political judgment did not concern them since at issue was a practical decision based on the ac-

205

knowledgment of value. But Grandin isn't interested in that; the main thing, for him, is that nothing should change; in this sense, generosity as exis must be deduced, as the manufacturer's objective being, on the basis of the exact sciences. In other words, knowledge must establish ideology—as a justification of its practice—by replacing being-in-question with being-in-itself, pure and simple. The point is, therefore, to deduce nonknowledge from true knowledge at the cost of false arguments, illicit extrapolations, an anomistic recourse to analogies, constant and camouflaged shifts from fact to privilege, from privilege to fact, and a hundred other logical contortions. Or, if you will, of submitting knowledge to an apparently rigorous treatment that wrenches it out of its true realm and transforms it into ignorance to give it the appearance of knowledge. If this is what ideology must be, if within this false totality the paired relations between differentials must be established by analogy with the type of relations that constitute the era's rigorous knowledge, it is clear that the fundamental structure of bourgeois ideology under Louis-Philippe, and even more so under Napoleon III, must be—as Grandin innocently observed—*scientism*, doctrinal nonknowledge constructed to satisfy the needs of the dominant class on the basis of *real* scientific knowledge.

It is obvious, by the same token, that the elaboration of ideology will be entrusted to the technicians of practical knowledge. They have learned to handle concepts and make use of their knowledge, combining rigidity and flexibility, to extend the conquests of science and industry. On another ground, their use and intuition of the *true* will make the construction of the false less onerous to them; they need merely apply their disciplines with the same severity, only this time to objects that do not originate in them. In other words, the bourgeoisie of 1840, unable either to reclaim Christian ideology or to preserve its negative humanism, orders its professionals to provide it with something positive: a scientific humanism. In this era, when despite the proliferation of social doctrines anthropology finds neither its real object nor its methods, when the earliest of the human sciences, psychology, wholly encumbered by scholastic entities and at the same time atomized by English empiricism, remains a simple metaphysical discourse or becomes the subject of futile "meditations," such an order means that science is required to provide a definition of man that might satisfy the dominant class by fixing rational limits to that object without, however, causing those capable of being *humanized* to fall forever into subhumanity. Let it provide a *realism* adequate to the bourgeois enterprise, a *hard-nosed optimism* that, without falling into Du Camp's inanities, exonerates the bourgeois as the pure product of a meeting of causal links, and at the same time—contradictorily—legitimizes him by representing him as the son of his works. Of his *work*, rather, for it is in progress: it is the industrialization of our planet. In short, let scientific humanism fix its Medusa's eye on that unknown, man, and let it transform him into *something known* by establishing, through experimental methods, the concrete content of human nature. Or rather—for the time of constants is passing—let it show his biological and historical evolution so as to assign him a future—which will be the *embourgeoisement* of the earth—and internal limits. There is no need, as I have said, to construct a philosophy, to propose a *Weltanschauung:* there will be a hundred philosophies, conceptions of the world will vary from one individual to another within a single class; the need is merely to put in place a system of relations that will allow anyone to see man through his product—through science and technology—or rather as the product of his product.

The fact is that the *capacités* had no mandate. Neither the bourgeoisie as a class nor the State apparatus had requested this service. As for certain individuals within the class, surely some of them must have clearly understood the legitimation that industry, daughter of science, expected from its mother. But for the majority of them it was a matter of an implicit need, sometimes experienced in the form of discomfort, and recognized only at the moment it was satisfied. If the professionals accepted the anonymous mandate to set the humanist wreckage afloat once more and patch it up again, as the bourgeoisie might have liked, it was to legitimize themselves, which they would not do without simultaneously justifying real property. In fact, as we have seen, science and technology are, in this era, *bourgeois.* And for the technicians of practical knowledge this means, first of all, that they will develop at the same pace as the dominant class, solicited by it and soliciting it. Their future, as far as anyone can see, is the future of the bourgeoisie and, more specifically, of the competitive economy; progress spurs their development because at each stage of industrialization it is an economic demand, the categorical imperative of liberalism, before it is a practical reality. Thus the professionals, in the very exercise of their professions, think they are—and are, in fact, for the present—dependent on private property. More concretely, their material existence is dependent on it as well. The greatest share of their resources comes from surplus value; their number will increase with the accumulation of capital, allowing all their sons to become technicians and scientists in their turn. So their mandate does not come directly from men but is rather a practico-inert imperative. Or, if you will, a demand of wrought materiality (manufactured according to their precepts and inventions, in factories that indisputably belong to the manufacturers, by wage earners subject to the pressure of competitive antagonisms on all levels of the market) insofar as it is their objectivization and consequently defines them *in their being* through their underlying relation to the mode of production and the institutions that characterize bourgeois society, and quite directly to the body of employers who produce them and maintain them to the extent that they are themselves a product of private property. The material imperative—their being put in question by their objective being—is therefore the categorical claim to an ideology that justifies them *based on the legitimation of private property.* If power has fallen into the hands of outlaws, if the wealth produced is generated by the exploitation of the workers, if the competitive economy finds its best definition in the pessimistic dictum: *homo homini lupus,* the enlightened elite will be prosecuted as accomplices. In the best case, it will remain suspended, rootless, incapable of making a value judgment on itself; it will know the discomfort that will trouble atomic scientists a hundred years later. If it must be the nerve of a society built on injustice, if its discoveries and their practical applications merely result in lowering wages and increasing the poverty and enslavement of the workers, this elite will be swept into an endless vicious circle, whose positive and negative reciprocally change places, where their Promethean pride will turn into shame. There is just one way to escape such a disaster: prove that the only society in which science and technology can be freely developed and dispense their benefits to all is a society based on private property, one in which economic liberalism, through the competition it engenders, is the objective and fundamental stimulant to progress in all fields of knowledge.

The fact is, this new humanism is not unambiguous. If the motor of progress resides in private property, it must be placed both at the bottom and at the top of the social edifice; and, as the rich would like, the bourgeois property owner, that empire builder, must be made the prototype of accomplished man, the exemplar of human nature at its highest flowering or achievement. Thus property is man, and the technician is wholly human only if he is a property owner as well. In a sense, if the dominant class adopts the ideology of the professionals, it is turned against them. But without touching the system, one can radically change its meaning by displacing the emphasis: what if private property were merely the most effective *means* of producing and accumulating concrete bodies of knowledge? What if liberalism and competition had value only as the sole conceivable *stimuli* for the development of technology? In this case, the scientist would be fully empowered man, and the plenitude of human nature would be realized without the acquisition of pure knowledge. The property owner would remain, of course, among the representatives of the species, but in a secondary position, worthy of esteem mostly because he sustains research and through it produces those real men, researchers. Thus, the scale of values is reversed according to what is valorized: knowing or producing. In the second case, the scientist is the lackey. In the first, the ideology of the practitioners is valid only for the upper strata of the middle class, and in this case the actual bourgeoisie finds itself out in the open, with no protective cover.

In 1840 this ambiguity does not arise from ideological indeterminacy; it expresses a factual contradiction in the real relations of the ruling class and the enlightened elite. Indeed, the elite is specifically designated to construct the humanism of the property owner, not simply because its members live off the property of others but also because most of them *are possessors*. They have, as we know, lands rather than factories; their goods are minimal compared to those of the dominant classes; be that as it may, they have property which directly demands legitimation. But at the same time these *semirich* are excluded from all political life; the exercise of their profession allows them fruitful investments, sufficient to compromise them and compel them to legitimize the dominance of the property owner, insufficient to allow them to accumulate the two-hundred-franc levy that would give them the right to vote. These men are well regarded by the ruling class, they are "received"; they are shown a certain esteem, and participate in egalitarian conversations during or after formal dinners. Nothing, in sum, distinguishes the semirich from the rich *in their own eyes* save that inexplicable prohibition which disqualifies even their knowledge: they do not participate in the affairs of their country. Here the vicious circle takes effect: if they are good enough to serve production or the producer, if the entire society depends on their knowledge, and if the organization of men imitates the organization of things—which is within their province—why are they kept from the ballot box? Saint-Simon, under the Restoration, had already conceived an answer to the question: tricameralism, which divided power between artists (the chamber of invention), scientists (the chamber of examination), and industrialists (the chamber of execution). But the doctrine had no immediate results, and property owners remained the only custodians of power. Even so, as man continues to be called a political animal—the full flowering of his *humanity* is thought to coincide with the actualization as praxis of his rights and duties as a citizen—the semirich find themselves cast down to the level of *submen* by the very class whose dominance they must legitimize. In other words, if they establish humanity on the basis of bourgeois property, they exclude themselves from the society of men and define themselves—like the proletariat—as merely the means demanded by the growth of production. But if, on the contrary, they define man as knowledge, society—which exploits them without integrating them— is deficient; it must be denounced rather than justified. In this case, it is a *challenge*—the very opposite of something claiming to be an ideology—and it may always include the revelation of its true origin, which is the *putting-in-question* of the questioner as an ontological structure. This means that they cannot question the property owners' right to deny them the political dimension without posing the basic question of their right to serve this dehumanizing regime. Especially since it is in their capacity as the semirich that they demand the right to vote. And the objective reason for this demand, far from putting in question the humanism of the property owner, can only reinforce it. In sharp contrast to the haute bourgeoisie, who in 1789 demanded political power because they already had economic power and wanted to free commerce from niggling irrationalities, the enlightened elite of 1840, knowing full well that the State, as Tocqueville says, "has taken on the appearance of a company in which all operations are aimed at producing profits for its members," wants to take part in the national administration in order to share in the spoils. Since power is in the hands of the rich and serves only to enrich them further, it will easily enrich two hundred thousand additional Frenchmen.

The demand of the semirich is modest: let the property requirement for the vote be reduced by half. A *hundred* francs—this is a far cry from year I of the Republic. And this curious demand integrates knowledge with the plutocracy: in order to vote, you must be rich. Of course. And if you are *very* rich, it hardly matters if you know nothing. But if you are *very* knowledgeable, you will have permission to go to the ballot box *even if* you are only half as rich. In other words, the principle of authority remains major ownership, the practitioner admits it by his very claim: the property requirement, lowered but maintained, means that my knowledge is worth two hundred francs. Despite its declared optimism, Maxime's text is curious to reread on

210

this subject. In a way, the "modernism" he vaunts in his preface is the advent of that Prometheus, the practitioner: "We are the century . . . in which *one* has found applications for steam power, electricity, chloroform, the helix, photography, electroplating . . ." We will, of course, admire the highly discreet impersonality of that "one." Be that as it may, what is affirmed with pride, in *this* century, is the application of science to nature through the mediation of industry; one discovers laws, one obeys them so as later to be in a position to command. Thus the value of the era resides, according to the author, in the practitioner's transformation of the natural environment into *antiphysis,* using physics as a starting point. Yet not one name is cited, and no mention is made, even collectively, of that enlightened elite, the necessary mediators between nature and antinature. In his verse, by contrast, Maxime makes a quick sketch of future society. We learn that it is built on the basis of universal Peace; the "Syntony" of this chameleon has limits all the same, since he sustains the pacifistic dream of the Louis-Philippean bourgeoisie under the military dictatorship of Napoleon III. And, even more interestingly, the social order, despite the disappearance of wars and the growth of production, has remained the same: the employer is the *general.* We already glimpse the martial and Faustian image the manufacturer wants to have reflected back to him. As for the laborer, he remains a second-class citizen. Of the semiskilled worker, there is no question: the reconversion is accomplished by itself, and howitzers are turned into plows solely by the providential grace of Peace. This absence, moreover, hardly surprises us—the custom of the time is to *keep silent* about the producer. It is more surprising that no one mentions the technician. Where do the inventors of the railway, photography, and electricity come in? Is Ampère a soldier, like the peasant and the worker? Or a captain in the Royal Engineers? And if this branch of the army exists, who commands it? A manufacturer who is chief of staff? Uncertain of this, Maxime keeps quiet, something even easier for him as the bourgeoisie has abdicated its political power in exchange for a consolidated security, and the only authority it preserves—*apparently*—is economic order. Be that as it may, this silence betrays an embarrassment; in the France of 1850, the practitioner's place and social dignity remain uncertain. In fact, he has entered unwittingly, despite himself, into a direct struggle with the property owner, beginning in 1840 when he demanded a share of political responsibilities. For the enlightened elite, it was a matter of a simple arrangement by the regime. By lowering the property requirement for the vote by half, the number of electors was doubled: 400,000 in a nation of more than 30 million inhabitants. But the *rich* see things quite differently. They have no wish to multiply by two the number of *eaters* when the number of the *eaten* has hardly increased, especially since the claim of the *semirich* immediately extends to larger and larger segments of the middle class. Behind the scientists and practitioners there is the matter of the entire *national guard:* 80,000 men, many of whom are not even semirich; they have enough wealth, however, to provide their own equipment. They demand the vote because the elite, made up of their brothers and cousins, has asserted its claim, and they have no other means of justifying their demand than to show their discontent at being forever the governed, fed up with gnawing away at bones or gathering crumbs under the table and yearning to sit down with the others and share in the feast. That naked demand—even more legitimate than the professionals' if it could be radicalized, but, as it is, *pure appetite for gain* because of its incompleteness, arrested by their class-being—which is stirred up beneath them by the *semirich,* and which disturbs and sustains them, becomes internalized by them as the truth of their attitude. Their *quality as homo sapiens* is merely a varnish: through them the middle classes set themselves against the dominant classes, and their political claim scarcely dissimulates their violent desire to share in the spoils, to become integrated with the process of accumulation.

The third estate bursts asunder in the final years of the Orléanist monarchy; what a hundred years earlier seemed undifferentiated at its core is now divided and in conflict. The bourgeoisie always claims to be universal by vocation, for its enterprise is to impose its domination everywhere, in short, to make men and the earth bourgeois. But in the face of it, sustained by the lower strata of the middle class, the professionals claim to constitute the milieu *of* the universal because the concept and abstract judgment are their products, their means, and because legislation (judicial, scientific) with its practical applications remains their own possibility and their particular function. When faced with the dominant class, how could these legislative specialists fail to demand the right to become legislators?

In fact, despite the support of their class, they remain in a position of weakness. First of all, these universalists are handicapped even in the ideology they construct by their denial of universal suffrage. In effect, try as they might to legitimize their claim through their elaboration of knowledge, they will still become suspect in their own eyes by their almost unanimous determination to limit education—except for religious instruction—to the children of prosperous families. We see the vicious circle: the masses will not approach the ballot boxes, their lack of cultivation prohibits them from making a reasonable choice; the masses must remain in ignorance, for concrete knowledge would impel them to become conscious of their situation. But lacking the rigor of argumentation, of the objectivity and larger perspective which are the patrimony that has been gathered and transmitted by numerous generations of thinkers and researchers either linked to or born from the bourgeoisie, the masses will let themselves be led by bad shepherds to embrace narrow and primitive ideas, incapable of comprehending that the necessary misfortune of the disadvantaged classes is integrated and takes on its true meaning in a much larger and, despite everything, more harmonious social context.

To summarize: If the workers haven't the right to vote, it is because they are ignorant; if they are maintained in ignorance, it is because, being poor, they would make poor use of knowledge. In short, if the worker remains a passive citizen, it is because he is poor. The professionals' argument—despite the mediation of the terms by the concept of concrete knowledge—is in essence plutocratic. By accepting the property requirement for the vote, they eliminate a priori any possibility of demanding its reduction; strictly speaking, it must be abolished or maintained at the highest level. Democracy or plutocracy—there is no other alternative. By rejecting one, they decide in favor of the other, which excludes them. Consequently, their thought oscillates between two conceptions of man. The first, the Promethean one, defines the human being as the inventor of fire; in this case, the only humanism is that of knowledge; indeed, the professionals consider themselves—not without reason—the mainspring of the capitalist economy. They put their talents in the service of an expanding society, which demands their enlightenment even more imperiously from day to day, and which, should they disappear, would become instantly paralyzed. But at the same time, the irresistible *conatus* that impels them to claim the right to vote as compensation contains—as its implicit meaning—a very different humanism: an antique eudemonism, of vaguely Aristotelian resonance, situates the reality of man in his full flowering; he will accomplish his essence by balancing his desires and his powers. The sole source of this wisdom is the internalization of private property. When they try to avoid that contradiction they merely fall into another; these *practitioners*, on more than one occasion, sense—rather than understand—the practical essence of all knowledge; for this reason they are filled with pride at

213

being indispensable to society. At the same time, however, the old quietist conception remains, which accords nobility only to contemplative knowledge—therefore without discernible relation to utility—and condemns *applied* knowledge, that is, technique, as vulgar. So the hero of our time would seem to be the poor and obscure scientist, pursuing his research with no other motive than his inextinguishable love of truth. Before 2 December, theory outweighs its applications. Well before the medieval intellectual—who contemplates the divine work through love of the personal God who created it—it is Socrates who serves as a model. Having already drunk the hemlock, he inquires: Can someone teach him the newly discovered proof of such or such a theorem? And when his astonished disciples ask him, "But you are about to die, Socrates—why do you want to know what they have discovered?" he answers: "In order to know." This admirable line is ambiguous; at the time, it was an unambiguous affirmation of *life*, for to live—even in one's final moments, if one's mind still functions—is not to meditate on death but to continue one's *own* life. A condemned potter wants to finish the work in progress; two lovers want to spend their last night making love. And even if we recall that Plato, a man of his times, defines true life by the exercise of the dialectic and intellection, it nonetheless remains that death is denied by the eternity of the true; and this idea which is false only because it was arrested and taken for the final term when it could be only an initial term—long represented (in fact until the end of the ancient world) considerable progress in the Objective Spirit: it humanized knowledge. It must be linked, moreover, to that democratization of reason which Socrates extends *even to the slave*. Man, singular and mortal, even in a servile condition, can become what he is at any moment, so that eternity changes him into himself *during his lifetime*—and not in death but against it—by the human appropriation of an absolute which seemed, in its universality, indifferent to our species. Of course, we must die in the body and shed our human particularities. Nonetheless, as a good dialectician, Plato gives us back what he had taken from us: in Socrates, intuition of the universal saves singularity. Or, if you will, thanks to the Platonic dialogues, Socrates enters into philosophic thought as its first *singular universal*. Starting here, a long movement could have begun, leading to *acquired* truth, to existence, to the historicity of the transhistoric, to history. That movement did not occur. As a result, those profound words of Socrates were understood in reverse; in the nineteenth century, he was made to say just the opposite: man, an ephemeral creature, has only a relative being, he represents the earthly means of knowledge. His death hardly matters, if through him and against him that knowledge actualizes and suppresses itself as intersubjective temporalization to the profit of impersonal Knowledge, of a practico-inert determination of the Objective Spirit. From this point of view, to know something concretely is to die. The Christian tradition, preserved despite lost faith, is at the source of this transformation of Platonism; it served the *capacités'* resentment of the rich. The enlightened elite proclaim that everyone pursues his self-interest—the utilitarianism of the dominant class—and, at the same time, that man's sole greatness is to realize his radical surrender to knowledge in all disinterestedness. In this perspective, which situates our merit in what will be called our "openness to being," the humanism of the *capacités* conceals a deep-seated pessimism, a declared misanthropy. If man is made only to manifest knowledge through his own immediate or long anticipated abolition, that is, *if he is made for Knowledge* rather than Knowledge for him, his only value resides in lucid consciousness of his relativity, and in the practical consequences he draws from it in religious terms, in his sacrifice, not to other men, who have no right to it, being made of the same stuff, but to truth conceived as something inhuman. In short, this rancorous elite, in the person of its members, defines man by his subjection to fetishized Knowledge, and so presents the human race with that raw subjection as a godless religion. Science is sacred; the scientist is its minister and martyr; the vulgar—property owners or not—have no other justification than to produce the props required by the cult and to support its priests. In this curious humanism, our race has in itself neither substance nor purpose (man, whether taken as a group or alone, can in no way be an end for man); it affirms its reality only by manifesting itself in its deepest being, which is a matter not of putting the self in question but of systematic self-destruction; it may well seem fitting that it annihilates itself willingly so that being, through its fugitive mediation, could replicate itself in a crude world, an invisible and ever mute referent, and in an immediately readable text that is never read. A paradoxical situation; according to their pride, their insistent hope, or their rancorous frustration, the *capacités* serve the property owner and through him the whole society; thanks to them, the Word and the Act pass into each other and through this indivisibility establish their right to share the power. Or else they don't serve anyone and never have done, certainly not themselves; what places them above the rest is their *disinterestedness*. Because of that, in the midst of

215

the vile multitude, their total abnegation, their self-forgetting, their sustained effort to sacrifice man to the inhuman—to hypostasized knowledge—within themselves and outside them should be enough to earn them a portion of the authority possessed by the property owners without any spoken or unspoken demand on their part. This is a difficult position and hardly a convincing one: give us power because we don't demand it. They are putting their self-interest in disinterestedness. We see the vicious circle: now man is the measure of all things, he is created to humanize the universe; in this case, the technician, who is measure and measurer, must share power with the conqueror; but he must be content with a secondary post—science is merely the means of production. And now the rejected elite, in its rage, makes the scientist the prototype of man and pure science the only properly human activity to the extent that all inductive and deductive work must be suppressed to the profit of a calm, inert knowledge always external to those who produce it or learn it. In this case, power should revert wholly to men of science; but by the same token authority finds itself disqualified, for they were exercising that power on a race they scorn and hardly recognize as their own, a race they condemn to permanent subjection in the name of sacrifices that they themselves freely made. In any event, and whatever the basis of their claim, the answer of the dominant class is always negative. It has no trouble catching them in their own trap: "Since human greatness manifests itself only through your abdication, to remain equal to yourselves and worthy of our admiration you must pursue your secular priesthood, which is well paid, incidentally, and not demand anything more."

Rejected, incapable of understanding that the scientist's bond to science simply expresses the bond of science to capital, the professionals return to their point of departure: as semirich, isn't it their goods that establish their humanism? Doesn't the relation of the possessor to the thing possessed give him—through slow infiltrations, through osmosis, through cementing—exquisite qualities, an unequaled sensitivity, formidable power, the internalization of great natural forces as they offer themselves to him filtered through his property? When Belaval wrote, "It is not man that is profound, it is the world," his maxim, which was quite apt, could serve as a principle for the property owner's humanism: by appropriation, an act that annexes the world to him, the property owner annexes the world's profundity, which becomes human. The property owner will therefore be the man through whom profundity comes to that flat race, humanity. From this point of view, the semirich, while less pro-vided for, would be as profound as the fully rich since profundity is attained by man's assimilation of the thing possessed.

Unfortunately, the question is no sooner posed than it is disquali-fied by the answer: it is land that is reputed to confer these eminent virtues—that very property, moreover, which the *capacités* acquire in bits and pieces, preferring earth to shapes. As a result, the *other* domi-nant class is justified; they levy judgment through their mouths on the bankers and manufacturers *on whom they live,* and condemn them in the name of a constant communication with nature—through the boundless continuation of proprioceptive synthesis—with the indi-visible unity of the divine creation. For the man of divine right, the aristocrat, the act of appropriation is the human correlative of the creative act of the Almighty. As we may well imagine, it is not only the wealthy bourgeois who are relegated to the status of commoners by this Christian humanism; it is also, and perhaps *especially,* their accomplices, the *capacités,* whose penetrating analyses destroyed the just privileges of the nobility and deprived Catholicism of its faith. By replacing as the basis of humanism the Faustian man of profit with the patriarchy of landed wealth, the enlightened elite condemned itself. The final turn of the screw shows us a new opposition: the practitioners, those specialists of the universal and of mechanistic materialism, are led by the very nature of their investments to redis-cover the organicist thought of feudalism and the Christian image of man it suggests. This *other* humanism, dated but still virulent, deeply contradicts the humanism they must seek to construct, since their system of thought—as well as the practico-inert imperative they have internalized in the form of an anonymous mandate—compels them to elaborate the ideology of the bourgeoisie. Even so, they are held to their practice of converting their share of the profit into private in-come just when the aristocracy begins to become seriously interested in joint stock companies.

As a result, analytic reason, so clear and distinct when it mani-fested itself—class against class—in the prerevolutionary period as the simple exercise of negativity, loses its bearings and its bite. In the final analysis, whether the emphasis is on his wisdom as a respectable family man or on his will to Faustian power, man under Louis-Philippe remains the bourgeois property owner. But humanist ide-ology is in the air; the elite did not know how to anchor it on solid foundations. So the *capacités* are uneasy: they see *themselves*—or rather they glimpse, they divine themselves, vague silhouettes—as nests of contradictions. Hence they discover their employers, barely, but still more than they would like. They discover that they are both accomplices and adversaries of the wealthy bourgeoisie, judging it and judging themselves through the eyes of the nobility; and judging these through bourgeois eyes, the eyes of their vanquishers; condemning the universality of capitalist domination in the name of the universality of knowledge, without which that domination would not take place; countering the *self-interest* of the rich with the guarantee of their political wisdom, the *disinterestedness* that establishes their own right to enrich themselves and to govern. Disturbed, however, by a vague awareness that their disinterestedness is interested, haunted in the very depths of their analyses by the phantom of totality—"a false dwelling instantly dissolved in mist"—that is none other than the rather unconvincing creation that effort manages to destroy, they grasp *through its results* another totalitarian and detotalizing process, the "trial [*procès*] of capital," the enemy force that may well ruin the entire society. But they are incapable of comprehending the synthetic development of these inhuman forces, both because they have attributed to them the human essence of man, posed as a property owner, and because their methods of thought, the necessities of practical knowledge, as well as their place in society compel them to exalt only analytic reason, a powerful instrument for knowing everything *exterior* but a radical solvent and murderer of syntheses which, where they might have seen true social beings, shows them only an infinite molecular dispersal. So they sink, despite bourgeois euphoria and no doubt because of it, into a pessimism that dares not speak its name and whose origin is, in short, the finally conquered autonomy of concrete knowledge (or, if you will, science positing itself as such), insofar as that autonomy defines the *function* of the scientist and technician but leaves their social *position* undetermined. What a problem! By keeping them at a distance, the bourgeois allows them to take their distance in relation to him, but this social character cannot in any case appear to them *objectively;* indeed, they are doubly in solidarity with his class, since they live on surplus value, therefore indirectly on exploitation, and their basic *conatus* pushes them to appropriate for themselves the goods of this world by using the techniques of knowledge. In other words, rediscovering in the bourgeois, as his realized interiority, the property that remains in them an inert lacuna, their potential interiority, they see him without seeing him and cannot judge him.

This situation, however paradoxical it may seem, contains in those very contradictions and the vicious circles they generate the germ of that ideology needed by both the bourgeoisie and the elite, namely capitalist humanism at the stage of accumulation. In the eighteenth century, the universality of humanism was established on its negativity since its primary function was the systematic destruction of any right that did not flow directly from human nature. Capitalist humanism must be primarily positive; no longer must the aristocracy be denied as an inhuman dream, but the humanity of bourgeois society must be affirmed. But couldn't this new ideology finds its unity in a radical and secret negation that would preserve the aggressive thrust of analysis by directing it against a new enemy? The professionals are suddenly going to discover the underlying identity of capitalist self-interest and their own disinterestedness. Certainly not in the fact—which they sense and want to conceal from themselves—that their disinterestedness is merely the form self-interest takes in them. But quite the contrary, in the fact that the bourgeois's real relation to his interest is the prototype and basis of all disinterestedness—somethng that must be taught to the working classes. But this fruitful revelation cannot be made to them in 1840; nor in the final years of the regime. After the massacre in rue Transnonain and the repressive laws against the press (1835), republicanism seems crushed; utopian socialism doesn't intimidate anyone—these are daydreams. The new barbarians, unsure of themselves, desire a collaboration of labor and capital. The dominant and middle classes are peaceful; prosperity, security—what more could they want? The general optimism does not allow the establishment of a *pessimistic* humanism, which is the only kind suitable to this society. For it to have some basis, there must be a catastrophe that tears away the veil of happiness and displays naked reality; fear must replace calm, and a terrible common threat must convince the rich and the elite that behind their differences they share a fundamental solidarity. Indeed, a combination of unpardonable mistakes and bad luck is needed to provoke the mystified practitioners' disgust with themselves and hatred of others. The requisite conditions will converge in February 1848.

Between 1846 and 1848, the difficulties begin. Scarcity in Europe: the potato is ailing everywhere. In France, bad weather aggravates the crisis. Hence, inadequate consumption; production is then reduced in key sectors (oil, cotton, metallurgy)—which has the effect of dangerously increasing unemployment. The working class is discontent. The bourgeoisie, irritated by a financial crisis that leads the bank to restrict credit, detaches itself if not from the old king at least from Guizot, who is the banker's man. Under these conditions— disconcerting, unforeseen, unforeseeable (the less serious crisis of 1837–39 had long been forgotten)—the middle classes, headed by the *capacités*, choose to begin their agitation. They hold forth at banquets: the cause of every trouble is the property requirement for the vote, which is too high. Let it be lowered by half, and the enlightened elite will take part in the business of the state; it will bring to the political arena its rigorous methods, its scruples, its precision, its rigor. No one wants the Republic—save some secret societies; the general wish is that Guizot should get out and that the regime, with a few adjustments, should endure as long as possible. We know what happened: just when the banquet campaign was drawing to a close—without the sightest result—the government made the mistake of prohibiting one of the final gatherings. Protests. In *Le National*, Marrast summoned to the Place de la Madeleine all citizens who are friends of liberty. He was summoning the people to a political demonstration. The people came, but their demonstration was social. The workers who overthrew Louis-Philippe hardly had in mind sending a new batch of rich men to the Chamber of Deputies. And while they supported the petty bourgeois republicans who fraternized with them in secret societies, universal suffrage mattered less to them than the *organization of labor*. In other words, they demanded the one in order to obtain the other. Weary of chronic unemployment, crises that cast them into the street with their families by the tens of thousands, of the implacable reduction of their wages due to excessively rapid mechanization (beginning in 1846, investments in industry were overabundant, which aggravated the crisis) and the carefully maintained surplus of manpower, they were ready to seize power and give it to whoever wanted it, provided the workers were given the right to their fundamental claim and the *right to work* was acknowledged in the new constitution. "Right to work!" declares a notice signed by Sobrier, "An obligation for the public power to provide work and, when needed, a minimum [wage] to all members of the Society not employed by private industry." The provisional government grudgingly concedes; in its decree, the right to work is not mentioned: it "is committed to guarantee the existence of the worker through work. It is committed to guarantee work to all citizens."

Respectable folk lived in terror. The Revolution, says Tocqueville, is "exclusively popular," it gives "absolute power . . . to the classes that work with their hands." He describes "the gloomy despair of the bourgeoisie thus oppressed," and he adds, with a naïveté that takes us by surprise: "It was an extraordinary and painful thing to see all that vast city, full of such wealth, in the hands of those who possessed nothing." They went to sleep the evening before, quite secure, and woke up "suspended over an abyss." We know what follows: the sabotage of the National Workshops—conceived by Louis Blanc as a first attempt to reabsorb unemployment and which became, in fact, a military organization—then their closure by decision of the Constitutional Assembly. The insurrection that was its inevitable consequence—foreseen by all the politicians and desired by some so they could put an end to it—was crushed in two days by Cavaignac. Four thousand dead on the side of the "reds"; twenty-five thousand arrested, fifteen hundred detained.

Among the rich and the semirich, fear is still rampant for all that. They distrust Cavaignac, replaced on 10 December by Louis-Napoleon Bonaparte, the prince-president. He was elected by bankers and industrialists; his coup d'état consecrates the definitive victory of the bourgeoisie over a sickened working class and over the great independent landowners who opposed the development of credit and public works. This battle, won on two fronts, does not reassure property owners; its effect, rather, is to consolidate their fear and hatred, which are transformed into that chronic malady, pessimism. The dominant class, in effect, feels mutilated; it sacrificed its political rights (of which it was so jealous that it refused to share them, thus initiating the February days), and made a gift of them to a military dictator who guaranteed their economic security in exchange. They will grow rich, that's certain, and since—after Saint-Simon—they know that the economy determines politics, they remain *dominant*. But they lose their title of *ruling* class since power escapes them and others govern in their place; in their interest, of course, but not in their name. Political life disappears, or rather takes refuge among the military; if man is still that *zoon politikon* we spoke of, the result of this abandonment will be, paradoxically, to send the rich to swell the ranks of the submen. In fact, they are *protected;* that is what they want, but their depoliticization can be experienced only as an emasculation. Curiously, the beaten aristocrats take their revenge: the bourgeois yield to a nobility of the sword—constituted, moreover, in great part by the sons of the former nobility. The vaguely antimilitarist pacifism evinced earlier by the rich yields to a masochistic cult of the uniform, which they exaggerate in order to mask their humiliation at having been castrated. *In appearance*, the Ancien Régime is restored:

the Third Estate is confined to its economic function, power is in the hands of a military aristocracy.

This is not true, of course; times have changed since 1789. There is no doubt, on the other hand, that Boissy d'Anglas was mistaken: a country cannot maintain social order when it is governed by property owners; social order requires that "the most sacred of interests, property" be guaranteed by force. This discovery explodes the optimism of the rich. Under Louis-Philippe, it seemed to them that a providential harmony allowed them to serve the general interest by pursuing their particular interests; this was an illusion, since the maintenance of order requires a repressive apparatus, or *continuous repression*. For the military dictatorship is nothing else: when blood ran and hatred was sown, it was either withdrawal or readiness to begin again each day; born of the June massacres, the imperial army is merely the perpetuation of the massacres within the country's borders. Certainly its bark is worse than its bite, but this show of force has only one purpose: to remind the poor of the repression of the summer of '48, and to make that past, if the troubles should be reborn, their inevitable future. The bourgeoisie did not have the strength to endure the hatred it had deliberately aroused, it hid behind the soldiers. But it knew quite well that the days of June made the institutionalization of force necessary. As Proudhon said, the *"secret"* was out: bourgeois society is built on the poverty of the working class; it needs that poverty, for, after all, it claims it cannot exist if the worker is granted the right to work. The Legislature demonstrated this tenet by suppressing the right to work, *which made the worker a man*, and by replacing it with the "freedom" of work, which transforms the worker into merchandise, forcing him to sell his manpower—himself—and to subordinate, in his person, human transcendence to malleable matter. The curtain is torn away: it is not "misunderstanding" that separates the classes, as Lamartine claimed, it is civil war, since the dominant class, at this stage of accumulation, can increase its capital only by compelling the worker to become dehumanized so that raw material can become something human. This would be negligible if the body of employers had perceived, alone and directly, that *its* society was built upon discord. One doesn't say such things; therefore, they are not said. In 1840, the bourgeoisie glossed over the matter of the worker; people calmly spoke of "working-class and poor neighborhoods" as if it was obvious that poverty was the lot of the manual worker. In short, the bourgeois forgot the worker because he seemed to have forgotten himself. It was still possible for the bourgeoisie to regard itself as the universal class.

After June 1848, the bourgeois felt *seen;* this time the workers exposed the paternalism of family capitalism; instead of regarding their relations to the boss in the singularity of the enterprise as relations within a family, they discovered the body of employers *in its generality as a class* during the conflict over the right to work. Of course, it would take them a long time to discover the real process of exploitation, but they felt it deeply nonetheless; they demanded to be no longer treated as merchandise, and they learned, dazed and full of hatred, that this demand was incompatible with the social order of a country governed by property owners, that the dominant class could not affirm itself without requiring them to respect their status as submen, and would drive them back to it with massacres every time they raised their heads. The factory demands the limiting of costs, technological unemployment, low wages; this is in the manufacturer's interest. And at the time, the working class is characterized by that *same limiting of costs* insofar as it endures that limitation as an external necessity even as it discovers its human intention. Destiny means to be subject to *another's will,* as to a natural catastrophe. By grasping the employers' general interest, which is to maintain the competitive structure of the economy and accumulate capital through it and through the work of the worker-merchandise, the worker of 1848 suddenly understands a blinding truth: his vague dream of a *federation* of capital and labor hasn't the slightest chance of being realized; the *self-interest* of the bourgeois class is the *destiny* of the proletariat.

The body of employers also discovers its unity, long masked by competitive antagonisms, but discovers it *through the eyes of others;* stripped of its universality, of the paternalism that gave it a good conscience, it feels constituted as a particular class *by the hatred of others.* By the hatred of others and also by what it has done. It has committed an irreversible act: it has killed. The memory of that ferocity would soon be lost if it had not become an unforgettable recollection *for others,* and had not thereby constituted the employers through their history as *other* than they feel themselves to be, other than they want to feel they are. Their false consciousness of themselves must vanish or be transformed, and it must integrate this butchery. Their ideological justification can never be constructed unless they assume and internalize this image they have given of themselves, reflected back to them by others, in order to dissolve and surpass it by preserving it in the service of a new legitimation. But their internalization of the hatred of others can be developed, to begin with, only in the form of a double hatred: one dedicated to themselves, as a subjectivization of objective hatred, and one they turn against those who hate them, a *counterhatred*. And so, curiously, this unbeliever, deprived of a divine cover, can be justified only by the valorization of man; but in 1850 the basis of his humanism can be only the most radical misanthropy. Since the dominant ideology is that of the dominant class, the ideology he demands will be fully effective only if it penetrates the exploited classes and leads the worker, fooled by this false humanism, to turn his abhorrence of the bourgeois against himself. In other words, this play of reflections will serve if the proletariat, denouncing itself along with its employer, is led to condemn not the bourgeois as such but human nature—its own and that of the bourgeoisie. And that cannot suffice; we would return to the abhorrent formulation *homo homini lupus* if we were to pursue this further—justification enough for any riot. The *positive* role of the new humanism must be to define man as a being whose greatness resides in sacrifice. The ethical basis of the ideology will be self-hatred conceived as the source of human enterprise.

The bourgeoisie does not, of course, have the intellectual means to elaborate that ideology. It is engendered by the facts themselves, or else by structures clarified by history, by a carnage illuminating class relations. But it appears at first only in the form of exigency. Yet the dominant class, which cannot produce it as an idea, manifests it as the underlying meaning of its exis; I use this word to designate the set of daily practices engendered by its situation and enterprise, and which give it, before any verbal explanation, a certain image of itself that is experienced rather than represented. This exis, beginning in 1850, can be summed up in one word: *distinction*. Monsieur Prudhomme is not distinguished: he is a grocer, the eternal victim of romantic jibes. Under Napoleon III, his sons or grandsons, big manufacturers, claim to have become distinguished, meaning that they incorporate a hatred of life, of lived experience, of vital functions and natural needs directly into their way of life. I shall recall briefly the genesis and practical meaning of this *habitus*, having described it elsewhere.

On the level of economic infrastructure, distinction is *already produced* as a practical imperative of the capitalist in the phase of accumulating capital; competition imposes abstinence on the bourgeois; he stints on needs and puts more into investments. Thus, the share of profit dedicated to concrete, organic life is conceived from the first

224

as his *cursed share:* puritanism and distinction have the same bourgeois origin—as Victorian *cant,* around the same time, rather strikingly indicates. However, beginning with Joseph Prudhomme, the normative character of these budgetary choices is masked by their manifestly utilitarian aspect. Utilitarianism, that morality which poses as an art of living, dissimulates the categorical imperative and its true meaning behind that strange object—half external, half internal—called interest. When it is declared that "every man pursues his interest," that interest is presented at once as an objective reality and as a subjective, though universal, *conatus.* In short, the property owner is pulled, pushed, carried, if you will, toward that external being, *his* objective determination; but before 1850 he rarely sees it as an imperious and empty expectation, a *duty* more than an impulse. He doesn't see it this way because he is not shown it through words, but there is no doubt that this is how he experiences it. He already looks to it, in some obscure way, for his justification: property is *sacred* only because it gives man the right to do his duty, which is the celebration of the humanist cult through human sacrifice. Beginning in June 1848, and increasingly in the years that follow, the bourgeois, throwing off his utilitarian disguise, wants to see himself and make himself seen in his double role of sacrificer and sacrificed. The dominant class being exposed, these ostentatious practices are meant to legitimize its power. It does not invent them, since they have their source in the mode and relations of production and are, on this level, intentional—that is, invested with meaning. (I have shown above that thought is born as a moment of praxis at the level of work, and that it grasps the world through the tool, in other words, that the mode of production is an immediate and fundamental structure of perception.) The invention is *to make a show of it.* Shall we say that this involved transforming it into a *gesture?* Not at all, since distinction, an obsession at this period, pushed the bourgeoisie to obstinate constipation, to frigidity. You had to act publicly, as if playing a role, what you really were. Sometimes you cheated—eating in secret before dying of starvation at the costly abundance of a formal dinner; but most of the time you only emphasized the economic conduct imposed by social structures. The bourgeois *represented* himself—to other bourgeois and to all classes—as the *heautontimoroumenos,* by living and making visible the rigorous imperatives of production as the a priori norms of an antinaturalist ethic. On this level, as well, distinction had two meanings: one negative, since it was antinature by the systematic denial of the *organic;* the other positive, since the bourgeois

225

was proud to produce *antiphysis* in his factory. We know what this meant at the time: it was a question not of escaping physical laws but, quite the contrary, of knowing and obeying them to create, as a function of those laws, objects—such as steel—that nature had never realized. The *distinguished* property owner produces himself as a real determination of antiphysis to the same extent that he escapes animality by strangling his needs. *Noblesse oblige:* the creator of antinature must demonstrate that he is its master, and that it obeys him within him as well as outside him. Thus is established the strict homogeneity of the manufacturers, free products of artifice, and the machined products they manufacture. But despite this glorious affirmation, the accent in distinguished practices is still on radical negation. First, because the economic maneuvers at their source are fundamentally negative; second, because the actual targeted public—the working classes—will be convinced to deny its needs only if the dominant class begins by denying itself.

Under the Ancien Régime the aristocrat, noble by blood and divine right, commands because nature made him superior. Nature, creation—it's all the same. So he is a naturalist. His needs are sacred because they are natural, because they manifest his nature; he guzzles, defecates in public, makes love as he can. More profoundly, as we have seen, this noble nature was experienced as the exercise of generosity, of the gift of self—not to things but to man. Or, more precisely, to certain men: it was the fidelity of the vassal to the lord, of the gentleman to the king, more, perhaps, even than to the monarchic principle, whose singular incarnation is still the king. These relations are concrete and personal, between concrete persons made in His image by a personal and concrete God. Their plenitude, moreover, dissimulates death; the gift of the self is military—a matter of dying for one's king. This potential death, always present, justifies privileges: born to destroy by being destroyed, the good lord, in the time of kings, designates himself a natural chef and pure consumer. And here comes a new nobility, the imperial Army, newly created in the middle of the bourgeois century, which establishes its right to govern France and to consume without producing on the solemn vow to die in order to kill. The bourgeoisie, terrified of the proletariat, its product, surrenders its political rights to that army; it is no longer the ruling class.

But if it wants to remain the dominant class, it must establish its rights to domination. This isn't easy; the truth is that it exercises a de facto power which can, it seems, become legitimate only *provisionally,* since it is denounced at once by the arrogance of the new masters—never have officers so scorned men in "civvies"—and by its own universalism. For the legitimists, the bourgeois are domestics; having tied up their masters, they sleep in their sheets, eat at their table. Are they any the less domestics as a result? For the Bonapartists, the bourgeois is merely a woman, since he doesn't fight.[27] Monsieur Poirier, the hero of the play produced by Emile Augier in 1854, represents a bourgeoisie that is already somewhat dated. This contemporary of Louis-Philippe rejects military violence on principle, and in particular the duel, that mini-war, which is not really *serious*. The serious business of life is the rejection of useless death as the extreme term of generosity, and, more profoundly, the rejection of generosity itself in all its forms. But for that very reason he internalizes the scorn of the nobility: when he weeps at military parades, he implicitly acknowledges the existence of a right to command, sinister and sacred, that challenges his de facto power, his economic domination; in short, he condemns it himself. It is a trap: if he surrenders to his *nature*, as he is adroitly invited to do, that domination will never be legitimate.

If, as a defensive maneuver, his domination calls upon his former humanism, it will play into the hands of the lower classes, who will challenge it in their turn. If, as this system of domination claims, class is dissolved into individual molecules, each of which is equally possessed of human nature, how could the right to vote be limited by the property requirement? The property owner is attacked on two fronts: indeed, the sole power that could legitimately be opposed to the military caste is that of the whole nation. The response of the rich will be revealed *in their practice;* since their nature condemns them to obey the lords of war or retire from their powers to the profit of democratic universality, they will justify their class domination by the systematic negation of that nature. The primary objective of this destructive and ostentatious practice is to counter the funereal generosity of the soldier, the basis of his right to command, with a no less funereal and *sacrificial* asceticism that is antithetical to the free gift of oneself. Gen-

27. In fact, all military laws between 1818 and 1868 allowed proxy conscripts, that is, the "replacement of the rich by the poor," as Rossel noted in 1869. The property owner exempts himself from serving and hence from risking his neck. One is a civilian institutionally. Thus, the relation of the bourgeois to military death is institutionally excluded. This results, moreover, in a reinforcement of the military dictatorship, since proxy conscripts created an army of mercenaries in the hands of noble or ennobled officers. So the institutions produced by the bourgeoisie produce it in its turn in the eyes of the masters of the day as a purely economic class, whose function is to manage and increase the national fortune.

erosity loves itself, it loves giving still more than it loves what it gives; sacrifice, born of hatred, hates itself as much as it hates what it sacrifices and the cost of that sacrifice. Faced with the soldier who offers his life, the bourgeois valorizes himself by the ostentatious sacrifice of his nature; in both cases, man exercises domination over his life. Only the officer, having given his once and for all, allows himself to live as well as he can and to satisfy all his desires while awaiting death. The bourgeois, judging violent death to be *unprofitable* and therefore *not serious,* makes his sacrifice a petty suicide: persecuting his needs, he lives in order to reject life as long as he can.

The other objective of this practice is to convince the lower classes; this is the *other* front, much more important than the first. Since all men are equal by right, power cannot be held exclusively by any social group as such. And since disorder would result from the exercise of power by all individuals, it therefore reverts by right to those among them who *distinguish themselves* from others. Since everyone has *nature,* organic life and needs, in common, the distinguishing factor can be only the denial of those common servitudes; if one were initially distinguished by talent, power would revert by right to the middle classes. Of course, an engineer leaving the Polytechnic is now a "distinguished subject," but in this case it is the dominant class that distinguishes him and so recruits him as an instrument of production. But the rich themselves—when they are bourgeois—can be distinguished only by *antiphysis:* living minimally, hiding one's body and persecuting it, frustrating its appetites, accepting neither its vulgar joys nor its exuberant fecundity; distinction produces and justifies Malthusian practices, which are increasingly—but still secretly —widespread among the bourgeoisie. It affirms itself as the hatred of all that is organic in the name of the inorganic purity of wrought materiality; its supreme and advertised, if unattainable, objective would be to give the bosses the cleanliness of the human thing. We shall soon return to this. In any case, on this ground, the denunciation of life as *vulgarity* is aimed expressly at the disadvantaged classes. It is a feature common to many ideological justifications to designate the effect as the cause: the excesses of colonial exploitation have the effect of imposing subhumanity on the colonized; that subhumanity, presented as a primary given justifying the colonial system, creates *racism,* the ideology of colonialism. In 1850, the bourgeois is so far from understanding this system that he does not know how to utilize newly conquered Algeria and sees it as a penal colony, a land of deportation rather than a market for his products and capital. He does not confront the workers with *racism*—which presupposes that the sub-humanity of the exploited is irremediable—but with that attenuated form, *distinction*, which considers subhumanity ("get rich by saving") *provisional*. Of course, one can rise above it, it's just a necessary stage; we, the rich, have all been there, if not personally then by way of our parents or grandparents. But the principle is the same: industrialization produced the proletariat and—until industrial expansion revalorizes manpower and raises wages[28]—constituted it *at the same time* the class of labor and the class of need. (Indigence produces work, otherwise why kill yourself on the job? And work produces indigence—by the competitive antagonisms created by an always limited number of jobs, or by the technological unemployment caused by the adoption of a machine, of work crystallized from other downtrodden wretches.) The proletarian, kept in unbelievable poverty at this time, lives in utter insecurity even if he finds a job, since labor is contracted most often on a daily basis and does not even guarantee the next day's work; hence his only obsession is the gratification of his needs. Thus, the entire economy rests on the fact that the worker, in his quotidian reality, is manifest as *the man of need*, he who works only to satisfy his gross appetites from day to day. Furthermore, this wretch shocks delicate sensibilities by his alarming fertility; the son of peasants or uprooted peasants, he has retained his forefathers' rural habits and regrettable lack of foresight even in suburban concentrations. In short, he manifests, at the gates of the city, a birthrate so grossly *natural* that, in conjunction with incessant need, it provides the rich with the nauseating spectacle of human animality, of their own animality. *Distinction*, deliberately taking the effect for the cause, justifies the inferior condition meted out to those unfortunates by the very fact that they have no notion of rising above the animal condition. When you realize, moreover, that most of them are illiterate and consequently good only for the unskilled labor they are ordered to perform, you come up against this sad truth: it is the proletariat that has created exploitation as its sole means of survival, and it is not, of course, exploitation that has created the proletariat. The fact is, in the face of the bourgeois and the professionals, men of *culture*, the proletariat represents *pure nature*. Not *human nature* but animal nature in its pure inhumanity. To be sure, distinction *says* nothing of this: it is not an idea but a practice; yet its meaning is to construct *culture* as the pure

---

28. This resurgence begins in the first years of the Empire, but it will be especially perceptible under the Third Republic.

negation of *nature*. For the bourgeoisie cannot take advantage of a positive culture because such a culture is produced, in capitalist society, by men of science, practitioners and artists, in short, by the enlightened elite; thus for the bourgeois, culture—as the legitimation of his powers—is like an ostentatious denial of human animality, that is, of life in all its forms. But to the extent that the worker is making demands at this time according to his needs and to those alone, and those demands are brutally flung in the face of the employers, what the dominant class detests and oppresses *in itself* is the proletariat, or more precisely their shared animality, which might authorize the demand for higher wages or that "federation of classes" which horrifies the rich. So the *man of distinction*—as we read even today on advertising posters in the United States—oppresses the worker in himself as universal animality, because he exploits him outside himself as the producer of goods. It is the worker he hates in himself when, ill treating his own body by his dress, by the punishment his clothing inflicts on him, by the abject ugliness of his stiff collars, by the disgust aroused in him by his own needs and the repressive practices he exerts against them, he displays that exemplary self-hatred which must serve as the basis for the new humanism. The silent abhorrence directed at him by the proletariat after the June massacres, and perpetuated by the dictatorship as a chronic evil of French society, can be internalized by the bourgeois only as self-hatred; but he uses his distinguished manners to turn this hatred back upon the worker by combating in himself the grosser instincts of the populace. He is disgusted with himself for being hungry, thirsty, sleepy, needing to urinate, etc. And he tries by his example to impose a negative cultural ethic upon the working masses; he seeks to arouse in them a vain aspiration to distinction as the essence of man, a disgust with their own needs that should make them ashamed and restrain their demands.

Such is the meaning of this practice, which aimed at legitimizing the economic domination of the bourgeoisie even as it was being stripped of its political powers. As a class behavior this defensive reaction constitutes the basis of a new ideology. At the same time it *requires* that ideology as its explanation through discourse and as its integration into a system of the world, a set of values. The bourgeois doesn't have the intellectual tools to become the theorist of his practice. In 1850, therefore, we find him in the same situation as in 1840: theoretical work can be undertaken only by the *capacités*. With a single but crucial difference: despite antagonisms, all elements are present to ensure his success. In other words, the bourgeoisie and the enlightened elite find a common ground in negation.

The unfortunate elite has been mistreated by the events of 1848. They are still in a daze and feel doubly mystified. What first dumbfounded them was to have been instrumental in a social upheaval they didn't want. It's true, they are somewhat responsible for the February days of unrest—didn't they demoralize the middle classes with the banquet campaign? And, again, didn't a banquet occasion the gathering in front of the Madeleine, for which Marrast gave instructions, and which was the beginning of the disorder? No doubt subversive elements took this occasion to foment the riot—there were demonstrations and barricades from the first day. But the national guard—80,000 men, the great majority middle-class—failed to do their duty: instead of launching a vigorous intervention, they stood by, doing nothing; worse, they often interposed themselves between the soldiers and the rioters. It wasn't that they shared the guilty intentions of the populace, but they refused to defend a minister who was obstinate in prohibiting their access to the ballot box. What did they want? The fall of Guizot and "reform": two hundred thousand additional voters. A hundred thousand Parisian mouths were heard crying "Reform," and not one voice was raised in favor of the Republic. On 23 February Guizot was recalled, and the triumphant national guard fell into each other's arms—what proud accolades! But these respectable folk did not know that subversion was taking its course in the neighborhoods of the populace, and that the barricades "were being mounted by new defenders." These new defenders did not intend the monumental Parisian insurrection to produce merely a change of ministers. The groundwork was laid for sparking a revolution. The leaders—let us say, the members of secret societies and surely some unknown leaders risen from the masses—were naturally responsible for the "bad mood" of the populace; but the real guilty parties were in fact the *national guard,* who—like their grandfathers in 1789—did not realize that an insurrection cannot be stopped when it is becoming radicalized, and that it is better to stifle it in embryo. They used the masses to intimidate Louis-Philippe; they got what they wanted and preached a return to order. Too late; the masses were now using them. At eleven o'clock there is the slaughter at Capucines; here again the national guard plays a suspect role as one of its lieutenants, Schumacher, involuntarily gives the signal for the massacre by parlaying with an intransigent colonel. From that moment, the chips are down: the streets are winning, the New Barbarians are the masters of Paris. From the enlightened elite to the republican petty bourgeoisie, everyone can cry, like Kaiser Wilhelm during the First World War: "That isn't what I wanted!" The semirich were not for the Republic; but they have it. The Republicans were not for communism: they are very much afraid they'll have it tomorrow. Universal suffrage, proclaimed under pressure from the masses, is no longer based on the eudaemonism of the rich, nor on the knowledge of the *capacités;* no one knows *what* it is based on now, when the ignorant and the poor, who are legion, come to mingle their ballots with those of rightful voters. The practicing elite, in a daze, makes a daunting discovery: the right to vote *is not a matter of merit;* either the ruling class arrogates it to itself and preserves it by force, or else it belongs to anyone. If they have unleashed revolution in spite of themselves, it is because their position was untenable. They had to resign themselves to the role of passive citizen or share with everyone the privilege that ought to have rewarded their knowledge. As a result, the professionals are disqualified even in the function they exercised with such pride. The rich do not admire them enough to grant them political rights; the poor don't give a damn: in their eyes, political rights belong to all men and are the means that must be used by the majority to improve the workers' quality of life. The elite no longer recognizes itself as an elite; there is talk of leveling by the lowest common denominator. In fact, all practitioners are acknowledged as having the right to vote, but by the same token they think it is denied them since it is simultaneously granted to millions of the poor, who will sink the reasonable opinions of the elite under an ocean of ballots.

These very same professionals, after four months of terror, will secretly organize the June trap and the massacres to follow. Their humiliation and feelings of culpability have made them hate the populace, which four months earlier they merely despised. Among them, Arago is an instructive case: this peaceable man opens fire on the defenders of the barricades in rue Sufflot. Brandishing his sword, he runs after the soldiers charging with fixed bayonets—a zeal all the more respectable as he is turning sixty-three years old. A witness reports dreamily: "A kind of frenzy propelled the old man forward." A carnivorous frenzy brewed of hatred and fear, shared by an entire class; what the professionals detest in those workers they massacre is less the danger of socialism[29] than the impertinence of submen who

29. Which, nonetheless, they are far from underestimating.

have declared themselves their equals. And the carnage they consent to—when they are not wreaking it with their own hands—they see, of course, as a means of suppressing the most dangerous elements and of avenging their own abject, humiliating fear. But to an even greater extent this slaughter seems to them exemplary because it will humiliate the survivors and return the masses to their subhumanity; if they cause blood to run, in short, it is to reaffirm the nonprescriptive rights of science against barbarism. Through humanism, in a sense, I say this quite seriously, for the ideology that is about to be born must not be seen as a simple play of concepts; born of a historic massacre, it must assume it and integrate it. This time the national guard rival the soldiers in zeal; after February, they were "heartbroken at what they had done." They charge, and thanks to the guard the forces of order make quick work of what Guillemin called a secessionist movement rather than an insurrection. By fire and sword the middle classes have forged themselves into a new unity.

But now they realize they've been swindled. When the professionals borrowed a sword to redeem themselves, they thought they were *reestablishing* the situation; in fact, the Constitutional and Legislative Assemblies wallowed in the joys of reaction. Without suppressing universal suffrage, they clipped its wings by using a ruse to eliminate more than two million voters. The elite could think that the new electoral dispositions, without being ideal, would allow it to participate in public affairs; of course, it was not said expressly that the right to vote was based on merit, but that was the meaning of the law: peasants would vote because they are led by the priest, but workers would not. So the real voters would be the semirich and the professionals. The 2 December coup left these good folk thunderstruck; solicited by the dominant class, the coup demonstrated to the practitioners that the bourgeoisie, rather than share political power with them, preferred to strip themselves of it altogether. The result was the same as in February '48, only in reverse. At that time, seeking to *advance* the regime, to make their rights worth something, they had been surpassed by the radicalization of the movement that owed its first impulse to them; now, heartbroken, they tried to back-peddle, to find and impose a happy medium. And now the reaction, which they initiated in June, proceeds without them, against them, escapes them, becomes radicalized and finds its truth in Napoleon III. They saw nothing, understood nothing, they believed they were acting and did nothing; or else, unleashing uncontrollable forces, they achieved just what they did not want. For these men and equally for the republican petty bourgeoisie, their hopes of '48 seem to have been "dreams"; the *reality* is their double failure, which suddenly reveals to them the truth of history, of societies, of man. A few of them—the star performers of '48—will not resist. As Mme Quinet writes some time later, "Those men, Lamenais, Arago, Michel de Bourges, Emile Souvestre, were devastated by 2 December. The bitterness that flooded their hearts made that quite clear to me." The old swordsman Arago died two years later. Lamartine let himself slip gently into senility. On foreign soil, discouragement and disgust with action increased among many of the exiles: to act is not to know what one is doing; the act escapes the hands of man and is lost unless it rebounds on its author, alien, unknown and yet recognizable, like a boomerang. Knowledge is less treacherous: Ledru-Rollin takes refuge in astronomy; Marc Dufraisse, an authentic republican who held forth to the Society of the Rights of Man, writes with bitterness: "I loved republican liberty passionately; today my virtue goes no further than the regret for what was . . . My presumption bows before the will of the greatest number and the designs of Providence . . . I have no more faith in France." And this strange republican—who loses his faith in his country and in the Republic when Napoleon is given a plebiscite of seven million votes—cannot help citing these words of Luther's, applied to the people: "He is a drunken peasant: he falls off on one side; you put him back on his donkey, he falls off on the other." We see that this partisan of the happy medium has understood nothing; and it is no accident that he cites Luther, that bourgeois monk who called princes to arms and condemned the peasant insurrections that his Reformation had unleashed. This bitter man puts himself—has always put himself—almost naively *outside* the people; he picks them up and puts them back in the saddle, and then is annoyed to see them fall off on the other side. He doesn't see, or doesn't want to see, that the radicalization of a revolutionary movement is not a fall but, on the contrary, its *evolved truth*. Nor does he see that the "fall to the right" is not the doing of the masses but the triumph of reaction, that is, of the dominant class. In short, he adequately translates the prevailing sentiment among the professionals. For the most part they are sickened by the apathy of the masses; in their innocence, they would have liked the working class to take to the streets on 2 December to defend the Republic that had affirmed itself by slaughtering them.

At issue here is not, or not only, an emigré's moroseness; this discouragement is shared by the professionals inside the country as well, giving the illusion that they've discovered the enduring defects of human nature. This grievance against the masses is real, but it has the function of disguising shame. Taine, *who has taken an oath to the Emperor*, can at the same time write: "Every day I find the human level lower." Or, which could be the motto of the enlightened elite: "Scoundrels above, scoundrels below, respectable thinking people are going to be crushed." Proudhon, who makes an approach to the new regime (the day after the coup d'état he asks for an interview with Morny to propose sending the deportees to agricultural colonies), also writes: "Rabble above, rabble below . . . Nothing is less democratic, at bottom, than the people." Renan, *who has taken an oath*, writes: "Since '52 I have become all curiosity, I believe that we must abstract ourselves from all politics." Sainte-Beuve, who rallies unreservedly to the Empire, later explains: "We needed a wall, we did not know what to lean on." There is also Fustel de Coulanges, a hundred others whose opinions we know through their correspondence, and a hundred thousand others who said nothing during the "years of silence" but for whom these outstanding men, sick at heart, are the spokesmen. The general opinion among the elite is that dictatorship is a necessary evil; the blind violence of the populace and its sheeplike resignation have provoked it and *justify* it; indeed, the masses have thus shown themselves doubly unworthy of the Republic, an ideal but unrealizable regime, for it demands virtue from all citizens. In fact, the social order must be maintained by force since human nature is bad; the Empire is a lesser evil because the unadorned reality is the mediocrity, meanness, unbridled egoism, malice of men, their incapacity to govern themselves, in short, radical evil. The practitioner, after 2 December, can tolerate his fear of '48 and his "cowardly appeasement" of '52 only by using the impotence of the human creature to explain them; mystified when he tried to act, he thereby concluded that action of any sort ends in failure. His historic—and specific—failure is transformed into a universal and quasi-metaphysical determination of the human condition. Man, a failure of nature, must founder in all his undertakings, that is his destiny. It is clear, in this case, that he must begin by giving up the illusion that he is the center of the world and renouncing the notion that he is an end in himself. If this monster has some reason for being, it is as a *means:* the human race sacrifices itself for the advent of a nonhuman reality. The elite uses misanthropy as a link with bourgeois *distinction* and so shows itself worthy of forging its theoretical framework.

The elite will achieve the necessary decentering by the abolition of the subject, that is, of interiority. Analysis and determinism will be used to dissolve transcendence and surpassing, the foundations of praxis. But this will be accomplished indirectly, by the exalting of scientism. It is no accident that during the years of silence the cultivated public becomes newly enamored of scientific works, sometimes by going directly to the sources, more often by reading popularizations. Of course, the desire for information is not peculiar to France; in Germany, Moleschott's *Kreislauf des Lebens* appeared in 1852 and ran through eight editions. Three years later, Buchner's *Kraft und Stoff* went into nine. But the Germans also experienced the great fear of '48, and like us they had their abortive revolution. In France, enlightened readers are avid, they swallow and digest "experimental" science, the name of Claude Bernard is famous.[30] Two years after *Madame Bovary*, Darwin's *Origin of the Species* is a best-seller. This interest in the exact sciences has numerous roots. Primarily, of course, it stems from remarkable scientific achievements in every field, from mathematical astronomy to electrodynamics, from physics and chemistry to biology. But on a deeper level this exalting of knowledge is compensation for the disappointments of politics. The purpose of scientism is to reduce man to minerality. Taine will own up to it when he writes: "Vice and virtue are products, like sugar or sulphuric acid." Darwin's considerable success can be explained in part by the fact that he reveals evolution to the general public in its *mechanistic* form and popularizes two deliciously inhuman and pessimistic ideas, the struggle for life and the survival of the fittest. The first provides a biological justification for the society based on competition; it gives the competitors their patents of nobility, since competition is none other than life itself. By stretching it slightly, it can be made to justify military dictatorship: why blame a powerful regime when all animal and human relations are relations of power? As for the exploited classes, their wretchedness is no longer disturbing: manual laborers are quite simply men who are less well equipped; certainly they don't deserve their sad condition, but one couldn't exactly say that it is unjust: the universe is such that they cannot be otherwise, for they haven't the means to raise themselves up. Let a son of the working class, moreover, manifest exceptional gifts and he will quickly be found at the top of the social hierarchy. As Valéry, an unwitting Darwinist, would say at the beginning of our century: "Is there any way of hiding a man of talent?" Indeed. If the best adapted, wherever they

---

30. It is not until 1865, however, that he will publish his *Introduction à la médicine expérimentale*, but in 1849 he began to describe the glycogenic function of the liver.

come from, triumph, our society at least has the advantage of not squandering its values; nothing is lost, and by the force of things every individual serves exactly where he should. The latter, apparently optimistic idea is merely another form of pessimism. Its primary advantage is to overturn social temporality: the aristocrat *descends* from ancestors who are more or less mythic, or in any case unattainable, and the best he can do is not to seem too unworthy of them. The bourgeois *ascends:* he ascends from the ape, and who knows if one day the superman will not ascend from him. This is progress become the law of nature; the best equipped survive, therefore machines must be continually bought and perfected. But Darwin doesn't hide the fact that *survival* by definition implies the disappearance of infinite numbers of species, liquidated by famine or simply eaten. In short, progress is made by massacres. So much the better; the necessities of life establish the iron laws of the economy; Darwinian evolution makes Nature's king a savage beast who achieved his power by the extermination or domestication of other animals. Obviously, he owes his victory to the superiority of his equipment; but the reader must beware of taking pride in that fact: this superiority comes neither from Providence, nor from a premeditated intention, nor from the organism's progressive adaptation to his milieu. It is just a matter of chance. Man is thus external to himself; his success necessarily derives from his nature, but that nature is fortuitous, he can neither internalize it nor totalize it by transcending it toward an objective meaning of human life. Moreover, Darwin merely finishes the job. The discovery of the glycogenic function of the liver in 1849 was soon followed by remarkable studies on the role of the pancreas; a little later the vasomotor nervous system was located. These accomplishments seriously eroded the Romantic belief—still very much alive ten years earlier—in a vital principle escaping determinism and governing the organism as a whole. The goal of scientism must be to apply to its object the methods of the pioneering science of physical chemistry. Temporalization disappears, replaced—in physiology as in psychology, still in its infancy—by physical time, continuous, homogeneous, inert, indefinitely divisible. The future is effaced; it can be foreseen only to the extent that it is the resurrection of the past. For in this era so intoxicated by progress, it is the past that dominates; not, of course, the historical past of tradition but the moment that immediately precedes the present. The concept is triumphant; freedom—it was high time—is relegated to the storehouse of metaphysical illusions; praxis, or practical temporalization, bursts asunder, pulverized

237

into an infinity of indivisible and juxtaposed presents. This was not said at the time—although Littré had owned up to it by eliminating from positivism the religion of humanity and reducing it to merely a "general theory of the sciences." But what everyone fully understands is that real man has left the scene, devoured by scientism. The operation has a double objective: to destroy the veterans of '48, those Illuminati devoured by the future; to replace politics, dangerous and too human, by external conditioning. The republican, the socialist of '48, liked to speak of the "human race" as if it were one species among others. But they thought that man was in fact isolated in nature by his transcendence; they were the first to discover that human reality is defined by the distant future, even in our remote past, and that we are creatures of the distance, who come to ourselves from the horizon, across the world. So we define ourselves by praxis and recognize ourselves above all by the political dimension. That is, by our *practical* relation to the human future, the determination of our acts as citizens, by the man we produce but can't see. The veteran of '48 defines himself, therefore, *internally* as a practical relation to future man; and by this definition that puts nonbeing, in the form of not-yet, at the source of existence, he gives himself a derisory power that makes him, depending on one's point of view, a perpetually-deferred-being or a pro-ject. No matter how you look at it, this optimism squared poorly with the analytic reason that alone reigned in France, with the mechanistic determinism, a legacy of the eighteenth century, that continued to infuse the professionals. The optimism, moreover, sprang not from the professionals but from persons born to or integrated with the people, who believed they were summoned to change the world by direct and *human* action on men. In 1852, nothing seems more dangerous than this optimistic vision; the elite hates the lies that did such harm to the people by persuading them that they had the power to modify the social order and escape their wretchedness. And since the optimism of '48, the primacy of praxis, and the political dimension of human reality are merely one and the same, the first ideological duty of the practitioners must be to discourage the popular classes and the bourgeois troublemakers by suppressing any possibility of praxis by means of a definition of human reality in exteriority. Reducing man to his pure objectivity as a mechanical system, the "enlightened" emphasized *at once* the radical impotence of so-called "persons" and the permanent possibility of conditioning the human body and the social body from the outside.

Legitimist romanticism made the body, with its mysterious power to be born, to give life, and to die, into a symbol of created nature; surrender to the passions was based on the intention of surrendering oneself to God *through* the impulses of a divine and ungovernable body. Under the Restoration, this literary and theological conception coincided with a temporary deceleration of medical studies; in the countryside the number of doctors was not increasing; for most bourgeois families, the birthrate mirrored the rural prototype: God gave children, God took children away. He took it on Himself to maintain the balance. This notion generated social romanticism, a vague kind of socialism which mistakenly treated the people the way the peasant treats his body. Fooled by aristocratic romanticism, which exalted the lower classes at the expense of the manufacturers, the bank, and the elite, too many people saw the populace as an organic totality shaken by the enthusiasms and upheavals that translated the movements of its inner genius; they believed that God passed sentence through the rumblings of the crowd, as He did through the Delphic oracle or the vatic poet. People must be demystified. With the triumph of the bourgeoisie, the idea of limiting births by contraceptive practices and deaths by the progress of medical techniques was already established in the upper and middle classes. The human body lost its mystery, it was an external system that must be conditioned externally; biological finality is systematically eliminated. Now, pushing the sciences and pushed by them, the *capacités* undertake to establish a new discipline whose objective is an exact knowledge of the social body. The analogy with the human body is preserved, determinism has simply replaced organicism. The principles of a social science must now be established that will subsequently institute a technique allowing the manipulation of social groups the way doctors manipulate the human body. This is the only way to avoid the return of riots and popular self-deception, as in '48. The social body, like our body, is external to itself, and its laws are *external* connections between concepts; to trigger a particular change in society, we need only find the law or function that determines those variations, then locate the independent variable and act on it consciously to obtain precisely the desired modification. The age of tribunals is over, the age of social engineers has begun. They will learn from the human sciences which factors condition social stability; knowing the optimal formula for balancing the forces in a defined society—the most appropriate type of power, the administration of goods and men which in given conditions will avoid the greatest number of conflicts, the limits that a necessary inequality cannot surpass without becoming a factor in disorders—the social engineers will use such knowledge to derive practical applications, which they will share with those in power. We see that *politics* is entirely disqualified. Why? Because even the Machiavellian sort is addressed to men and demands their approbation. Even an ambitious, dominating, and teacherous politician, who would impose himself by deceit or violence, depends on the masses or on a privileged social group; he must *persuade*. Thus the provisional government of the Second Republic was quite decisive about deceiving the working classes; but precisely for this reason it had to take account of their demands, at least in part, in order to subvert them. In any event, power, insofar as it remains political, emanates from a group that mandates it and protects it but at the same time controls it; relations remain human, even if deviated and falsified. In short, power is made by society: Guizot is the pure expression of the bank; history chooses him, realizes itself for a moment through him, and then suddenly discards him; in short, political man is *situated*. That is his weakness; the social engineer will not be. Renan is the perfect representative of the professionals when he writes in 1849, in his *Reflexions sur l'état des esprits:* "What is politics in our day? An unprincipled and lawless agitation . . . The mounting wave of social questions will force politics to confess its impotence . . . The Science that will lead the world will be philosophy, the science that researches the purpose and conditions of society . . . To organize Humanity scientifically is the last word of modern science."[31]

As conceived by the professionals, this scientific organization is destined to institute order without touching property. It implies that man in society is merely a molecular being, trained by laws calculated on those of physical chemistry. From this point of view, his consciousness is merely an epiphenomenon, his power of decision a vain illusion susceptible of being evoked from the exterior by appropriate procedures. Therefore, nothing could be more foolish than the vote, whether universal or selective: Why *request* citizens' assent *when it can be provoked,* that mirage whose causes are physiological and social? The scientific organization of humanity is not even the self-domestication of man, it is his abolition and his replacement by a robot.

The elite preserved all its ambition but, mortified by failure, transposed it; its hatred of politics, the result of frustration, is now unbounded. It no longer dreams of sharing power, it claims to advise those who command and so places itself above them, above every-

31. *Oeuvres complètes,* 1:225, 1:399.

one, *desituated*. This scientistic illusion is engendered by the real state of contemporary science. Much later, in the area of microphysics, when investigations will be made possible by new mathematical tools and by the extreme sensitivity of material instruments, it will be perceived that the experimenter is himself part of the experiment. In 1850, on the level of the great forces measured by the scientist, this idea would be useless and negligible, hence false; the experimenter is outside and content to observe the unfolding of processes he has isolated and released. And it is on macrophysics that social science, according to Taine and Renan, must model itself. Thus the social scientist stands outside; when he studies men in order to discover the laws that govern them, he will have no need to remember that he is part of the society under study, or even part of the human race. Toward the same period in England, another conception is elaborated which defines truth in terms of its practical efficacy and starts, by contrast, from the idea that all thought defines its thinker and situates him in a necessarily fragmented society. The French elite, clinging to analytic thought, misconstrue or are unaware of popular Marxist thought and its subversive tool, dialectical reason; to such a degree that Lachelier, several years later, goes so far as to prohibit the teaching of Hegelianism in the *collèges:* "As long as I'm alive, Hegel will not pollute French philosophy." During the first quarter of the twentieth century, Brunschwicg, the author of a weighty and outmoded work, devotes a dozen or so pages in one of his final books to the author of *The Phenomenology of Mind* and not one to the author of *Das Kapital.* Mechanistic scientism is so well protected in our country that it will penetrate working-class thought and for a long time disfigure it, opposing a nondialectical Marxism to bourgeois analysis. As a consequence, for the second half of the nineteenth century the enlightened elite practices *panoramic consciousness* and refuses to conceive of its own historicity; it discloses that vices and virtues and, similarly, works of art are historical *products,* but not for a moment does it wonder if pure theory—or what is proffered as such—isn't itself a product. It is striking that Taine, explaining the literary work by the mechanical action of race, milieu, and historical moment, doesn't for an instant wonder if the same factors do not condition his conception of criticism. It is as though he's not involved: a pure gaze, he contemplates the agitations of men and finds that in this species, whose entomologist he has become, the individual regards determinations and impulses communicated to him from the outside as his personal project. If only he could conceive of the dialectical process and understand that

241

men make history on the basis of previous circumstances—by assuming them, surpassing and preserving them—he would approach the idea of praxis. If he were to situate himself as a thinker inadequately disengaged from analytic positivism with regard to singular and collective realities, he would be able to grasp his own thought as an idea-in-motion, whose falsity appears only if it is stopped, would grasp the real as evolved truth, and would grasp the content of his doctrine, given that it is born within him and is stopped by him so as to become his ideological interest, as situating him, by its very limits, in his class and in a defined social setting, thus in his real relation to all other classes. But this is precisely what he is incapable of doing, at once because analytic reason has chosen him to mediate its application to social groups, and because he has chosen analytic reason as an exclusive instrument of knowledge and a corrosive weapon against any class-being, whatever his origins, against the enemy who attacks him on two fronts and perhaps three. This choice and these denials, therefore, rigorously define him. Not as an object—in the manner of the La Fontaine he describes for us—but as an object-subject, as a practical organism, both victim and accomplice of his society. For him, as for Renan, for all those panoramic consciousnesses, social science is inhuman. It requires the scientist who practices it and the engineer who applies it to first cast off their humanity; if they become accustomed—at least during their research—to practicing *impassivity*, they will elevate themselves to pure, transhistorical thought, which by definition escapes the singularity of anchorage and immediately situates itself in the abstract universal, above the humanity whose needs and ends they envisage *from the outside*. These universalists believe that one can perch on the peaks outside the self, and this is not surprising if we recall their preference—born of fear and resentment—for exclusively external human relations. Since Man, in them as in everyone, is external to himself as a mechanical system whose movement is communicated to him from the outside and who is restrained by external resistances, nothing is easier than to become external to the self; as a result, the substantialist illusion collapses along with that magic, sustained by passion, which makes everyone a magician to his fellow being; a system of laws appears in their place. Some decades later Brunschvicg will say, "To think is to measure." After 1850, the enlightened elite is already convinced of this. Man is a number. Social science will mark its maturity by the precision of its measurements.

The contradiction of scientism—as a bourgeois ideology elaborated by the *capacités* around the 1850s—is that it depends on the real gains of experimental science while depriving itself of the means to give an account of that experimentation. That is the business of the scientists and theoreticians of the Third Republic. As soon as they conceive that the unity of such experiments is the *experimental idea*, they will be obliged to reflect on the human power of unifying diversity through a synthetic perception that surpasses it and constitutes itself as an interrogation of being, absent or unrevealed, which defines itself precisely by a systematic reorganization of the practical field. Pierce, Whitehead, Brochard, Lachelier will return to Kant, to the categories, will attempt to win back from associationism synthetic judgments a priori, as indispensable conditions for the possibility of experiment. But at least on the level of specific knowledge this is a return to a certain optimism. *Homo sapiens*, in any case, will escape atomistic dispersal; he can accumulate his knowledge, surpass it and illuminate it by the putting in question of the self and of being that is the hypothesis. On the basis of this hypothesis, he can foresee a future which, far from being the restitution of the past, is rather its application; in this regard he is no different from *homo faber*, for the hypothesis is by definition the rule that presides at the material construction of the experimental system. In other words, science reveals itself as concerted action on the environment and, if possible, the scientist must be given back his praxis, man in general his prospective unity, his transcendence, his projects, as synthetic and revelatory surpassings of being toward nonbeing, his ends as significant totalizations of the means utilized to attain them. This is the last thing the enlightened elite of the Second Empire wants, set against itself, as it is, out of hatred of man. It has condemned action for evermore since it foundered, in 1848, in its timid political enterprise; it believes that praxis remains impossible. A dream, if you will. A nightmare. In any case, an illusion. If it had to be admitted, solely on the level of scientific thought, it would soon be found on all levels of human existence. The Bible of these misanthropes appears rather belatedly, it's true, for Taine doesn't publish *De l'Intelligence* until 1870. But this work merely makes explicit what the professionals have secretly been thinking for twenty years. Besides, its merely a hasty repair of associationism: consciousness is a flux of images bound together merely by external relations, such as resemblance and contiguity; let one reappear, another reemerges that often accompanied it in the past. Habit cements bonds carefully chosen for their nonsignificance; chance alone governs its sequences. In other words, no content of consciousness has its raison d'être in itself or in its intentional rapport with reality; it is manifest because another content, totally external to it, was produced externally a moment before. With Taine's work, the circle is complete, the physico-chemical world has entered even into thought, whose only laws are the principle of inertia and that of universal attraction. Taine's triumph is that he calls a book dealing with absolute nonintelligence *De l'Intelligence*, without any of his innumerable readers noticing it. In their frenzy to conjure away man, the scientists end by conjuring away themselves; these conjured conjurers deny themselves, in effect, the only possibility that exists to determine an object of science by the organization of an experimental field—namely, intellectual activity. This is their contradiction: if man must be their object, he must be reduced to inert external sequences, *even in them;* but if human science constructs its field of social investigation *through them* by defining the object by the methods and the methods by the object, it must be found, in studying them in their work itself, that there are two species of men: the uninitiated, who are governed by natural laws, and the men of science, who must escape these laws in order to discover them. Unless, of course, unity is reestablished by conceiving of *homo sapiens* as the firstborn of a species born to man and therefore superhuman. The idea of the superman, the inverse of a hatred of man, the site of a conjunction of mechanist transformism and the internalized myth of progress, appears—well before its Nietzschean expression—to be the falsely positive expression of the enlightened elite's disgust (it is clearer that man is currently a failure when one indicates what he *could have been* or what he will be later), and at the same time to be a solution to the scientistic contradiction and a new, more flattering presentation of subjection as a categorical imperative. Man is the means of producing the superman; his role is to suppress himself so that this new species might emerge. Unfortunately—and the work of Spencer bears this out—evolutionism, transforming passively acquired habits into passively inherited traits, *disguises* but preserves original inertia; by becoming an heir, man does not escape the fundamental rule of exteriority. So the contradiction of scientism leads to skepticism as well; meaning that we come back to the challenge of Hume and to pre-Kantian thought, with the aggravating circumstance that Kant has already made his contribution and these gentlemen do not want to acknowledge it. These professionals would very much like to have merely a "glancing acquaintance" with man, but they haven't even the resource of the pure gaze: the gaze is a prospective and synthetic activity, it delimits a field as a function of an enterprise, isolating a form from a background. Thus science—not only the science of man, which is still merely a dream, but also mathematics and physico-chemistry—is like a text without an author. Considering the *practical* features these exact disciplines require of the person who would exercise them—especially those based on experimentation—scientific discourse at this time seems self-generating and to be developing simply by the rigor of its sequences. And at this very moment the popularization of recent discoveries in physics, chemistry, and medicine were effectively presenting to the cultivated public the practitioner, that new (or rather previously little-known) man, whose exploits were being recounted, in whose name scientism was justified, and whom this ideology was finally inadequate to explain.

In fact, this major contradiction favored the builders of the new humanism more than it hindered them. Scientific anthropology might well have exploded it, but under the Empire that discipline was merely a dream. It was *The Future of Science,* to be sure, but a future conceived by a groundless extrapolation. Taine's literary criticism, while posing as an application of universal determinism to works and their authors, is more like a purposeful musing on what criticism should be in order to become an exact discipline. The same could be said of the oneiric decomposition of intelligence into psychic atoms. The future anthropology was *imagined,* its accomplishment was assumed, it was believed in, perhaps, but this changed nothing of the implicit but irreducible certainty that it did not yet exist. Moreover, those dreams themselves exposed its nonexistence; they were attempts to fill the gap abruptly revealed by the felt need to condition societies from the outside. The very insubstantiality of its prophecies kept scientism from discovering its contradiction; the theorist grasped himself, in the moment of conception and elaboration, as a *thinking activity,* and this proud consciousness of his praxis did not prevent him from imagining and articulating in his books an image of man as he would be seen by future anthropologists. Thanks to which man's subjection to knowledge received a kind of irrational justification in the eyes of the professionals; we might say that the human being's sacrifice of himself to science "in progress" is all the more valid the more incapable he is, as an inert succession of states, of practicing it. Shouldn't we set these nonmeanings that we are, each moment of our lives being merely the blind convergence of many causal series, against the universality of concepts and laws, the rigorous and intelligible succession of deductions, the exactitude of inductive interpolations? And consequently, having internalized already acquired knowledge, are we not convinced that science is made *through* man but without him? As if the first principle of scientistic ideology were formulated as follows: we are by nature incapable of contemplating the science we practice. Man remains the means of science, but he isn't even the *essential* means. Or rather, some active but hidden intention, *other than man*, conditions our states from the outside—like a social engineer—in such a way as to give us impressions and behaviors capable of organizing an experiment and transcribing its results, so that written knowledge would be objective reason without any corresponding subjective rationality on our part. In which case we would be the uncomprehending and highly unworthy mediators between divine intellection and its object. Or, as Brunschvicg so cogently remarked apropos of Hume, the scientist's pessimism touching the professionals of the human intellect can only be doubled by a cosmic optimism; in effect, empiricist man, a chance being, can be the means of knowledge on the simple condition that external constants are internalized by him as subjective habits. One would have to think, in this case, that the law of gravity *got itself discovered* by Newton, without the least initiative on his part or anything that resembles intellection, by establishing itself in him—the fruit of innumerable repetitions—as a conditioned reflex. This optimism, moreover, is merely implicit; it can be called the *necessary* counterpart of the original negation—in other words, of the abolition of praxis—but this counterpart is not the object of a positive affirmation. The professionals do not really believe in it; unbelievers for the most part, at the very least agnostics, these somber men neither can nor want to soften the shipwreck of the species with some preestablished harmony. Their instinctive pessimism extends to the universe; a remark of Renan's rather effectively articulates the general attitude: "And what if the truth were unhappy?" Science must have some foundation, so they transfer to the macrocosm the legislative activity they deny their fellow men and even deny themselves. In any event, their attitude toward science is ambiguous.

1. When they *practice* it, they preserve the proud certainty of 1840; they feel they are agents and subjects, their subjection to knowledge seems voluntary, they discover in it a deliberate intention to sacrifice which establishes their merit. But this merit is futile, it neither is nor pretends to be at the origin of any political claim, since politics is an aimless agitation and, more radically, the nightmare of a mechanical system that imagines it initiates movements that are actually impressed on it from the outside. The intellectual, however, continues

to claim power for himself. But he will exercise it as counsel to the dictator; he no longer imagines convincing men, but he is prepared to manipulate them through the intermediary of the secular arm. The enlightened elite, in short, envisage making a contract with the State apparatus and the employer; here we come close to what a hundred years later will be called *social engineering*, that is, mobilized sociology. Even at this time the *capacités* foresee calling themselves technocrats and establishing their new power on the separation of goods management and property. For the moment, their visions of the future serve only to increase their bitterness, for the time of monopolies and oligopolies has not yet come; as for the social sciences, they exist in the system of knowledge only as an empty position. The "luminaries" of the period know that they will die in mediocrity. Measuring the breadth and vanity of their sacrifice, those men-failures extend their hatred to the entire world, as much to the victorious soldiers, to the bankers and employers who gave them power, as to the workers whose arrogance unleashed the thunderbolt. They see the human race as a magnificent disaster, and their only unequivocal joy is in despising it. A sad panoramic pride, an imaginary attitude, since it claims to be based on knowledge that does not yet exist. The elite excludes itself from the species; and to manifest a superiority *that ought to be*, it borrows the *practices of distinction* from the bourgeoisie. These symbolic privations are the sign of its disinterestedness, its sacrifice, and above all its refusal to share human ends, with which its only rapport must be *knowledge by causes*.

2. But when the practitioners consider knowledge from the outside, neither elaborating nor applying it, they fall back into the common clay; it seems to them that one day they will be its objects, and in the name of the principles and teleological intentions of scientism they grasp themselves, when confronted by it, as fragmented pulverizations whose inert dispersal prohibits them from *producing* and *accumulating* it. Thus the practico-inert system of knowledge—as established in books or manifest in its industrial applications—seems to them, in its calm universality, like something neither they nor their peers could generate. Science has fallen from heaven, and even if nature has chosen to announce itself through their mediation, they deserve it no more than Eberfeld's horses, which were trained to stop in front of numbers or letters and appeared to be counting or reading when they were merely obeying instilled habits. In this case, their misanthropy extends to themselves. But it is accompanied by a boundless admiration for science, an infinite but anonymous enterprise,

247

which continually expands and deepens without any directing subject or, better yet, bases its radical objectivity (a certainty of scientism) on the destruction of all subjective interiority. Everything is then reversed: far from man's illuminating the multiple manifestations of being by the production of universal concepts and synthetic judgments, it appears that universality and the synthetic connection between concepts, of which mechanistic man is by definition ignorant, come to him *from the outside* as *other*, and that he internalizes them by doing an apprenticeship in objective knowledge. It is from accomplished science, in short, that the student or practitioner derives his cohesion: knowledge—according to them, *accomplished* knowledge coming to them like a stranger—is the only possible unity of their infinite dispersal. Through it, accomplished reasonings impose themselves, as habits and the matrices of new reasonings, on this flux of meaningless impressions—governed from the outside, disappearing and reappearing according to absurd principles of association—which represents the psychism of empirical man. In a word, science as an alien reality comes to structure human thought. On this level, the apt word is not even *alienation;* we are dealing with a particular case of fetichization. Man, in effect, does not recognize his product; misconstruing the human work crystallized in it, he takes his own praxis—or that of previous generations—for requirements of the object. The subordination of the producer to his product is total; his *reality as man* is conferred upon him by the human thing that issues from his hands. And such, indeed, is negation, which will serve as the basis of the professionals' humanization. Whether they see the value "man" as residing uniquely in the sacrifice that abolishes it for the sake of engendering knowledge as inhumanity, or whether man receives the human structure only after the fact, as a product of his product, and human nature as a repercussion, constituted by the internalization of the inhuman, scientism declares itself to be humanism when it can admire man as the being whose being proclaims his radical subordination to wrought matter.

By this definition, scientistic ideology, originally conceived to express the arrogant spite of the enlightened elite, is immediately designated the provisional ideology of the French employers. It will give meaning, after some elaboration, to the practices of distinction and will rather easily demonstrate that the disinterestedness of the professionals and the driving interest of the banks and manufacturers are one and the same thing. It must be observed that the infatuation of the cultivated public with scientific works comes also, perhaps above all, from its attention to the development of industry. In 1848, France is a nation that is three-quarters agricultural. The leading industry is still textiles. After 1870, metallurgy becomes the key sector. Between 1850 and 1870 there is a shift from one economy to another; during these twenty years—especially after 1860—we can see the emergence, growth, and consolidation of the first industrial revolution. Its contemporaries, as the poems of Du Camp have shown, are extremely conscious of its importance; if they educate themselves, it is not out of pure curiosity, for practical applications interest them *at least as much* as theories. They want to understand why the utilization of coal tar (1856) created such an upheaval in the dye industry; what kind of impact the Bessemer converter (1857) had on metallurgy; the extraordinary development of the railroad under Napoleon III, with the progressive elimination of cartage and earlier modes of navigation—something that stirred up public opinion. It may be in this last example that the public is best able to grasp the substitution of the machine for manpower, for antiquated modes of communication, for work animals. Just as scientism invites man, that self-consciously relative being, to venerate that absolute, science, it compels him to admire its products when it emerges from the laboratory to serve the manufacturers. Machine-made material, in effect, preserves something of the inhuman purity of knowledge for its own sake. But above all there is a reciprocity of perspective between the relation of the scientist to science, as it is conceived by scientistic humanism, and the relation of the manufacturer to his factory, between the fetishism of knowledge and that of merchandise.

In the beginning, unable to comprehend the demand of manufacturing or trade that comes to him as a practico-inert imperative, the rich man regards it as a general characteristic of human nature; thus he assimilates it, under the name of *self-interest*, to the order of a psycho-physiological drive, concluding that "everyone pursues his own interest." At first, then, the property owner, a particular affirmative essence, appears merely to be trying to realize himself in his individual being, and thus affirms *human reality* by saving and acquiring wealth. The only reason to import English theories is to indicate that the particular interest of the property owner coincides with the general interest, proof that the bourgeois economy is made for man, and not bourgeois man for the economy. After 1848 these pious lies explode, and under the Empire the working class and the employers are "increasingly impervious realities." Under the circumstances, it is impossible to maintain that fine English optimism—the boss's interest *cannot be* the same as the worker's. The employer's interest, stripped naked and reduced to itself, no longer seems to be a *conatus* born of some will to power, nor indeed the unfolding affirmation of his personality. The possessing classes, however, persist in identifying man with the property owner. But from this fact they affirm *at their level*, in the presence of the exploited classes but with no reference to them, subjection to the thing as constitutive of the human essence. The property owner's being exists outside him, in his factory, his bank or his lands. And when property is bourgeois and real, when the possessor is alone with the object possessed, without those human meanings that in feudal times inserted themselves between the holder and his holdings, he himself becomes a thing to the extent that the thing is found to be his unique objective reality. And scientistic humanism can indeed provide credentials to the human thing insofar as it is humanized by taking possession of the reified possessor. This operation can be conceived in two ways: either on the basis of real and scientific knowledge that will be utilized outside the sector in which it is valid, to establish ideological nonknowledge and demonstrate that man is merely a dream of the human thing; or on the ethical plane, by presenting the subjection of the scientist to knowledge as the very model of the sacrifice of man to the thing, of the property owner to his property. These two elaborations of the new humanism are, in fact, incompatible and could not coexist in the real system of knowledge. The purpose of the first is to give man the status of wrought materiality: nothing exists but things, some of which, produced by an annihilated demiurge, constitute what might be called the inorganic humanity of robots; in this case, the practico-inert imperative has no meaning, a sacrifice cannot be demanded when, along with praxis, the very idea of obligation has disappeared. The second conception, by contrast, tends to define a set of values in which subjection to the inhuman is the supreme norm, restoring man in his dignity as practical agent even if the operation is simply for the purpose of radically subordinating him to his goods or his product. But the characteristic of ideology—of any sort—is precisely not to be totalizable and, with its faulty structure, to be an undefined set of incompatible procedures which nonetheless coexist because they have the same objective. These operative schemes taken together are the skeletons of concrete thoughts that transcend and hence preserve them in the illusory unity of aberrant syntheses called *ideas*—vicious circles in the best of cases, more often multiplicities of interpenetration—which take on the appearance of thought. Thus the property owner, to the extent that he wants to *live* his right of possession, can borrow simultaneously from the professionals these two negative legitimations and even imagine to himself, in the fog of mental rumination, that they are mutually consolidating.

The first conception, by applying the methods of the most developed sciences to the human agent, the subject of *his* enterprise, by replacing praxis with inertia and pulverizing interiority, allows the bourgeois to refute the arguments of subversion as well as those of the aristocracy; the reign of real property conforms to the nature of things. It is true that the possessor, as he is defined *juridically* on the basis of established relations of production—and without even considering production in its concrete reality, which is none other than exploitation—negatively manifests his essence by forbidding all others to use the thing he possesses without his consent. It follows that by imposing a limit on other property owners as much as on the dispossessed, and equally by the seal it stamps on one's goods, thus collecting them and holding in a closed fist their indefinite dispersal in exteriority, the synthetic and continuous act of appropriation attempts to communicate to the thing possessed some inert interiority. The result is to manifest the impenetrability of matter by a social and institutional "No Entry." Conversely, however, this diffuse impenetrability is the physical basis of bourgeois property; in addition, it manifests itself as such, as the essential quality of possessed goods, only by continually absorbing into it the act of the property owner— the owner as agent—and making that its inert limit. Thus real property, as this institution defines the property owner, makes material impenetrability, underscored by the proprioceptive act it absorbs, the fundamental quality of the human essence and produces in human relations the exteriority that characterizes the relations between elements of a mechanical system. This is what is experienced as *incommunicability;* men fail to communicate among themselves, not only because they borrow *its* essence from the thing, but also because they confer humanity upon the thing in the form of a fixed determination, namely, negation. Language has two functions: in production, it serves as an imperative prescription for conduct, and in a more general way it manifests relations of production in the form of prohibitions. In the marketplace, words are exchanged like merchandise and money: in the course of a sale, they are *external* markers; employer and employee, seller and buyer have *nothing* to say to each other because the only relation between them is one of merchandise (involving a manufactured object or manpower) and price—which is established, moreover, independently of the contracting parties on the basis of general conditions that govern them in exteriority. Private relations are of a similar nature; among themselves, the bourgeois— except in periods of crisis—reaffirm the principle of the man-thing, without real interiority, by *talking and saying*, by treating language, by *common* agreement, as an external system having only external connections with the signified, or else as unable, for lack of internal bonds, to constitute itself in *signifying* sentences. Thus discourse, outside of technical terminology, can say only the unsignifying. Everyone at the time knows (and this endures in certain circles) that the loquacious silence of fashionable gatherings or formal dinners serves not only to censure the *secret*, to simultaneously repress the body in general, the genitals as a symbol of the needs of those who suppress other needs by satisfying them, and the man of need who is the proletarian; but more explicitly and more superficially to renew ceremoniously the "impenetrability of beings" as the basis and consequence of private property. Saying mere *nothings*, the bourgeois takes pleasure in manifesting his bourgeois essence. This is what scientistic ideology must articulate as theory.

And the task is even easier since the technical terminology of the practitioners and scientists, meant to condition external systems from the outside, is itself constituted as an external entity. This means, first of all, that the links between the terms are external to each of them, that the terms themselves are defined as references to other terms which condition them from the outside, and as false syntheses which, like the act of appropriation, release the quantitative dispersion of their content through the very unity of the conceptual act. The practitioners will have no difficulty establishing the reason for this in the new ideology: isn't it quite simply, on the human scale, the result of cosmic atomism? Bourgeois individualism is integrated with scientistic humanism; among themselves men are like atoms and stars, perfectly solitary and bound together in exteriority by strict laws that may be merely a specific instance of the principle of universal attraction.

Yet this dehumanization of man does not take account of the bourgeois ethic. If he is by nature inhuman, there is no need for him to sacrifice his humanity. The morality of distinction requires that the property owner is characterized by a *minimum* of humanity so that he can proceed to his permanent self-destruction. On this level the practitioners, by giving themselves over to knowledge, provide the bosses with a precious example: no longer, in this case, must man be defined by the *fact* of his inorganic materiality; now he must be defined by the fundamental *norm* that presents his subjection to wrought matter as his duty. Human relations are negative; they condemn the individual, as an example of the species, by a fundamental negation— of the *person*. Since the property owner allows himself to be defined by his property, he drops out of himself into the setting of the world and there becomes his own *material interest*, his well-being as it is constantly threatened by material forces, by usury and the competitive economy. We now understand the inevitable error of utilitarianism, which was to psychologize a necessity of an economic nature under the pretext that it is internalized and lived by the privileged. This psychologism, moreover, is itself the result of man's subjection to the thing possessed. The law of self-interest, in the bourgeois universe, is none other than the practico-inert imperative of profit: to possess is nothing, since in a competitive order one must change to stay the same, therefore reduce costs, increase productivity, economize, reinvest, or go bust. The manufacturer's subjection to his factory results in the factory's giving the orders. In 1840, when one weaver imports an English machine, another weaver's interest lies in the obligation to buy the same machine, or other, even better machines, to tackle the competition of a rival manufacturer whose costs have been lowered. In this sense, *his* self-interest comes to him negtively on the basis of another's, the simple threat of ruin which the factory absorbs and sends back to him as a positive requirement. An imperative that is *in principle* hypothetical, "If you don't want your property to vanish . . . ," is in fact categorical; since the manufacturer's objective reality is in the object possessed, the destruction of that possession would be equivalent to the annihilation of the human essence in his person. Self-interest therefore manifests itself to the property owner as a double subjection: to others through manufacture, to manufacture through all others; it is profit as the objective truth of man and inhuman necessity, and the ineluctable obligation to progress. And undoubtedly the myth of progress, as reworked by Maxime, can be integrated with an optimistic ideology. We see it as an a priori characteristic of capitalist economy, and we thereby conclude that it is always possible—"You must, therefore you can." This pious lie is frequently revived and repeated by the manufacturers, but they are not fooled by it; they have learned the truth from their daily struggles: history has taken the bit in its teeth, and that stupefying acceleration is continually paid for by individual disasters and a growing tension in the victors. Thus interest—that is, profit posited for its own sake as an absolute value—is *against man*, that is, against the property owner. He is inessential; what matters is the accumulation of the thing. Insofar as profit is the means and supreme end of capitalist production, insofar as it is not made to serve men but only for itself, to produce capital, human work at this moment of the bourgeois era is perfectly *useless*. And so utilitarianism appears to us in its true light. At first it seems to be a theory of human ends and an art of living based on the search for the *useful*, but we see now that its only purpose is to realize, on all levels of social living, the subordination of human life to the necessities of accumulation. Yet the reign of wrought matter, by suppressing human relations in favor of pure relations of exteriority, makes every property owner in the eyes of others an anti-man, the most dreaded enemy of our species, who manifests his diabolical hatred of the human by attacking every man in his very inhumanity, or if you will, in his being-in-the-world. Competition is a hatred revolving from one man to the other, and no one understands at this time that man is not the natural enemy of man, of himself, but that others' properties hate the property owner through his own goods. It appears, on the contrary, that man is hateful, and that his real merit will be to execute the sentence he has pronounced against himself by suppressing himself—utterly—so that the reign of the human thing can come into being.

This generalization of hatred could not be effective if it were limited to reflecting the property owner's subjection to property. On this superficial level, it could certainly be masked beneath a form of optimism; after all, the conflict of particular interests can become manifest only in the larger framework of class interest. This is why, in 1840, people thought they could see a preestablished harmony between the general interest and particular interests. The February revolution tore away the veils: the general interest is none other than the interest of the ruling class, and to a certain degree that of the middle classes. And after '48 it became evident that the interest of the bourgeoisie lay in maintaining the exploitation of the working class by any means at hand—including violence. It was understood that the workers perceived this as an intolerable destiny, and the interest of the exploited classes, it was feared, would become, like the abolition of exploitation, the destiny of the bourgeoisie. Thus the necessity for a new humanism that would be accepted by everyone as a tool of bourgeois hegemony originates in the hatred the manufacturers believe they read in the workers' gaze. The internalization of that hatred comes to define man by self-hatred as early as the unprincipled *habitus* we have

called distinction. The ideology of the enlightened elite must therefore be based on this definition; the privileged respond to the hatred
they awakened by the June massacres with fear and hatred; in the
light of this intolerable tension, competitive antagonisms seem to
them homicidal undertakings, and by the same token the *subject* of
this universal hatred becomes man in oneself, that is, the property
owner in his own self-hatred. It is indeed as if the system were spontaneously producing a strange justification for the regime that is first
presented in its nakedness but will be unconvincing without careful
elaboration. So that man might become completed in his humanity by
the legitimate exploitation of his fellow man, abhorrence must be the
sole relation between men insofar as it is based on every man's abhorrence of himself. We see that as in most ideological legitimations, the
terms are reversed here, with effects offered as causes. Be that as it
may, the essential thing is that the new humanism transcends *homo
homini lupus* by showing, on the level of accomplished man, the property owner, that man is a being who is posited in himself and in his
relations with others only in order to suppress himself. If humanity,
in each of its exemplary individuals, did not demand its own abolition
as its absolute aim and the meaning of its deepest impulses, how
would we justify the immense waste of human lives that characterizes
capitalism in its phase of accumulation? In this form, obviously, the
argument is hardly flattering and does not easily invite agreement. It
is up to the enlightened elite to dress it up, to adorn it with something
dazzling. Since there is apparent homogeneity between the relations
of the property owner to the thing and those of the worker to the
product of his work, all arguments will be valid if they justify for the
worker the "sacrifices" demanded of him in the name of the abnegation the owner imposes on himself. One produces, the other possesses: in both cases man is denied in favor of the thing and the end
in favor of the means. The dominant class provides the example: in
it, human reality blossoms without the constraint of need or ignorance; it is fully prepared to accede to the fullness of its essence
through property. And for this very reason, just when humanity is
posited for its own sake through property, in it, at the top of the social
scale, it reveals the secret of the species: man is a being who can affirm himself only to deny himself radically. Thus the hatred of the
Other—internalized exploitation—finds its justification in that imperative which tears us away from ourselves: "Behave always in such
a way that you treat the person in yourself and in others as the means
of realizing the human thing and never as an end." Thanks to this

rigorous norm, being and value are confused in the definition of human reality; self-hatred seems to be an a priori feeling—like Kantian respect for the law, which certainly isn't very different. In the name of this thoroughly universal moral law (Don't workers, when they sell their labor, turn it into a *thing?* Don't they oppose each other with all the violence of a competitive conflict?), the boss, if he sets the example, can ask the workers to sacrifice themselves without hope of compensation.

This is where the elite intervenes. Since bourgeois ideology must be constructed on an original valorization of man, it *recognizes* in the subjection of the manufacturers to their interests, that is, to their factories, its own sacrifice to practical knowledge considered in its inhuman being. In other words, from the time that man's objective is to destroy himself as man so that the thing other than man (or the human thing) can exist, the practitioner will undertake a self-imposed austerity so that the manuacturer can embrace a self-inflicted avarice as the subordination of human life to the necessities of accumulation. They've pulled it off, disinterestedness and interest are two ways of expressing this subordination—and those two expressions are reflected in each other. Undoubtedly, one accumulates knowledge in order to produce, but it must also be said that one produces in order to know, since the instruments of scientific knowledge progress along with industry and through it. The *fundamental value* for the new humanism derives from the fact that the essence of man seems to be the negation of a negation. Indeed, it admits a "human nature" that is at bottom merely a restrictive determination: reduced to itself, to the atomism of impressions, to the organic egoism of needs, to the weaknesses of a noticeably naked body without protective covering, without a shell or even a coat of fur, man's essence would be merely a vague natural existence which, to the degree that it would be inclined to affirm itself through the simple reproduction of its life, would make itself the negation of the universe in favor of a molecule's stupid perseverance in its being. But the new humanism, impelled by necessity, has injected into the heart of man a kind of instantaneous temporalization, let's say an outline of the dialectic process. For he is granted this existence that he might make himself man by denying it. Certainly, the inertia of his nature can be envisaged as the tendency of being to persevere in its being; but this tendency, which according to the professionals would be at the source of all his needs, and finally of his animality in general, seems really to be a *factual given* posited for its own sake, even for a moment, only to provoke a negation of *another order*, a negative *imperative* that binds itself to that tendency and eats away at it. And as this vulnerable creature's existence is as necessary to the dazzling products of science and industry as his sacrifice, it is as if he were produced in his physiological hideousness and fragility so as actively and continuously *to deny himself* in favor of an impossible universe made of platinum and cut diamonds, a macrocosm penetrated, confined, exploited in the name of *antiphysis*, whose only source is man's affirmation, then negation, of human nature in himself, or (a negation disguised as an affirmation) as it appears as an exemplary and local manifestation of nature in general. Man therefore has a mission—which, to be sure, no one has given him—to doom himself in order to produce an increasing number of goods, inert objects exterior to themselves but marked with a human stamp that only their perfect inertia preserves, and which thereby throw back the passive and false image of an interiority that is simultaneously reduced to nothingness by analytic reason. As if what the manufacturer and the practitioner had in common were that in them interiority denied itself except as an inessential, and inconceivable, means of producing externally and in the dimension of exteriority a deceptive reflection of what it *could* have been. This can be refined, if need be, and one can declare, for example, that man kills himself on the job because he cannot realize in himself the interiority that *ought to be* part of his essence, and so that wrought matter can *bear witness* to his unrealizable dream. The producer and the practitioner, the worker himself in the enlightened elite could make him open his eyes, would understand in this hypothesis that their salvation is in their doom. External systems haunted by an impossible dream—or, if you will, conscious of the impossibility of being man, of self-government in the unity of interior syntheses—they will at least have borne witness, in the heart of that shipwreck which begins at birth and ends with life itself, to their will to the impossible by destroying themselves to recreate matter in the image of their dreams, profiting from its inertia to compel it to bear the false interiority of a seal. A mechanical system, sickened by itself with the presentiment of what a synthesis might have been, annihilates itself to infect other mechanical systems with its dream and its aversions. The truth is that man and his product are homogeneous; in both, internal determinations are merely appearances. Merchandise, of course, is a capricious idol: it imposes itself, imposes its price, points to man with its dead arms, dictating his behavior to him by an imperative "operating procedure." It breaks down, however, and chiefly it wears out; this diabolical image of man soon gives us a glimpse of universal dispersal beneath its borrowed humanity. Scientific laws and technical precepts first offer the appearance of an act of thought uniting the diverse, and at this point a few men have identified with the knowledge they have produced to which their name is attached; in other words, they have entirely passed into knowledge, and their humanity remains as a designation of the inhuman. Yet these acts are false pretenses, existing only superficially like an afterimage of human sacrifice; the content of knowledge, in the form of a hypothetical judgment, is the quantitative connection of a so-called independent variable with one or several others, whose *measurable* variations are proportionate to those of the first; and quantity is the relation of exteriority in its purest form. Be that as it may, nothing more is needed to justify a social system in which the wrought thing serves as a mediation between men. Clearly, the human enterprise, born of failure, attempts to universalize it; paradoxically, inorganic matter tolerates the seal—or apparent unity—for a time, only to the extent that it is incapable of refusing it, and is therefore inert and dispersed. So a man can no longer be measured even by his efficacy; it is the conscious perseverance in failure that will establish his value. Bourgeois ideology in this era produces an ethic of effort. It is not the result that counts—that is not within our reach—it is the *effort*, the sacrifice of man to something he *knows* he cannot attain.

This ethic reveals too much of its underlying pessimism; it remains permanently at the disposal of the bourgeoisie and the middle class, but it is only a last resort. Scientistic humanism prefers another morality, which subsumes the first but conceals it beneath a superficial optimism. Of course, one must preach antiphysis, the subjection of nature internalized by the dominant class through distinction, man's sovereignty over his organic needs; and what is not said or even thought, but is *manifest* in everyone as the meaning of lived experience, is that this sovereignty, far from being a power man has over himself, is the ideological expression of the tyranny of the human thing. At the same time, however, antiphysis, as a recreation of the creation, is an enterprise in progress and far from accomplished, which it may never be. The human thing cannot be considered a completed idol, taking its fixed demands from its material fullness; it seems to be a *thing in production*, its reign scarcely begun, and every day it is consolidated by progress that will extend its reach to the entire universe. The structures of capitalist society are now in place; as a consequence, the subjection of *all* social classes to production is complete; the private property of machines, the competitive economy, the necessities of accumulation are *present* imperatives of the practico-inert that governs the classes, the form of their struggle, and their reciprocal positions as a function of the relation of forces, of an immediate and bloody past, and many other factors. But since antiphysis is merely at its beginning, it contains infinitely less being than nonbeing; thus *represented*, even its being-to-come seems to illuminate its present reign; so, for the practitioners and employers who borrow their ideology from the elite, it is the constant object of *projects* which are, in fact, dreams (these anticipations, even when prophecies of Jules Verne, are situated well beyond the field of possibles that measure contemporaneous *reality*). But these dreams derive their substance from the fact that they offer themselves as legitimate extrapolations based on progress, that guiding principle of *all* bourgeois ideology. So that an inevitable optical illusion reverses the terms and makes the distant future—the Earth finally conquered, the *embourgeoisement* of the world—appear to be the hidden purpose of all current undertakings. Competitive economy would then be a ruse of reason, the means chosen by antiphysis to realize itself at the expense of human lives. In this view, the employer's abstinence, his alienation grasped as obedience to an imperative and symbolized by distinguished conduct, and concurrently the worker's production of *merchandise*, hence the accumulation of capital which is the end of the process—all this seems to be the sacrifice of natural man, not to what is or will be in some near future (which manifests real demands and can be influenced by reorganizing the practical field), but rather to an infinite task that is unrealizable by a society or a particular era because it is a priori confused with the *norm* that pulls our species out of animality, with the mission of bourgeois humanity (insofar as industrial production seems to be the end result of a long odyssey and its meaning). For the bourgeois, the sole imperative really *experienced* is his *interest*, insofar as his objective reality, which is manufacturing, causes the manufacturer to see himself as proscribed a definite future by operations that are more or less short-term. But this *sole* imperative (How could there be others, since its only reality is as a relation of the practico-inert to the field of possibles?) is lived as if it were the manifestation, *here and now*, for *these* individuals, of an infinite imperative that will become manifest otherwise for others in future times, but whose form will remain the same in any circumstance, and whose variations of content will be strictly linked to each other as the phases of a vast development. In other words, progress—that *idea-myth*, in

259

Plato's sense of each term—is not in itself, and taken as transfinite, an imperative; but infinitesimal and current progress, which imposes itself on the industrialist and forces him to promote mechanization to cut costs, is by itself an absolute requirement. The bourgeois grasps the former through the latter as the ethical meaning of the species. He is thereby designated in his being by an infinite; and as this infinite is in essence nonbeing (to the exact extent that *this* manufacturer cannot bring it alone to being), the current and material imperative of particular interest is dematerialized. It seems to be the point of a pyramid lost in the future, and since it is also manifest as an ought-to-be, it participates in the infinite nonbeing of the idea-myth, whose content, conceivable or imaginable in some near future, escapes any conception and even imagination in the more distant future.[32] This inconceivable and nonrealizable nonbeing is therefore manifest as *immateriality* by every practico-inert demand. Man is bidden to doom himself so that humanity can fill that inert lacuna by a consensual alienation pursued indefinitely. Hence, scientistic ideology succeeds in disguising the practices of distinction by representing the bourgeois hatred of man, in others and in himself, as a sacrifice to the *ideal*.

This new notion has deep roots; it was in the second half of the last century, however, that it became a centerpiece of bourgeois ideology. It was still in use in 1939, and many in my generation heard bourgeois gentlemen, twenty years older than we, say of Hitler, "What do you expect? The man has an ideal." That ideal, as we know, was the sacrifice of the Germans (and of course other men, Aryans or not) to Germany's domination of the world. It is clear, moreover, that this notion—as such—was foreign to the Nazi leaders and was found chiefly among middle-level functionaries of the Nazi party. But it is striking that the dominant class in the bourgeois democracies could

---

32. It is like this even today. Modern economy tries to *conceive* of transformations in production at some years distance and to define, by a rational calculus, concomitant *demands* (for example, the demographic modifications that must make them possible). Conversely, planning grasps demographic transformation insofar as it is expressed as *demand* (obviously, this hypothetical imperative is manifest and categorical: the social order *must* be preserved, must be maintained), and insofar as it can be used to determine the number of new jobs to be created and, hence, changes that interest the national economy as a whole. Beyond this future accessible to conceptualization, *science fiction imagines* epochs that are linked to ours only by the idea-myth of indefinite progress in the sciences and their practical applications. But the ideology has changed under the influence of numerous factors which it would be idle to describe here, and future times, instead of justifying humanism, appear in most science fiction to be a condemnation of man and his epigones.

understand (and *condone*) the Hitlerian enterprise only by filtering it through its own ideology. The ideal, it was understood, is nonbeing conceived as spirituality. The sacrifice of man to the wrought thing cannot be legitimated as long as this thing, present and visible, allows itself to be grasped as pure matter or, if you will, as the eternal moment of dispersal. Christian habits, which persist in the agnostic grandsons of the Jacobins, dispose them to condemn materialism; the spirit is nonmatter. And of course they don't believe in it; they have rejected vital principles, entelechies, souls; they have made consciousness itself into an epiphenomenon; but their ethic, insofar as it is expressed negatively by distinguished practices, must postulate nonbeing as the foundation of values and pose the superiority of nonbeing to being as a motivation of moral behavior. For, after all, the soul, the thinking substance, God Himself, for want of direct intuition have never been defined in their being—for the majority of the faithful—except *negatively*, as that which is in principle distinct from matter and can be neither seen nor touched nor measured. For this reason, and for other, more profound reasons mentioned above, the bourgeois ethic begins by demanding of every moral agent that he bully and tyrannize his own organic materiality. But because it cannot reveal that the meaning of this bullying is the sacrifice of the organism to inorganic matter as it takes on the aspect of wrought material and, eventually, of merchandise, we have seen that distinction fails to deliver its purpose of itself, let alone its legitimation. This, as it is offered before being elaborated ideologically, is the sacrifice of life to *nothing;* and the sole, still vague justification the bourgeois could provide in this preideological phase of his class conduct is that *nothing* has more value than concrete and material existence, simply because its nonbeing is linked to the immateriality of the soul and the supernatural that is forever lost. Ideology goes to work on these givens. It is clear, in the first place, that nonbeing, a mute and fixed value, a rigid and permanent imperative, a norm devoid of flexibility, incapable of adaptation, is characterized—even before its ontological structure has been decided and a content found for it—by the inertia that characterizes inorganic matter. But at the same time its *lacunary* essence dematerializes it, since matter is by definition present and real. On this basis, the *capacités* elaborate the Ideal, which is simply this nothing transformed into humanity's destiny. Indeed, on the human scale, they provide as its content the demand of the cosmos, which insists on being transformed into antiphysis by the progressive enlargement of bourgeois domination. And this demand is simply the transcending of current self-interest toward the unrevealed infinity of future interests. Thus does ideology show us, by a sleight-of-hand, the *absence of matter* (as it will manifest its inert demands through the practical reorganizations of the human field) as the *pure immateriality* of bourgeois imperatives. This is quite a farce: what is absent is matter, or rather its future transformations; thus matter defines its type of absence—which has material inertia; the future still to come is, nonetheless, not spirituality but materiality-to-come. As a consequence, the ideal, as an unlimited field of demands, is workable matter imposing itself on men under the deceptive aspect of non-materiality; it is the present subjection of man to the human thing—lived *in fact* as an inert demand *and* a necessity—insofar as it is transformed, by a shift to the infinite, into that "always future void," the mission of humanity. Justified alienation is the prophesied advent of being-in-itself as a wrought totality, thanks to the consensual abolition of the for-itself. This in-itself, whose nonpresence alone preserves a lacunary immateriality and which, on the other hand, asks to be integrally converted into the human thing, in other words, to be informed by the objectivization of the worker and the owner as nonliving reality—this nonmaterial command to become a thing, to be finally inside the machine or merchandise, beyond the phlegm and secretions of the organism, finally changed by eternity into themselves—must be seen as one of the historical avatars of that "in-itself, for-itself" I spoke of in *Being and Nothingness,* which is indeed the ideal of every ethic of alienation. Absent, a pure appeal of nonbeing, its demand appears to be that of the spirit, an impalpable negation of the body, of concrete man; in this sense it seems to be a collective for-itself that would be reduced by an infinite pressure to two dimensions; at the same time its inert impersonality gives it, as a simple void to fill, the *future* substance of the in-itself. For the bourgeois ethic claims that men are mandated to communicate to things, through transubstantiation, the best of the human essence—which does not seem, a priori, unrealizable since the essence of man, as the past surpassed, is in itself a thing; and this can take place only by the death of existing man and the absorption of the for-itself by the thing produced that reflects it in reverse, defining itself as human by giving the act that stamps it in the cosmic continuum with the inert substance of a seal.

It is clear that this masquerade, which disguises future industrialization as an appeal launched from the depths of the future, matter disguised as spirit, allows bourgeois humanism to economize by doing without religion. In Luther's time, the bourgeoisie in Germany, in England, and to a certain degree in France opted for the reformed Church because Catholicism condemned lending at interest and papist ostentation was too costly. Thus the austere Protestant God was pleasing to the degree that, by the elimination of middlemen, he offered the best bargain. Yet the commandments of this hidden sovereign, not being transmitted and humanized by the singularity of a constituted body, tended increasingly to present themselves as anonymous prescriptions whose authenticity was guaranteed only by their rational universality. In 1850, costs were checked to the maximum by substituting the ideal for the will of the Supreme Being. The job was more than half done; the universality of the law, as early as the *Critique of Practical Reason*, had ceased to be a *sign* of divine will; it was posited for itself and *against man*, since the moral agent had to deny his concrete singularity. To finish the job, the nineteenth-century bourgeoisie merely needed to take impersonality and anonymity as guarantees for the imperatives of its humanism: mandates are legitimate precisely because there is no mandator. The particular essence of a known person can cast doubt on any command he might issue; on the other hand, if a command is self-contained, issued by no one and addressed to everyone without specification, it must indeed manifest the ethico-ontological structure of the cosmos and of man, who is its product. The ideal thus appears to be the infinite and rigorously impersonal field of the ought-to-be. A constant denunciation of man, a permanent demand for human sacrifices—we cannot complain of its cruelty since the ideal preserves in itself the inert anonymity of inorganic matter; nor will we reproach it for being an empirical product of human history, for it does not issue from men; its *imperative* structure is clearly alien to them and remains *other* than them, even when they internalize it. Moreover, it ultimately *demands* genocide; the species is prohibited from positing itself for its own sake as an end in itself; its only objective is self-destruction so that the Other-than-man (man as other, the diabolical and inert image of human praxis) might come to replace it. In whatever form it presents itself, the ideal appears in its infiniteness to be the denunciation of our finitude and our corporeal being; if it condemns needs, impulses, and desires, it is because it does not control relations between men— at least not directly. Its prescriptions are aimed primarily at the relation of our species to the *material-being* it appropriates or fashions, and which is also, beneath the deceptive manifestations of life, *its* being, its inorganic reality. It defines man in the world, but *on the ba—sis of the world*, as the worker whom the world demands in order to become *bourgeois*. And *on this basis* it imperatively defines human relations *insofar* as they are mediated by workable matter—in other words, insofar as they are reified by bourgeois property. This reification is not grasped as a fact, which would make it justifiable, but as the necessarily incomplete result of a fundamental imperative, the ideal (which requires a shift to the infinite to be imagined as completed). And this ideal is none other, finally, than the double process that gives the bourgeois property owner the essence of the thing possessed and partially transforms the producer into merchandise. But since this process is lived as an imperative (no others exist but those of the practico-inert—demands of man imposed on man through the passive fixity of matter), it is easy to notice its true character, which is *to be* the necessary product of a society based on *real* property, by its secondary aspect, another consequence of the mode and relations of production, which is to be generated *as if it were an ought-to-be*. The ideal therefore seems to be a coercive call from the *in-itself for-itself*, that spiritual nothingness, to the concrete men of bourgeois society to realize in themselves the mineralization of man for the sole purpose of producing, outside, the humanization of the mineral, in short, to do what they are actually doing. It is clear that the ideal is the supreme means—the means of all means—disguised as an absolute end. Its sovereignty comes from its very impersonality: it *is* no one and consequently *serves* no one. All things considered, even God is suspect: He made me for *His* Glory—Can't I challenge such theocentrism? Especially when He torments me to test me. I understand: His motives are infinitely more profound, I am neglecting the infinite love he bears me. Be that as it may, this absolute is an absolute-*subject*, and for that very reason must be challenged. The ideal's credentials issue from its status an an *absolute-object*; it neither loves its ministers nor detests them; it shows itself candidly for what it is, the naked demand for permanent and unrewarded sacrifice. In it, self-hatred, the basis of black humanism, is exalted as *idea:* it is the ethico-ontological structure of man, it defines him in his *pathos* (an impulse evoked and sustained by a value) as a being who can achieve being only by martyring his fleshly self to serve his work—wrought matter. It will be noted that this hateful inessentiality of human reality is determined at the time as an ideal in the form of a trinity: *profit for profit's sake* corresponds to *science for the sake of science* and *art for art's sake*. We shall return to this. What interests us for the moment is that, though disparaged after the fall of the Empire by the expansion of French industry and the revaluing of manpower that allowed the working class to organize for the first time, this humanism of the inhuman remains in diverse forms a central determination of the ethic until the end of the century. Gide unwittingly refers to it when he writes, fifty years after the first ideological babblings of the *capacités*: "I do not like man, I like that which devours him." An illuminating and utterly revealing maxim. One begins by passing sentence on the human beast, that bundle of carnal and repugnant appetites, *mediocre* aspirations to security, relaxation, and happiness, that viscid organism which lives to live, and most of all that *existence*, that transcendence of a facticity *by* itself and, through the world, *toward* itself. But man is no sooner denounced than he is reestablished in his dignity as victim: he *is eaten.* One doesn't even do him the honor of attributing real greatness to him as a naked feast. All honor goes to the eater, a real carnivore, who steadily wolfs down his prey. Yet it must be observed that we are not dealing with an animal; although the sentence refers to Prometheus and his vulture, Gide was careful to make the sacrificer *neutral:* that which devours him. In other words, it is the ideal; its gender is neuter. For this writer, this haut bourgeois, the contradictory totality alone manifests the *ethical* in its plenitude—man and his chancre, the former tolerated as food for the latter. We could say that insofar as the thing—remorse, misfortune, a transcendent goal—manifests itself in every moment of lived experience by contradicting and spontaneous movement, by continually and pitilessly undercutting life in the name of something *transcendent, impersonal and immaterial*, it is no longer even the result of alienation that matters here (the transmutation into a human thing), but alienation in its nakedness. (In this way, the thing dissimulates its ontological status as inert and *unrealizable* matter: endlessly devoured, man *subjected* to the ideal. Gide does not claim there is a way out, a means of putting an end to pain, for example, by *succeeding in the enterprise*, and in the legend that serves him as a symbol there is none. Prometheus has no opportunity to surrender himself to his rapacious familiar, it all depends upon the grace of Zeus, who takes his time.) This transcendent, of course, can exist only as a coefficient to what we call our trans-ascendence (the objective aim of our practical surpassing as it is revealed to our *pro-ject*). But after fifty years of "black humanism," Gide's implicit intention is to strip man of his transcendence, to transform him into suffering passivity, and to turn his own praxis against himself as an alien power, hostile and corrosive. Failure remains characteristic of human reality and its cipher, for it is none other than the bite of the transcendent. Of course, Gide is of the reformist persuasion; a certain religious puritanism undergirds his position. And there is no doubt that what devours him, what he calls *thirst*, is the unsatisfied desire to rise above the self to the level of pure artistic, moral, and scientific values. It is also a voiceless anxiety stemming from the contradiction of his sexual preferences—sensed, at the time, rather than known—and of religious and social law. Be that as it may, we can consider this aesthetic-puritanical moralism an extenuated and subtle form of the ethic of alienation. *Thirst*, in particular, ranks at the top of the scale of values, and gratification at the bottom, if it is there at all. Or, if you will, gratification, insofar as it is sought, seems to be the *means* of thirst; and thirst, which is desire and the sustained negation of desire, seems at this juncture of Gide's thought to be the internalization of a neuter, the person's moral qualification by privation, the insertion into the *conatus* of an inert lacuna which exalts it by tearing it apart. This eulogy to frustration—as the dehumanization of man—preferring a passively suffered negation to a praxis that attains its objective, recalls quite precisely the morality of effort founded on the necessary failure of man by the bourgeoisie, following the *capacités*, a generalization of the historic failure of the dominant and middle classes between February 1848 and December 1852. After all, Gide's progress from *Prométhée mal enchaîné* to his *Oedipe*, covering more than half a century, leads him systematically to dissolve these leftovers of an outmoded epoch, to liberate lived experience from that pit of inertia, the ideal, to replace dolorism—which puts human value on the way a person endures his mutilations—with *restored* praxis, making man not the supreme end but the means, and man's purpose creation. In other words, until his death Gide continued to evolve in the direction of a positive humanism. In the beginning, he might have said, like Renan, that God is the future of man—which implies that one maintains a merciless hatred for one's neighbor, as for oneself. At the end of his life he would have subscribed, I believe, to Ponge's formula: "Man is the future of man," which replaces the inhuman impersonality of the ideal with the concrete and specific activity of men on the human thing reduced to its function of *mechanical slave*, on themselves through wrought matter and directly with the establishment of human relations. The aim of this activity is to produce themselves, liberated, in the affirmation of all their needs and all their desires, as indivisibly an organism and praxis, against any imperative—against any priority of the practico-inert—and against alienation, that Proteus forever beaten down and resurrected in another guise.

Under the Empire, man cannot be considered his own end; the exploited classes—from utopian socialism to scientific socialism—already have their theorists, but after the June massacres they retreat into themselves, their consciousness deepens but is a mute, silent labor that takes place beneath the external semblance of passivity and resignation. The exploited do not yet have *their own thought*, the only effective weapon against analytic atomism on the level of ideas, that dialectical reason which is praxis itself as the source of all knowledge and self-knowledge. Their ideology remains what the enlightened elite elaborated for the dominant classes; it poses as a humanism—for since the seventeenth century the bourgeoisie have been claiming power and then gaining it, in the name of natural law. But as the bourgeoisie denies the workers the right to work and the right to associate; as it has despoiled itself of its political rights so as not to share them with the proletariat, preferring the equality of frustration and impotence to that of rights; as the repression of the summer of '48 henceforth proscribed the uttering of the word "fraternity" except in jest; as after that splendid coup, human relations, where they are becoming established, seem to specify man's hatred of man; as the ultimate objective of the new ideology is to justify the exploitation of one part of the French populace by another part, more restrained but equally determined, representing exploitation as a particular form of universal alienation—this strange humanism begins by establishing that man is a being devoid of rights and is defined only by his duties. This is an old tradition. As early as 1789, in any case, certain members of the haute bourgeoisie claimed that the preamble to the Constitution was an inventory of the "Duties of Man and of the Citizen." This godless theology reduced man to nothingness, pulverized him; his sacrifices alone would externally give him a provisional and wholly negative unity. He must always strangle his nature. Such a system was obviously superior to medieval Christianity; seriously elaborated as it was by the intellectuals to serve peasants and barons alike with its ambiguity, Christianity certainly posited that the human creature is in himself nothingness; but it added that God had created him out of love, and this bounty of the Almighty gave absolute value to His creature. This valorization by the Other was a clear expression of alienation, but as feudal relations remained, even in oppression and violence, relations between persons, the supreme alienation was *personalized*. This facilitated, even in those dark centuries, a "white humanism" in which, as the object of an infinite love, everyone respected his neighbor—at least theoretically—for the love that God bore him. In 1850 the humanism is *black;* the human thing—worked matter, workable matter—has replaced God. It designates men by fierce demands that give some substance to their scattering by the sacrifices it claims. The seal that contains the pulverized material within boundaries supported only by inertia is an imperative that provides individuals and groups with their synthetic and necessarily passive cohesion: sealed matter seals men. But the perfect indifference of the thing or its extrapolation, the ideal, having been substituted for divine love, there is nothing in bourgeois humanism to valorize human beings; every man, for himself and everyone else, is merely a means, and inessential at that, of accomplishing duties that enlist him from the outside; for the rest, he is born of dust and remains dust, dead or alive. Here we find an echo of Calvinist pessimism among the manufacturers of the Second Empire; when the bourgeois of Geneva spoke of the human soul, it was to denounce its infection and proclaim the disgust it must arouse in the Creator— save in a granting of His Grace. After which, without transition, they espoused the most arrogant optimism based on their bourgeois duty to conquer the earth and rework it to render it up to God more beautiful than He had given it to them; adding that divine favor, and consequently the chances of salvation, were measured by the success of human enterprise, as witness the rich man, a stern worker, providentially aided in his work, perhaps saved by his very wealth itself, proof of his labor, his austerity, his voluntary sacrifice, hence of his merits and—who knows?—a prenatal blessing. In 1850, God is dead, workable and worked matter has taken His place; but the duty of the bourgeois remains the same: to ensure the *embourgeoisement* of the earth, to divide it into private properties, to develop it, to turn it into a harmonious set of manufactured products. If the instrument, if merchandise, indeed if wrought matter, which formerly served to mediate between bosses and workers, between producers and consumers, between supply and demand, is posited as an absolute, mediation becomes the supreme end, and the mediated terms, shifting to a relative position, function only to suppress themselves so that mediation can exist, or to make themselves the means of the supreme Means, which even while affirming itself as a means establishes its power over the ruin of all human ends or subordinates them to itself as a means of the Means. Thus, freed from God, man continues to serve; and so much the better, for a vague family connection to Protestantism gives this despairing optimism a touch of reassuring religiosity. It is *true* that property is *sacred:* it was a right, now it is a duty. Better still, every property owner has the sacred right to make it his duty. By defining man as an *intermediary* in conformity with his class-being, by proposing to our species the *man-means* as a model, the elite of the *middle* class did not limit themselves to constructing humanism by mythologizing and fetichizing the social relations that characterize it (with the lower levels of its class, with the other classes of society); they legitimized the dominant class by representing it as capital's chosen means of accumulation and concentration.

A strange humanism, and in this it betrays itself. For Calvin, there was a heaven: God gave back a hundredfold what He had rarely allowed to be given to Him. The human thing takes everything and gives nothing back. Man, an inessential means, is justified by his sacrifices; he is made such that *his only salvation lies in his damnation.* Contemptible if he wants to live, love, and let live, his unique value resides in voluntary self-destruction. This is not necessarily a question of real death; he is only asked to let the thing devour his unstable and labile essence. Does the human thing have at least more value than its owner or its manufacturer? Sometimes that is implied, for man is seen mineralized in it, delivered from his shameful organic functions; in a way, the thing would be the antiphysis of man. But the hidden truth is that human sacrifices are gratuitous. The resentment of the enlightened elite made it propose to the bourgeoisie the humanism of the *counter-man,* even while claiming to honor the tradition of the eighteenth century. For the professionals, riddled with hatred, envy, and frightened contempt, the perpetual annihilation of the human conceals no "Loser Wins," confers no merit. When man dooms himself, he dooms himself for good. Having sacrificed his life to the human thing, having objectified himself in his product or his property; having accepted all mutilations, all frustrations; having practiced abstinence in the name of utilitarianism and having been stripped of his transcendence in favor of inert, inorganic materiality; having misunderstood and relegated his practical temporality to the penumbra of the inessential so as to force himself to live in the dehumanizing time of economic exchange and Newtonian mechanics; having experienced the reification of human relations and accepted his incommunicability, remaining with his most intimate friends in a reciprocal rupture of communication; having conducted himself, despite his forgotten life's confused protestations, as a *man of duty,* a martyr to alienation, pulverized a thousand times a day by turning the atomizing gaze of the mechanist toward himself; having lived his life unaware and without understanding of the obscure impulses of his heart, which thus unperceived became transformed, condensed, and fled into the shadows incognito—this loyal servant has no other reward, upon his death, than to become a thing in his turn. He passes wholly into the inorganic, his diabolical image has finally devoured him. At worst he will be one slab of marble among many; at best he will stand in the square, in bronze or some kind of chiseled stone, a *manufactured product,* a demand of the practico-inert, the passive symbol of a society whose members are merchandise and which is founded on human sacrifice.

In other words, the basis of bourgeois humanism is clearly misanthropy. We can be sure that the enlightened elite is conscious of it and has devised it out of some perverse pleasure. The trick works; the accomplished type of man, his archetype no longer directly the property owner but the man of duty—who can realize himself fully only through property—duty defined in his innermost mind as the imperative negation of man in favor of the wrought thing, the essence of humanity can be only a futile passion, one long human suicide or, with a little luck, the self-domestication of men in a farmyard guarded by machines. In any event, the humanism of the nineteenth century pretends to exalt man when it admires only his inexorable devourer, demonstrating that society is made to exalt members of the species. In its terms this means that society is built and preserved only on *their sacrifice,* in short, that it is inhuman and devours them all. But this doesn't prevent it from proclaiming its optimism; since the essence of man is to be eaten, bourgeois society, ogre that it is, is truly the regime that suits him best. Thus the resentful and lucid elite feels a brutal pleasure in concealing its nihilism beneath the rigors of a positive ethic, and concealing its misanthropy—born of a double historical failure and the hatred it thus bears toward all the other classes—beneath a prophecy that reveals to the human race its exemplary mission. This ideology is turned directly against the possessing class, which the elite holds responsible for the troubles of '48 and for the coup d'état (didn't it stubbornly refuse to share its political rights?); it is hateful to the workers as well, even more, perhaps, but less directly, less organically. Yet the class that is its chief target appropriates it, for the bourgeois and the professionals are *also* accomplices. By condemning the bourgeois to the suffering of Prometheus, the elite could not prevent itself from justifying bourgeois society; if the bourgeois "eater" eats out of duty and to the detriment of his nature, the thirty million "eaten" must sacrifice themselves to become the docile means of his ostensible sacrifice. This ideology must be widely disseminated among the disadvantaged classes. Aside from the fact that it provides a basis for their vague pessimism, as we have mentioned, the dominant class accepts and diffuses this humanism of hatred because it effectively persuades the exploited that the exploitation of man by man is the *primary* norm and *ethical* basis of the best possible society, since humanity's only purpose is to exhaust itself to ensure the advent of the sovereign thing, and that alienation is the supreme value. The foundations are laid; for half a century humanism and antihumanism, buttressed by the rites of cant and distinction, will impose themselves on French society. To be sure, this pessimism is *strictly dated*. From 1880 on, humanist ideology veers toward the optimism it will truly incorporate only at the beginning of this century. The reasons for this new metamorphosis are complex. Basically, however, there is the new industrial upsurge which revalorizes manpower. Salaries are on the rise. When they were consistently low and there was a disturbing increase in unemployment, the employers dared not claim that the purpose of industry was to raise the level of life for all classes, including the working class. It would rather have subscribed to the thesis of absolute pauperization, which until around 1850 seemed to follow from the facts. So it had to sustain the notion that man is made for industry. At the end of the century, unemployment gives way to full employment, it is feared there will be a dearth of manpower; the strength to work is still a kind of merchandise, but with demand about to surpass supply almost everywhere, the worker knows his power, he becomes organized, the working class produces its apparatus, the antagonisms that bitterly set men against each other in the labor market tend to disappear, and the possibility of replacing such antagonisms with collective contracts is already glimpsed. Until 1914, working class strategy becomes offensive; the majority of strikes are won. Sure of its power, anarchosyndicalism dreams of overturning bourgeois society by a general strike. Challenged, the employers and the professionals attempt to reconstruct a positive ideology; they respond with a magnification of *force* to the integration of violence into the system of working-class values. This is, of course, basically violence in the service of the existing social order. But it won't do, for the Empire with its swashbucklers did the same thing; the military must be brought to heel, and it will be demonstrated that the hero of our time, both creator and conqueror, is the manufacturer. Action, permitted the lone warlords, is restored in its dignity as praxis. Basic praxis, however, which is simply work, is opposed by the economic, social and political activities of industrialists and bankers—as if they derived their substance from themselves instead of being derived from it. The young employer at this time, Nietzschean without reading Nietzsche, is Hercules, Samson. In this brutal optimism, which relegates absolute pauperization to the storehouse of accessories but clearly remains silent with regard to relative pauperization, the pioneer would still be captain, even if, despite the good counsel of Du Camp, he doesn't yet dare to give himself the rank of general. After all, captains go into action and generals die in their beds. In the perpetual battle to lower costs, increase production, improve the product, and conquer or create internal and external markets, the employer's main concern is not to spare his troops, who remain in the breach day and night. But he loves them, just as a good captain loves his men. And if he doesn't spare them, it is for man, to improve the human condition and thus the human character. In a word, when capitalism is about to conclude its phase of accumulation, before pessimism is reborn, revived by new contradictions and the necessity to combat crises by means of monopolistic overconcentration and the imperialism that results from it, between the end of the "coal-steel" complex and the beginning of the second industrial revolution (by the massive utilization of electric energy), *two* antagonistic ideologies appear, united by their very contradiction. United, that is, in the sense that their opposition is situated in the doubling of a common notion, praxis, posed on both sides as the fundamental value and original determination of the human condition but immediately split into (a) productive work and (b) the power of dictatorial decision. In any event, between 1850 and 1870, despite certain isolated attempts, the time had not yet come to define man as that practical agent who makes history on the basis of prior circumstances. Abrogated Christianity left behind it "Christian ideas gone mad,"[33] which allow a pessimistic humanism to be founded on failure, useless and passively endured sacrifice, incommunicability, subjection to work, that is, to the practico-inert, unsuccessful effort, and, essentially, self-hatred. Clearly, ideology does not represent man as he is but as he must be to justify the hegemony of the dominant class. Thus the bourgeois themselves, despite their distinguished practices, do not adequately realize the concept that designates them. The expansion of industry, a certain liberation of budgetary options, and in spite of everything the silence of a proletariat they believe to be "checkmated"—all these things dispose them

33. [Sartre attributes this to] G. K. Chesterton.

behind the scenes toward a certain optimism; under the Empire, business *is going well*. But the pleasures of profit, of comfort and power, are *passed over in silence* even as they give the lie to the universal imperative that engenders man as a sacrificial being. This discrepancy between what the capitalists are and what they believe they are is normal; otherwise ideology would give way to a conscious grasp of the situation. Furthermore, whatever their joys, it is true that these are produced on a common foundation of alienation and frustration (they are threatened in their objective being, in their self-interest; they have abdicated and returned that political power they fought for during most of a century to the military caste). Thus, at the slightest danger, ideology is reaffirmed; they use it to think about man, to think about themselves, to conceive of human relations under the aspect of reification. The *capacités* have not profited, moreover, from the troubles they initiated; brought to heel under the Empire, they preserve under the cloak of an iron contempt the bitterness and remorse that has been seething in them since the autumn of '48. These men of resentment want to be the conscience of the rich. This is the public that the Postromantic artists—all born around 1820—will find, without even looking, after the June massacres and the coup of 2 December. These are the readers who will ensure their success, changing their neurosis into an objective expression of society.

It must be acknowledged, however, that the society of the Second Empire demands a *class literature*, a literature subservient to the interests of the upper classes. But the order comes, in fact, from the right-minded military who have taken power. In short, it expresses a double demand: first, that the work serve the religious politics of Napoleon III, who recognized the power of Catholic circles and played up to them; second, that the beautiful be *idealized:* a nude must represent the *eidos* of the feminine body, whose archetype the most splendid nudities do not even begin to approach. This literature on order *does not emanate* from class, it *is addressed* to it. Its social function is, in the first instance, negative; idealization presents the truth of man on the level where the beautiful and the good mingle, in short, on the *normative* level—which is in a sense what the cultivated public requires. But the norm is not the same; here it involves showing that the truth of man is *aristocratic,* in short, that bourgeois and ordinary folk become enlightened by following the military man and his fine wife, of whom they are the demoted hypostases. Here we see a return to a modified naturalism. Human nature exists, and it is the product of divine creation; only it comes to fruition exclusively among the

273

upper classes. And these are not—or not only—the property owners, they are the warlords who, giving their lives in advance, have acquired in return the right to calm enjoyment. Alienation does not exist in this academic universe; the soldier's *being-to-die*—under the class of highly superior officers—is expressed in generosity and narcissism; a gift of God, man gives himself, and this double gift is the very source of beauty—surely the finest of all gifts; this perpetual offering of his person to France must be lived narcissistically. Indeed, his consciousness of himself as a doubly offered gift can only be expressed as an idle admiration of his being—or if you will, of divine generosity internalized as his own generosity, which makes his physical person, the least of his gestures, his most fugitive thoughts a silent donation. Since in the person of the sovereign and the aristocracy *man is a gift to man*, being-in-the-world on the level of the great is in itself a donation, a donation that has, therefore, no need of particular specificity; the generals give themselves when they eat, drink, dream—a bourgeois puritanism compels them to forget themselves when they defecate, something the legitimate aristocracy did not formerly do. But these men of war indeed feel that in this they are sparing the sensibility of the lower classes. And of their wives as well, who have no pubic hair when represented in paintings, nor bodily needs in literature, but who, all told, especially in the customary exchange of partners, fuck appreciably better than bourgeois women. In short, the Court requires artists to manifest its being-for-giving to the lower classes by painting or depicting it alone, by offering the public a view of men and women that would be worth co-opting. There is no prohibition on depicting a woman of the people, a simple soldier; established by a coup d'état, this dictatorship is not yet hereditary and does not repudiate the practice of conferring nobility. But such characters, victims of an error of birth, must manifest the nobility of their sentiments—perhaps by dying. There are no other characters in this world; some awareness of their existence, yes, but only as possible *readers*, who have the right—for the period of a reading and in imagination—to identify with the great gift-givers. As for the middle-class readers, ugly and vulgar as they are, they never tire of giving themselves, if only by employing the lower classes—who also possess, in degraded form, the ferment of generosity. What complicates things is that they have no one below them to benefit from it: therefore they will give themselves to the classes immediately above them, who, out of a civilian's obedience and respect for the military, give themselves to the aristocracy. As we have seen, there is a double giving, from high to low, from low to high. The artist will take note only of the descending order of generosity, except when it is a matter of a soldier's loyalty to his captain, a domestic servant's to his master, a noblewoman's to her husband. They loved this at Court, an archetypal literature that showers flattery exclusively on soldiers—preferably not in combat—and depicts only the body of their ladies, dressed or undressed, indeed, the body they should have, that they possess preeminently in the eyes of the God who made them, and perhaps from afar in their petticoats, liveries of impotence with a mutilating beauty, in the eyes of the bourgeois.

There are authors—and sculptors and painters—who provide the public with the prescribed potions. Their works, penetrating the middle classes, offer themselves in their beauty (or in what is claimed as such) as variations on the same aesthetic-ethical imperative: "Let us not look at ourselves; let everyone in our class be blind to others and to himself; we are inferiors since art has neither the means, the taste, nor the right to depict us. But to compensate, by reading this book or contemplating that canvas we have the right to admire ourselves in our exemplary image, which through the artist's mediation is generously offered us by the class with divine right." We know that the Emperor horse-whipped Courbet's *Les Baigneuses*—and Merimée, the sycophant, reveals the official conception and his basic intent when he writes: "I cannot understand how a man would take pleasure in painting, *au naturel*, a dreadful woman and her maid at a pond, taking what appears to be a much-needed bath." These good women have no business in a picture, quite the contrary, they are shocking; the people (or rather the petty bourgeoisie) are flung in the face of Napoleon, who has nothing to do with them. And this flesh, still pretty but slightly worn, suggests that life is not an everlasting metal—the bets are off.

In short, official art, optimistic, idealistic, must at once reflect to the Court a beauty that photographs do not permit it to see (if you haven't leafed through albums of the period you cannot imagine the ugliness of this bunch—Eugénie de Montijo apart), and teach the bourgeois, more adeptly than did the Ancien Régime, that they should find their fulfillment and their completion as men high above their heads, that they are not, however, separated from the nobility by a difference of race but participate in their archetypal humanity and even emanate from it. Thus the social hierarchy is consolidated by a mysterious unity. Literature is full of fine sentiments, painting full of beautiful women. Art is simply the reproduction of natural

275

beauties to the extent that these discreetly demonstrate that the social order is in conformity with nature, with the designs of the Creator. This results, for official critics, in a *concretism* of the beautiful which dissimulates its profound antinaturalism. The artist, bidden to imitate nature when the hand of God has left Its imprint in the very perfection of Its work, is secretly urged to idealize landscapes or people because divine action is nowhere evident, and the objects of experience, without a supplementary turn of the screw, are manifest as particularizations of the concept rather than as incarnations of the idea. Right-thinking literature finds many an author to write it; it is read; the bourgeoisie lulls its remorse and regrets by discovering in such literature nobility without tears, ennoblement within the reach of its children. Then too, they find these books boring, and it is *distinguished* to be bored, to *endure* time, deny action, disqualify lived experience; this snobbery explains why even in our day bourgeois best-sellers are frequently quite boring. Between 1850 and 1870, moreover, the bourgeoisie does not want to be mentioned; it is happy not to recognize itself in these works, nor to recognize the aggressive arrogance of its masters, the officers. Reading becomes a superficial and trivial diversion once it is understood that fiction communicates no real information and that the reader does not identify with the hero of the novel or find any of his own problems in it. In a word, reading is a process of being *silent*. Writing is talking without saying anything, as one does in the salons. The written work is reassuring because it remains external and self-subverting: "It's only literature," as the saying goes. And happily so.

This means that the enlightened elite and the bourgeois who know how to read *are not expecting* art-neurosis. If this becomes *their* art it is because its satisfactions create their need for it. Indeed, scientistic ideology under the Empire is never entirely *explicit;* without being exactly clandestine, it likes to conceal itself; its radical pessimism would not suit the ruling aristocracy, so as soon as it appears in outline it hides behind the official optimism. Scientistic humanism cannot expose itself without becoming quite explicit, even down to its fundamental misanthropy. Thus neither the industrialist nor the practitioner has his social *imago* at his disposal, the *persona* that comes to him as his *Ego* from ideology, that false knowledge generated by the truth and still preserving bits of it. He is far from conscious of his role and his class-being; but he doesn't even have full use of the *false consciousness* he produces. Frequently atrophied or embryonic, this consciousness sometimes appears in its integrity like a bolt of lightning, and is almost instantly extinguished; a fugitive thing, its cohesion is in the movement of its coming and going; if it were stable, its contradictions would in the long run cause it to explode. Moreover, scientistic ideology is made up of countless bits and pieces: everyone has taken a hand in it, no one has taken the risk of turning it into a complete system. It isn't *singular* for anyone but rather involves multiple and differential relations between key terms: ideal, sacrifice, etc. The impulses that sustain it—particularly the hatred of man—do demand some satisfaction. But they mustn't become conscious. When the Knights of Nothingness begin to publish their first works in 1849, the cultivated public adopts them and makes them *its* poets and *its* novelists, not because these writers are purveying self-knowledge, nor because they consolidate its false consciousness by presenting its *imago* incarnate in a poem or in the hero of a novel. The truth is more complex. The artist imposes himself on the professionals and the wealthy both because he resembles them and because he radically differs from them, because they implicitly understand his intention and because they manage to misunderstand it; at once because they grasp the homicidal intention hidden in his unrealization, sufficiently, at least, to make it serve their ends, and because what is perhaps an inevitable misunderstanding defines him in their eyes as a hard-line realist. These strange and twisted bonds have had the effect that no writer has so scorned his public yet more completely expressed it, not in its historic truth but in the real pathos that is at the basis of false consciousness and ideological nonknowledge. Nothing will be so instructive regarding the writer's relation to his society, his class, the historical moment, and tradition as to examine the strange affinities that make scientistic readers a chosen public for authors who want essentially to dissolve the true in the imaginary. If one believes, as I do, in the dialectic that leads from infra- to superstructures and generates the latter from the former, how is it comprehensible that a practitioner, mad about Darwin and professionally convinced that one must "submit to the facts," should finally permit himself to be represented in the literary sector, not by Duranty, who preaches just this kind of submission, but by writers whose well-publicized dogma is that "nothing is beautiful but that which does not exist"?

At bottom, this strange harmony comes from the fact that the scientistic humanists and the knights of absolute negation belong to the upper stratum of the same class and reflect the same contradictions inherent in it. We must hasten to note, however, a kind of diachronic discrepancy: the practitioners and artists have neither discovered nor lived those contradictions at the same time. For both, the fundamental problem was *transcending class*. One had to escape the middle classes, where man was merely the means of the rich or, at best, of society. For the writers in question, this desire was quite often merely the internalization of the pride of a father or of practitioner-parents who based their claims on their *capacities*. But this is complicated by a conflict of generations that fostered in these young men an ambivalent attitude toward science and a frankly negative one toward politics. They could not, therefore, allow their elders to base their right to share power with those of greater wealth on a rigorous but disillusioning knowledge. Leconte de Lisle apart, none of them participated in the events of '48 or really took any interest in them. And when Flaubert, much later, refers back to the February Revolution in *L'Education sentimentale*, it will be to blame everyone. These are the men, however, who will procure the professional's patents of nobility and justification from his still smarting failure.

At the outset, the enlightened elite will recognize certain of its own fundamental conceptions in the first works of these writers. Both writers and readers have a horror of their *own* class—each for reasons of his own. They were not concerned with augmenting its privilege or power, but quite sincerely with removing themselves from it. Or rather, since they had nothing but contempt for politics, to *be* removed from it. They needed a good aristocracy that would choose them and raise them up to its own level. And since they became conscious of themselves just as the aristocracy was on the decline, they had the immediate feeling that claims and supplications, which made sense only if addressed to the aristocracy, were becoming imaginary beliefs, or structures of the imaginary. Thence, by a vicious and unrealizing negation of their class condition, they internalize the scientific overview. Indeed, the attitude of the scientist at the time, defined by Heidegger's *Nur vorbei lassen*—which would no longer suit modern science—is characterized as *desituating*. But as the young writers attempt to adopt a superior manner with respect to their class and ultimately to the species they cannot escape, their desituating becomes imaginary, and scientific behavior is thereby transformed into an *aesthetic attitude* through sheer unrealization, without any modification of its internal connections or its relations to the object. This attitude, imagined in its generality, is a sham desituating with respect to the world, which brings with it for the subject an unrealization of the external object and of his own interiority. On this level, the researcher's primary procedure, *observation*, is no longer possible, and no information can be received or transmitted. Still, the enlightened public becomes *permeable* to art to the extent that—neglecting the process of unrealization—it finds that the behavior of the technician and the artist *correspond*. In other words, the practitioners are the natural public for this literature, which regards the basic character of the exact disciplines as the primary structure of aesthetic exis. Moreover, the negation found at the basis of this art confirms the enlightened elite in its pride and the bourgeoisie in its practices of distinction. Just as the scientist observes the system under study from the outside, the artist, when he represents the human race, must refuse to experience its passions or share its purposes in order to grasp them objectively. The reader rediscovers his objectivity as a practitioner in the impassivity of the writer, who, awaiting the advent of the human sciences and social engineering, plays the role of the future anthropologist— isn't he the only one to speak of man *as an object?* By this very fact he raises himself much higher than a real transcendence of class would do, since he detaches himself from the species itself and, having no more than a "glancing acquaintance" with it, verges on the superhuman. And this *distancing* seems to the scientistic reader a magnification of his own attitude. The professionals, theorists or practitioners, are precursors of the total objectivization of man—whatever their discipline—since they perpetually practice that disengagement which is indispensable to the world's "becoming-an-object." Thus the new authors' impassivity and impersonality, insofar as these are passed off as scientific, represent to the enlightened elite its own superhumanity and confirm the idea that as a pure, knowing gaze the elite itself escapes universal objectivity—and subjectivity as well. The gaze, like light that illuminates but is not itself visible, becomes the mode of being of those supermen the scientists, technicians, and artists; that reflexive consciousness, unable in its pure translucidity to become the object of reflection, escapes knowledge even while establishing it. The apprehension of the real and the apprehension of the beautiful are united by a reciprocity of reflections. And no doubt the positivist reader is not unaware that his reading plunges him into a world of fiction; but out of habit he believes—a great tradition of classical literature—that the new authors "lie to tell the truth," whereas they present him as his reality a surreal myth they have conceived for their own use. Be that as it may, for the public of 1850 the writer is a prophet. He prophesies what Renan will call the "future of science," the integration of man with knowledge; and using his distance to reduce humanity to its essence as object, he depicts it *from outside* and

279

in advance gives a content to the scientistic ideology that makes man a being external to himself, moved by forces external to him. This is enough to gain him everyone's confidence; he will take the place of the sociologist and especially the psychologist. That impersonal gaze accumulates experience, and shedding light on the causal sequences that manifest themselves in daily life, it derives from these what might be called a provisional science—more empirical than experimental—that will serve as a basis for true science when the time comes. By a misunderstanding we shall have to probe further, this public, still quite influenced by English empiricism, sees the Knights of Nothingness and the Imaginary as "men of experience," who communicate information in a concrete and rigorous (though nonscientific) form.

And the cultivated bourgeois, without accepting their arrogant assertion of superhumanity, finds in the impassivity they display a justification of his distinguished practices. Rightly and wrongly. Rightly, because hatred is at the source of both attitudes; from this point of view, the refusal of organic life and the more general refusal to share the aims of the species equally express a savage misanthropy. Wrongly, for it must be asked of any misanthrope: With what milieu, with what social stratum, with what class do you identify humanity? What aggregate or particular group do you hate, *in fact*, when you claim to hate the human race in general? And clearly bourgeois hatred, exasperated since '48, is addressed above all to the working classes in response to an imagined hatred of the bourgeoisie. The hatred of the professionals, surfacing at the same period, as we have seen, is simultaneously aimed at the dominant class, which renounced its political rights rather than share them, and at the workers, who tried to steal their February victory and turned it into a disaster. As for the artists, however, their misanthropy is of longer standing; they have chosen art against science, against industry, against their families, and against the grand bourgeois who have received them. To be sure, they have no great love for the workers; but it is the middle classes they despise, and secondarily the bourgeoisie. They have hated them since childhood because they regard them through the eyes of a dead aristocracy which they blame the middle classes for killing; they reject organic needs and generally animality so as paradoxically to strangle in themselves the bourgeoisie and their class of origin. Around 1830, the rather uncultivated bourgeois and professionals lived stingily on a restricted portion of surplus value, the bourgeois to accumulate capital, the professionals to buy land with their savings; they denied themselves pleasures in the name of utilitarianism, which reduced the enterprise of living to the satisfaction of natural needs. Yet it must be added that their satisfaction was offered as a means. We are not far from Molière's bourgeois, who swears by this maxim: "One must eat to live and not live to eat." Eat to live and live to protect one's interests. During their adolescence, then, these artists could not tolerate either the materialist necessity of naked need—which they compared to the gratuitousness of luxury, of the "superfluous," to the excessive and, moreover, imaginary generosity of the murdered aristocracy—or that utilitarian avarice which dehumanized it by denying organic life the possibility of being its own end. *Distinguished before the fact*, they all tried to destroy nature in themselves because they confused it with their class-being, which they denied. But in this very effort to deny organic existence and its "base" natural ends, they found in advance the bourgeois ideal of the 1850s. By repudiating in himself the *old bourgeois* (his father, his older brother—professionals or part of the dominant class), the artist at this time is united with the bourgeois, who wants to tyrannize in himself the *worker* of '48—a being of need, hunger, fatigue, sleep, etc.—in other words, that nature they have in common. By internalizing the hatred others feel for him, the bourgeois confuses a hatred of nature, a hatred of the worker and of man, *self-hatred*. When he reads, he finds self-hatred again as a principle of art, and this is not false since the artist hates the bourgeois in himself as a universal image of man—a bourgeois, moreover, of a type that is daily more superannuated (the model proposed in their childhood), so that the reader does not feel targeted as a class individual but primarily as an individual representative of the species; and he grasps beauty as the artistic equivalent of distinction, or as its justification in this realm. The beautiful is distinguished to the extent that it is the very type of antiphysis as it appears in the particular sector of art. By denying passions and needs as sources of inspiration, the writer reflects his own *imago* back to the manufacturer, justifying his decision never to guide himself by the *pathos* of his fleshly being and to accept as a rule only his inorganic essence, subjected in the external world to *others* and to exteriority, *interest*. Thus, surprising as it may seem, when Flaubert as a poor student dreams of castrating himself, then as a young recluse imagines he is rich enough to kill necessity by delighting in the superfluous; when Baudelaire, out of a horror of natural fecundity, pushes his love of sterility to the point of choosing literary impotence; when in *La Fanfarlo* he shows his hero so alarmed by feminine nudity that he begs the young woman who is about to give herself to him to dress up again in the costume that unrealized her as Colombine; when he writes, "The woman one loves is the one who has no pleasure," or, under the influence of Joseph de Maistre, "Nature teaches nothing, or almost nothing; it merely forces man to sleep, drink, eat . . . Crime . . . is originally natural . . . ; virtue, on the contrary, is artificial, supernatural . . . since it required . . . gods and prophets to teach it to animalistic humanity, and since man alone would have been powerless to discover it"; when he practices dandyism; when Leconte de Lisle goes around the salons mimicking the radical minerality of the artist—these antibourgeois are inviting their readers to become even more bourgeois by pushing bourgeois distinction a little further each day. It is clear that for Leconte de Lisle, man ought to be a monocle, a vitrification of the absolute gaze nailing the scrutinized creature to the wall, like a butterfly to a cork. And although the bourgeois and the professional often surrender the monocle to the military man, it is also their ideal; the antinaturalist current that runs right through the nineteenth century braces them in the attempt at a *manufactured transparency* by the double human sacrifice of the worker to his product and of their own needs to a sterile impassivity. For nearly half a century the writers will quietly offer them, transfigured, the myth of antinature. And when the last of them, Huysmans, breaking with "naturalism" out of disgust for the body, shows his hero turning on himself and trying to create a biological antiphysis as a work of art that would be totally real and lived in its plenitude, engendered by external conditioning but *against the grain* of our organism and its environment, he will give the reader a decadent and shocking but perfect image of distinction. Since needs can be reduced and frustrated but not suppressed, why not transform them by themselves into *antiphysis* by a sham appeasement that will create purely artificial habits *ex nihilo*? Why not take nourishment by means of a tube up the anus—wouldn't this both satisfy the organism and permanently pervert it? Yet distinction, at least for the first generation of artists, is not the intended end; by denying animality, they claim only to die to be reborn, impassive sons of their works, practicing on themselves the ritual murder of both the dominant class and the class of the middle, their fathers. In this way they convey to their contemporaries (their older brothers, their younger brothers) a confirmation of scientistic ideology; through them the ethic of alienation acquires the justification it was lacking. That ideology used to sacrifice man to wrought matter, to knowledge; now, through the imperative universality of aesthetic feeling, it demands the sacrifice of the artist to beauty.

Art for art's sake is simply the set purpose of subjecting the writer to his literary production. He must doom himself so that a *beautiful* work, useless to men, can arise from his shipwreck. The project of the artists, here again, is in principle antibourgeois; to contest the utilitarianism that defines man by interest and determines each man's place in the social hierarchy as a function of his utility, they have decided to make themselves inhuman by making their lives a long sacrifice to that which can serve no one—not even and especially themselves. They have all more or less conceived the work of art, a small-scale product crafted by a single person, in opposition to the collective civilization of manufactured products, in which the anonymity of the collective product and its ugliness are as closely linked, in their eyes, as a principle and its consequence. The work of art is the superfluous, in the name of which they are trying to crush the necessary in themselves; it is the imaginary denouncing the hideous reality of factories and merchandise and devouring their own reality. For this reason they consider the very meaning of their writings incommunicable; later, they will be impelled to conceal it. But to the pioneers of art-neurosis, this operation does not seem necessary; to grasp significations, readers would have to be "art people," they would have to conceive of the dimension of gratuitousness that exists in all language and conceive a passion for an object that serves no purpose. That is possible only through a radical mutation of the person: the man who would devote part of his time to his interest and the rest to the disinterested activity of reading does not exist, according to them. In short, they write "for posterity"—without much hope, for why should their great nephews be any different?—or for a God who does not exist or gives no sign of his existence. *Precisely for that reason* these antibourgeois are, par excellence, the bards of bourgeois society. Creators of a pure, impassive beauty that never laughs or cries, a mute, inaccessible work that stands alone, readerless, beneath the empty sky, they give the ideal, that impersonal imperative of knowledge and profit, an aesthetic dimenson. The reason for their mistake is twofold. First of all, in wanting to escape bourgeois alienation, they had to set against it another alienation. But in an alienated society, all alienations—subjections of the self to something other—whatever their structural level, share a symbolic meaning. Even if they cannot all be reduced by regressive analysis to the dominant alienation conditioned by the mode of production, it's enough that they are produced under the influence of diverse and irreducible factors in the setting of this primary alienation, for them to be structured as a function of it and to become in the end—in their very independence—an expression of it, even and especially if they contradict it. Moreover, the ethical utilitarianism of the bourgeois under Louis-Philippe has hidden its true essence from them, as it has from all their contemporaries, which is to justify the subjection of man to the human Thing. They believed that man is defined by the impulse that impels him to seek his interest everywhere, without perceiving that this so-called impulse, fruit of the utilitarian imagination, has no real existence, and that bourgeois interest—profit—was posited for its own sake and in its autonomy was clearly useless to man; rather, the contrary is true: man is useful to profit. From that time, fleeing from what they took for humanity toward the inhuman, they chose to make themselves the means of the Thing, as did the bourgeois and the professionals. And there is no doubt that the relation of the artist to the work produced is not assimilable to the property owner's relation to his property: *doing* is not *having*. At the least it can be compared to the scientist's relation to knowledge. The man of science, in effect, produces concrete knowledge, and if he does not produce it *for men*, he produces it for itself, which in the last analysis—and since all knowledge is practical—means for profit. Thus, in that society governed by profit, the artist's inhumanity can only serve, through the intermediary of knowledge, to justify the inhumanity of the property owner; he anchors his public in the opinion that man's only *raison d'être* resides in his self-destruction in favor of the Human Thing. Indeed, when the work of art is isolated and posited for its own sake, it becomes the Human Thing in its turn. In sum, the artist's mistake is to reject the human condition in order to escape the bourgeois condition, without realizing that the essence of the bourgeoisie, at this time, is to establish the social hierarchy on the rejection of the human condition.

This will become even clearer if we note that when the artist rejects the public, he is serving the dominant class. He arrogantly declares that the meaning of his work is not communicable, and in a general way he denies that communication is possible between men as a relation of understanding and interiority. For him, of course, the work of art is a totality, which means that it is defined *internally*, and that the links between the whole and the parts, and between the parts themselves, are internal. But as a product of the author's pen, and so given its limits *from within* by a totalizing internalization, it seems to escape from the artist without yielding itself, for all that, to the public. At least this is what our authors think: the accomplished work shuts everyone out because its development was merely a process of folding in on itself. The reader does not enter it, the writer no longer does so. Isn't this simply a matter of investing works of the mind with the fundamental structure of private property? In many cases, certainly, there is a great difference between the two. The artist, by producing his work, excludes himself; the property owner, by the propriocep- tive act, encloses himself in his property. And even this is entirely true only in the case of real estate. On the other hand, what absolute art and real property have in common is that in both cases a synthetic act seals an inorganic multiplicity and unifies it *negatively* by the im- perative: "No entry." Thus the interiority of the property or the work is the illusory consequence of a practical reaffirmation of universal exteriority: they have an *interior* simply because the entire universe, kept at a distance, remains exterior to them. Again, it must be under- stood that the interiority of the work *exists*, not in reality but as a determination of the imaginary; that of real property is an appearance to the extent that it is constituted on the basis of arbitrary boundaries. Be that as it may, noncommunication as the artist conceives it con- solidates the ideology of the property owner; scientism, an extrapo- lation of a body of knowledge based on analytic reason, is entirely incapable of giving a content of interiority to the act of appropriation. On either side of these boundaries, these walls, he sees the same scattering of atoms, the same exteriority. But when the writer prohib- its the reading of his work, the cultivated bourgeois and the semirich, far from being scared off, are quick to take advantage. They *buy* the book, they open it—since *it belongs to them*—reading is confused with appropriation. Let access to the work be uncomfortable, let it require unceasing effort to understand the author's intentions, the connec- tions between ideas or events, and finally the meaning of this particu- lar piece of merchandise—so much the better. What they have acquired, all things considered, is a domain just vacated by its former master, still warm with his life; everything is in good shape, well maintained, furnishings chosen; the layout of the rooms, even the nicknacks betray his tastes, his distastes, his entire personality; in a word, the work of art, once *possessed*, provides them with the model of property's interior contents. Incommunicable, certainly, but for sale; penetrable if purchased. On this basis, the prohibition on entry is no longer valid except for others, the buyer has moved in and dis- covers that there are positive reasons for this impenetrability, that it involves a *true synthesis*, a totality that can be assimilated only from the inside. In a word, interiority is the objectivization of a man. Thus the artist is comparable to the property owner, and the property owner is himself an artist since he is objectified in a creative appropriation. If noncommunication is the rule between men, it is not because private property condemns them to exteriority but, quite the contrary, because the interiority of each one is so rich and profound that it goes well beyond what discourse can express. Under these conditions, appropriation does not create interiority—as an abstract negation of the exterior—but, on the contrary, interiority justifies appropriation as the unique means of realizing it. Thus, refusing to be read, the artist serves bourgeois readers by justifying their refusal to communicate. The advantage for these readers is that interiority, as the writer presents it through his work, is realized only by objectivization conceived as the sacrifice of man to the thing and permanent alienation; the interior exists neither in the property—before it is possessed—nor in the person; it is merely what comes to inorganic matter, in the limits of a negative determination, when the person is posited as the inessential means of the Human Thing. On this level, subjection to the work seems like a peacock who scorns the jackdaw while lending him his plumage. In effect, in a society structured by the private appropriation of the means of work, man's subjection to the Thing is realized—on all levels and fundamentally on the level of the workers—by the subordination of human ends to the absolute means. The artist has a vague intuition of this; offspring of the middle class, he specifically rejects in his class-being the inert imperative that enjoins him to be the means of the means. His position is therefore contradictory, since he reproaches man for seeking his interest and believes he is thereby contesting all human ends—which, according to him, manifest our egotism, our short-sighted pettiness, our dull materialism—while he grasps in himself the class individual structured as a means of the means, and tries to detach himself from this specific determination. Unfortunately, he has no instrument that would allow him to combat the reign of the Thing by proposing to reverse the terms and restore man's *existence* and his absolute primacy over inorganic matter, that *sovereignty* characterizing praxis in every individual and allowing him to define means in terms of chosen ends. For he is unable to posit himself as an end. Others did it at the end of Louis-Philippe's reign; others placed their hopes in a revolution that would create a society in which man would be the purpose of man or, refusing to be the product of his product, would finally be his own product; but they *were coming from elsewhere,* and then their failure blocked this exit for a long time. The artist is the man who chooses, if he must be a means, to be the means to a supreme end, to an end that is not the means to any other. Beauty is that end to the extent that it is useless, that it *serves no purpose.* It manifests itself, according to the Knights of Nothingness, as a cruel and gratuitous demand that derives its nobility from its gratuitousness. In short, it justifies its claims on man only by a radical negation. And a double one: "I do not serve men, they serve me; I am a demand that no one can fulfill, my servants perish at the task in order to generate a work, at best a bit of sealed matter in which I, a vague phantom and almost ineffable, deign to trail a blurred image of myself." But this double negation, together with the impersonality of the demand, gives this supreme end the same qualities that define the absolute means without stripping it of its finality. In other words, if beauty owes its teleological character to its *absolute uselessness,* the supreme means—or rebel means posited for its own sake—can rightly demand to be accorded the same dignity. Served by men, useless and perhaps harmful to the species, profit manifests itself for a whole society under the aspect of a categorical imperative. Beyond it, there is nothing. It preserves its structure as a means because this Proteas seems to be the raison d'être of objects man claims to fashion in order to reproduce and ameliorate his life; that is its weakness. Can a demand be made to sacrifice to the *means* the man who generates ends in the world? But by giving an authentic end the characteristics of a means posited for its own sake, the artist allows bourgeois ideology to take for an end *as well* the means that isolates itself as pure, separate exigency. Indeed, the subjection of the artist to his work, which immediately pays off if the work is beautiful, seems to be a living symbol of the ethical-ontological status of bourgeois man, that is, of alienation. Between the enlightened reader and the author at this time there is therefore, despite the latter, a reciprocity whose strength comes from the fact that they both define themselves on the basis of an identical context, and see the truth of man in his sacrifice to the Human Thing.

Yet when the artist's "natural" public incarnates and recognizes itself in the work, it always seems shocking. Under the Empire, art-neurosis is suspect, it is *scrutinized* and continually threatened. The official critics, of course, denounce it, and the powers-that-be institute repression in the name of the optimistic ideology adopted by the Court to please Catholic circles, and also because it is fitting for a dictatorship of greedy parvenus to pass itself off as a legitimate aristocracy. The *real* public protests: it will grant glory to that young unknown, Flaubert, just when the public ministry has decided to prosecute him because it wants partially to withdraw solidarity from the cultural politics of those in power. For the twenty years of the Empire, however, good books make an impression *although they are shocking* and certainly, too, *because they are shocking*.[34] Their readers never accept them without reservations. Never, in any case, without being *shocked* by them in the strongest sense of the word. This is nonetheless the art that suits them, the authors say what everyone wants to read; literature fulfills its social function: in an alienated society, it has chosen to edify its public by presenting it with an ethic of alienation in the external trappings of an amoral aesthetic. But the public cannot recognize itself in the work without sensing that it is the object of a disturbing demystification; for the writer, whether he is a novelist or poet, is pushed by his neurosis to the most extreme sincerity; consequently he reveals the unspeakable secret: the hatred of man he shares with his readers cannot be the basis for a humanism. Yet just when their scientism aspires to dissolve the human to demonstrate that "nothing will take place but the place," the professionals have given themselves a mandate to patch up bourgeois humanism. This contradiction, as we have seen, is at the core of their ideology, which—in its real movement of pure negation—expresses the disappointed ambitions, the bitterness, the rancor, the humiliation and fear of the middle classes; it uses this negation to justify the dehumanization of the property owner insofar as he is possessed by his possession. In short, scientism is above all a disguised dream of genocide. But with this misanthropy as its premise, the elite has taken on the mission of justifying the reign of capital by a humanism that shows the universality of bourgeois man, his audacious conquest of the globe, the progress of our species—namely, industrialization— that will bring our species closer to the moment when it will finally be master of its fate, that is, entirely surrendered to the Human Thing. The *capacités* have tried, and will still try, to surpass this contradiction by defining man in terms of his sacrificial self-destruction; but the malice is too visible; the elite live this permanent conflict in discomfort and bad faith, proclaiming that man is the king of nature but feeling obscurely that they have set him on his throne only after murdering him. The writers, too, live in a state of extreme tension and are torn by conflicting imperatives; but their fundamental objec-

---

34. *Madame Bovary* is an obvious example.

tive is not in doubt: their hatred of the human race is visibly revealed, and absolute art, the total unrealization of being, is established on the *radical negation* of the cosmos and of all the men it contains. No doubt this involves an imaginary operation, since it is by definition impossible to bring about. But that hardly bothers them; the shift to the imaginary is *by itself* this destruction. Moreover, the destruction of the world, were it concrete, would not satisfy them; it would have to be a *continuous destruction;* they will represent the world of men in its infinite, palpable richness, and unlike the practitioner elites, who out of necessity reduce qualitative relations to quantitative ones, they attempt to render the swarming of life in its irreducible diversity. But they do not hide from themselves that art is a dead gaze, cutting to the quick all this multicolored agitation in an attempt to reveal allusively its hollow nothingness. They manage to suggest to us that this universe, or rather this narrow model of the macrocosm that remains suspended in their works, is *already* gone forever, like Antiquity, so utterly beautiful because all its witnesses have vanished and it is therefore, in the midst of life, doubly dead. Beauty is death—this is the common thread running through the new writers. Radically and fundamentally denying what they seem to affirm, anything will serve their purpose; and particularly the procedure that consists of presenting lived experience as such—that is, as an immeasurable multiplicity of internal relations—as *pure appearance* for which nonbeing would be its truth. And this nonbeing, in their opinion, will approximate the metaphysical nothingness they think they have discovered, at the time, underlying the philosophies and religions of the Far East in a hasty reading of the *Upinashads* and the *Rig-Veda*, recently translated and very much in fashion, but equally underlying the very Occidental mechanism at the basis of scientistic ideology.

The fact is that both conceptions coexist in an intentional vagueness. Indeed, it hardly matters whether the illusion of living is an ontological determination, like the *Maya* (which they were a little too quick to see as a shimmering but insubstantial veil, a simple dream of the void), or whether it is permanently the result of a false evaluation. In the first case, the void is fundamentally the absence by default of a *definite* being, of that personal God who is characterized by his omnipotence and his perfect goodness, in other words, whose ontological determination is the identity in him of being and ought-to-be. And in the second conception it seems initially that the mistake comes only from the fact that value—the basis of all ethics, which reveals itself only to existence in interiority—is pure deception, since the truth of lived experience, a simple epiphenomenon, is mechanistic exteriority. Thus one might believe that nothingness, here, is merely relative, since one falls back on *pure being*, resistant to all evaluation, abandoning all hope of being governed by the representation of the law, since one falls back on the molecular pulverization that seems closer to *fact*. But in reality the reduction of the cosmos to mechanistic infinity leads on the level of truth to the elimination of a being that denounces itself as pure illusion and is none other than the *human person* as it dreamed itself, an ethical and practico-theoretical unity of the enterprise of living. And it is the *impossibility of man* that negatively qualifies the mechanist cosmos and makes it seem, if not pure nothingness, at least privation: pure being or molecular dispersal—proffering itself, through the disillusionment of *homo sapiens*, as the ontological determination that is poorest and consequently most akin to nothingness.

What the enlightened public clearly discovers is that these artists are quite far from rejecting scientism or contrasting the world of lived experience—of knowledge of the first order—which is their domain, to the cosmos of mechanist conceptualism. Quite the contrary, they depict man and life to expose them as illusions in the name of the wisdom of the "brahmins" and contemporary science. Their purpose is obvious: self-destruction. The reader once again finds himself in it; in the poems and novels of the new authors he recognizes a secret homage to his ideology; he knows that in the name of his own principles they depict his life as he has experienced it, as a mystification, and that the artist, in taking the bull by the horns and attacking concrete man, is contributing to the general dissolution of the species. He certainly does not make man a being exterior to himself, who must be conditioned from the outside—that is not his business; but approaching the very depths of his inner life, he reveals that *in its very interiority* it is a pitiful lie. He stops there; so what? He has cleared the way for others with a stronger stomach, who will finish the job by chasing man from himself through systematic atomization. The writer, approaching concrete reality, is content to restore it as a determination of discourse and trace its contours, indications of future operations for the anthropologist to come. Nowhere in his work shall we read that action is merely a dream of matter and that, even when it believes itself to be human, it is contradicted by the ontological status that universally assimilates being to exteriority. But we do read quite clearly, on the other hand, that every human enterprise is doomed to failure. In other words, action, insofar as it requires the dimension of interiority—which can only be oneiric—contains its own radical negation. The more the human dream—as we show it in the work—tries to affirm itself as efficacious generosity, the more surely and swiftly will it be contradicted; it will end in ruin, despair, death. The more man, by contrast, lets himself be absorbed by the dense, inorganic materiality that is his truth, the more he lets himself be governed from the outside, by inflexible laws, in short, the closer he comes to the Human Thing, the more he has a chance of escaping misfortune. To be happy, one must be foolish and limited, stupidity is the pure pleasure of exteriority. *Stupidity:* "to be matter," to coincide with it to the point of never dreaming. *Panoramic Contemplation:* to be nothing, to escape to the condition of object by awakening from the useless nightmare of subjectivity and becoming a reflexive consciousness of knowledge or an impassive intuition of beauty, of the dream itself grasped as unrealizable. These are the only ways out. To descend *below*, to glide *above*. Between the two extreme positions, there is that "dream of hell," man, human, all too human, who exposes himself as an oneiric creature by his irremediable unhappiness and his meanness, the immediate and permanent consequences of his fundamental determination, failure—the vain ambition of that nonbeing which aspires to the consistency of being. And *who* is dreaming of man? No one; as our clever intellectuals would say today, the human nightmare is a discourse without any subject, meaning comes to man and impersonalizes him on the basis of a false personalization. This is the only source of human suffering: the content of the dream exposes it as a dream, the perpetual failure of dreamed undertakings reveals them in their insane oneirism. Yet the sleeper—having no real existence—does not succeed in waking; differently put, every disaster is a waking but a waking *in another dream*, something that often happens to us all in the course of an agitated slumber, when you say to yourself, "I'm dreaming" to defend yourself against dangers, against unbearable anxiety, and when that lucidity remains gagged, when it is covered over again by the dream imagery and engulfed without delivering us, having at most slightly deviated the course of the phantasmagoria.

In all that, the professionals, while reading, believe they recognize a summons to science, the prophetic claim of an anthropology and a *human engineering* that will condition the sleeper from the outside without waking him and give him beautiful dreams, or simply a mysterious sleep. But simultaneously they discover the subversive invention of the artist and understand without words, in a blinding flash, that it is also *theirs*; if man is this awful nightmare, there can be no more absurd ideology than humanism. And should one define the species by its self-destructive rage, that rage could not be assimilated to a sacrifice and invested with the greatness and merit that would justify philanthropy, even negatively. The sacrifice is a *gift*. But if the human object is merely this painful illusion, if it is detestable and miserable, the obvious strategy is to abolish it as quickly as possible; such a purge is merely a police operation, and should men themselves demand it and execute the sentence they have passed on themselves, they would be no better for all that. By disencumbering the universe of a monstrous species, they would be forever delivered from their miseries. Indeed, the dolorism most of these artists display seems less something to their credit than an initial expiation; they are trying to efface the stain of living by punishing themselves, merely a negation of negation—which, as we know, does not always correspond to an affirmation. The suffering of dolorism is not the same as the immediate unhappiness that is the lot of our species; rather, it is reflexive, engendered by our horror of the human condition as we live it or see it lived by others; it is the permanent shame of being too human, it is the aim, made ineffective by that very shame, of a radiant and mineral inhumanity which humans most often perceive as merely the undetermined reverse of their dissatisfaction, and with which they coincide, in the best case, when they produce that impassivity in themselves which allows them to survey their individuality as man. Dolorism, in effect, far from confronting that arrogant absence, appears to be the practice that allows it to be achieved; the painful contempt each man has for himself insofar as he finds himself in the Other—and for the Other insofar as he finds him in himself—detaches one from unreflected passions and, more generally, from the entire human pathos insofar as one endures it; thus its final term can be only a divine ataraxia in which it will disappear. Nonetheless, no one can be entirely free of the self or of others; the Knight of Nothingness is suspended between the bitter humiliation of being man and the implacable anorexia of panoramic consciousness, rising and sinking like a genie in a bottle from one to the other, incapable of fully taking "Sirius's perspective" on his peers—which would incline him to serenity and entirely purge his dolorism of misanthropy.

We must go even further and recall (something that escapes readers, and we shall soon see why) that the impassive overview is a *role*, namely the unrealization of the writer as artist; and since the imaginary surpassing of a conflictual situation changes nothing of the terms of the conflict or the tension between them, since this dream of surpassing is entirely *constituted*[35] by what it claims to surpass, impassivity still reeks of hatred even when the author thinks he has risen above it. Better, just when he believes he is contemplating the universe with the rigorous impartiality of someone who is no longer part of the game, a pure gaze transparent to the self, impassivity *is* the hatred of man, no more, no less; hatred gives it its consistency and its true purpose. An icy scorn takes on the trappings of indifference; contemplation is not the calm inspiration of the surveyed cosmos, the enumeration of *facts* and their spatial-temporal relations, nor is it the disinterested understanding of human behaviors by their causes and their ends: it witnesses the debasement of our species with acute but silent pleasure. When the artist exposes our illusions, it is not for the sake of delivering us from them, like the Buddhist monk, but for the pleasure of exposing the traps and seeing us fall into them. No matter how high he has risen, he never tires of contemplating our baseness. To understand the singular traits of this generation—and the way that it will be challenged, after 1870, by the young idealists who want to put a humanistic optimism back in the saddle—let us imagine Sully Prudhomme, coming home quite stupefied after a visit to Flaubert, and jotting down, with more terror than indignation, this sentence spoken in his presence by his elder: "When someone tells me about some contemptible or knavish act, it gives me as much pleasure as if I'd been given money." In short, when the Knights of Nothingness claim to reject any norm but that of the beautiful, they are lying: their enterprise is entirely *moral;* a black, sadistic puritanism exalts them, they preserve the imperatives of the ethical to the degree that these allow them to cast their contemporaries into hell; they reject them, on the contrary, to the extent that moral law, based on a "You must, therefore you can," might contain reasons for hope, might return to man his reality as agent, allowing him to postulate the existence of an undemonstrable transcendent and giving him orders as well as the means to execute them. The best trick they can play on him, as we have seen, is to compel him *in every domain* to condemn himself mercilessly for having transgressed ethical rules he hadn't the means to observe. "You must, therefore you cannot" is the cornerstone of this Satanic morality, whose explicit intention is to inspire despair. And to believe their version of it, this morality issues

---

35. In *real* surpassings, the surpassed remains as their origin and their *conditioning,* but is transformed into a mediated determination.

from the oneiric texture of our existence, a ruse itself; it all comes down to the fact that man, exterior to himself, is simply an inert material system, and his oneiric essence, by the synthetic unity and relations of interiority it confers upon him, defines him *as a dream* through activity. This passive being, manipulated from the outside by alien forces, cannot escape judging himself as if he were by nature an agent, irresistibly induced, as he is, to assume that false consciousness of himself. This is the source of his damnation, and of the merry pranks that cause our artists to laugh among themselves. The fact is, this mechanistic system can be neither base nor vile; however, this is good reason and *with his own consent,* to tax him with baseness and vileness, and this because he yielded to the decomposition that is his true status when he should have been *composing himself* as a practical agent. And since activity is at once his essence and a mirage, he can only and forever be disappointing and disappoint *himself.* This is the moment for bringing calm to the tormented creature; he must be led by ascesis to that *consensual passivity* which is, in fact, simply the impassivity of the artist. (He does indeed *witness* as a spectator the unfolding of a history that doesn't concern him but imposes on him the order of its sequences; yet this self-conscious inertia becomes the active unity of dispersed passivity. On this level he might boast of being an *active passivity,* but his underlying psychology does not allow him to do so. So he must admit to himself more or less secretly that impassivity can be merely represented.[36] But there can be no question of this: the writer writes of man only to add to human unhappiness; he demystifies him only halfway since he shows him his torments and in a way justifies them by refusing to explain them by their causes. He does not say to him, You are neither sublime nor base, for these words have no meaning when applied to a mechanical system; instead he says, You want to rise to the sublime, yet because you are bound to fail on principle, you will always find yourself back in the ignoble. Literature, when posited for its own sake as an absolute, is not only useless to the human race, it is intentionally and fundamentally harmful; as a fundamental negation, something the reader-professional perceives too late, it pretends to fly to the rescue of scientism but only to bring out its basic ab-humanism.[37] For this kind of literature itself has its source in an antihumanism of resentment;

36. In any event we can regard impassivity, as it is conceived in 1850, as none other than the inert and ideal negation of inertia.
37. A word used a century later by Audiberti.

those young bourgeois want to achieve the death of man by killing their brothers because, among other motives, those brothers produced the irreversible death of God by sweeping out the remains of an already moth-eaten theocracy. Subjugated by analytic reason to the point of accepting scientism and seeing mechanism as the absolute truth, they have inherited from their older brothers, the Romantics, a shameful and quickly embittered love of irrational thought and an impossible organicism. Hence they are prey to two contradictory ideologies, and put all their zeal into exaggerating the contradiction to such a degree that these ideologies mercilessly devour each other without the slightest hope that one might prevail, indeed, with the avowed intention that this indecisive combat should perpetuate itself infinitely, extending to everyone so that their horror of themselves should be shared with all of humanity. The purpose of the literary enterprise is to reduce the reader to despair by infecting him with that romantic scientism whose permanent instability will not let him rest; not to waken the sleeper but to exaggerate his nightmare by giving it the false unity—the pole of everything imaginary—which is beauty. For beauty, as the unrealizable archetype of every synthesis and consequently the synthetic principle or supreme category of the imagination, is in their eyes merely the irrational organicism of the Romantics and the vain attempt to define man by the practical unification of the multiple insofar as this praxis, denounced by atomism, has gone to heaven and is now manifest exclusively as the a priori rule of the image and accessible only to the imagination. The shocked public discovers beauty as a *source of harm;* by putting man on the rack, by forcing him to turn endlessly between two hermeneutics of lived experience, neither of which immediately yields itself and each of which is generated by the death of the other, the artist shows his hand. In a bourgeois society, when human relations are based on hatred, humanism, the stratagem of misanthropy, can only be a weapon of hatred with no other purpose than to effect the self-domestication of man, or his submission to the Human Thing, by exacerbating his despair even while depriving him of all efficacy with that deceitful optimism which redoubles our miseries and compels us to accept them—the humanism of sacrifice and merit.

Thus art-neurosis is *real.* It does not reveal the world or society as it is constituted on the basis of its infrastructures; and even less does it reveal the "psychology" of eternal man—first because this transhistorical man does not exist, second because the artist has deprived himself of the means to understand his contemporary by the double postulation of two contradictory and equally erroneous principles, mechanism and organicism. What the artist in all clarity denounces (without comprehending its origins and so without seeing in it a *transitory* relation between social individuals) is man's hatred of man on every level of society. The artist denounces it by assuming it, by making it the reason for his art, by inviting the public to share it, to discover it in themselves as the guiding principle of their sensibility, as their fundamental project. He publicly reveals the man of hatred, both the one whose underlying impulse is the hatred of man, and the one whose conduct and motivation are illuminated by the sun of hatred. On this last point we must be more specific. In the great writers of the time, in Flaubert for example, there are profound intuitions, an admirable comprehension of certain behaviors and attitudes; but hatred, scorn, and resentment deform these intuitions imperceptibly, if not in their raw content at least in their *meaning* (we shall return to this when we attempt to "read" *Madame Bovary*). Or, if you will, those intuitions are completely valid only when applied to the always possible case of man as *hating-hated*.

But their truth lies not in the fact that universal man is a wolf to man—he is neither that nor the opposite, since he does not exist—but in the fact that society under the Empire seems to be a circuit of hatred. This is a matter of *national* and historical fact. The class struggle is bitter in England, but it is above all a praxis; it generates reciprocal animosity but does not find its basic incentive in it. For quite a long time Marx continued to think that the social revolution would begin in France, industrially the least advanced country, because the ground between the ruling classes and the working classes was strewn with *corpses*. For more than half a century the June massacres will give the class struggle its essential character as a permanent "civil war." Hatred exists, redoubled by fear; it rises from the worker to the boss who, as the object of hatred, internalizes as self-hatred the horror he arouses in others. It then goes back down from the boss to the worker, whom he wants to infect in return with a hatred directed against himself. Between them, the mediating classes, terrified by popular outbreaks and still bitterly resenting the mystification of which they were victims when the ruling class gave political power to the military, internalize this revolving hatred, directing it at once against themselves, for their failure in '48, and against the classes above and below them who conspired to turn victory into disaster. In this sense a work of hatred—that is, a work that takes hatred as its point of view—*speaks the truth of the times* at a certain superstructural level.

To be sure, this truth is also an error: it remains incomplete because it hasn't *evolved from*, been engendered by, the mode and relations of production; its profundity exists, but it is not the "profundity of the world," merely the rather superficial profundity of that dependent variable then called the human heart. Still, without art-neurosis it would have been lived beneath a veil and never brought into the full light of day. Dialectically—that is, from the point of view of histori- cal totalization—the interpretation of human behavior by baseness alone is never exhaustive. We must first ask ourselves—something the Knights of Nothingness are careful to avoid—how we can even *conceive* of the idea of baseness except on the grounds of a praxis which, as the producer of notions and values, is the very opposite of a dream. On this basis it seems evident that in every historical and concrete situation, every behavior must be simultaneously inter- preted from above and from below, provided that above and below are themselves defined as a function of the society in question, of its structures, of its manifest class struggles. As a result, anyone using uniquely negative values to qualify an action defines himself as a man of resentment, who is compelled, in the name of the law of the heart, to cut himself off ideally from the community, or finds himself con- strained to affirm, even in his own heart, the predominance of the ignoble. But in the singular case of French society under the Empire, the misanthropic artist, by privileging the basest motives, is merely telling the truth: not about what men are but about what they think they are at the time, and consequently about what they make them- selves into.

Obviously, in the hypertense atmosphere of hatred, under the ma- lignant gaze that spies out those base motives in others, and with the permission everyone gives himself to respond to hatred with hatred, to violence with counterviolence, behaviors of all kinds will them- selves be profoundly altered. Everyone internalizes the judgment of others—which condemns him—and out of defiance, out of disgust with their so-called hypocrisy, denies any attenuating circumstance, professes to be criminal, pushes to the limit an impudent boasting of vice born of hatred, which soon becomes one of the motivations of his acts. Hatred slips in everywhere: not even the pleasure the rich take in their rapidly growing luxury is without an element of malice; they enjoy it against the poor, against the worker with his "envious

297

mug." All this, no doubt, remains masked. There is Christianity, the eclectic optimism of the military dictatorship; there is above all, for the professionals and the bourgeois, scientistic humanism, that fine fakery, that false consciousness of themselves. But if they happen to read the work of an artist, no sooner have they finished the first chapters than the veil is torn away; they find themselves on familiar ground. The practitioners and scientists are not, of course, going to identify with Germinie Lacerteux, that young, all too imperiously sexy maidservant, or with Sister Philomène (their wives—and we will see why—are more willing to recognize themselves in Madame Bovary, who bears an exemplary hatred toward her husband). The *impersonal character*, invisible, omnipresent, never named, with whom they spontaneously identify is the author; that man, one "of their own," the son or brother of a professional, who would have become a professional as well if not for that fluke—gift, talent—which they attribute to some prenatal accident. Impassive, disinterested, austere, this superman reflects their own image to his readers; his sobriety, the discretion he exhibits by refusing to speak of himself, seems to them the transposition of distinction into writing, all the more noticeable as he often recounts, without anger or benevolence, banal stories of crude beings with gross appetites; nature stifled beneath the weight of style—what a relief from the vulgarities of Musset and his drunken confessions. But just when they adopt the author's point of view and contemplate the world through his dead gaze—so similar to their own—they are stupefied, shocked, and delighted to discover that he has borrowed their virtues to put them ostensibly in the service of evil, of death, of nonbeing. Sometimes the shock is not delightful, and the book is sent flying across the room. But most of the time the enlightened elite adopts the artists because they are its shadow brothers. Its shadow brothers, or its truth stripped bare? They are not content to depict man, they murder him. Gently, cruelly, by denouncing his lies, his deceptions, his flights, his base needs, his malice, his egotism. Hasn't the elite done this itself by refining scientism? And surely they are not very friendly, these beasts caught in the trap of humanity. But the elite feels a secret satisfaction when the artist puts him in possession of his hatred by inviting him to actualize the shameful genocide at the basis of his humanism. More precisely, the reader is pleased to execute this genocide himself, with the complicity of the artist, through the sole enterprise of reading, gluing words together, illuminating the past by the future, and gradually transforming the future into the past. He thereby reconstitutes that imaginary synthesis, the work, and conjures man out of nothingness, that *hating-hated-heautontimoroumenos* who is the *anthropos* as only art has the audacity to manifest it, in order to lead him gently by the hand, "like a bad angel," to inflict increasing pain on himself and to suppress himself, in one way or another, in the midst of atrocious sufferings.

Shall we even say that the reader is an *accomplice?* Isn't he the criminal himself? Can he claim that the artist has led him into temptation? Or that the vitriolic gaze that *constitutes* through reading the perfect world of hatred has slipped into his own gaze, and that by this presence in him of the *other* he has the same excuses as someone "possessed"? Yes and no. For him, this ambiguity makes the charm of reading. It is quite true that in the depths of the work, art is an expectation, that the author has worked the practico-inert in such a way that *meanings* demand to be awakened by the eyes of the reader, that *the* general meaning (the extermination of everyone by a suicide-homicide whose symbolic inventor is Samson) *begs*—like a silence beyond words—to be restored by the totalizing transcendence of the work. From this very reassuring point of view, readers decline all responsibility: we don't kill someone possessed, his demon is exorcised. They have been caught up in another's dream and compelled to enact it in his place from beginning to end. Exorcism is quite simply the awakening, that moment when the reading is finished and the whole work becomes a past-surpassed by its readers, integrated as such into their *being-in-itself.* But from another point of view, compelled or not, it is true that they have *enacted* this dream in the literal, *practical* sense of the term, and that without them it was nothing but an inert incision in matter. Above all, they have *enacted* it because they never *endured* it, because oneiric magic, when it is the purpose of reading, is obtained and maintained only through the incessant *operations* of the reader, who, far from limiting himself to a simple decoding, tries to foresee the interior of the fiction, and constitutues a future for every character by *inventing* the author's future intentions. This implicitly transforms the reader into the author, no longer through *possession* but, on the contrary, through a free surpassing of the given—which is here the materiality and superficial finitude of the work as a simple determination of reading.

From this point of view, whatever the period in which the work is situated, there is no doubt that the writer, great as he might be—I would even say, the greater he is—having indicated some surface demands, must abandon us sooner or later, often from the very first

299

line, and let us do the work alone. The work is a demand; it will go deep if it reflects back to us as its demands on us our own demands on it, that is, if it supports them, if the *given* was worked in such a way that it can be freely *created* by the reading. And the plurality of readings, insofar as this is always possible, are generated not from an indeterminacy of the work but, quite the contrary, from a free surpassing of necessity by the duality of its creators, the one *preparing* the work of the other, the other surpassing that preparation, regarded as the actual field of its possibles, toward a product-to-come. For reading is, among other things, the ludic image of work, when we are dealing with a *poetic* work (in the original meaning of the term). Thus the professionals under the Second Empire are in a sense the victims of a premeditated fascination, and to this degree the author *possesses* them like a demon; but in another sense, they freely *invent* misanthropy and the genocide that follows from it because these "ideas" cannot be written but only intuited as the meaning of lived experience. For this reason our professionals are as criminal as the Knights of Nothingness; they invent and assume the latters' pessimism; or, rather, in that pessimism they *recognize* their own. Thus, ever since they intuited the objectives of *this* literary enterprise, it has been their formal intention to unmask it. The reader turns himself overtly and freely into the *man of hatred*—he changes himself into himself— because this man is the only one at the time who can read the work of hatred and understand it. He turns himself into that man in joy and terror *to be able* to constitute his fellow creature as hating-hateful-man, and so to give himself every reason to murder him. He was doing evil timorously, giving it the appearance of good, or strictly speaking defining it as a lesser evil or as the unique point of access toward the good; reading, he gives himself the disturbing delights of doing evil for its own sake.

He recognizes implicitly that on another level the literary operation has the same objectives as scientism, thereby completing and justifying it. The essential procedure of scientism was, in effect, to reduce man to radical exteriority; but by awaiting the advent of the human sciences, the professionals were losing the malicious pleasure of submitting that monster to continuous destruction. They had dissolved him once and for all in the abstract, and all they had left of him was a collection of corpuscles whose dance was governed by the laws of Newtonian mechanism. This negation of principle deprived their hatred of its object and so freed their scapegoat, about whom there was nothing more to say until qualified scientists established the physico-chemical conditions of his behavior. In effect, they did not know how to invent the idea of torturing the being they had just atomized with the mirage of interiority in order to prolong that murder. They would have had to inhabit simultaneously the confused world of the *doxa*, neither true nor false, full of traps and hopeless muddles, and the clean and proper charnel house of scientistic certainties. They would continuously have had to compare lived experience and quality, as illusions, to the concept and quantity. And what they could not do they are now able to realize through the mediation of the writer, who, whether poet or novelist, could be defined at the time by this cultural function: in full knowledge he has made himself the guardian of the *doxa*. Precisely because he sees in lived experience a world of appearances without truth and of "consequences without premises," he pulls away from it and, regarding it from above, wants to show its inconsistency, its contradictions, its lies, its nonbeing revealed in the sliding and continued disappearance of the all, without ever *making visible* its mechanistic underside or ceasing to suggest it. The professionals, who long ago lost the habit of fixing their mind on what they take to be a phantasmagoria of sensibility, and whose gaze customarily pierces through quality to discover its conceptual other side, its measurability, are led by art to become conscious of their own carnal existence; they rediscover inconsequential daily banality, the trivialities of life, the irreducible color of an autumn leaf, above all their individual and collective history in its unbearable pettiness, and the "stench" of others, that destiny of failure inherited at birth by all the sons of man, which they discovered during the February days of '48. Everything they had wanted to forget and everything they had never judged worthy of their attention is engendered or resurrected before their eyes: poisonous flowers, flowers of evil. Now it interests them. When these were sensed as immediate givens, raw blooms, unauthorized and superficial beings, they knew how to abstract themselves; these things were manifestations of the relative which, behind its singularity, allowed the absolute to be glimpsed, then grasped, in the universality of the law; today these things are yielded up to them, retouched, condensed, mingling their wild perfume with the sulfurous odor of antiphysis. Their natural contingency has given way to a curious necessity, which is not that of the exact sciences; elaborated, they seem to take on the value and dignity of a finished product.

More flatly than André Gide, an antiquary named Ravier, Montherlant's mouthpiece, will say a hundred years later: "I do not like men, I like what they make." This discreet motto of all alienations could be claimed by all the readers of art-neurosis: when *lived experience* becomes wrought matter, when it passes itself off as the result of specialized labor, when without ceasing to constitute the uncertain framework of their existences it is synthetically reconstituted and offered at a distance by the technicians who processed it, it becomes itself an absolute, it imposes itself. Reading becomes the homage of one technique to another; the practitioners of knowledge, while busy dissolving the immediate, judge it good that other workers should devote themselves to the opposite task of extracting its essence and preserving it in all its opaque irreducibility; thus nature itself *as nature* becomes *antiphysis*. Above all, it is turned against itself by this false interiority given it by the artist, and instead of being dispersed in the calm exteriority of a perpetual present, it painfully devours itself. The result is that the reader, led into hell—that hell glimpsed when "society trembled on its foundations"—rediscovers behind his abstract detachment or disengagement the concrete hatred that is its deepest justification; by this I mean that hatred which was aimed at all men but *through* real, specific persons glimpsed for a moment—a manufacturer, fellow workers, women, a rabble-rouser. Of course, those proposed as the targets of his hatred have other faces, other names; but they need merely be singularized to restore to fear, to rancor, and to animosity the irreducible idiosyncrasy of lived experience. All the time he is reading, the professional experiences and relives his homicidal impulses, he rediscovers motives for those impulses in *his* history: it is there between the lines, folded in on itself, enveloped; illuminated by the reading, the reader's own history illuminates the reading as well. So we can say that at a certain level, this reader is reengendered with all his destructive passions and his desire for self-destruction. Through *one* life—the one told to him—he totalizes *his* life, that long, antipathetic unhappiness which can be neither known nor, he thinks, completely understood but only suffered. But even as he is *experiencing himself*, he is conscious of *making himself* through the synthetic act that organizes words and sentences into a work. The author is merely the rule of his operations. An internal-external rule, whose otherness is, for this reader, a guarantee of objectivity. Justified, partially embodied in the artist, he does nothing but *recreate* the world, *his* world, the one in which he has lived, in which he must surely live until the end, by deliberately giving it the characteristics of hell. In this sense he is reunited with himself, with his malice, his sadomasochism, his suffering. But as he produces himself and his environment by a free creative decree, by a *fiat* whose omnipotence he shares with the author, he does not enter completely into the created Cosmos; a demiurge beneath the glittering words, he discovers and engenders absolute negation as the law of refabricated life and the primary norm of beauty. As a sovereign and implacable worker, he thereby gives himself the free determination to produce the worst of all possible worlds because only this kind is beautiful. As a result, he legitimizes the man of hatred, the worst of all possible men, he justifies *himself* insofar as he is implicitly his own creature in the concrete cosmos of the book. Since the terrible unity of appearances demands that one *be* evil—as the part is the expression of the whole—that one must endure and enact it by harming and suffering, he is merely fulfilling the law; so much for his empirical character. As for his intelligible character, that is double: reading, he surveys the world he creates, a sinister and splendid fable that has no truth; when he closes the work, he will survey the knowable and real universe of the exact sciences. This second aspect of the overview—the calm sacrifice to the ideal—offers itself as the alibi for the first. While reading, he surrenders himself with even less remorse to the authorized pleasures of genocide since he intends, after reading, to forget the nakedness of evil and to return to scientistic humanism. More artfully, his unformulated but permanent bonds with scientism greatly increase his criminal pleasures as a reader; beauty gives lived experience enough consistency so that when his gaze, running across the lines, engenders those crazed and painful agitations, those insatiable and always frustrated desires, those endless massacres, he is delighted at the thought that man is a ghastly and vain nightmare of inanimate matter, and that all his sufferings, insofar as they are *lived*, are an absolute of wretchedness and, for the scientific gaze, trivial illusions.

Thus, thanks to the productions of art-neurosis, the reader can be reunited with himself and unveil to himself simultaneously at many levels of existence the genocidal nihilism, a spawn of hatred, that he generally forces himself to disregard and conceal. Although this unveiling is bound to be repeated at every new reading, it provides a nice shock—though less and less—and never terrifies him. This is hardly surprising. To be sure, when for the first time a "decent man" catches himself red-handed and discovers his unquestionably sadistic inclinations, he may be stupefied and thunderstruck; but this is because a *real* act has made him conscious of his *reality*. The professional, by contrast, has no sooner opened a book than he knows that he is being presented with a synthetic reconstruction of the world of the *doxa* in which he finds himself living, but which in his eyes resists all intellection, provides no certainty. The beauty of style and internal organization of the work give these phantasms enough consistency to fascinate him; he leans over them in order to admire himself, and discovers his cruel visage as *counter-man*. But this image, which is in his view a confused determination of an obscure world, possesses qualities that are neither clear nor demonstrably true. No more than it is clear or demonstrable that the principle of human relations is the reciprocity of hatred. Moreover, this is not said but only suggested apropos of a small group of characters, too few in number to generalize from their behavior. These persons do not exist, furthermore, and the events that confront them are in the fictional domain. Even when the author is inspired by a real story, he has chosen it according to his taste, therefore arbitrarily, and has interpreted it in his own way. To the essential unreality of the image is added the obvious project of *derealizing* the reader. Let him be led to embody himself in one of the characters or to identify with the author, he cannot awaken the words, give life to these lying sentences, sustain this plot and the unreal world glimpsed through it without himself becoming imaginary. So he will surrender himself without difficulty to the proposed game, having forgotten nothing except that it is *as himself* that he is invited to become derealized. But he knows that too. He knows quite well, as I said, that in order to understand what he is reading, what might be called the *Ecce Homo* of misanthropy, he must turn himself into the *man of hatred* and conduct himself, while reading, as if he were the abominable and sadistic creator of *hating-hateful-man*. But the necessity of being a demiurge only in the imaginary—since in reality he creates nothing at all—facilitates his conjuring away of the homicidal impulse that constitutes him *in truth* and *alone* allows him to put his reading into effect and unrealize himself as creator of the unreal world of misanthropy.

In fact, in these times and for different reasons, author and reader have internalized hatred, that general reification of human relations manifesting itself in the hypertense setting of "civil war." This hatred happened to them, it produced them, and we can say with some reason that they are its *creatures*. They don't think hatred—or at least not at first—they are thought by it, it is inside them as the desire to murder and a vision of the world; each of their impulses, each of their ideas surpasses it and contains it as a nourishing humus. They are the flowers of evil. But how could they recognize for the moment that their character as *free creator* is rooted in their truth as *creature*, when

304

the former manifests itself as the systematic negation of the latter? This, however, is the fact of the matter: in order to tear themselves away from the abject society that poisoned them with hatred, they have chosen in their dreams to make themselves its legislators. Everything they have suffered they play at producing, as if their freedom were at the source of the cosmos that contains and manipulates them. As the photographer said in *Les Mariés de la Tour Eiffel:* "Since these mysteries are beyond us, let's petend we've organized them ourselves." This is just the point: to produce, legislate, organize. Not an illusory universe in which men would love each other, in which virtue would inevitably find its reward, but *this very world;* being unable to escape it, the only way to bear it, in their opinion, is to imagine they have created it. If they succeed, it will seem to them that they have put their omnipotence in the service of the infinite idea they have conceived: evil—ignoble when they endure it—becomes, when they assume it, the unifying principle of the cosmos, its ordering arrangement. But what they sense, then, as a pure freedom, without further determination than those it gives itself sovereignly, must in fact be seen as merely the reexternalization of the hatred they have internalized. And when they legislate, when they decree that suffering and malice are universal, that virtue is always punished and vice rewarded, they are not content to assume on their own account the objective structures of society and nature as they thought to grasp them through their experience; they assuage in the imaginary the homicidal impulses with which society has infected them at this moment in history. The artists, of course, reflect on art, on their need to create; sooner or later they become conscious of their misanthropy, their desperate desire for inhumanity. Their readers haven't the time to imitate them; this means that they take reading for a free play of their imagination, or as the retotalization of a work scattered among disparate signs, for which the author is solely responsible. And most often, as we have seen, these two interpretations are confused: the reader is free and a creator, he submits freely to the rules of the game proposed by the artist and at the same time declines all responsibility. In this way he can calmly abandon himself to hatred, to the genocidal intentions that are really his own, pushing sadism and masochism to the limit and compensating for his political failure by substituting for the modest powers he was denied a demonic and unlimited power exercised, in the first instance, over the very persons who rejected him. This is merely a directed daydream and reveals nothing about him since he is surveying an imaginary world. The reading, in this case, has all the characteristics of the dream. Not continuously but from the moment the reader is *caught up;* during those moments of hypnosis, the reader satisfies his secret desires without really acknowledging them, as the dreamer does during sleep. And just as our nocturnal dreams are like brief neuroses, so the reading of "artistic" works will be a neurotic form of behavior under the Second Empire to the extent that the practitioner, collaborating with the author, producing what he is shown and fascinated by the black world of absolute negation, allows himself at last to coincide with his real and demonic inclinations because he has been made to regard them as unrealities.

The artist, by his hateful denial of any public, unwittingly gives himself the very readers he has turned away. It is true that he now finds them to be *other:* he began to write, under Louis-Philippe, to detach himself from his class, from his class-being, from his commoner's condition. Unable to transcend his class, he chose literature because in its abstract autonomy, constrained by that very abstraction to exist for its own sake aside from any content, it was transformed into an inhuman end and symbolized alienation as an absolute demand. To opt for art and reject his class, which was his "natural" public, was one and the same thing. Neurosis accomplished a triple rupture: with the social environment, with the artist himself, with reality. In this sense, art-neurosis, or art-failure, could also be called art-rupture since the artist forces himself to miscarry even in his art so as no longer to be at one with himself.

And his books, which he dreams of as powerful and solitary, simple, perfect stones erected in the desert by the dead, are published after 1850 when the class struggle, suddenly assuming the force of a civil war, became the public manifestation of the fundamental rupture breaking bourgeois society apart. That objective rupture, internalized by the middle classes as their own contradiction and thus making them the *broken classes,* becomes subjective in the professionals as the permanent divorce of the concept from lived experience—the former relegating the latter to the confused succession of random appearances and unfounded opinions we are pleased to call, today, the world of the *doxa.* The bourgeois has to internalize the hatred of the working class and then to reexternalize it, universalized, artfully camouflaged beneath a humanism that makes *rupture* man's essential relation to himself.

When the artist thinks of denying the satisfied plenitude of the

bourgeois or the vanity of the professionals both within and outside himself, it turns out that these characters are already outdated.
By legitimizing the exploitation of man by man, by basing it on the
deserving hatred each man feels, and must feel, for himself, the mutation of 1848–51 transforms the bourgeoisie in such a way that
to be bourgeois under the Empire, they must hate in themselves
the bourgeois of the July monarchy. So it turns out that the artist, the
bourgeois, and the practitioner share the same enemies. Behind the
scenes the enemies are, of course, those spoilsports, the manual
workers. On the level of ideology, they are embodied by the bourgeois of yesterday, that old man who must be cast off. Thus, when
the writer uses a permanent catharsis to deny himself so his work
might exist and do harm to the human race, he defines his public at
the same time, since to the wealthy and the professionals he represents
alienation lived as self-hatred, only *magnified*. And it isn't the subject
that matters but the impulse of hatred. By a flaunted puritanism—
which deliberately challenges the wasteful generosity of the arrogant
lions of Romanticism—the artist demonstrates that he sees his life of
flesh and blood as merely the means of accomplishing his work, subordinating in his person human reality to the unreal; moreover, in
the work itself, the all too human content becomes a pretext for the
form that devours it; the sufferings of the characters are the raw material of style conceived as the visible manifestation of a pitiless impassivity. The *black* literature of the 1850s is exactly suited to the
ruling classes because in the meantime they have been *blackened* by
the history they made; the reader demands that his reading allow him
to become unrealized through the imaginary appeasement of his hatred. Indeed, before becoming the flimsy instrument of scientistic ideology, and of the false humanism that is produced from it the way a
rabbit is pulled from a hat, that hatred is a reality suffered and constituted in everyone by the internalization of a universal and disembod-
ied hatred that is subjectivized as the secret desire for genocide. But
it makes the man who feels it suffer because it must be continually
hidden, kept in shadow, reduced to a succession of brief flashes, in
short, lived groping in the dark, prevented by continual distraction
from manifesting itself with the expanse and clarity of an exhaustive
totalization, an interpretation of the present and the past. The reader
assigns a precise function to literature-neurosis, which is to put him
in possession of his hatred without naming it, to allow him to enjoy
it in imagination without departing from a fierce objectivity. He does
not personally wish to play the role of inquisitor or executioner, just

to be shown the unhappiness and malice of men, and even more their mediocrity; to be witness to the torments they inflict on one another—all against all and everyman against himself; to be given the obscure pithiatic belief that "that's how it is, that's exactly how it is," and at the same time the feeling of living in a cosmic nightmare that is not entirely and yet is partially of his own making. His reading will be at once a sadomasochistic delectation and a *catharsis.* In this way he lets off steam *in an unrealizing act,* a passion so violent that without this safety valve it would explode into the light of day, or make him explode.

The paradox of these black novels is that through them the imaginary designates the reader in his truth *in imagination.* The absolute negation at the basis of art-neurosis is a cosmic annihilation, a pure dream of hatred. Lacking the power to sink the world into nothingness, the artist tries to derealize it through words; the work is, in his eyes, the pure unreal, and to the degree that truth is the unveiling of the structures of reality, the artist turns away from it. Conversely, the hatred of the bourgeois or the professional is translated in them by real and adaptive behavior, which nonetheless their false consciousness is prohibited from connecting and interpreting. When this highly realistic bourgeois enters into communication with one of these novels, whose meaning is the unreal annihilation of man, his devalorization, the novel provides him with the object he desires: a humanity one can hate because it is offered as hateful through characters who represent it. The reader's hatred is real and justifiable; and as we discover him from one page to another, man elicits that hatred by his behavior; or, if you will, contempt, disgust, abhorrence are the only means of *grasping* and *understanding* him. Consequently, the reader is no longer compromised by his own hatred, even as it is unleashed. This impassive reader is not a man of hatred; that passion comes to him from the outside as the only possible way of relating to such a humanity. *On the condition,* of course, that our species is really as the author portrays it. This indispensable qualification allows the reader's misanthropy to shift into the imaginary at the last moment; images have provoked it; others that might be more accurate would have aroused love. In the last analysis, responsibility devolves upon the author: he is the real misanthrope, and nothing proves him right. The reader, exposed in his deepest truth only a moment before, closes the book once again and falls back into ignorance about himself.

Yet that one moment suffices to establish the *veracity* of the work.

Produced through hatred, understood through hatred, its dual aspect makes it a real mediation between members of the upper classes in a society burdened by its crimes. If the dominant relation between two individuals is not reciprocal hatred, it will nonetheless comprise— whatever the other factors—a complicity of hatred against a third party regarded as representative of the human race. This veracity, however, which on principle distinguishes literature from ideology, must be carefully understood; if literature bears some relation to truth, that relation must remain *literary*. In particular, art-neurosis certainly does not aim to provoke the reader's conscious awareness. Moreover, having burned his bridges, the writer cannot imagine communicating to the public the least bit of information, and since art seems to be the final term of an ascetic derealization, writing is on principle the opposite of informing. "The marchioness went out at five o'clock." This sentence, which the ideologue Valéry *could not* write, is the very type of false information seen from the point of view of communication—of intersubjectivity. This marchioness is the person missing from all nobility, as for Mallarmé the rose will be the flower missing from all bouquets. On the other hand, when we put the false information back in its place in the totality of the work, it becomes *functional*, and its role is strictly determined on all levels of the discourse. The work is, in effect, conceived by these novelists as a system of structured relations that produce their terms, each of which refers to all the others equally as phonemes, morphemes, and lexemes. It does this either by being isolated at the moment when the reading revives it as a transient form whose content is nothing other than a specification of the whole system—which at the same time overflows the relation and sustains it as its substance, that is, as a nonspecific totality; or, when the reader's gaze turned away from it, by a falling back that reintegrates the relation into the totality it inhabits as an implicit determination of the substance, as a particular but veiled demand that will make new *forms* progressively *necessary*— those sentences and words that follow it even while legitimizing all those that have preceded it in the obscure nondifferentiation of the substance. The beauty of the work is defined in these authors' eyes by circularity: temporalization—which, though they don't much like it, is nonetheless the very essence of the narrative as a reported and read event—loses its irreversibility to the extent that any determination required by those that precede it is turned around to underwrite them, tightening their connections, even while becoming isolated as an expectation of a future that will fully justify it. In the ideal work, then, the first sentence of the first chapter would be fully grasped in all its depth only at the end of the book, when the reader would perceive that its ultimate objective was to produce the last sentence.

Thus the literature of the time, being uninformative and even disinformative, never aspires to show the truth insofar as it is known or knowable. It is no accident that the writer of 1850 chose as his literary *terrain* the world of the *doxa:* had the marchioness existed and indeed had she gone out at five o'clock—these would be matters of raw fact that could be established by witnesses but not demonstrated. Absolute art needs this irreducible and unnecessary facticity; this opaque slumber of things and men as they yield themselves to meanings is the only possible raw material of its rigorous and formal totalization. Aesthetic necessity as a false interiority of the exterior is the opposite of the mathematical necessity that grasps exteriority as a rigorous bond between terms (without seeing that the controlled movement of arguments and the unity of their logical sequence presuppose a dialectic vigilance, a true but hidden interiority). Beauty can only be the deceptive unity of a multiple, and the totalization of the world by the work is reduced at the outer limit to the totalization of the work by itself and for itself. If, however, *truth comes* to this deliberately forged fiction that aims to provide a diabolically beautiful and poisonous image of the necessity of our contingency, it is not because it was sought after or clearly conceived by the *artists,* even for the sake of denying it. Nor *especially* was it aspired to *through* the fiction. Certainly, the fundamental relation between the two notions Goethe called *Dichtung und Wahreit* has preoccupied generations of writers from the classical centuries to our own day; given that the intuition of essences could be actualized only by the free exercise of imagination, which engenders and consequently limits the field of possibles that correspond to one particular essence, total truth is necessarily poetry, and conversely it can be claimed that poetry itself is truth to a certain extent. But art-neurosis *rightly* does not enter into these views. It is not the truth but the *fable of the world* it wants to tell; appearance, which is moreover deceptive, is not surrendered insofar as being, despite everything, is manifest in it but, to the contrary, insofar as it is the negative of being and consequently of the true. The artist is veracious when he *puts into the work* its absolute negation, to the same extent that the war machine he is propelling becomes effective through the cooperation of the reader, who becomes what he is by enduring it as a passion and assuming it as a crime. Beauty as the mask of hatred is that concerted unity of stratagems which, patiently reconstituted by the reader, finally blinds him to its cold clarity. But the truth of that beauty is that it *has a hold* over its public; or, if you will, it is outside it because the reader can reconstruct it only by constructing himself as he is. This reader was not targeted either as a future reader or as a representative of humanity; the work meant to be a realm of the sun. But it conferred his ontological status when it found him; since he is transformed into himself in order to understand the work, and with no explicit motive but the search for aesthetic pleasure through the retotalization of this totalized discourse, he is *its truth*, that is, he makes it the means for becoming what he is. And while he constitutes it outside as an objective determination of the social imaginary, he internalizes it as the rule of the subjective movement of his praxis and the meaning of his attitude. The truth is that it can be understood only by certain social categories—those to which the artist addresses himself, unwittingly or grudgingly; this public can understand only this work, which appears in the intersubjectivity of readers as their serial and detotalized unity insofar as they are joined together in their admiration for it by a reified and masked complicity of hatred. In short, the dominant and middle classes have chosen this literature as their *tacit* expression. They do not claim to share its misanthropy, nor do they dream of denouncing it; yet through the comprehensive reading of the work, the wealthy and the professionals are driven to commit the constitutive act of misanthropy—genocide. They simultaneously produce their truth, which is the hatred of man, and make the author, who offered them a hateful humanity in his fiction, responsible for it. Thus fiction remains fiction; it does not claim to explain the origin of hatred—that is, the exacerbation of social divisions by an irreversible event; through fiction, the reader alone becomes true (although that truth is achieved in the imaginary), and for a moment he becomes the man of hatred (hating-hateful-man, who hates himself). And the strange ambiguity of this reading resides in the fact that it does not expose the reader to himself—since his attention is entirely absorbed by the reproduction of the objective imaginary. And while the fascination lasts he is incapable of self-reflection; exposure exists as a subjective certainty, nonetheless, but its setting can be only *lived experience,* that wide river washing along, pell-mell, actions and unconsidered attitudes, perceptions that are essentially confused or confused by affectivity, uncertain opinions, passionate internalizations of an unknown or unknowable situation, falsified feelings, false thoughts, a false consciousness of the self. And structuring this heterogeneous multi-

311

plicity, imposing a synthetic unity on it through practical temporalization, we have the meandering of teleological intentions that in essence slip away—to keep their purposes in shadow—and would be accessible only to the acute gaze of a noncomplicit reflection. In other words, what is revealed, though susceptible to being *known* by rigorous methods and on condition that all factors are made explicit, proffers itself here as *unknowable* and is indeed so, just as the very way it is given can disclose it only to life itself. Indeed, it is hatred insofar as *it must be lived* as a practical, nonconceptual unity of those two temporalizations that symbolize, between them, reading as a book's being-to-die, and life as the evolution of the reader between his past birth and his future death. That is all the reader needs to *live* a certainty. I have said elsewhere that hatred is a vow, like love. It never offers itself to reflection with the apodictic clarity of pure reflected consciousness; it retains a past which it interprets, it projects itself toward a future which it claims to define by its own constancy. The social hatred of 1850 does not escape this rule: the vow of others must be sworn, or at least internalized, as a practico-inert demand; and as it is customary at the time to conceal misanthropy beneath humanism, the vow takes a thousand indirect forms, the chief of which, moreover, is humanism itself. Not made entirely explicit, however, the commitment of hatred is never radical, it cannot satisfy the multiple isolated impulses that demand it as their unification and perpetuation; thus the rich and the professionals live in a state of constant frustration. By contrast, when they read a product of literature-neurosis, hatred makes itself live through them freely, without their having to make the slightest commitment. For the vow has already been taken outside them, in the work, which thus becomes the rule of their lived temporalization; an author has objectified his misanthropy, his vow is refracted in his book where it has become the totalitarian unity of the demands of a fictive past and the real expectations of an imaginary future; in short, it is at one with the imperative of beauty. The hated thing is the world as it is represented in the book, and man as he is shown in it, who guarantees the constancy of hatred since the writer has made him essentially hateful. Thus the unity of lived experience is restored in the work by reading, the reader's impulses are organized by themselves and lived in their plenitude without any subjective commitment that might make them *knowable* by showing them in too crude a light. That plenitude, the radical and momentary disappearance of all frustrations, violence accepted, tacitly legitimized—this is the content of the experienced certainty that underlies the reading. This is also the source of the ambiguity that characterizes these black works: on the one hand, even the reader's fascination does not lead him for one moment to regard them as anything but imaginary; yet on the other hand, while reading, he grasps *himself* in *his* truth. Indeed, we find in imaginary consciousness the mediation between fiction actualized in its objectivity and truth as a determination of subjectivity; for on the basis of subjective experience, that consciousness reconstructs the imaginary object by the *act* of reading—which is indeed real—and conversely gives lived experience the unity of an imaginary vow. But the instability of the fascination is such that this pithiatic consciousness (autosuggestion controlled by an objective structure of heterosuggestion) remains fragile and breakable; anything at all can *break the spell*. When that happens, the reader, taken out of his reading, no longer knows where to put the truth of lived experience because breaking the spell signifies the reengagement of the whole defensive apparatus—humanism, censorship. This vicious circle will be the cause of a memorable misunderstanding. Despite their protests, these nihilistic writers will be ranked under the banner of *realism*. This word, which official critics applied to them from the outside with negative intent, will be taken up by the public to designate their enterprise. In a sense, although their success proves that readers transformed the pejorative meaning of the epithet "realist," we could not be further from the truth. But to the extent that *realism* designates not the author's intent or the meaning of his project but the demands of a public, its contradictions, and, more profoundly, to the extent that it provides the reader's false consciousness with an account of the dialectic of the real and the unreality he is constantly living, the word is valid; the reader adopts it to reassure himself, to explain himself in his own eyes, and to present his own intentional hatred as an innocently *other* intention (of that *other*, the author) by unrealizing himself in the real, that is, by realizing himself in the unreal. But this is not the moment to describe this complex connection. We shall come back to it after studying *Madame Bovary* and its reception. Let it suffice that we have indicated here the underlying affinities uniting the realistic and scientistic public with the dogmatists of absolute-art.

5. Neurosis and Prophecy

We have just observed that the truth of art-neurosis is confirmed around 1850, when the reader is conditioned by a disguised hatred.

And we have further observed that the literary work is the ritual site where the public's misanthropy can be achieved and *realized* under a false name, claiming to be a pure contemplation of the *real*. But we know as well that the public's disposition is not simply a product of the structures of bourgeois society; the class struggle, understood as the fundamental contradiction of this society, cannot be internalized in the antagonistic classes without being lived as a reciprocal animosity. In a more general way, the conflict between the ruling classes and the exploited classes is a process that is temporalized through prior structures, and by deviating or breaking them, this conflict produces different structures that yet contain the product of their transcendence. When internalized, this temporalization produces all kinds of *hostility* in everyone. Not in a strict pattern of development that would become progressively more "conscious," say, for example, from the mildest form of hostility to its most intense, but rather according to the givens of the general situation and especially the historical moment. In other words, as hostility is merely the subjective expression of the conflict, its motive lies not in itself but in the vicissitudes of the struggle. There is an order to praxis—for example, the emancipation of the workers; as such it is at once the consequence and the motive of their organization. There is no regulated hostility differing in quality and intensity, depending on whether the conflict confines itself to the economic realm or spills over into civil war. And these are basic contradictions: they are the ones, for example, that set the forces of production in conflict with the relations of production—which, through the dialectical rigor of their development, ultimately determine the intensity of the antagonisms and the way they are experienced. When the Canuts of Lyon seized their city at the beginning of the July monarchy, they did not hate their employers, and this was their downfall. It was the bourgeoisie who did a terrified apprenticeship in hatred. Yet after several discreet massacres, they let down their guard a bit and dozed off on their money bags. Furthermore, as we have seen, the man of hatred is not the product solely of these infrastructural relations caught in their entirely relative immobility; those relations had to become exacerbated in the context of a singular history, and that history—*praxis-process*—had to produce an *event* through them and against them. The man of 1850 is no longer simply a boss or simply a worker; after June '48, as a boss he is in solidarity with the perpetrators of the massacres, and as a worker he is in solidarity with the massacred. For at any given moment the historical agent resembles Pascalian man, in that he can *never* be the

314

object of a concept. For Pascal, *human nature* as a pure essence existed when Adam left the hands of God; after the Fall it continued to exist but in perverted form, bumped off track by what may well be called the absolute event, and subsequently answered by that other historical absolute, the death of Christ. The consequence, for Pascal, is that man must be accounted for at once by conceptual universality and by the opaque irreversibility of a singular temporalization. The situation is the same for historical man: just like the creature of God, in the *Pensées*, he is the totalizing and totalized expression of defined structures in a society defined by its mode of production and by the institutions resulting from it; and at the same time he is an irreversible event that bears in it the mark of all prior events. Pascal concluded that man is not *thinkable;* he envisaged him only as the object of an impossible intellection. It is characteristic of dialectical reason, by contrast, to understand this man-event as someone who endures history and at the same time makes it.

If this is the case, if the reader of 1850 becomes manifest *even* in the demands of his reading as constituted by history made and endured, it is clear that in order for writers to find the truth of their work confirmed in that reader, it will not be sufficient for them to be the serene, unagitated products of the dominant or middle classes. Their evident hatred of man must be distinctly, as we say today, "trapped in events," or, if you will, must be an event itself, the product and temporalization of an event. The extent to which the novel as a general form expresses for the nineteenth century the infrastructural contradictions of bourgeois society as a *synchronic* constellation will be the subject of our study when the time comes to propose our "reading" of *Madame Bovary*. But what interests us here is a *diachronic* problem: since the author's misanthropy is an *event*, mustn't it derive from the same events as the reader's misanthropy to give it adequate expression? In other words, shouldn't the close connection between the reader and this fictional expression be manifest only in works in which the author turns to pessimism *under the shock* of the events of '48? As for the writers who kept themselves in the background of the Revolution and the Counterrevolution at the time because they were apolitical or for some other reason, couldn't their misanthropy, if they are indeed misanthropes, be explained by accidents of public or private history that are hypothetically prior to the February days? And, because of this, couldn't the convergence of that bilious mood with the great fear and hatred provoked by the resurrection of the Republic be merely fortuitous? In other words, if their neurosis surfaced under

315

the July monarchy, don't we have to acknowledge that it cannot conceivably express the pathos of the bourgeois and the middle classes in the 1850s, and that such writers should have included as an epigraph to each of their books the disclaimer customarily used by authors of spy novels on the first pages of theirs, "This work is purely fictitious. Any resemblance to real persons or events is merely accidental"?

The question is not so simple. It is posed, moreover, in one form or another, in every era. If, as I believe, the work is in some way representative of its time—of the very moment it appears—how can this synchronic homogeneity conceivably be compatible with the diachronic heterogeneity of temporalizations? Indeed, the multiplicity of coexisting generations involves for each of them—as a function of their age and development—characteristic and irreducible ways of living the same events. Family structures are diverse, as are socioprofessional circles and geographical regions, which suggests certain discrepancies within every generation, this or that individual's lagging behind in relation to the social whole, or, on the contrary, extreme speed, a burst of power that compels him, finally, to change course, to stop short, or to overturn. The diversity of the environment gives provincial life a meditative slowness whose flow—from one region to another—is a function of the means of communication, etc., etc. Yet the author publishes his first work at the age of twenty, at thirty he is already getting on well, he has lived history from the perspective of a certain childhood, which has constituted him as the bearer of a preestablished destiny and of a certain, perhaps already outmoded, subculture. How can he bear public witness to a historical catastrophe he has experienced with only the means at hand—the tools he was given in early childhood, which allude to a historical moment that might already be passed and may not be appropriate to help him understand the current historical moment, if not as it is (this would presuppose an impossible conscious awareness), at least as his contemporaries believe it to be? Or perhaps he hasn't experienced that catastrophe at all?

So it can happen that an agent of the Revolution, having participated in the February days, may hardly be capable, even if he is a writer, of depicting the joy and the subsequent disappointment of the populace, and that on the contrary, the meaning of those days may be more clearly expressed in a work whose author may not have lived through them but whose misanthropy derived from his early history. In this case, however, the deep and distant causes of this misanthropy must *also* be considered the causes of the February movement, or otherwise, clearly, the congruence of the work with the general French misanthropy "dictated by events" would be strictly accidental. To further our understanding of this phenomenon, we can take our pick among the authors of the second half of the century and choose someone who might really have taken part in the clashes, then compare him to Flaubert, who was not involved but who nine years later ranked among the best new writers with the sudden fame of *Madame Bovary*. Practically speaking, Leconte de Lisle became a misanthrope *after* the events of June '48, whereas Flaubert, as we know, was one as early as 1835. If, as we shall see, Leconte de Lisle is merely a minor representative of opinion, it is because his peevishness and his disenchantment, born *after the fact*, are merely anecdotal consequences; they reflect to the reader nothing but his own moroseness as anecdote. If Flaubert, by contrast, suddenly becomes prominent, he does so because his neurosis long prophesied the events of February and June, as well as the coup of 2 December 1852. This is what gives his first published work the sudden breadth and obscurity of a myth. On the other hand, if for Flaubert the misanthropic work is merely from the first the restoration of the *primal scene* as a prefiguration of the civil war of 1848–51 and conditioned by the same factors, the works of Leconte de Lisle, though explicitly—and quite truthfully—the consequences of political disillusionment, could neither be understood nor preserve the little value they have if they were not also, though more weakly, the projection of a primal scene into the imaginary. To observe the difference between these two types of authors we must go into a certain amount of biographical detail and compare the life of Leconte de Lisle, his elder by three years, to the life of Flaubert.

At the source of *Poèmes antiques* and *Poèmes barbares* we find all the themes of art-neurosis. There is nothing to suggest, however, that their author might have been neurotic. He was the son of a bourgeois gentleman, that is, of a mutant whose contradictions—analogous to those of Achille-Cléophas—surely affected the poet. Leconte de Lisle's father practiced the profession of military surgeon in Bavaria—which designated him, socio-professionally, as a one of the professional elite. In the life of the surgeon Flaubert, rural by birth, practitioner by culture and profession, it was professional skill that won out. The opposite is true for the surgeon from Bavaria: he departs for La Réunion, marries an aristocratic woman, acquires and administers his properties, returning *partially* to the landed basis of the nobility and

317

a private income, except for the fact that his lands are not inherited but bought in part with his savings—money earned in the exercise of his profession—in part with profits realized in La Réunion itself through trade. We do not know how he felt, this former practitioner smitten with the aristocracy, this merchant creating a coat of arms for himself by marriage and trade, and inventing his own feudal reality by the constitution of a domain, this veteran who chose the army of Empire as a chivalric order but who was associated with it as an auxiliary and not a combatant. We don't even know the nature and extent of his learning: after all, he was merely an adjutant in the Grande Armée. Latin and the rudiments of the natural sciences were probably his entire baggage. Certain evidence—somewhat suspect—seems to indicate that he liked Rousseau and Voltaire. It is clear, in any case, that even after choosing the particularism of privilege, he could not entirely free himself from the universality of acquired knowledge, or from bourgeois universalism. An untenable position, practically speaking. He surely had more difficulty crushing the universal in himself than Dr. Flaubert had in transcending monarchist ideology, the fruit of his rural childhood. As we know, the Rouen surgeon did not entirely escape his original background: he founded a family of the "patriarchal" type in which he reestablished the right of primogeniture. Conversely, we can easily imagine the gentle or sometimes blunt influence of that analytic reason developed by a bourgeois education in the man of independent means of La Reunion. Be that as it may, Achille-Cléophas bought lands with his savings, but the central thing in his life would always be his practice; the domain of the expatriot surgeon similarly had its source in the practitioner's earnings, but he left Europe *to remake his life* and disengage himself from his profession once and for all. The instability of this character is intriguing: Did he share the philosophical mechanism of his fellow practitioner, or, in order to save the ancient syncretisms that established privilege, did he surrender to vitalism? One thing is certain: he had few scruples about using slave labor. Did he see it as the resurrection of serfdom, an ancient and sacred custom, and thereby the reestablishment of feudalism, his vanished honor, his raison d'être? The contradiction between this vicious oppression and a certain learned egalitarianism surely did not occur to him, for he used to beat his slaves. It existed nonetheless; his words must have contradicted his behavior *for others*; indeed, his son Charles, born on île Bourbon in 1818, considered slavery a scandalous iniquity from early childhood.

Let us be clear about this. A happy child—a loved child—accepts institutions as laws of nature or eternal decrees. There were many sons of plantation owners on the island who adapted quite well, whatever they thought later, to the forced labor that existed before their birth—from their point of view from the time there were men on earth—which the grown-ups justified with the calmness of a conscience tranquilized from the cradle by a benign racism. This is the ideology most easily assimilated by a very young child, provided, however, that his parents belong to the superior race. Had Charles been loved, he might have been less sensitive to his father's contradictions; deprived of love but put in possession of an unambiguous racism, he would have found other outlets for his resentment. For slavery to have seemed so unbearable to him at such an early age, he must have understood the weaknesses of paternal ideology through his frustration at being unloved. He must have been taught the universalist demand of bourgeois humanism with no corresponding effort to hide from him the wretched life of the Blacks, or *above all* the corporal punishments inflicted on them. *"Above all,"* I say, because a rich child has difficulty conceiving of poverty; even if it is under his nose, he sees it as a kind of modesty, a laudable simplicity. But the pride of *nobility* inculcated in him by the father[38]—again a contradiction—made horribly palpable to Charles, not so much the physical pain, perhaps, as the humiliation of these men and their women, who had not been presented to him as animals merely parading as humans, and whom he endowed, as a result, with his own pride. We hardly know the circumstances of his Oedipus complex, but it is clear that he spent his life fleeing from his father and the memories of his early history. Horrified at an early age to discover that his father tormented his slaves, conversely he despises the father in all slave owners. We come here, I think, to the essential contradiction, the one *that made him what he was:* pride of privilege and, equally, a horror of privilege when it is based on oppression. This contradiction exists in Flaubert on another level, opposing the rational universality of the exact sciences to the irrationality of desire and pride. But as the sons are their fathers' opposites, the paternal contradiction is reversed in each of them. The son of a rationalist, Gustave becomes a great irrational dreamer devoured by the diastases of analytic reason; the son of a privileged father, Charles puts his aristocratic pride to work in denying irrational prerogatives in the name of reason. As we shall see, Flaubert's position, just because of its absurdity, is much stronger

38. Or, indeed, the mother, who was real nobility.

than Leconte de Lisle's. Unlike his insincere younger peer, de Lisle is inclined to consummate a radical rupture; with his friend Adamolle, he considers republican and philosophical sentiments to be "the truest, the noblest of human opinions." He later displays the hatred he then felt for slavery in a story entitled *Mon premier amour en prose*. In love with a young Creole girl, he hears her haranguing her slaves one day "in a voice that was bitter, false, piercing, abrupt, mean: 'Louis, if the *manchy*[39] is not here in ten minutes, you will get twenty-five lashes tonight.' He backed away and said to her, bowing: 'Madame, I no longer love you.'" A suspect narrative. It is true that around this time he was infatuated with his first cousin. But aside from the fact that she bore no physical resemblance to the young slave owner, he seems to have preserved until the end of his life a tender memory of his young love,[40] which would be unlikely if, as he claims, he had been disgusted to discover the slave owner in her. It is much more likely that this fictive rupture is the screen for another, much earlier one that he consummated with his father (perhaps with his mother)[41] when he discovered that the Blacks were beaten. Did the former surgeon affect a belief in God? Or did the young man harbor grievances against his mother, who was Catholic and an aristocrat? The fact is that this republican became anticlerical. Vehemently, like Gustave, but continuing, at least at first, to affirm his theism. The chief thing, in any case, is that by his political choice he denies his seminobility, the false aristocracy of the plantation owners, the privileges of colonial society. This society, the only one he knows (although he had stayed a while in Nantes early in his childhood), remains within him as his essential contradiction, for he both issued from it and hated it.[42]

39. A kind of palanquin carried by black men.
40. Cf. "The Supreme Illusion":

> And you are reborn, too, diaphanous phantom
> Who made my heart beat for the first time . . .
> O precious vision, you, who spread again . . .
> Like a melancholy and soft gleam of dawn
> Within what was a dark and frozen heart.

41. She had brought a dowry of lands and slaves; it was impossible to regard her as completely innocent.
42. In 1843, he goes back to La Réunion for two years. The letters he writes at that time clearly inform us of his feelings for his native island: "I am in one of my dark days today, and I suffer terribly, for reasons I will explain." Or: "I've been on Bourbon now for fourteen months: 420 days of unremitting torture—10,080 hours of moral poverty; 60,480 minutes in hell . . ." It is around this time that he breaks with Adamolle in a way that rather closely recalls Gustave's more cunning, never articulated rupture with Ernest: "I am terrified to perceive that I am disengaging from individuals in order to

As a young man he returns to France to go to law school. Transplanted to an unfamiliar world, which he interpreted—at least in the beginning—in terms of the one that formed him, he thought he was a radical. In '45 he convinced himself, not without some effort, that he was a follower of Fourier: "We all are, those of us who believe in a better fate for man and who avow the goodness of God . . ." This profession of faith remains rather vague: he attempts to develop it in several poems he publishes in *La Phalange*. Despite a notable zeal, his verses seem to display the major contradiction that set him in conflict with the disciples of Fourier. This thinker, who died in 1837, built this *Théorie des quatre mouvements et des destinées générales* on the most reckless and hence most profound optimism: universal harmony will find its foundation in the free play of unconstrained passions; when those passions are in conflict, it is because they are restrained, censored; they will coexist peacefully if nothing external obstructs their full development. There is no doubt this harmony will be lived *in happiness*; the admirable audacity, here, is to inform us that we are suffering from a *lack* and not from an *excess*; men will be happy and embrace each other as brothers when they are *whole*. To give these ideas their poetic expression, Leconte de Lisle curiously chose "The Robe of the Centaur." Hercules clothes himself in the poisoned tunic, it eats away at him, he climbs onto a wood pile and burns to the bone:

> O holy passions, unquenchable ardor,
> O source of sobbing! O brilliant fire . . .
> . . . On the holy pyre where your flames burn
> You consume a man and make him a god.

In short, Fourier's optimism is refracted through Leconte de Lisle's pessimism and as a result is considerably altered. In the first place there is no longer any question of *universal* harmony, that is, of a *social* accord among men; Nessus's tunic, glued to the skin, gives each man

---

act and live, through thought, with the masses only . . . How is it, then, that we must deny the friendship that it has not been given us to pursue as naively as in former times? The fault is neither yours nor mine, You married, you have lived a strictly limited life. For my part, I have ventured on a divergent path, and I have sought my greatest sum of happiness in the external and internal contemplation of infinite beauty . . ." The words "a strictly limited life" are admirable. Mediocre writers sometimes hit upon rare felicities of style. That is also the life led by Chevalier, and had Flaubert written Leconte de Lisle's phrase, he would have done his friend justice by condemning him with extenuating circumstances. Gustave, an incomparably "greater" writer than Leconte de Lisle, could not write that phrase; he preferred to condemn without recourse—as we saw in the letter to Madame Flaubert that I cited above.

his grandeur through the atrocious burns it inflicts. We are much closer, here, to an individualistic dolorism than to an act of revolutionary faith. Nor is this yet a matter of Flaubertian or Baudelairian *dissatisfaction*, and the poem as a whole is much more reminiscent of the conception of Musset. Yet the idea of pain-as-merit is not alien to Leconte de Lisle. Between 1843 and 1845, when he so carefully counted up his "minutes in hell," he added: "No God is possible if this doesn't count later," without specifying whether his sufferings were earning him heaven or earthly power—probably ignorant himself of the outcome. In any event, this panegyric to the passions is not so removed from misanthropy and the future practices of distinction. The "intoxicating torments" are flames burning the flesh, consuming Hercules entirely and "exhaling him into the heavens." No passion, therefore, is a carnal or corporeal blossoming; passions make the *denied body* the means of acceding to the ideal. In fact, Leconte de Lisle is a socialist—if he is one—only in theory and in the abstract. He had already said to Adamolle before his departure for Paris: "I am going to detach myself from individuals in order to act and live, *through thought*,[43] with the masses only." In another letter he explains to his friend that he wants to go to France to find a calmer life, more propitious to study. He adds this sentence: "I *always* despised the noise men make, and *them* as well."[44] This is an acknowledgment, like the one made by Flaubert, of a quasi-congenital misanthropy. But unlike Gustave, more sincere this time—or less burdened by contradictions—Leconte de Lisle, even while hating men, has no wish—at this period, of course—to disengage from humanity. "I would have to abstract myself from a blind or grudging world. Yet can a man, *whatever he is*, constantly abstract himself from humanity?" Humanity, an ambivalent notion, suggests two meanings to him. It is the concrete totality (or totalization) of all real men; in this case, it is not worth an hour's trouble, and one must abstract oneself from it, as soon as possible but not *constantly*, on pain of losing the humiliated but necessary consciousness of our facticity. The main thing, in this first use of the term, is Platonic ascesis, the renunciation of "love, ambition, friendship as they are conceived on earth" for the "love of imperishable beauty, ambition for the fixed riches of intelligence, the study of absolute justice, of absolute good, of what is absolutely real, all this to be abstracted from the false morals found here below." This letter,

43. My italics.
44. My italics.

written on île Bourbon at the age of twenty-two, dates from shortly before he set out again for France, and constitutes adequate proof that this Platonism—which preserves only the body's abstract facticity and makes it a *situated* relation to the ideal—is the antithesis of socialism, even the utopian variety, which must essentially affirm itself in theory and practice as the future of real men in the real world—"blind or grudging." But at the same time humanity, for this Platonist, is the nontemporal idea, a pure object of contemplation; it escapes duration because it contains its own future. The achievement of this archetype—which is inscribed in the idea itself—is expected the minute the real society and the ideal society mutually reflect one another. In short, through this second meaning of the term—so wildly prodigal in that golden age of socialism—Leconte de Lisle manages to slip from a Catharist pessimism into the temporal optimism of Fourier. In the poems he writes in Paris for *La Phalange*, we see him shift innocently—almost everywhere—from humanity, the collective populace, to humanity, the mediation between earth and the idea.

> Cease your dull complaint, and dream, Humanity,
> That the time is near when the shadows of iniquity
> In your heavy heart and in the gloomy universe
> Will be chased away by rays of happiness . . .
> . . . O Holy Creature of infinite desires
> What sacred treasures brought together at your feet
> As the price of your agonies and your holy courage
> Will at once redeem the long, stormy centuries.
> Fraternal labor on the devastated soil
> Forever nourishes the tree of freedom . . .
> . . . God, God whom you were seeking, poor blind spirit,
> God will stream out everywhere, and to you He will have spoken.

Is this socialism? In this homily it is not clear whether the time of "fraternal labor" will come at the end of an effortless evolution, whose "devastation" of the soil (the negativity of the term is curious—preserved to designate the shift from nature to antiphysis) will put the human race in possession of the abundance produced by its hard labor without changing the regime or the class system; or whether this golden age, whatever the labor involved in the relation of men to things, implies a praxis, the labor men perform on themselves through the mediation of things or on human things as they are man's inflexible predictors of his inhuman destiny. This uncertainty is typical of Leconte de Lisle and many of his contemporaries. However, evolution far outweighs the revolutionary idea, which is finally nowhere present. The fact is that humanity, enriched by savings and accumulated labor, leads, in the end, to God. Is this an image? Is God merely accomplished man? No; in this era—and this time under the influence of the followers of Fourier—Leconte de Lisle considers that God, whatever His existence, invested "human nature" with the strict rule of its development. The final happiness will therefore be man as *evolved truth*, recognizing the law of his Creator and contemplating the ideal that will be given to him directly. Progress seems here to be the development of order, and in this Leconte de Lisle appears to resemble Comte more than he does Fourier. Further, he is not in any hurry to reach that golden age, since around the same time he writes in "Le Voile d'Isis"—speaking of "obscure man, crowned by justice," that is, of himself (my italics):

> *In the distance,* happier and more beautiful,
> Ceasing to rebel against creative designs
> Humanity comes into his astonished view.

These curious lines are doubly interesting because they show us that under the influence of the times, Leconte de Lisle intentionally confuses prophecy and the vision of essences—at the end of a long journey, humanity will become what it is—and that even in his "socialism" he preserves the ambivalence of the human idea. Admirable in its future essence, which is nothing other than the "design" of the Creator, humanity is contemptible in its empirical reality because "the disturbing folly of human beings" makes man rebel against the will of God. This preserves intact the original misanthropy and abandons it only in the distant future when man, by his submission to his rediscovered essence, will dissolve himself in infinite divine will. Only once, in his poems from *La Phalange,* are we invited to believe that time exists—the irrational time of the "little tremor," of the violence that breaks chains. This moment occurs in "Niobe," the unhappy mother, symbol of the human race:

> Oh mother, your suffering will *one day* be over . . .
> You will break the marble of immobility,
> Your heart will make your fertile bosom quiver.

The unlucky Niobe, transformed into a marble statue, bursts out of the imprisoning stone by means of a *historical and dated* ("one day") movement that is suggestive of violence. This vague prediction is unfortunately presented to us as *poetic prophecy*—that is, as an irrational intuition wagered on beauty and faith. Moreover, in this text (omitted in the version that will appear in *Poèmes antiques*) it is less a question of establishing a more just society than of the denial of false gods. Curiously, moreover, and quite significantly, the poem's thought is muddled: Niobe's children, "the only living gods whom love multiplies," those martyrs of despised cults, will cure "the humans' disturbing folly." But how can that be? Aren't those children human? Proof is that Niobe, at the end of the last stanza, is called "Mother Humanity." All men are her sons. But among them, some are greater than others: those who were "struck down by the rejected gods," meaning "killed by the arrows of Artemis and Apollo." Translation: people martyred by Catholicism, whose hearts the Church has destroyed and who have consequently driven faith from those dead hearts—Leconte de Lisle in particular, I would even say singularly, since he knows no rival—are the true men; that is, *gods*. They go among the crowd composed only of humans, or rather hominids, and cure these beasts driven mad with superstition by raising them up to their level. We recognize several familiar themes here. Charles, by birth, was only half an aristocrat, one of the living dead; his sacrifice makes him a God, or let us say more modestly a superman. This socialist burns up the steps of class transcendence, bursts through the ceiling of the aristocracy, and plants himself in heaven, from where he agrees to enlighten his inferior brothers, human beings. The poet is vatic because he is a murdered child; vaguely, this confused mind assimilates—as Flaubert did around the same time—beauty as a way of capturing the idea, and death as the murder and renunciation of the body. Once again, a radical contradiction of Fourier's message: "*Vos fratres estis!* You are all brothers!" Perhaps Charles only valued the messianic pride of his avowed master. Provided he himself is that Messiah announced by Saint John: "a prophet for the industrial fatherland." In 1846, minds are overexcited. Charles's in particular, as he finds himself up against the "inexorable demands of matter"—translation: money troubles. At this time, moreover, he is in the anguished throes of stormy and difficult love affairs that end badly. His rage takes him out of himself. He writes to a friend: "This will not last, it must not last . . . With what joy will I descend from the calm contemplation of things to take up my part in the struggle." In the same week, in *La Démocratie pacifique*, he proposes this alternative: "progressive and peaceful renewal" or bloody Revolution. But a postscript to the previously cited letter clearly reveals where his preferences lie: "Take no account of all the incoherent things I just wrote you; my head is not yet on straight—I am suffering from fever and

325

spleen." In other words, this contemplative man, who sacrifices his rags to the ideal our of contempt for *lived experience,* feels an old hatred boil up in him in periods of agitation, a hatred born twenty-five years earlier on a distant island and whose violence terrifies him in himself and in others. We know, however, that unlike most republicans he takes the side of the workers in the June massacres. It has even been claimed that he mounted the barricades and gave the "insurgents" the formula for an explosive. However, it is not revolutionary brotherhood but mainly peevishness that radicalizes him for a moment. On 30 April he wrote to a friend: "They want to conjure away the Revolution. The Assembly will be composed of bourgeois and royalists. It will vote for thoroughly reactionary laws, leave untouched the social and political order as it existed under Louis-Philippe, and—who knows?—may soon impose other royalty on us." This lucidity is striking, prophetic, it could be said, since the bourgeois class will give France something better than a king—an emperor. But the following section of the letter is disconcerting: "Ah well," he adds immediately, "we have a lot to put up with. I do not despair, for my part, of dying at Mont Saint-Michel. What filthy and disgusting rabble, humanity! What a stupid lot, the people. They are an eternal race of slaves, who cannot live without a burden and a yoke. And we shall fight again not for their sakes but for our sacred ideal. So let them die of hunger and cold, those easily fooled masses who will be massacring their true friends before long. The reaction made me a furious communist . . . The French people need a little Committee For Public Safety to force them . . . to make a love match with the Republic."

This text is valuable because it is written by a fool; the sophisticates are better at concealing their contradictions. But what are we to think of "those true friends of the people" who soon risk getting massacred for them and, worse, by them? Leconte de Lisle ranks himself among them, there is no doubt, for he declares "*we* shall fight again . . ." What a strange friendship that makes the working class "an eternal race of slaves" and promptly condemns them to die—just because they are, according to him, "easily fooled." No, this new Marat, this "Friend of the People," doesn't give a damn for the masses, as "filthy and disgusting" as their masters since, like them, they belong to that "rabble," humanity. Humanity, as we see, has lost its idea on the way: the future, a few months earlier, should have freed man from his chains and allowed him to fulfill his potential, thanks to the teaching of a few young gods, the sons of Niobe. This future melts away forever; the chains will be eternal. And Niobe's children, abandoning their peaceful role as educators, suddenly reveal their plan: to impose the Republic *by terror;* heads will roll—some will be bourgeois heads, but most of them will be those of the people. Hatred explodes: this republican despises the populace and always has. He will fight for the *ideal.* Which means, as we have seen, that he wants to bind the working classes forcibly to the republican regime conceived as a *human thing.* Democracy—although formal—cannot be conceived in its truth, in 1848, except as a change in human relations. An *internal* change that would derive its meaning only by common agreement, only by a "general will" to emancipation. In other words, to an *authentic* friend of the people, the Republic is like the regime that, born of a free social contract, produces its institutions in order to maintain that contract's permanent reality. The political dimension of the citizen is confused with his free praxis as a sworn member of the group. It can thereby be *imposed* only on the privileged, who refuse it in the name of their privileges; if the people were compelled to submit to it, if it did not emanate from them as their fundamental claim, it would be merely a dictatorship calling itself a republic. This is where Leconte de Lisle gets tangled in his thoughts; but his confusion is revealing. In fact, the workers are not so enthusiastic. Less easily fooled than the poet believes, they feel obscurely that these formal freedoms don't amount to much as far as they are concerned. We consent to the Republic, they think, *if it really is the way* to make a *social* body politic. But their concrete claim—the only one that, without their even suspecting it, is revolutionary—is their claim of the *right to work.* And a month earlier they perceived that a bourgeois democracy can be as reactionary as a parliamentary monarchy; elections had just taken place, industrialists and gentry got elected by proclaiming they were republicans—that was the best way, according to them, of dissociating the Republic from "communism." Tocqueville will write: "The Constitutional Assembly had been elected to avert civil war." As a result, the workers lose interest in their political rights; what matters to them is the struggle against unemployment, the national Workshops, the stabilization of wages. This is what unleashes Leconte de Lisle's fury. This *abstract republican* abominates the provincials who brought the conservatives to power; but he equally despises the urban workers who, if they demonstrate *in the streets,* will play the game of the rich by giving them a pretext to abolish the regime. When he characterizes them, with a sweep of the pen, as slaves who need the yoke, it is precisely because they refuse to be slaves, and because real freedom for them consists not of sending to the Assembly a politician who will betray them, or whose voice, if he is loyal, will be drowned out by the shouts of "decent people,"[45] but *literally* of not "starving to death." This infuriated petty-bourgeois reproaches them with preferring the "social" to the "political," just at the moment when these terms are defined by their opposition. In this, our self-styled follower of Fourier unmasks himself: the ideal he wants to impose on the people by force, forcing them to endure their wretchedness quietly to save the Republic, is quite simply the claim of the middle classes—and particularly of the lower middle class to which he belongs. The petty-bourgeois want to take part in public affairs—some out of interest, others out of ambition or pride—and to gain the support of the masses, they have thrown them a bone to chew on, namely the ballot. Those who condemn the idiocy of the populace, which doesn't know how to be satisfied, are numerous now, crazy with anger and fear. Fear can be read between the lines of the letter cited above. Hatred is quite evident. And under a vile pretext: the poet reproaches the people with loving their chains because they endanger the schemes of the petty-bourgeoisie by refusing to do their dirty work for them; he condemns the workers to die in poverty because they are beginning to understand that the right to vote is not enough to pull them out of it.

Thus, when he gets involved in their struggle in June, he already hates them—as he hates the landowners, a typical position of the petty-bourgeoisie as Marx described it at this historical moment. Why, then, does he take the side of the massacred rather than withdraw, like a true son of Niobe, to take up the thread of his sacred meditations? Well, he tells us in his letter of 31 April, for the sake of the ideal. The fact is, this is a fight for honor; he will be seen on the barricades and spend forty-eight hours in prison, "the longest hours of his life." Be that as it may, this son of a plantation owner and an aristocrat regards himself as a gentleman, as we know. Against his birth and thanks to it, which indeed gives him the sense of honor that allows him to deny it. Honor, for Charles, is no longer the bond of man to the house but rather that of the sons of Niobe to "human beings." He thereby becomes individual and bourgeois; this attitude and the behavior that follows from it are no longer distinguishable, in the final analysis, from what we call "dignity." Duties toward others are only the consequences of duties toward oneself. The man of

45. The "Republic of decent people" was often spoken of at that time, as opposed to the "social Republic."

honor pays his debts: in June, he goes over to the side of the "race of slaves," certainly not out of sympathy for the wretched, for the louse-ridden souls he deigns to visit, and still less for their claims (he has long been, as he says, using a charming euphemism, "less and less sectarian with regard to socialism"), but to *keep his word*, to respect the earlier contract made in the secret societies, in the political gatherings, in the progressive clubs, between the petty-bourgeois republicans and the workers. He thereby breaks solidarity—this is the positive aspect of that fugitive visitation—with all the self-styled defenders of the Republic who shoot the men who brought them to power; he disavows the massacre by ranging himself symbolically on the side of the massacred, a stance that in his eyes allows him to preserve for the republican ideal—by such a symbolic sacrifice of his person—a purity that seemed highly compromised. The true democrat is going to get himself killed with the people, and by doing so in the name of respect for the sworn faith he shows that the executioners were never for democracy. But by the same token he frees himself; he has paid his debt to men he never loved and never even approached before the February days, whom he despised from the time they left their hovels to appear on the boulevards of the city, and whose behavior since then has continued to increase and consolidate his aversion to them. Now he owes them nothing; two nights in the slammer have given him the *quietus*. This sacrifice is simultaneously a rupture. Or rather it contains in itself the intention to make a break. Henceforth Leconte de Lisle is free; he will be able to show his iron contempt for the lower classes. Be that as it may, we find him for a time—let's say from March to July '48—in the strangest position: he defends a cause he detests—that of the populace—and one he *knows* to be lost in advance, against the false brothers who call upon the Republic to witness "its great sacred dream." He defends it *because he knows it is lost*; in other words, the future king of Parnassus enters literary life by making himself a *man-failure*. A short while before, from Dinan, he wrote to his friend Ménard: "None of that prevents me from continuing to live on the intellectual heights, in calmness, in the serene contemplation of divine forms. A tremendous tumult is going on in the lower regions of my brain, but the upper part knows nothing of contingent things." We might think—except for the style—that we were reading one of the letters in which Gustave, some years earlier, spoke to his friends of his underlying serenity and his extreme but superficial nervousness (the image is reversed, but we found two metaphors in Flaubert: sometimes the calm is at the upper level of the soul, and the young man "enters again into the Idea, becomes a brahman"—and sometimes it is his fundamental truth, masked in the eyes of others but not in his own by a superficial and meaningless agitation). The text by Leconte de Lisle is clear: the lower regions of his brain are in profound accord with the lower regions of history, and in a certain way with the dregs of society[46] and that contingency, poverty. What did he do in June but *accept the fall* by taking the side of a scorned populace; haggard, running through Paris—if the hagiographers are telling the truth—with the formula for Pyroxylin in his pocket, he wants to identify with the tumult of the lower regions of society and the lower regions of his soul. This is what Gustave did at Pont-l'Evêque, with the difference that society was not directly implicated by his "attack." Nonetheless, Flaubert wanted to surrender to the body and fall below the human to be reborn as an artist. Similarly, Leconte de Lisle, by taking the side of the massacred, makes himself the defender of submen and thereby becomes a subman himself. But this collapse is a Passion that must allow him to break all ties with "contingency" in himself and in that "idiot's tale" we call history. He makes himself all too human, dies of it, and is resurrected in inhumanity; the theme for Flaubert and for him seems to be the same. His double failure—emotional and political—seems to be a rite of passage that concludes his youth and prefigures the age of man.

What is certainly striking is the incredible alacrity of his aboutface. He renounces politics from one day to the next. The only conclusion he draws from the June massacres is that one must scorn the people, who "were swept off the boulevards by four men and a corporal [and] . . . who went home cold, indifferent, and inert." When we consider that the *official* statistics list 3,035 dead among the "communists," and that Normandy—who is not exactly a friend of the "reds"—declares on 6 July: "As for the losses to the insurgents, it would be difficult to calculate their extent with precision because many of the dead were thrown into the Seine . . ."; when we recall something that everyone knew at the time, that the Assembly was specifically elected to drown the popular demands in blood, and that it was very honestly engaged in doing so, preparing with the precision of a clockmaker the ambush that would provide at once a pretext for slaughter and the means to execute it, the poet's judgment is seen in its true light: it is an attempt—one that must surely be called ignoble—to make the victim

46. We shall later see another text in which the "lower levels" designate the working classes.

assume all the responsibilities of executioner. Flaubert would display the same sophistry a little later, when that respectable landowner, sickened by the passivity of the people who did not take a firm stand against Badinguet on 2 December, would explain that the workers *deserve* the dictatorship because they did not have the courage to oppose it. As Leconte de Lisle so succinctly put it: "I hate slaves who love their chains." And as there are no other kind, according to him, he joins Baudelaire and Flaubert in their icy scorn for the "vile multitude." He preserves Fourier's "great human hierarchy," but does so in order to put the revolutionaries at the bottom of the scale—and radically condemn *action* in all its forms. Louis Ménard, more honest or more consistent, condemned the June executions in *Le Représentant du Peuple;* he got fifteen months in prison and was fined ten thousand francs. He fled to Brussels.[47] Leconte de Lisle is indignant at his conduct and rebukes him from Paris:

> How can the Artist fail to see that all those men committed to the brutalities of action, to the banal digressions and eternal repetitions of paltry and pitiful contemporary theories, are not molded from the same clay as himself? How can he fail to perceive that those men seem disturbed by the realization of any ideal because they have more blood in their veins than gray matter in their skulls? Doesn't the coarseness of their emotions, the flatness and vulgarity of their ideas, wound him? Is the language they speak similar to his own? How can he live, he who was a man of delicate emotions, of refined sentiments and lyric conceptions, among those rude natures, those limited minds always closed to every clarity of a superior world? Doesn't a law of harmonic necessity envelop and direct everything that is? Those men have been confined by that law to the lowest rungs of the great human hierarchy.

Naturally, the blind artist who does not perceive his crushing superiority is, first, poor Ménard, who risks "descending forever into the lower regions of our unhappy era of decadence to waste away in sterile efforts, deplorable deviations . . ." But in a way he is also Leconte de Lisle himself, *before* the fall. For Ménard might have answered him: And you, why did you take so long to see it? The answer is given in the text itself—implicitly at least: I understood my failure better than you did, I made it a revelation. Political failure is at once excused and assumed; if the multitude is vile, loving its chains so much that it stubbornly refuses to be freed, if on the other hand *action*

47. A little later he too will come round to art for art's sake.

is brutal and mad, no matter how it is envisaged and what its objective, the political enterprise is doubly futile. Even if led by angels it would be disavowed by those who are its object and could only lead them to change masters; but its very coarseness prohibits it from fixing a strict objective. All "men of action" claim to realize an ideal, but they are incapable of conceptualizing it—brainless, sanguine fools that they are—and then, proof of their philistine foolishness, they do not even understand that an ideal is *in essence* unrealizable and that the man of the ideal must situate himself above all reality. Moreover, *action,* if we mean an enterprise defined by an exact objective and intelligently organized, does not exist; on the contrary, people leap into action *through lack of intelligence.* Intelligence, he says in the same letter, can be only contemplative. It is "of a value quite different from life and death." Meaning, clearly, from the petty problems of work and hunger. "Thanks to [intelligence] we shake the dust from our feet on this filthy, impassioned earth and rise up forever into the magnificence of stellar life." We see the fate this former disciple of Fourier allots to the passions so dear to his master: they pollute the earth. On the other hand, since intelligence cannot structure praxis, it is now nothing but passion itself, vaguely illuminated by an infirm brain: too much blood in the veins, too little brain matter. Action is the fantasy engendered by the passions when they are unaware of themselves and fail to grasp the nature of the agitations they produce. If that's the way things are, Leconte de Lisle has every excuse; this artist, gone astray in action, did not at first recognize the ideal for what it is, in essence *unrealizable,* and exhausted himself in sterile efforts. His first justification: his failure was inevitable since action is an illusion that reveals its insubstantiality as soon as you leap into it. Moreover—his second justification—he has displayed his supreme worthiness; he did not act, of course, but he sacrificed himself out of generosity to a lost cause, which—as we have seen—is the era's definition of nobility. He thereby unwittingly displayed the superiority of his views and his fidelity to the ideal, still poorly understood, that was already devouring him. Obviously he had to be betrayed by everyone, by the crude politicians who called themselves democrats and by the common people who refused salvation. This Christ, more fortunate than his predecessor, had the benefit of numerous Judases. But for all these reasons, failure has become beneficent: the prophet betrayed reveals man and the world in that same pitiless light. He *had to* begin with action, it is in the order of things; the progression is from illusion to truth. Far from blaming him for having entered—little as he did—into the political arena, he should be congratulated for coming out again so quickly. Indeed, his superiority over Ménard derives from the rapidity with which he chose failure as a cipher and transformed that pathos into exis. The moment he is disabused, in effect, he understands that he had to fail in his political enterprise because he misunderstood the preeminence of his nature as artist, which is the proud negation of all praxis. As a result, continued failure takes on the aspect of a *conversion:* taken as positivity, this failure to win becomes art. The artist, in effect, contemplates the idea, and the superiority of his being stems from the fact that he has acknowledged the universal incapacity to act.

Given these facts, we shall recognize in turn, sometimes obscured but always present, the great themes of art-neurosis. First, panoramic consciousness: with regard to humanity as bearer of an idea, the poet deigned if not to integrate himself with it entirely at least to lead the procession. Once it is reduced to its eternal wretchedness, he both abandons and contemplates it. The first thing he sees is "a process of degradation"; it took him no more than an instant to transform the progressive movement of evolution into the regressive temporality of involution. History is an agony: nature endlessly gives birth to creatures in order to destroy them; man is among them; his destiny is inscribed on the earth, living today, dead tomorrow. The image of our planetary fatalities haunts our night skies, we have only to lift up our eyes to see the prophetic moon, "in former times a happy globe," today a "monstrous specter." So it will be with this world below; the poet transports himself voluntarily to the end of time, describes in the present the face of the "utterly denuded earth."

> All, all has disappeared, without echo or trace.
> With the memory of the young and beautiful world,
> The centuries have sealed in the same tomb
> Divine illusion and the murmur of the races.

It is as though his corrosive gaze had dissolved the trees, the forests, the walls, and could now grasp through life's tumult the icy ground, the frozen oceans of the defunct planet that rolls in the night, "far from warming suns," alone in

> The calm abyss where lies the vanity
> Of what was time and space and number.

In other words, for him, as for Flaubert, panoramic consciousness is the point of view of death. His poems will repeat it over and over

333

again. Here are four lines that are comparable to the desire Flaubert registered in *Novembre* when he envied the fate of funerary figures:

> Forget, forget, your hearts are consumed,
> Your arteries are empty of blood and heat.
> Oh you dead, you dead, happy prey to avid worms,
> Remember life and sleep.

His wisdom, moreover—since "the worst is to live too long, and death is better"—consists of regarding his own life in its quotidian banality as if it had already reached its end.

> Life is like this, we must endure it . . .
> But the wisest man laughs at it, knowing he must die.

To survey, to die living or to live one's death is also what he calls *entering into his eternity*. To enter *living*, of course, to be "taken alive by death."

But it is in "Le Secret de la Vie" that he has best expressed the underlying connection he has made between life, death, fate, and beauty:

> The secret of life is in closed tombs,
> That which is no longer is such only, because it has been,
> And the final nothingness of beings and things
> Is the sole reason for their reality.

Trashy verse, wretched thought, or, if it *is* perhaps thought, thought dropped on a rockery of words. Be that as it may, the aristocrat must exert himself to grasp the universe and man who inhabits it *without resorting to anthropomorphism*.

Nature, perfectly indifferent to men, sometimes allows him this ascesis:

> . . . If disabused of tears and laughter
> You want, no longer knowing how to curse or to forgive,
> To taste a supreme and dismal sensual pleasure;
> Come! the sun speaks to you in sublime words,
> Endlessly let yourself be absorbed in its implacable flame,
> And slowly return to the lowly cities,
> Your heart steeped seven times in divine nothingness.

For him, in effect, "nature is empty" and the sun is consuming.

> Nothing is living, here, nothing is sad or joyous.

To merge with nature is not pantheism—at least not a positive pantheism. It is borrowing not its plenitude, which does not exist, but its *absolute emptiness.* We are not so far removed from Saint Anthony's vow "To be matter." The implacable justice of Noon, devourer of shadows, is the perfect equivalence of the copses, the barren fields it consumes, annihilation by the light of relations, of values, and finally (but symbolically) of all life; it is the discovery of *non-sense,* not as some shadowy opacity of being but as its dazzling and sublime explosion, as its glory. Absorbed "in the implacable flame of the sun," the poet borrows its power of annihilation, he makes the corrosive light his own gaze; in full daylight, in the heat of Noon, he joins himself to that future Night, to "the great shapeless Shadow in its emptiness and sterility . . . where lies the vanity of what was time and space and number." These all too human categories would be inadequate to qualify the true being that is eternity; it is man who claims to be the measure of all things, but he is mortal; he is dead, and the measure disappears with him. By identifying with the sun the poet rejects the cardinal categories of thought and at the same time thought itself; he returns to lowly cities to look at people and their agitations through the sun's eyes, from the point of view of nonlife, of nonthought, of nonknowledge, and, finally, of nonbeing. If he preserves the "divine nothingness that drenched his heart," he will use it to *dehumanize* men, to grasp them not as they think they are or live but as they *are,* that is, in that original non-sense whose surface has not even been scratched by their futile significations. We recognize in passing the techniques of derealization that Gustave refined as early as 1844, and that Mallarmé would perfect under the Third Republic. Leconte de Lisle—who owed nothing to Flaubert—used cruder techniques; yet, they issue from the same intention.

To dehumanize, to derealize, is to totalize; for Leconte de Lisle, totalization is above all temporal. Surging up out of nothingness, doomed to annihilation, humanity, a flash between two eternities, introduces time—which will vanish with humanity—and the ontological structure of time is nothing but *decline: before* is defined, in one and the same movement, as that which precedes *after* and as that which is superior to it. There was the youth of the earth, there will be its death, we live in its old age. There was the magnificent youth of man, Antiquity, gone forever: "Since the time of Homer, Aeschylus and Sophocles, decadence and barbarism have invaded the human spirit."[48] Then there is the advent of Christianity, an inexpiable crime: It "was nothing but a deplorable influence on intelligence and mores." At

48. Preface to *Poèmes antiques.*

least the Barbarians tried to struggle against this infamy. After their defeat, we get the hideous Middle Ages and then, skipping over the Renaissance and the classical centuries, Leconte de Lisle sets us down in *our* time, in *our* iron century, in *our* senile, devitalized humanity, which lives its ordinary life with trivial, pleasant passions while awaiting death:

> You live like a coward, without dream or design,
> Older, more decrepit than the infertile earth,
> Castrated from the cradle by the murderous century
> Of any vigorous and profound passion.

No salvation. Soon,

> . . . on a great heap of gold, wallowing in coin
> [They] will die, stupidly filling their pockets.

Leconte de Lisle, more sincere in this respect than Flaubert, does not hide his game: he is a Knight of Nothingness, an artist of hatred. Hatred detaches him from humanity; through hatred he sets himself against it. His poems would be full of fire: let them enter the reader through his eyes, the shame of being a man will burn him to the bone. The author, in effect, is no moralist; if he shows us the abjection into which he claims we have fallen, it is not to raise us up, to show us the right way. It is understood in advance that our baseness is irremediable; the very nature of time, a process of degradation, is against it; the species will fall still lower; it must; only a cosmic cataclysm, soon to come, will put an end to the collapse. From that time on, this active misanthropy has no other purpose than to plunge us into despair. A single restraint on this resentful malice: the autonomy of literature, which manifests itself in him, as in other artists, by a flaunted contempt for the public. He lives in financial hardship, lodges at first with friends, gives Greek and Latin lessons, looks for publishing work, does translations, finally accepts a pension of 300 francs per month granted by the Emperor and a private but rather meager income irregularly forwarded by his slave-owning family from the île Bourbon (it is true that slavery was abolished there, but the condition of the black worker was hardly improved). Anything—patronage and the aid of feudal plantation owners—rather than sell one's pen. Let's get this right: rather than sell it to those who alone have the right to buy it, one's readers. From the time of his literary debut, he declares quite firmly that he is not seeking success, that he will gladly die unknown rather than owe his notoriety to accommodation. This means, first of all, that in the name of a dignity very close to distinction he repudiates the "vulgar" confidences of his *bête noire*, Alfred de Musset. To complain even while weeping, as Musset does, one must have a little self-love and retain, even in the deepest orgies of wretchedness, a childish confidence in the tenderness of the reader, that "maternal father." Leconte de Lisle has no self-love, he will not sell his secrets: "There is vanity and gratuitous profanation in the public confession of heartfelt anguish, as of its no less bitter sensuality." But he gives his discretion an additional motive; he does not like the public well enough to tell it about himself:

> Ah wretched century . . .
> Should I be swallowed up for black eternity
> I will not sell you my drunkenness or my ills.

Thus Parnassian *impassivity*—like Flaubertian impersonalism—has complex roots. It is vile to prostitute oneself; the times are too abject to give oneself to the public. As with any case of overdetermination, these two reasons, far from being mutually reinforcing, tend only to weaken each other. Is lyricism always to be condemned, whatever the public? Or does the interdiction apply only to the poems of that "wretched century," in other words, those written after 1850? Indeed, the lyric poems of Greco-Roman antiquity are numerous; must they, too, be accused of prostituting themselves? The answer is complicated. In the first place, we might say, the thing that discourages lyricism midway through this vile century is hatred. Sappho could confide in her readers, both the old and wise, and the young and radiant; she could do it, Leconte de Lisle is convinced, because the primary bond between the Ancients was love; a confession—especially if it was the subject of a beautiful poem—was in no danger of being misinterpreted or ill judged; and besides, since the immediate relation was *already* intimate, no admission could be indiscreet. But Leconte de Lisle hates his public; he is convinced that they hate him; so the poet is forewarned: anything he says will be held against him. Moreover, what can the man of hatred find in himself that is not hypothetically hateful? Panoramic consciousness implies a death of the self that keeps lived experience at a distance without entirely suppressing it; that is the poet's human aspect, namely, the exis of failure. There is no question of disavowing it, but neither should it be endorsed; failure is the world denying man, revealing his impossibility; panoramic consciousness is born of failure. Once man is acknowledged in the lower regions as impossible, the poet emerges from this assumed im-

337

possibility; he defines himself by the ideal, by the *unrealizable;* the claimed nonbeing of man becomes the springboard that allows him to leap into eternity. For this reason, the meditation "Noon" ["*Midi*"] is eminently poetic for Leconte de Lisle since nothingness, the "sublime speech of Nature," is internalized in it and becomes the revealer of subjective nonbeing. But for this very reason the identity of external nothingness and internal nothingness prohibits him from preserving the anecdotal singularity of *his* individual failure. One must go from consensual and universalized failure to the properly poetic condition, and make oneself in every poem the harbinger of nothingness. From this point of view, nothing is more edifying than Charles's attitude toward love. We know very little about his amorous adventure—from '45 to '48?—and in the present state of our information we have no way of confirming or denying that it was intentionally broken off. We have only two indications, but they are crucial. First: between 1850 and 1855 the poet—cured or not of his previous passion—carries on two love affairs *at once,* one platonic, with a tender and frigid blond, the other sensual, with a passionate woman. This dichotomy was frequent at the time, and we find it in particular in Baudelaire, who spiced his revels with Jeanne Duval or some "frightful" prostitute by imagining to himself that a snow queen, whom he loves with an impossible love, is gazing at him with a mixture of repulsion and infinite sadness. This effort to derealize a sexuality which, because it wants to be unified, shifts to the imaginary and becomes a role nonetheless remains a need in the course of being satisfied; we know that for the stepson of Colonel Aupick this effort has more than one meaning, and in particular that it is meant to offend his mother, that forbidden and treacherous lover. But taken as a whole, this dualism—love of the soul, love of the flesh—is typical of the midcentury. It is born of a failure: needs cannot be integrated with the practical unity of the person, nor the sensual relations of the body with the human relations established between couples. This dissociation so frequent at the time is merely the result of the practices of distinction when they are applied to the particular realm of *sex.* Here again, need, denounced, strangled as vulgar, is satisfied in shadow, shamefully. This is the period of concubinage and adultery: There is a formal prohibition to "treat one's wife like a mistress"; one denies her, she denies herself pleasure, that consent to animality. But the mistress, usually a venal relationship, exists; lacking an ongoing affair, the brothel offers interchangeable companions—the fireworks of fantasy. It allows those who visit it to maintain a sustained culpability that reinforces self-hatred. Marriage and the licensed brothel are two complementary institutions. Leconte de Lisle seems to have internalized this division. Nothing would suggest that he made love with one woman in order to offend the other unreally; or that he secretly humiliated the first by claiming to give the other the best of himself—that is to say, the denial of any physical relation, the distinguished invitation to scorn the body. Yet he loved *here* and fucked *elsewhere*. As happened then, the senses lose out; the Preraphaelite virgin with the muslin body is triumphant. Yet Charles needed this equilibrium and this double, joint denial—the systematic devalorization of the flesh when it succumbs; the systematic frustration and *inattention* to the body as the basis of "pure" love. Yet even without recourse to explanations of sadomasochism—so clearly called for, in contrast, by Flaubert's sexual deployments—Leconte de Lisle's two simultaneous loves have a *derealizing* effect on each other: the one is lived as the dark shadow of the other, the other as its immaterial and luminous specter. We can only assume—as a simple working hypothesis—from the time he was suffering a thousand deaths in the stormy liaison that ended in '48, that the origin of his malady lay in this contradiction and in the *acquired* impossibility of simultaneously swearing to love the same person in two conflicting ways. In this case the calm dichotomy of 1850 would seem to be a *solution* corresponding to a conscious awareness that comes after the rupture and is caused by it. He would have understood that he would find peace only by projecting himself into two persons, who by merely existing would pursue the struggle between bodily need and the ideal, and would make that struggle at once *calm, simultaneous,* and *external;* whereas, in his failed affair he loved with pure love, desired, possessed, then hated the same person, and the struggle, necessarily successive, took place in remorse and rancor. *One* angel and *one* beast—this is Charles's ideal, understood at last. But if a single woman has been at once angel and beast, it is *she herself* who angelically regards herself with contempt when she opens her naked thighs; it is she herself, guilty of bestiality, who at other moments pollutes her angelism with dreadful carnal memories, and at the same time, through many anatomical particularities, revealing what is hidden under the skirts of that asexual phantom, she makes platonic love a frustrating role played in bad faith. Thus he successively detests the whore in the name of the angel, and the angel in the name of the whore. We are speaking, then, of a *conduct of fail-*

ure, since in bed Leconte de Lisle would contest her sexual conduct in disgust, while in a chaste boudoir his burning memories would contest her platonism and denounce his mistress's bad faith.

All this, of course, is mere conjecture. But we will be struck—our second indication—by the haste with which Charles amplifies and generalizes a story of unhappy love and turns it into the Unhappiness of Love in all its forms. Fourier would no longer recognize his disciple. Passion becomes a troubling source of unhappiness. It had already been that, to be sure, in the time of "Nessus," when the poet called it a "devouring tunic," but at least it continued to be a "mantle of hope" in the name of romantic dolorism. That's all over; take it off, don't allow it to "consume" you with a "ghastly" evil force. In *Poèmes barbares* it becomes a viper, and he who claims to love its bite is a coward:

> Tear from your breast the fatal viper
> Or be still, coward, and die, die of having loved too much.

Thus Leconte de Lisle reveals his profound misogyny, an infantile rancor, a grievance against the woman, the angel-demon he loved around 1848, an internalization of the misogyny of the times, that special variety of misanthropy that regards woman as a ghoul. She is Ekidna, the "horrible and beautiful monster," half nymph, half dragon (here again we have platonism grasped as pure appearance and behind it, sexual horror). She comes forth in the evenings and sings, splendid and pure, concealing her scaly hindquarters. Men "under the whip of desire"[49] are drawn into her cave, where she eats them raw. This is not, as has been claimed, a depiction of passion itself but of the monster who arouses it, for on 30 June 1862 the *Revue contemporaine* publishes an unequivocal poem by Charles: an "adorable child" possesses "a silky little dog"; she caresses it, hugs it, calling it "my love." Then this "large-eyed despot" bites the dog, drawing blood: "the humble groans" she tears from the beast "please her soul"; so she consoles her victim "with a quick kiss." A very predictable conclusion:

> And I saw that she was already all woman
> Love in caprice and cruelty
> As God made her, and for eternity.[50]

---

49. We might compare this expression to Baudelaire's "Under the whip of pleasure"—more beautiful and more paradoxical. What a lot of bogeymen among these poets!

50. Cf. his first disappointment in love.

In short, you would have to be mad to love those creatures who are expressly put into the world to devour you and are fundamentally incapable of improving. All told, this misogyny is worth more than Flaubert's: it translates the apprehension in face of the *other*, in face of our sexual needs; but Leconte de Lisle would never have written of woman that "she takes her ass for her heart." And Gustave, who hardly knew him at the time, makes fun of him—secretly aiming to shock the Muse—because he made it a principle never to have relations with prostitutes. We know his reason: prostitutes sell themselves, that is, they *are sold*; Leconte de Lisle sees them as slaves; unable to break their chains—something for which he surely reproaches them—he will never make use of them; if he did, he would become accomplice to the slave owners, accepting the white slave trade and consequently the trade in Blacks. His misogyny does not, therefore, exclude a certain respect for woman as a human creature. This respect is entirely missing in Flaubert, who is more radical and, moreover, far surpasses the worthy chief of Parnassus in his abhorrence of the male sex. If women take their ass for their heart, it is because they have no heart; it's quite right, in this case, to put those asses on the market; and Flaubert as an adolescent was not embarrassed to buy certain dissolute pleasures on the cheap. Indeed, this would be the only *truly common* memory that Frédéric and Deslauriers evoke together at the end of the second *Education*. But despite this challenge to the reader, these practices inspire Flaubert with great disgust; in Alfred's company he smugly makes crude jokes about it, but while he places whores above grisettes in order to irritate Ernest, who set up house with some amorous shopgirl, he confides to Ernest, and not to Alfred, his abhorrence of the poor student's life—drinking bad coffee, sleeping with ugly but cheap prostitutes. It is not the venality of love he deplores, it is that he cannot afford to buy the expensive kind. He would throw himself at the feet of a beautiful love slave, who would be the concretization of his millions, if he had them. At her feet, yes. But on her neck? Not so quickly, perhaps. We mustn't forget his serious chastity—which, although he occasionally frequented grisettes and brothels—would remain part of him all his life. And his hysterical castration during the 1840s; in particular we mustn't forget the "phantom of Trouville," that alibi which allowed him to resist platonism—especially when he was seeing Louise; platonism: that distinction, that recourse to the imaginary (particularly in this case), to the *real* if crude pleasures he finds in the Muse's bed.

I am prepared to say, however, that Flaubert's abject contempt for women and his envy directed at wealthy old men, or sometimes at the jeunesse dorée at Tortoni's, through the medium of their prostitutes' finery, are more authentic than the respectful errors that Leconte de Lisle flaunts in his poems. After all, Charles has finally got married: he is not afraid to live under the same roof with Ekidna. It is true that marriage is a way of setting yourself up for life; all his life, even after taking a wife, he never stops skirt chasing, and we even see him beginning a new love at sixty and rejoicing in it. "Women," said one of his intimates, "had a great place in his life." Indeed! But after 1850 it was the place he wanted them to have. They never irritated him; on the contrary, they gave him occasion to exercise, quite gratuitously, that generosity which defines the gentleman. For this titled commoner they replaced the king that he had banished from his republic, and even in his last days he had his horse saddled to accompany some beauty in the Bois when his age surely prevented him from doing her either good or ill. Formerly, the platonic nature of his conjugal relations—the religious boredom of coitus, the sacred refusal to give and receive pleasure (one does not treat one's wife like a mistress)—allowed him to calibrate his contradictory postulations by looking elsewhere for carnal pleasure. In short, sexually he arranged things rather well. So we are surprised by his decision after 1848 to regard Love, once and for all, as the most immediate expression of failure. On this level, his pessimism is a prejudice that his life does not justify; it would be fairer to say that he transformed his amorous disappointments into a poetic exis under the influence of his political failure and the pessimism of his contemporaries. Even though we cannot confirm that he himself destroyed his first liaison by conducts of failure, he certainly used the break-up as a pretext to declare that love is a torment containing its own corrosive virtue; hence, failure is the cipher of the world, it can be lived daily, even in sexual relations. On this level, the impassivity of the poet is meretricious: he proscribes lyricism for himself because, since amorous failure is a priori contained in the very idea of love—in the impossibility of *realizing* it through a singular liaison—the anecdotal confession of the poet's sufferings is of interest to no one and isn't worth an hour's trouble. But at the same time a judicious use of polygamy allows him to pursue a rather rich and peaceful sexual life with some stability. What he will never say is that as a consequence of his major contradiction—which in this fierce anticleric is curiously Christian—he discovered to his convenience that *Eros was double*. We shall compare these falsifications—which make the poems unconvincing—to Flaubert's depth

342

and power. Gustave—we shall return to this—has *never loved*, except for one time, the second year at Trouville, in the absence of Madame Schlésinger, through the pure exercise of his imagination.

In other words, Leconte de Lisle does not *suffer* failure the way Flaubert does; he takes it for a poetic theme and as a *conversion* to the ideal, to the non-real. He is not the man who would seek art, groaning, and would simulate impotence even in poetic composition. When Gustave writes with sly humility: "Genius is merely a long patience," Charles owns up and declares forthrightly in one of his poems: "Genius is pride." This is in fact what Flaubert *thinks* underneath—something he rarely *says*, something he regards as a truth best left unsaid. In Flaubert, moreover, pride is part of the "rebound"; it is a reaction to primal humiliation and, as a result, a fragile, untenable attitude that is posed as a role in numerous passages in his letters. It is a role for Leconte de Lisle too, of course. But a more comfortable one, more in conformity with his origins, with his early history. A republican, the son of a plantation owner, he regards himself as an aristocrat even and especially when he fights for the advent of universal suffrage. For this reason he is going to push derealization of the real to the limit, not, like other artists and especially Flaubert, because his superhuman inhumanity can appear to him only in the imaginary and upon the collapse of all reality, but because this god, son of Niobe, considers that the preeminence of his mind has revealed to him, at the time of his erotic-political failure, the truth that escapes most men: that the real is none other than nonbeing; that everything is illusion, and the vulgar allow themselves to be caught in the veils of Maya. This discovery began with a flight toward a dead world. When Gustave is set on "doing" Greek and Latin in order to escape his own century, Charles is translating *The Iliad* and finally restores Greece in *his* way, that extinguished light, so much less disturbing as it is doubly dead (it has vanished, and our criminal conversion to Christianity has cut us off from it; our memory and our traditions do not refer to it), and as he has never set foot on Attic soil. The apparent ambiguity arises from his seeking to totalize that vanished universe in the splendor of its antique *reality*. He will spare nothing in this effort. Like the other knights of art-neurosis, not content to borrow the impassivity of scholars, this surgeon's son asks for the assistance of the sciences. The poet is destined to "seek refuge in the contemplative *and scholarly* life as in a sanctuary of repose and purification"; but contemplation will be valid only if the (vanished) object of his attention is restored in its rigor by the exact disciplines:

343

"No more individualism. We must bring art closer to historical and archeological science." This methodological concern mustn't fool us, for the Antiquity thus invoked is merely a specter. Since "the final Nothingness of all things is the sole reason for their reality," Leconte de Lisle, distant descendant of those who survived the second flood, the invasion of Greece and Rome by the Christianized barbarians, ranges himself *on the side* of the "raison d'être" of antique things, on the side of that nothingness which is the secret of their vanished reality. Dead to his time, dead to himself, he revives the life of Athens insofar as death has seized it in flight and fixed it forever in its unreality. Or if you will, insofar as nonbeing is the secret truth of being. The ancient world is beautiful because it *no longer exists;* but the poet goes further in his systematic destruction of being: if the truth of being resides in its future annihilation, can we not say of that which no longer exists that at the time—now vanished—of its full existence, its secret truth was *not to exist?* If death is the truth of life, then all life, given a mortal blow, is already dead even at its most violent moment—just as the soldier of Marathon, according to Janet, was dead well before finishing his course, and without knowing he was a corpse proclaimed to the Athenians a victory that no longer concerned him. The sophism, here, is clear. Charles suppresses temporalization; given "being-to-die," an already highly controversial definition of human reality but one that at least has the advantage of giving man the irreducible existence of a *being-on-reprieve*, he makes this relation to the future the atemporal relation of the living individual to his essence; since he must die, it is because he is fundamentally dead. Already dead, from all eternity. Thus, at any imagined moment, the inner meaning of time—seen by the poet as an irreversible degradation—gives that vanishing humanity and the world around it, seen through the poet's eyes, experienced and measured, the value of a mere dream. Thus time is merely an appearance that hides the eternity of the void; and he who feels, experiences, lives, and believes he *exists* is already no more than a phantom that has been, a groundless illusion. Though we would have to presuppose at least an original moment of real plenitude, such plenitude is hardly admissible when it must be eaten away from within. So it all ends the way it must have begun; the world is merely an immortal mirage:

> Nothing is real but unique and dismal Eternity,
> Oh Brahma, everything is the dream of a dream
> For [says the God Hari] my Inertia alone is the source of Being,
> The matrix of the world is my Illusion.

344

He will add in 1876:

> Maya! Maya! *torrent of moving chimeras . . .*
> The centuries flown by, the following minutes
> Are lost in your shadow in the same moment . . .
> Lightning flash, fatal dream, lying eternity,
> Ancient Life is made inextinguishable
> By the endless whirlwind of vain appearances.

The source of this "brahmanism" is, of course, the *Bhagavad-Gita*, which Flaubert, some years earlier, was reading or pretending to read to flesh out the "Orientalism" of his oriental tale—and particularly the *Bhagavad-Pūrana*. But Leconte de Lisle interprets his readings for his own purposes: for him, the *Maya* veils at times the absolute void and at times the fixed plenitude of a featureless eternity that is absorbed in contemplating itself. Which is to say that Charles shifts from positive to negative at will, and vice versa. "Eternity lies," or else it is the absolute purity of being. We are on that elementary level where, as Hegel demonstrates, being and nonbeing, highly unstable notions, are constantly transformed into each other. For our mystagogue, mystification consists not in presenting this uninterrupted shift as movement but, on the contrary, in replacing it by a fixed ambiguity, that is, the metastable concept—*in repose*—of what might be called being-nothingness. Or, to approximate our previous descriptions, to affirm behind the insubstantial flux of appearances the strict equivalence of the nothingness of being (there is *nothing*) with the being of nothingness (nothing is; conscious of itself—nothing redoubled—it is God). The adept use of inertia in the above excerpt is obvious; not only are our actions dreams, dissimulating our perfect passivity, but—Flaubert did not go so far—inertia itself is the condition for it. To dream that one acts, it is necessary and sufficient to surrender to the fundamental characteristic of being, which is absolute repose. Or, conversely, the only dream inertia can generate is that of being as nonbeing and nonmovement, and through it the dream of those rigorously suffered passions, which, however, being unacknowledged as such by intellection—an impossible activity of being—assume the deceitful status of praxis. In other words, illusion—inertia denied in dream—can only have the false practical unity of an enterprise because it is appearance, flowing from being and contesting it. Gustave, who had no taste for metaphysical games, never pushed the argument this far; he denied action in the name of the passivity that was for him the very flavor of lived experience; it

345

would not have occurred to him dialectically to generate practice—as a *necessary* dream—out of its opposite, pure being, as the static surrender to nonbeing.

In any case, the deliberate preservation of the metastable concept being-nonbeing allows Leconte de Lisle to assuage his rancor at the expense of his unfortunate reader. In the celebrated poem "Noon, king of summers . . ." we have seen him listening to the "sublime words" of the sun; light is presented as a revealer of being. But what is in fact revealed by this crushing clarity is non-sense, the equivalence of all. In short, since language is *deprived of meaning,* silence. In the same way, nothingness appears as faceless power, the naked force that tempers the poet's heart, while in fact the annihilation of things by light must, adeptly imitated, serve as a model for his poetic techniques of annihilation. This gives many of his poems a very particular structure: he begins by *positing* what he intends to deny. The act of positing is the revelation of the object in its fullness. These motifs have caused him to be described as *visual.* And indeed he *makes visible.* But neither does he disdain to make audible:

> Happy globe, giving rise to the murmur of the living . . .
> With its waters, its blue summits, its swaying woods . . .
> Its million birds singing in the clouds . . .

The main thing is to reproduce the palpable richness of the *Maya,* the pseudo-plenitude that is its mystifying function—in short, to show man fulfilling himself at the center of a dense and infinite nature, full of lights, colors, movements and noises; this allows him to show more effectively, in the second part of the poem, the death that simultaneously—and from the beginning of the centuries—strikes the world and man from within. That globe—the moon, and soon our earth.

> Far from mild suns, far from any nocturnal nimbus
> Now rolls through the expanse of space.

We then perceive that this extinction of fires was given *at the outset* and *legible,* even as the poet was presenting us with the spectrum of palpable qualities. Indeed, while these qualities were being affirmed in their *reality,* one word had already paralyzed them with nothingness. In "Les Clairs de lune," the line that begins "Happy globe . . ." is preceded by

> Formerly clothed in its first grace . . .

346

And the single adverb "formerly" is sufficient to derealize the illusory plenitude by reminding us of the current aspect of the ice star; by the same token it implicitly predicts the fate of our planet. This generates the poem's unity. At other times, without leaving the earth and without foreseeing the return of the ice age, it asks nature itself to expose its nothingness. This plenitude *sounds hollow:* to the piercing gaze of the poet, Noon—the king of summers, exaggerated light and warmth —has the effect of revealing to us the perfect unreality of the heavy, concrete earth it illuminates.

> Noon, king of summers, spread over the plain
> Falls in silver folds from the sky's blue heights.
> All falls silent. The air flames and burns without a breath
> The earth is benumbed in its dress of fire . . .

The reader is convinced of the *realism* of this description: the warmth, the silence, the blazing of the air, the blue of the sky, and those folds of silver that spread over the hard terrestrial crust. He recognizes this *apperception* of an All (noon-on-earth-in-summer); those vivid words constitute more than an evocation—they are an invocation of his memory and of cosmic forces. But no sooner has he projected through the sounds of words the burning image of a summer, of a plenitude, than the terms chosen by the poet silently reveal the dissolving power they possess and for which they were chosen: everything *falls silent,* the light *falls,* the air burns *without a breath,* the earth is *benumbed.* Thus, confronted by the very moment when it imposes itself, absolute being, dense matter at a white heat, suggests the presentiment of its nonexistence. The subsequent stanzas need only present this premeditated unrealization as a lesson of nature: when the real has accomplished its fullness, it informs us of its unreality. This carefully maintained ontological ambiguity necessarily issues in a moral ambiguity. And just as he sometimes shows us the obverse side of the medals he is chiseling, being beyond all communication, and sometimes the reverse, nothingness—sometimes Leconte de Lisle presents the basic attitude of conscious man (he who has grasped the *Maya* outside himself and within him) as a long complaint, as a desire for death, pure pathos that derives its value only from its authenticity (Night! Silence! Forgetting of bitter hours! When will you absorb deceitful desire, hatred, love, thought, anguish and fantasy? When will you appease the ancient torment?), in short, as the bitter claim—nothingness acknowledged, things of the world *penetrated*—that the *Maya,* exposed, cannot survive that exposure

347

(but it does survive, that is the poet's misfortune). And *sometimes*, when the cosmos is unrealized in the name of the positive eternity of a being superior to all qualification, he exhorts the upright man— that is, the artist—to adopt the superior attitude of scornful stoicism, except when he is creating. In order to be stoical, you must *believe*. In God, of course, but in any form. For example, in the *absolute* importance of stoicism, in its conformity to the nature of things. Upon returning from his journey to the Congo, Gide, who then no longer believed in either God or the Devil, suggests that if he were being tortured by men or by an illness, he would not bother to stifle his cries just to deny pleasure to his torturers or to edify his followers. To scream at the right moment, to cry, to weep freely is an outlet; in torture or illness one can allow oneself this indulgence because there are *more important* things to save (a secret confided, or, if pain causes pathological troubles, a certain mental equilibrium); and stoicism, a perfectly futile attitude, may actually be harmful if the patient, stressed beyond endurance, succumbs. This is an eminently *human* position. The things you are held accountable for to your intimates and yourself are substituted for those we have too long been accountable for to a dead God or to His ersatz negative, the ideal, the absolute as devourer of men. Prometheus, too loosely bound, frees himself forever from his vulture; Leconte de Lisle kept his own. He joins the only poet he likes, the Vigny of "La mort du loup":

And then, like me, suffer and die without speaking.

Good god, what's the point? Vigny is at least faithful to a lost cause and offers an ethic of disdain to the shipwrecked nobility. But de Lisle? The fact is, this plaintiff adopts stoicism because he aspires to *panoramic consciousness*. This superaristocrat finds his preeminence in a living death. Death, the supreme derealization, reduces everything *retrospectively* to the game governed by imagination. Thus art and stoicism are one and the same: the latter places itself above the *Maya* and reveals its phantasmagoria; the former—surveying vanished worlds, meditating upon them, and thus grasping the pitiful nothingness of the world that surrounds it, reduces everything to the imaginary and makes itself the equal of an infinite but inert God by totalizing the dream of a dream exclusively through the exercise of imagination. We have already had occasion to mention Flaubert's pseudo-stoicism. But he didn't go as far as Charles; he saw only suicide as capable of making him God's equal: what He made, Flaubert thought, I can unmake with a bullet. Which implies, in short, that the world was its representation. But this argument for self-destruction was never made entirely explicit. His idealism, I think, was restrained by familial realism; in his early writings we saw him bitterly and despairingly mocking the work of the artist, that "aping of creation." Leconte de Lisle follows this position to its logical conclusion: since the Creation is merely a dream of being, a linked succession of images deceitfully persuading us that the world exists and that we exist, the work of art, a linked multiplicity of images, has neither more nor less reality than the Other, an illusory product of an eternal inertia. And the fascination of a beautiful poem is no different from our fascination with the *Maya*. For this reason, the artist is God. In any case, he has broken ties with the species; for the species, buttressed by realism, still believes that it exists, that it acts, that it suffers, that it really covets the good of this phantom world, dreamed through its mediation by a God for whom it is itself an insubstantial fiction. Rejecting human ends, recognizing the unreality of the real, the artist sets himself against God by knowingly using images to create a demystifying fascination that reveals to the reader its fundamental nothingness. For Leconte de Lisle, stoicism is the first step on the stairs leading to art. As a stoic, he already believes that the world is phantasmagorical; but he still appeals to being; as an artist, he has risen to the intuition of nothingness, and his poems are a curative *Maya*, for his images reveal the utter nonbeing of appearances.[51]

Such is the man: austere, sober, and monocled, uncontested head of his school but almost insufferable. Catulle Mendès, on the verge of the twentieth century, said of Leconte de Lisle that "the yoke of his genius . . . was rather hard and narrow for us. He was repelled by novelties, by personalities that might have contradicted his own . . . It could be said that he narrowly missed turning us into poets alien to ourselves; it is terrifying to imagine what contemporary literature might have been if it had bowed uniquely to his supreme will." By that excellent formula, "alien to ourselves," Mendès does not simply mean that the master may have opposed their particular inclinations and the singularity of their gifts; he also means that for Leconte de Lisle, the poet is essentially *alien to himself*, or, if you will, that the attitude of panoramic consciousness—in relation to oneself and to everything—in short, the specifically poetic attitude, is *estrangement*.

---

51. In this sense—although Mallarmé valued him very little—he ensured the Symbolist changing of the guard, since for Mallarmé, too, the subject of poetry can only be nothingness.

This schizoid (or pseudo-schizoid) rejection of any inner adherence to lived experience, contemplated from above as the illusion of living, similarly involved the condemnation of spontaneity as a source of literary inspiration: how can one trust illusion to provide the ambiguous images that will denounce it? Curiously, the art that must reveal the inertia of being and the wholly passive insubstantiality of our imagery must then be voluntarist: study, science, work, the search for the right word, the refining of exact combinations—these are what is required of the "stonecutter." Before leaving Parnassus for good, Verlaine explicates this point of view rather well in his *Poèmes saturniens:*

> What we need, we the Supreme Poets
> Who revere the Gods without believing in them . . .
> We, who chisel words like goblets
> And coldly fashion lines of heartfelt verse . . .
> What we need, in the gleam of lamps,
> Science conquered and sleep overcome, . . .
> Is Stubbornness and Willpower!
> What we need is incessant dedication,
> Tireless effort, peerless struggle,
> Night, the harsh night of work . . .

The master, however, tightly buttoned up, is becoming bourgeois. His disciples barely manage to enjoy a few discreetly silly moments in Nina de Villard's salon—people even go so far as to take drugs there, imagine! Best of all was when the mistress of the house ended by thinking she was dead: in her psychosis, poor faithful Egeria realized the dream of all the poets she loved: dead, she saw life, that future death, from the point of view of death and eternity. Leconte de Lisle left it to her to *live* that estrangement he rendered fascinating to others only out of poetic duty. He accepts everything, money from île Bourbon, from the Emperor; he takes a wife, presents himself three times to the French Academy—to which he is unanimously elected in 1886. And the Republic, while continuing to pay him the pension he received under the Empire, names him assistant librarian of the Senate.

This career is a surprise, hardly in keeping with the bard of the *Maya*. And if everything is illusion, why is this petty bourgeois so incensed at the Communards, those slaves who refused to kiss their chains, that he even *demanded Courbet's head?* Most of the Knights of Nothingness share his rage. The Commune is a call to arms; without ceasing to hate the bourgeois and the "ignoble" worker, they shift from the cult of art to the defense of property. Not so surprising since the former is founded on the latter. Courbet, I suppose, must have been Leconte de Lisle's bête noire. Like him, he belonged to the generation of the vanquished of '48; but he had reacted quite differently to the defeat, and his painting was called "realist" because it demanded universal suffrage: it denied the elite public for the first time and made visible *to everyone* the burdensome reality of the everyday. Not, of course, in order to dissolve it in the idea, but to contribute to the emancipation of the people by showing their original freedom. The Emperor was not in the least mistaken: when he horsewhipped *Les Baigneuses*, it was the Republic, crushed but not dead, that was his real target.

The sworn enemy of Courbet, the master of Parnassus appears, by contrast, to be an excellent supporter of the regime. To deserve his three hundred francs a month, he did not need to sell himself; it was enough to be what he was: the pure Knight of Nothingness, contesting any rebellion against the established order by striking at its root, dramatizing the vanity of action and systematically derealizing the real, finally making the reader and the poet himself the dreams of a dream. Taking as his principle "genius is pride," he served the designs of a hierarchical society. When the author has genius, the reader must be ingenious to follow him. Who, therefore, has the right to genius under the Second Empire but the dominant class and the enlightened elite? At the same time, of course, that vanquished author, infected by rancor, gratifies all the hatreds of the public, that hating-hateful entity; but his arid vanity puts the public's loathings in perspective: the lowest is shared by the populace—by the wretched who wallow in the abject illusion that this world exists, that they suffer and hunger in it; the highest belongs only to the lords, who, turning their dead gaze toward the *Maya*, reduce it to what it is, the insubstantial product of an inert nothingness, or, what amounts to the same thing, a being without qualities. Thus, even in this illusory universe where the individual is merely a dream, the social hierarchy is justified; it is based on lucidity and on the appreciation of beauty, which is nothing but the *Maya* itself, presented in the fascinating fixed movement that initiates its abolition, or if you will, nothing but the unrealizing totalization of the real. *Labor improbus vincit omnia*: the Parnassian poet resolves in his way the problem of inspiration— suspect since the death of God. The poet is not inspired: he is asked only to place himself on that level of estrangement—or, as we say, of depersonalization—on which the real reveals its profound unreality. After that, let him work: let him assemble words and chisel his verse

351

to encapsulate the greatest possible reality and, consequently, the greatest unreality. This denial of inspiration—which without God would be born of passions, carnal appetites, need—this impassive sacrifice of man to his product, this primacy of the ideal and of the human thing over the humble lived experience of daily life, is the exact tracing of bourgeois misanthropy, of the secret but impossible genocide dreamed of by those deceived in 1848—in a word, of that human sacrifice, distinction. Moreover, the leader of this school, authoritarian and secret, an impassive worker without confidants, guarantees his works with his life. Scornful of men, respectful of property—which he doesn't have—he lives in relative financial straits quite majestically.

This is a man of '48—the February Revolution made him what he is. He speaks to the men of February and June, to their younger brothers, to their sons. Engendered by a failure, his nihilistic poetry is the description of that failure; no other would be better suited to the duped republicans, those idealists who are still dazed to discover that they've massacred the people and are suddenly tyrannized by a military dictatorship they elected by plebiscite. He is the writer they need to explain this time when, as Marx says, "universal suffrage appeared only to be suppressed."

Why, then, is he unconvincing? Under the Empire, he was hardly read. And no doubt his semiobscurity did not entirely displease him. Being autonomous, poetry is written for its own sake, it exists without a public—let the public come to it. Furthermore, disciples were not lacking: there was Catulle Mendès, Glatigny, Leon Cladel, Villiers de l'Isle-Adam, Sully Prud'homme; later Dierx, Jean Lahor, Heredia, twenty others. On the publication (1862) of *Poésies barbares*, Sainte-Beuve cited Leconte de Lisle among the leaders of the school, along with Banville, Baudelaire, and Theophile Gautier. And Gautier himself noted in '67: "Withdrawn from success, in his proud independence, or rather from popularity, Leconte de Lisle gathered . . . a literary coterie . . . around him." Still, under the Empire, as one of its contemporary commentators remarks, "his hour had not yet come," and it only came under the Third Republic, around 1875, when memories of the Commune were fading and the bourgeoisie forged a new and *optimistic* ideology. With praxis reassimilated to ideology, the man of action par excellence became, to the detriment of the military, the captain of industry; the aim of our species was to tame nature by imposing *antiphysis* on the great physical forces transformed into "mechanical slaves," and on all members of the human group through judicious employment of the social sciences, self-domestication. Between socialists and conservatives a party was born, soon to be the largest party in France, radical socialism, offering progressive optimism to defend universal suffrage by combating "the cloth," by developing education, and—a mysterious wish at this period of accelerated concentrations—by greatly increasing the number of small property holdings. How could this period of euphoria be precisely the one in which Leconte de Lisle received recognition? And, above all, how could Hugo, optimist incarnate, the vatic poet recognized by God as his sole valid interlocutor, the courageous defender of the Communards (the rabble that Leconte de Lisle wanted to exterminate), that bard of the poor, the only one who was and still is read by the working classes, and whose final wish, puerile, histrionic, and sublime, was to be taken to his tomb in a poor man's hearse—how could this astonishing man, half priest and half anarchist, undisputed sovereign of the century, have expressly and publicly designated the cold-blooded Leconte de Lisle to succeed him at the head of poetic movements and in his chair at the Academy? How is it that fame, denied to this pessimistic misanthrope in a time of hatred, should have been granted him by the optimism of the nascent "Belle Epoque," at the dawn of the Symbolist movement he engendered and which affirmed itself—still respectfully—against him? Let's look, by contrast, at Flaubert, whose fame suddenly explodes—a tempest of scandal and enthusiasm—in 1857, and who, after *Salammbô* had been systematically thrashed by the new criticism, was finally affected by it—though still bewildered—and said, sadly: "I am an embarrassment." Indeed, he was embarrassing, not because of his exclusive love of beauty but because of the misanthropy that was its other side. And when his disciple published *Boule de Suif*, whose superficial psychology is cribbed from Gustave's, the indisputable success of the story was accompanied by a profound nausea: the Third Republic isn't averse to being shown malicious characters, but its political structure demands that it be given positive heroes as well. Zola was not mistaken there: hated, represented by caricaturists as a chamber pot, he always defended himself—rightly so—for being pessimistic. Poetic pessimism is shameful at the time: the Symbolists, the last cautious templars of nothingness, lacked the temerity to attack reality itself and reduce it to a succession of appearances; they pass over it in silence and escape from it into the dream. An example is Mallarmé, whose radical despair is magnificently hidden. If Leconte de Lisle triumphs, if his unpolished, malicious, aristocratic poems find admirers among the republicans of the new generation, it must be because his pessimism is not, in the final analysis, the main point of his poetry. I remember reading his *Poèmes* at the end of childhood, then rereading them during my adolescence; I thought them grim, I didn't like their crude solemnity or their somber pride. It would not have occurred to me, however, to use these poems to feed the real misanthropy I then harbored; Laforgue and his very personal vision of Schopenhauer were my food, and I was grateful to that young poet for dying of the pessimism that devoured him—at least he had *passed the test*. The other, for me, was a grandfather who adeptly developed the old, well-worn themes passed down from generation to generation: life is a dream, death is the truth of life; better to die than to live; rather than die, even in the cradle, better to have never been born; man is a wolf to man, pain is the lot of humanity. All that scarcely moved me, it was universal wisdom; I saw it as a pretext for literary developments that did not move me any more than the empty speeches made by my teachers when prizes were handed out. It is virtually certain that the young people of 1860 saw no more in his poems, except that they took some pleasure in the unmitigated hammering of the verses. In other words, before being assimilated forever to the objective spirit, Flaubert's pessimism appears under the Second Empire to be the very expression of its reader's lived experience, and under the Third Republic to be an outmoded but still shocking attitude which, after his death and before his apotheosis, got him several years of regulation purgatory. The pessimism of Leconte de Lisle, more radical, more contrived, hardly moves the pessimistic readers of the 1850s, who don't identify with it; it is not even recognized as such by the public of republican France, which sees it as a mere pretext—there will, it's true, be a second generation of Parnassians around 1880. But these are the latecomers, the provincials or hurried visitors, who are going to test the atmosphere of the group before joining the ranks of the Symbolists. After this, it isn't purgatory that awaits the leader of the school, or hell (that would confer too much honor), but a progressive and implacable oblivion: he is no longer read, he is *explained* to high school students. Balzac, a royalist and legitimist, found a public contemporary with his writing under the Orléanist monarchy; Stendhal, a Preromantic and anticlerical republican, dies incognito and wins his trial on appeal: Barrès and Taine, and a hundred other indolent professors of "energy" and the "me culture," resurrect him; he is anchored in glory and has never gone out of favor. Leconte de Lisle, a product of February '48 addressing the readers that '48 produced, awakens no echo; worse still, that old republican seems so tame that the Empire pensions him off, even as the police did not hesitate to murder unrepentant republicans in their beds. After the fall of the Emperor, he is teased a bit about his imperial pension; he protests, speaks publicly of killing himself. And yet this resigned imperialist causes so little embarrassment to the new Republic that it continues his monthly allowance—become republican—and adds a sinecure besides. He is finally read but without any shock, out of misunderstanding; he missed his true public both before and after 1870. Reading him, no one *felt* the wretchedness and beastliness of our species, the fundamental unreality of the real, nothingness as the glacial truth of appearances, the contempt for needs and passions as a sign of aristocracy. And at this time of hatred, of failure, and of distinction, no one said: "How true it is!" Yet what did he do, that disappointed veteran of '48, but reflect their disappointment to other veterans of '48? Was he lacking in talent? No, he knows how to work; he shares with Flaubert the art of shaping in marble a fixed, dense line, one that is eternal, whose marmoreal substance is subtly devoured by nothingness. So? Should we speak of injustice? A hundred years ago he published his major poems; after nearly a hundred years, when we are talking about a written work, injustice cannot be invoked. Even the poems that Hölderlin, while mad, signed "Nardinelli" were integrated into German culture in less than a century. In the case of Leconte de Lisle—whose pessimism was not recognized when it expressed the universality of hatred and was not taken seriously when it resisted a new optimism—we would do better, leaving aside the form of his poems, which is nonetheless inseparably linked to it, to investigate the authenticity of their content. This may lead us to better understand the true requirements of his contemporary readers.

The basic question, in short, involves *intention*. Did he experience 1848 as a *suffered* failure, that is, something imposed unpredictably and rigorously by history on his public action? Or are we to infer from his initial conduct a secret intention to run aground? Or, again, should his attitude be conceived as a function of other motives and other reasons?

There is no doubt that his political activity was condemned in advance by a historical development that can be reconstructed today in the light of subsequent events but that he, of course, could not foresee. Defeat came to him from the outside, as it did to all professionals; for this armchair socialist could not even imagine that new reality, unconscious of itself and terrifying, the proletariat. Because of this, of course—and we shall return to this question—he internalized his failure and gradually turned it into his eminent greatness, the source of his pride and his accepted destiny. Nonetheless, as a follower of Fourier, even in his innermost thought he never *bet* on it. But we can ask him—concerning what seems a simple distinction but is, in fact, crucial—if he *sincerely wanted* success. Or, if you will, what singular enterprise he wanted to succeed, and by what means. Indeed, when Baudelaire cries to the surprised rioters: "Everyone head for Colonel Aupick's house, and let's put it to the torch!" we can hardly suppose that his motive is the triumph of socialism or even of universal suffrage. For the young Leconte de Lisle, too, the February Revolution was equivalent, on the deepest level of his inner being, to the murder of the Father. Under the usurped name of the Republic, what fired his passion was the overthrow of white tyranny on La Réunion. In his eyes, his father is the symbol of that tyranny and responsible for it; long ago Charles assimilated paternal punishments to the brutality inflicted on the slaves. In one sweeping movement the Republic will deliver Blacks from servitude and Charles from the authority of the paterfamilias. That is all to the good: one needs motives to act, and the deepest motives originate in one's early history; it hardly matters if our most universal choices have their first source in our singularity—after all, in the best of regimes, man will never be anything but a singular universal. The important thing is to know whether the process that issues in a choice passes through all the requisite mediations, in other words, whether the initial singularity is not found quite crudely, at the moment of choice, beneath the cheap finery of lip service to the universal. To free the slaves—to abolish forced labor—is one thing; to give everyone, whatever his level of culture, the right to vote is quite another. Isn't Leconte de Lisle making an amalgam and confusing the two meanings of the word "liberty"? Is he really an "out-and-out republican"? This is surely doubtful; to demand universal suffrage presupposes an act of faith; you must at the very least be convinced that "good sense is the most widely shared thing in the world." You must believe unreservedly in Plato when he shows us Socrates teaching a slave to demonstrate a theorem. We know that the professional elite, jealous of their knowledge, mean to keep it for themselves alone; the development of public instruction, one of them has said, has had no effect but to increase crime. This is precisely the negation of the Cartesian formula. Good sense has become racist; it is shared among the members of the upper classes, and to teach the populace to read is to lead them astray, for they possess neither the discernment nor the moderation that allows the elite to distinguish true from false. Did Leconte de Lisle share this opinion? I'm afraid so—let's not forget "Les Fils de Niobe." In this poem, well before '48, he divides the children of that unfortunate woman into two groups—gods and humans. They are all men, if you like. But the first have the duty to lead the second toward the light. Are these gods anticlerical poets? Yes. But above all they are men of culture. Even in the framework of formal democracy, the masses must emancipate themselves; if their role is to follow their good shepherds, why should they take the trouble to vote except at long intervals, to provide a plebiscite for an enlightened despot? This should be seen, no doubt, as an objective contradiction of formal democracy; be that as it may, Charles internalized it. He certainly wanted to participate in political power, something his meager resources had hitherto prevented him from doing; he wanted it in the same way as the semirich, who during the banquet campaign demanded the lowering of the poll tax. Poorer than they, however, he had to be more radical: he was not unaware that he couldn't get near a ballot box until the poll tax was abolished. The outcome would have to be universal suffrage, but Charles did not really desire it for those uncultivated masses he had despised from the first; he resigned himself to it as he would to a lesser evil. We have seen how he swung between actual pessimism— humanity *today* is bad and foolish, therefore unworthy of taking its own affairs in hand—and a suspect optimism: thanks to the divine sons of Niobe, humanity will one day be the equal of its essence. At issue here is an idea. And at the first disappointments, his republican faith disappears; it is now merely an aristocratic loyalty to an ideal— to hell with the people, we are not fighting for them. These are just words, moreover, for despite his brief and legendary appearance on the barricades, he did not fight at all.

Isn't he confusing the Republic with the abolition of slavery? Let us not forget that his republican ideas were born around 1836 on île Bourbon, in his conversations with Adamolle, the son of a plantation owner who was to become a plantation owner in his turn, and with other Creoles of his own age. They all led the lazy life of sons of good families—hunting, riding, *idleness* at the center of the paternal domain, reading (books arrived for them from Paris, sometimes months late, sometimes years late). Already dead, Romanticism lit up their world like rays from a dead star; they never saw its monarchist and aristocratic aspect, for as sons of aristocrats they were aristocrats

357

already; they assumed lofty ideas and beautiful dreams from Romanticism. These young men were suffocating in Bourbon society, aristocratic and silly, closed in on itself, entirely conditioned by the utilization of servile manpower. When they received the news from Paris, it seemed to them that La Réunion was fifty years behind, that they were living in a world already abolished elsewhere, before the French Revolution. *Slavery,* in a way, was the core of their contradictions: demanding *freedom*—against the reactionary Moses who gave them life—and a society in which they could breathe and act, in which urgency and an intrinsic interest in tasks to be accomplished would put an end to their Creole apathy, they could not help but see that the little community of the islands of La Réunion was forever oppressed by its oppression of Blacks. And that consequently their own personal freedom—in relation to their parents, to the atrocious and stupid "milieu" whose offspring they were—was closely linked to the abolition of the slave trade and slavery. In other words, they dreamed of substituting free labor for forced labor, of replacing an outdated feudalism based on servitude with a bourgeois society of the sort defined in 1789 by the Declaration of the Rights of Man. Many of these young people knew how to assuage their anxieties, beginning with Adamolle; their contradiction lay in the fact that the paternal property, the generalized laziness of the Creoles—deprived of any possibility of *working* by the oppression they exercised—were precisely the basis for their generous ideas and the setting in which they were developed. To be abolitionist in La Réunion, one had to be the future heir of a father who possessed many slaves. The idea, simply a negative product of a still solid society but one threatened *from the outside,* disappeared along with the negativity. The son kills the father, inherits, and resurrects him by adopting his mores. In short, these sons of planters will become planters, too; they are the ones who in '48, in agreement with the preceding generation, will protest against Schoelcher—in vain, as it happens. But for others, for those who in the first days of the Revolution—under Charles's inspiration—presented the Assembly with an address denouncing their slave-owning fathers and swearing to support the provisional government, it is clear that they conceived the Republic through the lens of their childhood and the abject society of La Réunion; what they demanded of the new regime was, much more than the right to work, freedom for the worker—the freedom to present oneself to the agency of employment and be committed to a contract that both parties had to respect. Indeed, what had struck them in their colonial years was certainly neither unemployment, caused by a surplus of manpower, nor industrial poverty—that is, total neglect of the workman. Mistreated, wasting himself at labor without the hope of remuneration, the slave's only advantage in the servile condition—the very thing that makes it costly and not very profitable—is that he must be fed all year round, meaning, in those rural societies with seasonal crops, even in periods when he isn't working. Thus their experience, conflicting with that new fact which is incomprehensible in the colonial framework, namely the industrialization of the metropolis, led them to see French society as a central colony that would become free by abolishing forced labor. At the same time, taking the workers for Blacks, those illiterate "grown children" whose minds could not be developed beyond certain limits, they wanted to replace constraint and the whip by a gentle authority based on reason, on racial superiority, and not on terror. This explains the obscure symbolism of Leconte de Lisle's Niobe. The woman's divine children are poets, of course, who have suffered from that vulture, Christianity, and who have finally wrung its neck; but they are also, and in particular, the young plantation owners of Bourbon, who will soon generously renounce their rights over men and thereby find themselves confronted by a subhumanity that is free but scarcely emerged from an animal torpor, whom it is their mission to guide cautiously toward the fully human condition. On this subject, nothing is more characteristic than Charles's obstinacy in confusing the industrial workers with the black farm workers of the colonies; many times we have seen him give one the name better suited to the other; and when he claims that the masses need the yoke and the whip, when he declares, "I hate slaves who love their chains," the contamination becomes quite obvious. The workers, exploited and oppressed, have nothing in common with slaves; their fundamental demand is the opposite of that which the young colonials present *in the name* of servile manpower; they have freedom; they can magnificently choose *in the best case* between work and—literally at the time—starvation and death. This prevents neither a decrease in wages nor an increase in unemployment, generating antagonisms from which the employer profits; nor does it prevent the insecurity that plagues the heads of families, since the contract is generally on a day to day basis. What they demand, therefore, is a *right to work*, which, presupposing the intervention of the state, must also be a *duty*. The Creoles came to France in 1848 to accomplish the Revolution of 1789; they favor the law of *Le Chapelier*, they favor liberalism and not those governmental organizations—such as the National Workshops—behind which they glimpse the specter of forced labor. What Leconte de Lisle finds striking, and immediately disillusioning, is the lack of resemblance between the turmoil of the white workers and the discreet gentleness of the Blacks. He was not familiar—it must be said in his favor—with the great slave revolts, their unexpected violence, the massacres that resulted on both sides. He did not know that in the era of Toussaint-Louverture, the divine children of Niobe would not have had the slightest chance of making themselves heard by their "inferior" brothers. What enrages him, on the contrary, is that the white Parisian "slaves" mock his advice. He knew it from the first day: the populace is sure of itself; against the professionals and probably—at least in the beginning—against the leaders of the Secret Societies; it made the Revolution, it forced the provisional government to proclaim the right to work. Then, of course, it waivers, for lack of organization and a *minimum* program; this accounts for the strange uncertainty of the first months of '48: no one knows where he is going or even where he would like to go. But Charles felt that those still hesitant masses would not compromise on one point: they bear their destiny within themselves; for the moment, it is tragic, they sense it, but they will live it alone and without outside help; the only leaders they could accept would have to emerge, in the course of the action itself, from its ranks. This painful emancipation, still somewhat unconscious of itself, more negative—at the start—than positive, has the effect of sending the planter's son back from La Réunion to the place he occupies in France in the petty-bourgeoisie. That is his misfortune: there are no Blacks in Paris. This quickly leads him, as product of rural life, to despise all those bleached-out products of industry, those people who have the audacity not to regard themselves as slaves, those Blacks who don't know it. And the others, in fact, the Blacks conscious of being black, those who bear on their naked backs the indisputable stripes that attest to their servile condition—did he love them? When he became indignant at their mistreatment, was it in the name of liberty, equality, fraternity? Hardly likely; if he saw those illiterates as brothers, it could only have been, we have seen, as inferior brothers. And did he even honor in the slaves the sacred value of work? That is hard to believe; in that idle society, work was not held in high esteem. Moreover, the return on servile manpower was so negligible from the eighteenth century on that the planters in the American South thought of abolishing slavery. It was the appearance of the cotton gin that convinced them to maintain it. I believe rather—and the word *ideal*, in its abstraction, thus assumes its full meaning—that the young man condemned forced labor and corporal punishment because they relegated the landowner—that self-styled judge—and his executioners to the rank of their victims. The slave, a subhuman, seemed abject when he was so cowardly as to kiss the hand that struck him—something that happened every day. But no more nor less than those who reduced him to this extremity. In one respect, he did it to have the pleasure of condemning his father and all adults; in another it was an oath to liberate future planters from their slave owning; he wanted to restore innocence to his friends, to the heirs who abhorred or were enthusiastic about the same things as he. It is not so rare, indeed, for reformers, when they are the offspring of the privileged classes, to want to remedy the ills of the "lower classes" in order to liberate their peers and themselves from some original sin. With slavery abolished, you have property without tears, crime, or fear.

It will already have been observed, indeed, that the condemnation of slavery, far from being a path toward socialism, must have inclined Charles to valorize the bourgeois property that recruits its manpower from among free men and involves them in a free contract for work. Since the two dominant classes, the bourgeoisie and the nobility, were in open conflict, the bourgeois youth in the home country came to regard their milieu and their families through aristocratic eyes—as did Flaubert. But Leconte de Lisle, that quasi-nobleman breaking with his class, regarded his original milieu through the eyes of the bourgeoisie. When he was still living in La Réunion, the abolition of slavery was the overthrow of the old patricians by their sons; it was the metamorphosis of those sons into bourgeois, the simultaneous advent of the bourgeoisie and of youth. The Republic he dreamed of, then, was first this overthrow and metamorphosis; he demands universal suffrage but cares little about it. Of course, there is no question of giving the vote to emancipated slaves who don't even know how to write their names; once they have become free workers in the same plantation, their former masters, now free employers, will idealistically take on the task of educating them. This long-term project will extend over several generations.

So when he arrives in Paris, this young provincial has only one desire, rooted in his childhood: the abolition of slavery; and that desire, revolutionary on île Bourbon, has no bearing in the metropolis where slaves do not exist. Since work is free there, this same desire is silently transformed into approbation for the established order; Leconte de Lisle *adopts* bourgeois society. Or rather he would adopt it entirely if it would have him; his misfortune is to live in financial straits, respectably but acrimoniously. This condition reawakens his fits of rage and his revolutionary rhetoric; the bourgeoisie, his class of choice, took power in 1830, but he doesn't see it: he sees a king, a court, noblemen; these must be overthrown. As so often happens, in France, and especially in Paris, this ultraprovincial product of an outmoded colonialism found new words and some older words invested with new meaning, both of which were awakened or reawakened by an original situation and somehow designated the imperatives generated by it. He took the second sort—born at the end of the eighteenth century—with the meanings they were given by the Revolution of 1789, because they seemed to account simultaneously for his abolitionist demands and the aspirations of the masses in France. But the inner instability of those terms, the conflict as well as the interpenetration of new and old meanings, all contributed to lead him astray. Could he imagine, for example, that the conservative employers would invoke *freedom to work* against the demands of the working class, or that this class, through its representatives, would prefer organization to freedom? Hadn't "liberty," that magic word of 1789, that secret dream of black slaves, changed and become synonymous with oppression? Or wasn't it rather the proletariat who had lost the meaning of human dignity, and who had to be freed in spite of itself, by force if need be? His uncertainties pushed him, then, to borrow new words—from Fourier, Considérant, and others— which had suddenly appeared in the language by a sort of spontaneous generation, and to think through them the requirements of the moment. But they carry him well beyond what he wants, what he *can* want. Instantly he's a socialist—though as the product of a rural society, he is utterly ignorant about industrial societies and has had absolutely no contact with the masses. But he momentarily confuses the wretchedness of the proletariat with the unhappiness of the slaves. Wouldn't socialism bring the abolition of slavery for all the damned of the earth? After this, he no longer understands himself: he does what he thinks he is not doing, and does not do what he thinks he is doing; he vaguely realizes this, becomes increasingly disgusted, and from February to June *no longer recognizes* his action. He reclaims it again only because it is leading him toward a great collective shipwreck; he finds himself, through aristocratic pride, in the midst of a populace he despises, fighting for a cause that he knows is lost in advance and that doesn't concern him.

All right, he didn't *want* to lose; his defeat was not even the object of a veiled intention. But in the first place he had nothing to lose; for a few moments—perhaps—he figured on the side of the "insurgents," but he had really given his heart to the other camp. This so-called "socialist" had been led by the demands and limits of a primitive choice never to surpass the demands of the middle classes. In spite of the compulsory vituperations, he did not harbor the professional elite's abhorrence of the bourgeoisie—on the contrary, *he loved it.* After the coup in April '48, the bourgeoisie had realized his dearest wish and at the same time, with slavery abolished, had removed the real content from his primary demand. To be sure, he still grumbled that his Revolution was going to be conjured away; that's only because he was already on board, carried away by the current. But this absentee agriculturist has *nothing more to ask:* he begins to understand that he has nothing in common with industrial workers. The freedom of Blacks—well done! *They never demanded it;* the Whites, like good lords, *conceded* it to them. That decision honors those who made it; it manifests that generosity which until then was thought to be a prerogative of the aristocracy. But *for that very reason* he hates the popular turmoil and those masses—all-powerful for a moment—who claim to wrench from the government the kind of concessions that, according to him, have value only if they are granted. What counts for him is the gift, and so this seminobleman reveals himself to be an aristocrat of the same sort as the squires of 1789, who would have contributed to ameliorating the royal finances if French society had allowed this contribution to be free and voluntary. Curiously, however, this aristocrat despises the nobility and admires the bourgeoisie—and especially the middle classes—for a virtue rarely acknowledged and never vaunted, for the free exercise of its constitutional generosity. We see the source of his mistake: with his sole wish realized, this bourgeois gentleman could withdraw from politics. But our acts, integrated into the collective praxis, always stop either too soon or too late; the current that bears them along runs into a causeway or carries them beyond themselves to such an extent that they cease to be ours. After April, a letter from Charles informs us, he was trapped and dreamed only of withdrawing from public life while he still claimed to be fighting "for the Ideal." The power of words, of friendships, an aristocratic sense of honor compel him, in June, to take the side of the "vile multitude." But if he gave them the formula for Pyroxylin, it was a parting gift. The defeat of the workers was not *his* defeat. He had once demanded the "right to work" without really comprehending

363

what this demand implied. As far as he is concerned, he is satisfied: the liberation of Blacks, universal suffrage—he asked no more and this was enough to wreak havoc in La Réunion. We now understand the meaning of his April letter: "How can I, a satisfied republican, arrange to break with the masses and socialism?" The events of June solved his problem; by this I mean not only that he had nothing to lose but also, above all, *that he won.* He shows his loyalty to the unfortunate and guilty allies in one stroke by exposing himself— symbolically—to the massacre that will decimate them. A few hours of prison free him forever from those compromising alliances; he has paid, it's all over. And as the popular movement was crushed at the same time, its "leaders" murdered or deported, this extermination puts an end to Charles's obligations: *To whom* should he be loyal, since everyone has died or disappeared? *To what,* since the people, mute with horror, no longer demand anything, give a plebiscite to Louis-Napoleon, which amounts to kissing their chains, to revealing their fundamental baseness. It was not Leconte de Lisle, the heroic combatant of June, who betrayed the proletariat; after the 2 December coup it was the proletariat, as an entity, that betrayed Leconte de Lisle.

This analysis would suggest that for de Lisle, the conduct of failure is *playacted.* How can we say he fails in that adventure in which, in fact, he loses nothing and wins the freedom to adopt the bourgeois order? Moreover, how is he to feel *from within* the despair and humiliation of defeat when he courageously accepts martyrdom for a cause that is alien to him and he knows to be lost? He surely felt great pride—tempered by a healthy fear—in living his hours of captivity, "the longest hours of his life." Longest because he thought he was slated for summary execution. Perfect: when he leaves, he has paid his debt. Nonetheless, it is clear that the privileged classes have dirtied their hands a bit, bourgeois order is restored by a massacre, and universal suffrage—his *personal* conquest—is somewhat compromised by the dictatorship of Napoleon III. But curiously, Charles keeps quiet about this unpleasant aspect of the adventure; it's the workers he bears a grudge against—who is talking about massacres? One corporal and four soldiers alone managed to disperse them. Now those slaves "kiss their chains"; why waste time trying to save them in spite of themselves? In a way, however, the crime of the bourgeoisie is going to serve the interests of this petty-bourgeois: not only does it allow him to return to the contemplation of eternal ideas, but it gives him the chance to demonstrate an aristocratic and priestly scorn for a social order which he prefers to all others. We have seen that his passion for his peers was hardly his strong suit. Can we call him a misanthrope? Yes and no. At first he had little love for men, but he dared not condemn them outright—Charles passed judgment on his contemporaries in the light of an ideal humanity that would one day be realized. He was, of course, sacrificing living reality to the human thing; but it must also be acknowledged that he was giving the sons of Niobe a chance: if the species is one day to merge with his idea, it must even now, in the midst of its worst meanderings, carry this idea in it like a leavening. At the time, Charles represented his aristocracy to himself as a system of strict obligtions: Niobe had made him a God to lead her other children, simple humans, on the path of the Good. This is what he did, conscientiously, until the June catastrophe. In June, however, he couldn't help getting the message: his divine intercession was of interest to no one and served no purpose; everything happened outside him. If the young gods, shepherds of the human flock, were recognized by their powers and their audience, he had to admit that he did not belong to them, which infuriated him. Thus his humanism and the optimism he professed served merely to contest his superior quality as a leader of men and to make him despair. In this sense it would have been preferable to break forever with our vile breed, to condemn action on principle, and to invest his superiority in contemplative quietism. But to shift from the nobility of the sword to the priesthood, he would have had to abandon his idealistic humanism and replace it with a Catharist pessimism. And he dared not do this before the events of '48, for it would have meant breaking with his childhood, with the time in which the idea of human goodness, born by the winds to île Bourbon, intoxicated him twenty years late, giving that apathetic and gloomy adolescent the taste of a vanished century, a defunct revolution.

So I am not going to say, as so many have done—that the events of '48 made him a pessimist but, rather, that they gave him permission to be one. The individual interpretation of a historical disaster, in effect, is an option that puts into play the entire person, all his life until the moment of choice. And Courbet, a republican who experienced the fall of the Republic much more intensely, still never despaired of man. Each of them had to decide if his party, his class, had lost a battle or a war. Each had to explain the worker's defeat by a provisional reflux of the revolutionary movement or by the "impotence of the plebs." And he judges himself by this measure. As Glucksmann says in Le Discours de la Guerre, one does not *vanquish* the enemy, one

365

convinces him. Courbet didn't let himself be convinced; at the first skirmishes, Leconte de Lisle declared himself convinced. His pessimism and his misanthropy have no depth: they are not the fruit of accumulated experiences of disgust and anger; nor have hatred or horror ever tormented him; he played a peaceful Oedipus, there on île Bourbon, confusing the symbolic father and the slave owner, and at the same time working out his mission. Never was he swept by homicidal desire; never did he go home, like Baudelaire, stunned and enraged by the "tyranny of the human face"; never did he experience, like Flaubert, the desperate desire to do violence for its own sake, to beat just anyone, the first person to come along, even if he gets his face smashed in return. He had a little excitement in '48—who wouldn't have?—but it was countermanded by his prudence as soon as it was expressed. The truth is that he feels nothing for men—neither friendship nor disgust—because they are not his fellow creatures. This planter's son is fashioned by the very hierarchy he condemns, a hierarchy that places him, in his Creole idleness, at the summit of the social scale. While he believed in his duty to act, in contact with the followers of Fourier—who, moreover, did not act—he always more or less clearly preserved the hierarchy of colonial society, which assimilated praxis to slave labor or to subversion, and thereby put inactivity at the summit of the social scale. Rather quickly, as we have seen, his practical concerns—that is, politics at the time—fell into the "lower regions of his mind." What do young Creoles do? They chase women or game, they chat with their peers, they might read. Leconte de Lisle *contemplates;* this was not forbidden, far from it, provided you had dozens of slaves. In Paris the right to quietism is not measured by the abundance of servile manpower; if you want to cultivate an indolent superiority to men of work and action, you must ground it on misanthropy. 1848 came in the nick of time: this poet was going astray, looking for île Bourbon in Paris, not finding it there, yet failing to understand the Parisian situation; a poor man himself, he took the part of the poor when he should have taken the side of the bourgeois who fed him. The defeat was a source of happiness, the awaited illumination, the sign of his vocation and his recovered superiority. The workers are dogs who deserve their chains—the bourgeoisie is justified. It was wrong, however, to spill blood and especially to let itself be chained. This congenial and sensitive class is therefore to be condemned insofar as it is unified and defined by general enterprise. The poet—defined negatively by nonaction, that is, by his Creole nonchalance—is superior to all of humanity, whose aims he denies. But the calm contempt that compensates—in the name of childhood memories—for the real situation of the adult in the home country (which has made him a petty bourgeois without great resources), never has the violence of a true misanthropy, it is much more a *factor of equilibrium*. Indeed, let us not forget that the hatred of man—in Flaubert, for example—does not spare the subject himself, who feels hating-hateful. This anxious passion, when it is real, does not leave anyone in peace. Leconte de Lisle does not hate himself—why should he? From his childhood he kept his magisterial Oedipus complex happily sublimated in a generous ardor against slavery and in delicious memories—he will return to these later and sing the natural beauties of his island. If he made the mistake, for a time, of mingling with crude and vulgar politicians, it was at least with a generous intent; he withdrew when he understood that one cannot be more royalist than the king, nor more slave owner than the slaves themselves. But *not without paying his debt in full*. Therefore he is pure, he is clean, he has joyfully rediscovered what he has known since childhood: that the artist, a contemplator of ideas, a passionate lover of the beautiful, is superior to the men of French society, just as the young plantation owner of île Bourbon is superior to his slaves. Only the divine child of Niobe cannot put his gifts or his virtues in the service of men, because those men do not want them. So he is a man *apart;* no longer even an aristocrat, he is superhuman since he reduces to the minimum in himself the portion of animality that links him to human beings. He offers to his friends and acquaintances the image of perfect distinction, but that somber nonchalance, semibourgeois and semiaristocratic, while it has the rigidity of prejudice, is merely a matter of comfort. It does not express the hatred of the other in oneself, the hatred of oneself as other, the horror of the body as the common site of the species; Leconte de Lisle, innocent of any massacre, indifferent to the social order— meaning that he demands and accepts the order that favors this indifference, depoliticized imperial society—hasn't the slightest reason to direct his misanthropy against himself. On the contrary, misanthropy allows him to introduce a solution of continuity into the social hierarchy; suddenly the levels of the social scale are fixed; there is nothing and then nothing, and then nothing again; at the summit, without any access route, cut off from men, dead and quite alive, the poet comes into view. Leconte de Lisle is a misanthrope out of naïveté, in order not to be man, to prove by his flaunted contempt for the species that he is not part of it. He is too stupid and too cold to feel, as Gus-

367

tave always did, that the misanthrope cannot escape the human condition except through a directed dream, and that, on the contrary, he
is the man in whom our species has chosen to hate itself. In other
words, you can be forced to destroy either ants or grasshoppers, and
in certain cases that does not happen without anger. But to *hate* them
you must be one of them, and know it to your despair. Leconte de
Lisle hardly loves and doesn't hate: his odd bourgeois aristocracy,
which came to him from the cradle, gives him the curious capacity to
live his human experience calmly, as the expression of his radical inhumanity. Man is suffering and meanness; but how can one hate him
since he does not exist? Leconte de Lisle exists as humanity denied,
he becomes an ineffaceable determination of Eternity at that precise
point of reflection where this dream of a dream deciphers its oneiric
nature and denies it by a strange *cogito:* I know that I do not think,
therefore I am.

So for this ambiguous man, pessimism and misanthropy are just
conveniences; if the 1848 Revolution had not been threatened by the
rich and by popular demands, if it had given him a leading role—for
example, the ministry of Public Instruction, which the politicians of
'71 apparently wanted to offer him—he might have preserved the
scornful optimism that in feudal times was called generosity. If the
Second Republic, triumphing over its enemies, had affirmed its aspirations—the advancement of the middle classes within the framework of fully evolving capitalism—and if, besides, it had dispensed
with his services, no doubt this melancholy man would truly have
become a "black" writer; without going so far as internalized self-
hatred, he would have detested *his* public, which yielded to others
and not to him. But the failure of the Republic saves him. He will be
bitter all his life, of course; but since the society guided by the sons
of Niobe is impossible, and action is at once a dream and the lowest
level of directed oneirism; since literature, that dream denounced by
a dream, can have no effect on slumbering humanity and in fact
addresses itself only to other poets, those Gods dreaming on their
feet; since obscurity is the lot and in part the proof of genius, of superhuman status; since his poems, without attaining *La Belle au bois
dormant,* are read by the young people who become his disciples,
whom he, good-natured but tyrannical, receives in his modest apartment; since his pension from île Bourbon and later, after his father's
death, the monthly 300 francs from the imperial patron allow him to
write quite independently of any public and without dirtying his
hands with work for hire—he has been spared all opportunities to

hate, to hate *himself.* As a result, his pessimism is an idea; his system demands it as its logical foundation, as the mediation that will allow him to shift from the secular aristocracy to the superhumanity of the intellectual priesthood; but misanthropy, that stifling genocidal passion, is not the source of his thought. An aristocrat is never entirely misanthropic, even when he participates in the shipwreck of the aristocracy. Leconte de Lisle, in contrast to Flaubert, remains an aristocrat in the midst of bourgeois distinction. He is not noble, but his father has slaves; slavery, which he so violently challenged, was his birthright of happiness; only he was not loved *enough* to accept it. But neither was he despised. Pessimism and misanthropy came to him from the 1848 Revolution, from defeat, from disappointments. Men of hatred and fear—sullied by June '48 and so terrified by the popular silence that they threw themselves into the arms of an Emperor and made the army all-powerful, provided it became the state's internal police—should have recognized their own experience in his, which was contemporaneous with that of the men who committed the massacres, and in a way legitimized the massacre by the radical condemnation of human nature in the victim even more than in his executioner. Indeed, the same events forged the author of *Poèmes antiques* and those professionals—frustrated, ashamed, guilty—who should have been his readers. This much seems clear; after all, when he writes his *Poèmes antiques,* before and after the Revolution, isn't he participating in the general craze for things Greek that moved Gustave before him? And when in preparing the collection for publication in book form he eliminates any political allusion in those poems written before the defeat; when—as in the case of "Niobe"—he transforms an optimistic image of the future into a symbol of humanity's inconsolable lament century after century; when, more generally, he pulls himself away from his time and casts about for an attachment to brilliant imagery, Apollonian but spectral, of what was and never will be again—isn't he offering fodder to those defeated readers seeking their salvation in anachronism and depoliticization? Well, not really; the reader doesn't buy it. These works tell of *his* disappointment; they are born of the history he has lived, the years of defeat *together* produced the author's misanthropy and that of the elite who *should have* read him. The same adventure marked for all of them the end of illusion, a hatred of the humanism of '48, the desire to legitimize the cold-blooded murders of June and the notorious loss of 2 December by the ontological condemnation of action, the substitution of man as the object of the sciences and their applications for man as the subject of history. Yet de Lisle is hardly read. The same readers who in 1857 will grant instant fame to Flaubert will not buy the *Poèmes antiques* or the *Poèmes barbares,* either in 1853 or later. Let us recall that French society at the time did not underrate poetry: *Les Châtiments, La Légende des siècles,* retailed clandestinely or tolerated by the powers-that-be, are a huge success. Lamartine and Musset, though a little out of fashion, are much read and much loved. If it has a taste for lessons in stoicism, the public looks to Vigny, never to Leconte de Lisle. In other words, literature after 1850 is going to assume a cathartic role by investing the reader with its own images, by making him hate *hating-hateful-man,* and by constituting him as such in imagination; and, further, this image of the bourgeois as his implicit representation of himself is emerging under the influence of the historical events of 1847–52. But the public that *became* pessimistic and misanthropic will not seek that black imago of itself in the poet who lived with the same bad faith, the same hopes, the same contradictions, the same brutal shock from an implacable reality, and the same final catastrophe. One might have thought, however, that this public would welcome any "news from the front" retracing its metamorphosis. But not so; Leconte de Lisle himself, moreover, is careful to efface any allusion in his poems to what might be called the fall of the bourgeoisie.[52] This fall, this Original Sin, which appeared in '48 but was committed in every era—an a priori consequence of bourgeois praxis—was something everyone wanted to forget; people accepted the guilt, the shame, but refused to connect these with the event. They admitted the hatred but on condition that its historicity should be suppressed and that it should be made a general determination of the species—at once an explanation and an abolition of history. They preferred to hate *themselves,* to be *hated,* as man and *even* as bourgeois, provided the bourgeoisie was linked to certain eternal characteristics of human nature and not to a particular type of exploitation. Above all, they accepted Vigny's stoicism, whereas in the new poets they judged it

52. There had been many massacres since 1794. Each time, however, the bourgeoisie was able to deceive itself and preserve its facade as the universal class. During the Revolution, the necessities of war were invoked, making any internal opposition an act of treason. In 1830, the brotherhood of the bourgeois and the people brought gentle tears to Joseph Prudhomme's eyes. The Canuts were worrisome, but only to the very small group of big industrialists and their hired thinkers. The murders in rue Transnonain seemed at the time a hard lesson given to a handful of rogues by decent people. In June '48 the veils were torn away: the bourgeoisie fulfilled its class reality by means of a crime. It lost its universality and defined itself by its power relations with the other classes in a divided society.

insulting, outmoded. The rich man knows quite well that the wolf who dies, braving hunters and hounds by his silence, is the aristocrat, fatally wounded and not even deigning to look at the common man who slays him. But what the rich man allows Vigny, in the name of the respect that bourgeois menials have always granted, and still grant, to the nobility is something he will surely not accept from a bourgeois-gentleman like Charles, whose petty bourgeois status he unmasks, along with the false superiority the colonials generally assumed over the cosmopolitans in the name of their still feudal property. After the fall, moreover, muzzled by the police dictatorship it had summoned of its own free will, the bourgeois class was horrified at itself. The elite was as well—if we exempt those with a clear conscience, such as Montalembert and Falloux. It *demands nothing*, as I've said; a public expects nothing, a good book makes it conscious in retrospect of what it needed done without even desiring it. But if it must accept its hideousness displayed by someone else, it will do so only if that other person experiences it in himself as a basic feature of his essence, and despairs of it. The reader's self-hatred will accommodate a hatred coming to him from an author who hates *himself* first, and who hates *him* intimately *on that basis*, as his double, his brother. It is not that the reader finds, or tries to find, some self-pity in the depths of that hatred; no, hatred and fear have entirely desiccated him, the time for plaintive lyrics is over, and only much later will it come again. Simply, the reader will accept only a self-hatred that is the representation of his own; whether rich man or professional, he will tolerate only the misanthropy that is generated by the hatred a professional or wealthy author truly feels for himself. Leconte de Lisle hates men from too great a height, and as a result decks himself out in a phony misanthropy; he regards the bourgeois reader with a gaze à la Vigny, but not being a real nobleman, the member of a vanquished class, he hasn't *sufficient rancor*; in any case, if his poverty has endowed him with a certain amount of resentment, that emotion is weak and accidental, and does not translate the homicidal impulse of the downtrodden aristocracy. De Lisle is a commoner, too concerned with taking on the superiorities of an aristocrat, with affecting imaginary dignities, for his pessimism to be taken seriously. As a false republican version of Vigny, he has nothing in his favor: he will speak neither for the ruined caste of the privileged, to which he does not belong, nor for (or against) the bourgeoisie, to which he does not want to belong. Nor, above all, for the people. In other words, Leconte de Lisle, false nobleman, false misanthrope, petty bourgeois innocent of the sin of the bourgeoisie but converted to an affectation of pessimism just as the bourgeois class was falling into real pessimism, cannot meet the needs of the new public: he was not seduced in '48. His manners are irritating, his misanthropy is insincere; a republican who rallied to the Empire, he, like the reader, has made the mistake of being the product of a historical moment that must be passed over in silence. In his work we find all the themes of art-neurosis, from failure to derealization, but they are not convincing and fail to stimulate in the contemporary reader the brief fascination with evil, the directed oneirism, the nightmare that *reading-neurosis* had to be at this time. The poet's chance pessimism, which would not have been discovered without the events in question, repulses the public by its *accidental* character; the nightmare does not "take" because neither the reader nor, ultimately, the author wants it to. The failure of the republicans was experienced by the author as a stroke of luck, and his subsequent happy misanthropy *freed* him from any obligation; certainly he has to express it, since it saved him from ill-considered vows. But it is superficial, mere lip service; he wants neither to feel it nor to have it taken seriously. The bothersome thing for the reader, discouraged by the gratuitousness of the author's pompous pessimism, is that if the misanthropy had to be taken seriously, its only justification would have to be the original Fall, that month of June 1848 in which the rich and the professionals were banished from the paradise of bourgeois innocence; and as we have seen, *that* is utterly unacceptable to the reader.

In other words, we can say that Leconte de Lisle belongs *formally* to the Knighthood of Nothingness. Failure has transformed him into an artist by allowing him to accede to a more explicit understanding of absolute-art as the generalized negation of man and the real; the defeat of '48 caused him to shift from a still rough but real conception of *engaged* poetry to one of *poetic autonomy*, of the poem for its own sake with no relation to the public or, above all, the aims of the species. Failure has become a creative force in him, a way of seeing the world and seeing man in the world; it is the internalization—under the pressure of history—of the contradictory demands of the objective spirit, becoming art-neurosis through the synthetic unity of lived experience, as a man's personal relation to the being of nonbeing and the nonbeing of being, that is, to the beautiful. And yet this Knight is not really consecrated by the reader of 1850, for he is perceived as seriously deficient, as practicing art-neurosis without being neurotic himself. Conditions converge *on the outside* to determine his conception of the means and ends of literature *through the objective neurosis;* but while his poems are the rigorous products of this nihilism, of the derealizing intention, and of the explicitly recognized primacy of the imaginary, the internalization remains a purely aesthetic option. This is what clearly marks the contradiction between his public attitude and the meaning he claims for his art. For Leconte de Lisle, as for the other templars, the task at hand is the hysterical imitation of a schizophrenic vision of the world. Yet he is incapable of fulfilling it; fundamentally, he ought to manifest the incommunicability of the beautiful, the artist's maladaptation to the real, his solitude and his despair, his real and degrading fall into subhumanity. For it is not through ennoblement that the writer will raise himself above the species; he can only glimpse that elevation as a desirable and possible consequence of the shocking triumph of the ignoble.

And if this deserving, imperious, rather affected, somewhat pontificating man is playing a role, surely he hasn't chosen to play the buffoon who reaches the stars only by rolling in the muddy stream that reflects them. His behavior is unrelated to any secret notion of "Loser Wins"; his false failure (we know that he wanted neither to lose nor really to win) has freed him, and this melancholy but by no means devastated man regards himself, and makes others regard him, as winner of the trial. A coterie, zealous followers, a literary salon, a wife—the bourgeois life is accepted, even claimed; this planter's son manifests no oedipal hatred but that of slavery, which is in fact abolished. To be sure, the bourgeoisie institutes the reign of the golden calf. But for him it is also the reign of freedom. He settles in; it is the least objectionable social order; he will rise above avarice and lucre by making his voluntary poverty a patent of nobility. The role he plays publicly is not that of the madman burned by Nessus's tunic, the humanity he cannot detach from himself, but rather the role of Alfred de Vigny, the stoic, in the sense that stoic thought is the thought of the Master. A *normal* role—Who doesn't playact his being in order to recuperate it?—and perfectly adapted; relatively unknown—but didn't he reject his public?—he exercised indisputable power over his disciples. But isn't it obvious that this stoic morality, this spiritual dictatorship and intractable pride, cannot be based on "belief in nothing"? If we are mistaken about everything, even our existence, if being and nonbeing are confused and their perfect inertia produces the *Maya;* if man, an illusion, is merely a futile and polluted sufferance, many attitudes are possible, from Buddhist asceticism to suicide and even genocide—which Schopenhauer was the first to imagine. Only one attitude is foolish: precisely that moderate stoicism based on the idiotic pride of an image that takes itself seriously. In short, in his poems Leconte de Lisle denounces any absolute that would not be the void, or being without qualities, or the process of aesthetic derealization that dissolves material plenitude in nothingness. But in his behavior he implicitly admits that man is the measure of all things, and that the true absolute is the exercise of courage as practiced by a human and disabused pride.

This contradiction would be nothing in itself; when the reader revives a poem by his reading, he has neither the obligation nor often the means to reconstitute it and interpret it through the author's biography. But Leconte de Lisle's perfect and annoying normality is manifest not only in his behavior; to the extent that it determines him, it is *produced* concretely in every line of his work. Art-neurosis, harmlessly encountered by a young Creole with a limited but healthy mind, seems less like the unique hope remaining after the catastrophe than like the calm object of a doctrinaire choice. We could take the poems of Leconte de Lisle as examples. Indeed, although madness is an objective imperative of art-neurosis, nothing is more lucid and decorous than those model constructions in which mental aberration becomes a theme of the Parnassian problematic and poses the calm question of its integration, as an irrational component, with the constructed rationality of the poetic object. Unreason is inscribed as the dark side that gives greater value to the clarity of the poem, and in any case this poem will not seem to be the real product of unreason. No doubt the Master's impassivity, he tells us, remains aloof from those puerile contradictions: reason, madness; good, evil. But precisely for that reason, that peaceful panoramic consciousness of the disillusioned illusionist seems much closer to the gaze of the archaeologist than to poetic delight. Beauty, as the insubstantial nature of material opacity revealing itself to impassivity through words that produce the world and annul it at the same time, is *also* and *primarily*, according to Charles, ontological truth. And, no doubt, when Nina thinks she is dead, or when a man thrashes about on his madhouse bed, shouting that he doesn't exist, these proclaimed truths are experienced and clinically studied as the very expression of mental disturbances whose etiology is known or made the object of investigation. But these disturbances are in great part *suffered*. How, under the influence of a particular childhood, a particular prehistory, did Nina internalize impassivity—which is an *obtained* ataraxia for the Master, coming at the end of an ascesis—in its profound and *pas-*

sive, deathlike truth, and consequently disintegration? (Impassivity is merely a card player's poker face; only death is impassive, indeed, it no longer *is.*) We don't know enough about it to answer; but her psychosis—the reasons for which are certainly well within the poetic art of the Parnassians—borrows from Parnassus several *rhetorical* themes and transforms them by *living* them. They become her singular relation to the real and to the imaginary; by their characteristic singularity and inflexibility these themes reveal their irrationality *in Nina.* Moreover, she is not thereby transformed into an *artist.* Today, schizophrenics produce "works," no longer prohibited in this domain; it's been more than half a century since art lost that equilibrium of craftsmanlike traditionalism (or formulas) and genetic rationalism that required the work to be a *finished* product. In the nineteenth century, the negative work began; and it was certainly begun by the Knights of Nothingness through their contradictions. But Parnassus shows its limits and its fundamental contradiction if we realize that—though the Master calls for polishing the work through rational labor, which only a "healthy" poet can accomplish—to *live* Leconte de Lisle's conceptions was enough to rid oneself of any means of rendering them poetically. And of course impassivity is life denied: the artist *must* be impassive; but as we are nothing but what we *live,* impassivity must be *lived as a passion*—this is what Nina did—or impudently *playacted* (living at a distance from one's own impassivity). This dilemma is valid, of course, only within Parnassus itself, and because Leconte de Lisle chose to base poetry on histrionics. At first doctrinaire, he played at feeling nothing—several hours a day, a task made easier by the fact that his heart had dried up en route—but he would have gone mad the moment he felt it expressed his true state. He would find, in any case, that ataraxia (that mixture of anesthesia and anorexia) is totally unsuitable to poetic creation, while elsewhere he denounced the *passionnel* and hence suspect character of everything that claims to be *inspiration.*

In all fairness, however, our chief versifier gathered up the nihilism of the era and made it an aesthetic doctrine, modifying it to suit his needs. But this theorist of nothingness—unlike Flaubert, Baudelaire, even the Goncourts—never understood that art in this era, with its contradictory requirements, required neurotic determinations of the objective spirit; he didn't realize that its doctrine imperiously claimed that the truth of the world was madness, that *being* was putrefied by an ontological psychosis. He publishes his choice: the real is nothing but unreality; the imaginary, when it is exposed as such, achieves the highest ontological reality in pure appearance; and he does not even understand that that reality is *untenable* for anyone who does it in cold blood, for no one can find in the world around us *objective* reasons to practice *phenomenological reduction* [*epochē*] in any form whatsoever. This is an admission of his equilibrium and his moral health. It is also an admission of his limitations: in the course of his practices of derealization, as we have seen, he has raised himself above any singular determination, if only the singularity of a law—universal but specific—or of an instrument of thought, even of number, *to enter eternity.* On this level, being without qualities, the void, and the true are conflated; the poet, a simple illusion unmasked, is altogether merged with pure being and pure truth. We cannot deny that this disenchantment is at the same time the triumph of a mystical ascesis. But the poet is so limited that he comprehends neither what he undertakes under the banner of stoicism, nor what others will succeed in doing far more consciously and better than he. For the *true* Knights of Nothingness, those who truly depicted for the readers of the Second Empire the era of hatred and the man that era produced, the entire culture had to be denigrated and, along with it, reasoned reason, out of a pure abhorrence of the human. And their true misanthropic task, the underlying purpose of their "entrance into literature," was not simply the choice to have being swallowed up by nothingness—which Leconte de Lisle does magnificently and almost philanthropically, to deliver man from the error of his ways—but *originally* to reduce the reader to despair and madness by having *reasoning* reason—before his eyes but without saying so—devoured alive by universal unreason. The fascinating discomfort of reading is that every reader, his book open, is continually tossed between two contradictory statements of fact: the world is mad, I am mad since it produced me, my misfortune is to be conscious of it but unable to cure myself; or, the world is rational, everything that is real is rational *except myself,* and my madness, which is known and scorned by the crowd, has doomed me to failure, to subhumanity, to abandonment.[53]

Leconte de Lisle's foolishness and prudence prevented him from playing the madman; never would he agree, even for a moment, to replace his petty bourgeois distinction with a few benign aberrations. But what is striking in his first disciples is that many of them glimpsed the connection between art and madness: they took drugs at Nina's, which proves that these young people went much further

53. See, for example, *Bouvard et Pécuchet.*

than their Master. To be sure, de Quincey's *Confessions of an Opium Eater* was all the rage, and more than one of them bragged of taking hashish—or, like Flaubert, opium—when they probably did nothing of the sort. Still, Nina's salon was witness to violent crises or strange incidents, some disastrous, some bizarre, and if several of those in attendance exaggerated their eccentricity, keeping their heads cooler than they pretended, this was merely the homage good sense paid to madness. Those "artificial paradises"—very artificial and, at least at Nina's, hardly paradisiacal—were not worth as much, obviously, as a good and glorious psychosis—like Gerard de Nerval's—or even a declared neurosis. But that was the contradiction of these young people. According to them, there was a time for releasing the products of an artificial madness, a time for yielding, like goldsmiths, to the traditionalist and technically rigorous craft of *embossing*. Without claiming to be the equal of mental disorder, psychedelic illusion was not to be disdained; it had the advantage of provoking, by external and controllable stimuli, an oneirism that was partially directed, partially suffered, in any case self-conscious, which denied the real for a limited time through imagery that was simultaneously *imposed* as vision, inevitably suffered, and *exposed* as a simple mirage. The moment of provoked unreason (which could also signify the triumph of *antiphysis*) was certainly not the moment of invention—precisely because of its artificial character.

The state of intoxication, for those excessively calm young Parnassians, is not a premonition of the heaviness of existence in the midst of its lightness; they think, for the most part, that it is really an *adulteration* of their being conditioned by chemical factors, and in their eyes that is exactly its value. They do not become what they are not, the beliefs the drug imposes do not emerge from their depths but simply do not belong to them, that's all. Nor to anyone else. And the objects to which these beliefs refer do not exist at all; their greatest joy is to expose this nonbeing of apparitions while they are nonetheless powerless to prevent themselves from believing in them. They are *conscious madmen*, who have the privilege of *living* the dogmas of art-neurosis as a concrete aberration. In short, they can only *underwrite* the doctrine; starting from principles in which they disclose the hidden primacy of unreason, they attempt to guarantee its authenticity by realizing it in themselves in the form of a provoked psychoneurosis. In madness these nihilists can intuitively grasp the evidence of the doctrinaire cogito: *someone* thinks me, therefore *someone* makes me exist; I do not think, therefore I do not exist; I know

377

that I am not what I am persuaded of being, and that I do not see what I claim to see, therefore I am. I am like the madman who knows he is mad and cannot help it; I am the triumph of consciousness over phantasms and the incapacity of consciousness to dissipate them; I am the dreamer who never stops thinking; I am the dream of a dream and yet cannot manage to wake up. Yes, that is what one *had to be* to write the poems of Leconte de Lisle; and his epigones had such a lively conviction of this that they agreed to lose themselves in the short term and recover themselves later in order to ground the abstract teaching of the Master on a concrete and suffered determination of their experience. Indeed, these young men had learned that art is born of failure, of hatred and inertia—as the negation of praxis and its human subject. Going beyond these principles toward what they believed to be their immediate consequence, they deduced that absolute-art has the objective characteristics of a neurosis. But after seeing that neurosis—which Leconte de Lisle never mentioned—as merely a constellation of aberrant determinations of the society and its environment, they felt they could not make it the source of their poems without being affected by it from within, as by a subjective illness. This, in short, was a necessary mediation. The young Parnassians found no common measure between the doctrine, its arrogant nihilism, and the miscellany of their daily lives; for this reason they hoped that the intermittent neuroticizing of lived experience would allow them to find in those dogmas an equivalence of their private experience. As we have seen, of course, they would not have dreamed of drawing their inspiration directly from hashish or opium; but at least they had license to do so when they "embossed" their poems with all the seriousness of a *realistic* craftsman (who knew the *real* possibilities and resistances of their material), license to refer through memory to those moments of derealization and to see them as the subjective guarantee of their enterprise.

The fact is, their attempt was doomed to failure from the outset, simply because their felt need to find unreason in drugs proved conclusively that without it they would have been perfectly healthy, and therefore incapable *on their own* of derealizing the real and realizing the imaginary. Since it isn't experienced spontaneously and doesn't dictate their poems to them, their *pseudo-neurosis* is merely an imposture that is abandoned when they work. But since the motifs they borrow from doctrine, still entirely shadowy, are not initially pathological themes, obscure determinations of lived experience that have been surpassed, unified, objectified in their works, those motifs remain pure abstract and rhetorical determinations, even in the anecdote that would suggest them allusively. So it is clear that the young Parnassians' procedure is just the opposite of what they were hoping, however obscurely, to attempt. Although subjective neuroses, conditioned in everyone by early childhood and prenatal life, do not seem a priori susceptible of being surpassed toward an objective neurosis that originates in the structures of society, in their cultural expression, and in the practico-inert determinations of the objective spirit, the young Parnassian poets' dream had been to *feel* first, to exchange the internalized knowledge they tried in vain, in their deplorable normality, to deepen and darken for the confused idiosyncrasy of a pathological *lived experience; then* to produce their myths, as much to see them more clearly as to loosen the bonds of the self; and finally, by deciphering their works and comparing themes, to reveal *art-neurosis* as the still obscure meaning of all their attempts and the objective imperative of autonomous literature.

Our only interest in Leconte de Lisle is sparked by the fact that his "entrance into literature," following a false failure, was the occasion of a true conversion and turned this normal man of modest means into an objective and contagious madman without the slightest affect on his internal stability. And that metamorphosis comes literally from the fact that the writer of 1850, having no place in official society and no role to play, unless he were to renounce the autonomy of literature to serve class interests directly, can produce nothing but a work—an abolition that resumes the social body's denial of him and his own denial of the social body. For this historic form of literature—autonomy for its own sake thanks to a double antagonistic negation—to be inscribed through certain works as the practico-inert determination of the objective spirit, to be preserved and surpassed in the *evolved* literature it generated under the liberal empire and after the fall of Napoleon III, it was enough for the events that marked the course of the Second Republic to be vividly experienced by some adults who were mediocre writers, like the author of *Poèmes tragiques*. On the occasion of the civil war that bloodied Paris, sickened by the murderers they secretly regarded as their brothers, without sympathy for the massacred and liking neither their poverty nor their demands, it was enough for these men to discover, in that multiplicity of interpenetration of a syncretic intuition, the following:

1. *Misanthropy*, the only adequate response to the common infamy of victims and executioners. By which we mean the only hyperbolic ruse

permitting the acceptance of a social order based on exploitation by dissolving classes in the universality of evil, the most common thing of all.

2. *Disengagement*, an immediate and practical consequence of human wretchedness—there is no just cause, there are no unhappy wretches. It ratifies as well the resounding failure of every generous action (the Republic finds its grave diggers among the same folk it might have showered with its benefits), and more generally of our claimed activity.

3. And equally *the autonomy of literature*, too often betrayed in the name of so-called political or social ideals, simple masks for our passions and interests. Here autonomy reveals itself by the denial of human aims—a denial of needs and of the body, a denial of ambition, a denial of the public, a denial of spontaneity in the name of impassivity and of inspiration in the name of work—to be the fundamental negation of man or, if you will, the passage to the negative absolute.

4. The *nonbeing of the real*—as a consequence of that hyperbolic extrapolation—in short, the denunciation of our passions' cherished illusions, and the *being of the nonreal*, a valorization of the imaginary. We understand this to mean appearance offered as such and revealing, in the static evolution of a beautiful work, insubstantially as the ontological rule of cosmic totalization.

It must be observed, however, that this intuition, in Leconte de Lisle's terms and as a result of his double political and cultural motivation, could not by itself constitute a metaphysical *Weltanschauung;* without extrapolation, it does not go beyond the ethico-aesthetic sector. Man is bad; literature, far from serving the aims of this wretched being, affirms its autonomy by revealing the vanity of those aims. And this vanity must be defined *morally:* human aims are unattainable, their only purpose is to make those who try to attain them suffer in vain; illusion itself remains in the ethical sector: our passions make us believe in human goodness, in happiness, in love, and these great, hazy ideals simply reflect our blind, egocentric impulses. The deluded individual affirms himself in them as he would like to be, not as he is, or as he ever will be. This pessimistic *morality* does not, however, imply the negation of the real; quite to the contrary—and we shall see further on the misunderstandings generated by this prejudice. Official critics will dub *realistic* those works that claim kinship with this prejudice, thereby conceding that in their view, when reality is unveiled in its original purity, it can only be radical evil. Therefore art will be reproached for being *too* realistic, for attempting to render the raw being of materiality in its impenetrable contingency. This reproach, when addressed to the true Knights of Nothingness, is strikingly unjust and foolish. But it does touch upon the weakness of Parnassus: the scornful condemnation of human activities—especially following a historic crime—does not allow by itself, nor of course by its accompanying considerations, for an assimilation of the real to the veil of *Maya*, nor does it allow the literary work a mandate to *make visible* the unreality of the real through the realization of the unreal.[54] When Leconte de Lisle shifts from an acquired misanthropy to a metaphysics more or less inspired by Brahmanism, he is simply making what Camus called the "leap." He is leaving behind a still human stoicism, supposedly inspired by experience but in fact by the refusal to take the side of the proletariat, and throwing himself into an ontological and metaphysical adventure that no longer has even the guarantee of a poorly interpreted event, an idiosyncrasy, or a class attitude. Through his pseudo-failure, literature is revealed to him as the unique absolute; by that very fact it requires the foundation of being to be imaginary; only on this condition will its fictions define the ontological structure of the true—there will be no truth other than a lie designed to expose itself the moment it affirms itself. But the poet hasn't the means to fulfill this demand of the objective spirit for the simple reason that he is not *in himself* determined in such a way as to contest the reality of being, nor to submit to the imaginary as a heteronomy of the sensibility. In other words, he does what he must, but without *believing in it*; inevitably, the reader doesn't believe in it either.

Thus *art-neurosis* does not reject the services of the Creole minister; it consents to be internalized by him and then guides his hand. But that rigorous and abstract *internalization* is no *incarnation*. In him, poetry suffers from two fatal flaws. First, it is clear that his pessimism is acquired belatedly, a conclusion he drew from a historical event as recently as did his future reader. When he is accused in 1870 of having sold his pen to the imperial regime, he protests in *Le Gaulois:* "Since 1848 I have not written a single line touching on a contemporary event." One might respond that a writer also sells his silence. But that is not the point; what matters here is that he abandons politics forever just when the rich and the professional elite decide to abandon their

54. As an objective center of derealization.

rights as citizens—and *for the same reasons*. His misanthropy is at bottom merely a justification. But the new public is made up of men of hatred—hating-hateful to the core—who are also asking pessimism to justify them. And Leconte de Lisle's pessimism—I believed in men, I have withdrawn to my ivory tower because an inexpiable crime revealed to me what they are—serves only to condemn them. Since they did commit that crime, they want someone to relieve them of responsibility for it by removing its irreversible character as a historical event and seeing it—like the innumerable crimes of the past—as an inevitable and equally nontemporal consequence of human nature. Men of hatred—so be it, but from father to son and since the time of Cain. The pessimist will be received if he proves in his work that he already foresaw the worst in the good times, during the paradisal reign of the Citizen-King. Misanthropy will pay off if it is prophetic.

The other flaw of Parnassian poetry is that absolute-art, a determination of the objective spirit, cannot by itself force the creator to live his creation as a subjective neurosis. For that very reason, as soon as it is posited for its own sake the work is deprived of the quality it demands, namely *irreducibility*—and, in particular, irreducibility to knowledge. In this case it seems to be the pure reexternalization of schemes and techniques internalized in an *application*, that is, in a fable carefully invented (or selected) as a function of contradictory imperatives, and never as the always suspect objectivization of phantasms. In short, the two flaws of Parnassus are two aspects of the same deficiency: if Leconte de Lisle's misanthropy presents itself as a reasoned conclusion and is displeasing as a result, that is because it seems explicable and specifically dated instead of emerging through his poems like a muffled, indefinable evil, based as much and more, perhaps, on the horror of the self as on that of others, and certainly not on a comfortable contempt, impossible to date but surely originating in childhood.

This negative aspect of Parnassian poetry powerfully suggests the positive conditions which, united in a work of art-neurosis, whether prose or poetry, will give it the greatest chance of finding a favorable reception. For literature to posit itself as an absolute, not in theory but in the imaginary object it produces, we must be able to discover in the work a singular quality attesting to the indissoluble unity of an objective neurosis in the author—the internalization of contradictory imperatives and the surpassing of all these contradictions by art-failure—and of a clearly delineated subjective neurosis, with roots reaching down to his early childhood. If the creator is lucky, each of these determinations will reflect the other in a constant reciprocity, and it will be unclear whether the first simply facilitated the internalization of the second or whether, on the contrary, the second produced the first, in the course of its evolution, as an invented and universal consequence of its individual contradictions by projecting itself into the objectivity of a work to escape stewing in its subjectivity. Or whether, as a consequence of the original situation, artneurosis was able to *become incarnate* in a particular subject and, far from remaining a set of formulas and pseudo-philosophical aphorisms, to live through him as an endured delirium and as an accepted Passion. If anyone is to have a chance of moving this sullen society, its bitterness and anguish masked by its superficial fires, he must clearly be a member of the professional elite or must be wealthy and, as such, conscious of belonging to the most favored classes—those called, at the time, the bourgeoisie. This class consciousness must be the source of his malaise. Let him regard himself with the scornful eyes of the nobility: he will be all the more acceptable since at this time a depiction of the bourgeois as seen from below by the brothers of the massacred must be avoided at all costs. Thus hatred is more tolerable; for the reader, it is reversed—the author makes him experience that internalization of the sentiment the "lower classes" harbor for the murderers of June '48 as the internalization of a privileged disgust for the commoner's condition. With one proviso: that selfhatred appear as the burning core of misanthropy; the aristocratic gaze will not be the gaze the writer—in the manner of Vigny and, comically, of Leconte de Lisle—levels on his public, but *first and foremost*, to the contrary, the gaze he feels leveled from above on his own life, the vivid light from that dead star, the nobility. It is not anyone's gaze, yet it must be *endured*; that is the reflexive consciousness of the true nihilist—or, if you will, his reflexive phantom; in fact, reflection does not *exist* in this realm. Rather, whatever the reflexive scissiparity, the last reflexive consciousness does not grasp itself as the consciousness *of* consciousness but as a superior degree of the reflected; in other words, it refers by a transascendent intention to the reflection *of another*, and is thereby constituted *in its being* as pseudo-reflected, meaning that this other being constitutes it in that this other is *elsewhere*. Moreover, this consciousness, from the depths of its baseness, thereby reveals itself to the *scorn* of that dead eye as exis. And the pseudo-reflected feels constituted as an object by that gaze—which is identified increasingly with an illumination—without ever being able to enjoy that fundamental character of its objective essence: a contemptible-being-held-in-contempt. In short, he must first be discontent with himself, and he must not be able to *live* this discontent even while presenting it as constitutive of lived experience; in one respect this discontent must be nothing more than what haunts him, and in another merely his first *concern;* haunted by his insubstantiality, as contemptible-held-in-contempt, he must turn constantly toward reflexive scissiparity in order to coincide with the *absent* reflection of contempt. Nor must he ever succeed—obviously—and from this fundamental concern, from this never abandoned, never entirely successful effort to *realize* himself as the horror he inspires in the *other,* he must derive some metaphysical merit, owing entirely to his dissatisfaction with himself and to the profound failure that is his identifying mark—not primarily or even chiefly an incapacity to cast off his baseness but an incapacity merely to *see* it (or to *see* it *seen*). Given this self-hatred conceived as the mystical relation of the feudal to the bourgeois, which—insofar as it *does not have* its roots in an inexpiable and irreversible crime—is never altogether felt as real and remains in suspense, proffering itself as always future, always capable of pouncing on its man and leaving him struck by a blinding intuition (an intuition that is forever impossible, of course, but which, from the depths of the future where it claims to be hiding, seems to be the ever *realizable* meaning of lived experience); given this internalized and reversed hatred, the author has the perfect right to hate others. The public will believe this is only an incitement to each reader to win salvation by hating himself, but in fact this is not true. Here, all is alienation: its source is a hatred clearly proclaimed by the other (or believed to be so); this alienating primacy of the symbolic father, the aristocrat or any *other,* is not truly experienced—except as a Destiny—and so provokes a neurotic hatred of the other,[55] the intentional and dialectically rigorous displacement, masked by syncretism, of one unrealizable objective by another, which the reader is only too inclined to *realize.* In this sense the *misanthropy* of the neurotic author of 1850 is a realistic impulse aimed at real objects, although it is dialectically conditioned by an unreal and unrealizing—if true—hatred of oneself. *Hatred of others*—whatever its origin—remains at the center; and obviously in that society devoured by hatred one wants to satisfy hatred still more than contempt. But that hypocritical and puritanical public can give itself such license—and thereby welcome a

---

55. Not necessarily, of course, hatred against someone we believe we are hated by.

writer-witness, looking at the world in complicity with him—only if the work that invites him to do so presents itself initially as the product of a centripetal hatred whereby the author claims to discover *first the hateful universal*, namely our universality, human nature, in the contempt he inspires in himself or does his utmost to inspire. Thus we find the tendency, which is detectable everywhere at the time, to dissolve vulgarly historical crimes in the anguished metaphysical and nontemporal self-condemnation of the species in the heart of the man who committed them. They disappear, they are merely symbols, merely the necessary temporalization of intelligible character; the worst is necessarily and always certain, for it is merely the expression—in circumstances otherwise random and negligible—of radical evil as it is posited, sensed, sought, and never attained. And this evil is none other than the return in force of universality, the bourgeoisie posing once again as the universal class but this time *negatively*, by attributing to human nature the contradictions, conflicts, alienation, and hatred that are the products of bourgeois society in France in the mid-nineteenth century. This means, of course, that the chosen writer must *keep silent about the events of '48*; that is indeed Leconte de Lisle's strategy, and, as we have seen, he admits it freely. But this isn't sufficient; or, rather, it is too much and not enough: too much because it might be seen, *it is seen* as a *historic* silence based on a specific contempt (and on an equally specific fear); not enough because misanthropy must not remain abstract and rail against man without giving its reasons. It would be unconvincing; the only way to make it attractive is to give it content, which is to say that the optimal attraction at this time will be produced by the reading of a work that in its subject matter, and even in its form, engenders the man of misanthropy, a work that *makes visible* the curse of Adam and its eternal consequences. But it must do this through the ordinary anecdote, in the banality of *apolitical* life, so that abjection, discovered in simple, "habitual" lived experience, justifies in advance political crimes and depoliticization without *ever* recalling them. This last condition implies that the *atemporality* of the presentation is based, in fact, on a temporal discrepancy: if the author's manifest misanthropy is to be welcomed as "genuine" and presented as an actually felt sense of shame, and not as something coldly manipulated for promotional purposes (or as a denunciation of the bourgeois, tied to the events of '48), it cannot present itself—unlike the misanthropy flaunted by de Lisle—as the simple result, eternal and calm, of a stoical or "brahman" panoramic consciousness. In other words, it must be *generated at the time* not as a blind passion forged by accidental causes but as a *conversion*, as the discovery of the truth in the light of an individual event that is specific and yet archetypal; this event can only be failure. But it had to be felt by the author in his very marrow; Leconte de Lisle's failure was doubly defective in not being truly lived as such and in being related to the taboo date. The only way an experienced failure might have escaped the reader's suspicion, then, was to have taken place *prior* to the catastrophe of '48—not by much, however, three or four years would suffice, otherwise that particular defeat might have been explained by the previous regime (the stupidity of the Restoration, the violence of the Empire, the revolutionary Terror, the privileges of the Ancien Régime). And it had to leave visible traces: the meaning of that shipwreck would then be that man is impossible, a life had to be broken under the July monarchy, and only that living deadman, the artist, could survive this singular experience of our universal impossibility. A small, obscure disaster, inexplicable, irreparable, this shipwreck had to be lived as an irreversible degradation, the frigate had to sink into the lower depths of subhumanity. Through his martyrdom and through it alone, lived through *for nothing* and without compensation on condition that it reveal to him the indissoluble bond between misfortune and evil, between our total impotence and our original culpability, the victim can be *convincing*; dead and already cold, the public's welcome can raise him to the rank of *fascinating writer.* For this original failure—precisely because it is prior to the collective failure of 1848 and implicates only humanity—can be recomposed by reading and thus established for *this* public *as an oracle,* and—through a disaster that will become manifest in and through the work as a singular universal—as the symbolization of the advent of the Second Republic, of its impotence and its crimes, of its collapse and its death, crushed under the boot. For although that memorable historical moment distantly follows the individual misadventure of the author, it is nonetheless a singular universal as well. Through tens of thousands of individuals, something was begun in pain and blood, then broke apart, that bore general *significations* even at the outset, but its *meaning*—even in the midst of generality—is a singular temporalization, a lived and plural determination of the intersubjectivity that marks the era at least as much as the era marks it, and that "will never be seen twice." With this in mind, we shall more firmly grasp the prophetic character of personal failure—insofar as it is the meaning of the work and its possibility—for that failure, while utterly condemning *man*, relieves the *men* of '48, even the murderers, of all particular responsibility. Yes, unremittingly guilty. But guilty *by nature*, guilty of *being born*, pledged on principle wherever they come from, whatever they've done, whatever side they've taken, to a destiny of impotence, endured misfortune, and *ontological* culpability. Finding himself in the *anecdotal* wretchedness and abjection of a singular life, especially if an always possible universalization is never accomplished, if no conclusion is drawn from it, and mutely deciphering it as a free rendering of the abortive revolution, the reader will not necessarily be touched by a new innocence but rather he *will derealize* his culpability. He will strip it of its historicity; the fault is no longer specific, it is not engendered by certain immediately irreversible decisions that one might not have made; it is the human tragedy. Certainly one can distinguish between the moments of the act: there is a *before*—the crime is not yet committed—and an *after*—it is committed for all time. But this *before* and this *after* are fictive since in *any event* the act of deciding produces a crime (at once because our acts resemble us and because they don't resemble us, because—resembling—they betray our egotism and our foolishness, and because, derailed by the force of circumstance, falsified, misunderstood, their violence and their harmfulness become exacerbated. And more generally because human activity is an illusion, an appearance taken on by great cosmic and inhuman forces). This culpability does not seem to be a historicization but the a priori irreversibility of a process of inevitable decline; time and history are at once preserved and adeptly reduced to impotence. There is a duration, a flash of lightning that illuminates a fall—and there is no duration since the fall, which defines human action and enters into the definition of man, begun anew with every man, with every group of men; predictable and repeated, it takes place in the cyclical time of eternity. Failure will therefore be oracular if the readers of the Second Empire read into it their own political and social history and see it dissolved in an eternity forever begun anew. And since it is easier to succeed than to fail on command, as the voluntarism of defeat would have the immediate result (as we have seen) of changing it into a victory that dare not speak its name, the ascribed failure—as a universal singularity, as the *always possible* universalization of the singular—must be assured, shall we say fatal, *from the outset,* must become for the reader, after ten pages, the object of a certainty and an expectation corresponding to certainties lived by the author himself in the course of the process of degradation he is retracing. This forecast, imposed before 1846, before the decisions of the individual had been implemented even to

387

the slightest degree, like the anticipation of his death and resurrection, had to have for that individual the mysterious clarity and irrationality of a sibylline message; he would be able to ground it neither on his familiarity with the human condition (if he had experience of our impotence, of the lie that makes our illusory acts qualify us without belonging to us, why would he decide to act? Experience comes *after* the fall, that totalizing abolition) nor on a show of will which, while giving him no certainty (indeed, the worst is not always certain), would replace the anguished feeling of a fatal seduction with a cold, abstract determination. Indeed, it is *precisely* that anxious apprehension of a *suffered* seduction—without any justification—that must be *prophecy itself* as an indefinable quality of lived experience. Not only the prophecy that the future reader will find in the as yet unwritten work, but the prophecy that, passed over in silence, makes the *end* of an enterprise—as the radical condemnation by being of all praxis—the fatal meaning, *tasted* rather than understood, of its beginning. In this disturbing prescience, *denial* and *lack of awareness* are clearly marked by anguish: the destiny about to be imposed, whatever it might be, is abhorrent to the individual at any price. The shipwreck is certain but indeterminate, otherwise anguish would become horror and denial would become specific, defensive forces would be organized. The unqualified purity of the anguish reveals, here, that failure is grasped from within and in anticipation as though already *suffered*. But certainty of the worst, the flavor of lived experience, implies in a way that the victim is in on the secret being hatched against him; in other words, he *organizes* what he *will suffer*, not on the level of the more or less deliberate decision but on that of implicit intentions—by a refusal to know himself—which teleologically structure and orient the temporalization of lived experience. Prophetic anguish therefore finds its basis in these pithiatic depths where, for certain individuals, inventing oneself and enduring oneself are indiscernible. Furthermore, anguish is itself the bias of failure; to foresee it is to be affected by it first, not in the *active* form of wanting but in the passive and hysterical form of *belief*. In other words, the requisite failure, if it is to fascinate readers as their own historical failure and the eternal failure of man connected by the singular mediation of an anecdotal defeat that took place several years before, will result only from a *conduct of failure*, the apparition in some haunted young soul of a subjective neurosis whose origin is to be sought in the singular and specific givens of his early history. The objectives, in this case, are set by the Other; the young man affirms them as *his* because he cannot reject them, but they continue to seem alien to him, as evidenced by his defensive belief that he cannot attain them. Yet as he considers non-success to be synonymous with subhumanity—because the primacy of the Other confers on him the right to define humanism to his liking, so that the human race, in the eyes of its victim, continues to appear as *his other-essence*—the neurosis in this instance consists of the humiliating expectation of a fall that will deliver him at once from the mandate imposed on him despite himself, and from his destiny as man. The failure of 1848 will find its justification only in the narrative of prior facts inspired by the pathological metamorphosis of an ordinary man into a man-failure. Art-neurosis does not demand that the artist be *truly* neurotic; in principle, it is of little consequence whether he *is playing the role* of a mental patient or really affected by psychic difficulties; in one way or the other, the themes required by absolute-literature—noncommunication, the solitude of the artist, derealization, failure, panoramic consciousness, and nihilism—will become manifest and determine the meaning of the work. If, however, the best candidates for glory turn out to be two authentic neurotics, Baudelaire and Flaubert (both born in 1821); if *Madame Bovary* seems to the readers of 1857 to be *the book* of their times and, even more, *their* book; if they unwittingly find in Emma's destiny the image of the fatalities that gave birth, and dealt a dirty death, to the Second Republic—if all this is true, it is because beyond the practico-inert imperatives of the objective spirit, the public can admit only a work of fascination. As I have said, this is an era in which reading is either listless or neurotic; and in the second case it involves an oneiric satisfaction whose meaning is highly ambiguous. Each person assuages his hatred of all others and justifies his misanthropy—in the margins of a falsely humanistic ideology—while *unrealizing* his personal culpability and even finding an obscure merit in his sufferings, his abjection. And in order to be temporalized, this reading-neurosis requires that the general themes of absolute-art are presented through a true and unique experience that enriches them, veils them, deflects them, and above all, far from drawing all too obvious conclusions from them, *makes them palpable* as the very flavor of lived experience. This means that the public *wants to conclude nothing*, that it is afraid of changing concrete givens into ideas too quickly and of being obliged, after closing the book, to declare its own misanthropy. It means that misanthropy must inhere in the connective tissue of the book, as an *other* thought, a thought *of the other*, of the author, always on the verge of being formulated, always elusive; the public must be able to recom-

389

pose in secret, reading *another's* failure as an *other* failure and, reassured by this alibi, as its own failure. In a word, it must be appeased and protected against itself by the substance and authenticity of an experience that *cannot be* its own, and that is lived out before its eyes by a spellbound consciousness, a consciousness the reader reconstitutes in the process of reading as his product, and at the same time as an alien reality. This reader is not a man-failure: his defeat is historic and real, therefore it is not proof that the shipwreck is characteristic of man; quite the contrary, it *characterizes* this midpoint of the nineteenth century and defines the bourgeois and the professional elite. Others in other times could have vanquished their adversaries; in France, after June '48, there is no one but the vanquished—and so they remain defined indefinitely in the history books. To tear themselves away from the historicity that condemns them, they will recognize themselves in their writers only if they find in each one the survivor of a nontemporal, absolute shipwreck, in short a *man-failure* having lived his fall into subhumanity as the singular realization of the original sin, of the archetypal disaster, repeated daily, that gave our father Adam his true nature. The public of 1850, overwhelmed by real crimes, will heartily welcome the writer whose semisincerity will allow him more effectively to lie to himself, the writer who *really* believes in the "curse of Adam." But since this curse cannot be considered a truth, since the prophetic evidence of bankruptcy cannot, except in neurosis, accompany the establishment of an enterprise it so essentially contradicts, the reader in this era will recruit his misanthropic authors from among those who are authentically neurotic. A subjective neurosis of failure expressing itself in works conceived according to the objective imperatives of art-neurosis and communicating to them the opaque and convincing richness of lived experience—that is what will best support the lies of this society disgusted with itself, unable to recover its equilibrium. This society is not awaiting anything, of course; but *after Madame Bovary* it discovers in itself the need Flaubert awakened, and which for some years would be its properly literary demand.

It is clear, then, that in the 1850s the votes of a public inadequately recovered from its collapse will go to authors whose subjective neurosis consists *precisely* of an intention to fail, and who, apprehending it as *other*, see it as the manifestation of the *impossibility of being man*. In their works, *lived experience* prophesies *after the fact* and universalizes the disaster of '48. In this sense we can say that Gustave offered *this era* the image of the exemplary artist. Conceived this way, however, Gustave's relation to his times seems contingent; we have gone from the necessary and sufficient conditions for his welcome by the public to the proposition that he was, in effect, fulfilling them. But comparisons, especially this entirely empirical one, do not an *argument* make. The striking fact is that the public of the Second Empire *rejects* Leconte de Lisle, its worthy interlocutor, the man who, *like his readers and at the same time*, was determined by the *watershed* of '48— and that this same public, by contrast, adopts as *its* author a young man indifferent to all politics, *whose own watershed* was accomplished, for idiosyncratic reasons, in January 1844. That readers recognized Flaubert as *the exemplary artist* can surely be explained by the structures of the new society, by its historic pessimism, its culpability, its misanthropy. But this selective attitude applies exclusively to the public, which is so constructed that it can recognize itself only in *Madame Bovary*; there is no indication that Gustave's failure—produced and suffered at Pont-l'Evêque—was socially prophetic. Especially since that same public asks him *at once* to be the oracle of the metamorphosis and to derealize its sin by a universalizing lie. This last quality implies that thirteen years after the fateful night, Flaubert is chosen not for his *truth* but as the instrument of a self-deceiving lie; Gustave therefore seems to have been chosen *by a misunderstanding*, and in a way it is not his *truth* that reading obscurely deciphers but, quite the opposite, his insincerity. So it is hardly possible that Gustave's Fall of '44 can *authentically* reflect the general collapse in 1848 to the readers of '57. All neuroses are insincere; Gustave's seems to be a happy accident that is immediately *exploited* by the disingenuous of 1857; in this case there would be merely a fortuitous connection between the author and the public: the double insincerity and the diachronic time lag could not establish the organic bond of interiority that is regarded as indispensable when we say that a writer *expresses his times*. But it must be acknowledged that this rather awkward notion was simplified to an extreme by criticism—notably by the "scientific" studies of Marxism. We shall be able to grasp the truth and necessity of the reciprocity of *expression* that makes the work an illumination of the general praxis in a given society and makes that society a guarantee, a realization of the work as imaginary prophecy, only if, *on the one hand*, we assume that the book takes account of an entire collectivity, with its lacerations and its struggles, but from a partial perspective that confuses everything and belongs, *in general* (exceptions abound), to the writer himself and to his class of origin, and, *on the other hand*, we assume that what we call an era is the meeting place of numerous

391

generations that distinguish themselves from one another by different pasts and futures, while uniting in a contradictory synthesis because they *share the same present*—a present imposed on them by the force of circumstance even if they interpret it differently. Moreover, it is to this concrete and plural unity that the author must bear witness, though he can do so only *from the perspective of his generation*, that is, on the basis of a past and a future that are unknown to his younger readers. Class bias and diachronic discrepancy—which are, of course, not unrelated dialectically—have the effect of muddying the message and at the same time giving it a *plural* meaning. Engaged in an inflexible present, which he interprets through his projects (the double extase "past-future," which defines him), but thoroughly penetrated by anachronistic *meanings* born of futures and pasts that are not his own, the author can be the contemporary of his contemporaries only if he is both behind and ahead of them. Quite often, moreover, not to say always, what is ahead is determined by what is behind. And that is indeed the case with Flaubert.

Nonetheless, if the adults of 1857 choose this author out of *recognition* and not out of complicity in the lie, it is proper to end this chapter with a search for the answers to two complementary questions. *First*, since Gustave's neurosis is subjective, since it characterizes his idiosyncrasy and is generated by particular factors (the mutation of Achille-Cléophas, for example, and the structure of the Flaubert family that followed from it) lived in the opaque singularity of a childhood, how is it united with practico-inert imperatives and with the axiological system of art-neurosis? How do we conceive of the reciprocity of perspective that joins together the failure syndrome—as a neurotic response to a unique situation—and art as failure surpassed toward the dead contemplation of life? Without the concrete project of *human persons* synthesizing the imperatives of the objective spirit and at the same time exploding their contradictions, these norms, as we have seen, do not come to life, nor will they define the work to be done as the beyond of the impossible. And without the practico-inert objectivity of these imperatives—more or less clearly internalized through the reading of older or contemporary works—the young man would not be incited to surmount these abstract oppositions through the concrete totality of a work that preserves them in its very fabric by transcending their intended meaning in the direction they themselves indicate when they are brought into contact through an enterprise. But looking at it in this light—the enterprise of writing in its *partial* truth—we falsify the givens of that delicate adventure. It would seem, indeed, that the contradictory elements of the objective neurosis, internalized by a life, are what confer neurotic subjectivity on lived experience; in other words, we might believe, if we had to stop here, that slight torments, some discomfort, the "unpunished vice" of reading that transforms a *normal* adolescent into a bookworm (whatever one might think of it from the ethical and political viewpoint, the escape is much more often normal than pathological), would ensure that he live art-to-be-done as the future result of an induced neurosis, of literature revealing itself at once as the absolute and as the immediately foreseeable failure of every attempt to write.

Yet this isn't so: Gustave does his reading when he is, if not neurotic, at least in a preneurotic state, and for that reason his poetics will fully coincide with the requirements of art-neurosis. Leconte de Lisle, by contrast, internalizing the requirements of absolute-art, is nonetheless unaffected by psychosomatic disturbances; in other words, he lives that abstract madness of failure in complete health of body and mind. This is why he writes his work—and misses his mark. In Flaubert's case, then, there seems to have been a double determination or, as we say today, an overdetermination: Shouldn't the idiosyncrasy of his familial situation and his early history have been enough to cause a "nervous illness"? But how could that effect, so strictly individual, result in the internalization of art-neurosis? And how could art-neurosis, an axiological constellation of dogmas, norms and techniques, have become the *truth* of subjective neurosis? Is it permissible, moreover, to speak here of *truth*? Shall we say that *Madame Bovary*, that center of derealization, is the *truth* of the crisis of 1844? Why not? But it would then have to be established that Gustave came neurotically (or preneurotically) to literature-neurosis by way of subjective motivations that already contained it as an unperceived constellation of objective determinations. His given constitution and his family problems oriented him from childhood toward a neurotic solution; but in another era, that solution would have remained purely pathological, simply because what he would then have asked of literature the objective spirit could not have given him. Furthermore, this very hypothesis is absurd because it is clear at the outset that his neurosis is specific; in other centuries it would have been other, or, to be more specific, little Gustave Flaubert would not have existed. Under the July monarchy, it results in art-neurosis and thereby goes beyond itself because literature was such that it is *already* at the source of this preneurotic childhood, and in the 1840s the impossibility of being man and the impossibility of writing reflect one another and communicate with each other *within* the subjective neurosis. The question is, therefore, to understand how Flaubert's individual and protohistorical determinations can correspond to the practico-inert transformations of the objective spirit rigorously enough to allow *his* neurosis to be developed—without ceasing to be his singular adventure—in tandem with the contradictory imperatives that outline the face of the new art; to understand how, through the failure it cultivated at length, it is externalized and universalized by the doctrine of absolute-art in such a way that this doctrine, though inscribed in the objective culture, appears to his contemporaries, and not without reason, as the singular product of his genius. There is no question here of parallel developments; the only hypothesis we shall have to verify must be based on the idea that a man—whoever he is—totalizes his era to the precise extent that he is totalized by it. We shall have to ask whether Gustave's neurosis totalizes bourgeois society under the July monarchy *on every level*, and whether consequently it is *through him* that these levels reveal their correspondences and their reciprocal symbolization—as if the Flaubert family's adventure and that of French literature were expressing, each in its own way, the same evolution of French society. If so, then art-neurosis, as a surpassing of cultural problems could be lived and *constituted* by an adolescent as a solution to his familial difficulties; and the hysterical neurosis of failure could be developed on the basis of a very real familial failure, first as compensation for that failure through art; then as failure *suffered* within literature (not for lack of a "gift" but through the glimpsed structure of the objective imperatives of 1840); and finally as a radical content of failure, surpassing conjointly the impossibility of being man and the impossibility of writing through the intention—this time thoroughly neurotic—to realize man-as-failure as the only possible writer of literature-as-failure.

As I have said, two questions had to be posed. The developments of the first lead us to the second; for if we want an exact answer, we shall have to picture simultaneously—and illuminated by each other—the adventure of French society and that of young Gustave. And we must therefore propose that the former leads not only to a constellation of cultural determinations—contradictions inscribed in books and totalized by Gustave's neurotic adventure in art-neurosis—but also and especially to the catastrophe of June '48, a historic and concrete moment manifesting itself as a tragic destiny lived by thousands of lives, as the beginning of conscious awareness for hundreds of thousands of others, then in the multiple singularity of a real and endured hatred. In other words, June 1848 manifested itself as *history* realized through its formative structures, structures that it breaks and bruises in some places, reinforces in others, tears away from all conceptual knowledge, and temporalizes by its irreversibility as a moment of praxis and as the inevitable, inimitable orientation of lived experience. On a certain level the evolution of bourgeois society in France in the second phase of capitalist accumulation, when all of Europe is undergoing economic crisis, is experienced by its protagonists as a historic drama that leaves permanent traces in the history of the French workers' movement and in the exis of the ruling classes, at least until the First World War. Speaking only of the ruling classes, the rupture is manifest in them *as original sin* (they have actualized a disaster that did not formerly exist), *as a punishment a thousand times worse than the crime* (banished from paradise under Louis-Philippe, they fall into the Bonapartist hell, without the hope or the will to find their way out); and as a *transformation of the "honnête homme"* (much was made during the Republic of "honnête," or respectable, folk— property owners to the extent that property is, if not the basis of virtue, at least what makes virtue possible and even necessary) *into the man of hatred* (hating-hateful murderer, responsible out of terror of the "reds" for a white Terror that cannot abate without endangering him—he thinks). As we have seen, the public—the wealthy and the professional elite—have entrusted Gustave and a few others with the job of freeing them from this *historicity.* But the lie would have been instantly apparent to them if it were not sustained by some profound truth. Indeed, this dual relation of author's insincerity and reader's bad faith could not possibly constitute Flaubert's fundamental relation to the public. If it could, this relation would have appeared only after a fortuitous encounter and would thereby manifest its *contingency.* Instead of being that *cultural* relation which, as an anticipation of the city of aims conceived as the *evolved* triumph of *antiphysis,* transgresses for the "read-reading" pair the limits of facticity, *reading* would seem on the contrary to be a mode of noncommunication or nonreciprocity, the exploitation by an *other* reader of a text that did not admit, or not at first, the meanings the public found in it, or rather put there. In the dual rapport that awakens the work and actualizes it, this amounts to privileging the act of reading at the expense of writing, which is a manifest absurdity.[56] In other words, Flaubert's

56. And naturally this absurdity is *always possible.* More, it is part of every effective

relation to his readers cannot be uniquely or originally the lie. Certainly, bad faith can reveal in *Madame Bovary* a conception of the world, time devoured by eternity, a void without qualities, the nontemporal character of human nature, an archetypal fracture that *presupposes* succession so as immediately to dissolve it in the cyclical duration of repetition. For how should bad faith fail to find what hysterical insincerity put in? But this second and false premonition, having wanted too passionately to replace the *nonpareil* of history with a *déjà vu* that by degrees throws us back to the eternal return, would wilt in a moment if it had not become the parasite of a prior and *true* premonition that it continues to contradict and vampirize. This original prophecy is Flaubert's neurosis as *Madame Bovary* deforms and universalizes it but reveals, despite screens and precautions, to be a temporal process. It is clear that author and reader are working hand in glove; for their chief concern is identical: each wants to forget a *history* and have it forgotten by destroying the historicity of human societies. And the basis for their accord is that each has lived his adventure *historically;* they have both been temporalized toward a final cataclysm, intuited from the first day, prophesied but neither seen nor known; they have felt the implacable speed of the *praxis-process* that was carrying them along, they have seen themselves making and suffering their destiny, gradually etching their features by actions or passions—which amount to the same thing—that are irreversible. And then the day came when that great movement, the same and other in each of them, precipitated them into crime or subhumanity,

---

reading to the extent that this reading, facticity transcended on both sides, is also facticity preserved in the movement that surpasses it—which means that the most radical communication is *also* noncommunication. Noncommunication runs the gamut from *resonance* (a complex fact generated by egocentrism—the reader is concerned less with understanding than with resonating, he projects himself into the work to objectify his image and to have a presentiment of the affected pleasure of reinternalizing it) to *hermeneutics* (the reader simultaneously interprets the message according to *at least* two codes, one of which is explicitly utilized by the author and the other—unknown to him, perhaps invented after his death—is applied to him without authorization, as a *severing of complicity*). But noncommunication is conceivable in this domain only as a determination of communication. It is a shadow zone, and variable besides, which is displaced in the interior of a harshly illuminated field and is explained only by light, like those margins of obscurity produced by the interference of light rays and which might be called the darkness of clarity. What I am saying here, of course, is equally valid when it is the *author* who seeks noncommunication. We have seen this already—and shall soon see it again—when we described the Knights of Nothingness and their untenable ideal, the denied public.

in any case into hatred; their fall seemed to be the conclusion of all their actions, radiant and unbearable evidence that in a way killed them. It is therefore *on the basic assumption* of a historically lived history and *against it*—against the idea that "men make history on the basis of prior circumstances"—that they have connived to suppress *historicization* as a dialectic of necessity and freedom in human praxis, and in the final analysis, in order to disclaim all responsibility, contested that praxis itself. In other words, their primary accord arises from the fact that both have drunk their historicity to the dregs through the vicissitudes of a dramatic temporalization. And since the adventure of one is a few years prior to that of the other, the primal premonition arises from the fact that the first is the anticipated expression of the second. In each premonition—for reasons we shall have to clarify—historicity is revealed as man's misfortune and his profound culpability. Such premonition exists because this way of living the history one makes is peculiar to them; in other eras the historic dimension of man is not part of conscious awareness—one makes history, one doesn't feel oneself living it. In still other times, history *exists*, empires rise and fall, but either the hand of God guides history or events follow one another at random, the nose of a sluttish queen is reason enough to explain a world war. Between 1789 and 1794 the most authentic revolutionaries regarded themselves as Plutarchan heroes, others felt anxiety at being carried along by that irrepressible tide of radicalization which characterizes revolutions in progress, but they exhausted themselves in futile efforts to stop it with their bare hands. Sometimes circumstances can push people in the direction of historic optimism: history is the progressive victory of the good over the bad; and according to the time and place, it also happens that it reveals its true face to the historic agent. An ambiguous face: men make history, but nothing will prevent it sooner or later from stealing their acts in order to transform them into crimes, nor from "progressing by means of its worst aspects"; it *has a meaning*, which is the advent of man, but "the road that leads from evil to good is worse than evil.[57] In 1850 all these conceptions and quite a few others as well were current in Europe. In France itself, well before 1848, historic optimism was typical of those called the "forty-eighters." But, in stark contrast to this optimism, Gustave and his reader were united by their pessimistic view of history; and this was

57. Mirabeau.

a result not of their doctrinaire positions but of the fact that they lived their histories in profound unease, Gustave his anecdotal history, his reader the history of French society. For both, events offered the *fall* as the fatal meaning of their enterprise; for both, this mortal enterprise was imposed from the outside, they lived their action as a passion. But if the writer must *express* the reader's point of view *organically*, and not by a fortuitous encounter, the writer's subjective neurosis—in this case, Flaubert's—must be a *real* anticipation of the reader's social temporalization, such that this subjective neurosis is surpassed in the singular universality of the work in which it is recounted. Thus the crisis of Pont-l'Evêque and its aftermath until the death of Achille-Cléophas would be *Gustave's* February and June days, *his* coup of 2 December, and *his* plebiscite; he would have lived, not symbolically but in earnest and in advance, the defeat and cowardly alleviation of a class which, in order to complete its destiny and realize its secret primacy, agrees to renounce its visible praxis (political action) and go into apparent hibernation to retrieve its "cover," its irresponsibility as an eternal minor. In other words, the difference between the general evolution of society in the middle of the nineteenth century and the evolution of this microcosm should amount to the same process—passing from preneurosis to neurosis, refusing to become an adult, reclaiming under the authority of a cursed but "reliable" father the advantages of an indefinitely prolonged adolescence, and discovering, in June '44, art-failure and the "Loser Wins" that characterizes it. At the core of a movement of macrocosmic temporalization, microtemporalization as a retotalized totalization of historic totalization would differ from it only in speed; it might offer merely a contingent image of the larger history *unless* it is *that same history* constituting itself in certain individuals and micro-organisms as an *accelerated process*.

Before seeking answers, we must formulate our problematic more precisely. In particular, what do the words "for real" mean in the preceding context? It is clear that we are not using them here in opposition to some determination of the unreal or of the ideal but more particularly to any idea of reciprocal symbolization. But we must be specific: reciprocity of symbolism between a man and his era is often possible. But whatever the life and era under consideration, this reciprocity is valid only as a *rhetorical* illustration of the macrocosm by the microcosm (and vice versa), that is, as an image elaborated by an author and whose practical value resides in its convenience alone, *unless* history were *in fact condensed* in the era's *abridgment*, which a singular biography claims to be.[58] I am prepared to say that the life of Leconte de Lisle *rhetorically* symbolizes the history of French society, from the Three Glorious Days to the coup d'état, and that it *really does* express the historical moment that is made manifest by the events of the February days, the June days, and then 2 December 1852. Here the real appropriation is *synchronic:* the totalization of French society by the great contradictory movements that shake it *at once* produces the abortive 1848 Revolution and the conversion of Leconte de Lisle. It may even fashion his conversion directly and at the same time through the mediation of the Revolution.[59] And of course this conversion must be seen, properly speaking, as a surpassing of the historical moment by personal praxis, in short, by the reexternalization of the interiority-retotalization of the totalized—that is, a destiny, a free fall toward a new alienation by which the poet becomes the singular incarnation of every singular and contemporary surpassing, and assumes *in complete freedom* the general and concrete but infinitely near destiny of the whole society. This synchronism is, of course, infinitely broader than what we are describing here, and Leconte de Lisle sums up all levels of the society to the extent that he is *on every level* (infrastructures, mores, dietary regimen, fashions in clothing, etc.) a *signified-signifier.* The products of human labor define his class standing (he is a consumer, not a producer) and his general individuality (fashion or tools designate him as any individual of the French petty bourgeoisie of 1850); by consuming or utilizing those products, he *signifies*—that is, being signified as an individual of this particular era, he shifts to the

---

58. To be sure, it would be the same for any collective object of microsociology.

59. Leconte de Lisle is defined as *disposed to conversion* by his own contradictions, which arise directly from his internalization of the French collectivity's contradictory whole, and at the same time he realizes his conversion by the direct internalization of the *catastrophe* of June '48. Thus in every totalization in progress one must always envisage the dialectical relationship of the direct connection between the general totalization and the singular totalization (a totalization of the singular by the concrete generality), that is, of the whole to the part. And one must keep in mind the same dialectical relationship of the macrocosmic totalization to the microcosmic totalization *through the mediation* of the historical moment—of the *concrete universal* produced by it, retotalized by every part, and determining individual singularity at once by the historical event (the totalized incarnation of the totalization) and by the general face of the world (i.e. by the real relation among all the parts, not insofar as they directly express the whole but as they are distinguished from it by their movement to retotalize it—in order to reexternalize it as it was internalized by them). It is as if the Spinozist substance were producing its modes *at once* immediately, through the intermediary of attributes, and as a specification—incomplete and for its own sake—of the infinite mode. We must, of course, conceive of Spinoza's broad dialectical vision in terms of historical temporalization and not in terms of a substantialist ontologism.

rank of signifier of the unspoken and lived meaning of his time by his singular appropriation of the sign. One example will do, and the simplest one at that: de Lisle wore a monocle; so did the Goncourts. But if in their shared condition as *wearers of monocles* they are signified by this vitreous gaze imposed upon them to choose freely, if each of them fully expresses himself (*grosso modo*) by the way he wears this cyclops eye, it signifies for his contemporaries and for us, his descendants, an individual, opaque and *comprehensible* meaning of the whole era insofar as it is *also* the infinite depth of lived experience, an infinitely faceted totalization grasped as an irreducible and plural idiosyncrasy.

Whatever its scope, synchronous symbolization—as shown by the case at hand—is *real* but superficial and in a way *false* (in the sense that Spinoza defines the false idea as an idea that is true but incomplete) because, considering it in itself and without another temporal determination, it does not seem *evolved*. Certainly Leconte de Lisle does not escape the rule; for him, as for everyone, the chips are nearly down from childhood, and somewhere in the depths of his memory there is some "primal scene" always ready to reemerge and forcibly impose its meaning on events. But, as we have seen, the feudalism of île Bourbon and the young Creole's Oedipal relations with a slave-owning Moses are, for the republican of '48, an *other past*, the permanent source of *other motivations*. That *other* past is also *the same* but on a deeper, even global, level; experienced in 1848 *in Paris* through voluntary exile, it is the source of a permanent detotalization for de Lisle. When the event explodes, imposing on the poet—in the name of *other* motivations—a brief and thundering common destiny, then and only then is reciprocity of expression based, for the abortive Revolution and the false revolutionary, on the *real* relation of internalized totalization and retotalizing externalization. As we see, whoever would make the life of the Master of Parnassus into an abridged version of the history of mainland French society in the period under consideration would provide merely a *rhetorical* illustration of events; the *real* relation does not go beyond the level of the historical moment (or it returns us in depth to the totalization of historic humanity, which is indeed impossible to grasp except retrospectively).

On the other hand, if Gustave's *expressive* bond to this same history is *real* in its diachronic form, it must be understood that the collective past and that of Flaubert the individual are indistinguishable, and that an identical future grasped as an inevitable destiny illuminates an identical present on the basis of an identical *original* curse. Thus, as even synchronically—which everyone easily understands—the macrocosm can become incarnate in a microcosm, thereby becoming a signifier-signified (or totalization-retotalized), so *diachronically* a comprehensible temporalization—the general movement of a society structured one way or another by events that express it and become those structures—can and must become incarnate in the microtemporalizations it produces, in which it is resumed *before* arriving at its final term. Synchronically, the finitude of the person or the microorganism is immediately grasped; but, far from blocking comprehension of the total meaning, it is indispensable to it. Indeed, whatever its scope, the *historic event* is itself *finite;* moreover, its vast finitude is a guarantee of its reality;[60] it has boundaries that constitute its *determination* even as it transgresses them to become imperceptibly annihilated in an external zone of lesser sense or non-sense. These boundaries would still exist even if, in the One World created by the communications revolution, it involved all living men; for those men are finite in number, and although the event is a mingling and totalization, *within* this synthetic movement quantity determines quality; in other words, the fact that this number is two, three, or six billion is not an external characteristic of the event but quite the contrary, a mode of *internal* structuring. Thus the *real* incarnation of the macrocosm in a microcosm is based not on the fact that both are finite (which would be a fortuitous coincidence) but on the rigorous dialectical conditioning of the two finitudes *by each other* across the medium of the practico-inert.

But by the same token they also define the *possible* transgression toward non-sense, that is, the period in which it will be said—of a person or a small collectivity—that it *lives on.* In other words, it is clear that we always die too soon or too late, but if the "too soon" is a matter of chance (the interference of sequences on the level of detotalization),[61] the "too late" is determined as a function of "program-

---

60. Furthermore, one would have to choose—depending on the event under consideration—between the case of "unlimited finitude" and that of "strictly limited (circumscribed) and internally indefinite reality"; the structure of a historical fact cannot be defined (even synchronically) as that of an institutional whole, in short, it is impossible to provide an abstract and conceptual model of it.

61. If a political figure dies before completing his work, *it is not an accident* in that the mode of production generates dialectically and in close connection *both* the era's means of communication, the economic interests that can condition the safety of transportation (transportation being the greater risk in a capitalist society, in which profit dominates at the expense of prudence), and the social and political problems faced by that politician. More, we can say from this point of view that the contemporary society

ming." Meaning that the very efficacy of what one does marks the finitude of the enterprise, and this is not the date of its completion but rather the moment when the times will cease to support it, when it will be prolonged by inertia without being nourished by social life as temporalization and so necessarily doomed to sclerosis, to repetition, to stereotype.

But it must be admitted that the finitude of an individual or microorganic temporalization *can* incarnate the finitude of a macrocosmic temporalization, that is, the finitude of a *historical period*. In time, too, the global process produces its limits and violates them to become annihilated in non-sense. For instance, the July monarchy unquestionably ended in February '48, although it was prolonged as an increasingly meaningless survival under the Second Republic and under the Empire. The same thing happens with public figures or small groups that produce their determination from within, who, on the basis of the totalization in progress and, of course, without ever becoming clearly conscious of it,[62] define the period during which they will be said *to live*, the period in which their efficacy—slight as it may be—results from the fact that the general totalization, though continuing to perpetuate itself everywhere, really becomes incarnate in them.

---

produced both the politician and the jet plane. In other words, the death of this figure is not a meaningless chance event but a possibility realized and predictable (with a certain coefficient of probability) *insofar as* it is *signified* by the society through practico-inert structures. To the extent that certain people are *designated in advance* as possible victims of an airplane accident, they are also designated as victims as individuals of varying indications of class according to the societies in question. Beyond the distinction imposed between capitalist and socialized countries, there are national airline companies in which even the farmers travel by plane. From this point of view, *this death* seems to be a differential element of their destiny.

By contrast, the accident is a matter of chance—a perfect piece of non-sense and not a *variant*—if we consider the individual as *signifying*. To the extent that his praxis surpasses the contradictions of the society (synchronic and diachronic) by retotalizing them, its dialectic intelligibility can *and must* reveal itself in its full integrality without the possibility of this accident being contained in it (except in certain cases as an event alien to the enterprise but necessitating precautions—the choice of a substitute or, should the occasion arise, a successor). If he took the airplane in order to sign a treaty with a foreign government, the airplane represents *in his enterprise* the mode of normal and necessary (most rapid) communication; it is envisaged—implicitly and at the lowest teleological level—in *its positive aspect only*.

Thus by its very nature the *signified-signifier*, the individual, constitutes the characteristic chance events inherent in his life at once as the sense of non-sense and as non-sense of sense.

62. A *formula*, a "life plan," often becomes evident—at least for individuals—from the earliest moments, in any case in the protohistorical period.

Similarly, we must envisage the diachronic finitude of individual and historical temporalizations. In other words, the *internal* limits of the person embody the internal limits of the totalizing process to the same extent that the internalized boundaries of contemporaneous microcosms give the historical sequence its internal finitude. We must be more precise: if the sequence is finite, that is, if it has a beginning and an end produced from within (even surpassed toward the nonsense of survivals), this is because it is the enterprise—as praxis-process—of ever new generations who inject *solutions of continuity* into the perpetual historic *continuum,* or who detotalize the totalization from the diachronic perspective. Those who speak of a history of humanity have, in effect, an *identical subject.* From this angle we can certainly preserve the idea that contradictions are the driving force of history, but those contradictions take shape, explode—and surpass themselves toward a solution—in the unity of a smooth temporalization. Thus in the finite enterprise of a single worker, the object produced (as the altering of the individual practical field) moves toward its completion through a dialectic sequence of incomplete moments that contradict each other, are posited for their own sake, and are shattered within an *identical development* whose unity is assured by the worker's unwavering intent. History, that totalization in progress, is continually detotalized in the very movement of totalization and by it, for even if it were assigned one subject alone for centuries (the bourgeoisie from the time of Etienne Marcel, the proletariat from the time of the Commune, etc.), that subject itself would be *shattered,* broken into generations, each having as its past the future of the preceding generation—although they all meet on the *common site* of the present—and each deciphering the present made for it as a future denied (even when it is accepted, since it is accepted as other).[63] In other words, humanity *is not* and does not respond diachronically to any concept; what does exist is an infinite series whose law is recurrence, defined precisely in these terms: man is the son of man. For this reason history is perpetually finite, composed of broken se-

63. To simplify: what makes the problem of the generations so complex is that the notion of generation is in fact a mental construct. At best one can decide to set fathers and sons against each other at twenty years' distance. But there are older brothers, younger brothers, and cousins being born every day of every year, who reestablish a continuity—an imperceptible evolution—at the core of discontinuity. Hence detotalization itself is overtaken by totalization. This dialectical game of continuity and discontinuity is well known to historians but not to philosophers of history. I shall try to come to terms with it in detail and envisage its consequences in the second volume of the *Critique de la raison dialectique.*

quences, each of which is the *deviated* (not mechanically but dialectically) continuation of the one before, as well as the surpassing of that preceding sequence toward ends that are the *same* and *other* (presupposing that it is at once *denatured* and *preserved*). History is finite, moreover, because its agents "make" it from the perspective of its finitude (and theirs), even if they claim to strive for eternity. In fact, the proposition "man is mortal" is a purely inductive one—considered from the point of view of the future—whose only interest *today* lies in its rigorous application to all contemporaries; the extrapolation is facile since the law *never* allows any known exception. But as this synthetic judgment a posteriori does not provide *its reasons*, it is impossible in the present state of our research to know whether death is bound forever and by dialectic necessity to the human condition, and so it is equally impossible to give any meaning to this proposition on the basis of progress in biology and medical science. We can certainly show *today* that death is an event *of life* and from the first a direct consequence of it. But that is *for today:* tomorrow *antiphysis* can be extended to death itself. We can decide as well that man will conquer death or, quite the contrary, that it will remain his indefeasible law and his destiny; nothing is *logically* contradictory *today* in these ideas about tomorrow, but they remain opinions conditioned in each of us by class ideology and individual history. What interests us here, then, is not the *fact* of mortality but the importance of death and of the desire for death in the *imago* that the historical agent has made of himself and of others. In other words, if it is true that men make history on the basis of prior circumstances, we must determine to what extent the death of preceding generations, or their slow progress toward death, which is internalized as the conviction that one's contemporaries, too, will die and is objectively apprehended as voids *to fill, to await*—apprehended, then, not only as a personal conviction that *we* are mortal and as an extroverted desire that *they* die to make way, but also as an introverted desire that death should overtake us and explode the narrow and monotonous limits of our banality—we must, as I say, determine to what extent death can be considered by the historian as a *prior circumstance*. Indeed, death seizes the living; it seizes the living person because he feels mortal and can surpass the old deaths that crush him only toward his own death. Hence the enterprise of a life is defined *against death and by it*. By making certain choices it is easy to work *against death* in complete lucidity; I am thinking, for example, of the immortality Flaubert dreamed of. This is because survival through the work—provided that work remains an inert determination (a demand) of the objective spirit—is identical with death. The wish comes down to this alone: that an indefinitely prolonged public should reawaken the work by serving it (by *using it*). The work but not the man. The work at the expense of the man. Just as at the cemetery one reads an epitaph that assumes meaning and sometimes beauty only if one is conscious of its connection to a vanished life, so the author who aspires to immortality desires his work to *assume meaning* in our eyes as the epitaph of someone deceased. One more reason in our society for assimilating death and beauty. How many writers are there, how many have there been to kill words? Underscoring in this way the strict finitude of their real life and making their future nonbeing the aim and truth of their existence. In other words, art—insofar as it is not tied to a popular history (it is not *anywhere*)—is an enterprise that defines its own history and "prior circumstances" *by finitude*.

But what about enterprises that can be conceived only with the prospect of an indefinite or poorly delimited progress, in any case such that they have meaning only if they continue after the death of the present agents? The point is no longer to see them as *stases* perpetuated by inertia but, quite the contrary, as embodying a process that is pursued as a temporalized action *after* the demise of agents and by others who will suffer their demise, and is thus defined by the dialectic of *same and other*. Indeed, if this process were abolished or radically altered, it would expose the finitude of the *current* enterprise and reveal as illusory the future the enterprise assumed in order to define itself. On the other hand, it cannot by definition remain the same since *other* agents must pursue it whose past is indeed the former future of its originators, meaning that since the past is the metamorphosis of praxis into being (more precisely, into being-surpassed), what constituted the deceased originators as existences and their enterprise as praxis becomes, in their successors, the "rough coverings of being," which the project must deny by heading toward a new future. It is clear that the original enterprise, borne along in the course of things, in a historical world in perpetual *oriented* flux, must change, become *other* to *remain the same*, and that in these conditions, *even if these connections with the whole of the totalization could, by some impossibility, remain constant*, it would nonetheless be the case that the originators, should they be resurrected by some miracle, *would not recognize* the enterprise, which would still be *theirs*. For these two reasons—it is other because it is the same pursued by others and so imperceptibly but irremediably altered, it is other because it attempts to remain the same in another world—it exposes the finitude of its originators and thereby its own. In fact, the enterprise continues to escape itself, lose its own ends, die, become resurrected elsewhere, different, doubling itself, depending on whether agents transform it in fidelity to its original function, or whether they are stubbornly fixed on its original principles and objectives in order to preserve its *internal* structure without taking account of external changes (a preservation that fossilizes the enterprise, the *same* becoming *the absolute other* when the claim is made to preserve it as an isolated system).

Its current animating subject is not unaware of these *future* aspects of his praxis. Learning from his praxis the finitude he shares with the enterprise which results from the necessity of his death, he is led to take his enterprise even further by his ambivalent attitude toward his successors. On the one hand he takes precautions against postmortem changes by the most rigorous measures (the tightening of internal bonds, the choice of a successor, the balancing of powers), and thereby succeeds only in assuring for himself a mechanical and anachronistic survival in the world of tomorrow—until that world crushes him. In this case, no matter what he says, he has bet on a *finite* history and chosen immortality for his project (namely, a corpselike inertia), which effectively denies it survival, giving the project the boundaries of his own finitude. On the other hand, conscious of the fact that these precautions themselves will not suffice to protect his enterprise, he tends to imagine the significations of his project only insofar as he produces them himself, *in his lifetime*, and to consider as *non-sense* whatever will happen after his death, a constellation of transformations in which he knows he will not recognize himself and for which he does not take responsibility. From this point of view, he is still shaping his work for finitude, but instead of defining it as the immortality of a dead object whose singular structure is fixed once and for all, he confuses the finitude of the enterprise and that of his own life; hence, whatever his claim, the determinations of his praxis have only a limited scope; they are born of his life and are effective only for the duration of that real life. To his successors, these "prior circumstances" will seem like obstacles.

Thus the cyclical structure of history ("man is the son of man") makes comprehensible its continuity and the discontinuity of the sequences it totalizes; and as that structure is tied to birth and death, it is clear that the relative finitude of historical series is based on the absolute finitude of historical agents. Conversely, the finitude and singularity of an *era* (this is the name I give to any historical temporalization to the extent that it produces its own boundaries) rebound in turn on the agent, who is defined *not only* by general characteristics (the mode of production, relations of production, class, groups and subgroups, etc.) but also in his singularity as a certain moment of a greater but singular temporalization. Thus the diachronic finitude of an individual is particularized by the finitude of the social projects that include him and—by enlarging to constrict the field of his possibilities, therefore his options—give him his destiny as *finite* man with his particular alienations. In this sense, a life like Gustave's and an era like the reign of Louis-Philippe can enter into reciprocal rapport on a *real* foundation; it is enough that they are conditioned by the same factors, and that these factors totalize them and are retotalized by them in such a way that they present the *same curve,* the same profile of temporalization. Both must also, of course, be oriented toward the same goal on the basis of the same "prior circumstances," the same obstacles, the same intentions.

On this basis we can understand perfectly the effect of acceleration that transforms a life into an oracle, into a diachronic summation of the general evolution of society. There is no reason for the catastrophes of the microcosm and of the social macrocosm to coincide in time. Certainly the two finitudes are but one, since the smaller is a moment of the larger, and the destiny of the individual, in case of *real* identity, is none other than that of the era; better yet, since the individual is produced as an agent responsible for the destiny of the era to the extent that the era seeks to surpass itself in and through him. But the presence of the whole in each of its parts does not prevent each one from containing an irreducible finitude that distinguishes it, as a part, from the whole (a reality without parts but which can only exist by making itself total, through the parts, as the meaning of each and the unity of all) and from the other parts. In this sense—the example was taken from the realm of synchrony—the part is posited for its own sake in relation to the whole as a *compendium,* as the all itself seen through the large end of the telescope, and this cannot be done unless it defines itself in relation to the combination of the parts as *being partial*—that is, by the presence in it of the whole that is present in the other parts, and by the singularity of this presence insofar as its very finitude becomes its determination (and conversely). And what is the true for a supposedly inert totality (which is the very meaning of the synchronic object) is even more so for the temporalized totalization; individual lives—those, at least, that are temporalized from their protohistory (or from their prehistory) onwards as the

totalizing-totalized surpassing of general factors of the social movement toward the singularity of a destiny—are defined in their historicity as a *moment* of totalization to the extent that they produce their
own limits from within as a singular determination, and this determination is none other than the very rule of global temporalization
we have called the *era*. In this sense, the temporalization proper to
each of these lives is *in itself* their finitude. The macrocosmic totalization is manifest in it as a diachronic presence, just as the whole is
synchronically present in each of its parts, but what constitutes their
singularity is the way that each one, under the influence of equally
finite and singular factors (for example, the social environment as it
transmits institutional conditionings while particularizing them, or
again the singular relation to parents and to brothers and sisters to
the degree that their personalities make the Oedipal trinity experienced as a *unique* situation, and through it the infrastructures that
govern the slow transformation of the family), produces its internal
determination—speed, rhythm, duration—in the form of *programming*. In other words, biological, social, metapsychological factors—universals that make us live them in their singular reality—are
for each person at the source of a *life plan* that is generated by internalized contradictions, and that is restrained or accelerated by the
general movement of society.[64] Thus on the level of the individual,
historical movement is double: *on the one hand*, the person is irresistibly drawn toward certain particular rendez-vous (February 1848,
2 December 1852, 4 September 1870) arranged for him by the history of
others and his own history as other. So Gustave, through his frustrations, his impotent rages, his dreams of glory, his preneurotic failures
and his neurosis of failure, is *borne* along by the force of circumstance
and the praxis of men toward the February Revolution. But this *public*
rendez-vous might have rather little importance as *lived experience* in
private temporalization—even if it appears retrospectively, in other
respects, as crucial. *On the other hand*, the life plan based on circumstances similar to those that produced the global sequence determines
and governs the internal movement of individual lived experience,

---

64. Obviously, the deceleration of social changes or of global temporalization does
not necessarily have the immediate effect of slowing individual temporalization, any
more than a general acceleration is inevitably translated by singular acceleration. It is
the curve that counts. And life plans in themselves involve temporal schemes that
determine in each person a disposition (*open* and relatively flexible) to respond *in his
way* to transformations (speed, rhythm, deviation) of the historical pace.

and leads the person to realize—within a period of time that varies in each case—the diachronic totality of his era. We sometimes say of an actor that he "has one or two acts, etc., in him," by which we mean that he can *sustain* the exhausting tension of a role for twenty or forty minutes, but past this limit he collapses. Similarly, it must be acknowledged that an individual, as a function of the society in which he lives, of the mode of production, of the technical expertise at his disposal, of the family structure, of prior circumstances, of the historical future that is sketched out as his destiny, but also as a function of the singularity of his protohistory as well as his biological characteristics—inherited or acquired—has twenty, forty or sixty years "in him." And we have already understood that at issue here is not the "life expectancy" revealed by the statistics on newborns of a particular period, although these constitute the framework in which life plans must be determined, but rather the concrete duration of a human existence as it is limited if not by death at least by the collapse into the afterlife, and that this limit is the negative aspect of the surpassed surpassing we call a program. Some lives burn like nylon, others like candles, and still others like a piece of coal slowly burning out beneath the ashes. What counts for those that are diachronically significant insofar as they are retotalizing[65] is that whether short or long, quick or slow, they are the era itself in its entirety, gathered up in a program. Consequently, the era can complete itself in an individual well before reaching its social end. Brief lives, therefore, will be oracular; in them, the era has chosen *really* to reveal its meaning and the circumstances of its future demise. Moreover, from one life to the other the era continues to tell its story and to self-destruct. Lived from beginning to end, the era doesn't merely produce a symbol of itself: in opposition to serial detotalization it realizes itself progressively as a global totalization. In other words, these lives *make* the era, they act in it to retotalize it continuously, just as the era is present in each of them. *Praxis-process* is generated by the interaction of those lives that are in a dialectical relation of contradiction and complementarity to each other, which more manifestly unites the parts among themselves in an accomplished totality to the extent that they are all necessary to the whole, and each is posited for its own sake as an

---

65. Any real life—whatever its *insignificance*—is significant as totalized. In other words, the historian will find it signifying to the extent that in its own era it approached the pure signified.

incarnation of the whole. But since temporalization is the issue, it is easy to understand that these contradictions are a driving force of history: the era *invents itself* as the totalization of a society by setting up an internal conflict through the thousands of particular incarnations that battle among themselves to survive on the basis of infrastructural transformations.

BOOK TWO

Neurosis and Programming in Flaubert:
The Second Empire

If Flaubert's life is programmed, it could only be as a result of his neurosis. And if that neurosis is oracular, then in January '44 he definitively chose a social environment that did not yet exist but would become *his* society for some years. We shall first attempt to show that in its liberal period the Second Empire could be regarded as the *optimal* society for Flaubert; indeed, he considers it the high point of his life; whereas after 4 September he becomes one of the living dead, fossilized. He lives ten years more; but it is a long drawn-out agony, he feels like a stranger in the world around him. We must find out why this is the case, and so we shall try to imagine Flaubert's life in political and social terms in accordance with his own testimony. Our task is to understand what made him "the great writer of the Second Empire," what caused his death on 4 September and his survival in exile under the Third Republic, when he published only *one* book.

Like all his contemporaries, Flaubert had a rendez-vous with the February Revolution. He would be so conscious, under the Empire, of the importance of this missed appointment that he would use the word "fossils" to designate his contemporaries, the young men in their twenties at the time, and to compare them unfavorably to the twenty-year-olds in the last years of the liberal Empire. True, he would use the same word for the survivors of the Empire under the Third Republic. But upon reflection, the meaning remains unchanged: in the Commune, to his mind a sequel to 4 September, he sees a *repetition* of the June days. In both cases the precipitate and ambiguous proclamation of the Republic—something that *was not wanted* by the leading citizens—was followed by a plebeian insurrection. It was as if the 2 December coup had kept the nation for several years on the brink of the abyss, and yet this brutal jamming on of the brakes had clearly not prevented the final collapse of French society.

413

In short, 1871 is a replay of 1848. The real *rift* occurred when the populace overthrew Louis-Philippe, simultaneously destroying values, merits, and the social order. And consequently breaking Flaubert's life in two. According to Flaubert, historical time runs from better to worse, irreversibly; individual and social history is a process of degradation. Therefore, Gustave's finitude programmed as an internal struggle against the temporality of lived experience finds its justification in the disastrous orientation of general temporalization. At the same time, Flaubert's historicity is strictly defined: he is the man of the rift; a *fatal moment*—the shooting on the boulevard des Capucines—chain reactions, explosive and brief, and then nothing more: the after-life. Gustave, historical man, differs in this respect from a nobleman of the eighteenth century, from a writer of the seventeenth century, in that his life is deprived of a slow, continuous maturation by the general movement of society; witness and victim of a revolution, he is made of two isolated sequences which have no meaning except in relation to that event: a series *before,* a series *after.*

Yet, as I have said, he was not at the rendez-vous. To believe the author of *L'Education sentimentale,* to see his determination in reconstituting the February troubles, the June insurrection, the allusive insistence with which he persuades us that it isn't entirely Frédéric's and Deslauriers's fault that they have botched their lives, and that the *times*—the trouble of '48—play a large part in their failure, to note the icy sullenness with which he condemns all the actors in the drama, one would think he had hopes and was disappointed. Anyone unacquainted with his life would go even further: to be *fossilized* by an abortive revolution, wouldn't you have to take part in it? The fossils exist: Lamartine, Ledru-Rollin, Louis Blanc, a hundred others, and perhaps, too, the young men who mounted the barricades and whose enthusiasm, crushed by the defeat, gave way to apathy. But it would be absurd to imagine Flaubert lending a hand, or even praying for the combatants' success. His correspondence gives us a perfect picture of his state of mind during those years, which he will later call ill-starred and crucial. for this hermit, the February days brought no more inconvenience than the delay of the mailman. A letter from Louise took more than a week to reach him; yet even this wasn't much of a hardship as he had been cooling toward his mistress for some time; there was even a break of several months. As for the events themselves, he pictures them with great reserve but without disfavor because they flatter his misanthropy: "You ask my opinion on everything that has just transpired. Well, it is all highly amusing. It is a joy to see the discomfort on certain faces. I take great delight in contemplating all the deflated ambitions. I do not know whether the new form of government and the state of society will be favorable to Art. That is a good question. It couldn't be more bourgeois or more undistinguished. As for being more stupid, is that really possible?"[1] In other words, the new regime, in all probability, will be no worse than the last; there is very little likelihood that it will be better, since action, especially political action, is merely a delusion, and all social orders, insofar as they are established by men, are about the same (except for the feudal hierarchy, long since abolished). It is the change that delights him: we will see other faces, and those who were yesterday in positions of power will now begin to suffer. Resentment, misanthropy, sadism. "Existence—what a shabby business! I don't know whether the Republic will remedy this, I seriously doubt it."[2] That is all he can find to say; and from the point of view he has adopted, which is at once that of immediate lived experience and of its metaphysical meaning outside of any social consideration, it is quite clear that his skepticism is justified. *No*, the bourgeois Republic and the abstract rights it brings to the citizen cannot change *existence;* and when Marx speaks of changing the world or Rimbaud of changing life, they are putting themselves on another level. Rimbaud, that gruesome toiler, wants to elaborate the "terrible and tedious depths" which Gustave senses in himself without daring the descend into them; and Marx wants to transform concrete man, the man of need and work, by acting on his social environment. In short, for Flaubert, the Republic can only bring the French another kind of tedium. Never has he felt more removed from politics. Between February and May '48 he has distinctly other concerns: there are the quarrels with Louise and the breakup; then, at the beginning of April, Alfred dies: "I stayed with him for two nights, I gave him a parting kiss, and watched as his coffin was nailed up." *Saint Antoine* is marking time: "Since Saturday I haven't written a single line. I am stopped by a transition I cannot solve. I am eaten away by anger, impatience, and impotence." He is not, however, ignorant of the conflict ranging the Assembly against the Parisian workers, since he exhorts Maxime in the same letter, dated May '48, to "try at any cost to get the hell out of Paris." He adds: "You must do it to save your miserable skin. As a last resort, forget about your horse and get out just the same." These

1. To Louise, *Correspondance*, 1:79.
2. To Ernest, 10 April 1848.

bits of advice are entirely typical of him: when the pressure of history is too strong, there is no recourse but the most desperate flight. Maxime, too, acts according to type in his refusal to follow that advice; as a journalist with great curiosity, he will not leave the capital; he agrees with Goudchaux that Falloux and the party of order have decided to "hasten the dissolution of the National Workshops to engage in immediate combat." In sum, he wants to be there to report on the massacre. He does so, moreover,[3] and of course he aligns himself with people of property, which earns him a glorious wound in the right calf. Gustave's attitude during the June days is revealed to us in two letters written in July; one is addressed to his mother, in which he excuses himself for having been "so egotistical and foolish" the evening before. Art, of course, is to blame: "One cannot spend the whole day making desperate efforts to excite one's sensitivity without ending up with something too delicate." The source of the dispute, it seems, was Hamard's return to Rouen widowed and out of his mind. These family events absorb him entirely, as we can see in another letter addressed to Chevalier. "I spare you, my dear Ernest, a swarm of details *atrocious* for my mother . . . He is unrestrained and outrageous. *I* am going mad, too, mad with sorrow. If he doesn't leave in a few days . . . we will emigrate to Nogent." He adds a little further on: "As for me, I am . . . in hell." In other words, he is too absorbed by his private life to pay much attention to the June insurrection and its repression. A single sentence—a rather ambiguous one—alludes to it: "You know from the newspapers about the atrocities that have just occurred in Paris." Those atrocities do not seem to have been *committed* by anyone; they *have occurred*. Are we to understand that no one is responsible for them, and that Gustave, like Charles Bovary, thinks "it's the fault of fatality"? Absolutely. But this fatality stems from universal human wickedness; for him, everyone is guilty, the vile bourgeoisie and the ignoble workers; envy, fear,and hatred have pushed them to mutual slaughter. He will attempt to show this, twenty years later, in the second *Education*. Furthermore, he shares the anxiety of the rich, and on 3 October '48 he writes: "I have had the good fortune to be mobilized. A year from now, if there is war, I will leave. I will almost tell you that I hope for it, such is my need to get out, to say goodbye to my charming circle of intimates, to breathe freely. Whether I am killed or not, I don't really give a damn, and in the political uncertainty in which we are now living, I am busy in any

---

3. *Souvenirs littéraires*, "Souvenirs de l'année 1848."

case polishing a fearsome Vincennes rifle with a thousand meter range. Many people are quite disturbed, quite agitated, they imagine the future, they pale at what they see. Well, my dear Ernest, it seems to me that whatever comes along now, it's all the same to me."[4] An extremely valuable text whose apparent illogic—so frequent in Gustave—informs us better, in its insincerity, than the truest confession. It is scarcely credible that an adult man of highly superior intelligence could write *in the same sentence* that he doesn't give a damn whether he is killed and that, in these days of political insecurity, he has made preparations with a rifle that shoots a thousand meters. Who could attack him, in his fortified castle at Croisset, but the commoners, the socialists? And whom would he shoot but the urban rabble, come from Rouen en masse to attack him? Shall we say that this hermit, this philosopher polishing his weapons is entirely calm? And if he has armed himself, isn't it precisely to defend that life he claims to hold so cheap? Upon closer inspection, this contradiction dissolves somewhat: it is *in war* that he scoffs at being killed, an eventuality so abstract, so distant, so little a threat that he does not even imagine some *external* enemy attacking France. And if he takes a certain amount of pleasure thinking about his "leaving," it is against those in his domestic circle, Hamard, Achille, Caroline, even his mother; a national duty that would force him to "breathe more freely"—that would be an unexpected piece of luck. And what luck it would be, as well, to die: according to a now familiar procedure, he settles into his future demise and considers his intimates with satisfied resentment: there is no doubt, they are the ones who killed him; their gibes and quibbling have so sickened him that he has lost the basic prudence every soldier must preserve if he wants to come home on two feet. So much for *foreign* war.

The rifle, by contrast, is destined for *civil* war. To die by a Prussian bullet, okay; but he will not let himself be lynched by the crowd, that mob he has unmasked *in advance* and whose stupid cruelty he has demonstrated: they are the ones who hunted down poor Marguerite and forced her to throw herself into the Seine. Gustave has *always* been afraid of the crowd; in October '48 he dreads its violence and sarcasm more than ever. A deep infantile fear whose source lies in his "anomaly." Although he owns property and has a private income, property is not the *first* thing he is defending against the socialists, but rather his right to regard his anomaly as a distinction and to de-

4. *Correspondance*, Supplément, 1:71.

rive a sense of superiority from his idiosyncratic inferiorities. The advent of the commoners is his condemnation. In other words, he cannot defend himself—despite himself—from a certain historic fatalism: if the populace wins, they *will be right*; the rifle is to *prevent them from winning*, to make them wrong. And of course he is much more aroused at the thought that property is threatened than at the institution of the Second Republic; for him, universal suffrage would *already* be the triumph of the multitude. But that is precisely because this provincial, absorbed by private cares and bereavements, hasn't understood the meaning of the Revolution. Later, after some reflection, he will put in place a historic scheme that will permit him to understand the events of '71 and, retrospectively, those of '48. The triumph of the common people is a result of the deficiency or crimes of a degenerate elite (whatever it is), and universal suffrage inevitably leads to the "Social State." In that summer of '48 the June massacres *have already determined everything*, but the countryside is in the throes of a green funk not unreminiscent of the Great Fear of 1789—except that the funk of '48 has *no object* and survives its reasons for being. At this time it's as if Gustave were overtaken by the contagious terror, were filled with fright and rage, and had intuited the political scheme—as if he had thought confusedly that defending the right to solitude, the right to be *different*, and property as a defensive shell all amounted to the same thing, but this time making no distinction between universal suffrage, which he conceived as the rule of all, and the collectivization of personal property, which becomes its fundamental truth and will eventually topple the walls that protect his solitude, the solitude of a trapped and wounded beast. In short, fear of the *socialists* colors his view of the February events: he will dream of it during the long silence of the Empire. And *L'Education sentimentale*—at least in its social and political aspect—will be the result of this long meditation on an event he did not experience.

For he can shine his boots and polish his weapon as much as he likes, he is not *highly* aroused. The end of the previously cited paragraph refers back to that tranquillity we know so well and reintroduces the themes he amply articulated, beginning in February '44, in the letters that speak of his "nervous illness." He is calm; is this numbness due to an excess of earlier sufferings (let us recall the Numideans and their hot coals and "the hand I burned"), or is it stoicism (recall the first letter after the attack at Pont-l'Evêque: "Nothing can either disturb me or touch me")? The fact is, "whatever happens now, it's is all the same to me, I am becoming philosophical" (remember what he wrote to Alfred: "I am becoming a brahman"). We know that he has two ways of describing his state: the terms are the same but the emphasis is different: I vibrate like the strings of a violin, *but* deep down I am marked by ataraxia; *I am indeed profoundly serene*, but everything agitates and exhausts me on the surface. This paragraph seems to offer us a simultaneous articulation of the two points of view confused in Gustave's habitual syncretism: so many bereavements, so many failures, so many betrayals, and his final choice of the game of "Loser Wins" have all made him insensitive to any possible private misfortunes—even ruin, he says elsewhere, *provided it is an individual misfortune in the framework of an economy based on private property*.[5] Ataraxia is a great calm gulf in the depths of his soul. The void, tedium: he fears nothing because he expects nothing. But this "provisional morality," which is inseparable from his neurosis, is something he was able to practice in his *personal* life: he forearmed himself in depth against his frustrations, the Father's curse, the triumph of the usurper Achille, the *literary* impotence that he believed he was threatened with. This provisional morality protected him only from his anguish, his fierce jealousies, and his angry spite, *all other things being equal;* for we must understand that in order to prove itself, this morality required the stability of the social environment and the reign of private property. He has not, however, armed himself against an overthrow of society; when he foresees that the social structures of France are about to break down, he is tormented because he imagines that under the new regime once again, unable to find *his* coordinates so patiently constructed on the basis of determined structures and institutions, he will no longer be definable, even in his own eyes, and will be left spinning in the indeterminate abyss of the "social state," like Smarh in the void where Satan let him go. So we find in Gustave two simultaneous attitudes: the tranquillity of the hermit—as long as he is allowed his hermitage—and the distraction of a monk who dreads that his monastery will be secularized. Which of the two predominates? My guess is sometimes one, sometimes the other. The calm can be superficial, the anguish at the regime's decline can be profound; the words he uses to calm himself, then, are ineffective because ill adapted. Since his inner calm involves social stability, it is clearly not credible that he can allay his

5. This, of course, is my addition. Besides, he is lying: the prospect of ruin horribly torments this man with a private income, for whom time is a process of degradation; and when it does happen—always foreseen and totally unexpected—it will be the death of him.

anxiety in the face of public events by saying to himself: "Bah! I've seen this before." His private misfortunes were "stoically endured" only in the framework of an immutable society. And if he claimed to withdraw from the bourgeoisie, it was on the basis his strengths alone, at the price of a meritorious and solitary conversion; but this was on the condition that the bourgeois class remain outside him and even within him, like the vulture of Prometheus feeding on his liver, thereby increasing his merit and at the same time delivering him from all material cares. So in a way his anguish wins the day: it is *beyond hope*. But from another angle, when we read his letter to the end and find in it such wild imprecations against the family—on this point it would seem at first that he is much less stoical—we realize that his anxiety in the face of the avatars of the Second Republic cannot be very deeply felt; he is too *occupied*, literally, with Hamard, with the Achilles, with his mother and little Caroline, to be really accessible. There is a certain amount of posturing in the paragraph I have cited. How much truer this sounds: "Now on that front, things are rather calm [the conflict with Hamard], but the moment they begin again in earnest, look out! Oh, the family, what a bloody nuisance! What a mess! What a ball and chain! How you get swallowed up in it and rot, buried alive! Why wasn't I born a bastard with 150,000,000 in private income . . . It is hardly the money I want (though I would be quite happy to have it) but freedom, not the political kind but I mean real freedom, the freedom of a bird or a savage."

A man so easily tormented cannot indulge in private concerns *at the same time* as public ones, for the latter serve as a restful diversion from the former. And then, when he dreams—with what abstract violence!—of being a millionaire bastard, he reveals to us that deep down he does not *really* believe in the imminent advent of socialism. When a property owner senses a threat of appropriation gliding above his head, when he is convinced that the reign of private property is about to disappear, he can busy himself all day and wildly seek ways to save his goods, but he cannot seriously think of increasing them. To picture things this way, we would have to reverse the relation: Flaubert, exasperated by family difficulties, finds his ataraxia just then in his relation to the historical moment, and the reason for it is that as a provincial deprived of social imagination, he has not witnessed events and has not even the means of *inventing* them with enough force to be aroused. To which must be added that other motive: everyone—everyone who is *anyone*, of course—in Normandy is afraid; the gentry of Rouen, detested as much as the workers if not more so, "are deeply disturbed, deeply affected . . . , pale." Gustave's attitude is dictated by the need to resist the temptation to share their base cowardice, so he shores himself up against fear.

In short, the Little Fear of '48 hardly touches him, inducing confused, contradictory feelings. History is merely the backdrop to his family drama. He takes no clearcut position, neither with the gentry against the rabble nor with the rabble against the property owners; nor does he stand with the republicans or the conservatives. He's against them all, but feebly. He dismisses both commoners and bourgeoisie. Indeed, this hermit is consumed by his private cares and savagely apolitical (What will the new government do *for art?*—that is the only thing he's curious about. Yet that curiosity itself is quite mild, for he already knows the answer: *nothing*); he missed the February rendez-vous, perhaps because he had made his revolution in advance. We shall see. In any case, this neurotic who demands a hierarchical society in which he is protected against the masses by the Satanic power of the Prince of Darkness, of the Father, certainly cannot accommodate himself to the Republic.

Louis Bonaparte, by contrast, seems more amusing. For a curious reason: Gustave thinks he may be the Garçon incarnate. Flaubert left France in October; after a long journey through the Middle East, he returns in May '51 to find himself under the rule of the Prince-President. The misanthrope in him delights in the humbling of the French: "I feel as much a stranger amidst my countrymen as I did in Numibia, and I am seriously beginning to admire the Prince-President, who grinds our noble France under the heel of his boot. I would even kiss his behind to thank him personally if there were not such a crowd waiting to do the same." [6] Louis-Napoleon does not stay fixed in this position but quickly assumes the role of *demoralizer* that Flaubert wanted to play some years earlier: "I read of the travels of the Prince-President—truly splendid. What one really needs to do (and he does it extremely well) is to have no more ideas, no more respect for anything. If all morality is useless to societies of the future, which will be organized as mechanical functions and no longer need a soul, he is paving the way (I am serious, I think that is his mission). As humanity perfects itself, man degrades himself." The Garçon in power—what a rare windfall! Or perhaps he is a reincarnation of Nero, the callous emperor whose role Flaubert so often took pleasure in playing out of sadism, making imaginary heads roll by raising an

6. To Louise, 30 May 1852, *Correspondance*, 2:428.

eyebrow. This angry young man sees the events preceding the coup d'état as a vast enterprise of national demoralization and the debasement of the human race. Of the coup itself he says not a word. It is true that at the beginning of December 1852 he was terrified: Louise had informed him that she feared she might be pregnant; she disabused him only on the 11th. Be that as it may, Gustave's sole allusion to the replacement of the Republic by a reign of personal power comes three months later, on 22 April 1853: "When genius is lacking, will replaces it to a certain degree. Napoleon III is no less an emperor than his uncle was."[7] This remark, indeed, is introduced in a commentary by Buffon's aphorism: "Genius is merely a long patience." Blasphemy, says Flaubert, but not without some truth. Naturally—and the context proves it—Gustave is thinking in particular of art, consequently of himself. In the absence of genius, patience can produce a masterpiece, as witness Louis-Napoleon, who without any of his uncle's qualities has created the Second Empire. So here we find this Bonaparte compared to Flaubert, even representing him, his incarnation in another domain—the political arena where Gustave does not deign to descend—and we find his unfortunate coup compared to a literary masterpiece. This is clear evidence that the forced coup had astounded Flaubert. This wholly unexpected comparison of art and politics is pursued and specified in detail, at the beginning of 1854, in a letter of surprising incoherence:

> Hide your life—Abstain. The respectable man is he who is surprised by nothing . . . In following those ideas one stands firm in life and Art. Don't you feel that everything is now dissolved in *relaxation* . . . in tears, in chitchat . . . Contemporary literature is drowning. We must all strengthen our resolve to get rid of the Gothic chlorosis we've inherited from Rousseau, Chateaubriand, and Lamartine. This explains Badinguet's success. That fellow focused on one thing. He did not waste his energy in trivial, diversionary acts. He was like a heavy, relentless cannonball, headed straight for his goal. All at once he exploded, and everyone trembled. If old Hugo had imitated him, he might have done in poetry what Badinguet did in politics, something truly original. But not he, he let his whinings get the better of him. Passion dooms us all.[8]

The peculiar comparison of Hugo and the emperor can be explained *historically*. Louise acted as messenger for the exiled Hugo; Gustave

7. To Louise, *Correspondance*, 3:180.
8. To Louise, January 1854, *Correspondance*, 4:12.

helped her rather grudgingly. He had recently received two poems from *Les Châtiments*, accompanied by a letter from the *Crocodile*. One of the poems ("Stella") struck him as "fine," the other visibly irritated him as "stupid." Hugo's whinings are, of course, his political writings; the passion that dooms him is his hatred of Napoleon-le-petit. Nonetheless, Gustave always considered him a "Master," the greatest of the century, and after the Commune, when Hugo incurred the insults of the press—he had demanded amnesty for the Communards—Flaubert vigorously defended him *as a poet* against Raoul-Duval, one of his closest friends. His opinion on the exile can be summed up as follows: a great poet who made the mistake of holding political opinions as stupid as they were humanitarian. If he could have purged himself of his passions, achieved Flaubertian impassivity, he might have equalled the greatest poets of all time, even Shakespeare. And this is the man, this giant of letters, whom Gustave calmly and maliciously compares to his worst enemy, Napoleon III. In addition, the emperor succeeded in doing the kind of original work *in politics* that the other might have created *in literature,* had he known how to *limit himself* to the literary realm. Superiority therefore belongs to the emperor. Though not entirely. The art of manipulating men is, in any event, so inferior to that of manipulating words that it is more admirable to be a Hugo who sometimes misses his real mark than a Bonaparte who scores every time. Despite this hierarchy, which concerns only their arenas of action, it is still the case, taking them for what they are—two men defined by two enterprises—that the poet has failed where the politician has succeeded. Why? Well, he has managed to *limit himself*. A matter of long patience. But above all he has refused to be distracted. Buffon's definition becomes clear. Or, rather, we distinguish more clearly the way Flaubert interprets it. It should rather be said that genius is an obsession. Let it keep you continually occupied, let it free you from your internal pluralisms, from your resistances, from your superfluous tastes, let it concentrate and define you as a *program for life,* let it become the unique opinion, the principle of all selection, the unique destination, and then it will generate its own means of realization; the end will produce and define its intermediary moments from the depths of the future.

Flaubert knowingly defines himself by that obsession, which is the subjection of man to his enterprise. That may be why the Goncourts repeatedly sensed in him the secret dream of a frog who would have liked to make himself as big as Hugo. There is no doubt, in any case, that he recognizes Napoleon III as his brother in obstinacy. The Empire, an "original" political solution, is the equivalent of the literary coup d'état that Gustave, at the same period, was patiently refining. Undoubtedly the police officer prevailed through terror; he "suddenly burst upon the scene and everyone trembled." But Flaubert certainly doesn't resent him for it: hasn't he dreamed a hundred times, doesn't he still dream, of *inspiring fear?* And who did the trembling?—the populace and the bourgeois republicans, those harbingers of socialism. The reign of personal power is not at all displeasing to this solitary, excluded from the family and from his social setting because of his anomaly, who used to dream of avenging himself by imposing himself on everyone—either by launching his hordes against France, like Tamberlaine, or by making men jump into the frying pan of style. Isn't the artist at this time a solitary worker whose works, coolly but cunningly arranged, deftly condition the public and release in them all the passions—still imaginary but violent—that the author has denied? This is a *reign,* too, though the writer may be a capricious king who scorns and rejects his subjects, or sadistically accepts them only to lead them to despair. The comparison of the great writer exercising tyranny through the dictatorship of style, and the cold, solitary dictator of a police state presents itself to Flaubert quite naturally in 1854. As early as August '53 he let out the secret of his misanthropy: "Humanity despises us, we do not serve it, and we hate it because it hurts us."[9] However, his hatred of man—which is counterviolence, since he thinks the first violence was done to him by the human race—can be momentarily eclipsed; a month of sequestration, some flattering encounters, a conversation with "people in the arts" are enough to make him forget it a little. And he is convinced that this sole passion—the a priori of the artistic sensibility—is necessary to the impassivity of art, it is the effective structure of the *obsession.* The artist is all the more impassive before the catastrophes that ravage the people the more he despises the human race. A certain pleasure in hatred is not without its uses, in this case; it can easily be changed into aesthetic pleasure, and the artist will enjoy *contemplating* the bloody jolts of the hated beast, applying himself to rendering them through a work whose style will fix them in the absolute. Hatred would therefore be one of the sources of art. If this is true, the artist must never be distracted from it, on pain of miscarrying. "Modern torpor comes from the unlimited respect man has for himself." Therefore, from the "humanism" of the rich and the professional

9. To Louise, *Correspondance,* 3:294.

elite, as well as from the "religion of humanity" practiced by the positivists and—in an almost identical way—by the followers of Saint-
Simon; and quite as much, if not more, from the romantic politicians,
socialists, "Forty-eighter" idealists, from all those who proclaim that
man is the future of man, that the human species has no end but
itself, in short to assure the reign of man over conquered nature.

The ideal that Flaubert contests, which he judges harmful to art, is
the naive and spontaneous struggle undertaken under Louis-Philippe
to liberate man from whatever separates him from himself, that is,
from all *alienation* (alienations, indeed, are often more quickly revealed to a sudden critical consciousness than are the infrastructural
givens—exploitation, for example—that condition them). Gustave,
as we have seen, wants to escape his familial alienations and screams
this out by *subjecting himself to art*, that is, by presenting it as a nonhuman end, as an inhuman and ultimately antihuman imperative; he
cannot conceive of humanity establishing itself for its own sake and
attempting to define its task as the dissolution of the Other in the
bosom of the Same. Ruled and cursed by the Other, Gustave can admit man only insofar as his essence is outside him, in a cruel Other
who scorns and devours him. "I love to see humanity and everything
it respects cut down, ridiculed, disgraced, hooted at. That is why I
have some tenderness for asceticism." Here we find, reintroduced
obliquely, that minor asceticism which is the distinction or tyrannical
detestation of the other in oneself. Again, what's needed is a *visible*
society, which through its institutions and its customs shows man
subjected to counter-man. "I am thankful to Badinguet. God bless
him! He led me to scorn the masses and hate anything popular. That
is a safeguard against baseness in this time of rampant vulgarity. Who
knows? Perhaps now I shall write more clearly and trenchantly what
may be the only moral protest of my era." In other words, Gustave
reproaches himself—very gently—for having lacked vigilance in '48;
for a time he accepted the Republic—without enthusiasm, true, but
without protest. He reproaches himself for having indicated by his
indifference that he considered universal suffrage merely one regime
among others, neither better nor worse, and which in any case could
not be lower than the Orléanist monarchy, while in fact at issue was
the reign of the ignoble, which must be avoided at any price. Napoleon III *recalls* him to his scorn for the masses, just as Louise *recalls*
him to his pride by refusing to show *Bretagne* to Gautier. He took
power by force, and far from fighting for the Republic, the rabble gave
him a plebiscite, proving that they were made for slavery and that

425

they *deserved* this self-imposed head of state. As a result, Napoleon—who seems to Flaubert a composite of the Garçon and de Sade—is found to be perfectly justified: he came *at the propitious moment* to represent for the crowd *alienation* and *demoralization;* for Flaubert, power—the most effective form of action—is tolerable only if it is employed systematically to destroy, to degrade, to debase. If the world is hell, the worthiest sovereign takes his power only from some diabolic right—divine right in reverse; he must be, in one way or another, a hypostasis of Satan. And that is what Flaubert likes in Badinguet, I would even say it is what he respects in him: whether he likes it or not, the Emperor will play the role of Antichrist, of Antibourgeois, of Antipeople, he will be the exterminating angel. When Gustave "foams" at the mouth, nauseated by an article by Pelletan in the *Revue de Paris,* he no longer invokes the Devil, or Tamberlaine, or the Huns, but the Emperor: "If the Emperor suppressed printing tomorrow, I would make a trip to Paris on my knees and go to kiss his ass as a sign of acknowledgment, so weary am I of typography and the way it is abused." [10] We see, in effect, what he expects of Badinguet: at once the public exercise of evil and a kind of cultural revolution in reverse, in which the great liquidation of bourgeois and popular values, implemented at random by the caprices of an Ubu, might allow—though completely negative—a glimpse of an *elsewhere,* the possibility of a new beginning *for others,* and for Flaubert the radical impossibility of being man. I would not be exaggerating to say that Napoleon III, as Gustave conceives of him between the coup d'état and 1857, plays the same role in the Flaubertian *Weltanschauung* as Caligula did in the absurd world of Camus *before* 1945. What I mean is that while the two universes are different in every way, the relation of the imperial figure to the cosmic totality is in both cases almost identical. He is the revealer, the denunciator and the realizer of the human condition as abjection or absurdity, he is the one who brings scandal, who reveals the pure and essential shock of living to the arrogant and dismal Senators, to the pious bourgeois of rue de Poitiers; he is the one who, through his omnipotence, systematically ridiculing *people,* reveals that human *dignity* is an ignoble farce. In short, he has a mission to transform his reign into a work of art by tightening the always somewhat slack bonds of daily life in such a way as to radicalize the impossibility of living on the level of experience and force it unceasingly down the throats of all his subjects. I

10. *Correspondance,* 3–261.

will not say that in 1854 Gustave had the tenderness for Napoleon III that Camus felt for Caligula, for Flaubert is not tender; even when his characters are his spokesmen and his incarnations, he remains highly ambivalent toward them, and this is because he does not like himself. Still, this savage Antichrist amuses him. Or he is amused to see the Antichrist in Badinguet. At the same time, of course, he does not deprive himself of the pleasures of irony. When Dieudonné Bellemare fires two shots at the Emperor—without success—Flaubert pretends to be indignant, deploring the latest assassination attempt by such a "monster." "Thank God we have preserved him for the happiness of France. What is more deplorable is that this wretch is from Rouen. He is a dishonor to the town. We no longer dare say we're from Rouen." These rather heavy-handed pleasantries, the reference to Rouen, the labored irony of this "thanksgiving," all prove that Gustave, who was quite amused at the time by the pranks of the crowned Garçon, would have viewed the sovereign's disappearance with indifference.

For some time now, as a matter of fact, Napoleon III had not been entirely in conformity with Flaubert's constructed image. The Antichrist—like every dictator—took some time groping for the mainstays of the regime; during that period his speeches were pleasing to Flaubert—he was still only Prince-President. For Louis-Napoleon put a little of everything into them—including professions of socialist faith—in such a way that all his ideas contradicted each other and cancelled each other out even as they were articulated, just as they would do later in *Bouvard et Pécuchet*. But the goal of the Prince-President was not to create these delightful short-circuits—which for Gustave disqualified any political principle. At the outset he wanted to bring about unity through vagueness, through ambiguity. As Emperor, he was struck by the power of real property and the Catholic circles that represented it. He had to satisfy them if he wanted to accelerate industrialization. He began to play up to them rather early: the Church in particular became the dominant force in the arts and letters, and more generally on every cultural front. Instead of systematic demoralization, Flaubert perceives that his Nero is asking the intellectuals to institute a moral order. Which effectively strips the writers of nothingness of the sole freedom they claim, the freedom, in their work, to obey only the imperatives of art. More profoundly, the military and police dictatorship necessarily produces an embryo of optimistic ideology that is easily wedded to Catholic optimism. Flaubert, who unwittingly represents the pessimism of the middle

427

classes, feels directly threatened in his nihilism, that is, *in his being*. A short while later, moreover, his fears are justified when the regime thrice puts its intellectuals on trial: the Goncourts, Gustave himself, and Baudelaire are dragged before tribunals.

Flaubert will never forgive the government for making him appear before a court of summary jurisdiction. On the eve of the trial, he writes to Doctor Cloquet: "You will be able, by way of example, to cite [to the Emperor] my trial as one of his regime's most inept acts of turpitude."[11] But rereading this angry sentence attentively, we perceive that it is aimed at the regime and not the sovereign. To be sure, he is not *acquitted:* he has all the power, therefore he is responsible. However, the sentence indicates that Gustave reproaches him rather for being ill-informed; he still hopes that Napoleon III, once aware of the excesses of the priestly party, will have the firm will to put an end to it. So we see him conceive for the first time a *political* idea that he will subsequently develop: the regime of personal power, demonic in its essence, antibourgeois on principle since it cannot continue to exist without becoming strictly hierarchical from top to bottom, is, to state it baldly, the only kind of regime suitable to artists, or at least the only kind that does them no harm; and it is not the empire they must contest but its chosen supporters; he will fight *for* the dictatorship and *against* the clergy. The Emperor must not be the prisoner of his majority, he will say. Certainly beginning with the trial, the tone changes: he rarely speaks of "Badinguet" without an affectation of irony, sometimes even of contempt. But in the following years he will be received at Princess Mathilde's, at the Tuileries, he will spend fifteen days at Compiègne and receive the Croix d'Honneur. How did he live those eighteen years that separate the coup of 2 December from the insurrection of 4 September? The collapse of '44 made Gustave a fossil: his youth was dead, leaving only an impassive gaze. But how did this fossil adapt to the Empire, born of the collapse of the Republic? He came to it more dead than alive. But what did the new society make of him? Did its animating movement carry this inert thinker along without breathing life into him, or did the social milieu sustain him, nourish and revive him? The second hypothesis prompts us to wonder if Flaubert's neurosis is perhaps oracular, for it designates and claims the regime of personal power as the only one in which the young neurotic might *live*, in every sense of the term,

11. *Correspondance*, 4:156. Ten years later, having been decorated, he writes to a woman friend that, even so, he has not forgotten the offense of 1857.

that inert eternity he calls his aristocracy and which is the basis of his aesthetic attitude.

In order to know whether the hermit of Croisset and the society around him had, as he often declares, merely a relation of contiguity, or whether their apparent coexistence was not in fact a profound symbiosis, that is, whether Gustave was *made for the Empire* at a time when the Empire could not be foreseen, we cannot rely on Flaubert's positive confidences. We've known for a long time that he admits nothing. We must have recourse, as always with him, to the *negative.* In other words, as long as the regime is still standing, everything Gustave *says* about it is unreliable; as for what he *does*, the "compromises" that will prompt later reproach and cause Louise Colet to call him "Napoleon's valet," any meaning remains obscure unless we examine these actions under a new light—as we shall attempt to do. In contrast, when the Empire crumbles, when it is succeeded by the Commune, the Prussian occupation, and the Third Republic, Flaubert's reactions are highly significant. Again we find this survivor by vocation once more surviving a society; how is he going to enter the new society? Dead or alive? If he adapted to it, was it because it too was the object of his prophecies, that he defined it implicitly by his program for life? And if he could not adapt to it, wouldn't we be inclined to regard this lag an index of his finitude? In this case, the Third Republic would not be part of the program; the oracular neurosis would find its accomplishment only in the Second Empire, and the regime born of the events of 4 September would cause Flaubert's *social death* ten years before his physical death. That is, Gustave's adaptation to the new historical totalization would be purely synchronic; tossed from one moment to another, the man would have lost his diachronic relation to macrocosmic history.

Between 1870 and the end of 1871, Flaubert's reactions are erratic and violent; he declares he had never suffered so much, wonders how the sorrow hasn't killed him, reverts to his suicidal inclinations. In November '72, calm has long since been restored, the Prussians have departed, the Communards crushed, the moral order established. He then writes to Turgenev: "Since 1870 I have become a patriot. Seeing my country perish, I realized I loved it. Prussia can disarm. We can die without her help."

The rest of the letter, however, is highly ambiguous:

The *Social State* overwhelms me. Yes, it's true . . . Public Stupidity overwhelms me . . . The Bourgeoisie . . . doesn't even have the instinct to defend itself, and what follows will be worse. I feel the sadness of the Roman patricians of the fourth century. I feel the unstoppable Barbarians rising out of the earth. I hope to be dead before they have borne everything away . . . Never have intellectual interests counted for less. Never has the hatred of all greatness, the disdain for the Beautiful, the execration of literature been so evident . . . I can no longer talk with anyone, and I am infuriated by everything I read that is contemporary.[12]

He "despairs of France," prefers the Commune (because it belongs to the past) to the regime that succeeded it: "The Commune did not make me despair of France as much as what now exists. The convulsions of a raging madman are less hideous than the maunderings of an old idiot."[13] The old idiot is the clerical and royalist reaction. Reading this passage, one wonders if it is really patriotism that made Flaubert an "angry young man," as he calls himself, or if his fury and his despair are not motivated by the regret for a vanished era that would be, in sum, "*his time*"; and one wonders as well if, for example, beneath the previously cited line (in the letter to Turgenev) another message might not be deciphered. It would involve changing just a few words: "Seeing the imperial regime perish, I realized I loved it." To settle the question, we must examine the Correspondence and several testimonies that give us the complete record of his reactions to the public misfortunes from July 1870 until the end of June '71. Do these express—even negatively—a profound and suddenly declared attachment to the Motherland?

For several years now a confrontation between France and Prussia could be foreseen, in which the stake would be hegemony over continental Europe. Flaubert knows this, it is mentioned to him, he cannot entirely plug up his ears; but he refuses to see the imminence of war, even as an eventuality: no sooner is it evoked than he categorically thrusts it aside. In 1866, after a speech at Auxerre in which the Emperor claims to be the guardian of order and peace, Gustave exults: "I have always thought that *there would not be war*."[14] Then a brief but respectful nod to Isidore: "Well, I personally believe the Emperor

12. *Correspondance*, Supplément, 3:62.
13. Ibid., 3:68: Thiers had asked for a vote of confidence: 263 for, 116 against, 277 abstentions. The Royalists, at the time, formed the majority of the Assembly.
14. At issue was the conflict that threatened to erupt between Austria and Italy. The public—including Flaubert—did not know if France would commit itself to Italy's side in this war, and so it was not known what Prussia's position would be. In the same letter, Flaubert is delighted at the interview in Biarritz, which reunited those political sages, Napoleon III and Bismarck.

is stronger than ever." He also *believes* in the value of the French Army: "If we make war, we shall come out of it with the Rhine." He even *believes* in the genius of Badinguet with regard to foreign policy: "The Emperor holds Austria under his boot, and so far, with respect to foreign policy, I consider him enormously strong, whatever they say."[15] The French annoy him, he writes a few months later, because they are "fearful idiots: fearful of Prussia." At the last Magny dinner, stupidity is pushed to the limit: the only subject of conversation is politics. "All that mattered was Monsieur de Bismarck and Luxembourg."[16] The result is a double emotional reaction, typically Flaubertian: on one hand, a private and negative vow (rupture)—"I swore not to set foot there again"—and, on the other, a general condemnation of French society—"France, which was seized for a time with Saint Vitus' dance (as it was under Charles VI), now seems to be suffering from paralysis of the brain."[17] He refers to it again in a letter dated from 1867 (no further specification) and addressed to the princess Mathilde: "As for the fear Prussia inspires in French fools, I confess I do not understand it and feel, for my part, humiliated by it."[18] And here he is, in March 1868, instructing his niece in politics: "Everyone hurls abuse at the government, which doesn't stop me from believing in its solidity for the following reason: there is no rallying cry, no common idea, no flag of any kind to gather around." An argument well known to the Gaullists; the partisans of dictatorship defend it negatively by opposing the unity of its politics to the fragmentation and impotence of the opposition, which, should it triumph by some miracle, would plunge us into chaos. This indirect argument, leaving open the possibility of *condemning* the regime—as bad as it may be one *must* preserve it or sink into anarchy—must have been

15. All these citations are taken from a letter of May 1866 to Caroline (*Correspondance,* 5:214–16). Flaubert is expressing himself here quite freely, and we can neither regard as oratorical precautions the marks of respect he directs to the "Emperor" nor attribute to prudence his professions of political faith.

16. Much later, Goncourt polemicized with Renan: "I never said that Monsieur Renan rejoiced in the German victories or that he found them legitimate; but I said that he would consider the German race superior to the French . . . Well, for God's sake, the prevailing taste during the two or three years before the war, the taste of our great French thinkers for Germany was no secret to anyone, and the diners at Magny during those years had drummed into them the superiority of German science, the superiority of the German chambermaid, the superiority of German sauerkraut, etc., etc., and finally the superiority of the Prussian princess over all princesses on earth." *Journal,* vol. 10 (Editions de Monaco).

17. To George Sand. *Correspondance,* 5:282.

18. *Correspondance,* 5:332.

particularly pleasing to Flaubert. He specifies that "the question is no longer political, and a change of government would not resolve it." The *"only important thing,"* in his opinion, is to fight against clericalism. We have already seen what this meant: to keep the Emperor and modify the majority "whose prisoner he is." And abruptly, unexpectedly, we find this sweep of the pen: "As for war, with whom? With Prussia? Prussia is not so stupid!" Such a blunder is surprising. But Flaubert is an oracle only when he is playing the prophet of misfortune. The surprising thing is rather his stubborn refusal to resume his great role of Cassandra, which brought him such unequivocal and lasting success. Everything beckoned him to it, since, as he notes in the same letter: "The 'political horizon' is darkening." The ironic quotation marks are reserved for the cliché that is the subject of the statement. There are none for the verb, which is nonetheless a Prudhommesque stereotype as well. Flaubert really thinks that the evil is growing worse. What evil? Well, the opposition *to the regime* (which he euphemistically calls government). Consequently his thought reveals to us its implicit meaning: if the evil is the opposition—which by definition denounces the vices of the system and predicts, by way of logical consequence, an imminent disaster (which it alone can prevent provided it takes power)—then *the opposition* will play Cassandra. And all the more so because in the proposed alternative—run to the abyss or give us the power—the partisans of the regime do not know which outcome strikes them as more abhorrent. For them, if "the worst is always certain," there is no real choice: *first* will come disaster, and on the ruin of the country the triumph of the adversary party.

Whatever their ordinary disposition, then, they are constrained to profess optimism. In the case we are now considering, the paradox is profound. The bourgeoisie surrendered to the Emperor out of fear, out of hatred of man, because its experience in '48 taught it that the social order can be maintained only by repression. In sum—as we have seen—its choice of personal power is a declaration of pessimism. Precisely for this reason, Flaubert, whose pessimism dates from long before the February revolution, could rally around the Empire; the Emperor, to the extent that he embodied bourgeois certainty that the worst, in social relations, is always certain, seemed to him an Antichrist, the political equivalent of an artist. Gustave did not want to see that Napoleon III held his power from the bourgeois; in any case, he persuaded himself that this Nero-de Sade exercised the authority they acknowledged *against them*. As a result, he finds himself, like all the partisans of the imperial regime, forced into optimism to keep his faith in the future of a system to which his own pessimism drew him, and which he continues to sustain even as he has never ceased to regard the world as hell. This evil which requires and produces the good as the sole means of assuring its perpetuation, this good which, in consequence, attenuates or deviates the effects of the evil that produces it and is protected by it—might not this strange vicious circle be the accomplishment dreamed of by the prevailing evil power: to debase an entire society and destroy it? But this is the very thing that must *not* happen if the reign of the Evil One is to continue. Thus Prussia will not make war, or will lose the war if there is one. This is how we explain Flaubert's rages: he is only too tempted, by nature, to lend an ear to those who "hurl abuse" and, to an even greater extent, to adopt their declarations and carry them to an extreme. But now he execrates the prophets of misfortune he meets in Paris, being unable either to validate or to invalidate their assertions. We find the simple and profound reason for this attitude *in the same letter*, a few lines above: "Last evening I was so exhausted that I left my Princess in the lurch; this evening I am going to the concert at the home of her cousin the Emperor."[19] What has been happening for several years now is that Gustave's allegiance to the regime—at first a simple inner determination, a subjective and ludic acquiescence to an imaginary Antichrist—has changed in nature: Flaubert frequents the salon of Princess Mathilde, he is received at Saint-Gratien, at Compiègne, at the Tuileries. Of course, he hasn't been bought off; but this loner is not so uncomfortable at Court; the Goncourts will reproach him for his servility, and after the defeat Louise Colet will accuse him quite unjustly of having fawned over Napoleon III. The fact is that the sovereign rectified his mistake of 1857 and *distinguished* Flaubert; he is incontestably the great writer of the Second Empire simply because, as a great writer, he published nothing before the coup d'état, and for the not so simple reason that the Emperor enhances the artist's glory by recognizing it and appropriating it, using it for public relations purposes, and presents Flaubert to public opinion as if he were the product of the regime. The Empire becomes a matter of personal interest to Saint Polycarp.

The more so as our anchorite makes his debut in the "world" when the republican opposition has just reconstituted itself. No longer of importance, of course, are the "forty-eighters," his elders, who are

19. Ibid., p. 360.

433

either senile or defeated: under the liberal Empire, the political conflict overlays a conflict of generations; it is the young people who do
not support personal power.[20] Born in the 1840s, they did not see
their father's humiliating defeat. What they condemn in '67 is not the
bloody Republic that failed to turn into the Social State but, quite the
opposite—the reaction that followed, in short, Papa's infectious cowardice. Twenty years their elder, Flaubert knows they will establish
the future. If that future is republican, the author of *Madame Bovary*
will have no place in it. Absolute-art, pessimism, and the Empire—
everything is connected in some obscure way, he is sure, it's all bound
together; the dictatorship must endure or Gustave is ejected from history. As for those angry young men who will survive him, he feels
their very existence is pushing him toward decrepitude and death; his
enforced optimism allows his anguish to surface from time to time:
what if he were to be *forgotten while still alive?* Cassandra is not far off
when he writes to George Sand in 1867: "The men of our generation
have become real fossils for the young people of today. The reaction
of '48 created a gulf between the two versions of France." He is then
at the height of his fame, but even so, when he wants to speak of his
contemporaries, of himself, the word "fossil" is what comes to mind.
We shall find this word again, ten, twenty times. After 4 September,
in hate-filled and despairing tirades. In '67 the tone is calm; we might
think it's a simple observation, made with amused detachment. But
this myth of fossilization—which will become clearer after the defeat—translates a chronic malaise from its first appearance. Flaubert
feels compromised by his fame and by the sovereign who consecrates
him; it encloses him in the present; for that present to remain eternal,
the perpetuity of the Empire must be *desired*. But for Gustave, the
word "to desire" has only one meaning: to believe. Therefore he believes hysterically, desperately, that the regime is solid, and—since
the sole truly dreadful threat, in his eyes, is military defeat—he persuades himself that there will be no war, that Prussia cannot imagine
making war, that it is not stupid enough to take on the invincible
French Army.

We can easily imagine his stupor and his peevishness upon waking
up and perceiving that the conflict is inevitable. He expresses his

20. The typical representative of this new generation is Georges Clemenceau. But
Clemenceau admired his father and inherited his taste for practical truth as well as his
vocation of physician. Curiously but not fortuitously, the young man's political career
began in the dark days when Flaubert was convinced he would end his literary career
with a disaster; Clemenceau was elected deputy to the Assembly of Bordeaux.

horror in advance at the "appalling butchery in the making," and pushes prophetic indignation to the point of "weeping for the broken bridges, the smashed tunnels, all that human labor lost." We recognize that he has not accustomed us to such respect for works of civil genius or industrial labor. This is proof that he is keeping quiet, or trying to keep quiet, about the real reasons for his outrage. Curiously, it is occasioned by the French: "The good Frenchman wants to fight, first, because he believes he is provoked by Prussia. Second, because the natural state of man is savagery. Third, because war in itself contains a mystical element that transports the crowd." That, above all, is what exasperates him—"hats off to the gun." This empty enthusiasm hasn't a single idea behind it. He'd rather die than see more of it. The conclusion is a double judgment: he condemns "the stupidity of my compatriots" and the "irremediable barbarity of humanity."

This bitter exposé seems suspect. Why does the Frenchman *believe* he is provoked by the king of Prussia? Wasn't there any Prussian provocation? Any trap? Is Bismarck entirely innocent? And what about that "human butchery"? Did he get so worked up by the Italian and Mexican slaughters? Hasn't he written that the sufferings of his contemporaries moved him no more than the sufferings of the slaves of antiquity? Why would the massacres he dreads move him more than the Punic Wars? He has been convinced of the stupidity of the French since childhood; since childhood he has stigmatized the barbarity of humanity—and not without some pleasure. How will he make us believe that he has just discovered our defects? Furthermore, since man's natural state is savagery, here is an excellent occasion to show himself a *defeatist*, or rather confirm himself in his anchorite's impassivity: *Homo homini lupus.* Winners and losers alike will be wolves. Therefore, let us think no more about it.

But he does think about it, he does nothing but think about it. He is "won over by public anguish"; his "heart is wrung in a surprising way." He prophesies: "We are entering *darkness*." He does not restrain himself from teaching George Sand a lesson: "There you have *natural man*. Go spin your theories now! Vaunt progress, the reason and good sense of the masses, and the kindness of the French people. I assure you that here you would get flattened if you took it into your head to preach peace." A horrified Cassandra has a vision—always right when it is sad—of future wars, "a war of the races" in which "many millions of men will kill each other in one bout." Sometimes he tries to persuade himself—without much success—that the Germans will lose the war: "Perhaps Prussia will

435

receive a good thrashing, which was part of the design of Providence to reestablish European equilibrium." And sometimes he predicts the French defeat: "This people may deserve to be chastised, and I am afraid it will be."

Why all these outcries? Patriotism? His first impulse is to escape among foreigners: "Ah, why can't I live with the Bedouins?" And the hatred he vows toward his compatriots touches on madness. He spends two days in Paris and returns sickened: "Now I know the Parisian deep down, and in my heart I have made excuses for the most savage politics of 1793." He may remember this appeal to the Terror when he writes in June '71 that the treachery of the Parisians makes him inclined to admire the Commune. Certainly from the first days of the war, the theme of vomiting—which will be somatized after the defeat—makes its appearance: "My compatriots make me want to vomit." What is it about them that so violently nauseates him? That incurable "barbarity" of man, his homicidal impulses, a fanatic chauvinism? Not at all; it is their bellicose thoughtlessness, their certainty of winning; they think they are in the era of parlor warfare.

What stunned him, in fact, was that when the war finally seemed inevitable, he abruptly rediscovered what his optimism had been hiding from him. Since 1866 he had stubbornly pushed aside any possibility of a conflict with Prussia, which, after Sadowa, revealed itself to him for what it *was:* the most formidable military power in Europe. When in 1867 he swore never again to attend the Magny dinners, it was not so much politics that repulsed him as the guests' timorous admiration for Herr von Bismarck. And their evocation of the Luxembourg affair and the threats of war. For this man of the imaginary, Prussia is realism, the real. While the Empire was discrediting itself with the crazy Mexican expedition and Maximilian's lamentable end, while Napoleon III's foreign policy was revealing its almost oneiric unreality, Bismarck's "precise, rigorous," and, as they were beginning to say, "scientific" foreign policy was impressing more than one of them, especially Renan, who voluntarily predicts that a unified Germany is easily going to dominate Europe. This is intolerable to Flaubert; this is why he retires, profoundly shaken, to the solitude of Croisset and stubbornly repeats that war will not occur, that no one wants it, that Prussia "is not so stupid." He begins to convince himself that in case of conflict, France would be lost, which for him means, first, the disaster threatened by the opposition; second, the fall of the Empire; third, the advent of the Republic; fourth, the triumph of science over the dream; fifth, the accession to power of those positive and serious young men who have fossilized him in advance. In a word, his historic death or, if you will, his purely biological survival in a society that excludes him. What he *believed* to be impossible, *France*'s mad declaration of war on Prussia, makes him suddenly aware that he has been asleep on his feet for twenty years, and that he has been sleepwalking toward the abyss with the rest of imperial society. Napoleon III's decision is the last dream of the Empire, and it may be Gustave's last dream as well; the very criminal frivolity of this country that gaily commits itself to massacre for its own sake provides him with proof that the French armies will be beaten. How can anyone believe they will prevail, those imbeciles who "believe they are being provoked" by Prussia and are falling into the trap? This war should never have been waged, it should have been avoided at all costs since we were certain to lose. The evidence hits him with full force: Cassandra, resurrected, rediscovers the old fatalities that governed his life and the lives of his compatriots: failure as destiny. But this time it is no longer a question of "Loser Wins" but quite the opposite. To the extent that failure was an option in '44, a perverted choice to find glory in the depths of voluntary abjection, what he prophesies in 1870 might be called *the failure of failure*, a flat denial of his enterprise without the least compensation, a dead loss, a pure and simple abolition of the being he gave himself. And would we want him to love France? How could he fail to hate it when the government it chose is deliberately running headlong to its ruin and at the same time stripping Flaubert of his reasons for living by revealing to all eyes the criminal vanity of illusion. If the Parisians make him want to vomit, *it's because they are dreaming,* and they disqualify the dream since that dream, which ought to pull men away from reality, seems, on the contrary, like a ruse of the real, evoking it only to affirm itself by crushing it. If the Emperor had not pushed his dream so far as to take himself for a Caesar, the future vanquisher of Prussia, if his courtiers and ministers had not encouraged him to engage in the theater of war, if the "imperialists" had not wildly applauded, the brilliant society of the Second Empire would long have persevered in its oneirism, and Flaubert would have persevered in his. What infuriates the sleeper is that he has been awakened, and that daylight values will be the opposite of nocturnal ones. This abrupt explosion of hatred creates a profound conflict in Gustave; as is his habit, he ought to desire the shame and annihilation of the guilty. And this is what he does, in sum, when he writes of *his* populace (while detaching himself from them: "this populace . . .") that it deserves to be chastised. Adding: "I am afraid it will be." Afraid? We know Flaubert: this vaunted fear disguises a powerful desire; he wishes the French the worst humiliation. But at the same time, this wish terrifies him: he is in solidarity with the regime, and his particular dream is nourished by the collective dream. The chastisement of those wretches would be the collapse of the Empire and his own dismemberment. So quickly, off he goes again to dream: perhaps Providence has decided on the doom of Prussia. He hardly believes in this and remains tossed between hysterical hope that never quite *takes hold* and rancorous lucidity.

On 26 August 1870 he changes his mind. This fifty-and-some-year-old pacifist predicts the siege of Paris; he will take his gun and fire on the side of the Parisians. After several days the excitement abates, the gun is returned to the rack: "The siege of Paris is hardly likely." But for the first time he shows his rancor against the imperial family openly: "Good *riddance* to Prince Napoleon. We had some fine fellows governing us, let's face it!" Indeed, he has to face it, for he visited those fine fellows, among others Prince Napoleon. He hastens to add: "The Princess will stay in Paris. Until the end," to save his protectress from fate. After Sedan ("What a bashing, eh? But I think we are going to make a comeback, aren't we?") he is again won over by the vertigo of violence: "I have a desire, a *rash* of warlike heredity." Chosen sublieutenant of a company of national guard at Croisset, he will go so far as to declare to his men that he will stick his sword into the belly of anyone who flinches, inviting them in return to demolish him if he retreats. He—the internationalist, the pacifist, the scorner of all action—takes "lessons in military art at Rouen." His letters become more shrill, take on an extremist tone: "I'm exasperated at the very idea of making peace." He is so well aware of the transformation that he writes to Caroline: "Your old windbag of an uncle has struck an epic note." The optimism reappears—an optimism beyond despair; to Du Camp on 29 September: "We know that this is a *duel to the death.* All hope of peace is lost. The most yellow-bellied people have turned brave . . . I guarantee that two weeks from now, *all* of France will rise up . . . There will be no civil war. The bourgeois have become sincerely republican, first, out of fear, second, out of necessity. There is no time to argue: I believe the 'Social State' is deferred for a long time to come." There is only one exception to this magnificent unity, the peasants. "They are furious." Yet it is one of them who provides him with proof of the reawakening of French combativeness: "A peasant from the neighborhood of Mantes strangled a Prussian and tore him apart with his teeth. *In short,* the enthusiasm is now general." I have italicized that "in short" which is so alien to Flaubert (at least as much as the "enthusiasm"). Two months earlier, he might have found in this act of naked, almost animal violence proof that man is condemned *as a species,* and that our mores are merely a varnish. Now it does not even occur to him, he goes so far as to write: "The most open cordiality reigns."[21] Certainly he preserves his misanthropy; the bourgeois are republicans *out of fear.* But even so, he wants it understood—for the first time in his life—that in the extreme moment of danger, fear, original violence, interests, all the base passions elicit in everyone a surpassing of our original egocentrism toward disinterestedness, altruism, and the will to integration. "The Prussian army is a marvelous precision machine, but all machines break down unexpectedly; a straw can break a spring. Our enemy has science on his side; but feeling, inspiration, despair are elements to be reckoned with. The victory must go to the right cause, and now we are in the right." I don't think we should lay too much emphasis on the last sentence. Since when does this heir to de Sade believe that vice is punished, virtue rewarded, and that victory *must* go to the right cause? In fact, he has always *believed* it; that is the meaning of his "Loser Wins," but he has always stopped short of *saying* it so clearly; this sudden profession of faith gives the measure of his exultation and his distraction. However, special emphasis must be put on the deeper meaning of his hope, which so effectively leads us back to the time when, incapable of reading the Code—of *working*—he promised himself that in the final weeks before the examination he would make a special effort and study twenty hours out of every twenty-four, in an *emotional* paroxysm that would replace the impossible *activity* with an explosive violence. In 1870, pushing fifty, he still wants to believe, he does *believe* that a leap of passion provided it is desperate and Pantagruelesque—can effectively stand against the best organized praxis. Thus he can simultaneously engage in two contradictory enterprises: "drilling and doing night patrol duty," and "reworking" (*Saint Antoine,* which he had practically abandoned since July).

This same letter, so blatantly optimistic, is not lacking elements of pessimism; and they are more profound, if more allusively evoked. He has "witnessed exquisitely grotesque scenes"—without being saddened by them, for at such moments "humanity sees itself stripped bare." And he adds, without transition: "What makes me despair is

21. Like Homais speaking of the banquet at the Agricultural Fair.

439

the tremendous boorishness that will overwhelm us. All civility, as Montaigne would have said, is lost for a long time." The theme is introduced that is going to dominate all his correspondence for the years to come: "Militarism and the most abject positivism will henceforth be our lot." Henceforth: whatever the circumstances, we shall vanquish the Prussians only by borrowing their gloomy virtues— discipline, organization. Vanquished, we shall neither recover nor have the right to plot revenge without imitating our vanquishers. In short, *whatever happens*, the future is sealed. The first term of the alternative suggests that Corneille's hope "that a noble despair will come to aid" the French is chimerical and, despite a good pithiatic effort, consciously so. Whatever happens, the era of the organizers begins with the capitulation of Sedan. In forming the bourgeois of Croisset into patrols, Gustave has the feeling he is playing out a tragic farce, as he did in the forties, and of arranging for himself—despite himself but with his own hands—the very destiny he abhors. When he was a student, every successful exam was like an uphill march toward the boorish bourgeois condition and the utilitarianism that characterized it; as a sublieutenant, the patrols, the drills, the study of "military art," all those martial practices may contribute to preserving the integrity of the territory, but at the same time they combine to produce a republican and militarist society in which the bourgeois class will dominate without the screen of monarchy, and in which Flaubert will have no place. We shall soon have to ask ourselves why he spends so much energy combating the worst while knowing that it is always certain and that all of his efforts to prevent it are merely ways to make it happen. For the moment, he wants to avoid discouragement, to avoid the collapse of his nervous and partly factitious exultation. He quickly jumps on the bandwagon of optimism: "unless we emerge from it stronger and healthier." What is striking in this pious conjecture is less the absence of conviction than the chosen adjectives: *healthy, strong,* will the French be so different from the Prussians? Gustave explains that the Second Empire was merely an extended lie, a mirage-society concealing the real country. It is this lie that his compatriots are in the process of paying for; if being put to the test helps them to grow, it is because they will be morally healthy enough to want the truth, the *only* truth, and because they will be sufficiently strong—organized, balanced, realistic—to bear it. Is this really the society in which our Knight of Nothingness wants to live? Are the virtues he desires for his compatriots really the highest in his estimation, those he would want for himself? He is lucid where the future is concerned, but he is so divided, so confused when he must judge the past record of the regime he supported and witnessed that in order to take his distance, he finally identifies his works with *truth* and the imperial society with what is "factitious": "Telling the truth was immoral. Persigny reproached me all last winter for 'lacking the ideal,' and he may have been quite sincere." A surprising sentence: does Gustave hope to fool Maxime, to whom he so often insisted on his ammorality? Didn't he tirelessly repeat—hardly a different idea—that if the artist has an ethic, its only source is the impact of artistic imperatives on his mores and private life? As for *truth*, does he really dare to claim that he is seeking it for its own sake unless he confuses it with the long, nihilistic, and pessimistic dream that made death the absolute point of view on life and nothingness the abysmal depths of being? But since this dream itself provides the definition of beauty—as the totalization of the being of nonbeing and of the nonbeing of being—truth exists for Flaubert only as a hypostasis of beauty. A work is true when it is beautiful; of course, one can reverse the terms: to be beautiful, it must be true. But this means only that the unifying principle of the narrative, the guarantee of its irreversibility, is that abstract disposition to regard the worst as always certain. The characters will thereby have, in their dull present contingency, a tragic structure of the future, that is, a fate. In short, he is faking; he wants to clear his name as quickly as possible, out of prudence and especially out of rancor. Is that possible? And how can he condemn the duc de Persigny for his statements *all last winter* without acknowledging at the same time that *all winter* they frequented the same salons? Is this even desirable? From what point of view, in effect, can he condemn the verism of the society to come if he has pronounced judgment *in the name of truth* on the love of the factitious, the lie, the oneirism and verbalism of the defunct society? The sole result of this insincerity would be, if he stuck to it, the loss of any coordinates—of any internal and external orientation. A conservative solidly established in the past defines himself by his denial of the future. And similarly, a progressive defines himself by a future society, whether reformist or revolutionary. Even revolt—negative as it is or may be—bears some self-determination, a project. But Flaubert, denying *everything*, even the imaginary, risks fracturing his internal structures without replacing them with any restructuring, of severing his basic and objective relation to the practical field without acquiring the means to substitute another relation. The consequence is a double spinning—in the inner void, in the external void, Smarh revisited.

441

But *Smarh* and his pitiful defeat generated Gustave's neurotic option, and hence that literary future which is now *behind him*, from his preneurosis. Today, the immense void where he spins is generated, in contrast, by the simultaneous abolition of future and past. The present is secretly eaten away by the absence of the two other temporal ecstasies. In other words, Gustave's exultation is undermined from below: after the abject reign of the citizen-king, the grocer in power, French society of the past is a lie extending over a quarter of a century; in the present moment it is "naked humanity"—and we know that Flaubert does not find it attractive; tomorrow will usher in the reign of the republicans' foul positivism. We wonder then, since the national unity of the moment must give birth to a detestable society, *where is* the real country Flaubert is ready to defend? He wonders about it himself, since his enthusiasm cannot free him from a lucidity that is all the more disquieting to him as it is rare, and he is quite familiar with the trap he's fallen into. The ruse of history leads him actively to protect—against his native constitution, against his chosen dogma of quietism, and with weapons he doesn't know how to use—the early childhood of a society whose first order of business will be to forget him.

Sedan raised him to epic levels—rebounding pride; the surrender of Strasbourg plunges him back into inert prostration. He resigns—like many other officers—leaves his highly undisciplined troops (anarchy or the simple application of rules of the democratic game?), and abandons *Saint Antoine* as well. A single consolation: the Republic—that "poor Republic" he reluctantly defended—seems to him "to surpass the Empire in boorishness." In short, he allows himself the bitter and paltry pleasure of slandering it *in the present*. That does not prevent all from being lost. Cassandra triumphs: in a month, Paris capitulates. "The second act [of the drama] will be civil war." The theme of fossilization reappears, affirms itself in a desperate violence that no hope can soften: "Whatever happens, the world to which I belonged has been lived out. The Latins are finished." *Whatever happens*; this time, Gustave is explicit. He is a disinterested observer of the conflict since the stakes no longer concern him; whoever wins, the Latin world, *his* world, has been lived out, France will be *Germanized*. In his overexcited state several days before, we saw him dig his own grave; he had not entirely found a way to stop this stupid activity. This time he's won: as long as the structures of the new society seem to be a French product, one can only accept them while abhorring them; everything changes when it can be claimed that the

442

foreigner's hand is at work; then the Latin's duty is to refuse the Germanization of his fatherland *in the name of France*, even if he regards it as inevitable. And to sink, like Mallarmé's old man, in a noble shipwreck, "obstinately refusing to unclench his fist." What undermines the grandeur of this attitude in Flaubert is that he has, in fact, only one desire, and that is to escape. Anywhere, any time. Into time, first of all. He returns to the past. "It is impossible for me to do anything. I spend my time reliving my past." A usual procedure for him, to which he resorts effectively and increasingly—especially after Commanville's ruin—until his death. But as we have just seen, he has closed all the doors that would allow him to arrive at a retrospective understanding of his life—as the internalization of the external and the reexternalization of the internal—by detaching himself from the Second Empire. In addition, this "mute unwinding of memories" is a denial of all objectivization; an introverted, almost autistic thought pulls him away from the present, from the future, *and from reason* by sinking like a stone into the depths of memory. The past—although the regression to childhood is the basic intention—is not necessarily *the most distant;* in other words, its date matters less than the *way it is approached*. Gustave seeks its eternal aspect, the invariable foundation of that which no longer threatens to become other, that is, *of being* as a refuge from existence. He also defends himself against any temptation to interpret, to conclude or totalize, by demanding that memory be relived *idiosyncratically*, awakening in the event only the pure and "inarticulable" quality, the immediate as it is given, unique and therefore absolute, to the sensibility of a morning or evening. The anomaly *is saved* by denying all comparison; Gustave *saves himself from the future and the present* by taking refuge in his anomaly, which is experienced as unique. Perhaps he always did; and perhaps the false death at Pont-l'Evêque transformed a young man into pure memory and the surviving old man into the pure contemplation of that memory. No doubt. But the retrospective gaze has lost its impassivity: now when Gustave *remembers*, he is escaping from anguish into a surge of tender feeling. As a neurotic option, the crisis of '44 defined an aesthetic attitude and a literary art: impassive contemplation of the inarticulable past was accompanied by a radical departure from the usage of words that attempted to make writing capable of rendering its object, the inarticulable past, articulable. For the goal of this *return to childhood* was the *access to art*. In 1870, the escape into the past is totally unproductive. No longer can he exploit the unreality of mnemonic images—or their semireality—in order to represent a derealized reality in the work. The semireality of that rough autumn's evocations functions only to protect from the real by surrounding Gustave with a defensive environment that offers more substance than the pure imaginary. To produce such an environment, in effect, and to maintain it against its natural tendency to collapse, Flaubert as a "passive agent" had to develop a passionless and sadistic aggressiveness which required true solitude sheltered by real walls, the inviolability of Croisset, to become manifest. But Croisset *is no longer* inviolable. Gustave is no longer involved in imagining; he surrounds himself with a second system of defense, the ramparts of memory, reality's contesting of itself. This absorbing self-defense, conceived expressly to absorb him, provides us with supplementary proof of his adaptation to imperial society; it is what guaranteed the anchorite the security of his sanctuary and consequently his imagination's right to free play. Yet Flaubert also envisages escaping the Germanized world through sequestration. At this very moment he writes, in a letter to Caroline: "One will have to shut oneself up and see nothing." We might think we've returned to the 1840s, when the adolescent preferred a cell in the family prison to the bourgeois future they were planning for him, as if the individual destiny he then believed he had once and for all rejected, at the price of human sacrifice, had returned to lie in wait for him, inflexible, a quarter of a century later, through the catastrophic metamorphosis of the *whole* society. The sole difference is that truly vanquished, he is no longer up to exercising that conquering sequestration that produced *Madame Bovary, Salammbô*, and the second *Education;* having taken refuge in an uncertain sanctuary, he will to nothing but immure himself in his "dead life."

This escape in time does not prevent him, elsewhere, from continually dreaming of an escape in space: "Our lamentable country, how I wish I could leave it definitively! I would like to live in a place where one would not be forced to hear the drum, to vote, to fight, far from all these horrors which are even more idiotic than they are atrocious."[22]

"My dream is to go to live somewhere outside of France, in a country where one is not forced to be a citizen."[23] To George Sand: "Oh, if only I could escape to a country where one sees no more uniforms . . . where one is not forced to be a citizen. But the earth is no

22. *Correspondance*, 4:177, 28 October. To his niece.
23. To Claudius Petit, p. 185.

longer habitable for poor mandarins." The theme reappears at the end of December: "My sole remaining, if distant, hope is to leave France definitively." Unless France leaves him; after the capitulation of Paris, he confides his timid hope to Caroline: "France is so low, so dishonored, that I wish it would disappear entirely. But I hope that civil war is going to kill many of us . . . I shall abstain from voting, I no longer wear my *Croix d'honneur*, for the word honor is no longer French, and I am so comfortable thinking that I, too, am no longer French that I am going to ask Turgenev (when I am able to write to him) what it takes to become Russian."[24] A decision whose wholly verbal and foolish violence provides a temporary release of spleen. Is he really entertaining the idea of emigrating to Moscow, or will he be a czar's subject without leaving France? He does not say, and, moreover, knows nothing about it; that day he is dominated by resentment and is less concerned with living abroad, French or not, than with becoming a foreigner to France wherever he lives. He is still clearer in a letter to Mathilde. Declining the formidable honor of saving face and showing by her courage that under the Second Empire, the Bonapartes had preserved the virtues that had allowed them to establish the First Empire, she had fled to Mons. On 3 May 1871 Gustave writes to her: "After the Prussian invasion, I drew the shroud over the face of France! Let her roll henceforth in muck and blood! Whatever happens, she is finished." A very clear text, but one which the identity of the receiver makes rather ambiguous. For the princess, a cousin of Louis-Napoleon, France is guilty chiefly for having betrayed her Emperor and evicted the imperial family; and Flaubert tells her so because she wants to hear him say it. But doesn't he *also* reproach his country for having given itself, in the throes of abject fear, to those idiots who ruled it for twenty years and led it to military disaster? He has hidden this neither from Feydeau, from Maxime, nor from Caroline. He doesn't mention it to Mathilde because it's something *unsayable* to a Bonaparte. How do we know if he is flattering her or sparing her, prompted by his tender feelings of friendship? Consequently, how do we determine which of these two motifs of hatred Gustave secretly emphasizes? For me, the answer is clear: his position is that the two crimes, far from contradicting and weakening each other, can only be mutually reinforcing. He detests them, of course, the idiots whose blunders have hastened the end of the *Latin World,* and so he must also detest the French society that produced them and took

24. Ibid.

them as masters. But by the same token he hates it for that accelerated democratization and Germanization that seized it like a malign fever and pushed it, first, to overthrow the Emperor. That is the final word, for the Emperor is at once the soldier of *Latinity*, its guardian, and its gravedigger. He is therefore guilty of having made himself, through unpardonable inadvertence, vulnerable to *being dethroned*. But this doesn't excuse the French denial of their ancestors and Greco-Roman culture in the act of overturning his throne. The people are guiltier than their tyrant; they chose him inopportunely and for the wrong reasons; for reasons even more blameworthy, with a more intemperate frenzy, they broke the contract that bound them and threw out the dictator just when they should have kept him at any price.

Kept Napoleon III? After the capitulation of Sedan? Yes, they should have. Gustave is specific on this point. He gave his opinion in two letters, separated by only one month, both written to George Sand. The sentences at first glance seem identical, with a few differences that one would be tempted to overlook. Yet it is this minimum "differential" that will allow us to elucidate its underlying meaning. The first text is spontaneous, the syntax is simple and direct: "If one had been wiser, one would not have believed . . . that the word 'Republic' was enough to conquer a million well-disciplined men. One would have left Badinguet on the throne *expressly* to make peace, *even if* he were then thrown into prison."[25] The Empire led to the defeat, which a humiliating and disastrous peace must necessarily sanction; the shame should belong to those who were already responsible for declaring war. The new regime is not much more than word: since republican enthusiasm is powerless in the face of the Prussian army, the Republic must not degrade itself from its inception by signing the peace treaty in the Emperor's stead and thereby accepting the Empire's legacy of a fraudulent bankruptcy. So let us keep Badinguet on the throne a little longer, even if we send him to prison later. In short, very little is at issue: granting the imperial regime a few months' reprieve. The sole ambiguity of the text concerns the Republic. The apparent meaning is: the Republic—why not? And why wouldn't the republican system, with its austere positivism, *in the long run* provide a better army than this "factitious" and "deceitful" dictator? Flaubert's criticism would have bearing, therefore, uniquely on the literalism—a sequel to the Empire—that took the word for the thing. On

25. *Correspondance*, 4:216.

446

4 September the Republic was *declared*, it was not *constituted*. There was no *republican order* but quite simply chaos, whose cause was the decomposition of the former regime. Was it sufficient to *pronounce the word* to produce ex nihilo a new society with established institutions and a trained strike force? George Sand, a republican, could read his words to mean that the Republic should be given a chance by not being proclaimed before the peace. But is that the only possible meaning? It is not by accident that the Republicans are talking empty words; nor is it because the Republic is "even more stupid" than the Empire—4 March 1871 follows 4 September 1870 as a matter of logic, something Flaubert never stopped crowing about. Since universal suffrage, under its demagogic egalitarianism, is at bottom only the resolute choice of stupidity; since putting power in the hands of a stupid mob necessarily leads to the systematic extermination of thinking minds and of anyone of any merit, to the abolition of all hierarchies based on value, in short, *to the reign of stupidity*, of the "mad dogs"; since the Commune is the *foreseen* truth of the Republic, just as the insurrection of June was the truth of the foolish February Revolution, then 4 September is a fateful day, to be marked with a black stone. With better advice, the Parisians would have kept Badinquet to make peace; in other words, they would have *stayed home* and 4 September would be just an ordinary day; the word "Republic" would not have been pronounced. And even as Flaubert is writing to Sand, the French would still be living under the Empire. For how long? Until the signing of the peace treaty, certainly. And *afterward?* How are we to imagine they would accept such shame without revolting? Not only against the dictator but against the unacceptable conditions the Prussians have imposed. If they revolt, *in fact*, the Prussians will lay siege to Paris, the improvised Republic will try to fight and will be beaten whatever it does. Whence the Commune. If 4 September had taken place in May and 18 March in October, what would have been gained? And if they do not revolt, if they give a tacit mandate to the Emperor to submit to Bismarck's *Diktat* in their name, if those dogs—cowering rather than mad—demand peace *at any price*, where will they later find the strength, with Badinguet back in the Tuileries, to chase him out? Is this what Flaubert *means*? To help us make up our minds, let us read the second text and compare it to the first: "If we had been more enlightened . . . we would have suffered neither Gambetta nor Prussia nor the Commune . . . Ah, how practical it would have been to keep Badinguet, *in order to* send him to

prison once peace was made." [26] *Even if, in order to* [*Quitte à, afin de*]: it could be said that the nuance is slight. It is that nuance, however, that will allow us to force a confession from the guilty man. It is notable that the second expression of the idea, its heavy-handed, tormented form, awakens the suspicion that Gustave's thought, here, is at least as concealing as it is revealing. The time of prudence, the era of suspicion has begun—at least Gustave was convinced of this. Hence this odd sentence, full of precaution: Badinguet is kept *in order* to be put in prison. Is it therefore *insofar as he is emperor* that he will become a convict with ball and chain, in his finest uniform? And if you really intend to condemn him to hard labor under the sun of Cayenne, isn't overthrowing him the simplest and most effective means to that end? Not according to the construction of the sentence: the best, indeed, the only way to turn him into a convict is to prolong his reign. It will be objected, no doubt, that Louis-Napoleon was in Prussian hands, therefore out of danger. Disavowed by the new government, Bismarck regards him as a simple private citizen and has no reason to return him; on the other hand, he would return him as Emperor, that is, if Badinguet signs in the name of the French and if they honor his signature by keeping him in power. From that time on the criminal is in our hands: he would be prisoner in the Tuileries, just as Louis XVI was between the time of his flight to Varennes and 10 August 1792. Isn't it true, then, that if you want to bring him to justice, you have to begin by recovering him, and that can be done only by provisionally preserving his title? The answer is simple: if Bismarck, having signed with Napoleon, regarded him *as sovereign* for the contracting party, he would not tolerate Napoleon's being overthrown by the French. For this would be to disavow his signature; the king of Prussia would deal only with a worthy interlocutor; if he is the head of an elected government, so much the better, provided he is *representative;* if he is Emperor, past his prime, weakened by his defeats but accepted by the country without too much grumbling, the Germans will arrange to consolidate his power, and since the French did not take away his throne, the occupiers will see to it that he stays there. Naturally, in this odd *enunciation,* the meaning Gustave *wants* to communicate implies that the prepositional locution "in order to" [*afin de*] has bearing on the group of statements that follow; equally, we would have to read: "in order to send-him-to-prison-once-peace-was-made" (which implies "by him"). But aside from the fact that this turn of

26. Ibid., p. 219.

phrase borders on incorrect usage—which often happens when Flaubert tries both to tell and to withhold—the locution, having two different and nearly opposite functions (to keep Badinguet, *in order to* punish him so that he should take responsibility for signing the peace treaty), is overdetermined. This plethora of meaning has the effect of scrambling the sentence, and the reader is left blinking. It's all because Gustave takes *oratorical precautions:* whatever one thinks of Napoleon III, it is indispensable to affirm *first* and absolutely that he is a criminal who deserves a sentence of hard labor. And this outward indignation makes us forget that Gustave would rather see Badinguet a crowned assassin than a fallen emperor. This is quite a contrast with the preceding letter. In that case, Gustave dots his *i*'s: Napoleon would be kept in power in order to shoulder the responsibilities of the peace treaty, *even if* he were later sent to prison. *Even if,* a prepositional locution, signifies "at the risk of." It looks like rain, but I have to visit Pierre *even if* I get soaked to the bone. In this sentence, the eventuality of rain is not dismissed; it is one of the factors that determine, on that day, the index of adversity of the practical field; however, the subject declares that he is going on, whether he judges that despite the clouds, the storm is unlikely to burst here and now, whether the motive that prompts me to meet Pierre is stronger than the fear of inclement weather. In any event, I take responsibility: the *even if* rather effectively defines the politics of "calculated risk." In the light of the second locution and that surprising *in order to,* we suddenly discover that the first is not as simple as it seemed. How can Gustave—who, unlike certain of his contemporaries, knew the meaning of words perfectly well, and as a disciple of Boileau wished to use that meaning *mistakenly*—how can he write to George Sand, a convinced republican, and represent the Emperor's possible punishment, should he be kept, as a *risk to be run?* We might say that three meanings have been telescoped. The first—"The only risk we run is that of sending him to prison *afterward;* in short, of prolonging his reign a little"—is the esoteric meaning. But it is not clearly expressed. In fact, a second meaning, inseparable from the first and yet *other,* attempts to *compose itself* under the reader's eyes, never entirely succeeding by reason of the indeterminacy of the articulation, but for that very reason persisting as a perpetual solicitation without ever entirely decomposing. I think it would have to be explicitly stated as follows: "We should have kept Badinguet on the throne to make peace, *even if* he were made to pay for this undeserved prolongation of power with a *more severe* sanction. The events of 4 September merely resulted in condemning the imperial family to exile; if we had not deposed them, we might have condemned them later to prison." The *even if* would have bearing, in this case, not on the prolongation but on the sentence itself: the calculated risk would be excessive severity. Flaubert takes it upon himself: forced labor for a prince is perhaps cruel and unjust (after all, hasn't Gustave repeated a hundred times since adolescence, don't judge!). To bad! Better a particular injustice than the dishonor of a nation. Impossible that this meaning should not confound the preceding one; even more impossible that it could be realized. First of all, it is not adapted to the personality of the correspondent; and we know that Gustave's chief concern as a letter writer is to shade the same opinion in a variety of ways, according to the positions he attributes to the recipients of his letters. It is impossible to believe that George Sand would not be exasperated by the odd indulgence which this "reading" of the text implicitly reveals: exile was sufficient; prison is too much, but reasons of State demand it. Yet the second letter and its *in order to*—surely somewhat forced precautions but *in line with* the first articulation—show an *although* metamorphosed into a *because*. Prison, calculated risk, injustice accepted by reason of State, is transformed into an *absolute end*, that is, into supreme justice. Everything must be done to punish Badinguet, *even taking the risk* that he will remain on the throne. This intention must implicitly structure the first exposition: the coefficient of adversity, a negative force and a brake on praxis, can be posited—at thirty days distance, all things being equal (the same script writer, the same reader, for both a situation practically unchanged)—as a categorical imperative, the *positive* and supreme end of action, only if its negation contained from the outset a secret positivity, an implicit affirmation. What is this affirmation that is clearly the third meaning? What is this esoteric meaning that Flaubert, true to form, transmits like a contagious disease to the unsuspecting reader? Looking closely at the two texts, and recalling that for Gustave, form is the indirect expression of an idea, we are instantly mindful of the fact that if the thought claims to be the same while its form has changed, we must seek the *invariable* element—leaving aside variations, which "indirectly express" peripheral modifications of intention from one text to the other. We then realize that this element is that inviolable and already violated imperative, "we should have kept Badinguet." A hypothetical imperative in the first letter (implied: if we wanted the least shameful peace), a categorical imperative in the second (the *sanction* becoming the only human connection between the Emperor and his former subjects). But with that secret stubbornness that makes it persist as an inert demand, whatever the alleged justifications, this imperative—*passed, surpassed* (nothing can change the fact that the French of 4 September *should have* submitted to it and that the future, whatever it might be, will bear the mark of their disobedience)—reveals its character as an unconditional demand, one that is, however, impossible to satisfy today because of others and what they did yesterday, initiating an endless cycle of recriminations. In short, the third meaning, which sustains the two others, nourishes them with its pathos, and reveals itself beyond their position, could be expressed in these terms: "After Sedan, *the only thing not to do* was to overturn the Empire; this was done, and we are entering an era of *darkness.*" The oppositions—whether of right or left, provided they remain respectful—voluntarily position themselves just when the government *has no fault left to commit.* Cassandra always lives in the moment of no return, *after* the opposition has marked out clear boundaries, when those boundaries have been crossed, when the final transgression has been committed. On this basis she foretells the future as the fatal product of the irreparable past: prophecies are born of recrimination.

The basic meaning, then, is that Flaubert misses the Empire, and resents the French for overthrowing it. He lets George Sand glimpse some of his rage: too fast for anyone to notice, just long enough to annoy the good lady, whose humanitarianism exasperates him: "Ah, you have principles! You believe in the goodness of men, in justice, in civilization; well, look at the consequences of this phraseology. True knowledge is skeptical and pessimistic; it does not seek the Good—which doesn't exist—but the *lesser evil.* The lesser evil was the Empire!" Then all at once he closes up again. The main thing is that she should understand without being able to hold anything against him. If she had taken the cue and pushed him to the wall, he would surely have had little difficulty *rationalizing* this passionate and desolate regret; already strongly liberalized before the declaration of war, the imperial regime, after Sedan, was not at risk of becoming authoritarian; on the contrary, it would have needed to give proof of great wisdom to retrieve its lost credit. But Gustave hardly believed his own arguments. The truth is that he regarded the future—the egalitarian and militaristic Republic—with horror, and regretted the past—that is, imperial society—*for its own sake.* Something has materialized that he abominates; something has disappeared that he loved. The rationalization of his anguish and his regrets—"the Em-

451

pire would remain liberal, the process is irreversible"—must be reversed to understand its real meaning, which is irrational, and could be expressed in these terms: "in liberal and positivist France, a product of defeat, the Empire, preserved, would represent the minimum of madness I need to live." The dictatorship of Napoleon III was the *lesser evil*, certainly; but the lesser evil for a Knight of Nothingness is, in fact, the *best* solution: a social order that rewards him and which he has the right to slander. Such would have been the imperial Court for Flaubert, a man of resentment for whom nothing can compensate his original frustration.[27] It *rewarded* him in a certain way, but at the same time he preserved the power to ignore this symbiosis, to rise above it and denounce the *humus* from which he drew his sustenance. If a more radical Baudelaire regards his poems, and hence his poetic ego, as "flowers of evil," Flaubert, with his more cunning compromises, deserved the name "flower of lesser evil." His misfortune, in those terrible years, was to be unable to admit his bitter regret for the abolished regime without in the process proclaiming that he was its accomplice. This is the origin of his vomiting-as-denial. It is hardly his fellow citizens who *make* him nauseous, as he claims (always that cursed custom characteristic of the passive agent of projecting onto the Other responsibility for his own determinations); rather it is he, somatizing his denials since he is unable to declare them, who is determined to vomit republican France, to abolish it in imagination through a real but intentionally symbolic bodily distress. The Republic has given him cancer, he is tortured by its symptomatic nausea: it is killing him (cancer of the stomach), he is killing it (drowned in his vomitings). At the end of this tragedy everyone is dead, tragic equilibrium is established by the reciprocal annihilation of the contending parties. Better the Apocalypse than fossilization. In short, nothing is made of it, nothing can be made of it: through his oracular neurosis, Gustave determined his natural milieu in advance: this survivor of '44 defined at Pont-l'Evêque the *optimum* regime that would assure the reproduction of his survival; prophesying the Second Empire, he *surpassed* himself toward the establishment and flowering of imperial society, but as a result he is now forbidden to survive *alive*.

No, this man is no patriot. Not even a nationalist. All his life he has been proclaiming his hatred of France, and he hasn't lied; indeed, at the crucial moment he is only in a hurry to escape it, in any case to

27. Not that his desire, as he claims, is infinite. But frustration is by nature a deprivation of happiness that makes one incapable of enjoying it.

withdraw solidarity from it. France is dead, I have pulled the shroud over its face, he writes to an imperial princess in exile. Isn't this a declaration to the effect: let all the French perish rather than the Empire? For this reason he doesn't dislike the Commune as much as we might think: Parisians "made" the events of 4 September; let them all be punished by 18 March 1871, let the Capital, regicide twice over, burn down to the last man.

He obviously has no sympathy for the Communards, "those mad dogs," but he protests that he does not hate them. And he is not scared by the Commune. What is more, he foresaw it: beginning in October 1870, this provincial clearly registers the province's opposition to the capital and the threat it constitutes to national unity: "Metz's surrender will demoralize the countryside, I'm afraid, but anger Paris. Thence dissension. We are faced with a fine state of affairs." On 18 December 1870, he notes that "Achille Flaubert had (and is still having) great difficulties at the Municipal Council, which deliberated in the midst of gunfire initiated by the workers," indicating that he is aware of a more profound conflict behind the opposition of provincials and Parisians, the conflict of class against class. He clearly understands one of the reasons for this new tension, since he remarks upon the wretchedness of the refugees drifting into Rouen by the tens of thousands, half dead from cold and hunger. And this is what he prophesies: after capitulation, civil war. Then on 1 February 1871, at the announcement of the capitulation of Paris: "I hope the civil war will kill many of us." At this date, as we know, civil war had not yet broken out; but he is so sure of the future that he doesn't even need to predict it; he has already become part of it. His only uncertainty is the number of dead. He has therefore grasped many of the contradictions that will bring about the Commune: the opposition between Paris and to provinces that conceals those deeper conflicts between the rural and urban populations, landowning and profit; the pacifism of the conservatives—manifested by Bordeaux— intensifying the popular will to continue the war (and, of course, itself intensified by that will); the class struggle intensified by defeat and misery. This clairvoyance is shared by many of his contemporaries, but in Gustave—for whom *the worst is always certain*—it takes on all the qualities of revelation. What would pass in another's eyes for a strong probability he experiences as a sacred belief, the basis of which is not reasoned but rests, on the contrary, on the basic dogma of his black religion. The Parisian insurrection, *taken for granted*, provokes in him merely the bitter satisfaction of someone who "told you so."

In fact, the Commune seems to him the "mathematical" consequence of 4 September: from the moment the Republic was proclaimed and universal suffrage reinstated, the idiot reign of the many, of the multitude, the inevitable conclusion is that the common people should take power in disorder and once again demand the "Social State," that is, not the *right* to vote for everyone of its members—it already has that—but the dictatorship of the majority, that is, of the lower classes, the distribution of goods, the oppression of *quality* by *quantity*. This is what should have been foreseen *at the beginning of September*, he thinks with a calm contempt aimed more at the gentlemen who made the Republic than at the workers he thinks are in the process of destroying it: "All that's happened since the armistice is nothing. The worst thing was the first period of the occupation." And on 27 April '71—in the middle of the civil war: "Contrary to general opinion, I find nothing worse than the Prussian invasion. The complete annihilation of Paris by the Commune would cause me less pain than the torching of a single village by those 'charming' Gentlemen." Later, he writes to Feydeau: "I have no hatred of the Communards since I do not hate mad dogs. But what sticks in my craw is the invasion of Doctors of Philosophy breaking mirrors with pistol shots and stealing clocks—that is new to history." He so quickly resigns himself to the destruction of Paris, it almost seems he wants it to happen. In any event, the disaster will be localized. He never believed for a moment in the victory of the Social State. For the excellent reason that Bismarck's troops will not allow it. He mocks the people who are saying all around him: "Happily, the Germans are here." But he is doing to the same thing when he writes: "I admit that the [Commune] is beating the troops of Versailles and overthrowing the government. The Prussians will enter Paris and order will reign as far as Warsaw!" What determination in this pyromaniac: he insists upon the torching of the capital; either the Communards on the point of defeat are going to set it ablaze and lead the entire population to their deaths; or they will be the vanquishers, and it will be the Prussians who will transform the city into a heap of rubble. In any event, the countryside is, and will remain, calm. All they'll have to do is make Versailles the new capital. Flaubert claimed, however, to admire the heroism, of the Parisians during the siege. And he truly did, I imagine. *Provided they should all die of it*. His rage, when he learns of the capitulation, is significant: "I am angry," he is not afraid to write, "that Paris did not burn to the last house and become just a great black space." We should not be so surprised; this bourgeois landowner shares the sentiments of the residents of Versailles. This city of insurrections and revolutions is no longer loved. But in Flaubert, beyond the Neroesque *Schadenfreude* that allows him to taste as an artist—and in the imaginary—the systematic destruction of a city, of human labor, of its population *by men*, there is a tenacious and heated malice against the capital. Already in the preneurotic period of his youth he summoned Attila and his Huns to destroy Rouen and Paris simultaneously. He was then ravaged by irritations, humiliations; although his father provided him with a good allowance, he regarded himself as an impoverished student and fiercely envied the pleasures of the wealthy youth of the Right Bank. It was in Paris that he pushed his hatred of his studies, his horror of the Code, his anguish at the fate his father was preparing for him *to the point of neurosis*. For the attack, in fact, occurred in Normandy because he had gone there to escape from Paris and no longer wanted to return to his Parisian prison. Subsequently, as a celebrity, cured of his "nervous illness," he spent several months a year in the capital; but he liked it no more than he did in the era of his gloomy bohemianism. What he holds against it is that he, Gustave, is not rich enough to live in high style all year round. Not that he wants to live in Paris: Parisian life exhausts this great man of the provinces; he would like to be able to do it should he ever want to try.

Be that as it may, he has no sympathy for the insurgents. What exactly does he hold against them? Three things. First of all, *they are Parisians*. Then: "Those wretches displace one's hatred! One no longer thinks of the Prussians. A little longer and we will actually like them! We are spared no shame." Hatred for the Prussians, contempt for the commoners—that is his creed. But if "our brothers" rise up, we will hate the foreign vanquisher less; Gustave refuses to despise the Commune so as not to undermine his determination to despise Prussia. The other grievance he harbors against them is that, beaten by the inhabitants of Versailles, the fear they have aroused in the bourgeoisie might allow the triumph of "a strong clerical and monarchist reaction." He writes to George Sand: "We are buffeted between the Society of Saint Vincent de Paul and the Internationale. But the latter has been guilty of too much stupidity to last long . . . If it is conquered, the reaction will be furious and all liberty strangled."[28]

Flaubert is being torn apart by a paradox: he sees the disaster that is overtaking the Empire as the necessary consequence of imperial

28. 31 March 1871, *Correspondance*, 6:215.

policy. If only he could assume that the society in which he is implicated might have conjured away the dangers with *another* policy. But
no, he is quite lucid about it. Napoleon III's policy cannot be dissoci-
ated from the social structures of the Second Empire: "We are paying
for the long lie we were living, for it was false: a false army, false
policy, a false literature, false credit, and even false courtisans."
Sometime later this Latin will write: "[Defeat arose out] of our higher
education [its imperfections, its excessively "humanist," "Latin"
bent], September 4th out of our secondary education [those who proclaimed the Republic had done their baccalauriat], the Commune was
the product of primary education." Three grievances, in short,
against national education: there are *too many* baccalauriats, *too many*
schoolchildren in the municipal schools; educating the common
people only increases the number of the failed and embittered, and
gives the masses bad shepherds who will misuse their scrap of poorly
learned and poorly digested knowledge. But if the remedy in both
cases is easily imagined (merely establish a strict process of selection
at the nursery school level that takes account of both talents and
wealth), this is not equally so for higher education, which demands
a thorough reform: "Our enemy," says Gustave, "has a monopoly
on science . . ." If the French are beaten, it is because under Napoleon III public instruction neglected the exact disciplines and gave the
lion's share to the humanities. Less Latin, less Greek, and more
mathematics—that is the only way to take our revenge or simply to
pull ourselves up.[29]

That is all very well, but isn't this "humanistic" education, which
to Gustave is merely a particular expression of the "long lie" in which
his contemporaries have lived, precisely the same education he deliberately acquired? Didn't he try to read Theocritis, Virgil and Shakespeare in their original languages, to live intimately with Montaigne
or Rabelais, to keep company with them, incorporate them, so that
their finest and most profound ideas become, at four centuries' remove, the guiding schemes of his imagination and sensibility? And
isn't this just what the enlightened bourgeois mean, in this era, when

---

29. Gustave vascillates between two extreme positions, both of them negative and
misanthropic. *Before the Commune,* he deplores the *revanchist* atmosphere that he foresees—rightly—in a conquered and humiliated France. During and after, sickened by
the Germanophilia he detects in a good number of his friends, he reproaches the
French for no longer dreaming of revenge. These two contradictory grievances he
nurses against his compatriots—at several weeks' distance—seem to reflect his own
hesitations.

they say that they have "done their humanities"? If these are lies, then Flaubert is entirely their victim, for he is made up of those lies, and by condemning public instruction he is condemning himself in his *objective unreality*.

Actually, Flaubert's education, begun in the last years of the Restoration and pursued under Louis-Philippe, had just been completed by a "return to the sources," to the ruins of Egypt, to Greek and Roman antiquity, when Louis-Napoleon seized power. Not that Gustave subsequently learned nothing; but in general his culture was set: he had put together a system of references valid for all his life's circumstances on the basis of several fundamental choices. We have seen, in contrast, that public interest in the sciences followed the fall of the Second Republic and was, moreover, a consequence of it—even as it reflected the new imperatives of industrialization. Be that as it may, Gustave does not claim to be a product of the Second Empire; he considers that imperial society was mistaken in prolonging the education dispensed by the defunct monarchy beyond the limits prescribed by the evolution of knowledge, the same education he himself received at the *collège* before becoming "cultivated" according to schemes authorized around 1830. This education would barely remain valid in the first half of the nineteenth century, despite the admonitions of the Saint-Simonians and the positivists; scientific and technical progress made it completely inadequate after midcentury. Unfortunately, progress took place *among our neighbors*—at least that is how Gustave represents it to himself. The scientific challenge to humanism did not take place *at home*, thanks to the military dictatorship that establish itself by force and, ideologically, the lie, by the refusal to see itself objectively. This Latin who survives the July monarchy believes he would have been lost if the Second Republic had taken firm hold, and if it had reshaped general education to give the exact sciences their due. Flaubert's individual survival—of his crisis in '44, of the crisis in '48—cannot be reduced to the inert persistence of a fossil, because the coup of 2 December was a counterthrust to the country's real development. With a blindness paid for in 1870, the Empire presented itself explicitly as the preserver of an outmoded culture with sources in the world of antiquity and feudalism. In short, until Sedan, Gustave—rather consciously—enjoyed a *reprieve* because the dictatorship was a moratorium. Beyond the subjective and naked fact of the death-survival of the young hero of *Novembre*, he drew enough blood and substance from his environment to survive himself *alive* because the society around him was itself a survival.

457

Gustave sees a reciprocity of reflections between the austere, abstract support for humanist values by an enemy of humanity and the collective affirmation—by institutions and behavior—of those same values by an Antichrist. But this is only half true. It is true that France is equipping itself more slowly than England or Prussia, but the fault does not lie wholly with Napoleon III. Behind the *imperial facade*, the military hierarchy Gustave will contemplate, fascinated, for almost twenty years, there exists a *true* society that is putting in place its economic and social structures, and will suddenly seem bourgeois and modern, ready for the second industrial revolution, as soon as that facade has crumbled.

Flaubert and Badinguet are joined by a single lie, but their interests differ. Badinguet is paid handsomely by the bourgeois to act as their cover and practice in their name, without referring to them, an inoffensive but boistrous policy of pomp and prestige that distracts the attention of the masses. Even without the capitulation of Sedan, the self-assured bourgeoisie would have deposed him in the end, finding him too expensive. Flaubert quite simply asks this military—and feudal—hierarchy to represent the *relation of homage* and to make him forget the existence of the bourgeois. Nonetheless, whatever the truth of the matter, their destinies are bound together like their natures—that is, the *being* they have given themselves. For Flaubert, Louis-Napoleon will have been the *man of Destiny,* who forged a France in which the hermit of Croisset might have found a place of honor, in short, *Gustave in power.* But Gustave in power signifies—he has just learned—a backwardness that increases each year and, at the end of the road, collapse. Hence his disarray: how can he accept that final tumble, which resumes and totalizes a society by its destruction? Above all, how can he assume it and acknowledge that it was in the making? Yet how can he *deny* it when he has chosen failure for its own sake as the inevitable result of great demands, the condemnation of men, denial of life, honor found in abjection? How can he deny it when he has taken the dictator for an exterminating angel masked by a goatee, who came to accomplish what he had desired since childhood, the destruction of the human race? After all, young Gustave called loudly for Attila and his Huns; he entrusted them with the destruction of Paris and Rouen. Well, they came, topped with pointed helmets, better later than never, and seriously set to work. Who invited them, then, if not Badinguet himself—and the good people of France necessarily brutalized by imperial propaganda to the point of enthusiastically demanding their own extermination? But again, how can Gustave consent to the massacre if its final result is the elimination of the Latins? In this case, the most foolish of all would be the men of letters, the Mandarins, with Flaubert in the lead, for in advance of the populace they would have systematically paved the way to their doom with a lie of twenty years' duration. For this reason, Flaubert's letters sometimes present *Latinity* to us as a criminal madness (too much Latin in higher education), and sometimes as the unique source of human greatness. He sees the society that is to be born on the ruins of culture as doubly necessary: in accordance with the order of causes, since it is the product of defeat; in accordance with the order of ends, since there is no other way of reviving France. Even more fundamentally, he does not conceal the fact that this society was laboring to be born in the final years of Louis-Philippe, and that, all things considered, the Empire was merely a rearguard action, a desperate attempt to delay history.

Yet he vomits out this new society. Double necessary it may be—as a product of the defeat and as the means to our revival—but he prophesies its advent *with horror*. "What breaks my heart . . . is the conviction that we are entering a hideous world from which the Latins are excluded. All elegance, even material elegance, is finished for a long time to come." "A mandarin like me has no more justification." "One will be utilitarian and military, economic, small, poor, abject. Life in itself is something so sad that it is unbearable without great alleviations. What will it be like, then, cold and denuded? That Paris we loved will no longer exist." So at one and the same time Flaubert *condemns the Empire* and *declares himself negatively in solidarity with it*. For better or worse, it was his era, and he does not want to survive it. *"I am dying of sorrow* . . . Many others have more to complain of than I. But not one, I'm sure, is suffering as much. I feel as if it's the end of the world. Whatever happens, everything I have loved is lost." During the Prussian occupation he claimed to have noticed in himself symptoms of cancer. Since he relates those symptoms to his despair— it is certainly possible, given the context—he must have detected a hysterical somatization. Not that he considered cancer itself, that cellular madness, a psychosomatic complaint; let us say that he had come to a thorough understanding of things in the course of his lengthy concubinage with neurosis, and that he saw cancer as the *unreal* truth of his troubles. A letter to Doctor Cloquet, dating from the end of May '71, gives us some specific details on the nature of those troubles: "For two months I even believed I had stomach cancer, for I was vomiting almost every day." Gustave is addressing himself to a physician and cannot maintain the fiction—secretly cherished and sometimes clearly announced in his correspondence—that his misfortunes had brought about the onset of cancer. This time cancer is denounced as a pure *pithiatic belief,* and the vomitings shift to the primary level: they constitute Gustave's somatic reaction to events. They manifest a denial, a fundamental denial that engages Flaubert's entire person in his underlying materiality. Gustave "spits into the ashes," as pregnant women do when they are moved by a profound denial of their condition.

What is it, then, that he denies? A letter to Feydeau, written one month later, informs us: "Never, my dear fellow, have I felt such a colossal disgust. I would like to drown humanity in my vomit." But to the extent that he helped to prepare it, he cannot vomit up this "era of *boorishness*" without vomiting himself along with it. Hysterical somatization through vomiting has the function of expressing this *unspeakable* vicious circle: men are killing him, he internalizes the events of 4 September in the form of a hysterical belief in stomach cancer; the Republic is not only an external transformation of the environment, it is *himself as other,* it gnaws at him in his most organic intimacy as *his own life* and as a madness of lived experience that he must suffer in estrangement. The reexternalization is the "nausea"; it is also his revenge: he drowns his murderers by vomiting *himself* onto them. But if he vomits *himself,* it is because he considers himself guilty; in these moments of nausea, he denies both the world that denies him and his own Latinity.

Indeed, we see a curious convergence of his desperate attempts to get out of the game, to deny any responsibility for the disaster, to escape from France (in his imagination), or to let France roll, dead and bloody, in shit, doing nothing to avoid that supreme shame and the nausea whose violence is an index of the power of his involvement and complicity with the abolished regime. But between September '70 and May '71, we see clear evidence of his formal and deliberate intention to *cultivate* his sorrow. The theme first appears muted. In October '70 he notes that "certain persons endure our misfortune rather cheerfully. There are readymade phrases that console the crowd for everything: 'France will rise again! What good is it to despair! It is a salutary punishment,' etc. Oh, what humbug!"[30] In the face of these fools, he acts is if he can neither take heart (he is no longer young enough) nor resign himself (he isn't old enough); his

30. 28 October 1870, *Correspondance,* 6:179.

race is finished, he can no longer change *set*. Neither resignation, then, nor hope: he has no alternative but to dramatize his grief, to surrender to it and indulge it. This is what emerges from his imprecations of 30 October: "When I begin to have some hope, I try to suppress it . . . I am dying of sorrow, the real thing, and consolations annoy me . . . All the friends I had [in Paris] are dead or gone. I have no more center. Literature seems to me a vain and useless thing. Will I ever be in a state to take it up again?"[31] On 10 November he restates these declarations almost word for word in a letter to Caroline: "Consolations annoy me. The word *hope* seems ironic to me. I am morally quite ill; my sadness is unimaginable, and it disturbs me more than anything else."[32] So motivated a sadness could arouse this reflexive anxiety, this estrangement, only if rather than living his sadness directly he felt simultaneously as though he were throwing himself into it with all his strength and as though he didn't totally believe in it. Other passages indicate that he suspects he is perpetuating it himself and even forcing it: "I roll and plunge into my sorrow like a boat sinking into the sea. I no longer believed that my heart could contain such suffering without dying of it."[33] Of course, the image of the boat *sinking* into the sea has soon transformed intentional lived experience into a suffered determination: this lifeboat founders because it "springs a leak" or has taken on a huge quantity of sea water; the shipwreck overtakes him *from without*. But it must be noted that the comparison is introduced after the fact, and would be perfectly useless if it did not function here as a corrective. Indeed, if Gustave had merely written, "I roll and plunge into sorrow," the second verb would itself—under the influence of the word "sorrow"—evoke an intentional behavior. Those who would console someone use it in this sense when they invite a friend struck down by misfortune to "get the better of his feelings." "You'll snap out of it," etc., they say, adding with mild reproach: "You're wallowing in your sorrow." It is as if Gustave had first employed the word in its *active* sense, and then—no doubt fearing the *sursum corda* Caroline was so good at—had hastily thrown up the habitual smokescreen between himself and his correspondent by introducing the metaphor of the shipwreck. He returns to it, moreover, in January '71 and takes the same precautions, again toward

---

31. To George Sand, ibid., p. 183.
32. *Correspondance*, 6:186.
33. Ibid., p. 189.

Caroline: "My moral state, which nothing can pull me out of, is beginning to upset me seriously. I consider myself a lost man (and I am not mistaken)."[34] This time the corrective is not a comparison but a brief commentary in parentheses. "I consider myself . . ." taken alone, suggests something overly determined. When the head of the family scolds a nephew who is going off track, he is apt to say, "I consider you a lost man," and the verb is carefully chosen to inspire fear without closing all doors: *to consider* is not *to know*, the word designates an opinion; he is thereby alluding to a voluntary position: "I have decided the question, nephew; I, the paterfamilias, regard you as lost. This is not yet an obvious fact but in part a belief, in part a decision; it's up to you to persuade me by your conduct to change my mind." The same insolent willfulness is found in Flaubert's sentence: "I have decided to believe I am lost," he says. Which amounts to declaring: "I have decided to lose myself." But foreseeing Caroline's response ("It depends on you whether you are lost or not; if you are determined to believe it, your shipwreck is certain; to avoid it, you need merely decide it will not happen"), he hastens to transform his belief into certainty: "I am not mistaken." This psychologist, this subtle analyst knows himself: he suggests to Caroline that he draws his conclusion from classified evidence. In a way, however, it is not only, or even especially, his niece he would like to convince, it is *himself*. For despite everything, it is not his will that pushes him to outdo his pain, it is his enslaved will. He has too much experience of those preneurotic states; during the 1840s he kept catching himself "overdoing it" and would discover with anguish, almost simultaneously, that he couldn't help it; he has not forgotten the catastrophe of '44, a "mathematical" consequence of those suffered and desired beliefs he compelled himself to want. He is afraid of falling ill again. What if the nervous attacks should recur and flatten him as they did before? Yet at the capitulation of Paris he throws caution to the wind and in a letter, again to Caroline, he writes: "Proud souls are wounded to the quick and, like Rachel, do not want to be consoled." Once again he has been careful to present the general idea and introduce it by citing big brother Achille's suicidal rage and Raoul-Duval's ravings. But we know Flaubert's dialectic of the universal and the singular—and his real feelings for Achille. Further, we are not surprised to read this finally *explicit* profession of faith limited to his own case in a letter of 4 March '71, addressed to Mathilde: "I am astonished by how much

34. Ibid., p. 195.

one can suffer without dying. No one is more ravaged than I by this catastrophe. I am like Rachel: 'I do not want to be consoled.' I shall try to accustom myself to permanent despair."[35] To be sure, the tone is appropriate when addressing an imperial princess. And Flaubert, as a clever courtier, gives two reasons for his "shame." On 1 March the National Assembly confirmed the collapse of Napoleon III and his dynasty; the same day it accepted the conditions of peace dictated by Germany, in particular the Prussian march through Paris. This has just taken place; Gustave witnessed it. "How I thought of you, Wednesday, and how I suffered [because of the collapse] . . . All day [Saturday] I saw the Prussian helmets shining in the sun on the Champs Elysées . . . The man sleeping at the Invalides must have turned over in his grave."[36] What cunning! It would be easy to believe that the Assembly, in its baseness, had doubly betrayed the Emperor, first by taking advantage of his noble misfortune to depose him, then by accepting in cowardly fashion a *Diktat* that the heroic descendant of the first Napoleon would disdainfully have rejected. Or, rather, there is only one inexpiable betrayal: by deposing Napoleon III, the deputies were not content to commit a sacrilege, they revealed the crass commonness of their civilian souls, incapable of understanding military greatness, and by the same token committed a degraded France to total demilitarization, to the indelible humiliation of an accepted defeat. And so that Mathilde should have no inkling that after all, France was indebted to her imperial cousin for this march of pointed helmets, Flaubert conjures away Little Napoleon and substitutes Napoleon the Great: he turns over in his grave with anger, not against his nephew, however, but against the men of 4 September.

We are now prepared to recover Gustave's true sentiments from beneath these fawnings. It really is the Empire he regrets; he experienced that shame, "swallowed but not digested," in earnest on 1 September, for the Assembly confirmed *his own downfall* as a Latin and a Mandarin. We can thus give the lapidary formulas I have cited their full meaning: "I do not want to be consoled. Unalterable despair." They yield an experienced truth even as they are being written; they are the end result of a long process whose stages we have just reconstructed. This time, we would say that Flaubert opted for voluntarism. Should we infer that he *assumes* and takes responsibility for the obstinacies of his enslaved will? Certainly not. We are dealing with a

35. Ibid., p. 206.
36. Ibid.

463

denial; and his denials never have the inflexible firmness of a true negation. This one is no different: contorted, strained, ineffective, it is *lived* in a paroxysm of unwonted agitation; this perpetual upheaval is merely an *intentional* determination of pathos which, uncompleted by an act, exhausts itself in *somatizations*. When Gustave speaks here of his *will*, we should conclude not that he has gone beyond pathos by means of praxis but rather that his anxiety has disappeared; he has understood himself sufficiently so that this negative *conatus*, without escaping heteronomy or dissolving in the transparency of a voluntary decision, no longer seemed strange to him. As often happens, he has thought about these troubles, he has grasped their meaning and purpose; thenceforth, far from taking this alien spontaneity and guiding it toward his ends, he surrenders to it and allows it to guide him. But what has he understood? And what is he denying? We would not know how to answer these questions without attempting a phenomenological description of this attitude.

A widow is inconsolable when she does not want to be consoled. Marivaux demonstrates this effectively in *La Seconde Surprise de l'Amour*. "I am fond of my sadness," says the Marquise. "I must sigh all my life . . . there is no more consolation for me . . . I have lost everything . . . I want only to be left to my pain, [I] live . . . only by an effort of reason." If consolation achieved is purpose, it would result in the suppression of an inner determination. It would hasten that mental reorganization produced more slowly but irresistibly by the work of mourning. The inconsolable widow wants to maintain her state against this mute work of mourning and also against consoling friends. "Your pain, du Perier, will then be eternal?" Yes, that is its aim—eternity. Undoubtedly it is only a lived frustration, only the consciousness of a gap, of a lack; but this entirely negative relation to the "deceased" envelops a positive intention of *fidelity* which is addressed to the dead, to the past, to oneself. As we see, it involves a reflexive determination quite different from the upheaval that immediately follows mourning, though it originates in that upheaval and aims to perpetuate it. What is involved, in this case, is no longer only, or primarily, the relation to the deceased but the relation to the self. The mute work of mourning, which the widower obscurely feels in himself, can deliver him from his frustration only by a rearrangement that will turn him into *another*; and it is the *horror of being other* that compels him to fight all elements of change, inside and out. The widower will then decide that his life has stopped with his wife's death, which implies two contradictory determinations: I will never more be who I was (when my wife was alive); I will never be *other* (than what I am at present). The contradiction disappears, moreover, if we understand that he wants to perpetuate indefinitely not his conjugal life, which is definitively ruined, but a certain state of widowhood in relation to that life. In short, as Marivaux says, it is a matter of living only "by dint of reason," of considering all events following the mourning as potential consolations, and of existing now only to ponder a dead life. We shall consider this a double conduct of failure. First, the perpetual intention to evoke the past—the face of the beloved woman; her behavior, the sound of her voice, etc.—never fails to run aground, since the clearest memory manifests itself as pure absence; the inconsolable widower knows it, and it is this very absence to which he attaches himself, in other words, he seeks *for itself* the irritating disappointment that is the derisory result of his efforts. At the same time his whole life, from his birth to the disaster that brought it to a halt, seems to him a radical defeat since he can no longer see it except as a function of a union whose final wreckage is its truth. In exchange, he believes he is defined by a certain commerce with *being*; this is intangible, of course, but is nonetheless the point, since *what has been* is constantly aspired to *through absence* as the immutability of the past. Moreover, the refusal to change is accompanied by a feeling of lofty ontological dignity, of immutability. A sinking boat, a shipwrecked man who "plunges" into the darkness, immobile, determined to take a good look at the invisible being that is present at the core of its absence—that is the inconsolable widower. We have already noted that this attitude, taken in its generality, is familiar to Flaubert. In this case, however, it has a particular signification. Let us state, first of all, that Marivaux's inconsolable widower stiffens himself against the work of mourning and that, *already* consoled, he maintains his attitude—which has become an abstract *role*—only by voluntarism; in contrast, Gustave—in the seventies—feels that his voluntary decision is elicited, sustained, nourished by the heteronomy of his sensibility. But this observation is only interesting because it specifies the type of belief belonging to this inconsolable man in his inconsolability. The important thing is *first* to determine what it is he regrets. In other words, to bring to light the object whose abolition produces his widowhood. There is no doubt that it is the *Empire*. The Empire, meaning himself, since Napoleon III is the Garçon in power. Later, we shall reflect more fully on the central problem: *what is it he regrets* about the Empire? For the moment, the central question is related to *how* rather than why. How can Flaubert call himself a widower of imperial society? How *does he live* this widowhood? Why does he reject a possible reorganization that would integrate him into the new society? In short, what is the nature of his proclaimed fidelity?

He refuses, as we know, to resign himself and adapt to the course of history. Adapted, he would be one with the event; resigned, he would be a pure object, borne along by the current. But he wants to be neither the object nor the subject of history in the making; he demands that it drag him dead and protesting, forgotten, unforgettable, a phantom who comes, like a reproach, to torment the living. He will not be a Bonapartist. In 1871 Bonapartism is not a bleak regret, it is a collective praxis, whose objective is to restore a representative of the Bonaparte dynasty to the throne. The Bonapartists' reproaches against the new state are entirely different in kind from Gustave's: they are political and practical; they aim at weakening and discrediting the state to make it easier to overthrow when the time comes. But our passive agent is forbidden to engage in this *activity;* he can grieve, condemn a regime, but not join with those who want to oppose it. In his imprecations of 1870–71 we will not find one word to suggest that he wished to give the crown to a Napoleon. Moreover, in a way he accomodates himself rather well to the new government. After June '71, reassured by the repression imposed by the men of Versailles, he even goes so far as to *speak well* of the government; it is certainly the first time in his life that he has praised a head of state. Thiers is his man. He begins, like a good Cassandra, by imagining the aftermath of the Commune on the model of the consequences following the insurrection of June '48. Thiers is Cavaignac, he will be reproached for his softness, the clerical reaction will oust him from power, and some terribly devout person will take his place. In October '71, nothing has happened, Thiers is still in place; Flaubert exults: "I am not discouraged like you," he writes to George Sand, "and I like the present government because it has no principles, no metaphysics, no nonsense." And the next day, to Mme Roger des Genettes: "I think people are quite unjust to the present Assembly. What is happening suits me fine. This is the first time we've seen a government without metaphysics, without a program, without a flag, without principles, that is, without nonsense. The provisional is just what reassures me. So many crimes have been committed in the name of the ideal in politics that we should stick for a long time to the management of wealth." We shall observe that the Assembly he endorses represents in particular the provinces against Paris and, like the *Chambre Introuv-*

able, rural rather than urban interests, landed proprietors rather than industrialists. The Royalists are in the majority but dare not reestablish the monarchy. Even Falloux recognizes that "giving a third Restoration a third foreign army as escort would represent the most disastrous gift that could be made to the monarchy." Furthermore, these people are divided: the quarrel between the Legitimists and the Orléanists reduces them both to impotence. Thiers has promised not to broach the problem of the regime; he administers, that's all. The French State is, in effect, neither the property of a prince of divine right nor the expression of popular will: it is *provisional*, and the Republic is going to establish itself illicitly, shamefully, and *without a constitution*. This is what Gustave calls a "fortunate absence of principles." As to that "management of wealth" he approves of, it should be seen not as political planning but rather as the equivalent of the tasks that are to be fulfilled, according to our reactionaries of 1930, by a "government of technicians." Flaubert often appeals to liberalism, and it is from this perspective that the government has essential tasks to fulfill: the defense of private property, responsibility for "good finances," the establishment of a sound budget and rational taxation, the competent settlement of interest rates and tariffs. This fence-sitting minister is so occupied with things that he will no longer be tempted to concern himself with men—this in particular is cause for Flaubert's congratulations. If it should last, with any luck we would see reborn a system of values based on individual merit. This means, of course, that one "would humanize the brutal law of the majority,"[37] and artists would once more find their place in it. What he likes about this state that dares not speak its name is its ambiguity: "What is the difference between a modern republic and a constitutional monarchy? . . . The words republic and monarchy will make [our descendants] laugh, just as we laugh at realism and nominalism." On his good day he goes so far as to sketch out the plan for a future society: it will be the Republic of the Mandarins, in which the Academy of Sciences will replace the Pope. We recognize ideas that Renan developed twenty years earlier for the first time, and refur-

37. On this point, Thiers gave him every guarantee: 18,000 victims in Paris, 38,000 arrests, 270 sentenced to death, 13,000 to prison and deportation. These official figures fall far short of the truth; and the trials, by drawing attention to the legal condemnations, served to distract attention from the summary executions that were taking place by the hundreds and perhaps thousands. Gustave makes only one criticism of this impeccable settling of accounts: Courbet was not punished enough. We know that Leconte de Lisle, more radical than Flaubert, demanded that the painter be condemned to capital punishment.

bished at the Magny dinners; the Goncourts protested, but Gustave, bashful lover of the intelligence of others, drank in his words. In 1871 he added to these ideas personal variations on the theme of universal suffrage: all citizens should have the right to vote, but each should possess a number of votes determined "according to money, brains, even race, in short all the advantages." In this system, as we know from later reflection, Flaubert would assign himself twenty votes.[38] This is an even more arrogant reversion to the *program of the elite of '48*, a regression that seems to be a last effort to conjure away *in the imaginary* the egalitarian and positivist Republic he so abhors. Although, as a prophet of misfortune, he has little faith in the system, that doesn't stop him from participating in the legislative elections and casting his single vote at the polls. He does this, he says, "out of the pure instinct of self-preservation." We can believe it. By giving his vote to Thiers, he is defending himself as an *artist* against the clerical reaction and the censure of the moral order, and as a *landowner* against an always possible awakening of the "Social State." But the artist, in these hard times, is disabused; it is essentially the *man of independent income* who is protecting his interests.

This society, which seems more congenial to him and whose evolution he claims to influence by the abjectly egalitarian means the law puts at his disposal, must be recognized as the same society he fulminates against. At most we might say that Thiers' government "without principles" seems to lead a rearguard action suited to delaying an ineluctable collapse; he supports it so that the "provisional" should have a chance to become definitive, in any case to last as long as he does. By taking part in elections, however, he shows—for the first time—that he is a *realist*, that in this case he *accepts* social reality to the extent that it provides him with the possibility of consolidating his economic status and safeguarding his material interests. And of course it guarantees his dream: without Croisset, without its farms and its farmers, how could he preserve the "aesthetic attitude"? Yet this realism is still a betrayal of his fidelity; for this inconsolable widower of the Empire, the work of mourning has begun with a compromise. But his fidelity is not to imperial society and to Napoleon III but rather to *their failure*, to that moment of truth when a whole regime is totalized in a tragic and deserved downfall. Indeed, he never had many illusions about this dictator and his court. And after the capitulation the last scales fall from his eyes: how could he desire the restoration

38. "I am certainly worth twenty Croisset electors."

of the regime since he knows, now, that an infernal Providence had given it a mandate to lead the way, through a series of criminal and inevitable mistakes, through the lie that constituted its very essence, to the disaster that ineluctably brought about the emergence of the detested Republic? Until the final years of the liberal Empire it was possible to ignore the rigid direction of this path to the abyss, or at least to hide the truth from himself. But even if, by some impossible chance, a Bonaparte should ride again into the Tuileries and leap onto the throne, how could he accept the return of a past drunk to the dregs, *known by heart*, how could he find the courage to walk with his eyes wide open, in full consciousness, toward defeat, occupation, and universal suffrage? In short, Gustave resembles a widower who, having chosen to be inconsolable and henceforth to live only in his wife's memory, would energetically reject her return. Because he loves her less than he claims? No, but because he loves her less than his own failure. Or because his love itself, so abruptly exalted, contains the failure of his entire life as the condition of its intensity.

Around this time Gustave meets Maxime and confides something to him that will help us understand his obstinacy and define the object of his loyalty. "He regretted," says Du Camp, "having ended *L'Education sentimentale* too soon;[39] the war, the invasion, the capitulation at Sedan would have provided him with an ending, a final tableau, as he said, which he was sorry not to have had at his disposal at the time." Here is the tableau: the Emperor, deep inside his carriage, stopped by a column of French prisoners led by mercenaries. Some salute him. But one of the Zouaves leaves the ranks, shakes his fist, and says: "Wretch! You doomed us!" Ten thousand men start shouting insults, spitting on the carriage as they pass. And the emperor, "motionless, without a word, without a gesture," thinks: "And these are what they called my Praetorians." Flaubert adds: ". . . a rough final tableau for *L'Education,* I cannot console myself for having missed [the scene]. But I shall put it . . . in a novel I will write on the Empire, with the soirées at Compiègne, the field marshals, senators, and ambassadors, their decorations tinkling as they leaned down to kiss the hand of the imperial prince. Ah, there are first-rate books to be written on that era, and perhaps now the coup d'état and its aftermath will, in the universal harmony of things, simply have furnished interesting scenarios for a few good scribblers."[40]

---

39. Published in 1869.
40. Cited by Madame Durry in *Flaubert et ses projets inédits.*

These statements, faithfully reported by Maxime, we assume,[41] are rich in meanings that are developed on several levels. First of all, the regret expressed by Gustave appears to be perfectly justified on the artistic level. Obviously, one cannot *reproach* an author for not ending a work with the narrative of events that in fact took place a year later. But we can easily understand Gustave's bitterness at the bad luck that deprived him of an admirable *fall,* especially because this *historical* novel, beginning in the final years of the July monarchy and continuing through the Revolution of '48 until the Empire, would have found its temporal unity in the capitulation at Sedan. This was not artistically *necessary,* of course. But there is no doubt that the double failure of Frédéric and Deslauriers would have gained by appearing to be a historical fatality *as well.* Flaubert does not claim that illumination by history is fundamental. If life "betrays" these two young men and ridicules their dream of greatness by condemning them to the hell of self-conscious mediocrity, that is the doing of Satan, our master who exalts us with an illusion only to disappoint us doubly when we fall back into the common clay. And in the second place, it is the fault of human nature: we've known all that for a long time. Yet the two men, by the singular color of their failure, manifest the temporalized essence of the society around them, which produced them not *entirely* but on the basis of their qualities—that is, of the singularization *within them* from their early history, of the general features of the species through accidents—and which they contribute to producing more out of cowardice, out of inertia, out of inexcusable passivity (for Flaubert does not excuse it—even in Frédéric) than by their acts. History endured, in sum, is what one does not want to do and what others—who are, of course, idiots or scoundrels—will do. In other words, the defeat is predictable a priori since it is caused in each of them by the "curse of Adam," but its style varies with the epoch, the furnishings: there is the Directoire defeat, the Louis-Philippe defeat, the Second Republic or Second Empire defeat. And the colossal failure of the members of the National Convention is explained by passions other than those of Napoleon III. Consequently, the outline of the shipwreck, instead of delineating only individuals, might have gained—from this conclusion dreamed after the fact but never written—that singular scope which would make it applicable to forty years of history and to France as a whole. Purely allusive, mysterious

41. His most egregious errors concern Flaubert's *youth.*

affinities might have connected these two boats, sinking untragically into the nihilism of quotidian banality, into the disaster that tragically swallowed up the *Latin world*. In a way, these two individuals—yet sworn a priori, like everyone, to a petty hell—might have been presented retrospectively by this last scene as perfectly excusable for having no excuse. If they botched everything, of course, it is their fault, but after all, they lived in a world in its death throes that proscribed success. The boldness and novelty—for the time—of this failed conclusion is clear: introduced immediately after the final meeting between Frédéric and Deslauriers, it would have remained seemingly unconnected to the novel—which never proposed to depict the Second Empire—since Napoleon does not appear in the body of the narrative, and of the numerous characters it evokes, none would even have been named in the final scene. And, quite curiously, the book, a center of permanent derealization, would have been completed by a real event (or one that Flaubert regarded as such) concerning a character *so real* that he was still living when Maxime wrote these statements down. The paradox here, for anyone who knows Gustave, is that reality and fiction coexist in silence, and that fiction takes its meaning from reality. But even more striking is the fact that the fictive shipwreck of imaginary characters—whom the author wanted to be petty and bourgeois—might suddenly have displayed, in the black light of the real, an authentic and tragic depth. Mediocre imaginary and tragic reality, or, as we say today, "fact stranger than fiction"? Who would have expected to find this in Flaubert. For him, in effect, grandeur exists on the level of myth, and his basic subject remains *The Temptation*. Madame Bovary, who dies damned and filled with horror, is authentically tragic (and not dramatic as has been claimed) because her destiny is to live, through an unbearable experience, the radical impossibility of being human of discovering that her desire is too great to be satisfied by the things of this world, and at the same time that she is too small for her desire (that it does not become conscious except through silly nonsense—just as the religious instinct manifests itself only through the antics of instituted religion). Her suicide is tragic because it is inevitable and has been prophesied a hundred times over. Yet Gustave never stops groaning over the mean commoners who people his novel: in writing it, he judges the novel too close to that quotidian banality—his real environment—he claims to escape through the dream. And of course he took pleasure in writing *Salammbô* because, in the absence of any vestige or monument, he had to imagine the true. Thus the strange reversal he dreams of in '71, which might have given the final word to reality, must be examined with the closest attention, for it is surely laden with meaning.

All the more so since Badinguet is thereby elevated to the heights of martyrdom. His terrible defeat subsumes all the particular defeats of his subjects and gives them their meaning and their truth. Slumped in his carriage, mute, motionless, he is paying for everyone's faults—his own and those of twenty million subjects. Through his martyrdom he embodies everyone, in that deluded lie that has been their lives, by the sudden puncturing of his own lie, *of his being*. And before those other words, "The End," which sounding like a knell shroud them in eternity, the final words that resonate in his head—"and those are what they called my Praetorians,"—function only to denounce, bitterly and resentfully, the collective hallucination that made him emperor. It is noteworthy that he does not say "those whom I took for my Praetorians," but "those *they* called . . ." The collective and individual aspect (he shared it, he believed his objective reality was to be found in it) gives his *disillusionment* the quality of a singular universal.

Indeed, this martyr is also a hero. He never was one during his entire reign as Emperor, since everything about it was false, even the luxury. And here he is at the moment of his collapse, vanquished, guilty, a prisoner of the enemy, hated by his former subjects; with the Parisians prepared to overturn his throne he reveals himself as emperor—not, of course, in his own eyes but in the absolute—through what he represents for the first time in an ultimate totalization: the humiliation, the defeat, the contradictory lies, the errors and even the innocence of twenty million Frenchmen who dreamed him emperor and whose destiny he became. It should be noted that he is insulted *by each man going by* until the last row of prisoners has marched past his carriage. A military review in reverse, as is fitting in hell. We recognize the ten thousand ragged soldiers who insult him: they are the *mob,* the hideous mob whose insults pushed poor Marguerite to suicide in *Un parfum à sentir.* And they are also France. Stupid France, denying Badinguet just when he most represents them. It makes him emperor just as another mob, jeering in Jerusalem, made Jesus king of the Jews. It is clear that Gustave had this in mind, for in *La Danse des morts,* a story from his adolescence, he presented Christ as one of the vanquished, humiliated at having created the Earth and unable, despite his Passion, to wrench it away from the devil. But there are other intentions in this final portrait of a disappointed sovereign.

How does the Good Lord conduct himself under the rain of spittle usually reserved for poets? Well, we have to say, nobly. Just as Gustave imagines he would do himself in a similar instance, or like Baudelaire's Don Juan: "motionless, without a word, without a gesture," he "deigns to see nothing": scorn, a noble bitterness, a rebounding pride that leads him to survey the vile multitude and his own misfortune and to judge the entire human race by these faithless soldiers—stoicism. In a word, Badinguet the bastard, the false Bonaparte, the imposter, becomes a real aristocrat the moment his defeat exposes his commonness and incompetence. He is a criminal, he knows it, but this is not the time for remorse. That will come later—*not here, not now,* under base popular pressure. He will wait for solitude and will don Buffon's shirtsleeves to reflect on his vast and sacred crimes. And we cannot help interpreting this scene as a double symbol, whose meaning should be quite clear, for on the one hand it refers to the cabriolet of '44 and the impending fall, to Gustave's ennobling and chosen degradation; on the other hand, it is a kind of (retroactively) prophetic condensation of the evolution that followed the disaster and transformed France: those "Praetorians" who insult their Emperor are *at once* the scholars responsible for 4 September *and* the Communards (spittle). It will surely have been observed that this unwritten ending resembles the ending of *Salammbô,* except that Mathô, the defeated leader, walks between the two rows of his executioners, whereas the martyred Emperor does not move and it is the *others* who file past. In both cases the disaster of man is magnified by the impassive presence of an unattainable ideal: Salammbô, distant, mute, indecipherable, witness to Mathô's torture; and, in the spirit of Napoleon, despite bitter lucidity or disillusionment (those are what they called my Praetorians), the illusory Empire remains the impossible greatness of man, sustained by the very pain of the false emperor or, if you will, by the glorification of man through the stoic recognition of his own impossibility. We return precisely to that favorite theme of the Knights of Nothingness: nothing is more beautiful than the imaginary that denounces itself as such and imposes itself in failure, not despite but because of its unreality.

The series of statements reported by Maxime specifically confirms Flaubert's intention to invest the conclusion he imagined in '71 with this meaning. Since it is too late to use this "rough tableau" for the ending of *L'Education,* he imagines placing the scene in a novel whose explicit subject would be imperial society. And for the moment, this work's exclusive content will be the contrast between, on the one

473

hand, the brilliant lie (field marshals, senators, ambassadors, the tin-kling of medals at Compiègne, ostentatious respect for the imperial prince and, through this false prince, for the false monarch who is merely the dream of a slumbering France) and, on the other hand, the carriage scene in which, finally, the awakening and the return to reality serve only to reenforce his dolorism. The ontological dignity of the imaginary—this being of nonbeing—appears clearly when it is *suffered*. When the Court at Compiègne, the servility of the great, the etiquette and all the rest of this costly dream was financed by the bourgeoisie, it was just a rather pitiful game that no one took quite seriously. Massacred, bloodily ruined *through its own fault*, when this less than fabulous opera is revived in memory *even without indulgence*, it assumes its sovereignty from the siglum of failure. We might say that the norms of '44 are reversed: then, failure preceded the shift to the imaginary, which was its immediate consequence; in 1870 it is the reign of the imaginary that precedes failure and produces it. The first moment of the attack in '44 was the discovery of the impossibility of being a real man through a series of defeats arranged by a gentle, dark Providence; the neurotic option came afterward, presenting itself as the sole possible conclusion, as the choice of the impossible because of its very impossibility. The unrealization of the loser as artist is the continuation of the primary intention in other circumstances and by other means; since the harmonious plenitude of being is revealed as radical absence, he continues to aspire to it as absence, and he enters into contact with the nonbeing of being and the being of nonbeing through the permanent predisposition to take a leave of absence from oneself. Thus, *the image triumphs over reality*. After Sedan, this absen-teeism receives its punishment: the choice of the impossible is exposed for what it is, an impossible choice; *reality triumphs over the image*, and he discovers that it always has done: to be unrealized was not to de-tach himself from the real but, on the contrary, to surrender to it to the extent that he renounced control over it. In a sense, this is nothing new; Gustave was always conscious of his fundamental project: to choose the imaginary was *to take for granted* that the impossible was possible, in short, to assume the problem was resolved and simulta-neously to know that it was insoluble, and that a possible impossible, even on the level of the image, is a contradiction *in adjecto*. Therefore the mystical fall of the unreal was not only the consequence of prior defeats, even providential—intentional—ones, the leap into the imagi-nary bears *in itself* a commitment to end in nothing. The intention of failure is flagrant: victory never crowns being or nothingness—in other words, affirmation or negation—definitively; it is always appearance that is vanquished and, conversely, the loser, whatever he might be, is denounced by his defeat as mere appearance. The *blackest* thing about Gustave is his predilection to *lose for the sake of losing*, which is hidden beneath the religion of absolute-art. Beginning in 1844 he often said to himself: "Perhaps literature is merely the vainest of illusions," and not surprisingly he repeated this in 1870: "Writing seems to be a vain and uninteresting occupation." In fact, on a certain level it is a constant determination of his thought, and amounts to saying: I am damned in advance, and the surest instrument of my damnation is the Catharism by which I claim to free myself from it.

As long as the Empire lasted, however, his pessimism could be kept in check. First of all, there was the deeply held and opposing view that often succeeded in neutralizing it, not Jules's proud and dialectic "Loser Wins" but the humble, religious "Loser Wins" that originated in Gustave's conduct of failure, the cunning determination to surrender to God and tempt Him with his merits. And then we must consider the *works*, fixed centers of derealization that brought him sudden fame, the admiration of an undiscoverable and discovered public, and, after a few sulks, honors, the favor of the great. Isn't he led by the *real* consequences of these fictions to see them as an effective and successful effort? It's as if the whole society were giving the unreal—without *realizing* it—a kind of objective reality, a sort of ontological status, as if the society were assimilating *Madame Bovary*, as a singular universal, to the collective imaginary. After all, he is Gustave Flaubert, the purveyor of shadows whom the Emperor invites to dine and *distinguishes* with decorations; he is the man the sovereign heads of Europe want to meet at the Tuileries during the Exposition because they have been told he is the greatest writer of the Empire. Thus the a priori failure of his mad attempt to write remains veiled for almost fifteen years because *real* society underwrites his exercises in derealization.

But what if he were suddenly to learn that this touted reality were only a mirage? Wouldn't it surely mark the return to despair with a vengeance? Wouldn't he *see himself*, then, as a shadow purveying shadows to shadows? The effects of his work on the meritricious souls of actors—the admiration he thought to elicit, the demoralization he meant to practice—would be in fact merely ludic determinations by which each character would be affected as a function of his role; in short, his readers' reactions would not be prompted by him but would be *acted out*, mere gestures, imaginary feeling, for which his novels serve as pretexts. It would be in good taste, in certain circles, to disparage his books; in others, to praise them to the skies. And that is what happens at Sedan: at Sedan, Badinguet reveals that he was merely the appearance of an Emperor; as a result, like Charles Bovary reading Emma's letters, Gustave discovers that twenty years of his life were merely a "long lie." Sedan is Flaubert's capitulation. At the same moment, "Loser Wins" gently founders; it will later be recomposed as the central theme of the *Légende de Saint Julien*. But the catastrophe is so sudden, so boundless, so unforeseen even by the prophet of the worst, Gustave's unhappiness so far outstrips his hope that he abruptly wakes up, sees the rubble, senses the future, his own fossilization, and thinks he is *truly* in hell. *Before* 1870 an imaginary society evoked "the great writer Flaubert" as one of its images—a brilliant reign produces great authors; wouldn't this semblance of a reign produce a semblance of an author? *After* 1870, a real and impecunious society, enamoured of truth, unconcerned with dreaming, will discard him: "*we are superfluous,*" "there is no place for workers of art." *Who,* then, is he? What is his value? Did he ever have any? And what is the value, what is the meaning of literature?

We understand now to whom and to what he is faithful—and why he refuses all consolation. To be consoled is to adapt, to find a new equilibrium, therefore to become republican, in any case to become part of that Republic which can establish itself only by denying him. In short, it is an exercise in self-denial. By contrast, since there is a reciprocity of perspective between his lovely lies of art and the social lie that has just perished, Flaubert will endure almost unbearable tension in an attempt to preserve his fidelity to himself *through* his fidelity to the Empire. This does not mean simply that he regrets the imperial regime; we must see that he reestablishes it *for himself alone* in opposition to republican society. Indeed, he *institutes it,* in the way grieving persons, as Merleau-Ponty tells us, *institute* their dead through their more or less magical ceremonies, their feelings and behavior. Yes, the Empire has become an institution "made for one man," within and by which Flaubert will continue to live. Externally, by and for other fossils, he refuses to internalize his own fossilization: his "fixed despair," thus *sustained,* is certainly not a *negation;* but neither should it be seen as simple passive resistance. He escapes the present and the future because on a deeper level he succeeds in maintaining a fixed integration with the past. Again, we must understand that although for some time he has taken pleasure—as we have seen—in evoking intimate and singular memories (the most moving to him are those with least meaning, which thus best manifest the past in its absence and its being), the Empire he revives will have nothing seductive about it: Gustave wants to be faithful to the "long lie." Not because he could sometimes be taken in by it, but because he is no longer fooled by it or perhaps never was—we shall see in what sense. In short, he quite consciously restores the illusory Empire, the failed Empire, for himself alone. By identifying with the fallen Emperor just as this false sovereign, clairvoyant at last, receives the sacrament of failure and, by the loss of power, by a strange de-realization of the past (everything was merely a lie and a farce), *truly* becomes an Emperor and a great man, it is to his own failure that Gustave wants to remain faithful. He wrote novels he hoped would be immortal and which the society of the future is in a hurry to for-get;[42] might as well admit, he thinks, that they're bad, or that immor-tality is a meaningless word and fame a falsehood. Yet he has written these books that have missed their mark, that are only the *dated* dreams of a parasite nourished by a mirage society, and contrary to his most secret and fundamental hope, they never had the power to move easily from one society to another at the whim of history; in short, they could not survive him so that, once dead, he might yet remain in them, spiteful and beautiful, imaginary and mineralized. He has indeed written those triply illusory books that force the reader to resuscitate a fiction—false masterpieces that a false elite pretended to admire.[43] It is not that he is claiming to salvage something from the shipwreck—the labor, the effort, the suffering, for example, or, as he did as a young man through rebounding pride, the ethic of beauty, the virtues art demands of the artist. No, he seeks the negative in them in order to recognize himself in it and assume it. He seeks that moment when, like the other man in the carriage—stoic or despair-ing, it makes no difference—he thinks lucidly, "that bad writer, whom the Republic has now changed into his true self, fixed forever in his vain pretention, his real mediocrity, and the stories with which his mediocrity has been lulling itself, enclosed in those black years and slipping with them into a increasingly distant past, *c'est moi.*" Litera-ture is vain? All right, the imagination is merely a flight suddenly arrested; so the sylph colliding with "chill ceilings" knows his failure? Okay. But failure taken in itself, failure pondered then chosen in full

42. He is sincere, of course. But everything fits together: if he *believes* in this forget-ting—quite improbable in 1870–71—it is because he does not want to receive his fame henceforth from republican society. We shall come back to this a little later.

43. This is not what *I* think. It is what *he* thinks.

knowledge, the commitment to act the loser by betting on the impossible, finally the defeat, total and derisory but prophesied from childhood under the name of "the curse of Adam," *expected*, perhaps even provoked by intransigence—isn't this man's cipher, his secret, the only way his religious instinct can manifest itself without becoming mummery? The great thing is that Gustave had indeed written bad books believing they were good, that Napoleon had pushed France into a ditch believing he was imposing French hegemony on Europe, that the Court was sunk in the most vulgar servility believing it was recuperating the etiquette of the defunct aristocracy.

Flaubert is desperate; he means to be and wants to stay that way. We are not to imagine that he is quietly reentering a disguised version of "Loser Wins" by the back door; in fact he has never been more demonic; he reveals here, and reveals to himself, that he regards literature as a perfectly black religion, or if you will, he takes the mystique of unrealization to an extreme. The essence of the image is bad faith, the lie, the insoluble problem presumed resolved since, even in the simplest cases, consciousness has recourse to it in order to grasp in its concrete particularity an object *that does not exist* in its perceptual field. But if, in addition, the radical failure that follows reveals that this image bears in itself the ruin of its producer, even if this ruin is proferred as a punishment *deserved* by all those who leave the spoils for the shadow and let themselves be transported by the course of things, claiming to be unaware of it; if the imagination is in essence a self-deluding lie, if it claims to give us the impossible and the infinite even as it is confined to a few special effects and can only *signify* to the "religious instinct" the being-beyond-the-world of these two ideas, not through words but through its very failure to manifest them; in short, if in defeat the unmasked demiurge is revealed as a mediocre magician—then the imaginary achieves a most diabolical purity. Defined by the failure of man and image, it is no longer even what one imagines, lacking the ability or desire to grasp it or fix it in experience. Before the defeat it was (or claimed to be) the impossible manifesting itself in the unreal, or the infinite allowing itself to be approached through an unrealizing ascesis; now, untouched by the catastrophe, it affirms itself, purified, as the *beyond* of imagination or the very cipher of the routing of imagination. It is the image absent from every *image*—always "you must, therefore you cannot"—which constitutes the signification of every imaginative effort, since the impossible and the infinite *must be continually imaginable*, and these two primary categories together define the teleological intention that produces and structures the imaging disengagement. *But* insofar as the image is a *mediocrity* that sinks without ever manifesting those gigantic ideas, except by its painful inability to represent them, even outside of all reality, the ideal of the imagination, that is, the *imaginary world*, is no longer defined exclusively as the totality of that which cannot be realized but also, above all, as the totality of that which *cannot be imagined*. I would not say that this conception of the image—which he knew was already generated by failure and led to failure—as *itself* and in itself a failure, is entirely new for Flaubert. But he alludes to it at times, in moments of doubt, only to push it aside; if he really believed in it, he would have to declare that every work—including Homer's or Shakespeare's—is *always* a failure, and that the best it can do is to suggest allusively, silently, through that unmasked failure an *elsewhere* that authors have not merely failed to *render* but even to imagine. On this level, the real triumphs over the image not just by crushing the woolgatherer who believes he can escape it, but by becoming manifest *within it* as its limit and the determination of its possibilities: you can inflate this irridescent balloon a bit more, but sooner or later it bursts. That is imagination *realized*: it is none other than a real and limited *power*. The cult of the imaginary—of what man must and cannot realize, of that beyond of the real and of unreality—is a savage religion. For that hidden god, beauty, neither human sacrifice nor martyrdom will do; those who willingly sacrifice themselves must botch their death out of cowardice and perish, damned, under the ritual knife. Reality imposes itself on the derealization of the real as a determination, a limit, of the power to derealize: the discovery of the real as *already being there* in advance in the escape toward unreality, as the impotence and finitude of the imagination—that is hell. Pure hell. The trap laid for the best by Satan: by means of a calculated defeat, the Prince of Darkness teaches them that they are not of this world; he isn't silly enough to claim that an Other world exists, he simply invites them to imagine, both because he represents supreme beauty, and because faced with the choice between being and nothingness, the base vulgarity and hostility of being compels them to choose nothingness. But just when they commit themselves to it out of disgust with the world and its multitudes, he brings them up against their all too human limits: the Knights of Nothingness are men of flesh and blood, and their little imaginative disengagement—the *conatus* that seems to withdraw them from the weight of the species, from its materiality—is as strictly governed as their other behaviors, it defines them (variations from one to the other are infinitesimal but infinite in number in their individual *reality*) as much as the shape of their face or the color of their hair; in other words, the writer *realizes himself by becoming unrealized*. The radical evil is not that one cannot leave the world—in Gustave's view there are happy idiots who don't even dream of doing that—but that a diabolical mirage binds to the world the very men it has incited to tear themselves away from it. Mallarmé will state it clearly: once the dice were cast, nothing took place but the place. This chance occurence that is me, a contingent determination of time and space produced by an accidental inspiration generated by its limits and fortuitous circumstances, far from eliminating chance will only serve to realize it in the objective universe. Flaubert's religion (like Mallarmé's) is *black* when he wants to be inconsolable, because in all lucidity he loves this mirage. He preserves his fidelity to the mousetrap of the imaginary, the inaccessible ideal of imagination, not despite its harmfulness but because of it, because for artists, and especially for Gustave himself, it is pure evil. Let us imagine this: an extremely ugly room, Louis-Philippe furnishings, a fire has broken out, I am suffocating; there is a single way out, a door opening onto the void or onto some other room, I'm not sure because the smoke is blinding me. I get through the flames, run across the threshold, and find myself in the same room; disconcerted, I retreat, following the same course in reverse, I dash into another room, and that other room *is the same*. For Gustave, the imaginary is that door, that crazy false hope that invites me to escape the conflagration of this hideous world while really doing nothing but compelling me to plunge into it on my own authority, spontaneously to take responsibility for this horror, which hadn't the means to compromise me as long as I passively denied it. Does this door exist? Flaubert doesn't want to know; what he loves in this situation is the *deception*. As a result, the being of nonbeing is restored: in this base real world a certain reality must indeed pass itself off for what it is not. Thus the imaginary possesses a certain ontological charge: the door *is* a trompe-l'oeil, or by some satanic miracle it seems to offer an *exit* while it is really the one-way *entrance* to the room in which I am suffocating. Impossible, infinite, total, the imaginary is there: it is the infinite difference that separates *in* from *out*. But no on can locate it or enjoy it; the ideal of imagination, at first a mute invitation to imagine, affirms itself—like a lightning bolt—to the artist or the dreamer only in the moment of panic in which the unreal is revealed as *not other* than reality. Yet it is not directly graspable. In certain cases—for example, when the danger is extreme and one cannot conjure it away—all of the real is derealized for a few moments, no doubt the effect of a self-defense mechanism. We can then grasp the source of unrealization, since the environment loses its weight of reality for us and becomes a spectacle. And Flaubert, as we have seen, has had similar experiences, especially during his preneurotic period and in the first years of his neurosis—these experiences are at the basis of what he calls his "aesthetic attitude." In these states—false promises—he could glimpse the imaginary as a closed world to which he would have access when he had crossed the farthest boundary. But in 1870 a reverse movement transforms the lack into plenitude before his eyes, the unreal into reality. And when, to his confusion, he perceives that he has never left the earth, that he is suffocating in a leaden universe, without respite and with no way out, the imaginary can become manifest neither as an alleviation, a levitation of terrestrial things, nor as the final goal of an infinite derealization. What he sees, in fact, is the substitution of being for appearance; and just as God's omnipotence and total positivity prevents Him, according to certain persons, from conceiving of the weakness of his creatures, their "paltry reality," and their share of nothingness, so here the mystification stems from the fact that the new positivity of the real no longer allows Flaubert to find the dancing lightness of unreality in his massive, suffocating surroundings. Consequently, the imaginary is no longer before him as the future conclusion of a systematic derealization, but is behind him, in the past, as the reason for this visible transformation. Flaubert cannot manage to conceive of the imaginary now, since its images themselves are laden with reality; at the same time it is *something other* than the real since a *lie* was needed for Flaubert to get there. A strange lie, which, instead of making the usual offer of nonbeing for being, has chained Gustave to the being in him, presenting the whole world and especially his own psychosomatic reality as a "hollow musical nothingness."

In short, for the fifty-year-old of 1871, one doesn't imagine: one imagines that one imagines. He even said as much in his youth. He imagined himself a painter who understood nothing about painting, a musician who didn't like music; he didn't conceive of sonorous or plastic images but was merely playing the role of the composer or artist who conceived them. Now the idea has deepened and become generalized: the imaginary is the geometric site of all that we imagine ourselves imagining. It is what continually deludes and escapes us and continually returns to torture us. Its invisible purity denounces the imposture of our would-be images, which naturally have their share of nonbeing but are dragged down nonetheless by their all too real weight, like low-flying chickens. It is to this executioner—to *his* executioner—that Flaubert means to be faithful. Or, if you will, it is to the *image-failure* as it continually founders in positing itself. This can be summed up in a different way: for Gustave in 1870, the image is composed of nothingness and being; it contains too much nothingness to *produce*—in the way of intelligible intuition—the object it represents, but too much being not to be a real determination of a subjectivity and not to qualify in itself its idiosyncratic reality. To play a role, of course, is *not to be* the character one interprets; but it is also to reveal oneself *in one's being* as the good, mediocre, or bad actor of that role, that is, as one whose physique and manners, habits, tics, etc., *show through* the character as the real restraints of imagination. This real ambiguity of the image, which reveals the false duke or the nonbeing-duke of the actor, but also reveals the true actor through his failure to be a duke—this ambiguity is the object of Flaubert's dogged loyalty; futile as it is, its greatness being its futility, he wants to eternalize this evasion in the defeat itself. It is the impossible lie of the artist and of Imperial Society lived in the semilucidity of the 1860s and relived in the lucid despair of 1870 as a ruse of history—*accepted* as a ruse and blind alley or disaster, denied in its consequences, in the full flowering of republican knowledge. The false Emperor (who is never false enough) and his false court correspond to the false beauty of works of art. What does it matter that the lie of the Tuileries is more absurd and trivial than the lie of Croisset? What counts is the comedy of greatness and beauty, man's vain homage to what will be denied him to the end, this game of nonbeing and being (the impossible creation of the impossible, and thereby the consolidation and realization of the possibles inscribed in the real future by prior circumstances). The Empire was a sham? Well done! The unique greatness of man escapes him, but it is inscribed in the metaphysical heaven, being quite simply his conscious and necessary struggle against inevitable failure.

Does he love the Empire at last—as we know, it has not always inspired his tender feelings—*in its final failure* and just as it is about to be destroyed? Or must we admit that he was attached to the regime *before* the ultimate disaster? Numerous passages in his correspondence between 1870 and 1871 indicate that the second hypothesis is the correct one. He writes to Mathilde, 3 May '71, that "whatever happens, the Government will no longer be based in Paris. From that time on, Paris will no longer be the capital, and the Paris we loved will become history. We will never find it again, everything that made life so sweet."[44] So sweet? Life? In all his work and all his letters, Gustave has never said anything like this. And what has gotten into this provincial that he should suddenly love the sweetness of life in Paris—in that capital he so heartily despised? Isn't the explanation that he is writing *to Mathilde*? No, this theme can be found in his letters ever since the defeat. From 13 October 1870—to Mathilde, it is true: "Whatever happens, everything we loved is finished."[45] And again—still to Mathilde, 23 October 1870: "I feel as though it's the end of a world. Whatever happens, everything I have loved is lost." Everything "*we* love" (Mathilde, the imperial princess, and Flaubert, the great writer of the regime), everything "I loved"—it's the same thing, although the way of loving might be different for each of them. It is the Empire, or if you like, the *dolce vita* of the Empire. In fact, he reproaches the Prussians for "taking pleasure in destroying works of art, *luxury items*, when they encounter them, and for the dream of annihilating Paris because Paris is beautiful." So it is the luxury he regrets—for truthfully, art as he conceives it is unattainable. He is more specific, this time in a letter to Caroline: "My sorrow is not so much because of the war as its aftermath . . . Any kind of elegance will be impossible!"[46] *Elegance?* This is a word he doesn't often use. He sticks with it, however, for he takes up the idea in the following letter: "We are entering a hideous world in which the Latins will be excluded, any elegance, *even of a material kind*, is excluded for a long time to come."[47] This may will give us pause: at Croisset, Gustave enjoyed great comfort, but, as the Goncourts bear witness, nothing could have been less "elegant" than the furnishings and crude Oriental bazaar of trinkets. A lack of taste? Yes, but above all indifference. Moreover, this elegance is not only material, it is the Latin way of life: "The society built on our ruins will be military and republican, antipathetic to all my instincts. 'All civility,' as Montaigne would have said, will be impossible. The Muses will have no place."[48]

This is not only a matter of art, as these texts clearly show, but of a certain relation between luxury and art that can be understood as a

44. *Correspondance*, 6:234.
45. *Correspondance*, 5:166.
46. 24 October, *Correspondance*, 6:174–75.
47. To Caroline, 28 October 18709, ibid., p. 178. My italics.
48. To Caroline, 22 September 1870, ibid., p. 154. Cf. letter to Maxime DuCamp, 29 September 1870, ibid., pp. 159–60: "All civility, as Montaigne would have said, is lost for a long time to come."

reciprocal affinity—as when he writes that in the future Republic people will be poor, shabby, virtuous, and that workers of art will consequently be superfluous. But he goes still further, and on 28 October *speaks in his own name:* "Life in itself is something so sad that it is unbearable without great alleviations. What will it be like, then, when it is cold and denuded! That Paris we have loved will no longer exist."[49] This time it's clear: the inspired word *alleviation* covers everything. *Real* life as it is lived in the provinces is *truly* unbearably heavy: the hermit of Croisset knows it nine months a year in its "denuded coldness." He is merely a mushroom swollen with boredom, since boredom is nothing but the plenitude of being. Happily—at least until 1870—the capital existed, which allowed him three months out of twelve to *alleviate* his boredom. In black and white this means that Paris, the factitious capital, invited the great man from the provinces to stop struggling with his winded imagination and let himself live in the imaginary. Isn't alleviating the real a magical weightlessness that allows one to be unrealized by derealizing it? Or, rather, he holds the Parisians, the new Gentlemen, responsible for its derealization; all Gustave had to do was go along with it; they lied for him, he was only asked to believe in the lie. The sweetness of living, luxury, the universal alleviation of life was not the business of this Norman plodder; his business was only to knock himself out with his labor and produce those precision instruments, his works, fixed centers of derealization; but in the depths of his boredom in Rouen he waited all spring, all summer, all autumn for that fabulous trimester, winter, when in reward for his pains he was *given objective* unrealization.

What was it he found in that capital when he alighted after hours on the train? First of all, itself. He no longer despised it then. No longer and not yet. For him it was the capital of the fabulous. On 15 June 1867 he wrote to George Sand: "Paris . . . is turning into something colossal. It is going mad and growing huge. We are returning, perhaps, to the old Orient. It seems to me that idols are going to rise from the earth. We are threatened with a Babylon. Why not? The *individual* has been so denied by democracy that he will abase himself utterly, as under the great theocratic despotisms."[50] The ambiguity of the text will not escape notice. For Flaubert, the Orient is the death of the individual; but he has no objection to theocratic despotisms—didn't he write *Salammbô*? Furthermore, if this cataclysm comes about,

49. To Claudius Popelin, 28 October 1870, *Correspondance,* 6:179.
50. *Correspondence,* 5:308.

it is democracy and not the Empire that is responsible for it; the fault lies with June '48 and not with December '52. And then, although Flaubert is bourgeois, he is not—as we have seen—an individualist; if men are not to be exterminated altogether, it would not displease this Timon of Rouen to see them degraded one by one. Furthermore, he is writing to Sand, and these letters, beneath their hypocritical respect, are the most insincere in his entire correspondence. When she annoys him, he scratches her as if by accident; when she behaves properly, he dons a mask and retracts his claws almost entirely. He is coming from the ball at the Tuileries when he describes the modern Babylon—for alas, once more he is prey to the commonplace—he has seen "sovreigns," he exults: he has dreamed of a definitive abasement of the masses, of the "impotence of the common folk." He says all this to his *Chère Maître*, but emphasizes its dark side, feigning to prophesy misfortune to hide his jubilation. It is true that shortly after the capitulation at Sedan, he will say that he hopes the crumbling of the dictatorship will permit the rebirth of the individual; but he says it without conviction, between two homilies on the death of Latinity. In any event, his reflections of 1868 and his meditation on the gigantism of the capital are very close to a provoked oneirism. Paris no more evoked Babylon in 1868 than it does today, and the Second Empire was further than ever from a theocratic despotism, although it sought the support of the clerics against republican pressure. "Idols are going to rise from the earth"—that is the daydream of the commoner who has just left the Court and comes home in a fiacre; no need to reach for an undocumented evocation of the pomp of Carthage: Paris by night, obscure, indistinct, *inspires dreams* of a mad colossus; at the entrance to the Tuileries the jubilant guest of kings has stepped into the unreal; he will stay there effortlessly until the end of the night.

False, too, were those relations between peers that disguised bourgeois atomization and each man's profound solitude; false was that bellowing at the Magny dinners; when he entertained at home, no one quite believed in Flaubert's paradoxes, least of all he himself, nor in the awkward obscenities that everyone retailed to "make an impression." Yet all those stupidities beleagured him, overstimulated him, brought him to the point of violent and nearly intolerable aggression, which the Goncourts did not fail to observe but which he *suffered*—in the way that pathologically manic persons are painfully dominated by their irrepressible gaiety. Be that as it may, for a moment Gustave was living in the imaginary world of brotherhood, speaking, as he had wanted to do in his youth, "among people of

Art"; declaiming, gesticulating, he thought to impose himself on his equals as "the most equal of all," while he merely succeeded in stunning them; he thought he loved all those hucksters, when in reality no love was lost between them. Moreover, the mirage was collective; Flaubert didn't even take the trouble to invent it—it was enough to let himself take it in. In his presence, as in his absence, the Gentlemen of Magny regarded themselves as an Academy, spouting nonsense, false pearls of wisdom that, with the help of wine, they *believed* to be true.

And the relations of these intellectuals with the *demi-monde* were perfectly false as well. La Païva, la Lagier, at a higher cultural level Jeanne de Tourbey, Madame Sabatier—these women, especially the first two (and a hundred others as well), told all comers they were for sale, and named their price. One evening at Flaubert's home, in the presence of the Goncourts, Lagier, an actress of sorts, declares that "the theater is the absinthe of the brothel."[51] She astonishes the two prudes with her salacious conversation: "an obscene chatter of a scatological aesthetic . . . This woman has rubbed shoulders with everything in Paris that is dirty, doubtful, suspect, and sinister. She shines in the gutter."[52] Gutter, maybe, but she *shines* all the same, so obviously they are going to dine with her five days later, accompanied as always by Gustave, in a house that "resembles a *columbarium* of prostitution."[53] Flaubert liked her, not so much perhaps in any sensual way (he had her, as did everyone else, and probably for free) as by the coarseness of her conversation[54] and, "at the home of this old girl who is turning into an elephant," by the foul and salacious details she reported in such "down to earth language." For example, on the same 22 February: "We chat about actresses with stomach problems, soiled with shit, suffering from diarrhea, from the runs, women who wear their shit on their sleeves, according to [Lagier's] witticism: George, Rachel, and Plessy . . ."[55] Here is the *"petit fait vrai"* he adores: the great Rachel dragged down by the seat of her pants, all the more sublime as she is simultaneously "soiled with shit," and vice versa. It's delicious: in listening to her he surely has "as much pleasure as if someone were giving him money," but at the same time he is pleased—as are the others—to treat her with an ambiguous polite-

51. 22 February 1863, *Journal* (Edition de Monaco) 6:33.
52. Ibid.
53. 27 February, ibid., p. 34.
54. She said to him: "You are my heart's garbage can: I tell you everything."
55. 22 February 1863, *Journal* (Edition de Monaco), 6:34.

ness, half sincere, half ironic. These false members of the Academy love to imagine they are dining with Aspasia. It does not escape their notice that this "obscene language" is quite deliberate.[56] "The distance between argot and this language made of convenient nonsense, of sentences that have no more meaning, of oblique words, of superfluous locutions, is like the distance from prison to the army barracks. At least argot stinks of garlic; this smells like dirty socks," say the Goncourts, 22 February 1863. Yet *at the same time* they—and Flaubert along with them—believe that she is giving them a glimpse of the mysteries of Paris, that she is the expression and the symbol of the "sewer," of the underworld, of the lower depths, the awful depths of ordinary people and the human soul. Without risking their skin or their purse, they make contact through her with pimps, pederasts (who horrify them, of course), and criminals. This woman dazzles Flaubert because she serves his misanthropy by debasing the "artistic" elite ("Frédéric's nastiness was stirred up, mingled with a crazy spite . . . the belching, farting actor . . .") and exalting the gutter till it shines. Baseness manifests itself in her, surely, as the sublime below. The world is like that, she bears witness to it and totalizes it in the presence of these gentlemen, who are all, of course, persuaded that the worst is by definition the truth. At the same time, moreover, this lovely, exeedingly corpulant woman destroys Woman in herself by the crudity of her remarks. Like Rachel, *wearing her shit on her sleeve*, it is her own femininity she contests; this exhibitionistic self-destruction kills true desire while it excites, through the sadism of the men who listen to her, an imaginary desire that does not know to whom or to what to address itself. While she desperately exerts herself for them, they cannot ignore the fact that they are authors, and that actresses flatter them *at the slightest opportunity*, in the hope that such efforts will not be altogether lost and will—someday—land them a role in one of their plays. This does not stop Sainte-Beuve, old, bald, weary and skeptical,[57] from seeking her acquaintance and *paying court* to her, as though it were possible to win her as he would a virgin, timidly, ceremoniously, and with tenderness. Those were the rules of

56. To Nestor Roqueplan, for example, she says: "Your neck is so soft! It's like eighteen-franc satin! My ass is only fourteen!" That is a "witticism" made to please. Lagier knows what makes these flabbergasted intellectuals swoon: cynical truculence. So with brio she constructs and plays her character of depraved, venal vulgarity. The point is to drive them mad by showing them, continuously and simultaneously, that vice is the basis of money, money the basis of vice.

57. "As for me," says Sainte-Beuve, "my ideal is eyes, hair, teeth, shoulders and ass. Crassness doesn't matter to me. I love crassness." *Journal* of the Goncourts, 6:27.

the game. And Flaubert is correct when he writes of "false courtis-ans," when after the defeat he enumerates the "lies" of the Empire. What he does not say—but knows very well—is that the *falseness* does not come from these women; he and his colleagues, and many others, have all helped to impose it on them. Moreover, for him Lagier is the truth of the courtisan; the others, more decent, are the false ones.

With la Païva they almost reached their goal. Thérèse Lachman was a real whore and an authentic marquise: she was married to an im-pecunious Portuguese, the Marquis de Païva, whom the Goncourts—in a typical mistake—confuse with the Vicomte de Païva, the Portu-guese ambassador to Paris, a man who enjoyed wealth and power in addition to his noble birth. This ferocious prostitute got rid of her poor, unlucky husband (who ended by committing suicide) but kept her title, which she would exchange in 1871, after breaking off her marriage, for that of Countess de of Donnersmarck. Flaubert knew her earlier than the Goncourts, who were introduced only in 1867 to her "legendary mansion on the Champs-Elysées." What they notice immediately, once again, is the *falseness* of the place and its owner. She is "an old courtisan, painted and plastered, looking like a provin-cial actress, with a smile and false hair." The dining room, "with all its luxury and excess of Renaissance bad taste, resembles nothing so much as a very opulent private room in a great restaurant." In the midst of this false-true luxury (true if one considers only the money spent, "marbles, woodworkings, enamels, paintings, massive silver candelabra"—false if these heaps of tasteless riches are compared to the palaces and châteaux of the defunct aristocracy) "there is a halting conversation among embarrassed people, as if they were among a group of imposters." According to their account, "there is something unsettling about la Paiva, with her Russian accent, attempting to be gracious, something like a businesswoman . . . and her blond impas-sivity evoked a frightening past." Is it despite this fear or because of it? They return often. Here they are, on 31 May 1867, in the "famous salon which isn't worth the rumors about it." They take care, how-ever, to observe that it is "famous," just as the mansion was "legen-dary." Even though disappointed, they are attracted by the *myth;* and the disappointment is a large part of their amusement. The myth is somewhere in the air, rootless, it does not coincide with the perceived object and hence denounces itself; it is a vague, weak luminosity that illuminates the real, which in turn gives it the lie. What they come to find in "all this wealth" is the failure of imagination, and simultaneously a secret derealization of the real: the salon is not worth the rumors about it; this doesn't prevent it from *prompting rumors*. And these rumors, though given the lie by the thing itself, remain its property: it is a salon that doesn't live up to, and is therefore *undermined* by, its reputation. Moreover, there is suddenly a new transformation, a new contradiction: la Païva, that disquieting monster, a marquise, a courtisan, a businesswoman, and the German count, her keeper, are in truth nothing but a couple of bourgeois: "And we move into the dining room and we dine. Then there is the exhibition of the centerpiece,[58] the base, bourgeois invitation, so tasteless and immodest, to admire it endlessly. The price is not mentioned, but it is said that at the manufacturer's it would cost 80,000 francs. And everyone, his hand at his throat, gives voice to his admiration, to his compliment." Saint-Victor is the most servile. This must be true since Flaubert confirms it in 1871: "You haven't seen Saint-Victor paying his respects to la Païva!" Perhaps. But what were the Goncourts doing at her house? And Gustave? Were they fascinated by that other ambiguity, life unmasking death as its truth, death exposing itself as the realization of life? "The woman," says the *Journal*, ". . . I study her . . . A form which, beneath underpinnings of a courtisan still practicing her metier, is a hundred years old, and so at moments takes on the horrific aspect of a camoflaged corpse."[59] Good God! What enchantment for a Knight of Nothingness: this woman inspired passions, ruined the sons of respectable families; according to public documents she is still young enough to give pleasure; moreover, rumor has it—the two brothers have observed before meeting her—that the German who keeps her loves her to distraction. Yet she is ugly ("a pear-shaped nose with a flat Kalmouk tip, heavy nostrils, an expressionless mouth . . . surrounded by wrinkles that look black in the light on her white face"), which is a constant reminder, if one were needed, that love is another mirage; what is more, she is dead. Her life is merely an appearance; this is the moment to take the aesthetic attitude, in other words, the point of view of death on life. Gustave must have enjoyed these games, loving as he did to conceive of the living as bewitched cadavers. But the Goncourts emphasize that this defunct whore, reality disguised by the deceptive appearance of the lively marquise, reveals herself only *at moments*. A gesture is enough, a change of light, for the real to shift to the imaginary, and vice versa:

58. *Journal* (Edition de Monaco), 8:26.
59. Ibid.

the painted corpse is no longer the real being of their hostess; it is rather, let us say, her hyperbolic truth, accessible solely to the imagination of the artist. And given that at this moment life triumphs, given that the real, occluding all its fissures, fills the view, takes it over, prevents it from evoking the cadaver except by an empty and poorly explained intent, a guest of la Païva's, whether a Goncourt or a Flaubert, has the enervating pleasure of feeling his own *failure of imagination.*

If more materialistic reasons must be found, however, for the artists' visits to the "legendary" mansion, we will not have far to look. On 14 February 1868, the Goncourts, who have just come home from an evening there, note in their Journal: "A beautiful thing, wealth! It excuses everything. And no one who comes here notices that this house is the most uncomfortable in all of Paris . . . And in this thoroughly inhospitable house, beside that woman, jumping back for fear his cigar would burn her dress, Gautier endlessly mingled paradoxes, floated statements, original thoughts, the pearls of his fantasy."[60] What attracts them, basically, is money. And I mean money, not luxury, since this luxury is false. These writers are men of their times, their mores are austere; they live in bourgeois style, no more opulently. But when wealth—fabulous wealth, and especially inherited (Païva's German had received the title of count and silver mines from his father)—is consumed well beyond the necessary, consumed in the acquisition of the superfluous, they see merit in it, the basis of a new aristocracy. It was the Goncourts who declared that there are three ways of entering advantageously into life: birth, money, and talent. And Flaubert, as we have seen, meditating on universal suffrage, would fix the number of votes everyone ought to have at his disposal according to talent, race, and money. He will also tell his niece Caroline that he would prefer to see her dead rather than married to a pauper, even an inspired one. But for the Goncourts as well as for Gustave, money, while fundamental, can also be a delusion: for the rich do not know how to use it, and they are not what they should be. No one observes, however, that they lack taste, that they are incapable of managing a household; transfixed by the marble, the ceramics, the stone work, the "people of art" do not perceive that the famous mansion is the most uncomfortable house in Paris. A new and final illusion: wealth mystifies the guests, throws dust in their eyes, conceals the discomfort. Here they are, in ecstasy "in the con-

60. *Journal* (Edition de Monaco), 6:87.

servatory, where one goes to smoke after dining, half-frozen by the draft from above, half-suffocated . . . by the hot-air below." They sweat, catch cold, completely unaware. The Goncourts, however, are quite aware of it and mock their naive colleagues. And Flaubert knows it, too. How is it that they frequent this Trimalcion household? Well, for the same reason others do, they come to gape at money. But these Knights of Nothingness have the highly aesthetic pleasure of stripping it of its artifice; they admire it as naked power, ill-gotten and ill-used. Here again, it's a *double* game: acquired goods are distinguished from buying power. These goods are false; those who *believe* they are seeing marvels are dupes, victims of their imagination; in fact, with no greater expense one might have created true beauty, given the guests true comfort. Thus these costly objects are signs of wealth because of their high price; and at the same time they are not because, for people of art, true wealth must enhance its possessor's slow maturation, exquisite and subtle sensitivity, and taste, which are its truest sign and bestow the eminent right of possession. If such is the *eidos* of the property owner, here is a new and final ruse: Are la Païva and her sugardaddy husband false possessors, or, having failed to mature them, isn't money so foolishly spent false? In any event, lucid or not, the guests are all dazzled, they all come to profit from this golden river, if only for a few hours, to find its source and plunge in; simply, the most cunning taste the nihilistic sensual pleasure of *not being able* to grasp the costly and hideous fantasies surrounding them as the external signs of wealth, but consequently discover that money, deprived of these mediations, is an abstract and ineffable power. Reclining on the river bed, they perceive that this golden stream is a phantom. Yet for all that they must really be serious about these "alleviations of life," for Flaubert, braving Mathilde's rages,[61] is a regular attendant at la Païva's dinners!

In fact, the Knights of Nothingness far preferred the mansion in the rue de Courcelles to the one on the Champs-Elysées. But they certainly meant to be present at *both*. These contrasts charmed them; the Goncourts in particular were fond of sudden changes of setting, which gave them the feeling of living a dangerous and varied life whose pluralism was marvelously adapted to that pluralistic Paris, in which the various social strata—each with its own language—hardly

---

61. Mathilde, feeling her salon threatened, had almost as much hatred for this honest whore as for the Empress. She had declared quite clearly to her circle, with a sullenness that makes one think today of the furies of Mme Verdurin, that if she met one of her friends in the company of la Païva, she would not invite him again.

communicated.[62] For Gustave, it's a little different. He has never felt that indiscriminate curiosity that made the "two Lapdogs," even more than Maxime, such remarkable diarists. And what he is looking for in Paris after nine months of boredom are the alleviations of a worldly and even socially marginal life. From this point of view, far from betraying Mathilde with la Païva, he would not have thought of visiting the one if he hadn't regularly frequented the other. Like his peers, he was dazzled by gold, but when later, in a rage, he prophesies the disappearance of all elegance, *even material* elegance, it is clearly not the Marquise's furnishings he will so bitterly regret. As a provincial, he allows himself to haunt the demi-monde and the powers of money because he is received in high imperial society. Without Mathilde, he would have gone to Paris each time feeling like a sailor who, after the noble solitude of the high seas, tacks into the first port of call. He comes to the capital not to go slumming but to claim his proper rank. And his basic alleviation, the one that allows him all the others, is that there, with the concurrence of a whole society, he can play at "moving up socially," changing class. In fact, he would express his real regret in 1871 when he writes tenderly to "his" Princess: "I hold dear the powerful and charming memory of the hours I spent near you at Saint-Gratien and in the rue de Courcelles. Once again I see all those places where you come and go, seeming to spread light and goodness around you."[63] The elegance was there: at rue de Courcelles, at Saint-Gratien, at the Tuileries, at Compiègne. The *dolce vita* he leads at the Court. During the exposition of 1867, when the czar, the king of Prussia, and the king of Italy come to Paris, he is invited to the ball at the Tuileries. He writes to Caroline with a satisfaction scarcely veiled by irony: "The Sovereigns desire to see me as one of the most splendid curiosities of the regime." He returns full of enthusiasm. To George Sand: "Quite honestly, it was splendid . . ." To Mathilde: "The ball at the Tuileries remains in my memory like a splendid thing, like a dream." The banality of the comparison—"I think I'm dreaming," "it is a beautiful dream," etc.—should not foster any illusions. Flaubert is, of course, somewhat given to stereotypes, and it is on the occasion of this ball that he features Paris as Babylon. But he is writing to Mathilde, whom he loves tenderly, and seeks the exact terms, taken in their strongest sense, to convey his

62. 9 February 1863. *Journal*, 6:63. "Yesterday we were at the Princess Mathilde's salon. Today we are at a public dance . . . I love these contrasts. It is climbing society like the floors of a house."
63. To Mathilde, 3 May 1871, *Correspondance*, 6:233.

impression and to let her know his gratitude. And we shall observe that the two last parts of the sentence seem contradictory since the first gives the evening a *material* weight: he turns this ball into a splendid *thing*—a scattering of lights and sounds, shimmering ceremony, an escape from time. The adjective reinforces the realism of the substantive as well: the splendor is almost palpable, it is a flame with the density of stone. By contrast, the second part of the sentence insists, more banally but more accurately, on Gustave's feeling of unreality about the ceremony, which lingers in his memory. What estrangement it is when the younger son of Doctor Flaubert has been presented to the great sovereign heads of Europe—this is the ceremony of ennoblement. He regards it as such, and at the same time it is exposed for what it is: an illusion that is entirely subjective in origin. Thus, far from contradicting each other, the two *likes* are complementary. That is indeed what he seeks in Paris: consolidated illusions; an event that is compact and dense *like* a thing, that encloses and exalts him from the outside but that *in itself* already bears some kind of ludic structure. The density exalts him, revives in him the primitive compensation and old dream of feudalism, but he immediately internalizes its objective meaning and profound unreality by transposing them in his inner universe. We might compare this sentence with one he was to write much later, on 18 February 1871, again to Mathilde: "It seems to me that this war has been going on for fifty years, that *all my previous life was but a dream,* and that the Prussians will always be on our backs." [64] Yes, of course, "life is but a dream"; this is the title of a play by Calderon that Flaubert may have read; in any case it is a Catholic commonplace. But taking it literally here, as the context requires, the meaning is singularly richer: the waking state and reality are the Prussians: the war has gone on for fifty years and will go on forever; Flaubert's hell is a victorious Prussia that condemns him *never to dream again.* There is no way out except in the contemplation of the past, which hasn't even the solidity of what was but is merely an aborted dream lived without truth, loved *as such.* In short, this false past, the desolate memory of a dead, unrealized fable, is precisely one man's internalization of the "long lie" of imperial society. Oh yes, *everything was false,* so Flaubert was dreaming with his eyes open, but it is to this objective and subjective mirage that he remains faithful. No doubt the war and the defeat charge this imaginary life with a lack of substance. But the comparison of the two texts proves that Flaubert, even

64. Ibid., p. 200.

as he allowed himself to be lulled by dreams, was aware of their unreality. And since he regrets this life, we can see that he loved it.

Everything was false in this facade of a regime supported by the bourgeoisie for the sake of quietly developing its real power. But if the war had not taken place, the bourgeoisie would have gotten rid of the regime sooner or later, when the installation of its own structures or their consolidation would have made this costly dictatorship obsolete. Indeed, in the final years of the Empire, the republicans scarcely resembled those described above who mingled with the workers in the Societies of 1840. They were the sons of the rich or the elite, with no connection to the "Social State," who wanted the bourgeoisie to take power because they judged it adult and mature enough to produce a government whose ministers would be of the same class—or at least selected and formed by it—and would prove less expensive. The struggle between landowners and industrialists was played out in this second half of the century: the latter were aggravated by the favor the Emperor showed the former, and desired to accomplish their enterprise by imposing themselves without any intermediary on the class of former aristocrats, which was still strong but in decline. The mechanization of agriculture allowed the bourgeois to undertake the concentration of rural goods and to attack the old feudal gentry on its own ground. No more war, no more hemorrhaging of blood and money; only one aim: profit. Universal suffrage no longer frightens the bourgeoisie; fifteen years later they have finally understood Lamartine's reasoning: the demographic structure of France is such that it will democratically justify domination by the privileged classes while giving the disadvantaged classes a safety valve, the means to externalize their rancor safely through a minority vote. For the clerical aristocracy, by contrast, which the Emperor courts as an opposition to the republicans, Napoleon III will always be a usurper and his court a pack of commoners; they deal with him to restrain the disturbing rise of the bourgeoisie, but deep down they have contempt for him and sometimes hatred; and for them this miscreant is an emissary of the Devil. There is no one, moreover, who thinks, like Marx (who is quite unknown in France), that history repeats itself, but that what was once real tragedy is reborn as farce. Hugo would take on the task of teaching those unaware of it: after Napoleon *le Grand*, Napoleon *le Petit*. Everyone knows that the nephew is filling Europe with the useless tumult of his wars so as to imitate his uncle's triumphant expeditions. False wars, in short— except for the blood spilled—led by a false nephew. Rumor at the time has it that Badinguet is not a Bonaparte; the dates seem to indicate that during the king of Holland's absence, Queen Hortense played him false. False nephew, false emperor, false war, false court, false aristocrats, who were merely upstarts decorated with stolen titles. They were aware, moreover, at the time, that Badinguet was the greatest dreamer of them all. A product of France's collective dream, he was certainly the only one to believe in it completely. And since great reigns are accompanied by a development of arts and letters, he asked his cousin Mathilde to play the character of Maecenas—in part to imitate his Latin ancestor, Augustus, in part to cement first-rate public relations should the occasion arise. She took it on, for good or ill. She collected all the known writers. Can we assume they were tricked? Hardly, when we read in the Goncourt's Journal that one day Edmond declared to her—after 1871, it is true—that her devotees would all have been hostile to the Empire of *"she had not bought them."* He adds, of course, that it was not favors or money but a graciousness and civility that seduced the sourest among them. It is hard to believe, however, that she was particularly gifted at patronage, for Mathilde was hardly an enlightened enthusiast: "With this woman who has never opened a book, with this woman who, in occupying herself with painting, is only pursuing a moral activity, a bit of exercise, a soothing balm and repose from the effort of her thought; with this woman distracted by a myriad of things but deeply impassioned by nothing, one must continually invent distractions, playthings, and maybe arguments as a buffer against boredom, which takes the form of irritation and ill humor. What an indefinable being is the Princess, a being quite impossible to portray in writing which, depicting certain features of her childish side, her incomprehensions, the wretchedness of her nature, would prevent you from believing in the virile qualities of heart and mind that are so thoroughly mingled with her complex nature."[65] This unsentimental, somewhat mannish woman, whose "down to earth language" corresponds in high society to Lagier's in the demi-monde, has a vivacious wit but little intelligence; she is quite closed to the arts and especially to letters. When an author—in accordance with the deplorable practice of that century—gives a reading of his latest work, she dozes. Yet Flaubert found pleasure in her company; her salon seemed to be the entrance to the Tuileries. Of course, he could not entirely convince himself that at her salon he was like Voltaire paying a visit to Frederick the Great

65. *Journal,* 10:265.

or Diderot to Catherine; but neither was he convinced of the contrary. He came there *to play the role* of a great writer recruited by the nobility; in the person of Mathilde temporal power paid homage to the representatives of the powers of the mind. In a sense he did not doubt that the newly privileged, upstarts for the most part, had neither blue blood nor literary taste, and as a consequence could neither communicate a *mana* that birth alone can confer nor *distinguish* people of the arts according to criteria that would be alien to them. But wasn't he only asking the real to derealize itself and to remain indefinitely suspended, slipping between the being of nonbeing and the nonbeing of being? In daily life he needed solitude to maintain his "aesthetic attitude" by a costly effort; he continually transformed the perceived, the lived, into a neuter "visible," which at best he could grasp for a moment as the pure play of appearances. At Mathilde's, at the court, the event jumps him like a thief, but this aggression, though losing none of its brutality, is derealized by itself, bringing with it a simultaneous derealization of the victim. It might be better to say that relations between true and false, real and imagined were constantly shifting. At Compiègne, at the Tuileries, and even at Saint-Gratien there was only one necessity: to observe etiquette. Those who would not comply with the rules of the ceremony would risk real disgrace: the celebration of ennoblement would be finished forever, they would not be invited back. For this reason, the imposed behaviors take on the substance of *imperatives;* their reality comes, moreover, from the fact that they express respectful obedience to power, which—though it is basically just the screen for bourgeois domination—claims to derive its legitimacy from the overwhelming consent of the French people. Flaubert, a courtier and subject, must conform his behavior to this double character. A passage from the Goncourts' Journal illustrates the pleasure he gets from internalizing these external constraints. Princess Mathilde gives a reception; the Emperor has come as Prince Napoleon. Goncourt and Flaubert, standing in the middle of the salon, are conversing; suddenly Gustave takes Goncourt by the arm and turns him part way around, "so as not to turn his back on the Prince." In fact the Prince, returning from the back of the room, finds himself behind Goncourt. This is accidental, of course and Prince Napoleon hasn't the slightest desire to approach them. Be that as it may, one does not turn one's back on a member of the imperial family. It is proper, therefore, to keep constant watch in all circumstances for the evolutions of sovereigns and their relations, and never to be found lacking; a constant attention, ever vigilant, an unfaltering exploration of the "practical field" should prevent the guest from letting himself *be caught in violation of polite behavior*. Goncourt is rather surprised: does he regard Gustave as too much the courtier or does he admire him for being so well versed in the practices of the Court? The fact that he took care to note down this trivial episode is enough to signal a surprise that seems not to have escaped Flaubert at the time, since he hastens to add: "You know, he would not hold it against you." What is striking here is the double system of references he employs. His first movement is to warn a friend of impending danger: court etiquette seems to be a categorical imperative, it has the inflexibility of a system of real norms (that is, of mores actually practiced by a real society and whose violation is really sanctioned). The element that sets things in motion being an unpredictable event in the external world, it is the perpetually changing reality around him that demands appropriate responses. We are at the court of Louis XIV. But this necessity is immediately derealized: Prince Napoleon "would not hold it against" Goncourt. This simple remark puts everything back in perspective: first of all, the precaution was useless, since the interested party attaches no importance to it; and, second, Flaubert's words point out *a contrario* the absurdity of this etiquette: it really would be "henormous" if Mathilde's brother should resent someone for turning his back on him when he has forced him by his own movements to do so. Flaubert, however, does not seem to perceive this "henormity"; he would probably expect a Highness to be offended by such poor form, and if the Prince, according to him, does not hold it against Goncourt, it is out of good nature and simplicity. In any case there was no need for Goncourt to observe it: being useless, it is derealized and transformed into a *gesture*. This Napoleon's indifference demonstrates rather well that this "court" is bourgeois, and that after ten years of its reign these upstarts—unlike the aristocrats of the Ancien Régime—have not yet made its etiquette second nature. But Flaubert judges it indispensable to conform to such still uncertain, poorly established usages; he made the *gesture*. Why? To show Goncourt that he knows his business and that he is in his element at the court, like a fish in water? No doubt. But that isn't sufficient. The truth is that he delights in this false situation in which another's theater affects him as a constraint without ever ceasing entirely, in his eyes, to be theater. In the men and women he approached—bowing, kissing hands, showing his respect by his expression—he suddenly saw reality disintegrating; he is conscious of being an actor in a fantastic and boundless opera with no audience and, as a commoner, of

497

giving the cue to all those commoners who by tacit agreement regarded themselves, and had others regard them, as noblemen. Flaubert's role—like that of all bourgeois in contact with the court—was
to use his conduct and convictions to persuade (a little more and depending on his strength) this false nobility that it was real by showing
that the common people, in his person, were thoroughly convinced
of it. In exchange, that aristocracy, more certain of its rights, distinguished him from the bourgeoisie, raised him to the heights by making him, if not an aristocrat, at least a worthy interlocutor of the great.
His election was testimony to the effect that talent is as valid as birth.
And that, in a way, every genius is "well born." I have said that every
reception revived Flaubert's old but not forgotten dream of changing
class. The dream was satisfied each time, provided he was ready to
believe; each time it was *his* celebration; removed from his class of
origin, he acceded amidst murmurs and lights to the exquisite heart
of sovereignty. He bowed low before a woman who was the Emperor's qualified representative, and sometimes before the Emperor
himself. This was the ultimate consummation: the aristocracy had
crowned him as its greatest poet, conferring upon him a marginal
nobility that immediately liberated him from the bourgeois he was,
beneath his skin. He was satisfied by this para-nobility that thrust
him out of his class without enrolling him in another, preserving *his*
solitude, the ecclesiastical solitude of the mind. And, of course, his
enthusiasm and his overstimulation at the celebration itself did not
last long; after a few days, or even the morning after, it was no more
than a marvelous "dream," but this loss of weight was counterbalanced by the certainty that this ceremony of initiation would be endlessly repeated many times each winter; like family holidays, this
homage, the reciprocal acknowledgment of the lord by his vassal and
of the vassal by his lord, derived its substance from its eternal return.
Every time the archetypal event was repeated, strong hands grasped
him and raised him to his true place—as the Father, a legitimate king,
God, should have done long ago. By his complicity with the imperial
family, Gustave finally succeeded in what he had tried in vain to do
since adolescence: to change his birth and being. Between his labori-
ous sequestration at Croisset and the public assumption he came to
find in Paris three months a year, a deep internal relationship was
confirmed: his work and his long martyrdom gave him not only
absolute merit, the right to dubious divine favors, but conferred upon
him as well the relative and tangible right each year, from January to
March or May, to be the interlocutor of the sovereign or his qualified

representative. The nine months of long patience were preparation for access to the luminous Eleusian mysteries of Paris, to the repetition of his death and resurrection. One evening in January 1844, he summoned this alternation of monastic life and the ceremonies of initiation it earned him by sinking into illness; now he had won, it structured his life: writer at the Tuileries, he was a nobleman at Croisset. Thus the *alleviation,* sustained by memory, persisted even in the viscous tedium of his sequestration; *lived experience* remained heavy and monotonous, but there were moments of escape.

The alleviation, however, exposes itself as essentially unreal. As nonbeing. In the work of art, the image unveils itself as image but always remains *proposed* because the artist has done real work on matter to constitute it as a fixed center of unreality. In contrast, the ceremony of initiation—at least the ceremony in which Gustave takes part at Compiègne and even rue de Courcelles[66]—continually collapses even as it unfolds. In other words, he both believes in it and doesn't believe in it. He knows the false noblemen are not convinced of their own nobility; nor is he unaware that the legitimate aristocracy, which alone might actually remove him from his class, has forever lost its power. He loves it *in the past,* under the Ancien Régime, in the sixteenth century rather than the seventeenth, and has no illusions about its nature: it was then an order between men—birth, gift, hierarchy—instituted by centuries of history, that is, by the avatars of a precapitalist agricultural and craft society. The men he meets at the Court are not *real* noblemen, they always disappoint him, if only by the vulgarity of their manners—though it must be said that the *real* nobleman under the Ancien Régime would have seemed equally vulgar in the simple way he displayed his life and his needs. Each of them, moreover, refers to the Emperor, who refers to nothing; no Supreme Being has named Badinguet monarch by divine right. That too is missing, religion as the guarantee of hierarchical order, which, if it did exist, would give his change of class a metaphysical dignity beyond its *social reality.* The daily repetition of the event would manifest its eternal being; we can assume that this is how a poet of the Ancien Régime represented fame to himself, that is, his permanent election by the representatives of a reigning family, each of whom knew that a very particular Providence kept watch over the permanence of his reign, *in saecula saeculorum,* for the good of France. Thus

---

66. Obviously the rites of passage are real in every real society in which they represent factors of integration.

lasting immortality was accorded the poet in his lifetime to the extent that it was guaranteed by the House of France, therefore by God. Gustave can believe that Napoleon IV will succeed Napoleon III, but as we know, he is lacking in the faith of the simple man; if God torments this failed mystic, it is rather by His absence. In any event, the Almighty does not intervene in terrestrial matters: He is not politicized. In short, the House of Bonaparte will last as long as circumstances *will tolerate* it; the opposition grows ever bolder during the very time that Flaubert is "received," and we have seen that Gustave is well aware of this; it is a threatened sovereign who honors him with his favors. Threatened *by the Republic*. This pseudo-aristocracy, far from being preceded and followed by centuries of history, has, on the contrary, only just emerged from nothingness, and soon, perhaps in Flaubert's lifetime (he believes it, fears it, we have seen his efforts to mask it from himself), it will surely reenter that state. A mirage in the desert persists even when exposed as such; the difficulty is in not believing what we *see*; the mirage of the court is just the opposite: the impossible thing is to believe in it while no one else in Gustave's circle is doing so. Hence that affected "servility" for which the Goncourts enjoy reproaching him: he takes literally Pascal's advice: "Go down on your knees and you will believe" (except for a small thing that makes a world of difference—that he goes down on his knees to prevent himself from *seeing* that he does not believe. He is so mad about etiquette—yet unable to avoid contesting it—because it requires perpetual tension, a zeal that exhausts him and compels him to survey the environment rather than descend into himself. This introvert is entirely outside himself; he becomes extroverted to protect his introversion; he *falls* from one gesture to another to distract himself from all reflexive consciousness, to prohibit himself from making explicit the deep meaning of lived experience. To save appearances he makes himself giddy.

His relations with Mathilde, as well as the particular tone of the letters he writes to her before and after the war of 1870, must be understood in this light. At the outset, it is true, he exaggerates, expressing his admiration for this strong woman whose caprices, violence, stubborn ideas, and indifference to "matters of art" so often contradict the aristocratic patronage she represents. Because she is, or he believes her to be, admirable? No, but in order to hide from himself the fact that he does not admire her enough. He reveres the Princess in her because it is *the Princess* who disappoints him. He was said to have been in love with her, that she perceived it and may have waited for him one evening at Saint Gratien. The sequel to the story is predictable: naturally, he did not turn up. This anecdote, if apochryphal, remains perfectly plausible. That he believed he was in love, in any case, and meant to suggest this to her is evident not only in the previously cited letters but by the sentence he wrote in one of her albums: "Women will never know how timid men are." To be sure, Mathilde was bound to please him: he found in her, only more accentuated, that slightly masculine brusqueness he had loved in Madame Schlésinger, which we find in Mazza and in Emma as well. Unlike the other women he loved, she was not older than he,[67] but if she lacked the superiority of age she possessed through her powerful connections an often despotic and guaranteed authority that could not fail to ravish him. Yet what he loved in her was the Princess of the blood; not that she was truly royal but, quite the contrary, because in this she disappointed him. So his frustration itself became the source of an ardent surpassing of the nonbeing of being toward the being of nonbeing. Thanks to this pithiatic love, he *could no longer see* the defects of the loved woman or, if you will, he affected this passion pithiatically so as not to see them. In consequence she became what Kierkegaard, speaking of fiancées, calls the "infinite"—that is, the indefinite field of virtualities in the name of which the lover ignores the real behavior of the beloved woman. But more conscious, in this case, then Kierkegaard, Gustave is not unaware that this infinite is imaginary. For this very reason he becomes ardent: through autosuggestion he arrives at what would be impossible for others—the Goncourts, for example.[68] As we already know, he can love only absent women, because the nonpresence of the object makes it a docile, unreal image, which he covets to become unrealized. Here, this more complex self-manipulation also aspires to an absence: through Mathilde, present as she is, too carnal, too fleshly, he addresses himself to Mathilde the princess, who is missing from every Mathilde just as Mallarmé's rose is missing from every bouquet. In consequence, as in Madame Schlésinger's time, his feelings for her in themselves constitute a factor of derealization. The end of the story is instructive. Maybe we shouldn't take it seriously, maybe the princess never "waited for" Flaubert; we are certain, however, that he never pushed his advantages further. Mathilde was no imaginary princess; if she

67. Or by only a few months—she was born in 1820. When he made her acquaintance, she was scarcely past forty.

68. Edmond, however, as his Journal proves, was far from being insensitive to the "charms" of the princess.

had given herself, surely it would have been for diversion, and especially because she would have expected pleasures from him that would be only too real. That, indeed, is the reason he did not come or—in any case—did not shed his reserve. He wanted her to know the passion she had aroused in him—it was the best way, in Gustave's view, of giving that passion a certain substance. But if he loved Mathilde, it was truly *so as not to possess her;* the thighs and breasts of a princess are never royal enough except for the man who abstains from touching them and is content, like Flaubert, to desire a glorious body, an abstract, unrealizable image, the simple place where *all woman*—conceived as the idea of femininity—and *all aristocracy* converge. Still, the actual body of Bonaparte's cousin served as the correlative of the image; that is, Flaubert made a concerted effort to envisage, through the cellulite of this "once pretty woman,"[69] the seamless space that contained her glorious body. Through the brutal vivacity of "this person who certainly could have been a woman of easy virtue,"[70] dubious and rather shopworn, he had to make the futile attempt to reach that "blue blood" which seemed to him the imaginary essence of the ordinary red blood that ran in the princess's veins. He effectively derealized Mathilde's flesh and behavior by the very desire supposedly provoked by her grace, a desire that in fact fed on itself and whose primary aim was to *surpass* too common a reality.

This bold maneuver offers another advantage: false desire will soon be sustained by real tenderness, which will foster a play on words. For example, aristocracy of birth will be conveniently confused with nobility of heart. And to avoid any dispute, the little Saint-Gratien coterie, with Flaubert in the lead, will solemnly recognize Mathilde Bonaparte as its sovereign. After this reversal of the fundamental relationship, the question of birth no longer presents itself. Talent, the Good Lord's aristocracy, has consecrated the nobility of its Maecenas. Never mind what the vulgar think; whatever she represents to them, *objectively* she is a princess, chosen for that office by those made exceptional by their exquisite sensibility, and she *effectively reigns over them* at their own behest. This fakery will be exposed *after* the defeat and the fall of Napoleon III. Flaubert returns to it several times. The date is uncertain, but sometime after 4 March 1871 he writes: "And you, now, you are a simple citizen? But for us you will always be our

69. That was the first impression the Goncourts record of her.
70. Another impression of the Goncourts', noted the same day.

Princess, our dear Princess, whose hands I kiss with devotion."[71] Perhaps he cold hardly do less, and we shouldn't look for any calculation in these few words dictated by a former lover's delicacy and feudal loyalty. It's true that Gustave, who is insincerity itself, has rarely demonstrated greater sincerity. The point, however, is not to deny him this but only to determine whether this first reaction originates in a fakery established in the good old times of the Second Empire. And on this matter he is quite explicit in his letter of 3 May 1871: "Since the government (or the Commune, I don't know anything about it) has stuck its nose into my epistles, I don't see why I should be so restrained; therefore I am going to resume my habits and call you, as before, by your real name, because for me you are always Your Highness and, better than that, 'our Princess,' as Sainte-Beuve used to say. This is a title which, among my acquaintance, belongs only to you. It is unique, as is the sentiment I bear you."[72] Our Princess: meaning both the Princess who is ours and the one we have chosen to be princess, the one whose title endures, even if the Republic treats her like an aristocratic-has-been, because it alone can define our relations with her.

The advantage of this ambiguity is obvious: as a simple citizen, she will nonetheless always be "Her Highness" to these artists. But when Sainte-Beuve, well before the war, so dexterously used the possessive adjective, it could not have been in anticipation of the Emperor's future overthrow; *before* the coup d'état, Mathilde was not of the nobility, as Flaubert naively admits; in other words, she did not possess the right to reign that reverts, directly or indirectly, to all members of the aristocracy and might be called the *power of the nobility.* In fact, it was the emigrés—the only legitimate aristrocrats—who put an end to the First Empire, coming home in the wake of the foreign enemy, certainly, but reestablishing their caste against any imposture, with its rights intact and the king on his throne; and his cousin, little Mathilde, like all the nobility of the Empire, had merely lost privileges that were not really hers. Was it enough to overthrow the July monarchy, and soon thereafter the Second Republic, for these false titles to become real? Conversely, if they had been real, would a military defeat and even the fall of the regime have been enough to annul their reality? A simple citizen before 2 December 1852, Mathilde becomes one again after 4 September '71. And what was she in between? The

---

71. *Correspondance,* 6:218.
72. Ibid., p. 233.

answer is given in the text itself: elevated by the coup d'état to the dignity of "Highness," this rank was conceded to her only subject to verification and provisionally; the Empire had to endure, the dynasty had to remain in power for several generations: then the future would determine the past retroactively; once dead, Mathilde would become "Her Highness" in earnest because her cousin's descendants would have been, from father to son, emperors of the French. Meanwhile, her title was "pending," and all her faithful followers knew it; for this reason, Sainte-Beuve's maneuver was indispensable: "pending for others; for us and by us, princess." An excellent means of legitimizing *all* the nobility of the empire indirectly: if Mathilde is accorded noble birth, can it be denied to her cousin?

Here the ambiguity of the consecration acquires its full importance: we are given to understand that the aristocracy of the "patroness"— the name all the faithful give to Madame Verdurin—exists only in the more or less enamored hearts of her writers. But simultaneously another meaning suggest itself: and what if aristocracy—by contrast, something quite real—were entirely perceptible only to hearts? What if the gentle lady's rapport with her guests were indeed the feudal tie of the gift and homage, the only bond that can now unite a lord and his men? In this case, the whole aristocracy of the Empire would be consecrated through Mathilde alone by the love she inspires in her subjects. Flaubert will always hesitate between the two meanings. He cannot adopt one without smuggling in the other: she is a princess, she is *worthy* of being a princess; I love her because she is a princess, she is a princess because I love her; I love her because she is not a princess and so that my love might make her worthy of being one; devoted to that absence of a princess, my love is imaginary and Mathilde the commoner is merely a pretext. Yet, tenderness and respect were consolidated in each of them by the simple fact that these sentiments were manifest simultaneously in all the others; in them, somehow the *role* seemed like a real action; so Gustave had the odd feeling he was *playacting the truth,* as if, for lack of fully existing or, better, of being fully realized, he could seize the real only through imaginary behaviors.

Marvelous moments: when Flaubert managed to convince himself of it, this interpretation fulfilled all his vows: the princess really inspired respect and love, therefore she was a real princess. Gustave could feel these emotions only in a factitious exaltation, proof that this Knight of Nothingness, like Jules in the first *Education,* had cut loose the moorings that bound him to the world and had become pure panoramic consciousness, basing his profound knowledge of human nature only on eidetic intuitions aspiring to passions, which he would naturally push to the limit but which affected him only in imagination. It was all there: the aristocracy is solidly reestablished, with Gustave's unreality placing him, even in his clearly attested respect for Mathilde, above the noblest lady (and certainly above his colleagues, whose veneration of her is trivially real); and in particular that curious rapport is reestablished, affirmed a hundred times since adolescence, between the imagination and the real, the truth revealing itself only to imaginary beings as the meaning of their derealization. From this point of view, it is evident that Gustave's love for the princess is also a paroxysm provoked by competence. At Saint-Gratien, they all vied with each other in respectful marks of attention, striving to be the one who pleased most, the one most demonstrative in his desire to please. We know Gustave: his incredible provincial pride always drives him to extremes; he must impose himself and always be best in all things. Here we have a complementary explanation of his servility: if others flatter, he must fawn; if they prostrate themselves, he throws himself flat on the floor. But this may also be one of the reasons for his amorous theatricals: the good giant must surpass his friends' real (or what he judges as such) but tepid feelings *with the gigantic*; he cannot do less than love. What overexertion, what debilitating overexcitement, the cause and effect of extreme nervousness! He must keep running or collapse. So Gustave runs, hemmed in on one side by the imaginary and on the other by reality. When people are surprised that he doesn't prolong his visits to Paris or even move there, he answers that he hasn't the resources to lead such a life more than three months each year, or else that he can only really work at Croisset. It's true. But the resources he is referring to are not only financial; this backbreaking imposture in which he fools himself so as to fool others, fools others so as to fool himself, always engages all his physical and mental resources; three months of it is all he can take.

Be that as it may, the Second Empire is *his milieu, his society,* the only Carnival in which Jules can decently live—a Lenten Sunday of false Highnesses, august masked idols one must pretend to adore. Men no longer exist, or rather they have disappeared behind their disguise. An inhuman and turbulent solitude; the writer, honored by the people in fancy dress he feigns to revere, pays with intolerable tension for his place at the border between image and reality, one foot here, one foot there, like Charlie Chaplin in *The Pilgrim.* The *social imagination*—wholly employed in sustaining this impossible dream of the resurrection of feudalism based on universal suffrage in the heart of a bourgeois society—becomes the *setting* of his own imagination. But as if that were not enough, this unreal aristocracy, which lifts him out of his class (which invites him to derealize the real environment by using real trees or real furnishings as elements of decor for his personal theater in the earth of the universal theater), is as much the Devil's as the true aristocracy was God's. The guarantee of the entire system, under the Ancien Régime, was the monarch with divine right. Certainly the so-called nobility "of the sword" based its privileges on blood given or spilled; certainly Boulainvilliers, in the eighteenth century, made this class a more valorous and warlike *race* than the class of rogues and boors. Nonetheless, since the misfortunes of Charles X, the nobles were more willing to emphasize their fidelity to the unlucky monarch God had imposed on them; destined to disappear altogether in a heroic and futile sacrifice, this class saw itself—at least through the eyes of its poets—as the chosen of a providential failure that would manifest its superiority to being, whatever it might be, by demonstrating that it had existed only to be destroyed, proclaiming in death the necessity and impossibility of fealty as the only kind of *valid* relationship. In short, they were white and clerical. The imperial court was black; for all these courtiers who posit in principle the superiority of the gesture to the act, there is one exception—and a big one, since it is the only real foundation this facade of an aristocracy can attempt to claim: the military operation. Flaubert cannot conceal from himself the fact that this false nobility is a real soldiery, that these dukes have earned their titles with their blood. Discreetly relegated to the background but virulent, the bouts of carnage give the carnival of the Empire its always somewhat sinister sheen. Especially as they effectively demonstrate to this antimilitarist that the aristocrats of the Ancien Régime were merely the descendants of military parvenus. By giving a title to a fortunate soldier, Napoleon III believed he was imitating the first Capetians and thereby denounced the origin of *all* aristocracy—as Flaubert, in any case, could conceive of it in the past—by assimilating the nobles to the officers in a professional army. Nothing could be more sickening to him. Especially as he surely sensed the trap being laid for him: the nobility, in effect, and the type of feudal property that corresponds to it are institutions that agricultural and craft societies naturally establish for themselves. Whatever the importance of the nobleman's military contribution— from this point of view, the nobleman was originally defined as *he who possesses a horse* and will soon be *he who possesses a castle*—the dominant consideration here remains a type of appropriation, in an endangered society, in which the gift is the reward for homage. The *real* legitimacy of the past aristocracy does not reside in God but in a society that has very generally defined its structures by going beyond infrastructural conditioning toward the questions constantly put to the society by these conditionings. Flaubert would certainly not have used these words, but his entire work proves that he felt the *thing*. As do his letters. It is the *times* that legitimize privilege, he is fond of saying. And it is also, of course, the fact that they have had to consti-tute over a long period attachments to *definite* social services, the best or the only solution conceivable to urgent and specific problems that had meaning only *in that era* because their only function was to ex-press its contradictions. In this sense the true *authenticity* of an order or a caste would be marked for this shameful bourgeois of the nine-teenth century by the fact that its present members would be clearly its *survivors*, and the entire institution would seem slightly outmoded by events and hence dated; in short, it *would survive* its former efficacy.

Yet Flaubert can only see the methodical carnage by which Napo-leon III made his reign famous—at once to imitate his uncle and to reestablish the principle of a new social selection—as a satanic image of feudal wars; they are *too real*, of course, *horribly, stupidly real*, but as a selective principle they are instantly derealized. First, they are buffoonish and neurotic imitations of the wars of Napoleon I, and their goal, utterly senseless at the height of English hegemony, on the eve of German hegemony, is to impose French hegemony on conti-nental Europe. Moreover, the pithiatic character of this foreign policy is outstandingly manifest by the degree of *unpreparedness* of that vaunted army so necessary to prop up those overweening ambitions, as well as by a succession of conflicts whose motives are increasingly suspect and whose outcome is increasingly doubtful. *Present and in-effective*, these massacres are doubly common, and in any case they suggest the *voluntarism* that is the source of this imperial nobility. They send foot soldiers to be butchered so they might have an oppor-tunity to convoke a batch of newly created noblemen at the Tuileries. Real death, real suffering are unrealized to produce the insubstantial image of an impossible aristocracy. Isn't this substituting hell's right for divine right? Once again, men will slaughter each other and con-demn themselves for the false coins of Satan. All the same, when Gustave half opens his pouch, he cannot help finding beauty in the dead leaves he discovers; false money, real leaves, real blood spilled for the chimeras of *others*, and so for nothing. When he sees the pirouetting and bowing uniforms at Compiègne, and when he calculates the number of dead and wounded it took to justify this ridiculous mascarade, it takes on a certain meaning for him: real and savage violence gives a sinister radiance to the whole ceremony; Gustave can assume the "aesthetic attitude" and contemplate this nobility—a failure from the point of view of the young people who died for that nobility without knowing it was the only thing at stake. After all, what he loves in the defunct aristocracy is not its languid decline in the previous century but its *black power,* its sadism and its passions. Isn't that what he was dreaming of as a young man, when he tramped around Brittany with Maxime? Didn't he envy and admire Gilles de Rais, whose black religion dazzled him: "He made sacrifices, burned incense, gave alms and carried out rituals in his honor . . . Those caves glowed red under the incessant wind of magic bellows, those walls were lit up at night . . . , they invoked Hell, they feasted with death, they slit the throats of children, they experienced dreadful joys and atrocious pleasures; blood ran, instruments played, everything echoed with sensual pleasures, with horrors and delirium . . . I would rather have contemplated Maréchal de Retz's knickers than the heart of Madame Anne of Brittany; there were more passions in the one than grandeur in the other."[73] What enchants him, in short, is the low Middle Ages and the Renaissance, the race of *true* noblemen— who are at the same time "old troopers"—extinguished, according to him, around 1598, who would be the victims of absolute monarchy. After this date, there would be no more "La Tremblaye coming home with the head of his enemy in his fist," all those "beautiful and terrible faces" disappear: "Who has dreamed of depicting those violent provincial rulers, hacking away at the crowd, raping women and carrying off gold, like Epernon, the ghastly tyrant of Provence and perfumed mignon of the Louvre, like Montluc, strangling the Huguenots with his bare hands, or like Boligni, that king of Cambray who read Machiavelli in order to copy the Valentinois, and whose wife went into the breach on horseback, in full armor and helmet?"[74] Their sole descendant, the last to represent them, to save the solemn honor of his class in the era of bourgeois triumph, not so much by his acts as by his philosophical reflections, is the divine Marquis de Sade, making his "sadism" a philosophically conscious stance of his class at the very moment of a long prepared and providential shipwreck. There

73. *Par les champs et par les grèves* (Conard), pp. 78–80.
74. Ibid., p. 288.

508

is no doubt that beyond the thousand reasons that bring him to declare himself a "sadist," Gustave respects "the Veterans'" acknowledgment of evil as the basis of aristocracy. Under the Second Empire
he is caught between two nobilities: one is authentic but outmoded—
authentic *because* outmoded—and though its mawkishness, shabbi-
ness, and cant repel him, its greatness, after its failure, is at once *no
longer to be* and retrospectively to designate Sade and La Tremblaye,
dead but still virulent, as those who during its lifetime best embodied
its noxious splendor and its divine mandate to debase humanity,
"hacking away at the crowd" and tormenting the bourgeois in his
baseness; the other's falseness cries out, it is rejected by the very
bourgeoisie on which it depends, which agrees *faute de mieux* to keep
it a while longer, without a future and without a past, without roots,
but whose bloody military cruelty and power of demoralization are
indeed *present*, as were those of Epernon in days gone by. Thus the
first is real, but its past virulence can be evoked only by the imagination; the virulence of the second is imposing, but its class-being,
through this dreadful actualization, can take on only the unreal meaning of the directed destructions it is pleased to produce. These two
nothingnesses are mutually consolidating: the *being-no-more* of the authentic nobility, insofar as it lives it as a survival, allows the *not-really-
being* of the Empire's nobility a certain substance to its inauthenticity.
The false aristocracy does not affirm itself but rather maintains itself
for lack of *valid reducing agents;* at the same time, the imposters of
the imperial Court render to the feudal lords of the Ancien Régime the
homage that vice renders to virtue: since it is blood that ennobles—
the blood that runs in the veins of the "well-born," the blood passed
on from father to son—they will spill their blood to acquire the sper-
matic power to transmit blue blood to their offspring. All things
considered, this is borrowing from those vanquished by history the
general rule of aristocratic selection, and so recognizing that they
alone possess real authenticity. Flaubert asks no more of them: the
solidity of the imperial mirage fulfills him to the same extent that its
unreality disillusions him; but in any case the false and the true nobility equally incarnate the discretionary power of man over man, that
is, evil and, indirectly, beauty. Flaubert easily shifts from one to the
other: their contradictions do not concern him since at issue is really
two kinds of nonbeing. But, given the way he is put together, despite
his earlier regrets, if he had to choose now, he would give preference
to the false nobility: a whole criminal society changed into an image,
what could be better for a Knight of Nothingness? In truth, he did

love in the Empire what the Goncourts reproached him for loving: "In the Ancien Régime, everything is of a piece, there is a legendary government, a divine right, nobility of noble blood; all that was questionable. But today we have democratic government with a legendary Emperor on top, the principles of '89 beneath, the idolatry of one man, the Church kissing the feet of Caesar. Stupid and odious."

Two images in collusion: one, totalitarian, noble, and satanic, is produced by bourgeois society's dreaming of being "legendary"—an onerous oneirism, which they will pursue to their cost. The other, maintained nine months out of twelve in the solitude of Croisset, is Gustave's *image* of himself based on a primitive connection: genius— ennoblement[75]—and imagination becoming entirely totalized as the correlative unreality of a disengagement from being. In Paris, in Compiègne, the singular image offers itself *in its singularity* as a determination of the social *image:* it dreams it is *produced* by the *whole* society that dreams, as a differential term in an ultimately closed system. Thus, as part of a dream, it participates in its nature and so cannot contest it,[76] becoming the site of nervous irritation; when Gustave has returned to Croisset, the image has lost its substance even as it accentuates his singularity. But he has a permanent choice between two modes of conduct.

1. He is effectively free to attribute the insubstantiality of the *imago* to the fact that the imperial celebrations that produced it a few days, a few weeks before *are no more*—or at least are no longer taking place *for Flaubert;* thus the *imago* would be experienced as a remembrance, and the sharper, more frustrating feeling of its nonreality would originate solely in the transformation of lived experience into memory, the transformation of plenitude into absence that is only *aspired to*. This is the first possible attitude. It has the advantage of prolonging in solitude the mythic presence of the great imperial dream in the sin-

75. Compensation for the curse: anomaly-exclusion.
76. Simply because the part cannot question the whole, which produces it and is its inner fiber. That does not mean it can *affirm* its reality. Everything depends, naturally, on the systems. In a real totality, a part can objectify the whole by an act. In an imaginary totality, like the one we have described, the part has in any case no more reality than the whole, and so possesses neither the means to affirm nor those to deny it; it can only *live* it, that is, *believe* in it. But although the belief, in the absence of any *specific reducing agent* (of any *evidence*—in whatever area—revealing some kind of *truth*), can never be questioned by an undeniable intuition or by the apodicticity of a deduction, it does not pretend to *be* anything but a belief. This means that it cannot be lived without implicitly denouncing its secret insufficiency. You would have to understand nothing about that strange scissiparity we call *existence* to imagine for a moment that a belief can *make itself take hold* in someone and become a certainty.

gular image: the ennoblement *has taken place;* Gustave, in his prison at Croisset, *is* noble because he *was* ennobled. The vast and marvelous nightmare *has taken place:* he was one of its nocturnal creatures; once the product of a dream, he escaped from it, thus losing his live substance, so he could go off and continually ponder it rather than live it; for a man of quality, even if a dream is at stake, must prefer nonbeing to everything, in this case, the bitter regret of a phantasmagoria that has dispersed without ever having been. *In any case,* this first option preserves the umbilical cord linking the singular imago to the generalized witches' sabbath that produced it. The sabbath continues, moreover, and thereby helps to sustain its creature *from a distance,* the genius whose nobility is none other than the ceremony of ennoblement conceived as a frequentative. This ceremony, in effect, can take place at any moment, even in the absence of the exiled image of the all; Princess Mathilde has only to speak to her faithful about Gustave or think of him silently; even this can be dispensed with—let the salon at boulevard de Courcelles persist and let Gustave's place be marked there, let *things* await him. His upward change of class, inscribed in matter, is not only lived by the hermit in his hermitage as regret for what was and the absence of what is still pursued but elsewhere; it is also that expectation of himself, *over there,* his princess's slight frustration, what that dreamer is missing to complete her dreams with ease. And above all the future is certain: eternal return, destiny; the newly ennobled man of yesterday is the newly ennobled man of next winter. From this point of view, voluntary absence and reclusiveness are perhaps the best ways of masking the inadequacy of being that characterizes the umbilical cord linking Flaubert's image to the mother-image: one nothingness is replaced by another. Gustave *is not* the product of imperial society—since he was constituted as he is even before it was conceivable; that society itself cannot sustain its being, and escapes collapse only by running to keep ahead of itself. But when walls and a hundred and twenty kilometers separate the hermit from the court, the brutal negation hides the inadequacy: how does he know if the umbilical cord is pure fantasy since in any event it is *cut,* and whatever its true nature, it must be lived at Croisset as past (*already-no more*), present denied (out of reach), and distant future (not yet)? This triple nonbeing of temporal ecstasies has, rather, the effect of sketching the reverse of a being. In fact, for a *real* absence—for the absence of a reality—and for an imaginary absence—for the absence of an imaginary—the categories are the same: already no more, out of reach, not yet, characterize equally well my relations with my friend Pierre (whom I haven't seen in a year) and my relation to *Hamlet* (which I have neither seen performed nor read in ten years, but which I can always reread or see again—if only as a highly singular and dated image such as Olivier's screen version).

2. But Gustave can *equally well* profit from his reclusiveness to present himself, in contrast, as the creature of his own *imago*. In other words, the ennoblement of the artist is a self-determination. In this case, as in the other, the nobility of the empire is necessary to him. But the defect of that nobility does not reside in its unreality; he reproaches it, on the contrary, for being *too real* to satisfy him; every aristocracy, even one legitimized by secular traditions, is tainted with vulgarity by the fact that it plays an integral part in reality. From this new point of view, he sees the imperial court no longer as a false nobility that makes a laughing-stock of itself but as a true nobility whose manifest inauthenticity comes only from the fact that it *is*—or, more precisely, whose inadequacy the artist discovers through his sublime and permanent dissatisfaction. He needs it in order to surpass it by the radical movement of imagination, that is, by the futile disengagement toward nonbeing. Alone, he could not even conceive of the idea of nobility, since the determinations of the imaginary can be aspired to only through a negative surpassing of real determinations; thus the real Court becomes the analogue of an imaging intention, which aspires through it to authentic nobility, or the nobility absent from every nobility. But although the objective is rigorously defined, it is still not attained; for he aspires to the "elsewheres" that are nowhere, the aristocracy as it must and cannot be. What Flaubert experiences is not imaginative power but the proud impotence of the imagination. The invisible aristocracy is not only beyond all reality but above all beyond any image; it is the imaginary pure and out of reach, a sign of the peerless grandeur of exigency, and consequently of its inevitable failure. The gloomy and haughty satisfaction of the artist who feels too big for the world, too big for himself. His dissatisfaction is infinite; not that it seems to be at first, but whatever the given, it contests it and denounces its inadequacy without being able, for all that, to produce absolute nonbeing in the unreal, to produce the being of nonbeing, which, as the totality of all negations, seems to be the inaccessible ideal of the imagination, or the imaginary. But through the infinity of his accepted failures, the artist places himself *above everything*, since even his images are incapable of satisfying him, still containing, as they do, a scrap of reality that is their very finitude (they deny and surpass *that* particular reality, but it is to that reality,

taken in its singularity, that they owe their determination—each one is the beyond of *this* being but not of total being). His own *imago* appears to him as a result: far from demanding his ennoblement from others, he is *the Good Lord's aristocrat* even in bitterness and wreckage. In other words, since nobility is defined by its divine right of superiority over the human race, supernobility belongs to those who are elected or coopted by the true and only possible nobility, and raised above the feudal caste in the name of that imaginary construct, feudality as an impossible purity. With this attitude, the artist consciously produces his own *imago:* ennobled or distinguished by the true nobility, he is placed above it by the dissatisfaction that provokes imaginative disengagement. So he will be the man who derealizes himself toward the absolute, knowing that his superiority, which resides in the simple choice of the imaginary, is doubly unreal. On the one hand, as far as the content of the option is concerned, it is complete unreality; but on the other hand the option itself, having no practical result and permitting neither the attainment of the ideal of imagination nor the avoidance of the vulgar exigencies of the body, must be considered an unreal derealization. But the artist's greatness resides in the fact that he is determined, in the heart of reality, to *act as if* his metamorphosis into a pure image of himself were possible.

Flaubert, in his hermitage, adopts these two attitudes by turns— depending on his whim or the needs of the cause or event. In Paris, of course, only the first attitude is possible. But whether he adopts one or the other, he must be in complicity with the imperial aristocracy. And perhaps even more so when it comes to the second. What pleases him when he dreams of that black knighthood, which reigns by diabolical right and degrades the human race, is that it *is false,* even as some Satanic trick allows it to possess the solidity and efficacy of the true; in this case, a dream of a dream, he makes himself *imagined* through the objective dream of the French people. But if he collects himself in solitude and goes so far as to scorn the honors lavished upon him, *including* the ceremony of ennoblement, *he must* regard *the whole thing*—aristocrats and recruitment from above—as a system of real determinations. Otherwise his dissatisfaction might change signs before his eyes, and he would suddenly find himself scorning the nobility of the Empire *because it is not real.* Moreover, this leads to an unstable state and to the constant shift from one attitude to the other: no sooner does his doubt blossom, no sooner does high imperial society seem to him a mirage, than he rebounds from the second to the first. The reverse is true as well. This circular movement

513

is made easier for him by the fact that in both cases, the dukes and princes of the Second Empire are at once *titled* and *vulgar*. But he sometimes regards this vulgarity as proof that the titles are false, and at other times as proof that they are *too* real—for we might say, to parody Hegel, that everything real is vulgar, and everything vulgar is real.

Gustave is so conscious of this complicity that one of his first reactions to the defeat of 1870 *will be shame*. He writes to George Sand, 10 September: "My brain will not recover its equilibrium. One can no longer write when one has no more self-esteem,"[77] and to Feydeau on the 22d: "The worst thing is that we deserve our fate, and that the Prussians are right, or at least were right."[78] This sentiment is quite rare in Flaubert's comments on public affairs, and seems quite unjustified (he despised the army and militarism, never missed a chance to denounce the narrowness of the nationalist and "imperialist" views, and congratulated the Emperor for having declared in one of his speeches that the Empire desired order and peace; far from letting himself be won over in 1870 by the martial enthusiasm of the French, he issued a horrified condemnation of the declaration of war—so at first sight he ought not to have acknowledged any responsibility for the disaster). In order to understand this unusual stance, it will be useful to examine Gustave's odd behavior with regard to the "red ribbon," first when this was bestowed on him by Duruy in August 1866 at the request of Princess Mathilde, and then, after the capitulation at Sedan, when he decides not to wear it any more.

A hundred times over he has repeated firmly and correctly that "honors dishonor." Yet he is proposed for membership in the Legion of *Honor*, which means letting a minister he hardly admires decide whether the artist Flaubert is or is not "honorable." Duruy's perfect incompetence is betrayed, in Gustave's eyes, by the simple fact that Ponson du Terrail is in the same contingent. After this, how can he claim that such a government has the quality to judge art and reward its devotees? For this nomination is also a *reward:* by allotting it to the creators of *Madame Bovary* and *Rocambole*, the regime co-opts them; by claiming to serve their glory, it makes them serve its own. Flaubert knows all that by heart; on other points, on other occasions, he remains faithful to the proud refusal of his youth: the Academy, for

77. *Correspondance*, 6:148.
78. Ibid., p. 156. Flaubert explains elsewhere the meaning of this qualification: Prussia ought to have made peace after Sedan, and Bismarck's mistake was to invade France.

example, like the Legion of Honor, is an institution; after *Salammbô* he enjoyed such prestige that had he deigned to apply, he would have had a strong chance of being elected; but he had too much contempt for the Immortals to lower himself to canvas for their votes. Baudelaire was weak enough to present himself as a candidate, Goncourt was to ponder all his literary life a project for a Counter-Academy composed uniquely of the "truly valuable," resulting in that institution we all now know, [the Académie Goncourt, which awards the Prix Goncourt] Gustave, their contemporary and friend, was irreproachable. Judging himself without peer, he staunchly refused to enter that assembly: it was good enough for Maxime Du Camp. And not even for him: when Maxime, under the Third Republic, solicited and obtained a chair at the Academy, this "humility" made Gustave "muse": "How odd men are!" The "men," here, are not the thirty-nine kindly mummies who received him, but Maxime (and those like him), who thought it worth making thirty-nine visits to obtain the right to enter that venerable body. He knew Maxime, however, and had not severed his ambivalent relations with him, in which a kind of affection, a vestige of their former friendship, prevented neither irritation nor lucidity. The most curious thing is that he is surprised in 1880—after all, Maxime was worth more than the Academy—when he was not at all surprised in 1852 to see his friend promoted to *officer of the Legion of Honor*. In his letter to Louise of 17 January 1852, he is categorical: that opportunist is getting what he deserves, well done!

> News! Young Du Camp is an officer of the Legion of Honor! How that must please him! When he compares himself to me and considers the path he has taken since he left me, he is certain to find me far behind and think he has made his own way (on the outside). You will see him some day grab a place and leave this good old literature behind. It's all confused in his mind, woman, cross, art, boots, all this whirls around together, just as long as it furthers his career, that's the important thing. An admirable era (curious symbolism!) . . . in which photographers are decorated and poets are exiled (look at the quantity of good pictures he had to make before getting that officer's cross). Of all the decorated men of letters, there is only one worthy of knighthood, Monsieur Scribe! What a huge irony, all that! And how honors abound when honor is lacking![79]

79. To Louise, 17 January 1852, *Correspondance*, 2:352. The photographer (cf. above) is Maxime; the poet is Hugo.

Here it is clearly stated: Gustave, by condemning Maxime in '52, rules prophetically on his own conduct in '66. When poets are exiled and photographers are rewarded, an artist must refuse to enter into a fraternity in which the highest dignities, among people of letters, are reserved for the real grave diggers of literature, for those who—as we would say today—have never produced anything but works that are mere commodities. And he will not even have to refuse it; if he is entirely pure and solitary, if he makes art a religion, no one will dream of inviting him. I have already said that the worst thing Maxime did was not to canvas for his cross but to deserve it. Well? Did Gustave *deserve* the distinction they would grant him under the liberal Empire? When he accepts it, has the Legion of Honor changed its meaning? It seems not. Certainly, Scribe is dead. But Ponson du Terrail replaces him. Hugo remains an exile; Maxime the photographer is still in the fraternity. So? And great as the humility of "young Du Camp" may be, doesn't Gustave carry his own to excess by sporting the *ribbon* fourteen years after his friend received the *cross?* Indeed, there is only one alternative: refuse to enter the game or play by the rules; if Flaubert protects the virginity of his buttonhole to the end, then he can scorn Maxime's decoration and, whether Maxime holds the Legion's highest decoration, the "great cross," or remains merely a "commander," Flaubert can see it as proof of mediocrity. There are two orders: the temporal order, which is highly inferior; and the spiritual order, the aristocracy of failure, which is superior to the rest, *provided you stick to it.* But if Gustave allows himself to be decorated, he becomes part of a certain system in which his friend is superior to him. It is impossible to consider the rank of *knight* as a sign of *value* without consequently recognizing the rank of officer as the mark of a *higher* value. Regarding the ribbon as a valid distinction and simultaneously Maxime as a mediocrity coopted as such by a legion of mediocrities, Flaubert is left with nothing but a vicious circle in which his decoration is devalorized, though he is worthy of it in terms of the value it confers on the unworthy Du Camp, and at the same time Du Camp's decoration is revalorized by the fact that it rewards Gustave's real merits.

Yet here is Gustave, thanking the princess on 16 August 1866: "I do not doubt the good will of Monsieur Duruy, but I imagine the idea was suggested to him by another. And to me it is more than a favor, almost a remembrance." This passage proves that he did no canvassing: otherwise, Gustave would not speak this way to Mathilde. Shall we say that she took the initiative in the process and that he did not dare, after the fact, to disavow it for fear of offending her? What makes this believable is the tone of gratitude. Flaubert glosses over the "favor" and fixes only on the "remembrance": the public honor disappears, what remains is the discreet and feminine attention, the mark of affection. "I had no need of that," he adds, "to think of my Princess."[80] In short, Mathilde herself becomes his boutonniere. Thus he gives himself license to collect this testimony of tenderness without acknowledging the official distinction to which it testifies. It is inconceivable, however, that Mathilde would have taken it upon herself to have him decorated without first being assured that it would not incur his disapproval. In other words, at Saint-Gratien, in rue de Courcelles, when he roared out his paradoxes, he never let himself maintain that honors dishonored; it is even likely that since he saw it coming, he let it be understood discreetly, without insistence, that the project did not displease him. In a general way it is true that he shows little enthusiasm. As a response to congratulations, he found this formula, which he repeats complacently in each of his letters: "What gives me pleasure in the red ribbon is the joy of those who love me." Is that all? He is a little more explicit with the Goncourts: "Well, and what about you? I was so disappointed to see Ponson du Terrail in your place! And my joy is troubled since I do not share it with you. My delirium is mediocre in any case. *I am strong-minded* and I will still agree to greet you. Never mind! It bothers me that my favorites do not have the star."[81] This vicious circle is explained by Gustave's delicate situation with regard to his less fortunate colleagues: since the two brothers are not decorated, he cannot be too blatantly joyful; but since they would love to have the star that eludes them, it would be equally indecent to proclaim his indifference. A modest contentment is more appropriate, and he won't forget to mention Ponson du Terrail and recall in passing that public favors are a random lottery that sometimes favors the deserving and sometimes the unworthy. To be sure, he still says he is "*bothered*" not to see "his favorites'" names on the list; he overdoes it, of course, and this bother is not his own but what he senses in the two brothers. But he can represent it vividly

80. He is more specific in another letter, undated but written sometime after August 16: "I was so moved, Princess, reading your last lines . . . announcing a little gift (the medal), which is sweeter to me than the thing itself. For the honor is shared by many, but not your gift! *Correspondance*, 5:232. What is vulgar is the public distinction, which as such hardly gibes with the artist's idiosyncrasy. What is unique is Mathilde's gift, which is addressed directly to the *singular universal*, that is, to Gustave.
81. 16 August 1866, *Correspondance*, 5:225.

enough to claim to share it, because he would have felt it in their place; clearly, there is sufficient justice in the choice of those elected so that certain oversights can seem unjust. Moreover, when he writes, "My joy is troubled since I do not share it with you," he is taking it for granted that this nomination *gives pleasure*. In short, he recognizes that he is pleased. A mediocre transport, to be sure, for a man of his quality, driven by pride and the noblest ambition, deems himself far above such marks of esteem. But neither does he judge them insulting; he tolerates, and even finds some satisfaction, in the public authorities' recognition of his merits—and sighs softly: "Ah, if only one had received this at eighteen . . ."[82]

All this is merely an attitude. Flaubert behaves well, that is a fact—but he is behaving, which is quite clear in the bitter line I just cited. At eighteen, that is, under the highly scorned reign of Louis-Philippe, Gustave would have spat upon any favor granted by the citizen king, that is, by the bourgeoisie in power. If he claims in '66 that the Legion of Honor was one of his adolescent dreams, he is simply lying. A passage from the letter to Amélie Bosquet sounds a more honest note. In congratulating him, she had said to him, no doubt, that this promotion was fair compensation for the legal actions brought against the author of *Madame Bovary*. He answers almost brutally: "As to forgetting my trial and dispensing with rancor, not at all! I am like clay when it comes to receiving impressions, and like bronze when it comes to preserving them; in me, nothing is effaced; everything accumulates."

This time we have found our Gustave again, the prince of recriminations, and his subterranean reactions are more accessible to us: he nurses a deep and abiding bitterness against the Emperor, his government, and the official moralism. Under these conditions, he will allow himself to be decorated, but he is no fool: if this maneuver is meant to reconcile him to his erstwhile persecutors, it has missed its mark; he takes the red ribbon cynically, because it never hurts, but he will not sell himself for this meager trim. No present kindness will efface past wrongs; Flaubert's fidelity to his dead life is above all never to forget offenses. Let Napoleon III crown with his favors the innocent man he dragged to the bench of infamy, his victim laughs to himself while making a bow: he knows the sovereign thinks he is forgiven, and knows he never will be.

We recognize this ambivalence, it is how Gustave feels about *every-*

---

82. To Amélie Bosquet, 20 August 1866, ibid., p. 227.

thing. But far from enlightening us, it merely deepens the darkness. If Gustave considers the *Bovary* trial one of the great villainies of the Second Empire, perhaps the greatest,[83] since it is a crime against art in the name of moral order, in a word, the "taint of intellectual blood" that dishonors the reign of Napoleon III, how can he, who is on principle hostile to conferred distinctions, accept being decorated for his eminent value as an artist by a government that nine years earlier, on the occasion of his first work, showed its incomprehension of beauty and its principled hostility to workers of art? And how can he tolerate being recuperated with a cross? In the privacy of his innermost thoughts, he knows very well that he is not recuperable. But for others, for his friends whose joy gives him such pleasure—beginning with Amélie Bosquet—for his readers, the maneuver has been entirely successful; being liberal, the Empire clears its name by adoring what it has burned. Yet if Gustave has only a fraction of the resentment he expresses to Madame Bosquet, how can he lend himself to such manipulation? How does he hope to profit from it? In a way this modest honor does indeed compromise him: the young men have no great love for Mathilde's protegés and made this clear to the Goncourts when the Comédie-Française performed *Henriette Maréchal;* Gustave was in the first loges, he saw it all, and we know that this mocking inspired his first variations on the theme, "I am a fossil." Was it necessary to risk open unpopularity to serve the politics of a government that had offended him? And wasn't this the worst possible way for him, apolitical as he was, to become politicized? No doubt Gustave, like the Goncourts, would answer: "I am not an 'imperialist,' I am a Mathildist, that's all." But Mathilde was the emperor's cousin; shouldn't he have been more careful, and since all her faithful followers were "bought" by the woman's kindness, was it necessary, through the princess's mediation, to sell himself to Badinguet for a decoration? Gustave's attitude surely remains a mystery. To illuminate it somewhat, let us return to his letter of January '52—which he seems entirely to contradict by his conduct in '66—and ask ourselves if we have read it correctly.

Taking a closer look, we notice at once that Flaubert does not question the practice of *distinctions*, that is, of a selection made from above and conceived on the model of ennoblement; essentially, he condemns the choice of the elect and the distribution of honors. If the

---

83. Cf. *Correspondance*, 4:156: Doctor Cloquet will be able to cite to Napoleon III the *Bovary* trial as one of the turpitudes of his regime.

photographer were exiled or at least forgotten and the poet were decorated, everything would be in order. Since Gustave finds it absurd and revolting that "Monsieur Scribe" should hold the rank of commander, that high dignity must indeed inspire him with some respect. If chance were decisive in every case, indignation would cease to be appropriate; invented fortuitously to meet the needs of a particular policy, the titles would have no value and, drawn by lot, cause no surprise. Gustave's irritation proves that he sees things quite otherwise: the Legion of Honor, an august institution, is falling into decay; it was a palace built for princes now dead, it has been invaded by the rabble, and sullied, half-ruined; the rabble foolishly imitates the customs and ceremonies of its first inhabitants without comprehending their meaning. Clearly, the Legion of Honor instituted by Napoleon I was meant to reward the fanaticism of man for man, the devotion of the soldiers of the Empire. *Honor*—which is indivisible, omnipresent under the first Empire—is therefore fidelity. We should not be surprised that Gustave makes a cult of it, if a negative one, weeping for it when it is lost. We know he has little self-esteem and despises those who do not despise themselves; despite his flights into gigantism and truculence, which so often make him the victim of his ego, he dreams only of getting rid of it, of debasing it, his own and everyone else's, of constituting the ego simply as the means of establishing or sustaining the reign of the Other. In doing so he is merely improving upon the basic structure of his "character" and his destiny. His early history subjected him to the diabolical Other, to his father, and this subjection would prevent him all his life from being the *same* for himself, that is, from approving and assuming the self. So he looks for the remedy in malice: he will overdo that subjection and respect it wherever he encounters it in its feudal aspect. Clearly, he wants to replace subjection to the thing with subjection to man, or more precisely, to man insofar as he is boss and owner of the thing. *Honor* is that accepted subjection of the individual to the *House* (to the family as patrimony, to ancestors and descendants), and through it to the sacred person who manifests familial unity, to the paterfamilias. It is also fidelity to homage, which in feudal times rarely opposed itself to the first and often, on the contrary, through devotion to the father the vassal assumed his vassalage in advance and pledged himself to the second power, so that not only was the Supreme Other the Other of an Other, but fidelity itself was lived *as other*. For this reason, honor seemed to be neither a virtue (exis) nor an enterprise (praxis) but a being-other in the heart of existence as interiority: at once *property* to be maintained, to be preserved by entirely negative acts (one does not enhance *his* honor, merely his power), and a household God, the lofty object of a subjective cult. Gustave's ethic, that implicit valorization of *pathos* constituted especially for him,[84] has its foundation in the debasement of the Ego demoted to the rank of means, the dominant aim being the Other as other, whatever that Other may be; and we might even say without exaggeration that the devotion will be all the more noble the more undistinguished and mean the master, which restores a demonic clarity to this ethic of hatred. In the realm of Satan, the unique moral bond between men must be this inhuman devotion. When a society is structured as a hierarchy, when it is heavily integrated, in the full throes of expansion, in short, in its "ascending" period, *honors* are useless: honor is one and indivisible; although everyone has *his* honor, the constellation of these subjections is none other than the hierarchical structure insofar as it is present in everyone, like the whole in its part. In other words, it is the general principle of man's subjection to the Other, that is, to man as inhuman. Thus when Gustave affirms, well before Maxime's promotion, that *honors* dishonor, this phrase, taken in itself and without prejudging anything, is simultaneously a condemnation of all social distinctions and a reaffirmation of the feudal ethic: the red ribbon would not dishonor if honor did not exist in everyone, even as an inert and dizzying lacuna. In the letter to Louise, the relation of causality is reversed: it is the disappearance of honor that has the direct effect of multiplying *honors*. There is no contradiction here, just circularity. This means, quite simply, that the Legion of Honor was fine under Napoleon I because that imperial society offered the best example of a military hierarchy. What Flaubert reveres in this institution is the seigneurial gift as a counterpart to homage. The distinction has grandeur, first because it is earned on the battlefield, and second because it is the prize of blood; its dark grandeur derives from the fact that it rewards fealty to the death. Certainly Gustave does not like war. Yet how can he help admiring all those wars sustained against all of Europe, and all those battles inexorably won? Imperial glory illuminates all those crosses fastened to the chests of amputees and cripples, or sometimes, after death, to corpses. They are dazzling because, after all, they derive their luster from an amputated arm and

84. I have already shown that for what is called "human reality" every determination of fact is *at the same time* a value. For the facticity of existence reveals itself only to the project it elicits, and which surpasses it.

521

the genius of an invincible captain. They would not pluralize honor, which is the fidelity of the whole army to its chief; they simply *manifest* it here and there, and with even greater luster since in every particular case the impulse is to recognize in a single hero the unquestionable valor of *all*, for such a veteran decorated after Eylau could not have shown his heroism without the obscure sacrifice of all those who lost their skin. Under the First Empire, the Legion is merely an image of the social hierarchy; inferior to the nobility of the sword since it is not hereditary, it nonetheless represents a recruitment from above. Any civilian whose civil virtues bring him the incredible luck to be admitted to this military knighthood must be considered a participant in the soldier's sacred essence; in other words, the distinction is not—at least in principle—accorded to the industrialist or the scientist who, in pursuit of particular objectives, interest, or glory, may have served the general interest in the process, but to civilians whose self-abnegation, devotion to the Emperor, and personalization of the French Nation would have demonstrated that they were *first faithful* to the lord of war, and that, conducting themselves in peacetime as on a battlefield, they deserved this sovereign gift transforming them into *soldiers of honor*.

If the Legion had not degenerated to the point of coopting Maxime, Flaubert would judge himself worthy of it, since he is a *man of honor*. Isn't he characterized—in his own eyes, at least—by self-abnegation? Entering literature to escape his class, didn't he choose subjection to the impossible, to beauty? And didn't that require an atrocious renunciation, the rending revision of '44? Didn't he deprive himself of everything, deliberately, isn't he *dead to his body* without even expecting literary success, without even knowing if he will ever publish? Wasn't that the finest example of the ego vanquished, mortified, the very type of hopeless enterprise and futile perseverance? Shouldn't it be seen, above all, as a matchless fidelity, repeated and sustained each day, despite everything, from morning to night? There is only one drawback: *subjection*, integral as it is, does not subject Flaubert to a Lord; for him, the *Other* is not man as other but *the Other than man*, an impersonal ideal—despite its diabolical cruelties—useless to men, to the nation, the artist himself, the *pure imaginary* as a denial of the real and consequently of our species. Gustave knows it; let's not imagine he boasts about it. On the contrary, he would have preferred, even while continuing his futile quest, that his permanent sacrifice should be *recognized* by an all-powerful Master. In other words, *behind* the fidelity to art and to the imaginary, he would have liked a bond of fealty to attach him to an *individual,* and he would have liked to create his *works* for that person, as he used to dream of putting his fame at Doctor Flaubert's feet, saying: "I earned it only to please you." What makes him indignant in '52 is that the Legion, in the hands of bourgeois liberals and utilitarians, has lost all meaning; without the somber guarantee of the "Man of Destiny," the *devotion* that established it disappears; under Louis-Philippe, this elite of the faithful becomes a corporation based on the very principle of utilitarianism. Those who belong to it are people who, by attending in the usual manner to their particular interest and strictly defending it, find they have served the general interest. In short, the Legion of Honor cannot exist in a bourgeois regime since the bourgeoisie, having reversed feudalism and replaced the fanaticism of man for man with the double negation in exteriority that is manifest in real property, is par excellence the class bereft of honor. Gustave reproaches Du Camp, in short, for deserving and accepting a medal that has become bourgeois. It must be observed, indeed, that Maxime obtained the red ribbon from a bourgeois government, and that another equally bourgeois government put him on the first waiting lists. Meanwhile, the prince-president took power, but apart from the fact that the *senatus consultum* that made him emperor was not yet promulgated, the singular goal in awarding this particular crop of decorations during the Republic was to reassure the bourgeoisie by demonstrating that behind the change of regime there was continuity of values and norms. In fact, through Maxime, the first photo-journalist, always ready to celebrate new inventions and through them to reaffirm on all occasions the bourgeois myth of progress, the new dictator is really rewarding the bourgeoisie itself. Flaubert senses this so clearly that he *is not jealous* of Maxime. We know that he never passes up the chance to envy his neighbor; but in Du Camp's place he would reject so discredited a distinction: offered by men without honor, it *dishonors* him by revealing that he is theirs. These men, moreover, have just proved their status as common rabble by pushing Badinguet to seize power. Flaubert has no tender feelings for the Second Republic—no peevishness either, or not much, as we have seen. But the coup d'état allows him once again to proclaim his misanthropy. Those cowards—the rich, the elite—did not even know how to stay faithful to a regime they themselves had established; now they are prostrating themselves and licking the dictator's boots; as for the common people, they showed their baseness by failing to mount the barricades; indeed, all of France has dishonored itself. Gustave is showing his irritation—for

523

he is obviously irritated—not because he feels frustrated; he is simply annoyed at being unable to open his friend's eyes and denounce the false pleasure Maxime feels. Maxime is happy, that is the shocker; this unworthy happiness should have been transformed into shame, into a horror of the self.[85]

If Maxime is an officer of a false Legion of Honor, Gustave in '66 can hardly be humiliated at being made the knight of a *true* Legion of Honor. Is it true, then? And *since when?* Under Louis-Philippe and under the Republic it was false currency; so how is it that when the bastard Badinguet distributes these false crosses, they recover their truth? Quite simply, he is the lord of War, unlike Louis-Philippe, who was the guardian of a bourgeois peace. Under the Second Empire, there are conflicts; blood is spilled, France is involved in a politics of prestige: Napoleon III commands a professional army that is devoted to him and is called his praetorian guard. Under the July monarchy, soldiers lost their prestige; they recovered it with the coup d'état; officers again took pride in looking down on civilians; a new aristocracy was forged on the spot. Or rather it was revived—the aristocracy of the First Empire reanimated and expanded by the second. Louis-Napoleon may not be a Bonaparte, but the ennobled military men who surround him are the real or spiritual descendants of those who surrounded the first Napoleon. After all, we have to admit that wars

85. Clearly, Gustave is much more severe in 1852 on Maxime's account than he will be in 1880 upon Maxime's election to the French Academy. In the first case, Du Camp is not *guilty of demeaning himself:* it's worse, he is decorated because he demeaned himself long ago. In the second, he *is worth more* than the chair they are giving him: Gustave dreamily reproaches him for selling himself cheap. This is because since 1848 and, more precisely, since the reading of *Saint Antoine* to Maxime and Bouilhet, Flaubert holds a deep grudge against Du Camp; they will become increasingly distant from one another until 1857—Gustave's resentment stoked by his censor's inept and rather cheap advice. It seems the breaking point was reached around the time of the trial of *Madame Bovary*. But Gustave's new-found fame reverses the situation: now it is Maxime who is jealous of his friend. This is not at all displeasing to Flaubert, who, knowing from experience the pangs of envy, is fond of proclaiming that it is better to be envied than pitied. For this reason Flaubert is the one who, without much illusion, paternalistically proposes a rapprochement. They will remain somewhat connected until Gustave's death—as we can see from the final scene of the second *Education*. The author does not disguise Deslaurier's opportunism, but finally the failure of his two heroes lets them profit from a tender indulgence. For God's sake, Deslauriers was too big for himself as well; if not, would he experience such deep melancholy, or turn during the shipwreck, as Flaubert does increasingly, toward their common past? Maxime's confidences have left his friend suspecting a secret disenchantment. No more is needed for him to be dumbfounded by learning of what he calls—significantly—Maxime's "nomination" to the Academy. Since Maxime is conscious, like Gustave, of having wasted his life, what need has he to exchange this sublime disenchantment for the satisfaction of being recognized as a peer by the manufacturers of bad literature?

are no longer what they were in the time when the "straight-haired Corsican" made and unmade kings; they are never lost, to be sure, but they are never definitively won. Be that as it may, France has regained its honor—its military honor. And when the princess has him decorated, far from feeling "dishonored," Flaubert believes he has been elevated to a soldier's honor. In this way, his fidelity to art becomes a fidelity *unto death*. Or, if you will, there is an affinity between the *gift of death* through extermination by the enemy on the battlefield and the *point of view of death* as the basis of the aesthetic attitude; and the somber insolence of the fine officers of the Empire—who live with death, for it and by it—bears some resemblance to the proud *survival of the self* that constitutes the artist: both regard themselves as having *already perished*. In this sense, and thanks to this real affinity, Gustave saw his necrosis magnified; if those rude warriors—who said to the Emperor, *"Morituri te salutant"*—accepted him into their ranks and treated him as an equal, it was because this play-acted death, which established the basis for his art, had the same sinister grandeur as their very real sacrifice. The artist dies and kills, he dies to the world in order to kill more surely, just like the Praetorians; Gustave's abnegation, even before Caesar had acknowledged it, was the presence within him of a somber collective honor that in the army takes the form of devotion to *a single* man who incarnates the French nation. Gustave's loyalty is not *directly* to Napoleon III, though to the first Bonaparte it certainly would have been; but the decoration makes him indirectly participate in this "subjection of man to man." Loyal by way of interposed persons, he benefits from the fanaticism and the grandeur of the field marshals and other superior officers. He has never deigned, nor will he ever deign, to sacrifice himself to anything but art—the fixed and glorious destruction of everything. But the red ribbon teaches him that the very inutility of his works serves the regime and, in consequence, the person of the Emperor, as do those gold-braided killers he detests but whose emptiness he respects—that sinister lacuna, that *absence of everything* establishing their *right to everything,* which a hundred years later Genet's homosexual whores will admire in their pimps. So much the better if he can unite sainthood—the permanent sacrifice to a nonbeing—with heroism, a sacrifice *in honor* of oneself to *another* who is very much alive. So much the better, *on condition* that it has never been conscious, that he has never *aspired* to that fealty and is certain, after the nomination, of remaining faithful to the impersonal ideal that constitutes the imaginary. He will live, as in the past, *in sainthood;* or, if you will, trans-ascendence, as a mystic elevation above being, and the derealizing struggle against language will remain his unique concern. That is his only way of internalizing the external and reexternalizing it; but he does not scorn the fact that professional heroes, by admitting him into their ranks, consecrate from the outside as heroism what he, personally, can live only in the form of saintly abnegation. In any case, since he has become *one of them*, this valorization can no longer remain *external*; it is his essence *as a legionnaire*; yet, as he would not know how to *live* it, it can only haunt him inside, as the impossible other face of his sainthood, his *being-for-the-other*. A fleeting consecration, delicious frustration at *being sacred* without ever being able to *realize* it, the marvelous license to accept or deny, in the silent intimacy of lived experience, the charismatic power of the sovereign—now Isidore, now Badinguet, now the Emperor—because sainthood does not derive from Caesar; it is inevitably recuperated by him and becomes a *secular version* of heroism, honor, and fidelity. Not being responsible for this promotion, the Saint can simultaneously rise above it, by the mystic movement that carries him above everything, and accept it—even if he is unable to enjoy it—as the *century's* only possible recognition of that ascendant movement.

But we may well ask what proof we have of the accuracy of this description. It can be true phenomenologically, that is, on the level of *eidos* and as a disclosure of the artist's general relation to the cross of honor under the Second Empire. How do we know it is applicable to the individual case of Flaubert? My answer is that we have evidence. And substantial evidence, at that.

We said previously that on two distinct occasions, Gustave behaved with surprising inconsistency with regard to the red ribbon. We have just examined the events of 1866, and we have provided a partial answer to the unavoidable; question, Why did this man so contemptuous of honors accept the cross? Four and a half years later, on 1 February 1871, after the capitulation of Paris, he writes to Caroline: "I no longer wear my cross of honor, for the word honor is no longer French." [86] Upon closer inspection, this behavior is so discreetly peculiar that it is appropriate to question its motives. Of course, it is merely a *gesture*—and, as usual with Flaubert, a negative one. We are impelled, however, to discover its symbolic meaning and its motivations: why does Flaubert remove from his buttonhole in 1871 the rib-

86. The above-mentioned decision to become a naturalized *Russian* follows.

bon he stitched into it in '66? If we can answer this question, we shall be able to determine the underlying nature of the ties that bind him to the collapsed regime as he experiences them in the horror of the defeat and through the frenzy of lived experience, ties that were gradually forged during the ten last years of the Empire.

Gustave is exasperated: his letter is full of sound and fury; he insults France, takes pleasure in declaring that he would have preferred the annihilation of Paris to its surrender. This violence is the triumph of hyperbole; he searches for criminal words because he is paid to know that words do not kill. Yet in the midst of these vociferations there is something surprising, a single *constant:* he did not invent the line about the red ribbon on the spot; we recognize it at nineteen years' distance, having read it in the letter to Louise from 17 January 1852, "How honors abound when honor is lacking!" At that time, the Legion was merely a "tremendous irony," since honor had disappeared with the fall of Napoleon I. Fourteen years go by; in the meantime, honor has been revived since Gustave allows himself to be decorated. Four years later this inconstant virtue once more abandons France. After a new military defeat, Gustave refuses to wear his decoration. From Waterloo to the 2 December coup, honors swarm over French dishonor. From the time that Napoleon III takes the title of emperor, and as long as his armies are victorious the "tremendous irony" is over, a man of quality is *honored* by the red ribbon. After the war of 1870, France is again plunged into its old shames, and the farce of honors is going to be replayed. What is there to say except that the honor of a country is bound to a charismatic power that depends upon a military hierarchy, is reinforced by constant bellicosity, and does not survive defeat? Gustave's rage is thus a confirmation of what I have just proposed; in '66, he pretends he's letting his arm be twisted, he thanks Mathilde in a slightly offhand way, he dwells on how little enthusiasm he feels—this is strictly theater. He is, in fact, fiercely proud of being *ennobled,* assimilated to the caste of officers, transfigured by their common acceptance of death, fealty without knowledge and without obligation. After the defeat, honor disappears, both the army's and Gustave's—it was strictly one for all. Distraught, Flaubert finds himself in Maxime's situation—that of 1852: What does this bit of red string mean without the vast guarantee of an Empire? Nothing but opportunism or delusion: those who declared him their peer are cowards and scoundrels. Since he didn't reject their favors, doesn't he share their vulgarity and cowardice?

527

And if we share Flaubert's taste for clichés, isn't this the moment to say that birds of a feather flock together? Quick, it's time to break with them.

The fact is that this interpretation, though not entirely false, is still too simple and partial; Gustave's behavior is richer, more secretive and ambiguous. For us to take better account of it, let us put the line we have isolated back in context:

> The capitulation of Paris, which we nonetheless should have expected, has plunged us into an indescribable state! We're choking with rage! I am furious that Paris was not burned to the last house . . . France is so low, so dishonored, so demeaned that I would wish for its complete destruction. But I hope that the civil war is going to kill many of us. May I be included in the number. In preparation for the thing, they are going to name deputies. What a bitter irony! Naturally, I will abstain from voting. I no longer wear my cross of honor, for the word honor is no longer French, and I am so sure of no longer being [French] that . . . [etc.][87]

A surprising passage; for, after all, by what association of ideas is he led to impart to Caroline his refusal to wear the cross? Is it because he was awarded it by a false emperor, the false head of a false army and keeper of a false honor? And because someone who could have compared the Prussian officers to ours could have predicted Sedan *in 1866?* Does he say he was tricked? That after this, France hadn't a single drop of honor left in her veins, or hadn't had since the fall of the First Empire? And that consequently Badinguet, by decorating him, was bestowing what he did not have? No; Gustave is not saying any of this. Not a word about the Emperor. Moreover, if Flaubert had meant to condemn him, he should have thrown his cross in Badinguet's face five months earlier, after Sedan. Yet he refrained from doing so, and, quite to the contrary, before the capitulation but after some very serious reversals he wrote to Ernest Commanville: "Well! We're in a fine fix! The *Empire* is now just a matter of days, but it must be defended to the end."[88] Around the same date he writes to Madame Roger des Genettes: "What a heap of curses on Isidore's head." But the evils he prophesies, the Revolution, squalor, are not shameful in themselves; they are cataclysms, that's all. No, dishonor comes *with*

87. *Correspondance*, 6:197.
88. *Correspondance*, Supplément, 1864–1871, p. 241. The undated letter is probably from 18 August 1870.

the capitulation of Paris. Flaubert is not unaware, however, that Napoleon is doubly guilty since he unleashed this war and then lost it. He knows, too, that, by contrast, the new State began by refusing defeat, that it did the impossible to raise armies, that Paris—Republican Paris of 4 September—refused to surrender and decided to fight to the end. He knows it so well that he wrote on 30 October: "Poor Paris, I find it heroic . . ."[89] And on 18 December 1870: "Poor Paris is hanging on as ever, but eventually it will succumb! And between now and then, France will be thrown into utter confusion, lost."[90] And on 19 December—a day when this interminable war overwhelms him, when he wants to see it end as soon as possible: "This ghastly war has no end! Will it end when Paris surrenders? But how can Paris surrender?"[91] We sense in this paragraph the glimmerings of a slight impatience with that stubborn capital which is determined to resist in the face of all evidence, and will only succeed in prolonging the conflict. After all, couldn't someone answer Gustave that this futile obstinacy, assured of finally being crushed and not wanting to know it, is—using his own concepts as he understands them—the honor of the Parisian people, their fidelity not to a prince but to their own history? That would be their pure destruction: for Gustave, the populace has no honor; its dominant passion is envy. Still, he admired the courage of Paris; like everyone else, he foresaw that the enemy would take the city, and that since this was the inevitable outcome, he allowed himself to wish it over as soon as possible. Still, in the same letter in which he curses the capitulation of the Parisians he acknowledges that it "should have been expected." Clearly, he expected it. Yet there is no doubt that it was the anticipated surrender of a starving, bombarded city[92] that ravished France's honor. This is what makes Gustave say: "France is so low, so dishonored, so demeaned . . ." Shame has fallen once more on an armed civil population, which fought to save a nation that the professional army had lost. But this should not surprise us. This populace destroyed the honor of the French the day it overthrew its sovereign, the legitimate representative of France and repository of its glory. Observe the sequence of ideas: the civil war is at our gates; they are *preparing* for it by naming deputies, a "bitter irony"—these two words echo, after many years, the "tremendous

---

89. *Correspondance*, 6:184.
90. Ibid., p. 188.
91. Ibid., p. 192.
92. In January 1871, he writes to Caroline: "Poor Paris will not long be able to resist the terrible bombardment it is enduring.

irony" of 1853; in short, the new regime will be republican, the Assembly will be elected by universal suffrage; consequently, Flaubert decides he will not vote. Why? Because he "is worth twenty voters from Croisset," and because he does not want to play the game of a state that summons him to mutilate himself by removing nineteen of *his* voices and benevolently offers him the use of the twentieth to legitimize this brigandage—whoever the beneficiary and by the sole fact of going to the polls. The Republic, born of envy, has to be egalitarian: it will equalize from below; number will kill quality, hence "the word honor is no longer French." Nothing is more striking than the juxtaposition of these two consecutive lines: ". . . I will abstain from voting. I no longer wear my cross of honor . . ." It will not have gone unnoticed that the France-without-honor that dishonored Maxime by making him its "knight" is the France of the bourgeois-king and the Second Republic; just as the France without-honor of '71 is republican and, without even touching it, simply by existing, changes Gustave's red ribbon into a dead leaf. It is no longer Sedan that dishonors the French, it is 4 September, the implementation of the republican idea and the suppression of hierarchies of merit based on the gift of the self.

This absurd thought has a certain logic; it clearly demonstrates that Flaubert accepted his cross when it came from above and consecrated him. He rejected it when it made him a member of a group chosen in the commonality by commoners. Whatever he may have said about Isidore, Gustave stands behind that red ribbon *he owes to Napoleon III:* it is a personal bond between vassal and Lord. After 4 September, the deputies will receive their mandates from the plebe and will be, by definition, inferior to the artist. For example, Flaubert does not despise Thiers as a politician; but he considers him an execrable writer. How could he allow this scribbler to reward him for his merits as an artist? And in a way, he knows, that is what will happen: the uncertain Republic that is about to emerge from the disaster will preserve certain institutions of imperial France, in particular the Legion of Honor. For those decorated it is confirmation of the validity of their decorations; thus with Badinguet fallen, Gustave will hold his ribbon from the new regime, he will immediately be a member of the vile elite that will be designated by *those people.* Indeed, every new *republican* day, the old guard of honor will be challenged by the elect of the republic, and in the end it will be lost in the midst of a popular knighthood recruited from below. An anecdote reported by the Goncourts indeed expresses Flaubert's sentiment. Some years later, he had agreed to wear his ribbon again; then, to his unhappiness, they were going to decorate Lévy, his former publisher whom he cordially despised because he was a Jew[93] and because he regarded him as rabble. This was all it took for the red ribbon to disappear once more from his buttonhole. He did not want, he tells Edmond, to take part in a social body in which a Lévy was admitted. When Lévy died, Goncourt announced the news to Gustave and saw him fiddle with the lapel of his jacket; the following day, the ribbon reappeared. This story—which is not in doubt—shows that Flaubert took his order of knighthood quite seriously and thought himself compromised by those of the new members who did not possess the requisite conditions: Lévy had no honor, being a Jew; isn't this clear evidence? Therefore, his nomination tainted all the legionnaires with subtle dishonor. This was Gustave's sense of things before the question of decorating his publisher arose: the imperial institution, fallen into the hands of the vulgar, could only destroy itself. How could representatives of the common people or the utilitarian bourgeoisie recognize in certain of their fellow citizens a merit they hadn't the faintest idea about and would condemn, if they did, as a residue of the aristocracy? It would be futile to answer that while Flaubert might have refused this cross if Thiers, an appalling author, had offered it to him, he wasn't

93. I am not going to expand on Flaubert's anti-Semitism for two reasons: in his time and place, everyone was racist; Gustave is just like everyone else, no more so. In this sense I see nothing in such criminal foolishness, entering him by hearsay and remaining inside him, stagnant, like those blocks of stupidity that crush him and which his thought tries in vain to dissolve; I see nothing in it that characterizes his particularity, nor do I see that he had personally internalized it so as to reexternalize it in his books and his conduct. Unlike the Goncourts—especially Edmond, whose racism is so virulent that it deserves an explanation, to be sought, no doubt, in his early history—Flaubert is a peddler of anti-Semitism rather than an active agent and inventor. And it is an unpleasant but not very serious stereotype that he invokes with his mania for calling Lévy the "son of Israel." I am not excusing it; I have said elsewhere what I think of these carriers of microbes, who are more contagious than really infected, who perpetuate a genteel racism—which can, when circumstances are propitious, become a murderous rage. Yet I maintain that his "opinions" in this matter were merely reflections: the age is incarnate in him, as in everyone, with that hatred of the "Youtre" that is so precisely *dated*. (This is not yet the anti-Semitism of Drumont. Nor that of the anti-Dreyfusards. Nor that of the National Socialists. In the mid-eighteenth century it was still a defensive reflex of an active collectivity that refuses to assimilate—or regretfully assimilates—the new members who the Revolution of 1789 gave it.) But he doesn't overdo it; to despise the Jews one must necessarily be a misanthrope, but only to a certain point. Past this limit—and Flaubert passed it by some distance—one despises men too much to be able to establish a hierarchy of one's aversions: everyone is equal, everyone is vile, everyone is damned. Without believing, for all that, in the superiority of the non-Jew, Gustave is only too happy to pose the inferiority of the "children of Israel" in principle, and particularly when his publisher is involved.

531

ashamed to accept it from the hands of Duruy, who was hardly an adept of absolute-art, on the recommendation of Mathilde, who understood nothing about it either, and in the name of the Emperor, who favored insipid, edifying literature.[94]

The important thing, under the Empire, is not the *taste* of the person who decorates, but his charismatic power, which confers sacred power on the recipient. In order to *distinguish* Gustave, it was enough for the Emperor to be well counseled, for Sainte-Beuve, for example—whose writings Flaubert esteems and whom he thanks as a precaution—to have supported the Princess's application. A sensitive and artistic advisor might also, under the Third Republic, guide the choice of Monsieur Thiers. But to *consecrate* him, to recognize and make manifest the *numinous* aspect of his sacrifice by a sign, requires no lesser person than the chief of a black and bloody knighthood, of knights *already dead* and faithful against winds and tides in that very death that made them servants for eternity. What is needed, in a word, whatever the motives, is a person who himself possesses *mana* (*coming simply from the willing sacrifice by others*) and the power to communicate it. For this reason, Flaubert swallows the insult of Ponson du Terrail in '66, and rejects the insult of Lévy under the Third Republic. For while regretting du Terrail's nomination—which testifies to a certain lack of discernment—he does not feel truly compromised; it is a shame that *Rocambole* should be consecrated, but that enormous dark power of spilled blood redeems everything. Flaubert is the brother at arms of great soldiers; too bad about *Rocambole*—its just a *mistake* of the kind that any constituted body might make; the nomination of Lévy, by contrast, is not an exception in the Republic, *it's the rule*. It is tempting to respond, perhaps, that the Third Republic also decorated military men. Of course; and the Fourth Republic too; and the Fifth. But they are named hastily by ministers who come and go, vulgar commoners. Imagine *lay persons* investing priests! This is conceivable only in an absolute monarchy, because under these conditions the Sovereign is in principle a hero and a saint.

A truer objection, and one that cuts deeper, is that Flaubert could not accept an honor given to him by Isidore the Bastard unless he saw him as someone possessed, ridden without respite by Napoleon the Great. Here again we find the play of mirrors, since the first Emperor

---

94. Let us add that Flaubert considered Napoleon II the *author* a wretched scribbler. On 11 May 1865 he writes: "I have not even opened our sovereign's *Caesar*, which seems to be a mediocre thing." To Mlle Leroyer de Chantepie, *Correspondance*, 5:175.

of the French was the only one who could recruit Gustave for the Legion he created. When he accepts the ribbon, the "Solitary" knows quite well that it is given to him by a usurper, the lazy head of a false army; he must therefore return to the unreal: from the arm of a false Bonaparte, the true one, long dead, unreally rewards Flaubert's merits. The cross is false; it could not help but be. Had Flaubert lived in the time of the true Bonaparte and—an absurd conjecture— had he written *Madame Bovary* and *Salammbô* at that time and in that society, he would have been neither read nor decorated. Napoleon I, a man of action par excellence, certainly wanted his reign, like that of Louis the XIV, to be made illustrious *also* by a pleiade of artists; but when he created this new order in 1802, he meant to reward *services rendered*. And for him these words necessarily meant a certain political commitment, support given *even in works* to the regime, if not to the government. He could allow himself to decorate adversaries if they *counted* in his eyes, and if credible reports led him to understand that they were only waiting for a favor to rally to his side. But this *realistic policy*, which made the cross into a sign of a *practical reality*, would on principle have excluded Flaubert, the imaginary, from the number of the chosen. *What good would it do* to decorate him? What purpose would it serve? What advantage would the Subject of History derive from it? The ribbon would have been compromised by decorating a stubbornly apolitical woolgatherer from the provinces, even if his novels were read, unless he first changed his conduct, swore to *serve*, and accepted wages. Neither the Corisican nor his times could imagine that a man might serve a regime by taking to an extreme the refusal to serve anything. The Hermit of Croisset—from the realistic perspective of praxis—stood no chance of being decorated: he was useless, he did not harm; there was nothing to reward, no reason to win him over. To understand the importance of *disinterest*, of the *inutility* of a work that was meant to be an indestructible mirage, one would have to be a mirage oneself. Only Napoleon III, as the false resurrection of Napoleon I, could distinguish Flaubert and integrate him into an illusory knighthood; from him alone could Flaubert accept this phantom and discreetly Satanic distinction, which consecrated him in everyone's eyes but illusority, without committing him to anything, or better, invited him to persevere in the refusal of all commitment—and first and foremost the commitment to respect the Emperor. It required a false society conscious of being so, and wanting to be so, to understand that the best service literature could render it was not to serve it. In fact, the government first favored the vulgarities and servilities of official art. But beyond these academic productions (which were of interest to no one except perhaps the Empress), everyone among the Prince's advisers was aware that the literature of the regime associated with its name, like a certain style in dress or furnishings, was being forged in the work of the misanthropes of absolute-art—perpetuating the hatred of man against man, and shunting him off toward the imaginary. Flaubert is named Knight of the Legion of Honor insofar as he is already a Knight of Nothingness. He understands this and rejoices in it; the death of his body *in the imaginary* is that *illusory* death the decoration consolidates by defining it as Gustave's honor. His honor: his illusory fidelity to nonbeing, illusorily assimilated to the *real* fidelity of soldiers to their Emperor. *Real?* It would take less than five years to show what it was worth: when in '71 Gustave imagines that parade of clenched fists before the carriage of Napoleon III, *he too,* with the inner voice of the vanquished, is speaking of his profound disappointment: those were the men they called *his* Praetorian guards, he thinks. For he needed everything to be false *except* the devotion, courage, and competence of the military: this *reality* allowed him to unrealize everything; in rejecting the bourgeoisie, his bourgeois antimilitarism required the army to be the last refuge and guardian of the only human greatness in his view—fealty. *The Empire pulled him out of the bourgeoisie, in the imaginary,* because it seemed to him to rely on the *virtu* of its generals. When this is revealed in its inanity as a comedy of courtiers, and when at the same moment in Paris the bourgeoisie gets rid of the Empire and takes power itself, Flaubert throws away his cross. Out of anger at this Napoleon who has been revealed as a Badinguet? Not at all. It's true that he doesn't much like him at this moment; but his curses are not very potent. Since the real object of his hatred is bourgeois France, the meaning of his gesture is the opposite of what it first appears: it must be seen as a gesture of allegiance, something like the symbolic sacrifice of the liege man on the tomb of his master:

> From the time he had the trappings of the Sacred, he gave me honor by *consecrating my anomaly,* and as along as the collective dream endured that raised him above men, I kept that *other* consciousness of *myself: holy from day to day, in the throes of mediocrity,* I knew I was a hero in the dreams of others. Now that he has lost everything, even honor, I no longer want to keep from anyone else the gift he made me, the gift he continued to make me as long as he reigned. Not from anyone, and *especially not* from those wretches who have had the audacity to awaken.

It is striking that in the same letter he informs Caroline, almost in passing, of his refusal to vote, his decision no longer to wear the cross, and his desire—entirely imaginary but all the more violently felt—to make himself the subject of the Czar. Despite their monarchical regimes, he has opted neither for Italy, which bears too close a resemblance to France, nor for England, which is too democratic in his opinion.[95] In order to flee bourgeois egalitarianism, he hastens to choose the most autocratic regime, the most unfavorable to the necessary freedoms of art, one whose army, even more mediocre than the French, was beaten not so long ago in the Crimean war. For in Russia one finds *real* nobility, an ironclad hierarchy and serfdom; it unites all the requisite conditions for him to become integrated, in his lifetime, with a *real* feudalism.[96]

This vow—absurd as it is—reveals to us the underlying contradiction that makes Gustave's position untenable. Before the war it required a collective lie that had the perenniality of the real, a society derealized but more solid than the real itself. A false army capable of vanquishing real armies, or rather supported at great cost, like a dancer, which strikes terror in the enemy by its pomp without ever risking itself in the field. The correspondence indicates that beginning in 1865, Gustave slowly convinced himself that Prussia was militarily superior to France; he never admitted it. Only this terrible conviction provoked increasing anxiety; somewhat indifferent until then to the wars of prestige waged by the Emperor, he was gripped by an ardent desire for the peace to be maintained. This means, concretely, that in order to preserve *in the unreal* his belief, shared by all the French, that the French army was the best in the world, a confrontation with Prussian troops had to be avoided at all costs. We have seen him swear not to return to the Magny dinners and *keep his word*, because Renan, in the name of science and truth, affirmed the superiority of Germany and foretold its hegemony over Europe. He was deliberately shutting his eyes. But this ostrich-like policy is a clear indication of his discomfort and his bad faith. He demands that imperial society should be an opera—everything is false; Gustave himself, at the Court, took

95. It must be said that he harbors a certain rancor against both countries because they did not come to the rescue.
96. It must also be said that Russia, in his eyes, seems to take on the characteristics of Turgenev, whose charm and "civility" had attracted even the Goncourts. But conversely, we shall not forget that this charming aristocrat dazzled them especially because to them he represented the ideal of a great writer who was an authentic nobleman.

a caustic pleasure in being falsely ennobled. But unlike techniques of individual unrealization—which according to him pull the artist out of the real world and (see *La Spirale*) suppress a priori, through consensual failure, any risk of a confrontation between the imaginary and the real—collective unreality, far from pulling the Empire away from the real, entangles it a little more each day. Indeed, this society acts out the drama but acts it out *in the world in which it is anchored:* it does not claim the superiority of dreams, it dreams it is superior in earnest to other societies that actually exist and with whom, through its facticity, it finds itself maintaining *real* relations, which it is unaware of or misconstrues. Napoleon III plays the role of Napoleon I, his officers play the role of the marshals of the First Empire, but to give substance to this theater, an army must be supported, real men must be summoned under the flags, real rifles must be loaded, real conflicts engaged in, and thereby France made into an enemy to be demolished for a conquering and truly organized nation, which, with no vain concern for prestige, wants to pursue the policy its economy requires and assure itself outlets for its industry by establishing its hegemony over Europe. Certainly, in this second half of the nineteenth century we witness the rise of nationalism everywhere: the industrial revolution cannot go forward without new markets; thus Bismarck's policy is, in effect, the policy Napoleon III should pursue. And that he does pursue. But pursues in dreams, acting them out without providing himself with the means to realize them. That is Flaubert's theater: unrealized by failure and a perpetual contention of the spirit, he needs an unreal but solid society to sustain his effort, to nourish him and reward him; he finds it, it welcomes him, he becomes integrated with it but he takes account of the fact, after some time, that this *other solidity* of the collective dream comes from reality itself. In other words, the imperial drama can "take" only to the extent that it is tolerated by the constellation of dominant classes, which, being strongly realistic, see in the military dictatorship an effective (therefore real) force of repression and a dream of glory whose effect (quite as real) is to deter the disadvantaged classes from becoming clearly conscious of their lot. And this fine opera is, in another sense, a pernicious reality because it cannot help but lead to an immense collective failure that will overtake not only the actors but the whole country.

Sequestered, ailing, living off his property, Flaubert was able to live safely in the imaginary because circumstances were favorable to him, and above all because he chose failure *from the beginning.* The Emperor and his Praetorians began with *success:* this could not be otherwise since it was a matter of social fact, of the establishment of a regime, in short of a *real* transformation produced by concerted actions. The dream begins *afterward,* upon the advent of the plebiscite and the senatus-consultus. As a result, the Empire has its failure *before* it, which is necessary since this dream, far from radically questioning being, tries to pass as reality; this means that it integrates the real— as it is produced in historical temporalization—as its support. In other words, for lack of a catharsis through voluntary bankruptcy— inconceivable here—and of an ascesis, the dream is not a negation of the real but an *error* concerning reality; therefore it bears its own ruin within itself from the outset since this protracted error is given the lie by the reality it tried to integrate and whose disparate elements appear sooner or later in their essential heterogeneity. Flaubert, a specialist in "Loser Wins," sensed the "Winner Loses" of the imperial theater from the outset; we can even say that this fatality seduced him: society took the same road he did, only *in reverse.* So he remains irreproachable insofar as, coming to success through failure, he loves in the Empire that demonic success that must be completed by a failure precisely because it filled its images too full with its inordinately heavy reality. That is just what one ought to expect of a power in hell. But Flaubert's situation compels him at the same time to desire the solidity and permanence of that society as imaginary. In a way, we might say that he finds in the Empire the perverse charm of a bad dream, that he is conscious of dreaming—as we often are when sleeping lightly—but that he would like to prolong the dream over years and die before waking. *In this respect* he is guilty—according to his ethic as an artist. In this respect he is complicit with the regime whose continuation he desired *to the very end* out of complaisance with the opportunities of collective oneirism. We might say that he recognizes that the Empire is condemned to a shorter or longer term of expiration, that he rejoices in it but demands, for his part, an indefinitely prolonged suspension of the sentence. The final failure must be *in* the regime, like a worm in an apple, as the underlying feature of this appearance vampirizing reality, as the destiny it bears in itself; it must not *be produced* as an historical event, at least not *during Flaubert's lifetime,* for he needs the Empire so that his own failure—the fall beneath the human—should find its reward in a false but indefinitely repeated ennoblement. And of course his principled pessimism requires that this false reward be itself a future failure—through the collapse of the regime; thus, for Gustave himself, the failure of the beginning becomes absolute. The society that made his fame reveals itself as a mirage, the game of "Loser Wins" reveals itself for what it is: a permanent, pitiless shipwreck giving way to the horror of living and, more secretly, to the more humble and authentic "Loser Wins." God must exist; *He* cannot deal me the blow of not existing. But it is enough that the fatalities of the Empire should be lived in advance, as prophecies: no need for a real collapse. The contesting of failure-neurosis by neurotic success in a mirage-society, the contesting of this success by the very unreality of a regime that reveals itself as condemned more or less in the long term, the perception of the future failure of the society that welcomed him as the pitiless *meaning* of his individual failure of '44, the absolute despair that follows from it and engenders or surreptitiously restores the believer's "Loser Wins"—this whole dialectical game (which can, moreover, be reversed) may induce one's surrender *under the Empire* at any moment. More, *the Empire is necessary* for Gustave to preserve a ludic quality to this vicious circle of contestation. As long as it is maintained, it is an incubus whose quality of pure appearance can be denounced, a midnight vampire that will certainly vanish at the first cock's crow. Abolished, it will give way to *being:* vampire or not, it will have been; the *no longer being* will mask the *not being,* which is manifest at present as the being of nonbeing and the nonbeing of being. By desiring the perpetuation of the mirage, it is of little consequence that Gustave was more conscious of its vanity than Napoleon III; he is no less complicit; what is more, he *makes himself* a man of the Empire. Everything whose falseness he would denounce in 1870 he loved for that very falseness for more than ten years—the best years of his life—and because that deceptive greatness of France seemed to him the Satanic caricature of another authentic but impossible greatness, to which imagination itself could *aspire* but never attain. He loved to act out the drama within the larger drama until that exhausting and delicious moment verging on madness, always on the point of taking gestures—everyone else's and his own—for acts, always subtly disappointed, feeling that he can no longer drop his role and also that there is a boundary he cannot cross without finding himself in an asylum. But he senses that this dangerous frontier is *in fact* unbreachable since the unreal is in essence impossible to confuse with reality, and so the transport impels him to leap into the mirror—motivated by the frustrating but *reassuring* certainty that this mirror does not exist—and impels him not only to assume *a* role but to play the role of someone who takes his role for reality. That is all it takes for him to *be ashamed*. If the

Empire is a ruse, if the Praetorians are merely cowards or traitors, if Prince Napoleon "flees," if Bazaine betrays, what is the *honor* of the Legion worth then? And what is Flaubert's honor worth? Behind his imprecations we sense uncertainty. On 1 February '71 he writes to Commanville: "I have revoked the red ribbon, and those who continue to wear it seem to me haughtily impudent. For the words *Honor* and *French* are incompatible."[97] This text—written, however, the same day as the letter to Caroline—betrays a slight dislocation of his thought: "I no longer wear my cross of honor," he said. To his nephew he writes that he has revoked it; this curious turn of phrase seems to indicate the Gustave did not freely decide to get rid of a degraded symbol but that he acted as representative for the reckoning of an Other, of an almighty judge who, if he existed, *would have revoked his right to the Legion of Honor.* For a single conceivable reason: Flaubert appears to this supreme magistrate as *unworthy* of this distinction. The rest of the sentence confirms this interpretation: those who still wear it are hautily impudent, meaning that they have the impudence to believe they are still worthy of it when the event has just proved that a *Frenchman cannot have honor.* Gustave's sole superiority over these blind Legionnaires is to have taken account of the fact, *himself,* that the collective and indivisible honor in which he thought he participated has been destroyed. Gustave is French, *therefore* he has no more honor, and he will have none *as long as he remains French*—hence in the letter to Caroline the far-fetched idea of becoming a naturalized Russian. From one letter to the other there is a back-and-forth between the two formulations, each of which is essentially meaningless except in relation to the other. For Caroline, Flaubert refuses the shame of being French and shifts his allegiance to the Czar, for he himself *has honor;* if he gets rid of the red ribbon, it is to avoid ignoble promiscuity with the dishonorable men who wear it. At the very least he thinks that if the source of honor is military, if in order to participate in it one must be made the object of a choice from above, and if the conquered head of this operetta army no longer has or never had the charismatic power that allows the *consecration* of merits, it is up to him, Gustave, the solitary aristocracy of sainthood. Being integrated into a hierarchical society is enough for a sovereign's favor to allow his mystical self-abnegation to recover its heroic dimension for others. In the letter to Commanville, sainthood is not even allusively evoked; there is shame, that's all. No way out: Gustave is

97. *Correspondance,* Supplément (1864–1871), p. 254.

French, therefore he has no honor; he does not even seem to think that naturalization at nearly fifty would change anything. As we see, his sentiment swings between these two extremes: the French do *not* have honor and I am leaving them because I, Gustave, do have honor; the French *no longer* have honor and, like all my compatriots, I am *dishonored*. It's all there: do the vanquished of 1870 *not* have, or do they *no longer* have, the right to wear their crosses? In the first case, the overthrow of the regime and taking power by the multitude created an entirely new France, which does *not* have honor since the plebes who govern are by definition deprived of it. this must lead to the conclusion that the veterans of the Legion, those of the Empire, were rightly decorated: if they reject the ribbon, it is because they are faithful to a dead Legion, *their own*, and refuse to be sullied by its caricature. But if the vanquished *no longer* have the right to wear it, it is the defeat that is at issue. And the capitulation of Paris—which provoked this delirium of rage—is an adept *cover* that allows him to protest his shame: he can finally externalize it, the rage that gripped him after Sedan, and condemn the Emperor's capitulation without saying a word about him or the lords of war. When the plebescite capitulates, he speaks of dishonor. But it is the other, hidden capitulation that spoils everything: there is *no more* honor in France because the guardians of that virtue—the sovereign, the aristocracy—have failed at their task. Consequently, all those whom they had *honored*, by a retroactive effect of the military defeat, see their decorations reduced to *what they are:* neither signs nor symbols, they are nothing but material objects. But if looked at closely, were the Lords of the Empire *ever worthy* of distinguishing between men and promoting the best? If Napoleon III has no charismatic power and the Praetorian guard no fidelity, they are not good judges, and those crosses distributed so indiscriminately can only refer—except by improbable accident—to a false honor. Behind the *no longer being* is a *not being*, which is revealed to be much more radical than the first: since Waterloo, as much under the Empire as under the Republic and the two monarchies that preceded it, the words "Honor" and "French" have been incompatible; Flaubert's honor is *imaginary*.

These different attitudes in Flaubert mask each other. Gustave insists above all on the first (honor disappeared when the Republic was proclaimed) so that the second and especially the third might never be entirely explicit; it would be intolerable to him, in effect, to think that the *dignity* granted in '66 was an illusion. This attests to a considerable evolution in his attitude from '57 to '66: his rallying to the Empire, at first only ludic, was transformed into pithiatic belief: the Court was merely playacting; the red ribbon, however, is a serious matter. Flaubert's honor is *true*, it has been *truly* acknowledged; therefore, the regime must finally have some truth. He has not pushed further. But that is enough for the crumbling of the system to reveal his double culpability: he was wrong to stop at the dazzling images of this society, as heedless as the powerful of the moment, and to let real forces secretly decide the true destiny of the French community; he was wrong—paradoxically—to have taken military notoriety seriously and to have believed that our army really guaranteed the honor of France. Through these two contradictory but easily overlapping errors, he made himself the *man of the Empire* and could readily identify with the loser of Sedan. That is why, in the first days following the defeat, this admission escapes him: "One can no longer write when one no longer has any self-esteem." He was touched in the deepest part of his being by the events of 1870, which destroyed the surly courtier in him as well as the change of class from above—which he took in general as fictive and *believed* to be true in August '66—and plunged him back into his intolerable reality as a bourgeois "living on his income and occupying himself with literature."

This collective failure is lived by him in his singularity as the denial of his whole existence and the abolition of the failure-catharsis that he chose in '44. The imaginary child learns, half a century after his birth, that the real is a plenitude that cannot be abandoned; externally it is his dungeon, internally his very constitution: between the bars of his cage and his internal skeleton, there are such affinities that the structures of inside and outside are practically interchangeable, and all evasion is impossible except death. This infinite nonbeing, that glittering lacuna he thought he was made of, was merely a ruse of being, a means real enough to lead him, twenty-five years after his conversion at Pont-l'Evêque, to coincide with his finitude, with his facticity. After this discovery we understand why he is constantly vomiting. He is vomiting the defeat, of course, and the Republic and Prussia; but above all he is vomiting himself, he is trying to vomit this invasion of nothingness by being which I will call—in contrast to that half-century of derealizing effort—his *realization*. A terrible awakening; his old obsession, forgotten for twenty-five years, buried in the sand, is pulled out and resurrected: suicide. Sometimes he feels that he is going "to croak," he surrenders to "death by thought"; and sometimes he wants to blow his brains out. Unless he is pondering the project of taking his rifle to the aid of the liberated Parisians and getting himself killed, winning at the same time *in earnest* that military honor falsely attributed to him and which can be bought only with blood. This unexpected violence—even if its expression is sometimes hyperbolic—can be surprising: Isn't he first and foremost an artist, the greatest of the Postromantic writers, the most famous? When the war took him by surprise, he had undertaken to recast his *Saint Antoine* entirely in order to give it a definitive version; he was seriously thinking about that *Histoire de deux cloportes* [*History of Two Woodlice*] he had mentioned to Gautier beginning in 1869, which would become *Bouvard et Pécuchet*. As we see, he was not lacking for projects; and he would return to them when his rage subsided. However, during the first months of the occupation, he finds no comfort in the absolute-art that ought to have consoled him for everything; he feels incapable of writing for lack of self-esteem. As if, in a certain way, honor were the source of genius. As if his previous books had gone down with the shipwreck of the Empire; as if, products of a false honor, crowned with haloes of false glory, they were in themselves, in their content and their form, corrupted by an intolerable falsity. Did Flaubert go so far as to condemn his works? I don't know; but certainly, in the first moment of madness, this refusal to write and the refusal to live that is bound up with it clearly designate the Second Empire as the "natural setting" for absolute-art. At times, then, Gustave concludes that the works of the era and the society that loved them must disappear together, condemned by the same sentence to defeat and oblivion—and at times it is the new society on which he pronounces judgment: in this Republic without honor there is no place either for the flamboyance of an imperial Court or for "workers of art" still more flamboyant than the sovereigns who favored them.

In the early days, beneath the hatred it is shame that prevails; it will diminish little by little but never wholly disappear. He feels *culpable*, which is worse than a defeat; in effect, failure can be experienced in solitude as the destiny of great souls, it is possible to take pride in it. Culpability comes to the culpable from the other, it is an aspect of fundamental alienation: to be *wrong* is to be ineffective, inessential, it is the other who matters, who is *homo sapiens* and *homo faber* all in one because he *is right*. And because—by the necessity of the discourse or by the evidence of successful *praxis*—he compels the vanquished *to grant that he is right*, to treat *himself* as a condemnable pretext, as an error: before the defeat I *believed* I existed; afterwards they demonstrated to me that I did not exist at all, or rather that my sole reality—hidden from me until now—is that which the *other* concedes to me if I denounce my views and enter into his. In most cases what is intolerable is that I denounce them without bad faith but without ceasing to believe in them. Such is Flaubert's case. Men demonstrate to him in 1870 that he has always been wrong, and that the defeat of the Empire is his own defeat, that of the Latin world. The sudden irruption of the real into his dreams coincides with the invasion of France by the Prussians. As real men rooted in their times, they affirm the superiority of praxis to the dream. While the Emperor, his court, his artists abandoned themselves to the "civility" of the directed oneirism they called *living*, the Prussians were preparing themselves; they had taken the measure of France and the imperial army, and knew they could easily gobble them up. For them, Badinguet's dream, Gustave's dream, was not the product of a free imagination but a somnambulism they would turn to their advantage, when the day came, and strike the sleepers as they slept. They knew everything, they observed; for them, the imaginary, far from being a surpassing of all reality, was merely the passage from one state of the real to another, a technique governed by notions that self-destructed with the final outcome; if posed for its own sake in their neighbors the French, it was a reality insufficiently developed, a truncated and therefore false idea, arrested in its evolution by very real men, whom this choice defined *in their reality*—they were cowards, lazy good-for-nothings, etc. In fact, as we have seen, from 1865 on, the writers have *reason* to worry: unversed as they are in military art, they have the means to measure the strength of their future adversary. And it is true that they are a bit worried. But intermittently; bored by secular complications, they quickly return to their usual sublime *distraction*. This pithiatic *diversion* implies an unfounded confidence in the invincibility of the French army. These good monks have to believe, not so much out of nationalism—they hardly share such sentiments—but because it protects their dreams. They take shelter behind the regiments in order to derealize the world, just as the bourgeoisie takes shelter behind the imperial facade in order to *realize* France's industrial development as soon as possible—that is, to complete the accumulation of capital. This belief, shared by Emperor and inculcated in the masses by government propaganda, is a crime, the intellectual taint of blood for these artists. It is not a matter, here, of cultivating beautiful fantasies for their own sake and feigning to believe them to the extent that faith is clearly impossible; it is a matter of stupidly believing, like everyone, in an elusive *reality* so as to stop thinking about it. For when all those talkers at Magny—Renan apart—base

543

their easy paradoxes on the implicit conviction that the French soldier is the best in the world, this conviction concerns our troops' *real superiority*. The imagination is utilized here as it is by the technicians of Prussia: it precedes knowledge and opens a path to it. But instead of resulting in a hypothesis requiring verification, it is arrested by a dazzling image—the choreography of uniforms, military fanfare—which it entrusts with symbolizing French *invincibility*. The Prussians know it; to them, this mistake represents a deficiency of imagination rather than an excess: can't these French apes, steeped in their arrogance, imagine for a moment that the Prussian army is an awesome adversary? For the men who surround Bismarck, this mistake and the deficiency of invention are negative but perfectly real entities; they will know how to use them to manipulate the Emperor and his ministers, first of all, then the French generals. The dispatch from Ems, for example, would not have been a successful ploy with English ministers, or with Cavour; its attempt depended on our arrogance as visionaries, on our penchant for panache, on our honor, all the more sensitive as it only existed as a dream. In short, by correct and precise calculations in which French politics as theater figured as a real and measurable given, Bismarck revealed to Flaubert, and doubtless to many others, that the other side of the dream, its face *for the other*, is its finitude and its reality. Moreover, the impossible escape outside of being is perceived by the enemy as a real choice of impotence; that fabulous panoramic consciousness appears from the outside to the Prussian, the true subject of history, to be a simple bankruptcy, condemning these woolgatherers to being forever his objects, and through their own fault. What is Gustave's sin? To have opted for the imaginary by forgetting that one cannot escape the real, that the real recovers everything? Or just the opposite, to have given his pledge to *realism* after his failure by basing his tranquility as a hermit and his pleasures as a courtier on a few basic images he hysterically took as substitutes for reality? It hardly matters; in both cases, it is *the Other's existence* that comes in the end to ruin every enterprise of derealization. If we cannot escape the real, it is because, whatever we do, we are *realized* by the other, man is the living being through whom *objective-being* comes to man. As a result, to imagine is to surrender oneself to the other, to put oneself at his mercy. And if the purity of the dream is never perfect, if one cannot practice it as the being of nonbeing without being compromised with the real by another employment of the imagination, it is precisely because one cannot choose impotence and surrender to the manipulations of others like a simple object, without any assurance against anguish through autosuggestion; nor without convincing oneself to believe—in the realistic sense of the term—in a security that in fact doesn't exist since one is at the mercy of unknown executioners, with no defense but death. In both cases the woolgatherer who chose his own failure, and on that basis the failure of the imaginary, does not comprehend that he opted, in fact, for the triumph of reality. And that this option—as the total truth of his choice—objectively characterizes him insofar as it is grasped as such by others. Choosing the image, Flaubert has opted for the triumph of the Prussian realists in complicity with the Ancien Régime; he learns his objective truth from the Prussians themselves and from their contempt for the vanquished.

What has become of his arrogance? From the time he dreamed of writing *La Spirale*, hadn't he been proclaiming that the dimension of *for-others* should not be taken into account, and that in order to be a subject in the imaginary, one had to accept becoming an object in reality, that is, for the other? Shouldn't the hero of the novel attain the most exquisite joys, the height of imagination, at the very moment when he is shut up in an insane asylum, manipulated, doused, force-fed, beaten by attendants who oversee the regulation of his natural functions? Isn't it *as the very function* of this total resignation, of this perfect submission to the *Other*, that he can know the supreme sensual pleasure of a total derealization—in other words, of a *total absence of the self*? That is no doubt the idea. And as we know, one of Gustave's neurotic intentions at *Pont-l'Evêque* was purely and simply regressive: he wanted to return to his early childhood, to that nursing baby kneaded, manipulated, made passive by hands that were too expert, not tender enough. But what strikes him in these dark days is the discovery of the failure of his techniques of derealization. It is true that one attains the unreal by making oneself an object, but only to a certain point; beyond that point, the object-being of the dreamer forbids him the dream. The hero of *La Spirale*, manipulated by attendants—who for Gustave are inferior beings, ignorant brutes—can abandon his body to them: he may be an object *for them*, but he can deny them with his dreams; for the chosen and suffered defeat is not complete, and in any event, the mad painter is superior to them; *accepted* inferiority can degrade him only in appearance. But when the Other is the subject of history, when he is superior in essence and his superiority is recognized *in advance*, the man who voluntarily becomes a thing for and by that recognition loses all access to the imaginary: the degradation is real. In other words, he cannot dream *when he is an object for the Prussians.*

This observation leads us inevitably to ask ourselves, *who* are the Prussians? What do they embody? What do they symbolize for Gustave? Why does their victory and their presence make *impossible* the evasion that since adolescence, and until the summer of 1870, Flaubert has always regarded as practicable *on every occasion?* Why is literature *itself* put in question by the occupation? To answer these queries, which send us back sooner or later to Gustave's early childhood, we must first describe the nature of his relation to the occupying soldiers. He hates them, there is no doubt on that score. Before they've reached Rouen he writes: "As for me (if necessary), I have decided to flee anywhere rather than lodge *them.* That would be too much for me." And on 18 December, to Caroline: "I did not think my heart could absorb such suffering without dying of it," and: At Croisset (we are lodging) seven soldiers, plus three officers and six horses. Until now we have not had anything to complain about regarding these gentlemen. But what humiliation, my poor Caro! What ruin! . . ." And also: "Do you know that at Croisset they are occupying *all* the rooms? We would not know how to live there if we wanted to return." He is highly rebellious at this profound attack upon the meaning of *yours* and *mine:* "Croisset has lost all its charm for me, and I would not set foot there now for anything in the world. If you knew what it is to see Prussian helmets on one's bed." One day in January '71 he writes: "In what state will I find my poor study, my books, my notes, my manuscripts? I could find a safe place only for my papers relating to *Saint Antoine.* Emile still has the key to my study, but they ask for it and often enter to take books, which lie about in their rooms." When the Prussians evacuate Croisset, it is again the property owner who speaks through the patriot's mouth: "When everything is cleaned up a bit, I will go and see that poor house again, which I no longer love and dread returning to because I cannot throw out all the things these gentlemen appropriated for their use. If it belonged to me, I would certainly demolish it. Oh, what hatred, what hatred!"[98] On 16 March he will find the perfect phrase

---

98. To Caroline, *Correspondance*, 6:197–98. We know the arrangement: Flaubert lived at Croisset, which belonged to Caroline Commanville. In fact, his reaction remains that of the property owner: the Prussians have sullied his property insofar as it is a life of

in a letter probably addressed to Goncourt: "The Parisians, who have suffered greatly, haven't an inkling of a real invasion. Having those people *in your own home* is beyond any anguish."

When he is able to envisage returning home, this frightful anguish is calmed. On 31 March he is "resigned to come back to his poor lodgings, where [he] is going to try to work and forget France." And a few days later: "Contrary to my expectation, I find myself *quite comfortable* at Croisset, and I do not think about the Prussians any more than if they had not come! It seemed so sweet to find myself again in the middle of my old study and to see all the little projects again. Since Saturday evening I have been back at work . . . The garden is going to be very beautiful: the buds are coming out . . . What calm!" We know that the insurrection of the Parisian people began on 18 March. He makes mock of it: "I would be very surprised if the Commune lasted beyond next week." It does, however, and he splutters:[99] it is the Ligue, it is taking us back to the Middle Ages. He recognizes, however, that he *"sees it clearly"* and that he *"*is no longer in the awful state in which he agonized for six months." And it must be added that he does perfectly well without Paris: "Do you know the worst of it? *That one gets used to it.* Yes, one does. One becomes accustomed to doing without Paris, to no longer being concerned with it, and almost believing it no longer exists." This exercise in pithiatism must not be very difficult for the hysterical Hermit of Croisset; his speciality is techniques of derealization, and then the setting is favorable to it: the trees are sprouting new leaves, the Seine flows on, eternity returns to his study through the window. The insurrection *has taken place.* Paris is dead. This ascesis bears its fruits: on 30 April he concludes by deciding that he is fed up with it and that he will turn his back on events: "As for me, I've had enough of the Parisian insurrection! I no longer have the courage to read the newspaper. The continual horrors disgust me still more than they sadden me, and I plunge with all my strength into good old *Saint Antoine.*" Such efforts will be very quickly rewarded; on 3 May he has recovered his impassivity and writes to Princess Mathilde:

---

the interior sustaining his inner life; they have penetrated *inside him.* Obviously, he is quite pleased in his frenzy to demolish Croisset, to recall that "the poor house" does not belong to him. But that is an abstraction. The real bond, here, is organic.

99. Even this unexpected "prolongation" does not worry him. Since 18 April he found the explanation for it: "The outcome of the Parisian insurrection is delayed because they are using political means to avoid spilling blood."

For eight months[100] I too have been choking with shame, with rage and sorrow, I have spent nights crying like a child. I have been close to killing myself.[101] I have felt madness taking hold of me, and I have had the first symptoms, the first signs of cancer. But by distilling my gall, I believe that it was purified, and I confess to you that I have now become nearly numb to public misfortunes. As to personal misfortunes, the misfortunes of those I love, it is quite the opposite: my sensitivity is exacerbated and the idea of your sorrow devastates me. The callus has hardened over the wound.[102]

Here again, as in 1848, we have the comparison of public misfortunes to private misfortunes. Of course, the politeness, the affection he feels for Mathilde compel him to mention only the personal concerns of the Princess. But a few days later to Mme Schlésinger—the Commune is in its "final agony"—he writes in better faith: "I have gone back to work, finally, to forget the public misfortunes and *my*[103] particular sorrows. The greatest is the company of my poor Maman. How much she has aged! How weak she has become! May God spare you from witnessing the degradation of those you love." Already in 1848 he contrasted the Parisian insurrection to his family troubles, Hamard, Achille, and *above all* "Maman," who acted as an amplifier. Today, his irritation goes much deeper: his mother is senile, she is deaf as a post, and Flaubert's only distraction is to "drag her" twice a day around the garden. In short, he can no longer bear living with her. Thus when danger subsides, the contradiction between public and private life is reinforced and stabilized: privately, daily worries exhaust him, his nerves are like the strings of a violin; ataraxia is manifest in the public sphere: Gustave has recovered his impassivity in relation to history. This is how Goncourt finds him again, on 10 June. Gustave has come to Paris—a lightning journey—to seek

100. No, he said it himself on 27 April: "I am no longer in the awful state in which I agonized for *six* months."

Curiously, twelve days later, writing to Mme Schlésinger on 22 May, he writes that he "suffered horribly for ten months; suffered going mad and killing myself." This accordion-like suffering is an adequate indication of his insincerity: eight months, meaning since Sedan until 10 May, in short it is his patriotism that suffers. Six months: from the threat of occupation until the departure of the occupiers.

101. We find again, of course, three complementary motifs, each of which reflects the two others: madness, death, senility (here represented by the *callus*, which is also one of our old acquaintances). But *suicide* is never evoked in the preceding letters; he says that he wanted to die, that he will die of sorrow, never that he will kill himself.

102. *Correspondance*, 6:233–34.

103. My italics.

information for *Saint Antoine:* "He is just the same, a *littérateur* above all. This cataclysm seems to have passed over him without detaching him one iota from the impassive fabrication of his little book." The "fine psychologist" lets himself be taken in by appearances. First of all, this impassivity is quite new. Then, even during this quick trip, it masks the disgust and contempt the Parisians inspire in him. Upon his return to Croisset he writes: "I am *overwhelmed* less by the ruins of Paris than by the enormous stupidity of its inhabitants." He gives Mme Roger des Genettes the reason for his being overwhelmed: "Would you believe that many 'reasonable people' excuse the Prussians, admire the Prussians, want to be come Prussians without seeing that the torching of Paris is the fifth act of the tragedy, and that all these horrors are imitations of Prussia and quite likely incited by her." In a way, this is stripping the "mad dogs" of the responsibility for the torching in order to concentrate all blame and all crime on the Prussians. In a letter to Feydeau he goes still further: "Two weeks ago I spent a week in Paris and 'visited the ruins' there; but the ruins are nothing beside the fantastic stupidity of the Parisians. It is so inconceivable that one is tempted to admire the Commune. No, the contradiction, the stupidity, the idiocy, the mental abjection of the 'most intellectual people in the universe' surpasses all imagining."

Since the Parisians admire the Prussians, he admires the Commune that tried, he believes, to destroy Paris and all its inhabitants, and was—at least—a patriotic movement against the shameful capitulation to Prussia *as well. Two* men only (his italics) *have kept* their heads. Renan and Maury. He does not mention Goncourt. This is understandable, moreover, if Goncourt talked at the dinner on 10 June the way he wrote in his Journal on 31 May:

> It is good. There was neither conciliation nor transaction. The solution was brutal. It was pure force. The solution pulled souls out of any cowardly compromises. The solution has inspired the army with new confidence, which learned, in the blood of the *Communards,* that it was still capable of fighting. So the bloodletting was a complete bloodletting; and such bloodlettings, by killing off the combative part of the population, defer the new revolution for a generation. This will give the old society twenty years of calm if power dares all it should at this moment.

Such statements are disgraceful even for Edmond, and if they were advanced, Flaubert must have prudently opposed them with his Mandarin's apolitical stance: "It's all the same to me because I am writing *Saint Antoine.*" In short, his impassivity remains wholly relative. And his work is surely a flight into the imaginary *as well*. In fact, on a deeper level he is inconsolable: he hates the Parisians and all the French for not hating the Prussians enough. This hatred is an *emotional imperative* for him: every Frenchman owes it to himself to hate Prussia, and the Communards, those mad dogs, were only wrong to deflect that hatred, to confiscate it to their advantage. And especially to transform the occupying armies, in the eyes of the terrified rich, into a support for the forces of order. This Germanolatry—which compelled him to abandon the Magny dinners—grew visibly: Prussia is admirable because it has conquered the French, it is revered because it protects sacrosanct property—solely by the presence of its troops. When Gustave sees a pointed helmet on his bed, when, having taken flight so as not to see or hear the officers lodging in his house, he learns that these "gentlemen" sometimes ask for the key to the library to borrow a book, which "then lies around" in their rooms, he feels his right as proprietor is being violated *by the Germans*, not by the Communards. The first of April, indeed—the Parisian insurrection has scarcely begun—is not a day of anguish for Flaubert as it is for wealthy Parisians and for the residents of Versailles; it is the day when he comes back to Croisset, where any trace of the forty occupying soldiers has been carefully eliminated. This first of April is the holiday of *reappropriation*, the ceremony by which Gustave reclaims his rights and is reinstituted as property owner. Consequently, he is thinking of writing again and claims that he is thinking no more of the Prussian occupiers than if they had never existed. We shall see that he is in fact still thinking about them. But it is true that the worst shock was for him to have "those gentlemen at home." He goes so far as to maintain that the sufferings of the Parisians during the siege—famine and bombardment—are nothing compared to those felt by a Rouen landowner whose house is filled with garrisoned soldiers. A scarcely credible, indefensible lack of awareness which, however, I do not think should be made light of; to be sure, it is the result of Flaubert's egocentrism, his radical incapacity to imagine the sufferings of others (if not his sadism and his pleasure in them). But we must see, too, that this loner, for whom property, sequestration, the inner life, the mysticism of the imagination and literary creation are inseparable, must have found the garrison less tolerable than other bourgeois. The soldiers' presence, in effect, beyond the right of property, put *his very being*, his fundamental options, in question. On this level we may well ask whether it wouldn't have been the same whoever the occupiers were, or whether his desperate radicalism stemmed from the fact that the garrison consisted of Prussians.

The occupation of Croisset, whatever it's nature, was bound to provoke Gustave's outcries. First of all, it was the *realization* of the defeat; humiliation, fear, and misfortune are the common lot of all occupied peoples. Moreover, we have long been familiar with Flaubert's nervous state: how could this old fellow, who loses his head when he has misplaced his pencil, fail to go berserk when faced with the violation of his life of the interior, or, as we have already understood it, his interior life? The acknowledged irruption of the *Other* into the prison that protects his dreams was bound to provoke a lasting and violent trauma, *even* if, for example, the war had not yet been lost and military accident had compelled him to lodge French officers. Certain passages in his correspondence, however, clearly indicate that beyond the general reasons, a particular circumstance—the nationality of these undesirable lodgers—pushed his despair to an extreme. Indeed, he is not content to hate the Prussians: he is terrified by their hatred of the French, now wondering, in a daze, "why they despise us so powerfully,"[104] now answering his own question, overwhelmed: they despise the beauty of France, the 'graciousness' of our Latin heritage.[105] Yet if the Prussians were insensitive and the occupation quite harsh—no more so than any other occupation: the presence of a foreign army living off the inhabitants and imposing *its* order can only arouse rage—the German victors, who hadn't suffered many losses, did not really hate the vanquished enemy. It would be fairer to say that they were somewhat scornful of the French—and Gustave sometimes acknowledged this. Bismarck's realpolitik was aimed not at destroying France but at permanently weakening it, as we see some years later when he refused to support the monarchist pretenders, thinking, as a sincere enemy of democracy, that a republic would be more divided and therefore less formidable than an authoritarian monarchy. Be that as it may, for Gustave's anguish to be raised to the highest pitch, evil must triumph; jealous of our incomparable culture with its roots in Greco-Latin antiquity, in the eternal Rome that civilized the universe when the forests of Germany shel-

104. To George Sand, 30 October 1870, *Correspondance* 6:184.

105. "How they hate us! And how they envy us, those cannibals! Do you know that they take pleasure in destroying works of art, luxury objects, when they encounter them! Their dream is to destroy Paris because Paris is beautiful." To Mathilde, 23 October 1970, *Correspondance* ibid., p. 172.

tered only barbarian tribes, the enemy is particularly determined to destroy the *Latin world:* the horror is that *he succeeds in doing so.* Like Valéry, Flaubert would no doubt say that "civilizations are mortal." But he would add: "It is the barbarians that kill them." This suggests the extreme fragility of culture—which dooms it to annihilation—and the destructive will of the Barbarians, which is in a way *legitimized* by that very fragility. The Latin world bears its death within itself as the subject of history, doomed to future annihilation; the Prussians merely carry out the sentence, they are the agents of destiny, and in a way we can say that their destructive hatred was foreseen and summoned by the mortality of Latin civilization, which had to perish *beneath their blows.* Its fault was that, having provoked such hatred, it was unable to overcome it. The imaginary in momentary confrontation with the real was incapable of *persevering;* at reality's first counterattack it must have sunk into an absurd nothingness, never to rise again. And the Latins' greatest fault lay in failing to understand that their reign was only a moment of history, that their slogan, "power to the imagination," was merely a mystification; for the imagination is in principle *powerless,* and its advent had not produced an abeyance of reality but in fact corresponded to their determination to ignore the real, and particularly their own insertion in universal reality. In this sense, the Prussians, soldiers of being, are right, and the grand French illusion is wrong; they have always been right to the extent that the Greco-Latin "humanities" have never been anything but vain rhetoric, in which culture—letters, arts, philosophy—is reduced to the deliberate cult of make-believe. For in the final analysis are they really jealous of that sublime and tragic French beauty they so despise? Don't they rather despise it as an arrogant mirage, a verbal lie that the liar himself tries to take seriously? If this were the case, wouldn't we have to allow that at the moment of the neurotic option—and indeed both before and after that moment—Gustave acknowledged his guilt in choosing nonbeing, *faute de mieux?* His entrance into literature, the vows he makes, the accepted martyrdom, and the long patience are *assuredly,* on a certain level, the quest for complete success as an alternative to the mediocre successes proposed to him in another domain and by other means. But who knows whether Gustave was implicitly aware, either deeply or marginally, that the choice of the tonsure, of mystical quietism and the unreal, far from lifting him out of his original inferiority, only served to consecrate it forever. In this case, the Prussian victory merely reestablished the true order of values by manifesting everything that was hidden by Gustave's supposed saintliness: his consent to the conceded status that made him a passive citizen, a relative and secondary being, almost a woman. At Pont-l'Evêque, his brutal fall allowed him to avoid the fate of an excessively clever bourgeois prosecutor like Ernest; accepting dishonor, winning the right to glory, to the primacy of the artist over everyone else by his false death and risked madness, he would have continued, under the cover of an imaginary hierarchy that made him "the Good Lord's aristocrat," to preserve a secret *chin*, inculcated by the paterfamilias, which placed the scientist at the summit of the scale, well above the "man of letters."

Let's look at his reproaches against the Prussians: "Those officers in white gloves breaking mirrors, who know Sanskrit and throw themselves on the champagne, who steal your watch and then send you their visiting card, this war over money, those civilized savages are more repugnant to me than cannibals." [106] ". . . What sickens me is this invasion by Doctors of Philosophy, breaking mirrors with a pistol shot and stealing clocks; that's a new twist. The armies of Napoleon I committed atrocities, no doubt, but they were made up of the lower ranks of the French people, while in Wilhelm's army *all* the German people are guilty." [107] At the same time he recognizes that the "Prussian army is a marvelous precision machine." [108] The words "civilized savages" effectively express his feelings. On the one hand, these men *are reality* irrupting into France through their agency. And they bring it with them in their baggage because they are *realists*. Flaubert does not intend this as a denunciation of what he formerly called a grocer's materialism. No, these men are characterized in his eyes by the choice of efficacy: for them, the *real* is everything that can be known by exact methods and modified by rigorous techniques. Reality reveals itself to Flaubert as that which is most alien to him and most repels him, pure praxis. Scientists in the service of an integrated society, an inflexible discipline and hierarchy, a faultless civil and military organization, a government that treats politics as a science, generals who make war like engineers, nothing improvised, their imagination iron-shod, saddled and bridled in the service of action, with the sole function of exploring the field of *real* possibles before any practical decision is made—these are the factors that, in Flaubert's view, have ensured the Prussian victory. As a result, since re-

---

106. To George Sand, 11 March 1871, ibid., p. 203.
107 To Feydeau, 29 June 1871.
108. *Correspondance* 6:161.

ality is defined on the basis of the principle of *output*, he can assimilate praxis in its pure state to the operations of a "precision machine," thus effectively dehumanizing it. There is one hope: "All machines break down unpredictably; a straw can break a spring. Our enemy has science on his side; but feeling, inspiration, despair are elements that must be taken into account." Once more Flaubert can counter *activity* only with the most violent forms of pathos. Feeling, if extreme, despair, if intensely lived as the annihilation of all hope, of any way out, can *inspire*; we have to understand that this unleashed passivity can transcend itself toward the invention of the missing way out. Thus, in 1842 the young Gustave daily postponed the *decision* to set to work and was counting on the *energy of despair*; two weeks before the examination he would grab his copy of the Code and devour it. The method, at the time, was hardly successful, and later he chose to attribute his masterpieces not to this vague violence but to his long patience; indeed, didn't he condemn inspiration, which has its source in passion, in the reflections on the art of poetry that conclude the first *Education* and in all his correspondence besides? Why does the worker of art, detached from human ends and polishing his sentences with the impassivity of a precision instrument, return at the moment of defeat to the Romantic pathos of his adolescence? One word from the text gives us the key: "Our enemy has science on his side." In the final analysis, the Prussian victors represent the triumph of science, theoretical and applied. Their victory revives the symbolic Father and his curse; excluded from knowledge by an iniquitous preference and the intrigues of a usurper, Gustave, in the absence of exact knowledge, has taken it into his head to base a rigorous art on the exactitude of imagination. This was dreaming: he dreamed his "surgical gaze," dreamed that his images were memories of other lives or distinct and precise anticipations of future experience. The defeat shows him again what he has always known, that the real and the imaginary are not symmetrical, that they are not to be seen as two panels of a diptych but rather the imaginary must be regarded as a porosity of the real, or as pockets of nonbeing continually hollowed out and refilled in the bosom of a dense and closed world. In other words, the artist is no more the scientist of the imaginary than the scientist is the artist of the real.

This is why Gustave, rejected by the *measurable* world of adults, is returned to his childhood dolorism. For a moment—the time it takes to write it—he recovers the ancient challenge that made him a writer: on one side of the scale there is science, the vast, patient conquest of all men since the appearance of the human race; on the other he throws his heart, his great dripping heart, which bleeds so much it *deserves* to win the day. If military genius were drawn in the wake of its vast misfortune and France had improvised an army for which a dolorist Caesar would serve as improvised generalissimo, and if, on the strength of their affliction, these new legions had kicked the Prussians out of the country, imagination would conquer reasoning reason; the rediscovered spontaneity of the poet and the artist would rise above the scientific disciplines, the organization that changes a million men into a "marvelous machine." A vain hope: science is not a machine, and Gustave knows it even as he seems to confuse the two; no chance for the straw to break the axle. Science is the demonic gaze that cuts lies "to pieces" and leads the hysteric back to his reality; in short, it is the *realizing* gaze of the Father and his power to decompose imaginary orders, to pin his younger son down, reduced to his naked impotence. What Flaubert cannot tolerate in 1870 is the surgical gaze of the Prussians, inherited from the paterfamilias, which is fixed on naked France writhing in the mud, *reducing it to what it is*. When Nature imposes her reality on us, we hardly have occasion to feel shame because *it does not think us*. But, as in his childhood, Flaubert *realizes himself* through the gaze and the manipulations of others; beneath the eyes of the Other—who is at once Bismarck and Achille-Cléophas—the great choices of his life are revealed to him as *other*. They were basically flights: he fled into nothingness from the implacable superiority of the Father and the older son, and only managed to acknowledge that superiority by his useless gestures; he had chosen the imaginary to escape the human order, where his place was marked in the lower ranks, and so even his fame, should he achieve it, would be second-class and never equal to that of the captain and the scientist. Indeed, this escape into the imaginary was itself merely an image of escape; he had neither fought nor fled, he was affected by a strange paralysis and stupor, and found himself *because of that* beaten, chained, a prey to men, that species which despised his misanthropy and merely reintegrated him at the lower level he'd never really left. At the age of thirty, Gustave entered into literature *against science*,[109] namely against the curse of the Father and the unjust choice of the usurper; he thought he'd won: with Achille-Cléophas dead, Achille was just a mediocre provincial surgeon; the

109. Both to lay claim to the sector that naturally tended to escape scientific investigation, and to succeed in this by applying exact methods *transposed*.

555

younger son, on the contrary, with his international reputation, his cross of the Legion of Honor, his familiarity with heads of state, constituted his family's honor. Sedan sufficed to overturn the situation and restore the primal scene: the chief surgeon, resurrected, leans on his older son's arm and considers with icy scorn the poorly endowed child he had condemned in advance to the birthright of a younger son; science wins, it crushes the artist, or rather it *sees him as he is* and condemns him to see himself as it sees him. The defeat reinstalled the gaze of the Father in Gustave—or rather reactivated it, for it had always been there—and Gustave's *character* collapses. It is impossible to dream, to dream himself under that cold eye, the unreal is disqualified; on 30 October 1870, Gustave groans: "Literature strikes me as a vain and useless thing." This can only be the case because beneath the figure of Bismarck, the paterfamilias looks ironically upon this futile occupation. And if art is useless and futile, what about the artist, who has rejected the human condition in order to dedicate himself to his work? Note the abrupt reversal of signs: the inutility of art was his title of nobility in the 1840s and until 1870; upon waking, it is his original sin. Isn't this brutal shift from positive to negative the best proof that a triumphant Other has reinstalled himself in Flaubert? In the face of his unjust father, Gustave had wanted to gain glory, to lay it at Achille-Cléophas's feet, and make him weep with remorse. He does have fame; resurrected, Achille-Cléophas contemplates it, but instead of tearfully repenting he scorns it, just as in former times he scorned all his son's activities. Gustave will always be a slightly backward old fellow, the family idiot. To whom should he appeal henceforth? To his public? To that collection of the vanquished who share his fate today because yesterday they shared his illusions? To his future readers? He won't have any: Prussia is the future. "For *whom* shall we write?" he wonders. "We are superfluous."

How he hates those Prussians! But he hates them *as someone vanquished*. "So what is the purpose of science? Since this people, many of them scientists, commits abominations worthy of the Huns, and worse because they are systematic, cold, deliberate, and haven't the excuse of passion or hunger." This time, he does not breathe a word about their hatred of France: this would be giving them "passion as an excuse"; and he knows only too well that these meticulous and practical men are not encumbered by any sentiment. In the previous passage, Flaubert forgets himself and designates the true object of his resentment; Prussia is merely a cover for his real target, *science*. He is not afraid to ask, What *purpose* does it serve? Does this misanthrope reproach science, then, for not moderating mores? To some extent, but the point is that he makes it seem he is accusing that scientific culture of impotence, when, though intrinsically positive, it couldn't have prevented the extortions of the Prussians; when he describes those extortions, however, we perceive that far from being rooted, *despite* scientific knowledge, in the ancient barbarism of the human heart, they correspond precisely to the typical behavior of the scientist. What is experimentation if not a systematic, cold, deliberate, and passionless procedure? And what about the systematic, deliberate, rigorous practice of civil, political, and military engineers, specialists in the applied sciences? In other words, the Prussian is the scientist, he is modern man formed increasingly by the exact disciplines he exercises. *Homo sapiens, Homo faber;* he is the father Gustave thought was dead, changed into himself by eternity and become the archetype of the new human race.

He only knows these abominations, moreover, by hearsay: the German troops have "devastated Vexin," he reports, offering no further detail. At night in Rouen the occupiers behave so badly that it is better to barricade yourself in your house—which is just what he does; so he hears about nocturnal disturbances during the day. On the other hand, he can testify that the soldiers lodged at Croisset have shown themselves to be quite correct: forty men lived in his house and did so little damage that when he comes home he finds it intact and can forget his guests. It is noteworthy that during this entire period Flaubert does not speak once of the brutality exercised against the civilian population or military prisoners. We know that there was some, but we know it from other sources. First of all, since Rouen decided not to defend itself, the occupation was less severe; and then, our misanthrope has so little interest in men that he confines himself to condemning the victors for atrocities committed *against things.* The symbolic object is a looking-glass, now broken by officers "in white gloves," now "with pistol shots." The glass: the mirror that is carried as one walks along the road; this wholly military violence against reflection seems to symbolize for Gustave the destruction of works of art in the name of technology and science. And he was specific about this well before 1848: democracy, perhaps even socialism, was prevailing in a country that would become increasingly austere, concerned only with becoming industrialized as quickly as possible. What he instantly detested in the railroads and factories were the applications of science. From then on he would dub "civilized savages" the men who under Louis-Philippe were attempting to replace the world of quietist contemplation with the rigorous universe of technical applications. Of course these *capables* were civilized—they had their ceremonies, their mores, and their terrifying power, acquired by centuries of research. They were nonetheless savages to the extent that, well before the Prussian army arrived, they had "devastated" much natural beauty, ravaged the countryside with factory smokestacks and train tracks, condemning human beauty and the ministers of art in the name of their costly inutility. The factory, be it in the suburbs or in open country, testified to the new epistemology, breaking the unity of the macrocosm; it symbolically substituted specialized research, the quest for precise detail, for the calm, contemplative intuition of the all. For these barbarians, the *how* was replacing the *why*, the mark of the true idea was no longer its pantheistic richness but its success, that is, its confirmation by experiment or its practical efficacy. In this sense, wasn't Father Flaubert the first of the civilized savages, that hacker of cadavers who had never read novels—except, in his youth, those of Voltaire—and who would fall asleep when his cursed younger son would read him his works? Wasn't the usurper Achille such a savage as well, that flattened image of the chief surgeon from whom he had inherited science but not intelligence?

In 1870 they return, wearing helmets and boots, to finish their work and destroy the rhetorical world of the Latins; in the name of their indisputable superiority they take the paternal curse to its conclusion by exiling Gustave from the only refuge he had found against *their* reality and *their* science, and by sleeping in his bed at Croisset while he wandered, broken, between Dieppe and Brussels. Severe, correct, impeccably gloved, they break all the mirrors, deliberately depriving the French Latin heritage of the vain empire of reflections, of the play of reflecting mirrors, of the fabulous world of images. For science— which traffics only in objects—is in principle hostile to reflexivity. And scientists, those crude mercenaries, know the details of things but do not know themselves except as external objects. This is why Gustave, prostrate, overwhelmed with horror, calls the first scientific army in the world a "precision machine"; he was lacking the term "robot," which would be invented in our century. But he is conscious of his bad faith: the symbolic Father and the Usurper escape mechanization through the exercise of pure intelligence; he alone, the younger son, brother of idiots, children, and beasts, has been denied scientific understanding. Incapable of forming rigorous concepts, he tried to replace them with vast, vague images; Achille-Cléophas, the mercenary, and his lieutenant Achille draw near on horseback, con-template and analyze him—as they did before; since his childhood, nothing has changed; they seek and find specific, real causes for ev-ery movement of his imagination. His unfortunate, inconsequential consciousness is merely an epiphenomenon; far from surveying the world, it is crushed by it, determined in its slightest variations by the fortuitous encounter of several infinite and disparate series, some physico-chemical, some physiological, others historical and social. For someone acquainted with these sequences and their points of contact, his escapes themselves would be predictable. His dreams, gestures, and theatrical poses would be predictable too: there is nothing, even in his most secret counsel, that is not determined ex-ternally and is not external to itself at the very moment of actualiza-tion. In short, *he* is the robot. And, of course, Achille was a robot as well, a simpleminded, scrupulous, unauthoritative physician, who was in despair at the defeat, spoke of leaving his patients and taking up a gun or hanging himself; but this was not the *true* Achille. The *Other*, the pompous and fearsome usurper, who died along with the Progenitor, basked in his brother's sheets, resurrected by the Latin defeat.

Yes, Gustave was certainly the first victim of this memorable and devastating defeat, which seemed to him the cataclysm he had always secretly expected: the Father's revenge for his audacious behavior in 1844. At Pont-l'Evêque a cycle was initiated; at Sedan, it was com-pleted. Led back to his childhood in which he was humiliated as "lit-erary," lost in a family of practitioners, Flaubert understood that to choose literature was to accept his inferiority from the outset, believ-ing he would compensate for it by an imagined superiority. He al-ways knew and always suppressed what the Prussian occupation of his refuge revealed to him: that for him, imagination was actually resignation; he claimed to conquer the unreal in order to sweeten the pill and accept paternal authority—power based on knowledge—which chose to transmit itself, knowledge and power, to a usurper and leave Gustave to his original and total impotence. But you don't conquer what neither is not, was not, nor will not be: you playact conquering and know it all too well, disgraced by the fact that this sublime theater is a *means* of accepting the power of others and, for yourself, the condition of object they impose on you. There is a single resource for this son and brother of clever men that has long been denied him, which is to receive a portion of sovereignty from a power based on imagination. This is why the fall of the younger Flaubert son into the imaginary required the sovereignty of Napoleon III as the basis of his individual power.

The Republic, he proclaimed a hundred times over, was the rule of commoners. But he sometimes wondered if this regime would not become the oligarchy of the *capables:* after all, the source of the Revolution of 1848 was the ambition of the professional elite. In this case, he wondered, where will I find my place? Well, clearly, such a Senate composed of Flaubert brothers would only sleep through the reading of his works; Gustave would remain an object, worse, the dream of a woodlouse. A frightful dream, penetrated by the gaze of the powerful, who would discover behind its flimsiness the foul, somnolent, defenseless beast. The coup d'état, the return to the Empire, was, *in the last analysis,* pure theater: the dictator knew nothing, was worthless except as a rather palatable AntiChrist in the black hierarchy; this cold-eyed dreamer was holding his power from a collective dream. Yet that power was *real,* and consequently so was the power this charismatic autocrat delegated *at whim* and without taking account of bourgeois criteria. It might have been fine that he chose his elite *at random*—humiliating scientists and practitioners, half misunderstanding their capabilities, except in two areas, war (a dream of death, glory, and an identification dreamed by everyone and himself, of the nephew to the uncle) and art, that is, the creative imagination— the very imagination that put him on the throne. At first amused by this black sovereign who degraded his subjects, Gustave suffered the ghastly disappointment of being "led to the bench of infamy" on the orders of a false Emperor who had himself derealized France, all for having written a work of derealization. He had understood this, however, two or three years earlier: if the Emperor exercised his power by virtue of a dream, he would preserve it as long as the tale was a fairy tale; the literary lie would be rewarded if it was academic. Happily, with better advice, the false Napoleon began at the onset of the liberal period to buy good writers, some quite crudely for money, like Renan,[110] others through the intermediary of Mathilde or by judiciously

---

110. In 1860, Renan was planning to make a journey to the Orient, specifically to Palestine. The Goncourts claimed that the Emperor summoned him and asked him how much the journey would cost. Without hesitation, Renan said: "25,000 francs," and Napoleon provided them. The anecdote is not persuasive: sovereigns do not ordinarily enter personally into these transactions; they think it is lowering themselves and may humiliate the man who is for sale by tactlessly revealing his character to him as merchandise. There are intermediaries for this sort of proposition, and the merchan-

distributed honors: the Academy, the Senate, the Legion. Flaubert then forgot or repressed the feeling of being merely a pure object of science; the imagination in power consecrated in him the power of imagination. Since Napoleon, a fiction, *really* governed the French, the creators of fiction—when he distinguished them—were *really* superior to the realists, to those silently ignored researchers who wanted to know the real in order to dominate it. Of course, such theatricals were exhausting. Gustave kept vacillating between these two extreme views: on the one hand, that the Court, the nobility of the Empire, the marshals, everything was false, and it was their falseness that made them attractive; and, on the other, that the false Napoleon was a real dictator, at his orders real blood was spilled on battlefields, and the honors he accorded were real. But these variations of whim and vision did not prevent Gustave from harboring the *vital* belief that under the real dictatorship of unreality—when appearance imposes its domination on being—I am *the most real*, meaning the most effective agent of subversion, when I carry to their limits both my creative unrealization and the derealization of the world. This sovereign reality comes to him from the supreme Other regardless of any concern he might have, any desire or ability to live it, but simply because by fixing dreams, he participates in the collective dream and the real power that, born in sleep, prevents the French from waking.

After the Prussian victories, what happened? Flaubert suddenly perceived that the power of imagination was merely an imaginary power: Napoleon was reigning over a nation of sleepers, his claimed sovereignty had its source in the shutdown of their nervous systems. For the Prussians, who kept their eyes open, this droll civilian in military disguise had no prestige. They were waiting for France to ripen and were prepared to pluck her. There is a science of dreams, and there are engineers who manipulate them. Bismarck held the real power. Mathilde's associates never had a shred of it. In 1860, as in 1844, Flaubert was an inert object: a rigorous politics would maneuver him since it would scientifically maneuver the image of Emperor that

---

dise is generally approached by an honorable colleague who has already been bought. Moreover, until 1860, if Renan was not utterly hostile to the Empire, he maintained extreme reserve. Prudence and circumspection would both vanish when he agreed to travel as *chargé de mission*, and the imperial government took care of all expenses of that expedition.

he had taken as a guarantee. The Prussian minister was charged with realizing the paternal curse. What had happened since the holocaust of 1844? Nothing. "Skewered" by the paternal syringe or decorated by a shadow ribbon in the realm of dreams, Gustave was still the unworthy and feminized son of a family in which all the males, from father to son, practiced medicine.

Not only for the Prussians. Wilhelm's armies had long had their accomplices, even in France. Men had awakened in the provinces, in Paris: they looked at Badinguet and saw him naked; and so, too, they saw Gustave. For a long time, as we have seen, he had sensed a split between the Knights of Nothingness and the younger republican generation. It was not only a political rift; in the sacred domain of literature, the new writers wanted to change the relations between art and science; the "experimental novel" would appear only after the defeat, but the idea was in the air. Herr Von Bismarck suddenly justified these presumptuous brats—whose importance Flaubert had tried to minimize: they were not vanquished. Nor was the industrial bourgeoisie. Nor were the French scientists and engineers. The facade alone had crumbled, burying Flaubert beneath the rubble. All these people were right, moreover; only Flaubert was wrong—like the Emperor, his black Lord, who would die of his defeat three years later. In his letters from this period, Gustave takes three different positions without worrying about contradicting himself—now blaming the Prussians for destroying the "Latin world," now condemning the Empire for preferring Latin civility to science, now prophesying in horror that the Third Republic would undertake a systematic reform of education and of the way of life he reproached the Emperor for not even attempting. He continually repeats that he has "a feeling it's the end of a world," and that "whatever happens, everything I loved is lost. We are going to fall . . . into an order of things that will be intolerable to people of taste." But "this order of things" should have been established long before if war was to be avoided or won; the mistake was let to words buy you off: "You afflict me with your enthusiasm for the Republic. Just when we are vanquished by the rankest positivism, how can you believe in phantoms?" [111] Republic, Empire—words. The French lost because of their addiction to words. A little later, he is more specific: "Is this the end of the *joke*? Will we be done with hollow metaphysics and received ideas? All evil comes from our enormous ignorance. What ought to be studied is

111. To George Sand, 10 September 1870, *Correspondance* 6:148.

believed without discussion. Instead of scrutinizing, we affirm! The French Revolution must cease to be dogma and come under the sway of science, like all other human things. If we had been wiser, we would not have believed that a mystical formula is capable of making armies, and that the word 'Republic' alone could vanquish a million well-disciplined men." [112] To his niece he is more explicit: "I am deeply irritated by people who speak to me of hope, of the future, and of Providence. Poor France, buying herself off with words to the last." [113] He perceives the Commune itself as a product of this addiction to words and decrepit beliefs that we have still not shaken off. "Poor France, she will never disengage herself from the Middle Ages! She still drags herself along on the Gothic idea of the commune, which is nothing but the Roman *municipium!*" If the Commune of 1871 is a resurrection of the Medieval commune, which is in turn nothing but the survival of the Roman *municipium*—which, I must say, makes no sense—we have to admire to what extent our history, even in its bloodiest tumults, is rooted in Latin antiquity; what better proof than the Parisians' determination, despite the presence of a Prussian army and the troops at Versailles, to shed their blood to resurrect an institution of ancient Rome. Yet Gustave condemns this "Latin heritage"; in this time of positivism, it has led France to its doom.

Words! Words. One word, the Republic. What is the difference between a republic elected essentially by property owners and a constitutional monarchy? For Gustave, these two designations are homonyms, which, despite their identity of meaning, elicit conflicting passions and represent two contradictory mysticisms. For Flaubert, then, mysticism is merely a contradictory attachment to the *sign* independent of the signified: future, Republic, Providence, Commune, so many words that killed France; Prussian positivism is interested only in things. Very well, but what about the word "Empire"? Was it attached to a reality? And weren't those who bought themselves off with this word the guiltiest of all? It is clear, in any case, that the *writer* Flaubert cannot condemn verbal inflation without passing sentence on himself; not that he'd stuffed his works with long, vague, resounding words; but he thought that "style is the absolute point of view," [114] and while choosing his terms with the greatest concern for

---

112. Ibid.
113. To Caroline, January 1871, ibid., p. 196.
114. To George Sand, 24 April 1871, ibid., p. 224.

precision, he was determined, as we have seen, to derealize language. Far from using it to designate an external signified of the Word, he employed his art to make the thing pass into the materiality of the world, so that the sentence, sonorous and closed, cut off from its references to the world, tended to be posited for its own sake, to become what we call today a *text*, referring entirely and exclusively to language. Isn't he implicating that art—absolute-art—when he portrays a broken-down France, "surfeited with discourse," murdered by rhetoric? Or, more precisely, doesn't he have the sense that positivism—which he reproaches the Empire for not developing—was *indeed incompatible* with the subtlety of absolute art? When the objective of literature is the derealization of language, there must be some historical reason why the society that adopts it needs to buy itself off with words. Napoleon III is guilty of not banishing the "humanities" from higher education and replacing them with the study of the exact sciences because the *Latin world*, whose end Gustave thinks he sights in 1870, was *already dead* when the Prince-President took power. When Flaubert indicts "our enormous ignorance," his use of the possessive is no accident or stylistic formula: as a Latin, the son of the chief surgeon possesses a fine classical culture, but when it comes to the exact sciences, he shares the ignorance of his compatriots. he is even more ignorant than the new bourgeois—members of a *real* society he does not frequent. He has hardly shared the public enthusiasm for works of popular science some time later, while writing *Bouvard et Pécuchet*, he will gulp down at a random enormous amounts of undigested knowledge and promptly vomit it onto his contemporaries. Yet, as this ultimate revenge on the paternal curse was not meant to help him learn the sciences but to make his contemporaries unlearn them, he would have carried it to its farthest extreme in vain, he would die as he was born—in ignorance. Unlike Flaubert, the new writers, Zola in particular, would have no difficulty acquiring exact information and would know how to amass a scientific capital to invest in their works; the point was no longer to contest science but to assimilate it. Flaubert kept company with them, they shared their projects with him, and that was enough to make him conscious of knowing nothing; it is indeed himself, it is *also* himself he condemns: the Latin heritage having died, no doubt along with the Ancien Régime, it is a mistake and perhaps a crime to insist on remaining a Latin. What should be done? On 29 April 1871, he repeats to George Sand:

So what should we believe in? Nothing! That is the beginning of wisdom. It was time to get rid of "principles" and enter into the realm of Science, into the examination. The only reasonable thing (I always come back to that) is a government of mandarins, provided the mandarins have something to show for themselves, and even know a lot. The populace is an eternal minor, and it will always be . . . at the bottom since it is number, mass, unlimited. It hardly matters that many peasants know how to read . . . but it matters infinitely that many men like Renan and Littré can live and be heard. Our salvation is now in a *legitimate aristocracy,* by which I mean a majority that will be composed of something other than numbers.[115]

Would Flaubert be one of these mandarins? What relations would the "legitimate" aristocracy have with the "aristocracy of the Good Lord"? It is difficult to know; Gustave was long since indoctrinated by Renan; what he serves up to George Sand are ideas that Renan had been cultivating since 1848, as we have seen. But if he puts Renan in power, it is for choosing reason rather than art, and Prussia rather than France. Of course, Renan is not a scientist: he is a *mandarin.* This former seminarian, however, has a few rather un-Flaubertian ideas. Gustave must value his concept of chauvinism; and certainly he admires Renan's hatred of Catholicism and systematic doubt; when the author of the *Life of Jesus* declares that science is nothing but an endless questioning, Flaubert thinks he has found in another man that "belief in nothing" in which he has made a profession of faith since adolescence. This is why the passage cited above he assimilates wisdom to skepticism: believe in nothing, *examine.* But in his opinion, the only effect of examination is to abolish illusions *without replacing them with positive knowledge;* from this perspective, science would be solely negative. Gustave's interpretation falsifies the thought of Renan, who is really a positivist. His vague pantheism must please the writer who ends his *Saint Antoine* with the words: "To be matter!" And for all these reasons, Gustave tolerates Certain bizarre notions held by his friend Renan, in particular the opinion that the French language was permanently shaped in the seventeenth century, and that for a modern author this language is the only instrument. But can he accept Renan's literary and artistic tastes? Does he agree that Chateaubriand *writes badly,* or that Saint Mark's cathedral in Venice *is*

115. Ibid., p. 228.

ugly? He could accept them even less, I imagine, as these judgments rest on a principle that he permanently rejected during his Romantic adolescence. Beauty, says Renan, faithful to himself, rests on the *rational element*. Renan rejects the Baroque and Romanticism in the name of Classicism, submitting imagination to the dictatorship of reason. And of course in Flaubert, the imagination—at least when he writes—is not free; but the "form" he requires to structure it is not rationality, as we know; at most we might say that for this sadomasochist, who assimilates beauty and evil, it is the black, diabolical reflection of reason, the loan evil makes to good in order to "compose" itself and do more harm. Most tellingly, however, Renan sees an order in historical sequences; he seeks meanings in them, where Gustave sees only confusion and upheaval. To be sure, they share a contempt for politics. But Renan is counting on the moral engineers' application of the human sciences to the task of governing men. If by some miracle he were called to the presidency of the Council, he would not look for his ministers—with the exception of Berthelot—among the guests at the Magny dinners; he would surely surround himself with scientists and technicians. What would become of the "artists" when this "legitimate aristocracy" took power? They would hardly be favored, I imagine; their exquisite sensibilities, their neuroses or, if you will, the extreme delicacy of their nervous systems, their nihilism would be of little account in the eyes of a new power born of knowledge, which conceives of art, in the fashion of the seventeenth century, as a universalist naturalism based on reason. When he votes for the Mandarins, Gustave is giving his vote to Bismarck, to Achille-Cléophas, to Achille. These people will not decorate him—nor will they decorate the Goncourts, Baudelaire, or Leconte de Lisle; they will not call on him to take part in their labors, they will not invite him to their private dinners, they will forget him and the other "workers of art" in favor of younger writers formed by the same positivism; without favoring him or hurting him, they will silently ignore him and await his death. In other words, Flaubert cannot cast his vote for the new mandarins without condemning himself, and he is wholly aware of this. Of course, he will try to extricate himself from the fate of the guilty and present himself as a victim of the imperial lie: "For a number of years, France . . . was living in an extraordinary mental state . . . This madness was the consequence of excessive stupidity, and that stupidity came from an excess of cant, for so much lying made people idiots. They had lost any notion of good and bad, beautiful and ugly. Recall the criticism of those last years. What distinctions did it make between the sublime and the ridiculous? What disrespect! What ignorance! What a mess! . . . And at the same time, what servility toward the opinion of the day, the current fad!"[116] With Caroline he is more explicit: the French lost the war because they failed to recognize its sincerity—"Everything was false: false army, false politics, false literature, false credit and even false courtesans. To tell the truth was immoral. Persigny reproached me all last winter for "having no ideal,' and he may have been serious."[117] He presents himself here as Huron, the Peasant of the Danube, who tells the truth in the midst of the universal lie, and whose ideal (beauty as useless and even hostile to our species) is misconstrued by the materialism or the received ideas of those in power. But does he believe in what he is saying? At Mathilde's, at the Tuileries, Persigny could indeed have reproached him for having no ideal: to Courbet, just to chose one example, he would have been inhibited from making the same reproach. Naturally, since Gustave was "received" and Courbet was not. What could be done about him? Horsewhip his canvases, prevent him from exhibiting, imprison him, perhaps; all these measures would only result in underscoring his break with the regime. If Persigny could speak man to man to Flaubert, if there was no gulf of political repression between them, it was because Flaubert was *lying* too. Less than the others? No, just in a different way and for different reasons. In any case, without denouncing their lies, thus implying that he assumed responsibility for them. Littré, Renan, the youth of the prestige schools might well have regarded him as an accomplice of the regime. The fact is that Renan himself, a martyr in 1862,[118] had begun by selling himself, and in a sense continued to do so.

The very concept of "mandarin," moreover, remains quite vague in Flaubert. According to the text we have cited, he seems to have excluded himself from this category: the mandarin is a sage, whose positivist philosophy prepares him to command scientists and recruit engineers to rule civil society. This "legitimate aristocracy" will rule over a ruined country and distinguish itself by its austerity: no more festivals, no more humbug, the reconstruction of the country and the

116. Ibid., p. 229.
117. To Caroline, 27 September 1870, *Correspondance* 6:161.
118. After the publication of the *Life of Jesus*, the government suspended Renan's lectures. Napoleon III made his excuses to him in a personal letter, claiming that the measure was imposed by the Catholics; he was even offered a sinecure that would allow him a continuing salary. He took offense, refused, was broken. But after these minimal conflicts, he was again found visiting Mathilde, who loathed him at first. The war of 1870 began while he was crossing for Spitzberg with Prince Napoleon.

manipulation of the masses in conformity with the scientifically established laws of sociology; in short, *human engineering* in the service of an economic resurrection of France, politics replaced by the conditioning of citizens. But other letters, in contrast, inform us that Gustave claimed the status of Mandarin *for himself*. Let us look, for example, at a letter he wrote to Caroline on 28 October: "All elegance, even material elegance, is over for a long time to come. There is no longer any place in the world for a mandarin like me."[119] Flaubert as a judge of elegance? That is not said, of course—I have already noted that the logical connections of discourse are practically absent in the correspondence. Be that as it may, the contiguity of the two terms necessarily results in the interpenetration of their meaning. A mandarin—*among other virtues*—is characterized by his love of luxury and his taste. We have seen more than once Flaubert's disturbing juxtaposition of "luxury objects" and "art objects,"[120] on the erroneous principle that "he who can do most can do least." This means, in the case at hand, that since the artist is capable of producing literary works and passing sovereign judgment on their internal cohesion, the aesthetic affinities that connect the parts to each other and bind them to the whole, he must be all the more capable of judging the value of a piece of clothing or furniture. Flaubert was mistaken, I agree, and in October 1863, on the occasion of a trip to Croisset, the Goncourts confirm it: the art of selecting sentences does not necessarily imply the art of selecting furnishings.[121] But what matters to us here is that if the mandarin is characterized by his taste for elegance and luxury, for the useless, the gratuitous, he cannot be the austere sage who will reconstruct France by restoring order through the application of the rigorous laws of anthropology. It would be unjust to accuse the mandarin of the Renan type of utilitarianism, but his enterprise nonetheless has human ends, which entail reviving a portion of the race, the dead or moribund French nation. He is interested only in what furthers his practical design: luxury is not his business; he needn't even be acquainted with it—and, indeed, everyone knows that neither Renan nor Littré was. The other kind, the mandarin of the Flaubertian type, is a flower of evil; he is born on a dunghill—an *already* constituted society—and puts all his efforts into distancing himself from that society's ends. The paradox, of course, is that he needs the work

119. *Correspondence* 6:178.
120. Cf. in particular ibid., p. 172, to Mathilde.
121. *Journal*, vol. 6, pp. 140–42.

of men, their wretched needs, institutions that regulate the distribution of goods, the forces of order, to continue his subversive effort in peace, his radical destruction of the human order by the production of that aggressive inutility, the work of art as a center of derealization.

But while he may need this society he denies, while he may need it *in order* to deny it, his specialization makes him incapable, however willing he might be, of contributing to its reconstruction when it fragments in the wake of a cataclysm. Flaubert the mandarin—since he defines himself by the "aesthetic attitude"—will never participate in a real, practical power. The portion of sovereignty he has retained for several years came to him, as we have seen, from a deceitful and ineffectual power, from Napoleon III, that expensive slut, that high-class whore that the bourgeoisie, forgetful of the days of June 1848, was already weary of supporting. Gustave gave Louise a definition of this mandarinate well before his journey to the Orient: it is the cult of the superfluous and the forgetting of the necessary; it is the mystical contemplation of the all and the denial of action; it is the break with the human race and, more radically, with reality, in favor of an unreal beauty; it is misanthropy and, consequently, a sadistic conception of the fine arts. A dependent of the established order, this vampire would be the first victim of social disorders, but he has denied himself on principle the means to remedy these disorders or even to know about them. Thus the double signification of this word reveals Flaubert's profound malaise: sometimes he regards himself as Renan's peer—haven't they spoken as equals at Magny's?—and he likes to imagine that Renan, after taking power, will invite him to share his responsibilities. Flaubert enters the government, or some Senate constituted by all the great men of the nation; *along with the scientists and even for the same reason,* he is fully an aristocrat. A fallback position, since under Napoleon III he was *above* them, an eminent member of the "Good Lord's aristocracy." He would accept this equality, however, without hesitation as the sole means of escaping the triumph of the Father and the Usurper, the crushing of the artist by Prussian positivism: art and science are equally worthy, their ministers constitute the new aristocracy, whose role is to serve the nation and work for its regeneration. And sometimes, returning to his first definition of the mandarinate, he understands that the new society, not content to dispense with his services, will only be established when it eliminates him. In fact, since poverty, the necessities of reconstruction and those of national defense demand the spirit of seriousness, realism, a scientific management of finances, the sobering of the French by the injection of massive doses of the truth, "sad as it might be," as Renan himself says; since the country must deny itself any *superfluous* expenses and will agree only to those that are really necessary, Flaubert, the product of luxury and producer of deliberately useless luxury objects, a pure consumer, a parasite of a society that produces merchandise, seems to be a remnant of the Second Empire, a derelict of the condemned luxury that led to Sedan. "There is no longer any place for us!" he cries. But what must be particularly galling for him is that he himself has outlined the program of the very society that rejects him. It is not only the Third Republic that practices such ostracism; if the mandarins—like Renan—came to power and followed his advice (no more lies, no more foolish beliefs, truth, science), they too would begin by banishing him from their city, as Plato banished the poets. As a quick look through the correspondence reveals, the future he prophesies and condemns ("they will be utilitarian and military, economical, small, poor, abject," "They will be utilitarian, military, American . . .") will in no way differ from the future he advises the mandarins to prepare, should they come to power. Now he bellows with fury at the thought that a new world is coming into being *that will reject him*—and in this case he is prolific with pejorative epithets; now he insists in particular on the qualities of a "majority based on something other than number." It's as if he were sentencing himself unwittingly, condemning himself to annihilation by scientists and rationalist thinkers in the name of truth, dangerous and dated old illusion that he is; and at other moments it's as if he were trembling with rage, fear, and disgust at seeing the sentence he could not help pronouncing against himself come to him *as other* and *taken up by others*.

Curiously, well before basing his prophecy on a strict sequence—the Commune, the great fear of pious folk, and the violent reaction that will ensue—he prophesies the powerful return of Catholicism: "We are going to enter into an era of Stupidity. People will be utilitarian, American, and Catholic, very Catholic, you will see." This premonition is dated 30 October; Paris, besieged by the Prussians, is still holding firm, and in the same letter Gustave agrees that this is "heroic." If Faith emerged from the rubble, it was not resurrected by the civil war; those who empower it are the new barbarians, the scientists, the organizers. And above all the Prussians, by the very victory they accomplished and deserved, by the suffering they provoked in the French: "Misfortune makes the weak pious, and everyone is now weak. The war with Prussia is the end of the French Revolution." This is meant to suggest the end of the dechristianization begun by the Jacobin bourgeoisie, and perhaps the restoration of a very Christian monarchy. This reaction to a knowledgeably organized defeat would be accompanied by a self-defensive reflex toward our science, that is, toward a knowledgeable preparation for reconstruction and revenge. Under the police dictatorship of Napoleon III, it was still possible—if one granted Caesar the legitimacy of his power—to struggle openly against the Christian conservatives. The Emperor was a priori neither for them nor against them; he was seeking a majority, that's all. In Flaubert's view, the politics of the 1860s, instead of contesting the Empire, might have provided Napoleon III with a replacement majority that would have been more liberal and more competent in the literary domain—the only thing that could have interested the artist. But under the regime that had just emerged and dared not speak its name, the struggle would become impossible because positivism itself determined a change of minds; before the harsh realities revealed by science, before the pitiless principle of exact research itself, before the shattering of the humanities, the bourgeoisie would seek refuge in the dark, beautiful temples of a religion more encumbered than ever with fetishes and mummery.

Once more, Cassandra is right; we might say Gustave *sees* that meringue, the Sacré-Coeur, on Montmartre. Curiously enough, he perceives here, that victorious science will be counterbalanced by a renaissance of faith. Not that he wishes to contrast *one* group of conservative bigots with one group of audacious mandarins. "*Everyone* is weak," he says. And this presupposes that the confrontation is not simply external: in everyone the dry, sad will to know in order to change is balanced at least by the *temptation* to believe. Has Flaubert known this temptation *once again?* He doesn't mention it in his correspondence. But I would be inclined to think so. On 29 September 1870, after being broken by the capitulation, he found hope once more, for reasons that are debatable but in part self-consciously rational. What matters most to him, however, and gives him heart, as we have seen, is that he wants to believe for a moment in the triumph of feeling over reason, of pathos over praxis: the French will surprise and combat the civilized barbarians with those reasons of the heart unknown to reason itself. And in the same vein he exclaims: "Victory must belong to the right, and now we are in the right." But *who*, if not the Almighty, can guarantee this miracle, the victory of right, even disarmed, over organized force? We would never have expected such childish confidence in Flaubert. Deep down, since 1844 he has believed, of course, that his suffering has *earned* him genius; but we have already seen how he dissimulates his "Loser Wins" in certain dark corners of the soul. On the level of historic events, he gives proof of cynicism and might subscribe to that celebrated witticism "Everything has always gone badly wrong,"[122] and also to Pascal's thought on Cleopatra's nose. A sequence of bloody disorders in which the good are punished and the wicked rewarded, that is what ordinarily satisfies his sadism. We may therefore assume that, in the face of this unaccustomed attitude, he had for some time sought refuge in religion. At any rate, the implacable unfolding of events would set him straight: the Prussians would enter Paris. No pity for the just, this world is indeed the hell he had imagined at the age of fifteen. He is thus doubly excluded: from the strict, necessary, and *stupid* truth (scientific research involves detail and never has the amplitude of what he calls the idea), and from the tender chiaroscuro of belief (equally stupid: *credo quia absurdum*).

The old myth has reappeared: Flaubert is Madame Bovary, moribund and damned; Monsieur Homais and the parish priest Bournisien doze at his bedside. These two adversaries—positivism, or the stupidity of intelligence, and obscurantism, or the materialist stupidity of rigid dogmas—already confronted each other in the first *Saint Antoine*; neither of the two prevailed, faith reeled under the blows dealt by science but never disappeared. The opposition of concepts was deepened by meditation on the disaster, and a dialectic emerges: the idiotic and mystical irrationalism of the Second Empire provoked a catastrophe that gave rise to scientific positivism, and in reaction the dryness of that rational pragmatism reanimated religious beliefs in the Jacobin bourgeoisie, who then strove to "crush the villains" and win all the battles, never the war. This pair of allegories was reborn in 1870, not only because consequences resurrected it, but also, and in particular, because the new situation reanimated the old myth, which in Gustave's eyes resumes and symbolizes the curse of Adam: from childhood, his father's scientific unbelief has got the better of his mother's vague theism. As a mechanist, the philosophical practitioner stripped his younger son of any possibility of believing without being able to suppress his need for God. This is why Flaubert denounces scientific *vulgarianism* as well as the idiotic Church, which furnished him with neither arguments nor men he could oppose to

---

122. A sentence in general quite fair but superficial and static, whose underlying and dialectical truth is captured in Marx's thought: "History progresses through its worst moments."

the terrible Doctor. And the prophecy of Cassandra—technocracy balanced by theocracy—is merely the oracular evocation of his own life. More, it is at once its totalization and its conclusion. For the defeat of 1870 and the invasion are like a practical demonstration of atheism; Achille-Cléophas revives to prove to his son that he must *believe in nothing*, condemning both the religious instinct and the pithiatic belief that is the basis of the aesthetic attitude. By the same token, however, he solicits the religious instinct he condemns: fanaticism, too, is a gilded fruit of the defeat. Doubly condemned, jealous of knowledge and of faith, Flaubert can indeed say to his father: "You scientists throw us back onto the silliest superstitions, for you debase our divine dissatisfaction with being man but give us nothing in exchange"; yet he continues to tread water, abandoned, and the eternal pair will go its way without ceasing to bicker or to draw strength from this indispensable discord. On a single point realist positivism and Catholic reaction are in agreement: both forever condemn the artist, positivism because it incarnates the victory of the real over all fiction, Catholic reaction in the name of ethical idealism. In *Madame Bovary*, Emma alone is religious; she seeks God groaning, and is forever unconvinced by *representations* of Him that others try to give her; and she dies damned—this is the law of hell. At this moment in his life Flaubert reserved the game of "Loser Wins" for the author of the book, saved by the despair he had known how to derealize in his work. In 1870, "Loser Wins" is eclipsed, and it is the author himself who is damned, who was damned before birth, and who is deprived of his fame by the event, stealing upon him like a thief, consigning him to the *oubliette* of history. Returned to the bitter impotence of his childhood, a collective failure reveals to him the vanity of his personal strategy of failure; the literature of nothingness is denounced as a nothingness of literature, and absolute-art as a trap; meditating upon an impossible derealization, he has chosen the shortest road to realize himself in his finitude as a Frenchman vanquished by praxis and stranded in the hands of his worst enemies.

Such is Gustave on the morning after 4 September, so he is again after the crushing of the Commune: a defeated man, in solidarity with the Second Empire down to its most extreme faults, at once guilty and scornful, despairing and clinging to his despair, to his shame, by that proud vassal's loyalty that "does not want to be consoled." When peace returned, would he maintain this frame of mind? France has hardly changed, after all, even as it has claimed to be republican; monarchists and even Bonapartists made its laws; there has been little damage, no austerity. When Flaubert goes back to Paris, he sees the same faces again and visits the same salons. Indeed, he rediscovers his taste for work: he completes *Saint Antoine*, takes notes for *Bouvard et Pécuchet*. If he interrupts his work for a time, after Commanville's ruin, it is to write the *Trois Contes* and to reaffirm the game of "Loser Wins" in the *Légende de Saint Julien l'Hospitalier*. Over the years, however, he has remained haunted by the memory of the Second Empire. To such an extent that he repeats to whoever will listen that he dreams of writing a novel he will call "Under Napoleon III." [123] When he speaks of it, he seems somehow to have shed his remorse and his loyalties at the same time; all that's left, it appears, is rancor. In 1875, when Zola—who is writing *Son Excellence Eugène Rougon*—wants some documentation on Compiègne, Gustave, "in his dressing gown, gives Zola his version of a classic Emperor, shuffling feet, one hand behind his bent back, twirling his moustache, with idiotic sentences of his own. 'Yes,' he says, 'that man was stupidity itself, pure stupidity.'" [124] All ties are broken between the trusty vassal and the man who was for a time his black Lord. And this was not the picture of Napoleon he evoked for Maxime, enhanced by defeat and by the insults of the masses. The novel, in any case, seems conceived to bring liberation from the imperial lie: denouncing it is a way of publicly announcing that he was never its accomplice. He seems to have sounded the theme quite early, for on 29 September 1870 he writes to Maxime: "Everything was false: a false army, a false politics, a false literature, false credit, and even false courtisans. Telling the truth was immoral . . . Well, there are some whopping truths to be told; *that will be a fine story to write!*" [125] This is an idea he develops and elaborates seven months later: "Everything was false: false realism, false credit, and even false sluts. They were called "marquises," just as great ladies familiarly called each other "piggy." Well-known prostitutes like Lagier, who followed in the tradition of Sophie Arnold, were held in horror. And this falseness (which is perhaps a result of Romanticism, the predominance of passion over form and inspiration over rule) was applied in particular to the manner of judging. An actress would be vaunted, but as a good mother. They demanded that art be moral, philosophy clear, and vice decent, that science situate itself within

123. The last allusion to this project dates from May 1878: "The subject of 'Under Napoleon III' has come to me at last . . . It will be called 'A Parisian Household.'
124. Goncourt, *Journal*, 7 March 1975, vol. 10, p. 244.
125. *Correspondence* 6:161. My italics.

reach of the people."[126] In these two passages, Flaubert is already trying to put himself out of firing range; the falseness comes, he says, from the predominance of passion over form and inspiration over rule—two mistakes he severely condemns *as an artist*. And he is the one they accuse of immorality, of course, when he has only told the truth. But he goes further and shows that the false grand dames and the false whores are interchangeable—quite naively citing Lagier as a unique example of authenticity, the woman we have seen *playing* the role of good-hearted whore with a dirty mouth. And in particular he says that the falseness—whether lie, mistake, or hypocrisy—had infiltrated even the *manner of judging*. Here lies his real subject for the projected novel, as he would tell Zola after 1875: decency in vice as the symbol of the lie of a whole society. In *Les Romanciers naturalistes* Zola tells us: "He had finally found a subject, which he conveyed to us in too confused a manner for me to speak clearly about it here; it was the story of a regulated passion. Vice made bourgeois and satisfying itself beneath respectable appearances. He wanted this to be done with 'simplicity.'"[127] These indications by Zola are quite accurate, insofar as we can judge from the *scenarios* Madame Durry has so patiently restored for us.[128] But the subject that Flaubert "had finally found" existed, at least sketchily, in letters dictated by his despair and rage after Sedan. He hesitated over the plot: will it show "the degradation of Man by Woman"? Actually, this was a private preserve: after *Charles Demailly* and *Manette Salomon,* the Goncourts thought they had exhausted the subject. Gustave returns to it, however; in a letter to George Sand he makes two observations *in the same terms:* "A Catholic actress, a highly praised wife and mother. In contrast, the classic good-hearted whore (Person-Lagier)."[129] Essentially, he is tempted to return to the interchangeable nature of feminine *roles* by showing parallel "degradations": "Parallels· abjection caused by a woman of easy virtue and abjection caused by a respectable mother."[130] A short while later, as Madame Durry writes, "Flaubert attacks his subject for the fourth time . . . ; the demoralizing woman has become three characters." Indeed, we find in his notes: "3 sisters who all demoralize men, 1st as Catholic grd dame, 2 as whore, 3 as bourgeois and

126. To George Sand, 29 April 1871, *Correspondence* 6:229–30.
127. Zola, *Oeuvres complètes* (Bernouard), p. 169.
128. Marie-Jeanne Durry, *Flaubert et ses projets inédits.*
129. Ibid., p. 271.
130. Ibid., p. 272.

restricted. Relegate the 2 last as accessories, emphasize the moral Struggle in the soul of the Hero caught between his love for the Catholic and his philosophic-republican faith . . . First she does not love him—and attracts him in order to convert him. When he has become riffraff (a Catholic reac), he no longer loves her and she, disgusted with her world, loves him—to establish that, in principle, two beings never love each other at the same time.."[131] Under the Empire, the agents of *demoralization* (let us not forget that he'd wanted to be a demoralizer since adolescence) were chiefly women. As early as the first scenario he observes: "At the beginning of the war with Prussia, demoralization (cowardice) caused by feminine insistence. Those women finish . . . all the acts of cowardice committed under the Empire, caused by the same influences."[132] So women were responsible for dooming the Empire and for the loss at Sedan: the imperial Court is Man degraded by feminine insistence. He is thinking chiefly of the Empress; Mathilde had no qualms about denouncing Eugénie's pernicious influence on Napoleon III, and the Goncourts described her in their *Journal* as a false-Marie-Antoinette with a hint of commonness about her, the vulgar dignity of a woman of easy virtue. Napoleon III demoralized by Eugénie—just Flaubert's cup of tea. The man in himself is not a coward; he is a real emperor, whose sin—an inexplicable one at that—is having submitted to "feminine insistence" when he married. Following this logic, we can no longer hold him responsible for the imperial lie. The false pretence of France under the Empire was the inevitable result of a palace revolution that put woman in power. We shall not forget, of course, that Gustave, rightly or wrongly, had finally been convinced that the false prudery of the Empress was at the source of the trial that "dragged him to the bench of infamy." In a way, he was saving the honor of the regime and his own cross of honor if he could prove that these soldiers and legislators, despite their initial good will, were led by their wholly carnal weakness to be seduced *gradually* and dominated by beautiful intriguers greedy for power. But in particular this idea, which flattered his misogyny, awakened old beliefs that he had complacently offered to Louise in the form of *axioms* or *maxims*. For him, woman is the lie, the illusion par excellence. Her being is the pure materiality of the flesh; she has a very realistic sense of her own interests—organic, economic, and social—but can neither transcend this vulgar positivism nor raise

131. Ibid., p. 308.
132. Ibid., p. 258.

herself to the heights of the idea because of "something essentially exasperating and limited in the feminine character."[133] Stupid and stubborn, a whore by nature, she sells herself to transient clients, to princely keepers or a husband—Gustave makes no distinction between the two, for in either case she earns her living in bed. But in response to the demand and especially to the idealism of her clients, who want her to be flower, water sprite, and sylph, she tricks, she tricks *herself* and, coarse organism that she is, falls at last into her own traps, into words. She thereby transforms the needs of her sex, for herself and for others, into reasons of the heart, hiding her odors beneath perfumes and her body, "impure twelvefold," beneath silks and satins, changing the most material of beings into a symbol of immateriality with her gestures and discourse. If we are to believe Flaubert, woman is a costumed beast playing a role, or, if you will, a female creature perpetually in the process of derealization. Beneath the "Catholic *grande dame*," beneath the "bourgeois" and the "woman of easy virtue," which are merely roles, we find the same exasperating and limited animal. Following this argument to its logical conclusion, every *grande dame* is false, as false as respectable bourgeois women and whores; and any female, depending on the circumstances, will be Eugénie or la Païva or big brother Achille's wife. The only authentic women are the truculent "sluts' like Lagier, who not only do not dissimulate but derive their genius from the exhibition of their animality; these women cause dismay under the Empire because Woman reigns, and she forbids any yielding to nature, any search for the truth, for fear she will be unmasked.

If this is how it is, if there are no real women but only a theater in which certain creatures play the role of women, if illusion comes definitively to men through them, so that these females vampirized by nonbeing are necessarily the agents of demoralization, what argument would a Knight of Nothingness have with them? Isn't the artist someone who demoralizes by inscribing on the surface of the lens permanent centers of derealization? We can imagine what Flaubert would answer: these peddlers of illusion don't know what they are doing, they are unaware that they don't even exist except as vehicles of the imaginary, they fool themselves; leaping into the theater, they regard as hard currency the reasons they give for their behavior, and mask from themselves the sordid interests that dictate their actions and discourse. This is why the imaginary is not pure in them, first

133. Ibid., p. 361.

because they are not conscious of the nothingness that underlies the imaginary and do not seek in it the denial of being and the impossible advent of the impossible but, quite the contrary, a very real and effective way to be well furnished or to earn money; and, second, because in any event they do not make it the supreme aim of their enterprise but subject it to realistic objectives—like the man of action only in a different way. Unlike the artist, who has freed himself from passions and surveys them in imagination, these females, crushed beneath passion's weight, endure it uncomprehendingly, and drag themselves along the ground. What is more, they are *stupid:*[134] their desire for respectability—found equally in the patrician and in the woman of easy virtue—pushes them to conform; they propagate received ideas, and when the artist rises to the ideal, they counter with a conformist idealism. These sirens will degrade him if he allows himself to be taken in by their ruses, and they will make him sink from that summit, fiction posited for its own sake, into the muddy sea of fable that takes itself seriously. Such, indeed, was the imperial Court: colliding passions, conflicts of interest, struggles at knife-point, a desperate increase in servility dissimulating itself beneath a strict conformity,[135] all gilded with hypocritical pomp, with theater unconscious of itself, or at least played in bad faith. Here imagination was merely a diversion; they playacted, they spun out stories so as not to see the sordid struggles taking place, man against man, every man against all, so as to leave the field free for the sordid maneuvers that a remnant of dignity might have restrained if they had been in the open. In short, the Court was woman; not only did woman—that nonbeing unconscious of her nothingness—impose her dictatorship on the Court, but the narrow universe of the Tuileries and Compiègne was by its very nature a singular and collective realization of the eternal feminine. A mirage cultivated not for itself but as a dazzling mask, it was nothing

134. The hero, slowly degraded, "in the end perceives that she is stupid." Ibid., p. 271. He notes in the same paragraph the "false science of women" drawn from works of vulgarization. He is putting imperial society as a whole in question, for we know he reproaches it for this "false science" that is supposedly available to everyone. Not only is it supposed to be accessible to the multitude—ignorant and limited by nature—but it is dispensed to the most limited beings of the masses, to women, who, no matter where they come from, are naturally inferior to men of the same milieu, however stupid they might be.

135. "They had so lost all habit of thinking for themselves that they no longer ordered their own dinner! They followed *the menus of Baron Brisse*! Newspapers told you the selection for the day." Note on the back of a page in one of the notebooks on projects for "novels of the Second Empire;" ibid., p. 273.

but imagination held captive, humiliated, misunderstood, in thrall to the most materialistic passions.[136] Not the reverse of art but art in reverse. It is not accidental that the degradation of man by woman, in Gustave's novel, must be the transformation of an unbelieving republican (*or agnostic*) *into a Catholic reactionary*. Woman is doubly corrupting: she changes a male into a swine because she herself is merely a sow, and her reality is nothing but the ass she silently offers; but even as he realizes his masculine bestiality through the desire she provokes, she compels him to exchange his dearest convictions for the most vulgar kind of idealism, for the mummeries of religion, which are merely a screen for money. For woman, the fable of the world, that polluted imaginary she takes for reality, is Catholicism. Here again, Flaubert takes the high-minded line and justifies himself without much cost: didn't he claim under the liberal Empire that Napoleon III should be kept in power, and that the only useful policy was to defend him against the influence of Catholic reactionaries? He comes full circle: it was the Church that doomed France, the Church that was vanquished at Sedan; it was woman, natural accomplice of the priestly party, who doomed the Emperor. So the great mirage that fooled French society for twenty years, the vulgar and unhealthy dream that burst like a bubble at Sedan, was not the Empire itself, with its false nobility and its false army; it was the dream of all French females—the Empress in the lead—who, to seem like women in the eyes of men and in their own eyes, had to impose on everyone, and especially on themselves, the outdated mummeries of Catholicism.

But Gustave has other projects in mind; the one we have just analyzed satisfied his misogyny but not his misanthropy. If Woman is guilty, Man, her victim, is innocent. Flaubert doesn't intend his sex to get off the hook so easily. We find in his notes several sketchy versions of a second scenario, which he sometimes calls "Monsieur le Prefet."[137] This time he attacks the government itself in the person of one of its representatives. "The book," he writes, "must inspire the Hatred of authority and highlight the official element." Here again, the chosen theme was announced in his letters of 1870. Shortly after 4 September, in effect, he writes to George Sand: "The war (I hope) will have dealt a great blow to the 'authorities.' Will the individual

---

136. "The modern Parisian novel mingles as much ass, as much money, as much piety (*St Vincent de Paul,* etc.) as possible."

137. I am not referring to that play sketched out by Bouilhet, which Gustave termed, so lamentably, "The Weaker Sex."

thus denied, crushed by the modern world, take on importance again? Let us hope so."[138] A comparison of these two texts, however, suggests that he will assign blame less to the *regime* than to *power*, whatever it is, and so to the State. Flaubert an anarchist? Yes and no. When he leaves the Tuileries one night and dreams of the modern Babylon, idols rising up from the earth and the State-Moloch that alone can govern the contemporary world, it is with bitter joy that he predicts the disappearance of individuals in favor of authoritarian communities. After all, heads of state asked to meet him, he is on the winning side, with those who debase men, and not on the side of those who are debased; his misanthropy enjoys these daydreams of the self-domestication of man. A day will come when a handful of autocrats, perhaps surrounded by a few mandarins, will reign over the lower animals; they will have saved themselves the trouble of a genocide, and yet our hateful species will have disappeared. This prediction hardly gives him pause since he has never valued bourgeois individualism. And yet here he is, faced with the collapse of the Empire, wishing for the resurrection of the individual. This contradiction is all the more peculiar since, in 1871 or perhaps 1872, in the notebook containing the first sketches for "Under Napoleon III," he writes: "frenzy for individualism in proportion to the character's weakness. Portraits at the Salon and on the front of books (Feydeau). 'Have someone do a caricature of me,' biographies, autobiographies."[139]

This apparent contradiction is easily resolved if we are willing, first of all, to recall that after the ball at the Tuileries, Flaubert still regarded the Empire as a malign, gigantic, unshakable, and sacred power. Passive as he is, he does not dream of questioning power; it is evil, certainly, but it seems to him that all is as it should be, and that it is only fitting to admire the destructive power of authority. When he writes to George Sand, by contrast, the imperial regime has fallen on its back in the mud. For Gustave, authority is respectable only if it based on force; were it invincible, unvanquished, hereditary, the Empire would no less an agent of demoralization, but by the defeat of its enemies, internal and external, it would prove that it is an emanation from Satan and has a mandate to realize the destiny of France, that is, the suppression of the French through self-domestication. To the extent that Gustave believed in this, he revered that awesome idol, the Emperor. If he ceased to believe in it—and he had to, for the idol had

138. Mid-September, *Correspondence* 6:252.
139. Marie-Jeanne Durry, *Flaubert et ses projets inédits*, p. 393.

fallen—authority lost its consecrating efficacy; far from being the destiny of France, it was nothing but an ephemeral accident, a bad fever; that fine destructive fury succeeded only in destroying itself. From this point of view, the evil it did endured. It is true that the subjects of the Prince debased themselves; but their debasement, far from reinforcing power, was turned against it: the cowardice of the French, resulting from systematic demoralization, caused France to lose the war and Napoleon III his crown. And certainly one cannot imagine anything worse than this debacle, but its author was Bismarck, not Badinguet. The Empire hasn't decided the destiny of its subjects; rather, it's the Prussians who will take charge of it. Thus power, prey to its fatalities, has managed to prepare for nothing but its own destiny; as a result, it stands naked, absurd, condemned. Guilty: not of the evil it did in full knowledge, not of that incomplete degradation, but of the cataclysm that threatened for five years, of that evil which it did not, of course, want to call down on the country's head but which it failed either to foresee or to deter. Flaubert would respect authority if it emanated from some gorgeous monster, from those Tamberlanes, those Gengis Khans who peopled his adolescence; their authority, indisputable, unquestioned, based on genius, force, magnetism, and ferocity, would seem to him authentically charismatic. What is it, indeed, but the discretionary power of man over man, in short, radical evil if we go from high to low on the social scale, and, conversely, the only good that Flaubert will allow—honor, or the fanaticism of man for man—if we go from low to high? Authority must therefore be exercised by a prince of evil supported by a black feudalism. Let it fall into the hands of a mediocre dictator and it is degraded, contaminated by his own mediocrity. At the moment it is stripped of the sacred character that commands obedience, it is no longer anything but a constraint morosely endured.

We understand, then, that Gustave condemns the individualism of imperial society and desires the rebirth of the individual. In the text of the notebooks, the individual under the Empire is a ruse, an *ersatz of characteristics*. *Men of character*, we have understood, can be found in all regimes except in democracy: they are defined not by their egotism or by the cult of the individual but, to the contrary, by their relations with the monarch, their hierarchical superiors, their family, principles, the enterprise that transcends them—art, mysticism, war—and to which they are entirely subjected. So we come back to honor, to an aristocratic ethic. And, in Flaubert's view, that is just what has disappeared under the Second Empire: characters are broken by conformism, "the fear of comprising oneself," the need to play the courtier, etc. People no longer think for themselves, they deliberately resemble each other, men finally become interchangeable. Hence each man, feeling frustrated in his *originality*, tries to replace it by emphasizing his *singularity*. The substance is abandoned for the shadow: incapable of differentiating themselves from others through acts, opinions, ideas, they tend to fix on inessential and insignificant differences, which merely express the accidents of facticity. I have blue eyes, yours are black; so what does it matter if we articulate the same commonplaces and both eat the same meals, "following the menus of Baron-Brisse"! Yet those eyes, that hair, that nose will be painted or photographed as if these *individual* details replaced a certain intimate relationship to everyone else and to oneself that made each person "the most incomparable of beings." Flaubert seems to have anticipated the advertising techniques that, a century later in our "consumer societies," persuade consumers that each of us will be "more and more ourself" if we all buy the same products. In 1972, "personality" has the same enticing function *individuality* had a century earlier." [140] These remarks suggest that in the letter to George Sand, Flaubert—who has not adequately thought out the problem— is using the word "individual" ("the individual denied, crushed by the modern world") in the sense of "character." A little later, when he returns to the question in his notebooks, he will distinguish between the two notions. What was lost under the Empire, what he would like to see reborn in opposition to the "authorities," is the person of character, the aristocrat with his opinions, his aversions, and his loyalties.

But isn't it paradoxical that Flaubert expected this postwar rebirth when the imperial regime indeed claimed to be based on the devotion of a military aristocracy? We already know the answer: Flaubert reproaches the Empire for being a democracy in disguise. He never formulated this grievance before the defeat, but the Goncourts certainly did, and they were undoubtedly open with him about it. These "aristocrats," enamored of the *de* they appended to their name, were denounced and contradicted by the imperial regime, which, on the one hand, had a sacred, charismatic authority that in the final analysis could come only from God, and, on the other, sought popular consultations, in particular those plebiscites in which they chose to see

---

140. From a fashion magazine: "Discreet or audacious, but more and more yourself."

only the resurrection of universal suffrage, that is, the radical destruction of valid sources of power (which could be generated only by qualitative superiority). "Monsieur le Prefet" would have depicted this contradiction, or—on this point Gustave diverged from the Goncourts—this lie, in a single man, a highly placed official possessing a portion of power. We would see the tinsel, the trinkets, the dramatizing, in short, the appearance of authority, that false image of the sacred, which poses as its own source and which, in fact, is *playacted;* and then behind the facade the real man, he who directly or indirectly derives his power from universal suffrage, who cannot be the elect of each man unless he resembles everyone, in sum, the geometric place of commonplaces, the mediocre chosen for his mediocrity, so that he confirms others in theirs. In another "project," Gustave says of one of his heroines that she is married to "an imbecile of an official—and a considerable one." He is surely not thinking, in this passage, of "Monsieur le Prefet," but this is how he sees this representative of the executive when he thinks of him: the more considerable, the less competent he is. Indeed, these are the faults he attributes to officials and, ultimately, to all Frenchmen: the fear of compromising oneself, of thinking for oneself, of having one's *own* opinions, preferences, use of time, the failure of character—namely, the radical absence of those two opposed and complementary forms of transcendence: fidelity and the spirit of initiative. Today, we would see in all this—should we be obliged to observe that these faults characterized a given community—a group of distinctive but secondary features of a *bureaucratic* power structure. Hence, to the extent that they existed under the Empire, they were generated by an administration that was becoming bureaucratized in response to the growing demands of an increasingly complex society. The bureaucracy of the Second Empire was recruited *from above;* its sclerosis was the result of the need to multiply cadres, hence to sacrifice quality (knowledge, initiative, character) to obtain the required quorum, and, in particular, the result of the incompetence of a dictatorial government, which despite the plebiscite of 1852 had not, in fact, been chosen through universal suffrage but had been imposed by force with the complicity of the advantaged classes and was vampirizing the great nationalist myths of the First Empire to *consecrate* its power in the eyes of the masses. Flaubert comes very close to understanding this dialectic since he emphasizes on several occasions that bureaucratic imperialism corresponds to the requirements of the modern world—which mean that the complexity of the economy, the ever more extreme division of

583

labor, class conflict, the diversification of problems require at this historical moment an unquestioned power of decision at the summit of a strict hierarchy. Dictatorship would impose itself as the only conceivable unity on the multiplicity of men, functions, and interests. The "modern world" would be the era of empires, and authoritarian governments would spawn their own bureaucracies, a body of officials defined at each level by their refusal to decide and their referral of decisions to the next level up. Gustave, however, cannot help reversing his position at the last moment: it is not the bureaucracy that makes everything banal, it is democracy; the reign of the "We" crushes the small minority of people with "character." So we have "Monsieur le Prefet": an actor who claims to be adept at commanding because he possesses a portion of charismatic power—therefore claiming the dark grandeur of a lesser demon—and who is, in fact, in his deepest being, the creature of universal suffrage, a *false monster*, and actually a decent, rather banal and vulgar man who is like everyone else and does what anyone would have done in his place.

He chose as his model Janvier de la Motte,"[141] "one of the typical prefects of the Empire," an energetic man who unscrupulously fixed elections, in short, a good servant to the sacred power, a perfect antidemocrat. This person was arrested in 1871 for embezzlement. The minister of finances of the new State, Pouyer-Quertier, a big industrialist, testified in his favor, as did Raoul-Duval, a rich friend of Flaubert's, proving that the September "Republic" readily accepted men of the former Empire. Janvier was acquitted; but democracy, now consolidated, indicated still more clearly that it recognized him as one of its own: universal suffrage confirmed the choices of the dictatorship, and he was elected deputy in 1876, reelected in '77 and '81. Flaubert knew Janvier and no doubt regarded him as both common and decent—he had been prefect of Rouen and had invited Flaubert in 1864 to "a dance followed by an epic feast." Gustave had not gone: he visited princesses but did not deign to compromise himself with minor potentates. At the time of the trial, he calls him that "*poor*" Janvier and, like Raoul-Duval, perhaps under his influence, declares that they "have nothing much to reproach him for." Coming from Gustave, we should recall, this certificate of honesty is no compliment; Janvier is a small-time scoundrel, a true democrat; when he had power he didn't even use it to commit great crimes, unlike those wild,

141. I am indebted for the following information to the work of Marie-Jeanne Durry (cited above), which provides many other details on the man and on the trial of 1872.

pleasure-seeking mastiffs of the Renaissance whom Flaubert so admired. Here, however, we find an anecdote about the prefect of Rouen, reported by *Lapierre*, that might show him in a different light: "A midwife from Evreux attempts to raise her daughter very properly—she is condemned to six years in prison for abortion. J. proposes to the father that his wife will be freed if his daughter comes to the Prefecture. She does come—is nearly raped—and the mother is not released: instead of six years, she does five. The father, a drunk, drowns himself. The daughter rushes into prostitution and becomes an actress in the little theatres." This, Flaubert decides, will be the subject or, rather, "the point of departure for the action of 'Monsieur le Prefet.'" In short, pure evil: the man in power blackmails some wretch, forces him to commit suicide by (nearly) raping his daughter, in any case by perverting her, and to complete the torture he is inflicting he doesn't even keep his word, cynically keeping the mother in prison. We might call this a rather dark melodrama of the kind Flaubert imagined writing in his adolescence, for which the sketches still exist. This Janvier smells of the devil. De Sade would certainly have been delighted with him; evil triumphs, and the consequences of the act are not unworthy of the initial intention. When it is so difficult to recognize and assume the consequences of a "well-intentioned" action, the diabolical prefect has the satisfaction of seeing the developments of his sadistic project confirming its own destructive power and giving it a perfect ending: the father drowns himself, the daughter becomes a whore. What could be better, or what could be worse? This is "sacred" power, the power that comes from Providence in reverse—namely, Satan.

Now Flaubert chose to treat this *black* subject precisely to show that beautiful, pure evil is merely an *appearance*. Janvier does not have the aristocratic greatness of the divine Marquis or Gilles de Rais. Just after the schematic narration of the anecdote, we read: "Despite everything, the Prefect would have to be an honest man—take away the monstrous side—, the daughter with respectable instincts would gradually become a whore. The father's suicide should *later* be explained by a motive other than his daughter's dishonor." The word *later*—my emphasis—shows clearly that Flaubert meant "at the outset of the action" to present the facts as they *ought to appear* to the indignant, frightened consciousness of the reader. Perhaps he even pictured the novel beginning *after* the crime, and presenting that black diamond as an event remembered by public opinion. The actual plot would then take place several years later, since he adds: "The

585

daughter and the Prefect must meet again—help each other, she helps him make a good marriage." Thus the underlying purpose appears in all its simplistic clarity: the men of the Empire must be shown unworthy of the evil they do. We will learn that the tragic father was only an old drunk who jumped into the water on an alcoholic binge, or perhaps fell in one day when he was drunk. The daughter had respectable instincts, of course, but it was not the rape—not only that, at any rate—that led her to the gutter: the demoralization was progressive; it was *things,* the world, the society as a whole that slowly did the work. The criminal attempt—which wasn't entirely consummated—was only the initial prodding. And the girl is surely to some extent responsible; her "respectable instincts" must not have been very profound, for she holds no grudge against the Prefect and later renders him a service. And a little further on, contrasting the Prefect and his supposed victim to two other characters, Flaubert adds: "The Prefect and the daughter are content with things as they are—the *grande dame* and the democrat dream of something different. The first group represents the present, the second group the past and the future." The daughter, having become a slut, seems to enjoy a respectable living; she is raised by her keepers to the height of the demi-monde, since she has acquired enough diplomatic skill to help the Prefect make a good marriage; not only that, she plays in the little theaters. She is a combination of Lagier, Person, and others, content with *what is,* without a moment's regret for lost "honor," as if her "gradual" demoralization had led her, in short, to find herself, as if happiness, for her, were to give pleasure for money. Thus our Prefect is at least partially acquitted. What we were first led to believe were the awful consequences of his act now seem clearly to have been caused *elsewhere.* So he may be an "honest man": the blackmail was almost self-generated, it unintentionally became the irreversible meaning of things done and said; the rape was attempted because he got carried away, the flesh succumbed. His affinities with the girl, moreover, are notable: both of them are satisfied with *what is,* living in the present; these creatures of the imperial regime are totally adapted to the society of the Second Empire and want nothing more.

Are they to be congratulated? Certainly not; the Knights of Nothingness admire only the great malcontents. We might even recognize in these stalwarts of the Empire that materialism for which Gustave had reproached the grocers, that is, the bourgeois, since his youth. For this is the true fault of the imperial regime: its facade is the charismatic austerity of evil in power; its reality is bourgeois plutocracy and its utilitarian puritanism. The Prefect's real abjection is his opportunism and his contentment, his hideous mediocrity as a decent man. A decent man: he knows neither hatred nor burning jealousy, he has never felt the desires to kill, to bash someone over the head, that so often torment Flaubert, nor that wickedness Flaubert boasted of in his youth and for which he recovered a taste after the defeat. How could the Prefect know such things since he has never known Great Desire, its attendant frustrations, disgust with the real, the love of death and nothingness? The lie of imperial society is to hide the de facto power of a basely hedonistic bourgeoisie beneath the mirage of a black feudalism. We need merely to recognize that the *malcontents* Flaubert contrasts to the Prefect and the daughter are no more worthy than they: if the *grande dame,* who regrets the past, is not the Catholic trickster who demoralizes the republican hero to make him a tribune for the forces of reaction, she is her sister; as for the democrat, he might be the father of the demoralized republican. We know, in any case, that he cannot claim Gustave's sympathies. What does he want, then? And what is this future he is preparing if not the moment when the bourgeoisie, tired of so costly a mirage, will simply shrug it off and govern openly? Underlying regret and discontent, as sordid and calculating as the opportunism of denial. In any case, the chief concern of this Republic the democrat wants to restore would be to purge Janvier of his crimes and make him the most honorable of democrats, whitewashed and redeemed. A prefect under the Empire, a deputy under the Third Republic, Janvier makes a clean breast of it. The first of these two regimes is not much more than the necessary and provisional disguise for the second: before as after 4 September, the basis of all power resides in mediocrity.

Returning some time later to "Monsieur le Prefet," Gustave confirms his thought by retracing the career of this notable. The future deputy of the republican bourgeoisie "began as a subprefect" under the abject bourgeoisie at the time of Louis-Philippe, and became "prefect of the first rank at the end of the Empire." We see that he was supported throughout his career by his class of origin. It is true that he "ends up destitute and poverty-stricken," but that is because "the book must highlight the official element"—the State, a variable and deceptive apparatus that both dissimulates and serves the true power, which has everything to gain from staying hidden. The true power: the hegemony of the bourgeois class that breaks the people's resistance by making it bourgeois in such a way as to resurrect the myth of the bourgeoisie as the universal class. "As the official party

587

changes, the Prefect must experience upheavals in his own situation." *Socially* a fixture, he can be victim, nonetheless, of the fluctuations of *politics* presented here by Flaubert as a superstructural activity. In this scenario, Janvier is the "model prefect." He "maintains a balance between the clergy and democracy. Blocks everything . . . , [maintains] discipline in the newspapers, in the elections, in public opinion, everywhere." Disinterested "in relation to money," he has only one passion, and that is order. Naturally, he is a criminal: he betrays his friends, delivers his wife to Morny, denies his own brother, has a former mistress imprisoned—or allows her to be—and so forth. But on this subject Flaubert is explicit: "*must* commit all crimes out of a love of order." This imperiously underlined verb indicates that the Prefect's exactions do not come from some deliberately malevolent intent; quite the contrary, they impose themselves on the representative of the established order at once as the strict consequences of his fundamental bias and as categorical imperatives. These observations allow us to understand that the second scenario is merely a variant of the first, more systematic and elaborated. Here again, evil seems self-generated; it is everywhere, the intention to do harm is nowhere. Subjectively, the goal remains positive to the end: the established order is embodied in the person of the Prefect, who reveals his affirmative and singular essence in his passion for order, that is, in order itself demanding to be maintained regardless of the circumstances; objectively, an inflexible force produces the negative from this thorough-going positivity: betraying his friends, repudiating his brother, making himself "voluntarily cuckolded by Morny"—these are his crimes. But what is a crime that has not been willed as such? Monsieur le Prefet had no criminal intention, he merely chose; as for his repudiations, he simply saw in every particular circumstance the most economical means of avoiding disorder. And if in certain cases he may have *taken some responsibility,* if he had regrets—no one is perfect—his peaceful conscience was undisturbed by remorse: the order that was incarnate in him was pleased to be maintained, even at the sacrifice of a few human relations, because it was not made for men but men were made for it.

Gustave appears to have had a presentiment, nearly a hundred years before the events, of our amazement at men like Eichmann and other Nazi war criminals. They had been caught, irrefutable proof was gathered, they had clearly organized the systematic extermination of the Jews. Faced with the vile grandeur of this genocide, we expected to see before us if not princes of darkness at least defiant

criminals, people we could hate. We discovered, instead, niggling officials, bureaucrats who, without shame, didn't even take satanic
pride in what they had done, mediocrities, dutiful types who didn't
really understand the accusations, who kept trying to explain their
actions by referring to hierarchical discipline, to obeying superiors,
and to the need to save Germany by maintaining the established order. The evil was undeniable; the responsible parties appeared before
the tribunal, yet no one among them had committed it. This uncon-
sciousness hardly seemed an excuse, however, but rather aggravated
their case, provoking in us a mixture of uneasiness and contempt.
Contempt, for we would have preferred them to be wicked; uneasiness, for they were neither exterminating angels nor submen, simply
ordinary mediocrities, our neighbors, bureaucrats subject to the bureaucratic order—something each of us was or could be. Hugo's celebrated line seemed appropriate: "No one is wicked, whatever evil one
does." But only if the vatic poet's vaguely soft-hearted optimism, his
benevolent pity, had become a profound and almost misanthropic
pessimism. Evil is in essence intentional; if men always commit it unintentionally, they must be in such a state of permanent distraction
or giddiness that the judgment of things on persons—what I call elsewhere the practico-inert—is internalized by them, therefore *intention-
alized* in the absence of any subject. Evil must happen to them, and
precisely as the practical meaning of the established order, that is, of
disorder maintained by violence. This infinite and profound meaning, which would not exist without them but remains unthinkable in
each of them, unrealizable due to the simple fact of human finitude,
must become the rule of their actions, or, if you will, of human relations, while systematic *diversion* produces a false consciousness in
them. This is sustained by bad faith all the more easily when evil as
the meaning of a society is "unrealizable," and such a false consciousness presents the subjection to disorder as a fascination with order,
and presents the malevolent intention to treat men as things as the
imperious duty to preserve the present structures of the community,
even at the price of human sacrifice. This, indeed, is Flaubert's point:
whatever evil we do, we are not even wicked. The Prefect, for example, is a disinterested, decent man; the evil he does is not his own,
it is an enormously harmful thing, without a subject yet intentional,
and he *does not deserve* to be called its author. Unless that very thing
is merely pure appearance, as in the first scenario. Let us imagine that
the repudiated brother is extricated, that someone high up intervenes
to extricate the abandoned mistress, etc. Evil, praxis without a sub-

589

ject, would immediately lack an object as well. This is not what *I* think but it is probably what Gustave was then thinking. Evil is beauty, it is the impossible totalization of the cosmos; the Empire was merely a beautiful dream of evil and hatred that cradled the woodlice of bourgeois democracy for eighteen years.

"Under Napoleon III" was supposed to recount the demoralization of man by woman. The story of the rape at the beginning of "Monsieur le Prefet" was supposed to seem, at least in the first chapters, like the demoralization of woman by man. It is likely that these two excessively unilateral scenarios coexisted for a time in Flaubert's thought, and that from them he conceived the idea for a more exhaustive novel, "A Parisian Household under Napoleon III," which would unite the two subjects and treat the reciprocal demoralization of a husband and wife. Flaubert had already dreamed of doing this but in a less systematic fashion when he planned the writing of *L'Education sentimentale.* "Mme Dumesnil loathes her husband while in public she is always cajoling him—base character of D., he beats her. But she sleeps in *billows* of lace, it's all there. Love of dress and material elegance pushed to *heroic* proportions." [142] The idea is already there of sordid relations—the truth of the household—dissimulated in public by a comedy of tenderness. This is what becomes of the scenario after 1875: "At first they love each other. Madame surprises Monsieur in the act, then Monsieur surprises Madame. Jealousy. Everything gradually calms down—end of their love. 2d, they tolerate each other. The husband exploits his wife. The place becomes a business operation. 3d, but they still have a little good in them, a little individuality, spontaneity in passion, and as they are not utter scoundrels, their fortune fails and they are punished by their vices." [143] No doubt, for this is the narrative Flaubert alluded to when he confided to Zola his intention of writing "the story of a regulated passion, vice made bourgeois and satisfying itself behind highly respectable appearances." This household devotes itself to preserving a reputation intact: in public, Madame exaggerates her modesty a little, Monsieur his jealousy; their furtively exchanged gestures of tenderness per-

142. Marie-Jeanne Durry, ibid., p. 135.
143. This last phrase is surprising: didn't Flaubert make a mistake, and shouldn't it read: "punished by their virtues"? We are just told, in effect, that they have lost out because of the little good they still have in them. Moreover, this is a favorite theme in de Sade and Flaubert himself: Virtue is a punished, Vice rewarded. Unless Gustave wanted, ironically, to remind us that spontaneity and character were considered vices in imperial society.

suade friends and neighbors that this couple is happily united by love. This is a guarantee for their clientele, a clientele made up, no doubt, of "well-known personalities" who highly value the advantage of being announced to the husband, then fucking the wife, and leaving without anyone the wiser; these people do not balk at the price. We imagine the decency of the conjugal couple, their reserve very slightly tinged with austerity, the sobriety of their dress—good manners are preserved.

In what way is this excessively open household typical of the "Second Empire"? Aren't there whorish wives and obliging husbands in every era? We have to admit that the story, taken in itself, isn't very significant; Flaubert cannot be unaware of this, since he has long dreamed of writing short variations on the theme of the classic "triangle," and so did not originally link the couple's reciprocal demoralization to a regime but rather to the constants that, taken together, constitute his view of human nature. Things look quite different if we put "A Parisian Household" back into the context of that larger operation Gustave undertook, beginning in 1871, which was an attempt to give novelistic shape to the theme of "falseness under Napoleon III." In the first scenarios, it is the ideal that it is false, and woman, a pure mirage, dissimulates a female in heat or basely self-interested. In the scenarios related to "Monsieur le Prefet" it is power that is falsely charismatic and supports that beautiful and terrible illusion, evil: France is already secretly demoralized, it is the country of satisfied mediocrities, of honest folk whose hateful respectability has its source in fear, in conformism, in the taste for *what is*, for the established order, and in that permanent abyss resulting from it, the lack of imagination, of the taste for what is not. In the third group of projects—those concerning the couple—good manners, by contrast, are maintained to keep up *appearances*, and vice is presented to us as reality.

Gustave insists on situating his novel in the Second Empire—in other words, on giving this anecdote a historical dimension—because he sees the couple's adventure as expressing the experience of an entire society. Conjugal demoralization seems to him the product of a much more general demoralization originating in the coup of 2 December, and the singular failure of the household symbolizes the collapse of the Empire, since they share the same causes. This time the imperial regime has no other reality than *vice*, which here takes the form of sexual debauchery and the basest interests but which in other circumstances might equally take the form of self-deception, arriv-

591

ism, servility, repudiation, and betrayal. The mirage is respectability: they are all crooks pretending to be decent folk. The Prefect, too, sold his wife—he pushed her into the arms of Morny. But he did not do it with any malevolent intent, it was out of a love of order that he became so obliging. The young couple, by contrast, is as criminal as can be: the two spouses profit from the vile desire of lecherous fifty-year-olds to make love with beautiful, venal women without losing their reputation; they profit from it knowingly: "the husband exploits his wife, the place becomes a business operation." Their crime is playing upon the vices of others: in the society they represent and which produced them, each person treats his fellow with respect, confides in him a priori; there are no Cains among the privileged classes, only Abels by the thousands—all virtuous, all benevolent. For greater security, vice is unspoken; austerity, chastity, courage, and altruism are the only possibilities for man. How could they speak of that radical impossibility, evil? We cannot find words to name that which does not exist. Language is purged of all negative words, which are in essence suspect; ever benign conversations are stamped with a gracious positiveness: edifying behavior is reported, and everyone, even those absent, is given a certificate of good conduct. But ethical evaluations, whatever precaution is taken, have a double-edged quality, a secret violence that might provoke a negative reaction; and if everyone is good, we must not commend the good actions of others too often, for that would make them think that virtue is not natural. And it is hardly fitting to name virtue; one need merely show it through friendly gestures, the mildness of one's assertions, and through distinction; conversation will give preference to material facts that are indisputable and if possible insignificant, like the length of a bridge or the height of a mountain. This theater is played without respite everywhere by actors who, in their most secret counsel, despite their profound inner mutism, never for a moment lose the consciousness of being swindlers in the process of swindling other swindlers, or of getting swindled themselves. This would be Flaubert's picture of the Second Empire: a cave of brigands who would act like angels.

It is clear that Flaubert is attacking here the official moralism, the benevolent optimism, that represented the ideology of the imperial government as opposed to bourgeois misanthropy. In the name of a conventional aesthetic and a conformist ethic they had sought to condemn the author of *Madame Bovary*; inspired critics, guard dogs of the regime, systematically vilified his books. When he savagely evoked this stupefying lie, Gustave was close to thinking that the Court, the government, the imperial family, beginning with Louis-Napoleon, were nothing but a gang in power, and that these hooligans conscious of their hooliganism were throwing dust in the eyes of the people and persuading them of their virtues by censoring works of art in the name of the moral order they themselves were violating constantly in their private lives. "They were asking Art to be moral, vice to be decent, and Science to make itself accessible to the people," he wrote to George Sand at the beginning of April 1871. And in another letter he recalls with rage that "to tell the truth was immoral. Persigny reproached me all last winter for 'having no ideal.'" We observe the curious enumeration that sandwiches vice between art and science. This shouldn't surprise us: Flaubert loves vice and its dissatisfaction, the meanness of great desire frustrated, and the practical imagination of the vicious; he loves it to the extent that it is the negation of man, the destruction of the human. As a result, we discover the true meaning of "A Parisian Household." For a moment we believed that good manners were only the appearance, that vice was the reality of this society; and it is true that under the Empire, behind a facade of morality, there was great dissipation. But the comparison between vice and art enlightens us: it is not vice that sickens him, it is *decency in vice*, a contradiction *in adjecto*. Those who, out of servility or arrivism, accept the imperial demand and try to produce moral works, not only constitute *apparent* morality but *apparent* art as well; it is not a question of prudently concealing a true masterpiece beneath an edifying varnish, which is quite impossible, but of endowing an appearance of morality with an appearance of beauty. Hence the "false literature" he denounces to Maxime, which is not an absence of literature, since books that claim to be literary works are written, read, criticized, and sold, but rather a false literature: the objects exist but they contain a mirage sustained by their materiality. The author has objectified his theater in them; he *pretends* to be an artist, to choose words, to construct the book with respect to aesthetic norms; as a result, the product on a certain level will offer itself to him as a pretext, the result of this research, that is, in its inert being-there it will reflect the gestures of a pseudo-artist. Similarly, the science that claims to be accessible to everyone is a *false science* (based on the odious democratic principle that regards good sense as the most common thing in the world). The resulting book or discourse is found to have correctly imitated the external features of a work of true science: austerity, precision in the definition of concepts, rigor in deduction or in the account rendered of an experiment; everything is there *except*

593

knowledge itself, which does not communicate itself to just anyone and, once approximately figured in metaphors or in comparisons drawn from daily life, turns frankly into error. Vice, for its part, is shocking in itself, indecent by nature; it destroys the ethical conventions that make a society possible; it runs toward death, utterly devouring both the depraved man and his victim. The thing that allows the young couple to try and pull this off is precisely everyone's studied intention to *submit* vice to decency; simply stated, people in quest of this accommodation are now neither depraved nor decent. The sole desire to *keep up appearances* imposes limits on vice that *falsify* it (that destroy it as vice), since its greatness and its truth demand that it be *unbridled.* At the very heart of their basic intention, then, is an underlying mediocrity; they are resigned to make vice an everyday matter, on the cheap, in short, to give themselves the illusion of vice with a few prudent orgies while allowing others the illusion of that virtue in which they can no longer believe. Thus vice and virtue are mutually annihilating: neither can be the truth of imperial man, which resides rather in an unhealthy moderation of two great, contradictory demands. In effect, it is not a consciousness split between two infinite postulations, one ascending to God through holiness, and the other through the desire to destroy, to be destroyed, and to annihilate being, descending even to the Devil. No, imperial man finds accommodations with Heaven because he has lowered his claims, in both senses and simultaneously; in fact, he is but a small nature, *satisfied with what is,* and his only desire is to enjoy the real goods of the earth, to plunder a venal beauty weekly, without running the risk of letting his activities be known, preserving the scrap of power that comes to him, in this outwardly prudish society, from his good reputation.

So the theme of "A Parisian Household," which at first seemed to contradict the theme of "Monsieur le Prefet," actually broadens it. Monsieur le Prefet, despite his crime, is a decent man because he never adequately *willed* what he did; he merely got carried away for a moment. But in his deepest self he was incapable of postulating evil and insisting on it. The same for our young married couple, and especially their clients: these products of the Empire are in reality fabricated by universal suffrage, which necessarily privileges *the man without quality,* the man who is most like everyone else, whose countenance and bearing seem to everyone a mechanical portrait of anyone, one's own portrait. Opinion will choose the man most dependent on opinion, the man who is fearful by nature of *what people will say,* and he will be chosen and doubly obliged to respect the judgment of the public. These officials have a sexuality, however, that sometimes discreetly torments them; they would secretly enjoy the quite fleshly reality of a callipygenous female (men liked them that way in those days), provided their security was guaranteed. These doomed unfortunates demand very little of themselves, and even less of Satan, who serves them; not only do they want to preserve *what is*—though pure evil must be subversive—but they accept the loss of their honor and their self-esteem for so little: an ass in the dark. And thus they make the good absurd (an ample drama with a hundred different acts) without contributing, for all that, to the fearful enterprise of hastening the advent of evil on earth. False vice screened by false virtue. True vice, for Flaubert, is always sadistic: Gilles de Rais sodomizes young boys, then cuts them to pieces while still alive; true virtue is a quietistic mysticism and subjection to an inhuman ideal. This falseness is the lie of the Empire; but that lie—whose underlying purpose is the pleasure in *what is*—although it cannot be done without the concurrence of imagination, implies a narrow limiting of the imagination and its submission to the real. The minimal and contained hypocrisy of imperial society is generated, in this hybrid regime, by universal suffrage much more than by charismatic power; it produces lies we might call realistic, since they are simply the means of enjoying conflicting realities: the flesh, which gives itself in secret, and authority, which depends on reputation. This hypocrisy paves the way for the advent of total democracy, for the triumph of realism. The Empire is a false Empire; in reality it is a predemocracy. In "Under Napoleon III," only ruffians and rotters without personality succeed. Observe that our young couple run aground: despite everything, they have too much character. "As they still have a little good in them, that is, a little individuality, spontaneity in passion, and they are not utter scoundrels, their fortune fails." The scoundrel is a calculating machine: he determines his interests precisely in terms of the abjection of others—posited a priori. As a result, he is entirely unoriginal; it is not only that to fool others he must be like them in all things, but also, in particular, that a singular trait, an inclination or personal preference, would be enough to condemn him. It is not enough to deny himself all spontaneous movement, he must be deprived of all spontaneity from birth—or at least very early. Swindling is pure reason: the swindler must treat both his dupe and himself as the means of amassing a fortune; he must regulate his behavior with respect to universal principles. That, at least, is what Gustave thinks of "scoundrels," who are, after all, not so different from scientists as he conceives them. Spontaneity and individuality in passion, however, remain minor qualities in the eyes of the artist: hasn't he proscribed improvisation for himself, hasn't he condemned passions when they are real, save in the degree to which Providence transforms them into stations of the cross that lead the martyr to Golgotha, whence, perched on his pain, he surveys the world? In this young couple, then, we are dealing with the only quality that can be preserved by those who have chosen being and are satisfied by it: a temperamental spontaneity of choice. This is not, of course, *autonomy* but what today we call inner-directedness. In a society manipulated from the outside, all inner-directedness is an obstacle to perfect integration.

These are, broadly, the three major themes in the scenarios on the Second Empire: nauseating Good, a Catholic mirage sustained by females; phantom Evil, bound no doubt to Authority but committed by no one and having no real existence; the phantom couple Vice and Virtue annihilating each other in the same shipwreck, like Fantomas and Juve, enemy brothers who drown entwined, leaving space only for being and a few moderate dissipations. In other words, the death of imagination. In a way, what triumphs in the three themes, along with *reality*, is the mediocrity of the species. That practical, shabby little world doesn't even know how to dream: the *grande dame* doesn't demoralize her young lover for the pleasure of doing harm—that would still have a little grandeur—but to attract him to her party; and the Prefect never dreamed of systematically making a decent girl into a whore, he simply let himself be tempted by a very real body, his earth-bound imagination going no further than divining shapes under a dress. Well and good. But has Gustave really *felt* what he wants to *show*? Now he reproaches the Empire for having been the rule of the mediocre, a disguised democracy, the triumph of *being* and positivist assurance. Is *that* really what he is complaining about in 1870? He hastens to take his distance: he quickly condemns satisfaction with what is, conformism, servility; he has the right to do so, of course, being a provincial original, a malcontent, a peasant of the Danube (yet the Goncourts suggested repeatedly, not without irritation, that this false bear knew how to show the rather vile eagerness of the courtier when he had to), who frequented Mathilde's with no ulterior motive, in all disinterestedness. But indeed, if he merely denounced the vices of the regime *in which he shared no complicity,* he would never make us understand what attracted him to Compiègne, to the Tuileries, which effectively *evoked his complicity.* If this solitary was prepared to bow before sovereigns *for no opportunistic reasons,* it was for the dreamlike aspect of their sovereignty, as I have shown, and to relax from his tension as a dreaming anchorite by surrounding himself with the black mirage of the court, to internalize its consolidated nonbeing by taking part in its theater. There is not a word of this *in the scenarios*. What we find is an old contempt for man—conceived here strictly as bourgeois. In fact, he makes the Empire responsible for a mediocrity he had denounced well before the regime was really established. And isn't the Prefect—who *cannot do evil* because the girl he rapes cannot even die of shame, because her drunk of a father makes a mockery of family honor—the younger brother of the lover Flaubert imagined for Graziella in that enraged letter in which he denounced Lamartine's idealism? That character was equally heartless, the idle, weak son of a respectable family who sleeps with a fisherman's daughter, then abruptly abandons her—and Graziella does not die of it, she consoles herself and marries, which is worse: her seducer *could not* do evil simply because one does not die of love. But what happened to his fascination with the regime of absolute power, the witty conversation he would have accepted from all the regimes he had known, precisely because it was *simultaneously* a lie? *Everything was false,* he says in his letters of 1870–71. And this is what he claims to show in the scenarios. He does not say that he knew it, and that the *falseness* pleased him as such. It is true that *on one point* he was fooled and in good faith: like everyone else at the time, he thought that the French army, foremost in the world, was a steel rampart guarding the tender imperial society. His profound resentment against the Empire, against the Emperor, comes from his disappointment: "a false army," he says; yes, and he believed it was real. But he has no other grievance against the abolished regime. Its official art was abject, to be sure, but honors also went to real artists; the Empire, a center of derealization, should have rested on a *real base*, just as the work of art, an eternally objectified derealization, owes its perenniality to the matter it informs—bronze, canvas, or paper. If the army had been that *real base*, the Empire might have been a work of art living itself out through the consciousness of its subjects. He doesn't mention any of this in the plans he writes between 1871 and 1877. He must show the "falseness," however, of the imperial world; yet the denunciations we find in his letters from 1870 seem to lose their meaning when he wants to give them fictional form, and this hallucinator of the Empire no longer manages to understand what he loved about that hallucination, and what he held against it when it disappeared. He attains the height of *vulgarianism* (this is the word he uses to characterize the Republic) when, imitating the dethroned and deceased Emperor, he declares to Zola: "Napoleon III was stupid." The word is heavy with meaning in Gustave's mouth, and we know the repulsion and dizzying attraction he felt for that incredible density, for that quiet, dark power, the stupidity of others. Applied to a political position, it no longer means much. And since the point is, in fact, to characterize a man, the host of Compiègne, Flaubert demeans himself—something Edmond and even Zola felt strongly—by too easily hanging up his hat, reducing his Lord to the minerality of a village idiot, without saying what—what secret dematerialization, what dizzying loss of gravity—mesmerized him, Gustave himself, changing the very real Lord into a prince of clouds. It is impossible to write "Under Napoleon III" without preserving that ambivalence of the letters from 1870, in which he reproached Isidore on a number of counts, condemned the "long lie" that was the imperial dictatorship, and yet in the same letter, or in one written the next day, cried that this was the end of the Latin world, elegance and civility would disappear, all that we loved was lost. Impossible to denounce the Empire in the scenarios as a false autocracy, dissimulating the reign of universal suffrage, and to be terrified, as he was when the 4 September coup established democracy *in earnest* (he believed). In sum, impossible to judge the Empire or to absolve it without judging himself or without absolving himself by the same stroke. The novelist here cannot feign a position *outside,* surveying, contemplating, creating characters in which he does not embody himself; he is judge and witness, he is *inside,* burdened by the weight of things done and said; his characters must all be—and all together—himself and the other. Each must contain the good and bad use made of the Empire; each must surely contain the hidden bourgeois like Monsieur le Prefet, the little household that lends decency to vice, even the democrat and the *grande dame;* but each must also display that detachment from the bourgeoisie, which, fictive as it was, had enough substance for Gustave to experience every one of his sojourns with princes or the Emperor as a new baptism, as a death followed by resurrection that he surely found ennobling.

We might say that as those (for him) happy years become more distant, Gustave loses the initial meaning of his project. His confiding remarks to Maxime must then date at the latest from the beginning of 1871, since at first Flaubert merely regrets not using the *capitulation at Sedan* as the conclusion to *L'Education sentimentale,* which appeared in 1869. He seems to have moved from this regret to the idea for a whole novel devoted to imperial society, for in the same conversation he declares: "I am inconsolable at having missed the scene (the Emperor cursed by the prisoners), but I shall place it somewhere in a novel I will do on the Empire . . . Ah, there are great books to be done on this epoch, and perhaps, after all, the coup d'état and what followed will, in the universal harmony of things, simply provide interesting scenarios for a few good scribblers." What we have here is the project in its primitive form, barely distinguishable from a regret. The prospective novel seems spun out of a desire to compensate for a missed opportunity: I have not been able to place my scene; I will write a whole book around it. observe that the projected work must bear directly on power and the court: Gustave is certainly not thinking of replacing Napoleon III with that shabby agent of power, Monsieur le Prefet; he will put him in the scene as well. Flaubert's sincerity is evident: the capitulation at Sedan, by contrast, gives him a chance to evoke his own memories, to describe those servile marshals he saw at Compiègne, who lost the war of 1870 and those soldiers insult the fallen emperor. That is what must be told; and in this still abstract evocation there is one concrete element, the memory of a sound: Flaubert still hears the *tinkling* of medals. And he recalls it so clearly because he was there, beside those courtiers, a courtier himself, waiting his turn, perhaps, to bend over the prince's little hand. In other words, when he reports these facts and his intentions to Maxime, he knows *very well* that the novelist of the Empire cannot be that impassive witness who surveyed both the Carthaginian empire and, with the same detachment, the history of contemporary France from 1845 to 1852. Nor can he be its judge. Unless he is what Camus calls a *judge-penitent*. But this function—quite common in today's world of letters—hardly existed in the time of absolute-art; and, as we know, Gustave's predispositions are hardly propitious to such acrobatics. Never guilty, because he was made guilty to the marrow by the paternal curse, he knows only how to pronounce sentence. In this text, however, we sense at once that he is touched by discomfort (what the devil was I doing there?), and that he has found in a single stroke an *inspired* way to justify himself. The Empire—from 2 December 1851 to 4 September 1870—was *false*: the servility of the Pretorians at Compiègne was false. False emperor, false Pretorians. That is why, in this conversation, Flaubert places the marshals bent to the ground alongside the prisoners shaking their fists. But the "falseness" itself exposes its nonbeing by its radical inefficacy. The false Empire is nothingness in that it has made nothing but noise: it has the appearance of being only to the extent that its very inefficacy is indirectly efficacious, allowing the real forces hidden beneath its mirage to act in an entirely different sense from the way this comic-opera government *claims* to orient its politics. The Tuileries, Compiègne, are ruses; under their protection, the bourgeoisie slowly assembles the conditions for a power grab; when the time is ripe, the other force, Prussia—which is patiently pursuing another goal, ensuring the development of its economy by establishing its hegemony on the continent by force of arms—will give it a hand, or rather the necessary nudge to overthrow these imperial puppets and break their worm-eaten theater. That is the hidden tragedy: the objective complicity of German militarism and the French democrats, who would receive the Republic from the hands of the Prussian king.

In this light, the Empire and its court, which are perfectly separated from the real, are purely imaginary, and if the artist agrees to participate in the imperial *myth*, it is to recuperate that myth through a work that will return it to the absolute purity of imagination. This collective hallucination cannot be true history, for we have seem that history is forged elsewhere; neither is it a work of art, since it has no author—we know that for Flaubert, art begins with the rite of passage that creates the newborn artist, who is necessarily *a* person. The greatness of this image, however, lies in the fact that it is *purely unreal*, though for every dreamer it possesses an indestructible solidity because it is *also* the dream of others. It will all end badly *because* of that very solidity:[144] without ever being real, something is going to end in bloodshed; after the collapse, those foolish years will reveal, from the past, their arrogant and tragic unreality. Even in its shipwreck the dream will postulate its salvation by a specialized dreamer, by an artist, who will make it the subject of a work. This systematic derealization of French society by itself and through the intermediary of an unconscious demoralizer, much more a *medium* than a dictator, is the *rough* equivalent of the goal art sets for itself. The medium in this last case, however, cannot exist without a reflexive consciousness radicalized by *what it does,* and hence by what it *is*: the worker of art gripped by a useless passion, exclusively concerned with inscribing a little demoralizing nonbeing in being itself. In other words, at the moment he is conversing with Maxime, Gustave is quite conscious of what he wants to do: he claims he will approach the imperial world head on,

144. That is, because of the imaginary as it is socially instituted by the series and insofar as it derives a certain being from the *separation of the dreamers.*

directly. Later, he will lose this understanding of himself and will resign himself to illustrating the fact of the dictatorship *obliquely*, through its influence on midlevel civil servants of the Interior, on bourgeois families, on the monarchist and republican opposition. But at the outset he proposed to depict the high dignitaries of the regime; he dared to give a glimpse of the Emperor, that "historic" personage, and to convey his internal discourse; Gustave had understood that the subject of a so-called historical novel aspiring to reconstruct the dream of French society "under Napoleon III" could only be absolute-art taking itself as its subject. In a way, *Madame Bovary, Salammbô, Saint Antoine*, and—although to a lesser extent—*L'Education* do just this. For example, just as Emma is escaping banality through the dream, she sees her dream overtaken once again by banality; art fixes this vicious circle forever by inscribing it in the objective realm as a beyond of the imagination, or, if you will, as the absolute equivalence of the necessity and impossibility of the imaginary. We have also seen how, for lack of monuments or vestiges, the *past* real and the *pure* unreal—an empty ambition, ambition for an absence filled by the materiality of words—mingle in *Salammbô*. In this reconstructed Carthage, he was not afraid to make historical characters act and think; time had so profoundly engulfed them that they could not be evoked except by pure imagining. This is an *aesthetic* conception of absolute-art as an abolition just consolidated from below by the inverse and *magical* belief through which the technicians of imagination—considered as an exact discipline—somehow attain the real through fiction.

But in *Salammbô* the author claims to resurrect a *real* society as it was in the time of its reality. The true subject remains esoteric: it tempts the artist on the level of conception and structure, that is, reflexively, as a problematic of art and its techniques. Certainly Carthaginian society, like all societies, had its structures of the imaginary; but Flaubert wants to resurrect not only these but also the lived experience of daily life, with the *flavor of reality* it had for those living it, the materiality of work and war; the author is attracted by the difficulty—belonging to the singular subject, Carthage, but of a *literary* order—that I shall call the obligation to imagine without *analogue*, or, if you will, the necessity, for clarity's sake, to prophesy retrospectively without fortune telling. *Salammbô* is the image beyond the image, that which no longer retains the least materiality, and which one cannot imagine but can only imagine that one imagines. Conversely, Flaubert charges Emma Bovary with *realizing* in his stead the autobiographical theme of *Novembre:* I am too small for myself. Her moments of elation and disappointment underscore human finitude, the drama of facticity, the triumph of the real in relation to a particular creature for whom the ideal is merely a perpetual and futile effort to tear herself away from her powerful carnal materiality. In this dreamy and lucid woman, the dream never *takes* for long. In neither of these novels are the characters or, still less, the society that produces them conceived as fantasms; fictive, yes, but with the contradiction frequently found in novelistic works, that the fiction attempts to resurrect them in their reality, at least on a certain level of the writing.

In "Under Napoleon III," by contrast, Flaubert would have tried to render first the confused but dense oneirism of a mesmerized society. Its subject was the social imaginary during a pathological epoch when it devoured the real. Or rather, lost in shadow, canceled out, masked, the real still exists: when the false marshals grovel on their stomachs before a false prince, in a false transport of vassalage, the tinkling of their false medals is nonetheless real. But the art of the "good scribbler" would be to suggest it allusively, or to show it without commentary within the dream, caught in its web, an almost imperceptible menace, the mute and nearly unperceived denunciation of the internal *falseness* of everyone's gestures, statements, and thoughts. Reality, in this novel, in its swift and discreet appearances, would have had the same function as the *signs* sown with such profusion in *Madame Bovary:* it would have prophesied the final disaster. But in *Madame Bovary,* despite their poetic depth, these signs can seem somewhat gratuitous: it is not necessary, after all, for the blind man to reappear at such a moment, in such a place. In contrast to reality, these signs represent the *imagination,* an aesthetic tightening of the internal bonds of the cosmos that allows for oracles. The "tinkling" of the medals is superior because, on the contrary, it would have predicted the necessary defeat of the dream *from the point of view of reality.* An inversion of the first importance: that incredible monster is revealed, a mirage that resists, a lie more solid than truth, a theater that derives its obtuse inertia from its ubiquity; in short, a society that has nearly succeeded in the unlikely project of *realizing the unreal while preserving its unreality.* And the purpose of the narrative would be, without ever leaving this dream, to give a highly detailed inkling of its coming rupture, at first very distant, then increasingly imminent, never present to the clear consciousness of the sleepers, yet increasingly so to that of the reader, as an inexplicably ominous allure of the most brilliant celebrations, as a secret baseness of the most exalted personalities. And then all at once, turning a page, from one chapter to the next, we are on *the other side of the catastrophe*, in a reality that seems suddenly nightmarish, in the midst of a wild-looking mob which after eighteen years of slumber does not even understand it has awakened. This time the fiction and its subject are homogeneous: the men presented are invented as fictions in themselves; this false magistrate, that false general who did not exist, are drawn out of nothingness and placed among false judges and false military men whose existence is consumed to produce unreality. From this point of view, one can speak and think of Louis-Napoleon and Eugénie without leaving the realm of imagination, which would be risky if either of them were real. But apart from a little tedious flesh, an indispensable concession to facticity, there is no more *truth* to the Emperor than there is *truth* to the Empress; indeed, they are a double imposture that is not sustained by an imperial *reality* and so is played according to imaginary rules. Badinguet's thoughts have neither the unpredictability nor the dialectic necessity that characterizes true thought and makes it a double message, inimitable and doubly difficult to decode; what we can piece together of him is not lived experience but the way he played the role of a living Emperor and took up thoughts that were merely the internal part of his imaginary discourse—the part that dramatic authors of the time indicated by the words "surreptitiously" or "speaking to himself." True, the *real* man could have been shown a single time, or rather the man realized by catastrophe: there is no more Emperor, no more conqueror, just a prisoner "sunk" in the depths of a carriage, shorn of title or even name. But Flaubert would have shown this anxious awakening in its undeniable generality as dis-illusion; in other words, we are not dealing here with a *singular* disappointment—whose meaning would be determined by the singularity of the individual and the situation—for the good reason that the individual had disappeared twenty years before, absorbed by the character; and Flaubert would have shown merely the return to individuality—not to any particular identity, for we still know nothing of who remains, who has vanished, who has crowded together, hardened, impoverished, or worm-eaten—but with the abolition of the charismatic figure, the totalizing embodiment of society by the unique person, we have the simple return to individual dimensions. Condemned to passivity, the man in the depths of the carriage sees images of soldiers marching past; these handsome Zouaves, now in rags, can shake a fist at him: they are powerless objects, like him; the only subjects are the mercenaries who guard the troop. Is this awakening in earnest? Is he dreaming that he is waking up? No; he feels that the *anonymous* anguish and alarm are real enough, this man who has lost the habit of being himself and was playacting the Other, for everyone and above all for himself. We might say, rather, that the awakening comes to him *like another dream*, and that his ragged army marches past, as fabulous in its wretchedness as it was in its false glory when he reviewed the troops several weeks earlier; yet to his distress he knows that he is no longer playacting, that his role is finished, that he has no more *dialogue* to speak, that he has lost both his pasteboard Empire and language, the empire over which he claimed to be master, the language he imposed on the collectivity simply by using it himself, and which functioned only as the *text* of the universal theater. In fact, his alarm—the alarm of a man who would awaken in another body, narrower, punier, infinitely small—is immediately translated by the contesting of a word (which characterizes Flaubert more than it does Badinguet). The awakening—or rather what Gustave has resolved to show us of it—is reduced to this: the word "Pretorian" cannot be applied to that tumultuous horde shouting its hatred at him, which is nonetheless the *reality* of this army, though he was told only yesterday that everything was in order with these soldiers, down to the buttons on their gaiters. The language of the artist, by means of an unknown, a bad actor who has finished playing the man of destiny, performs its self-critique and exposes the bankruptcy of derealization by the Word, the great epic of the *throat* only discovering the truth of signs—their practical appropriation to the signified object—in order to suppress itself and end in a mutism that is at the same time the provisional asphasia of the imperial Hamlet ("The rest is silence," a belated response both to the derealizing enthusiasm of "words, words," and to that supreme unrealization, the play within the play), the prophetic announcement of his coming death, and the conscious, deliberate silence of the artist. He throws away his pen after this final "Pretorian" lie and its ultimate contestation, and invites the reader to throw away the book, to consecrate in one stroke the failure of that directed oneirism, reading, while recognizing that this failure is the very meaning of the book, a deliberate invitation to the abolition of the real by the dream and, more profoundly, to the abolition of the dream by reality.

But even as this final mutism is a deliberate assassination of the reader, plunged once more into his muddy reality, hence a success in failure, a tragic and proud "Loser Wins," it also represents Gustave's humble, panic-stricken awakening and his piteous vow never to write again. To make art, one must have self-esteem; but art implies an oneiric setting, the artist's hysterical belief in realized unreality, thus art is guilty by its very nature. Denounced by those tormenters the *practitioners Flaubert*, crushed by the extent of his deficiency, Gustave has no trouble breaking his pen: in 1870, language no longer permits itself *to be derealized*. Thus the asphasia of the false sovereign who dies a slow death on the road, the proud silence of the artist or the concerted triumph of nothingness, and the *awakening of language* in Flaubert; a worker of art condemned to silence by the disappearance of "knickknacks of sonorous inanities" and their replacement by real signs, computers of reality; writing as a refusal to act, the denial of writing as a fundamental failure required by absolute-art; the impossibility of writing as an experience *suffered* by the artist just when the false Emperor senses the impossibility of pursuing his theater: all this must be seen as what I have called, in *Question de méthode*, the *multidimensional unity of the act*. The act here, of course, is the totalizing conception of a scenario verifying the Second Empire as the vampirization of a society by the dream. Indeed, it is not difficult to see the dialectical relationship that governs the polyvalent unity of these facets and makes each one reflect the others. But what interests us here in particular is the play of reflecting-reflection that connects the Emperor and Gustave, their double agony, which is at once the punishment and the unique source of their greatness. Surely, when he conceived this first scenario, Flaubert had little desire to be purely a witness to the disaster. Certainly the principles of this art ordered him to rearrange it with the impassivity of a panoramic consciousness. But at the same time, the creator was living the passion of his creature, or, more precisely, Gustave embodied himself—as he did in Marguerite, in Garcia, in Mazza, in Emma— in the false, fallen Emperor. As if the author, invisible and omnipresent in the texture of his work—his crime, in effect—were punishing himself for his demonic pride and his malign preference for the imaginary in the person of his hero, Napoleon *le Petit*, another man too small for himself. There is no doubt that the novel, had he written it, would have been *diabolical*—what a vicious circle! A creator whose ubiquitous invisibility gathers itself together and contests itself—yet without ceasing to exist—in this precipitating agent, a mean and wretched hero who is his *creature* yet isn't even invented, whom Gustave chose to resurrect among his *real* contemporaries in order to lodge in the depths of his work as his incarnation, like a dark and singular ray of light, the representation of his original sin, of his artist's wickedness and his deserved punishment. Conversely, his hero is a conquered man caught out in his crime, just as his defeat publicly reveals his imposture, and in his overwhelmed, almost contemptible impotence—the impotence of the passive agent Flaubert always remained—he saves the impassive author, who has taken him on, silently testifying that there is greatness only in dissatisfaction.

A new turn of the wheel: the sublime unrealization of the artist to the profit of that derealizing center, his work, is denounced as a crime by the inexpiable sin of a politician who for twenty years has preferred the ideal to Machiavellianism, has preferred a dreamed-of greatness to practical efficacy, dragging the society that had given him its confidence into a disaster that was foreseen and accepted from the first. And let no one say that the intellectual is innocent because he is an intellectual, and that he would betray himself by showing a concern for praxis instead of contemplating ideas, while the man of power, who chose efficacious action, is a traitor if he prefers the gesture and a good role to rigorous *practice*. For the artist—while often priding himself on his quietism and claiming "to become a brahmin and enter again into the idea"—does not take part in a contemplative order. Truth interests him very little; his function is to produce the imaginary as a permanent triumph of nonbeing over being and the systematic destruction of the human race through techniques of unrealization. On this level, and since the intention of this misanthrope is clearly revealed, he cannot doubt that the insults of the "guard" and the fists brandished by the vile multitude are really addressed to him through the mediation of the humiliated Politician. Napoleon has harmed men by preferring his dream to them; if we allow that his Pretorians hate him, if, despite the misanthropic contempt of the masses, we find the captives' hatred of him justified, what can we say of the artist, who himself claims to prefer his dreams so as to do men more certain harm? As long as the Empire was left standing, any harm the dream did was itself a dream: whatever their intentions, when the Knights of Nothingness fabricated or published their works of art, they were harming no one; on the contrary, reading provoked a joyful liberation of hatred, too delightful to know it was imaginary. At the same time, the Court, a brilliant theater, a radical but ineffectual subversion, offered itself as a flower of luxury, unreal, a flower of evil born on the dungheap of the established order. But when disaster reveals that the most fearsome efficacy of the imaginary resides in its radical inefficacy, how are the artists, who number among Napoleon's victims, going to condemn this unreliable fellow for the evil his lies have done without condemning themselves? The misanthropes have reassimilated into the human race, they dread the occupation, the garrisoned soldiers, the physical violence, the depredations, the ruin, and some of them, like the Goncourts, discover a streak of chauvinism in themselves. They are sharing the aims of the species, or rather recognizing that they always shared them. As a result, the scale of values is reversed: the imaginary falls to the bottom, property rises to the top; from the point of view of that morality, the worker of art will not condemn Isidore, first wool-gatherer of France, without condemning himself. This is a recognition that "under Napoleon III" the established power got the writers it deserved, and the writers deserved the prevailing power. His honor and his property wounded, the artist sees that absolute-art—or the absolute preference for appearance—is turned against him as an enemy force. He senses, in any case, that the Empire and art for art's sake, sharing the same underlying source, are going to vanish together. Will there be another art—despised in advance? Or will literature and art disappear forever? Can an aesthetic exist that is based not on images but, of all things, on truth? The artist poses these questions for himself, but he knows very well that he will find no answer. If one day another kind of writing should appear that involves other aspirations, other verbal instruments, Flaubert is convinced he will not be the man for this literature: he condemns himself to the silence of the "fossil."

The wheel turns again: and what if the *purpose* of the coup d'état and "of all that followed" had been only to provide material for a good book? Flaubert does not actually say "purpose" but "result." He preferred the order of causes to the order of ends. But that is just a facade; and we know that beginning with the first *Education*, the order of causes providentially guided Jules toward his accomplishment. We are speaking here not of providence but of "universal harmony"; nonetheless, this single word, which is so Flaubertian, reintroduces the notion of finality. Jules's misfortunes have *chosen* him; the misfortunes of France are going to inspire some "good scribbler"—why not Gustave?—to write some interesting scenarios. We have already discovered this orphic conception of literature in Flaubert, a conception in which the world has no function but to provide material for a book, or, as Mallarmé would say, for the Book. But it did not issue so clearly from a rebound of pride; the moment he condemns the politics and aesthetics of appearances *together*, he suddenly turns around and reaffirms that the only justification of reality is found in the fictions one generates from it. That is art, in effect: a demand for universal harmony, or, rather, that harmony itself insofar as it produces the real as a pathway to the imaginary. To write a novel is to conform to the vast designs of a providence that has realized the world only to offer material for derealization. Derealization, the supreme negation, destroys nothing, leaves everything in place, and even, in a way, restores what has been abolished, only to transform this plenitude, through a subtle transubstantiation, into a *vacuum* that shimmers out of reach, the inaccessible place where harmony is universalized as an ideal of the imagination. We see the immediate application of this metaphysics of the beautiful: at almost the same time, Louis-Napoleon has created a reign of false appearances, and Gustave has created the literature of appearances. Their reciprocal adaptation is not fortuitous, for identical historical motivations produced these two epiphenomena. To this Court, an empty mirage consumed in designating an absence, a clumsy, ugly cavalry march at top speed that nonetheless issues from beauty in that its ugliness transcends itself toward the unimaginable image of the eternal Court, comes the artist to nourish his profound conviction that nothing is beautiful save that which does not exist. So he is complicit; worse still, he belongs to the regime, and when that collapses, we may well wonder whether absolute-art is not going to disappear along with it. In fact, the worker of art, that noble dreamer, has been buried beneath the ashes, and all that's left is a man who wakes up just as the false Emperor does: the one opens his eyes on a highway, and the first object he perceives is a fist, a real fist held to his face; the artist comes to his senses in the middle of his room, standing, and discovers that he is in the midst of contemplating a *real* Prussian helmet set on his bed.

This is the moment of despair and silence, which in a sense will never be transcended. And yet this transcendence exists: the despairing conviction that art is dead through its own fault, and that the positivist world will be able to reconstruct itself only by denying art forever—this conviction is suddenly inverted and becomes a tranquil certainty: victory lies in defeat, within reach. *It is true* that the Latin world has disappeared along with its product, the artist. But as a result, a miracle has happened: appearance and being have coincided for all eternity. The imaginary is *a denial of being*, but the past, whatever it may be, must define itself as *what has been*. It is true that that evening at Compiègne was one of a hundred different acts in the imperial theater, and it buried the real beneath a jumble of gestures and tirades; it is true that Louis-Napoleon, though grumpy, dull, and silent, surrounded by glittering medal-holders, invited one *not to see* him as a morose, scowling man who dragged his feet in the salons, but to see through him a phantom that the artist saw only by making himself a phantom as well. Well, precisely—*it's true*. On a certain day of a certain summer gone by, for this dreamer who awakens with a start and turns toward his past, the *truth* of Compiègne was only that particular theater, interpreted only by particular actors in the troupe. Truth or *being:* that charming, vague smile of a false duchess was false because it was addressed to a false Sire, and because the impudent woman was pretending to smile. Yet today, on this summer day of 1871, a smile *really* has come to those lovely lips: has the false Gustave perceived or imagined it? The question is meaningless; he perceived it, but insofar as he was surpassing it toward a divine invisible smile, insofar as he was pretending to take it as real although when it fluttered at the corners of her mouth it was false, we can say that this perception was imaginary. Today it is *real*: it *really* was Gustave's eye contact with the duchess, who really curtsied to Napoleon and really contracted her zygomatic muscles to give herself a certain look, which was true in that she knew her physiognomy and produced it according to proven empirical methods, but did so in *false* if precise and catalogued circumstances. Thus, after the disaster the Second Empire no longer appears as just a ruse but, rather, as a period that becomes a true recollection when resurrected by memory; and as it is evoked, the theater of the Empire miraculously becomes that moment in the past when being and nothingness were interchangeable. A moment when the nothingness of those courtiers' fawnings, fixed in being as *that which was,* a dead butterfly, a death's head in dazzling colors, was equivalent, as a real determination of lost time, to the being that imposes itself on lived experience now cast in the bronze of the past as a *no longer being* (it will *never more* be lived, save through memory; the future will be able to alter its meaning but nothing can modify certain structures, and particularly the immediate—perceptible and affective—aspect will remain forever protected).

We have observed that memory partially transforms memories of moments fully and really lived into images; and that is true even when Gustave evokes a visit by Louis Bouilhet shortly before his death. But when we are dealing with twenty years of lying, it is the opposite: memory gathers up every scrap of *being* in the theatrical production (the *real* tinkling, etc.) and makes it sustain the former nonbeing and its real ontological determination, making the past in essence surpassed-being. If this is so, then the Empire, the moment it is overthrown, becomes in some sense the absolute subject of art.

609

Indeed, it is the justification of absolute-literature. It was produced at a moment that can be reconstructed only by making the historic reconstruction coincide with the most radical imagination, in which, when we consider them retrospectively, the epiphenomena of history and especially the dreams it has engendered are a part of history itself and serve to characterize the epoch. Inefficacy and the vow of impotence that characterize this oneirism appear, in fact, as a ruse of reason meant to lead the Latins to their doom and, merely through the Satanic passion for the worst, to demoralize other men by submitting them to the yoke of Prussian science. Consequently, a study of that moment is indispensable to a realistic knowledge of our own epoch, and without it we should understand neither the Assembly of Bordeaux, nor the siege of Paris, nor the peace treaty, nor the Commune, nor the government of Monsieur Thiers. But such a study—which realism, the narrowest positivism, requires to be done strictly within the framework of the exact disciplines—calls by its very subject, which is the imaginary, for imagination to insist on playing much more than an auxiliary role, yet itself to be the exact science that all the others submit to. For by the identical imperative it addresses from the depths of the past in which it is engulfed to the ideal of imagination, which is beauty, and to that of reason, which is truth, this moment reconciles art and science, and as a function of its secret essence, which led in real history to the defeat of art and the triumph of science, it reestablishes as an object to be reconstituted—through its very disappearance—the preeminence of art over science. A moment, in other words, that pure science cannot conjure up and that will surrender only to a *learned* art. A moment that can be rendered and fixed only in a work. A tragic farce, whose *futility* can be communicated only by a gratuitous book, whose basis can only be the superb inutility of absolute-art. Certainly, the artist has died with the Empire, and 4 September signifies the death of literature *for everyone.* Yet there has to be a death certificate, a requirement all the more necessary as art is nothing but life contemplated by the imaginary gaze of death. As we know, the artist is a living person who regards himself as dead; he is now asked to tell us about that slow death that was his life under the Empire from the point of view of its last avatar, that catastrophic destruction, which, far from killing a man to give birth to the "imaginary" worker of art, has destroyed art and the artist in order to produce that barking beast, a man *awakened,* raised up from the underworld. "Under Napoleon III" is for Flaubert, at

first thought, absolute-art producing posthumously, as an eternal announcement, a final work that consecrates its death. It is what musicians call a "commemorative work." If the good "scribbler," rising
from his ashes to die ceremoniously in this novel, succeeds in scientifically reconstructing eighteen years of imaginary death, concluding
with the conflagration that suppresses art and the artist, he saves
himself through a spectacular suicide. By his compromising presence
at the Tuileries, his courtier's fawnings at Compiègne, he has given
up any claim to innocence, to the function of independent witness,
he has clipped the wings of his panoramic consciousness; but if he
tells about the theatricals he acted in along with so many others, if he
surveys to the second degree, through memory, the fatalities that
killed the Empire and absolute-art in one stroke, then, far from being
an accomplice of imperial society, he becomes its providential guest.
For it is none other than providence that has transported him to the
high moments of the theater because it needed him and his death to
pass into the eternal. He was the only one (provided he played a
double game as artist and courtier) who could reconstruct its criminal
and grandiose gratuitousness through the criminally harmful effects
of art; the only one who could trim, patch, tighten the raw material
and so render—beyond the depravities of individuals, their servility,
their arrivism, the universal ugliness—a profound aspiration toward
beauty, pervasive if obscure to itself, in its unsustainable brilliance
and its harmful, useless effects. In this exact and grandiose book, in
which imagination ought to detect being, art, *realizing* its death, an-
ticipates the judgment of posterity. This work is definitive, nothing
after it will ever again be worthy of artistic *treatment:* perfection is
attained when the very material of the work—in other words, being,
history—is imaginary and simply demands to be totalized by the
imagination. Resurrecting this false Empire, art *dies as beauty.* The silence that follows must not be seen as shame nor as a judgment pronounced against imperial lies by the September Republic; it is rather
the mutism of the great artists; they have taken leave of the public
in a final work. Then they have imitated the stoicism of the wolf,
"Suffer and die without speaking," refusing to use language to practical ends or to waste their time extracting an extenuated quintessence
of unreality from the real. "If one day they bother with literature
again . . . ," Gustave writes in '71. For him, it's all over: the work
of art is eternal, art is not immortal. At certain times, like ours, it is
eclipsed; in a decade, in a century, of course, conditions may again

emerge that will allow its resurrection by instituting a new connection between the real and unreality. *In any case*—whether provisional or definitive—"Under Napoleon III" had to *put the final period* to the work of the workers of art by revealing their surpassing ability on the occasion of a unique subject. Just when the artist would have piously murdered art, then immolated himself, he would have felt he was the executor of an imperative that emanated from universal harmony; by taking leave of the reader, he would have offered him the *Truth* of Napoleon III, the usurper in person, changed into himself by imagination.

There is not a shadow of a doubt: Flaubert had no sooner recovered from his disarray—not totally and not for long—than he felt he'd received a mandate. He tormented himself so intensely and so long—almost to death—trying to find an appropriate scenario for "Under Napoleon III" because for the first time in his life he wanted to write it, not out of fidelity to his dreams, to old themes, but to accomplish a mission: saving the Empire in a work seemed to him the unique justification of his courtier's fawnings. Or rather—for he was fleeing from the ghastly culpability they were attempting to bring down on him—he now felt that he, the artist, had been placed there, that he had been dispatched to Compiègne and to the Tuileries to be in a position to begin the work. Saving the Empire, of course, was not justifying imperial politics but quite simply—and whatever he may say—showing the homogeneity of the dream of the French collectivity and the labor of art, that is, of demoralizing derealization. Despite the beauty of the enterprise—the most totalitarian Gustave had conceived—he appears not to have had sufficient ardor to implement it. In his conversation with Du Camp, at least as it is reported, he manifests a certain enthusiasm; but, as I have said, this is clearly the earliest mention of the scenario. When he expresses in his correspondence his disgust with writing and vows to keep silent, he says he will take up the pen just one more time so as to drown his contemporaries in his vomit; but he is thinking of the Two Woodlice, not of Napoleon III. Subsequently he refers in his letters and his conversations to the "novel of the Second Empire," but not joyfully, rather as something that needs to be done. On 31 January 1876, Edmond de Goncourt listens with amusement to Alphonse Daudet, who evokes his memories of the duc de Morny; Flaubert and Zola are present. Zola, who has just written *Son Excellence Eugène Rougon* on the basis of secondhand reports, suddenly exclaims:

"That would be a marvelous book to write . . . Don't you think so, Flaubert?"

"Yes, it's odd, but there is no book in it."

"But what about you, Flaubert, why don't you do something on that period?"

"Why? Because one would have to find the form and the way to use it . . . And after all, now I am such a *bedolle!*"

"A *bedolle*, what's that?" asks Daudet.

"No, no one knows better than I what a *bedolle* I am . . . Yes, a *bedolle*—what's that? An old sheikh . . ."

And he ends his thought with a vaguely despairing gesture."[145]

To be sure, 1876 is Flaubert's darkest year: Commanville's ruin dates from April 1875. Yet he has set to work, and the *Trois Contes*, begun at Trouville, would be finished in February 1877. *Bouvard et Pécuchet*, though interrupted for a while, will not be abandoned. It was only *this novel* on the Empire that frightened him; he had not "found the form" and then, when he had to grapple with it, he felt too cowardly, too worn out for such a vast enterprise. Zola, referring to later conversations,[146] writes in *Les Romanciers naturalistes:* "He remained hesitant, the task *alarmed* him, for with his system he would have had to leaf through all the documents of the epoch; perhaps, too, he did not feel very free after his sojourns at Compiègne . . . But it must also be said that this novel on the Second Empire . . . was not something he felt inclined to do. Other ideas kept intruding, and I doubt that he ever would have written it." Indeed, around 1877 he started dreaming of an Oriental novel, *Harel Bey*, and declared until the end of his life that after *Bouvard et Pécuchet* he wanted to do a novel on "the Thermophyles." Meanwhile he returns, morose but zealous, to his notebooks, and jots down a few notes on demoralization, "Monsieur le Prefet," "A Parisian Household"; he seems to do this out of a sense of duty but without much enthusiasm, and his last scenarios charge the Second Empire with responsibility for all human stupidity and all bourgeois mediocrity. Must we consider, with Zola, that he "was not feeling very free after his sojourns at Compiègne"? As we have seen, the facts indicate quite the opposite: first, he makes no mystery of these "sojourns," and Goncourt does not miss the opportunity to insinuate that he flaunts them. And, further, they do not

145. *Journal*, vol. 11, p. 71.
146. That is, after January 1876, since neither Zola nor the Goncourts knew then that Flaubert already intended to write his "novel of the Second Empire."

prevent him, when he is asked, from declaring that Napoleon III was an idiot or from caricaturing him in public. From this point of view, on the contrary, it is Compiègne and the Tuileries that compel him to show the crumbling of the Empire in a suicidal work, in this way eternalizing the shipwreck and making it the symbol of human failure. What, then, holds him back? Well, when it comes down to it, Zola is right: Gustave has visited the Court; it's not that he feels embarrassed about it now, but simply that he *loved* imperial society; a rebound of pride whispers to him a command to bury it with his own hands, yet his imperative repulses him. He was in solidarity with the regime, he does not want to survive it, even to accomplish its interment. This hypersensitive soul owes his only years of happiness to the Empire; when it crumbles, Gustave feels touched by a mortal lassitude. A little earlier we saw him leaping with pain, vomiting, shouting out his hatred of the Prussians, proclaiming his willingness to die—but these things were not so serious. Such convulsive emotions still involved some violence, some life. Then he seemed to grow calm, to set to work on *Saint Antoine*, on *Bouvard et Pécuchet*, even the insurrection in Paris did not penetrate his tranquillity; with peace reestablished and a return to order, he seems out of danger. In effect, *nothing* has changed, the Prussian phantoms no longer even haunt Croisset; in the capital he is admired, respected, the young people, far from turning their backs on him, attribute some disturbing doctrines to his patronage. His dear princess has recovered her apartment in Paris, her property at Saint-Gratien; no one reproaches him for his past visits; after his ruin, the government of the Republic would come to his aid with good grace; and upon the publication of *Trois Contes*, republican criticism would reserve a triumph for the man who for so long had been dragged through the mud by the dogs of the imperial guard.[147] Be that as it may, during this period the whole extent of his malady was revealed; it was "that lassitude of soul that is the death of genius," as was said of the final years of Rabelais, a writer he loved.

Yes, the old sheikh has become a *bedolle*: he is dying of exhaustion and sorrow. He would explain this to George Sand at the beginning

---

147. It was the public that ensured the success of *Madame Bovary*. After *Salammbô*, official criticism, despite modest praise, was muted. *L'Education sentimentale* was a burial. With flowers and wreaths, to be sure, as Goncourt bitterly notes. For he had become a "received" writer in the meantime. During the entire period from the imperial defeat to his death, Gustave published nothing but the *Trois Contes*; and this was the only work the reviewers were almost unanimous in dubbing a "masterpiece."

of 1875, *before* the ruin, with that admirable sentence: "I was vaguely quite ill this winter." But as always, it is by projecting himself into another that he best informs us of his own state. Around mid-april 1872, Théophile Gautier begins to decline. Flaubert is deeply disturbed: "Another one!" and from letter to letter we see his anxiety grow; there is no doubt about his identification with Gautier, whom he charges with dying in his place. Gustave writes to George Sand: "My poor Théo is very ill. He is dying of tedium and wretchedness! No one is left who speaks his language! We are like a few old fossils left behind, lost in a new world." [148] It is striking that he says *my* poor Théo to George Sand, when "our" was the obvious choice; he is withholding Gautier from her, denying this republican the right to weep over his comrade in fossilhood. The mandate to die in despair is renewed on 3 August 1872: "All of my old friends are on the way out! When shall I follow their example?" At the same time he takes possession of the dying man—whose closely watched death throes drag on—and decides: "No one will weep for him more than I." On 23 October, when Gautier finally dies, the transubstantiation is effected: under the guise of Théo, it is Gustave who is put into the earth: "The death of my poor Théo, though foreseen, has crushed me . . . I was at Rouen . . . and I met three or four people from Rouen. The spectacle of their vulgarity, their frock coats, their hats, what they were reading, and the sound of their voices made me want to vomit and weep at the same time. Never since I've been on earth had I so choked with disgust for men. I was constantly thinking of the love Théo had for art, and I felt as if I were drowning in a tide of impurities. I am certain that he died from prolonged suffocation caused by modern stupidity."

A striking text. Théo's death allows Gustave to grasp his own love of art *as other*, it is no longer a subjective sentiment, it is an objective virulence, not only a pathos but an ethos that, in its corrosive absence, spontaneously disqualifies the bourgeois of Rouen. but while he thus devalorizes the obtuse stupidity of respectable people, he has first to be killed by it. Here Gustave is crucified, dead, and resurrected, like Narrator #2 of *Novembre*. In fact, it was not Gautier who *first* suffered from modern stupidity; Gustave gave him his illness and the other succumbed to it—like Alcestis descending to hell instead of Admetus. Still, the cause of death, in this passage, remains quite general: Gustave had never stopped suffering from stupidity and de-

148. May 1872, *Correspondance* 6:373.

nouncing it since his first letter to Ernest. On 28 October, writing to Mathilde, he is more explicit:

> He died of disgust with modern life; the 4th of September killed him. That day, the blackest day in the history of France, inaugurated an order of things in which people like Théo have no place . . . I do not pity him, I envy him . . . In these matters, one must respect the opinion of the dead; one must continue his *idea* as far as possible, that is why, if I had had to deliver Théo's funeral oration, I would have told what caused his death. I would have protested in his name against the Grocers and Hooligans. He died of a long-sustained internalized anger. I would, therefore, have exhaled some of that anger.[149]

As always happens, the identification reverses itself: now it is *Théo,* a dead man, who gives Flaubert the mandate to continue his *idea* and "exhale" his own anger as if it belonged to the deceased. In subsequent letters he develops the theme of *envy:* "As for him, I do not pity him; on the contrary, I envy him deeply. If only I were rotting in his place. For all the pleasure we get in this base world (*base* is the right word) we should bugger off as quickly as possible. That 4th of September inaugurated a state of things that no longer concerns us. We are superfluous. We are hated and scorned, that's the truth of the matter. And so, good night!"[150]

That "And so, good night!" is magnificent—it reflects all of Gustave's insincerity. People hated Gautier, they scorned him, the new society refused to integrate him. *And so,* he withdrew. Like the young hero of *Novembre,* the old poet has died by thought, an internalized anger has undermined him, accompanied by the will not to be consoled. But by negligently tossing in "we," Gustave insists upon this voluntary departure: he explains it as a decision common to all "fossils"—a highly restricted category since he declares a little later that he has lost the only person he could still chat with since the death of Bouilhet; in short, there are two of them, Flaubert and the Other, decorated posthumously. Théo is elevated to the dignity of *alter ego.* The Other is the one who dies, of course, but for reasons common to them both and which seem so convincing that they *must* have warped the same mortal woof in Gustave and caused the same death. And so, good night: the two buffoons, ironic and desperate, one at the front of the stage, the other somewhat behind, bow with the same

149. Ibid., p. 435.
150. To Feydeau, 28 October 1872, *Correspondance* 6:436–37.

movement to the hissing public, and retreat with the same step, interrupting their routine. We are convinced, moreover, that Gustave is already underground. Better, if there is only one dead man, it is Flaubert, buried by mistake under the name of Gautier. Isn't he the true, the only goldsmith, the pure anchorite who has sacrificed everything to art (when the new alter ego, who was married, a father, and impecunious, was wasting his talents on perfunctory but remunerative efforts)? Hasn't Gustave felt since childhood the anger that killed Théo? Wasn't he the first to decide to die by thought? Didn't he *refuse all consolation* after the 4th of September? Didn't he then feel washed up, senile, *bedolle*? Didn't he *know* he would die of it, and didn't he want to? There is only one answer: it hardly matters who plays the role of the deceased in the funeral ceremony; the *metaphysical* truth is that on this day of 23 October, Flaubert died, eminently if by proxy. That day it was not *a* dead man he installed inside himself, it was *his* death, not as a future event but as a logical and already drawn conclusion to his life—all the more obvious as it is *other*, drawn by another, and as this otherness gives it the inflexible force of an imperative.

But we would be wrong to see something buffoonish in this peculiar recuperation. if Gustave says "we," it is not only to parade in the dead man's plumage, or to persuade his comrades of the gravity of his state. The truth is that he *feels he is dying:* he sees the fatigue and dejection that grip him not only as the results of a catastrophe but, *in particular,* as ineluctable causes that will hasten his death; he recognizes in them the symptoms of that serious and vague malady that prophesies his imminent demise. We might say he has been doing this since childhood. Yes—only this time, it's true. One more blow, the Commanville affair, and it's all over. Again, he regards this blow—the ruin of a country gentleman by a man in the import-export business as the bourgeois Republic's triumph *over him*. The events of 4 September 1870 have killed Flaubert.

It is clear that without deluding himself about the sins of the Second Empire, Flaubert identified with that society and for almost ten years (1861–70) was as happy as he could be. Under the Third Republic he is nothing but a "fossil," idolized but no longer really existing. The vital literature of the time (naturalism) may claim kinship with him, but this is a misunderstanding. *Trois Contes* would be a critical success but not a public one. *Bouvard et Pécuchet*, that absurd effort, would appear, incomplete, only after his death. Let us try to see how the requirements of literature-to-be-written (practico-inert, or literature-written) necessarily led him, like a certain number of his contemporaries, to choose art-neurosis; and how, in opposition to Leconte de Lisle's republicanism—or disguised abolitionist sentiment—the attack at Pont-l'Evêque, as the realization of neurosis, summoned and prophesied the Second Empire.

The young bourgeois generation (*the one that was born around 1820* and lived through the entire "July monarchy") *perceives* the bourgeoisie, its own class, *almost* undisguised: the environment—their parents—is revealed as ignoble, the expression of utilitarianism. The denial is *total*. Yet it must be understood that this generation cannot bear *utilitarianism,* that is a fact. These young men, however, cannot *see* the bourgeoisie unless they adopt the (realistic) point of view of the disadvantaged classes; and while a few of them will love the people from afar, the majority merely have contempt for them. They are passably reactionary bourgeois, which for them corresponds, even before they formulate it, to opting for an order maintained by a hierarchical power. This feeling is deeper and more precocious in Flaubert than in many of the others. The son of a practitioner, he is denied by his family and his studies the possibility of being a scientist or a technician of practical knowledge. And the crisis of the bourgeoisie is manifest for him as an exclusion of utilitarianism and reality. He is therefore compelled to choose the *unreal* and panoramic thought—which claims to see the bourgeoisie from above, as it *is.* But this choice—a forced hand—is accompanied in him from the first, as we have seen, by guilt: he will be a conjurer of shadows, he says bitterly. Furthermore, choosing not to be useful is choosing to *do* nothing; later, he will make a small change and say he is doing *nothing.* Disgusted by utilitarianism, he chooses not only to be useless but to be harmful. All this hides a deep wound: not only is he disinclined to leave his class, but, since that class is the source of all evil, he would also hope it would compensate for its evil through the acknowledgment and selection of an elite to which he would belong. He enters into literature on this basis, that is, solicited from this point of view, literature-already-written (eighteenth century, Romanticism) is about to reveal its contradictory (practico-inert) imperatives to him. He wants to become a writer *so as not to take up a profession.* That is the possible choice for a small soul already penetrated by classical culture but still rather vague. The rest comes from things, inert objective demands that reveal themselves in considerable tension when seized from this angle. Certainly for another bourgeois, more reconciled to his class, for Maxime, for Augier, such demands are scarcely, if at all, apparent: those men want a bourgeois art against their class, which does not consider it necessary to have an art of its own and *for* itself. But from the moment that the Father, physician and lord, categorically condemns art in the name of science, the young apprentice wants art to be the reverse condemnation, the condemnation of the bourgeoisie—of the real—in the name of an imaginary feudal order, the aristocracy of the Good Lord. As a result, art-to-be-done reveals its triple objective demand: the failure of the man, the failure of the artist, the failure of the work. Which necessarily implies an objective neurosis. Flaubert and Baudelaire are the first to have understood this, precisely because their early history disposed them to become neurotic; the purpose of Flaubert's subjective neurosis is the same as that of the objective neurosis (demanded by the requirements of the objective spirit). We can even say that the imperatives of the objective neurosis universalize and objectify what remained singular and subjective in him: the failure of the man (of his bourgeois self) involves the denial of the real and naked bourgeoisie, and the creation of an imaginary *consolidated* man. He alone can conceive of art for art's sake and realize a work as its own end. This means that art is a treatment imposed on the totality of the imaginary by a man who has himself become imaginary: art and the artist are homogeneous. It goes without saying, however, that Gustave, subjected to the will of his father (who conducts himself in a typically bourgeois fashion by choosing his son's profession), can imagine changing his being only by changing his subjugation. Impossible and even harmful art (demoralization) becomes his daily task. Objectively, then, art for art's sake seems to be a black feudal order whose principle, beauty, is hidden, but whose artists are, in the imaginary, the Knights of Nothingness. Flaubert's relation to the (bourgeois) real is *imaginary destruction.* We thereby understand that art for art's sake, an unreal feudalism, is in truth the "cover" that writers and artists draw in advance over the bourgeoisie, which is dangerously exposed. An imaginary cover, to be sure, but one that appeals to another cover, also imaginary, that nonetheless *consolidates* it by *distinguishing* the Knights of Nothingness in the name of another knighthood, the chivalry of death (the military). Pushed by his family outside the bourgeois world and into anomaly, Flaubert's deepest, most intense desire (without admitting it to himself) was always to be reintegrated into the elite of his class

619

(inhabited, naturally, by his father and brother) as a mandarin, but he disguised this unrealizable desire with his (equally unrealizable) wish to *change class*.

So we must see that Gustave's profound intention in 1844 is not to *liberate* himself from his father but, quite the contrary, to become reintegrated with his family and live in it under the authority of the black Lord. The complexity and ambiguity of this *subjective* decision rests in the fact that Achille-Cléophas, who was a country gentleman and a bourgeois, a prince of science, appeared simultaneously to be a member of the bourgeois elite and a *modern* aristocrat. Flaubert therefore conceives hierarchy in civil society as an ideal, families being dominated by the paterfamilias, which necessarily implies, in his case, that to guarantee this dream, political society must be a black dictatorship creating an imaginary nobility all of a piece (as the result of a voluntarist selection). Gustave demands a cover because he wants to veil real *property* and self-interest, the basis of utilitarianism (which is this same property insofar as it objectively develops its requirements), with an impossible object, the beautiful, something one does not possess and that must be realized only occasionally as a presentiment, in the work of art. In short, at Pont-l'Evêque, by the realization of the objective neurosis through a subjective attack, Gustave demands an objective cover for his being-as-property-owner four years before the bourgeoisie sought one. He would continue to *possess* but by means of an alienation that made him forget it; he would be the bourgeois-gentleman, like the Goncourts or Baudelaire, because after 1840 the requirements of autonomous art compelled them to desire the reestablishment of patronage. It was the princes and dukes of the Empire who ought to have taken the place of that false nobility which achieved the appearance of changing class. We know, however, that under the authoritarian Empire, the ideology of this borrowed aristocracy was rosy and benevolent. There was misunderstanding, and certain trials took place as a result. But from 1861 onward, the Empire was liberalized, and it more or less understood its cultural mission. To a degree, political society and the writers become better-suited to meet each other's needs. But the liberal Empire was the bourgeoisie triumphant: in it, writers found their class and their public. Until 1870 they would be sullenly attached to the Empire that hid reality from them.

It is clear, then, that in 1844 Gustave was struck down by an attack whose motives were subjective, and whose objective meaning—coming from the conflict of two bourgeois generations and the requirements of the objective spirit grasped from this perspective—was a prophetic summoning of the society of the second Empire, the only society, strictly speaking, in which Jules the Hermit could live. This society, which the bourgeois would choose on the occasion of real events originating in the class struggle, was an imaginary society, the waking dream of the bourgeoisie of the 1850s, with the advantages and inconveniences attendant upon such a social accident. For the proponents of art for art's sake, there was indeed a kind of diachronic progress. Gustave, in particular, had already constituted himself a subject of the Second Empire in 1844. This is why he missed the rendez-vous in '48. It's as if *his* February revolution had taken place in January of '44.

All the artists were attempting to do this around the same time, with more or less success, whether dandyism was taken as a substitute for the defunct nobility, as it was for Baudelaire; whether they really believed in their nobility, as the Goncourts did; or whether an affectation of republican zeal dissimulated pseudo-aristocratic memories, as was the case for Bouilhet and Leconte de Lisle. That was art under the Empire. All these men, haunted by the idea of "nervous illness," read each other's work and confirmed each other. By their communion and solidarity they consolidated the unreal in themselves, that is, aesthetic perception. It remains to be shown how the bourgeoisie of the Second Empire would support them because it preferred an apolitical art for art's sake to any manifestation of *engaged* art.

Art for art's sake, however, is not a school. Each of the writers considered here is doing something unique. Flaubert, in particular, is absolutely not a poet. If he wrote some verse in Alfred's time, none has survived. He also declares that he *is not* a novelist, yet he wrote only novels and *La Tentation*. "I am a writer," he says. What does he mean by that? How shall we explain that the common idea of pure art prompted him to produce *those* particular works? We shall try to answer these questions by rereading *Madame Bovary*.